TECHNOLOGY AND HEALTH

TECHNOLOGY AND HEALTH

PROMOTING ATTITUDE AND BEHAVIOR CHANGE

Edited by

JIHYUN KIM
Nicholson School of Communication and Media,
University of Central Florida,
Orlando, FL, United States

HAYEON SONG
Department of Interaction Science,
Sungkyunkwan University,
Seoul, South Korea

ACADEMIC PRESS

An imprint of Elsevier

Academic Press is an imprint of Elsevier
125 London Wall, London EC2Y 5AS, United Kingdom
525 B Street, Suite 1650, San Diego, CA 92101, United States
50 Hampshire Street, 5th Floor, Cambridge, MA 02139, United States
The Boulevard, Langford Lane, Kidlington, Oxford OX5 1GB, United Kingdom

Notices
Knowledge and best practice in this field are constantly changing. As new research and
experience broaden our understanding, changes in research methods, professional
practices, or medical treatment may become necessary.

Practitioners and researchers must always rely on their own experience and knowledge
in evaluating and using any information, methods, compounds, or experiments
described herein. In using such information or methods they should be mindful of
their own safety and the safety of others, including parties for whom they have a
professional responsibility.

To the fullest extent of the law, neither the Publisher nor the authors, contributors, or
editors, assume any liability for any injury and/or damage to persons or property as a
matter of products liability, negligence or otherwise, or from any use or operation of
any methods, products, instructions, or ideas contained in the material herein.

Library of Congress Cataloging-in-Publication Data
A catalog record for this book is available from the Library of Congress

British Library Cataloguing-in-Publication Data
A catalogue record for this book is available from the British Library

ISBN: 978-0-12-816958-2

For information on all Academic Press publications visit our website at
https://www.elsevier.com/books-and-journals

Publisher: Nikki Levy
Acquisitions Editor: Nikki Levy
Editorial Project Manager: Barbara Makinster
Production Project Manager: Bharatwaj Varatharajan
Cover Designer: Matthew Limbert

Typeset by TNQ Technologies

Working together
to grow libraries in
developing countries

www.elsevier.com • www.bookaid.org

Contents

I

Theory and its application for health promotion

II

VR + AR: Technology for health in virtual world

III

MHealth: Mobile technology for health

IV

Social media: Networked technology for health

V

How technology changes our mind and behavior

List of Contributors

Laura Aymerich-Franch   Pompeu Fabra University, Barcelona, Spain

Jeremy N. Bailenson   Stanford University, Stanford, CA, United States

Nicola Brew-Sam   University of Erfurt, Erfurt, Germany

Rebecca K. Britt   University of Alabama, Tuscaloosa, AL, United States

Christopher Calabrese   University of California, Davis, CA, United States

Pamara F. Chang   University of Cincinnati, Cincinnati, OH, United States

Arul Chib   Nanyang Technological University, Singapore

Mark Chignell   University of Toronto, Toronto, ON, Canada

Emily M. Cramer   Howard University, Washington, DC, United States

Sandra Diehl   University of Klagenfurt, Klagenfurt, Austria

Géraldine Fauville   Stanford University, Stanford, CA, United States

Jacob T. Fisher   University of California Santa Barbara, Santa Barbara, CA, United States

Jameson L. Hayes   University of Alabama, Tuscaloosa, AL, United States

Heather J. Hether   University of California, Davis, CA, United States

Jeong-woo Jang   Korea Advanced Institute of Science and Technology, Daejeon, South Korea

Shaheen Kanthawala   University of Alabama, Tuscaloosa, AL, United States

Subuhi Khan   VSP Global, Rancho Cordova, CA, United States

Isabell Koinig   University of Klagenfurt, Klagenfurt, Austria

Kai Kuang   University of Pennsylvania, Bloomsburg, PA, United States

Chul-joo Lee   Seoul National University, Seoul, South Korea

SongYi Lee   Temple University, Philadelphia, PA, United States

Benjamin J. Li   Nanyang Technological University, Nanyang Link, Singapore

Tony Liao   University of Cincinnati, Cincinnati, OH, United States

Jessica Maddox   University of Alabama, Tuscaloosa, AL, United States

Alexis K. Marsh   Washington University, St. Louis, MO, United States

Henry Moller   University of Toronto, Toronto, ON, Canada

Swati Pandita   Cornell University, Ithaca, NY, United States

Jorge Peña   University of California, Davis, CA, United States

Macarena Pena-y-Lillo   Universidad Diego Portales, Santiago, Chile

Anna Carolina Muller Queiroz   Stanford University, Stanford, CA, United States

Rabindra Ratan   Michigan State University, East Lansing, MI, United States

Stephanie K. Van Stee   University of Missouri - St. Louis, United States

Ningxin Wang   University of Pennsylvania, Bloomsburg, PA, United States

John A. Waterworth   Umeå University, Umeå, Sweden

René Weber   University of California Santa Barbara, Santa Barbara, CA, United States

Andrea Stevenson Won   Cornell University, Ithaca, NY, United States

Qinghua Yang   Texas Christian University, United States

Biographies

About the Editors

Jihyun Kim (PhD, University of Wisconsin-Milwaukee) is an Assistant Professor in the Nicholson School of Communication and Media at the University of Central Florida in the United States. Her primary research interests are focused on (a) social and psychological effects and implications of new media/communication technologies for meaningful outcomes (e.g., health, education, enjoyment) and (b) a theoretical notion of presence (particularly, social presence) in a technology-mediated environment.

Hayeon Song (PhD, University of Southern California) is an Associate Professor in the Department of Interaction Science at Sungkyunkwan University in South Korea. She studies ways to use new media as persuasive and educational vehicle in the context of health. She is particularly interested in the psychological effects of virtual reality, artificial intelligence, and social media focusing on the theoretical concept of presence. Her most recent research focuses on the artificial agent helping seniors manage their mental health.

About the Chapter Authors

Laura Aymerich-Franch (PhD, Autonomous University of Barcelona, 2010) is a Ramón y Cajal research fellow at Pompeu Fabra University. Before that, she was a Marie Curie IOF postdoctoral fellow at EventLab, Barcelona University (2016/17), and at the CNRS-AIST Joint Robotics Laboratory, Japan (2014/16). Previously, she was a Fulbright postdoctoral scholar (2012/14) at the Virtual Human Interaction Lab, Stanford University. Her research focuses on the applied uses of virtual reality and social robots to enhance psychological well-being.

Jeremy Bailenson (PhD, Northwestern University, 1999) is a Professor in the Department of Communication and founding Director of the Virtual Human Interaction Lab at Stanford University. He studies the psychology of Virtual and Augmented Reality, e.g., how virtual experiences lead to changes in perceptions of self and others. His most recent research focuses on how virtual experiences can transform education, environmental conservation, empathy, and health.

Nicola Brew-Sam (PhD, University of Erfurt) holds a PhD from University of Erfurt (Germany) in cooperation with NTU in Singapore on "empowerment as an antecedent of app use for diabetes self-management." She conducted several studies with diabetics in Singapore and Germany. She worked in the field of mobile health interventions for type 2 diabetics in cooperation with ROCHE Diagnostics (2012/13). She holds a BA/MA from LMU in Munich/University of Zurich.

Rebecca Katherine Britt (PhD, Purdue University, 2012) is an Associate Professor at The University of Alabama. Her research focuses on eHealth and new technologies to develop health interventions. Dr. Britt's work has been published in journals such as *Health Communication*, the *Journal of Medical Internet Research*, and *Technical Communication Quarterly*, among others. Her work has been funded through local, state, and federal agencies.

Christopher (CJ) Calabrese (MPH, University of California, Davis, 2016) is a doctoral student in the Department of Communication at the University of California, Davis. He is primarily interested in health and science communication. His current research mainly focuses on health promotion, HIV prevention, social and communication networks, and persuasive technologies.

Pamara F. Chang (PhD, Cornell University, 2016) is an Assistant Professor in the Department of Communication at the University of Cincinnati. Her research examines communicative processes underlying how people manage stigma information and identities with the use of various information and communication technologies.

Arul Chib (PhD, University of Southern California, 2007) is an Associate Professor at Nanyang Technological University. Dr. Chib investigates the impact of mobile phones in healthcare (mHealth) and in transnational migration issues and is particularly interested in intersects of marginalization. He was recipient of the 2011 Prosper.NET-Scopus Award for the use of ICTs for sustainable development, accompanied by a fellowship from the Alexander von Humboldt Foundation. Dr. Chib has been the Principal Investigator of the SIRCA (Strengthening Information Society Research Capacity Alliance) programmes since 2008, mentoring emerging researchers from Africa, Asia, and Latin America.

Mark Chignell (PhD, University of Canterbury, New Zealand, 1981) is a Professor of Mechanical and Industrial Engineering at the University of Toronto, where he has been on the faculty since 1990. He has a PhD in Psychology and an MS in Industrial and Systems Engineering, with a minor in Artificial Intelligence (Ohio State, 1984). He is interested in empowering people through better user interface design with a particular interest in assessment and activation technologies for people who are aging.

Emily M. Cramer (PhD, University of Wisconsin-Milwaukee, 2014), an Assistant Professor at Howard University, examines how advances in new media can promote and enhance health in communities disadvantaged by access, income, or other sociodemographic inequities. Her work can be found in *American Journal of Men's Health, Women & Health*, and *Patient Education and Counseling*, among other outlets.

Sandra Diehl (PhD, Saarland University, 2001) is an Associate Professor at the Department for Media and Communication at the University of Klagenfurt, Austria, and Board Member of the European Advertising Academy. Her research interests include intercultural advertising and CSR and (m- and e-)health communication. She has published in several journals (e.g., *International Journal of Advertising, Journal of Business Research, Media and Psychology, International Marketing Review*) and authored and edited several books.

Géraldine Fauville (PhD, University of Gothenburg, 2018) is a Wallenberg Postdoctoral Fellow at the Virtual Human Interaction Lab at Stanford University, where she investigates how virtual reality can contribute to environmental and marine education both inside and outside school. She also holds two Master's degrees, one in Marine Science and the second in Education, Communication, and Learning.

Jacob Fisher (MA, Texas Tech University, 2016) is a PhD Candidate in the Communication department at the University of California, Santa Barbara, a researcher in the Media Neuroscience Lab, and a trainee of the National Science Foundation IGERT in Network Science and Big Data. He conducts research at the intersection of neuroscience, media psychology, and big data. Current work leverages functional neuroimaging and behavioral measures to investigate the relationships between various digital technology habits and neurodevelopmental changes in attention networks in the brain.

SongYi Grace Lee (MA, University of Georgia, 2014) is a doctoral student at Temple University. Her research mainly focuses on how people manage health through emerging media technologies. Her dissertation is about the relationship between VR technology and health management behavior and how human actors utilize VR in order to achieve specific health management goals.

Jameson Hayes (PhD, University of Georgia, 2012) is Director of the Public Opinion Lab at the University of Alabama. His research specialization is the intersection of brand and interpersonal communication within emerging media and has appeared in *Journal of Advertising, International Journal of Advertising,* among others. Hayes spent 6 years in the production side of media in radio and television and 3 years in advertising at the Snowden-Tatarski Agency.

Heather J. Hether (PhD, University of Southern California, 2009) is an Assistant Professor of Teaching Communication at the University of California, Davis. Her research interests focus on digital media in the health and education contexts, public relations, and innovative pedagogy.

Jeong-woo Jang (PhD, Michigan State University, 2014) is a Visiting Professor of the School of Humanities and Social Sciences at Korea Advanced Institute of Science and Technology (KAIST), in South Korea. Her research focuses on the social and psychological impacts of computer-mediated communication and communication technology.

Shaheen Kanthawala (PhD, Michigan State University, 2019) is an Assistant Professor in the Department of Journalism and Creative Media at the University of Alabama. Her research lies primarily in the arena of health communication, information, and technology.

Subuhi Khan (PhD, University of California, 2018) is a Senior Market Analytics Specialist at a private company in California. She is a research collaborator with researchers at Virtual Interaction and Communication Technology Research Lab (VICTR) at UC Davis, on research projects related to a mental health self-help application she designed during her PhD. She has published in journals such as *Journal of Computer Mediated Communication, Computers in Human Behavior, Communication Research Reports, Cyber Psychology, Behavior & Social Networking,* among others.

Isabell Koinig (PhD, University of Klagenfurt, 2015) is a Postdoctoral Researcher at the Department of Media and Communication at the University of Klagenfurt, Austria. Her research interests predominantly concern pharmaceutical advertising and related areas of health communication (social media, mHealth, health for sustainable development, and wearables), intercultural advertising, organizational health, as well as media and convergence management.

Kai Kuang (PhD, Purdue University, 2015) is an Assistant Professor in the Department of Communication Studies at Bloomsburg University of Pennsylvania. Her research program focuses on risk communication within health, science, and environmental contexts. Current projects examine uncertainty in risk communication, including psychological mechanisms associated with and communicative responses to scientific and illness uncertainty.

Chul-joo "CJ" Lee (PhD, University of Pennsylvania, 2009) is an Associate Professor in the Department of Communication at Seoul National University in South Korea. His research focuses on the interplay between communication and social determinants of health.

Benjamin (Benjy) Li (PhD, Nanyang Technological University, 2015) is an Assistant Professor at the WKW School of Communication and Information at Nanyang Technological University. He studies the effects of virtual embodiment on human behavior and attitudes. He also has a keen interest in the use of virtual reality technologies as a digital intervention (e.g., weight management, mental health) and in parental mediation of digital media.

Tony Liao (PhD, Cornell University, 2014) is an Assistant Professor in the Department of Communication at the University of Cincinnati. His research examines how augmented reality technologies are developing and how people utilize augmented reality technologies in everyday life in ways that affect their perceptions of space and place.

Jessica Maddox (PhD, University of Georgia, 2018) is an Assistant Professor in the Department of Journalism and Creative Media at the University of Alabama. Her research focuses on advancing qualitative methodologies with digital cultures and Internet studies.

Alexis K. Marsh (MSW, Washington University in St. Louis, 2018) facilitates social–emotional learning and community service opportunities among middle school students. Her professional interests include mental health promotion and understanding how community systems, particularly those affected by discrimination, impact the development of young people and families.

Henry Moller (MD, University of Toronto, 1996) has been involved in applied health science research, combining neuroscience approaches to sleep, wakefulness, and consciousness with immersive virtual reality methodologies, since completing training in neuropsychiatry at McMaster University and University of Toronto. His prior focus was on human performance. His current area of interest is developing medically applied meditation approaches for optimal well-being across cultures and the human life span.

Anna Carolina Muller Queiroz (MS, Universidade de São Paulo, 2013) is an Assistant Professor at Universidade de São Paulo and a Lemann Visiting Research Fellow at the Virtual Human Interaction Lab at Stanford University, where she investigates cognitive and affective implications of new media and technology in education. She holds an MS in Cognitive Psychology, a Behavioral Medicine degree, and a certificate in Education.

Swati Pandita (MPS Information Science, Cornell University, 2016) is a doctoral student at Cornell's Virtual Embodiment lab. Her research focuses on the clinical applications of virtual reality, centering around effects of technology use, identity, and embodiment on mental health.

Jorge Peña (PhD, Cornell University, 2007) is an Associate Professor at University of California, Davis. He is director of UCD's Virtual Interaction and Communication Technology Research lab (VICTR). He studies the persuasive uses and effects of video games, avatars, and virtual environments. He has published in journals such as *Journal of Computer-Mediated Communication*, *Journal of Communication*, *Communication Research*, and *Communication Theory*, among others.

Macarena Pena-y-Lillo (PhD, University of Illinois at Urbana-Champaign, 2016) is an Assistant Professor in the School of Journalism at Universidad Diego Portales in Chile. Her research focuses on health communication campaigns and health disparities.

Rabindra (Robby) Ratan (PhD, University of Southern California, 2011) is an Associate Professor and AT&T Scholar at Michigan State University. He received his PhD from USC's Annenberg School for Communication and Journalism and his MA and BA from Stanford University. He conducts research within the field of media psychology on how interactive media (e.g., video games, avatars) influence meaningful outcomes (e.g., education, health).

Stephanie K. Van Stee (PhD, University of Kentucky, 2012) is an Assistant Professor in the Department of Communication & Media at University of Missouri, St. Louis. Her research focuses on health communication, including health message design and health campaigns/interventions.

Ningxin Wang (PhD, University of Illinois at Urbana-Champaign, 2017) is a Lecturer in the Department of Management and Organization at the National University of Singapore in Singapore. Her research focuses on computer-mediated communication and interpersonal communication in close relationships.

John Waterworth (PhD, University of Hertfordshire, 1984) is a Senior Professor of Informatics at Umeå University. His research takes a psychological perspective, focusing on the subjective reality of living with information technology. Technical areas of focus include speech interaction, hypermedia, embodied interaction, and virtual and augmented environments. Human aspects include the sense of presence, emotion and embodiment, experience of time-in-passing, memory and attention, creativity, and aging.

René Weber (MD, RWTH University Aachen, 2008; PhD, University of Technology Berlin, 2000) is a Professor of communication at the University of California, Santa Barbara, and the director of UCSB's Media Neuroscience Lab. His research focuses on cognitive responses to media content. His research has been published in top-tier communication and neuroscience journals and in three authored books. He is an elected Fellow of the International Communication Association and was founding Chair of the association's Communication Science and Biology Interest Group.

Andrea Stevenson Won (PhD, Stanford University, 2016) is an Assistant Professor in the Department of Communication at Cornell University. She directs the Virtual Embodiment Lab. Research areas include the clinical applications of virtual reality and collaboration, teamwork, and learning in virtual environments.

Qinghua Yang (PhD, University of Miami, 2015) is an Assistant Professor at the Texas Christian University. Her research interests lie in health communication, new media, and quantitative research methods.

Foreword

Gary L. Kreps

University distinguished Professor, George Mason University, Department of
Communication, Fairfax, VA, United States

We live in an exciting communication era, an era of information evolution and revolution, where the advent of new advanced digital information technologies is advancing many important communication capabilities. Digital information technologies afford many important and exciting communication opportunities. Many of the advanced digital systems have evolved the basic communication functions performed by earlier media channels (such as books, newspapers, telephones, radios, and televisions) to provide increasingly easy and powerful access to relevant information, news, entertainment, education, and support. These digital tools enable communication interactions with a wide array of relevant others, even across potential time and space barriers. The digital systems are designed to store and process complex repositories of data to help inform many of the challenging decisions we make on a daily basis, from helping us navigate our way from point A to point B, enabling us to access desired goods and services, guiding strategic investment of our resources, and even providing us with opportunities to meet and establish interpersonal relationships with attractive others.

Nowhere in modern life, however, are digital communication tools of more importance than in seeking health care and in promoting personal and public health. Promoting and maintaining health is a tremendously complex and challenging task imbued with high levels of uncertainty (what Karl Weick would call high information equivocality). It is difficult to know all the possible risks that may impinge on our health and well-being, to prepare for times when we might get ill, and to respond appropriately for preventing and addressing challenging health problems. Timely, accurate, relevant, and up-to-date heath information is needed to guide important health decisions, to influence the adoption or discontinuance of health-related behaviors, and to coordinate the delivery of health care services! The best health information technologies are robust communication tools that disseminate relevant information, enable analysis of options and courses of action, and empower health promotion, providing the relevant health information needed to help demystify health risks and responses.

Yet, the rapid development and adoption of information technologies has not always resulted in tools that adequately met communication needs of health care providers and consumers. Unfortunately, there is not uniformly easy access to digital communication tools and information for all segments of society (the digital divide). Even when there is adequate access to technologies, digital tools are not always very user-friendly, especially not for those individuals who are not digital natives who possess high levels of digital competence. The ways that information is provided (messaging) via health information technologies are not uniformly easy to use, especially for those who are ill, incapacitated, and/or frightened (Health information technology developers must note that levels of health literacy are influenced by both trait and state conditions and digital tools must be responsive to these conditions).

Health information technology developers have often been more enamored by the technical sophistication and elegance of digital systems, rather than focusing on promoting the broad usability of health information tools. Moreover, as soon as information technology adopters learn how to use digital tools, it seems that newer more complex technologies are introduced to replace the more familiar systems. As a result, many health information technology users do not know how to fully utilize the digital tools available to them and many users are totally confused and frustrated by new technological equipment and software programs! There is a long way to go to design health information technologies to adapt to the unique needs and digital communication competencies of different users, especially across different demographic groups (based on age, education, income, and culture). We need help to get a better handle on understanding and using health information technologies!

Gratefully, this book takes several giant steps toward helping readers make sense of the communication functions of new health information technologies. The book covers a broad range of new digital health information tools and applications including interactive technologies such as interactive websites, virtual human agents (avatars), mobile applications, virtual reality systems, video games, augmented reality systems, online forums, narrative (storytelling) applications, social networking sites, and multimedia systems used for health promotion and education, as well as mental health well-being. The chapters in the book examine the innovative use of usability testing, communication campaigns, interactivity designs, persuasive messaging, gaming, social support, user-generated/participatory designed content, storytelling, data mining, empowerment strategies, immersive systems, and digital embodiment processes to achieve health communication goals. I admire the strategic use of clear commentary, theoretical analyses, and empirical research data to examine the uses of new health communication technologies in the different book chapters, helping to enrich understanding of new digital health information applications. I hope you enjoy reading and using this important book as much as I have!

References

Alpert, J., Desens, L., Krist, A., & Kreps, G. L. (2017). Measuring health literacy levels of a patient portal using the CDC's clear communication index. *Health Promotion Practice, 18*(1), 140−149, 1524839916643703.

Amann, J., Rubinelli, S., & Kreps, G. L. (2015). Revisiting the concept of health literacy: The patient as information seeker and provider. *The European Health Psychologist, 17*(6), 286−290.

Chang, B. L., Bakken, S., Brown, S. S., Houston, T. K., Kreps, G. L., Kukafka, R., Safran, C., & Stavri, P. Z. (2010). Bridging the digital divide: Reaching vulnerable populations. *Journal of the American Medical Informatics Association, 11*, 448−457.

Kreps, G. L. (2018). Communication and palliative care: E-health interventions and pain management. In R. Moore (Ed.), *Handbook of pain and palliative care: Biobehavioral approaches for the life course* (2nd edition). New York: Springer Publishers. https://doi.org/10.1007/978-3-319-95369-4_5.

Kreps, G. L. (2017). The relevance of health literacy to mHealth. *Information Services and Use, 37*(2), 123−130.

Kreps, G. L. (2015). Communication technology and health: The advent of ehealth applications. In L. Cantoni, & J. A. Danowski (Eds.), *Communication and Technology, Volume 5 of the Handbooks of Communication Science* (pp. 483−493) (P.J. Schulz & P. Cobley, General Editors). Berlin, Germany: De Gruyter Mouton Publications.

Kreps, G. L. (2014). Achieving the promise of digital health information systems. *Journal of Public Health Research, 3*(471), 128−129.

Kreps, G. L. (2011). The information revolution and the changing face of health communication in modern society. *Journal of Health Psychology, 16*, 192−193.

Kreps, G. L. (2009). Applying Weick's model of organizing to health care and health promotion: Highlighting the central role of health communication. *Patient Education and Counseling, 74*, 347−355.

Kreps, G. L., Burke-Garcia, A., & Wright, K. (2019). The use of digital communication channels to enhance environmental health literacy. In S. Finn, & L. O'Fallon (Eds.), *Environmental Health Literacy* (pp. 265−283). New York: Springer Publications.

Kreps, G. L., Gustafson, D., Salovey, P., Perocchia, R. S., Wilbright, W., Bright, M. A., & Muha, C. (2007). The NCI Digital Divide Pilot Projects: Implications for cancer education. *Journal of Cancer Education, 22*(Suppl. 1), S56−S60.

Kreps, G. L., & Neuhauser, L. (2013). Artificial intelligence and immediacy: Designing health communication to personally engage consumers and providers. *Patient Education and Counseling, 92*, 205−210.

Kreps, G. L., & Neuhauser, L. (2010). New directions in ehealth communication: Opportunities and challenges. *Patient Education and Counseling, 78*, 329−336.

Neuhauser, L., & Kreps, G. L. (2014). Integrating design science theory and methods to improve the development and evaluation of health communication programs. *Journal of Health Communication, 19*(12), 1460−1471.

Preface

Aims and purposes of this book

With the advent of various applications of innovative health technology, scholars from various disciplines, health practitioners, and health industries seek to find better ways to use new technology for health promotion. This book examines how various technologies can be used for attitude and behavior changes for health promotion. Specifically, this book is focused on technology as a tool that delivers media content based on an understanding of distinct features of each technology. It covers why and how specific technology (e.g., virtual reality (VR), augmented reality (AR), and social media) is effective in promoting good health and also suggests how it should be designed, utilized, and evaluated for health interventions.

This book provides unique perspectives. This book's focus is not only on the media content (e.g., what the health-related contents on the media do to people) but also on the distinct features of media/technology for health. In this book, world-renowned experts share their understanding of each technology as well as their experiences with using the technology for health promotion. We hope that the readers receive valuable information from this book that will help them design health technology interventions or research projects.

In all, the primary goal of this book is to provide an overview of how technology can be used to enhance health. Importantly, this book synthesizes theory-driven research with implications for research and practice, covering a range of theories and technologies in the diverse health contexts.

Intended audience and field of study

This edited book is primarily written for academics who are interested in using technology for health promotion. Considering the interdisciplinary nature of the topic, this book is not limited to a specific discipline. Rather, it can be beneficial for academics in diverse disciplines, such as Communication, Public Health, Information Science, Computer Science, Medicine, and Psychology.

Additionally, this book also has value for health practitioners. This book provides meaningful implications for practice, and they are discussed throughout the chapters. It can provide valuable information to practitioners, who are looking for theory-driven health intervention strategies using technology.

Scope of this book and content

This book provides an overview of how each technology can be used for promoting health. Specifically, there are five parts in this book. Part I is focused on "Theory and its Application for Health Promotion," in which four chapters provide theoretical frameworks that promote the understanding of why and how technology can be helpful for promoting health. Part II is focused on "VR+AR: Technology for Health in Virtual World," in which three chapters provide an overview of VR, AR, and how and why these technologies are helpful for health promotion. Part III is focused on "MHealth: Mobile Technology for Health," in which five chapters introduce the use of mobile technologies for health from both theoretical and empirical perspectives. Part IV is focused on "Social Media: Networked Technology for Health," in which two chapters provide how social media can be used in the health context. Part V is focused on "How Technology Change our Mind and Behavior," in which three chapters provide empirical support for the importance of technology for both physical and mental health.

Jihyun Kim
Hayeon Song

PART I

Theory and its application
for health promotion

1

The use of interactive technologies in health promotion and education: Theorizing potential interaction between health message content and message modality

Kai Kuang

Department of Communication Studies, Bloomsburg University of
Pennsylvania, Bloomsburg, PA, United States

Technology offers exciting opportunities for health promotion and education. In recent years, Internet-based public health intervention communication initiatives (e.g., e-Health) and mobile-health technology-based interventions (e.g., m-Health) are gaining more attention (e.g., Bennett & Glasgow, 2009; Fotheringham, Owies, Leslie, & Owen, 2000). Health promotion and education delivered via new media, or information and communication technologies (ICTs) in general, could offer highly interactive experience for target audience, with distinctive and innovative technological features on the interface through which health messages are presented (e.g., Kreps & Neuhauser, 2010, 2013; Rafaeli & Ariel, 2007; Strecher, 2007; Strecher, Greenwood, Wang, & Dumont, 1999; Street & Rimal, 1997; Sundar, 2007). Theoretical advancements as well as empirical investigations on computer-, Internet-, and mobile technology—based health communication focus extensively on the construct of interactivity (e.g., Bucy & Tao, 2007; Kim & Stout, 2010; Rafaeli & Ariel, 2007; Sundar, 2007), located at the "confluence of mass and interpersonal communication" and "poised between traditional and innovative media" (Rafaeli &

Technology and Health
https://doi.org/10.1016/B978-0-12-816958-2.00001-0

3

Ariel, 2007, p. 378). Systematic reviews and meta-analyses have been conducted to examine the effectiveness of interactive interventions in health promotion and education initiatives (e.g., Foy et al., 2010; Free et al., 2013; Lustria et al., 2013). These reviews suggest that interactivity in health promotion and education has the potential to improve health outcomes as well as the effectiveness of communication. One goal of this chapter is to synthesize extant research with regard to conceptualizations and operationalizations of interactivity in health communication and review empirical studies that tested the effectiveness of these interactive health interventions.

In addition, research in health communication has theorized and tested the effects of different message content constructs (e.g., susceptibility, severity, self-efficacy, cues to action). Narrative and systematic reviews within different theoretical frameworks have also been conducted. These reviews synthesize the effects of different health messages and appeals on health outcomes and perceived message effectiveness (e.g., fear appeals, Witte & Allen, 2000; the extended parallel process model, Maloney, Lapinski, & Witte, 2011; the health belief model, Carpenter, 2010; the risk information seeking and processing model, Yang, Aloe, & Feeley, 2014). With the increasing popularity of health communication initiatives delivered via interactive technologies, it is important to consider these health message content constructs together with the key feature of interactivity in mediated health communication initiatives. Therefore, another goal of this chapter is to review literature on message content constructs and present an initial theorization of how message content constructs may influence health behaviors and message perceptions together with interactivity. In the following sections, literature on both interactivity and health message effects is reviewed.

Defining interactivity

Conceptualizations and operationalizations of interactivity

As a defining feature of online technologies and a key variable in understanding the uses and effects of media technologies (especially new media), interactivity has distinct conceptualizations adopted by different research traditions (e.g., Heeter, 1989; Jankowski & Hanssen, 1996; Rafaeli, 1988; Sundar, Kalyanaraman, & Brown, 2003; Walther, Pingree, Hawkins, & Buller, 2005). Most of the definitions in the literature focus on an exchange of information, processes of reciprocal communication, responsiveness, and some variation on user control (e.g., Walther et al., 2005). For example, earlier interactivity researchers define interactivity as existing when users have the potential to be not only the recipients but also the sources of content; in addition, interactivity relates to the interaction that takes place on a medium (December, 1996). This perspective focuses on processes of reciprocal influence between the users and the medium (Pavlik, 1996).

In a similar vein, interactivity can refer to the proportion of user contribution to existing activity on the site; that is, "the ratio of user activity to system activity" (Paisley, 1983, p. 155).[1] Heeter (1989) introduces six dimensions of media interactivity, including available choice, user effort, the extent to which the medium is responsive, system use monitoring, contributing information, and whether the medium facilitates interpersonal communication. These six dimensions are closely related to the technological aspects of the medium that enable interactivity. For example, a medium that allows users to leave comments and engage in live chat will be considered having a higher level of interactivity compared to a medium that only allows user to receive information (but not contribute information). Following this conceptualization, the corresponding operationalization of interactivity focuses on the technological aspects of the interactive features on the medium, including the number of functional characteristics such as hyperlinks and e-mail links, comment boxes, feedback forms, and chat rooms (e.g., Kiousis, 2002; Massey & Levy, 1999).

Further problematizing the construct of interactivity from a dichotomous state to a more sophisticated conceptualization, Steuer (1992) defines interactivity as related to how much a medium allows users to modify "the form and content of a mediated environment in real time" (p. 84). Other conceptualizations highlighted how much users maintain control in the process of communication. For example, scholars like Jensen (1998) and Newman (1991) define interactivity as the extent of user control afforded by the medium, specifically, the "potential ability to let the user exert an influence on the content and/or form of the mediated communication" (Jensen, 1998, p. 201). William, Rice, and Rogers (1988) define interactivity as the extent to which users maintain control and exchange roles in the process of communication. In Bucy and Tao's (2007) mediated moderation model of interactivity, the scholars extend the focus on the processes of reciprocal communication and exchange of information between the users and the medium or between users through technology. They conceptualize interactivity as technological attributes that enable such reciprocity and exchange and afford interaction. The focus on reciprocity in the conceptualization of interactivity is commonly adopted in research on online health communities. For example, in their investigation of interactivity in health support group websites, Harrison, Barlowa, and Williams (2007) conceptualize interactivity as the elements of the site that allow users to participate in online communities and interact

---

[1] This chapter focuses more on user versus system interactivity and less on peer-to-peer interactivity commonly found in social support literature and virtual health communities (e.g., Matzat & Rooks, 2014; Wise, Hamman, & Thorson, 2006).

with other users. In fact, interactivity has been identified as one of the key attributes of online support groups (Walther et al., 2005).

While some conceptualizations of interactivity focus on the nature of information exchange and the reciprocal processes, others highlight user's perceptions and actions of the medium (McMillan & Hwang, 2002; Sundar et al., 2003; Tremayne & Dunwoody, 2001). Indeed, some researchers would argue how users utilize the functions presented on a medium is more important that the media features themselves in determining interactivity (e.g., Kayany, Worting, & Forrest, 1996; McMillan & Hwang, 2002; Walther, 1994). For example, Newhagen, Cordes, and Levy (1995) conducted a content analysis of 650 Internet mail messages sent to NBC Nightly News about the impact of new technologies. Their findings suggest that the levels of interactivity of a medium are dependent upon people's perceptions. McMillan and Hwang (2002) argue that most of interactivity literature focuses on the communication processes or functions of a medium, while not much attention is paid to interactivity as a perception; that is, the extent to which users actually perceive the communication environment as interactive. In explicating an operational definition of interactivity that is perception based, they define interactivity as related to three overlapping constructs, including direction of communication, user control, and time (McMillan & Hwang, 2002). Interactive media allow users to engage in interpersonal, two-way communication, provide a range of navigational and content tools to allow for user control, and enable users to navigate through information in an efficient manner.

More recent conceptualizations of interactivity incorporate some combination of the different aspects reviewed above (e.g., Kiousis, 2002; Liu & Shrum, 2002; Sundar, 2007). For example, Sundar (2007) explicates the concept of interactivity and suggests that three forms exist: medium (modality) interactivity, message interactivity, and source interactivity. Medium or modality interactivity refers to the features, tools, or modalities available on the medium that allows users to access and interact with information. This is also referred to as the functional view, which focuses on the breadth of functions offered by a medium such as sliders and zoom features that allow the users to have more control over the interface compared to a webpage that does not have these functions (Xu & Sundar, 2014). In addition, message interactivity is related to the nature of information exchange that takes place between the user and the medium and between the users. Specifically, this kind of interactivity is operationalized by organizing the information on the interface into different layers through the use of hyperlinks and navigation tools (Sundar, Jia, Waddell, & Huang, 2015). This is also labeled as the contingency view. Last but not least, source interactivity refers to the extent to which users serve as the sources of information in mediated environments, as they have control over the flow and nature of content on the interface.

In sum, conceptualizations and operationalizations of interactivity in the literature focus on distinct aspects of the construct. Some emphasize the nature of information exchange, reciprocal communication process, mutual discourse (i.e., two-way communication), and user control (e.g., Jensen, 1998; Newman, 1991), while others highlight functions and features on the interface (e.g., Massey & Levy, 1999; Sundar, 2007). Some approaches propose that user perception of interactivity is a crucial part of the construct, in addition to message and modality interactivity (e.g., Kiousis, 2002; McMillan & Hwang, 2002). Based on these existing conceptualizations of interactivity in literature, interactivity can be summarized as given below.

Interactivity refers to (a) the degree to which users maintain control by making decisions among the available choices they have on the interface; (b) the extent to which users can both consume and contribute information on the interface by using navigational and content tools, accepting and processing responses from the medium, and modifying the form and content of the medium; (c) the extent to which reciprocal influence and mutual dependence are demonstrated in the process of interaction between users and the medium, and between users; and (d) the degree to which users themselves perceive the mediated communication environment as interactive.

Effects of interactivity

Although defined with distinct conceptual and operational foci, researchers have consistently detected significant main effects of interactive intervention in the literature, especially within health communication research and practice. This section reviews literature on the effects of interactivity on information seeking, learning, persuasion, and health outcomes within areas related to health communication.

Several theoretical frameworks in the interactivity literature have explicated different ways through which interactivity can generate effects. Sundar's theory of interactive media effects (TIME; Sundar, 2007; Sundar et al., 2015), for instance, proposes that the three forms of interactivity may function in related but distinctive ways, all of which will lead to higher levels of user engagement. Specifically, modality interactivity (i.e., functional view) would lead to greater engagement by enhancing users' perceptual bandwidth (Reeves & Nass, 2000; Sundar, 2007). In other words, the interactive functions can help individuals expand and envision the range of things they can do with the medium (i.e., perceptual bandwidth). Message interactivity (i.e., contingency view) leads to greater engagement and elaboration of the information by enhancing the interdependency (contingency) in the message exchange process. In comparison, source interactivity can positively influence engagement by enhancing users' ability to contribute content (e.g., customize and create content as a source).

Bucy and Tao (2007) further problematize the processes through which interactivity generates effects. In their mediated moderation model of interactivity, the scholars identify the roles of technological attributes of a medium, user perceptions about interactivity, and individual differences such as Internet self-efficacy in influencing the outcomes of interactivity. Their model proposes that interactive attributes of an interface would influence affect, behavior, and cognition through user perception. This process, however, may be moderated by individual differences such as Internet self-efficacy (e.g., Eastin & LaRose, 2000). For example, users with varying levels of Internet self-efficacy, defined as "the belief in one's capabilities to organize and execute courses of Internet actions required to produce given attainments" (Eastin & LaRose, 2000, p. 611), may evaluate interactive technological attributes in different ways. Those with higher Internet self-efficacy may favor interactive technologies, while those with lower Internet self-efficacy avoid them (Bucy & Tao, 2007).

Empirical evidence of interactivity effects

In the interactivity literature, researchers have examined the effects of interactive versus noninteractive health interventions (e.g., classroom lessons vs. brochures, Burger et al., 2003), as well as interventions with varying levels of interactivity (e.g., interactive computer-based instruction programs vs. video vs. pamphlet, Champion et al., 2006; telephone tailoring vs. print tailoring, Champion et al., 2007). Empirical evidence in health communication literature, in general, supports the effectiveness of interactivity. For example, in a nutrition intervention with rural low-income women, researchers found that the interactive intervention group had significantly improved performance on nutrition-related information 3 months after receiving nutrition information, compared to the control group (Tessaro, Rye, Parker, Mangone, & McCrone, 2007). In another study, Stevens and colleagues (Stevens, Glasgow, Toobert, Karanja, & Smitha, 2003) found that participants who received an interactive, computer-based intervention showed significant effects in reducing their dietary fat intake and increasing fruit and vegetable consumption compared to the control group. Their 12-month follow-up data suggested the effectiveness of their interactive intervention on all dietary outcome variables, providing evidence for the effectiveness of interactivity. Similarly, De Bourdeaudhuij, Stevens, Vandelanotte, and Brug (2007) evaluated an interactive, computer-tailored fat reduction intervention. They found that the interactive intervention was significantly more effective in decreasing participants' fat intake compared to the generic intervention group and no-intervention control group 6 months after the baseline data collection. In fish consumption advisories context, Burger et al. (2003) study compared the effectiveness of a brochure and an interactive, classroom lesson. Their results suggested that participants who received the interactive lesson had a significantly better understanding compared to those who received the brochure. Lustria (2007) conducted an experiment to examine interactivity's effects on comprehension of health information presented on two interactive websites on skin cancer and attitudes toward the websites. Results of the experiment suggested that participants in the high interactivity group had higher comprehension scores. They also had more positive attitudes toward the health websites. Such empirical evidence supports the effectiveness of using interactive medium to communicate about and promote health.

In addition to comparing interactive versus noninteractive health promotion initiatives, researchers have also sought to understand the mechanism through which interactivity generates effects. For example, some researchers argue that interactive, computer-tailored interventions are better at providing participants with personally adapted feedback about their current health conditions, behavioral determinants, and personally adapted suggestions to change behaviors (De Bourdeaudhuij et al., 2007; De Vries & Brug, 1999; Kreuter, Farrell, Olevitch, & Brennam, 2000; Ryan & Lauver, 2002). In a similar vein, Block et al. (2000) focused on using an interactive CD-ROM for nutrition screening and counseling and found that nearly 80% of the participants reported learning new information about health and nutrition or their own dietary habits. A posttest 2–4 weeks later showed that more than 50% of the participants experienced behavioral change and put some of their dietary goals into practices. The researchers concluded that the interactive program was useful for dietary screening, feedback, skill building, and motivation. Related to motivation and goal setting, Booth, Nowson, and Matters (2008) evaluated an interactive, Internet-based weight loss program and examined the effectiveness of online interventions that included individual goal setting and feedback. Specifically, they assessed two online weight reduction programs: one included dietary advice plus exercise (ED) and the other was an exercise-only program (EX). Their findings suggested that both groups increased their daily exercise after participating in the interactive programs.

Burger et al. (2003) findings suggest that interactivity may contribute to message effectiveness and behavioral change in that it allows refinement for specific local conditions. In addition to highlighting the potential of interactive media to tailor information to users based on their needs, scholars propose that interactive presentational format increases user engagement with the message as well as their decision-making, improves learning, and increases attractiveness of the message and the interface (e.g., Bucy & Tao, 2007; Walther et al., 2005). Indeed, one of interactivity's advantages lies in its ability to expand perceptual bandwidth (Reeves & Nass, 2000; Sundar, 2007; Sundar et al., 2015) and promote cognitive flexibility and constructivist learning (e.g., Cairncross & Mannion, 2001; Spiro & Jehng, 1990). According to Spiro and Jehng (1990), cognitive flexibility is the "the ability to spontaneously restructure one's knowledge" in order to adapt to changing situations (p. 165). Constructivist learning theories suggest that users are actively involved in the information processing and have the power to construct their own meaning of new information (e.g., Cairncross & Mannion, 2001; Jonassen, 1999). Interactivity can, therefore, enhance information processing and learning as users utilize the technological attributes available on the interface.

The proposition that interactivity has the potential to enhance both information processing and learning has also found empirical support in health contexts. For example, Kim and Stout (2010) developed a theoretical model of website interactivity and proposed that interactivity would have significant impact on information processing, involvement with communication, as well as individuals' knowledge and attitudes. In this study, interactivity was manipulated based on two dimensions: coherence and relevance in user control over the message sequence. Specifically, in high interactivity condition, participants were able to choose topics of their interest and read information relevant for the topics they chose. In contrast, participants in the low interactivity condition viewed the information in a random order. The authors tested their model within the context of mental illness (i.e., schizophrenia). The results of their experiment suggested that interactivity did enhance message comprehensibility and involvement, while reducing mental illness stigma and increasing perceptions of severity of mental illness. This shows that interactivity could impact not only proximal outcomes such as message involvement and processing but also distal outcomes such as beliefs and attitudes about a health condition or health behavior.

Inconsistent findings in the literature

While much of the literature supports the proposition that interactivity can and should be effective in health promotion, some inconsistent findings do exist. Reviews of interactive information and communication systems, for example, have found that these were at times "superior to and at times no better than other media with respect to educational and health outcomes" (Street & Rimal, 1997, p. 9). The distinctive ways in which interactivity is conceptualized and operationalized reviewed above, in part, contribute to these mixed findings. Interactivity scholars have also suggested that other factors such as technological efficacy or communication efficacy may influence the learning and comprehension processes on the interactive interface (e.g., Aldrich, Rogers, & Scaife, 1998; Narayanan & Hegarty, 2002). In addition, individual characteristics such as cognitive skills and ability to search information on an interactive medium could also influence learning outcomes (e.g., Newhagen & Rafaeli, 1996).

Indeed, in the interactivity literature, there are cases where interactive presentational formats are not more effective, or even less effective than noninteractive presentation formats. For instance, researchers have compared the effectiveness of an interactive, computer-based fat reduction intervention and a print-delivered version of identical content (Kroeze, Oenema, Campbell, & Brug, 2008). Their findings suggest similar short-term effects on fat intake in the interactive versus print-delivered computer-tailored interventions. However, the effects of the print-delivered tailored feedback were maintained in the longer term compared to the interactive intervention. One possible explanation for this unexpected finding, according to the researchers, was that participants may be more likely to keep and reread print-delivered information, which tended to be read and saved more often (Kroeze et al., 2008; Oenema, Tan, & Brug, 2005). Compared to on-screen information, printed information may enhance memorability and/or cognitive processing due to ease of reading.

In a meta-analysis that quantitatively synthesized the association between interactive, computer-based communication, and learning outcomes in health professions (Cook et al., 2008), researchers have found that compared with no intervention, interactive instructional methods had large positive effects on learning. However, compared with noninteractive instructions, the effects of interactive instructional methods were generally small and heterogeneous. All of the inconsistent findings reviewed above suggest the need for more research to better understand how moderators (e.g., message features, individual characteristics) may influence the effects of interactivity in health promotion. This chapter focuses on the potential interaction effects between interactivity and message content constructs, which will be discussed next.

Message content constructs

Building on and extending persuasion theories and social learning theories, health communication research in the past decades has identified key constructs in health communication and promotion (e.g., Bandura, 1998, Rimal & Real, 2003; Rogers, 1983; Witte, 1992a, 1992b). Different theoretical frameworks put varying emphasis on which constructs matter more in health promotion initiatives. Among these constructs, threat and efficacy have been identified as two key constructs in influencing individuals' health behavior across existing theoretical frameworks, such as the health belief model (Janz & Becker, 1984; Kirscht, 1988), the EPPM (Witte, 1992a, 1992b), the protection motivation theory (PMT; Rogers, 1975, 1983), and the transtheoretical model (Prochaska, DiClemente, & Norcross, 1992).

For example, the extended parallel process model (EPPM; Witte, 1992a, 1992b), one of the most widely used theories in fear appeal literature, proposes that individuals' perceptions about a threat determine whether they would be motivated to engage in risk preventative behaviors. In addition, their perceptions about efficacy determine what they would do about the threat. A threat is defined as "a danger or harm that exists in the environment whether individuals know it or not" (Witte, 1992a, p. 114). Specifically, two types of threat have been identified in health communication literature: actual threat and perceived threat (e.g., Fischhoff, Slovic, Lichtenstein, Read, & Combs, 1978; Slovic, 1987; Slovic, Fischhoff, & Lichtenstein, 1982). Different from actual threats, perceived threats are individuals' thoughts and cognitions about a threat or a harm. Research has shown that it is the perceived threat that drives individuals' motivation to protect themselves, not the actual threat.

Theoretical frameworks such as the EPPM and the health belief model operationalize perceived threat into two dimensions: perceived severity of the threat and perceived susceptibility to the threat (e.g., Rosenstock, 1974; Witte, 1992a). Perceived severity refers to the magnitude and significance of the threat, while perceived susceptibility to the threat refers to one's belief about the probability of them experiencing the threat.

Efficacy, on the other hand, refers to individuals' perceptions of their ability to produce an outcome and to perform a behavior, or the ability of an external entity (e.g., a course of action) to achieve the outcome or behavior (Bandura, 1994). In health communication research, the general sense of efficacy is operationalized as self-efficacy and response efficacy (e.g., Rogers, 1983; Witte, 1992a, 1992b). Self-efficacy refers to "people's beliefs about their capabilities to produce designated levels of performance that exercise influence over events that affect their lives" (Bandura, 1994, p. 71). In comparison, response efficacy refers to one's belief that to perform a recommended response to a threat can indeed avert the threat. In many cases, response efficacy is a prerequisite for an individual to consider whether he/she is capable of performing the recommended behavior, and furthermore, for her/him to carry out the recommendations. Consistent with the EPPM, the PMT proposes that individuals' health behaviors are influenced by their evaluations of (a) severity of the event, (b) probability of the event occurring, (c) belief in the efficacy of a coping behavior to remove the threat (i.e., coping response efficacy), and (d) the individual's perception about their ability to carry out the recommended behavior (i.e., self-efficacy). Empirical evidence in the PMT literature suggests that perceived efficacy of the recommended health behavior to achieve the desired outcome is the key predictor of behavioral intentions and actual behavioral changes (e.g., Struckman-Johnson, Gilliland, Struckman-Johnson, & North, 1990; Tanner, Hunt, & Eppright, 1991).

Persuasion theories such as the EPPM and PMT suggest that individuals initiate two appraisals after they read a health promotion message: they first appraise the threat of a risk and then the efficacy of recommended health behaviors. One's appraisals of these two aspects will subsequently influence their belief, attitude, and behavior (Rogers, 1983; Witte, 1992a, 1992b). That is, only when individuals perceive great threat (severity and susceptibility) would they be motivated to begin the second (efficacy) appraisal. If the threat is perceived to be trivial or irrelevant, individuals will not be motivated to process the message any further. That means the second appraisal (i.e., evaluation of efficacy) will be superficially examined or the process will not be started at all. In general, perceived threat determines whether health promotion messages will be accepted or rejected and whether they would process the message (e.g., Witte, 1992a). After an individual perceives higher threat, their perceived efficacy will determine whether cognitive or reactive processes are initiated; that is, the nature of the reaction depends on perceived efficacy (Witte, 1992a).

Empirical evidence in the literature provides support for the important roles of threat and efficacy. For example, a meta-analysis synthesizing the fear appeal literature suggests that fear appeal messages impact perceived severity and susceptibility. Specifically, compared to low fear appeals and weak fear appeals, stronger fear appeals lead to higher perceived severity and susceptibility and are more persuasive. Moreover, messages with strong fear appeals and high efficacy produce lead to the greatest behavioral change (e.g., condom use, smoking cessation, flossing). Messages with strong fear appeals and low efficacy lead to the greatest defensive responses (e.g., defensive avoidance, denial, wishful thinking).

Message modality (interactivity) and message content (threat and efficacy)

As reviewed above, a significant body of research has provided support for the effectiveness of interactivity in health communication, both in terms of communication among care providers (e.g., primary care physicians and specialists) and effectively changing public health behavior through interactive interventions (e.g., Foy et al., 2010; Lustria et al., 2013). Importantly, the literature has recognized the importance of including threat and efficacy in messages to promote self-protective health behaviors (see Maloney et al., 2011 for a review; Witte & Allen, 2000). Scholars, however, have not connected research on interactivity with threat and efficacy, with only one exception (Kuang & Cho, 2016). That is, does presenting threat and efficacy messages on an interactive interface make a difference in terms of their impacts on message involvement, acceptance, attitude, and health behavior? If so, what kind of difference does it make? This section seeks to answer this question.

Interaction between message content and modality

The literature suggests that threat and efficacy are two crucial components to effectively communicate health information and further motivate change in health behavior. While these are psychological constructs, communication scholars are interested in how to communicate threat and efficacy information to the target audience. This line of research would suggest that a highly effective health promotion message should persuade people that they are susceptible to a severe health threat, that the recommended action would be effective, and that they are able to perform the recommended action, which will in turn help to reduce their level of risk for the health threat (e.g., Witte, 1992b). In health communication and promotion literature, much has been done to understand persuasive strategies such as message framing (e.g., gain vs. loss; see O'Keefe & Jensen, 2007 for a meta-analysis), emotional appeals (e.g., fear appeal; see Witte & Allen, 2000 for a meta-analysis), or one-sided versus two-sided messages (see O'Keefe, 1999 and Allen, 1991 for meta-analyses). However, not much attention is paid to the question about how to present threat and efficacy messages on an interactive medium, a powerful interface that has the potential to enhance user control, two-way communication, and reciprocal influence and expand users' perceptual bandwidth (e.g., Bucy & Tao, 2007; McMillan & Hwang, 2002; Sundar, 2007). Given the power and prevalence of interactive, computer- or Internet-based health interventions, it is necessary to examine and better understand how message content constructs can be translated into effective health promotion message presented on interactive platforms. Importantly, the literature also suggests that factors that influence persuasive processes and effects tend to be multiplicative (cf. multiple roles for variables; Petty, Wheeler, & Tormala, 2003). Health communication and promotion literature has not focused much on the multiplicity between message content constructs such as threat and efficacy and message modality constructs such as interactivity, and this chapter proposes a theoretical framework that highlights the interaction between message content and message modality and proposes that more research needs to be conducted within this area.

Specifically, in order to better understand how to utilize new technology for health-related cognitive and behavioral change, more research is necessary to unpack what is the "right information" to be presented on interactive interfaces for health promotion purposes (e.g., Kreps, 2017; Kreps & Neuhauser, 2010). The advancements of technology have brought exciting opportunities for health communication and promotion research and practice, and the feature of interactivity offers unique power to engage a large number of audience easily and the potential to tailor information to specific individual needs. In fact, some scholars suggest that interactivity could be the communication attribute that has the greatest power to improve health promotion (Rice, 2001; Street & Rimal, 1997). The effectiveness of interactivity can be realized because of the technological functions that allow user participation in both the communicative process and the content creation, modification, and exchange, yet we do not know how interactivity may function together with different message content. To address this void in the literature, the theoretical framework of interaction between message content and modality is proposed (see Fig. 1.1). At this stage, the framework offers an overarching conceptual model for research in this area, with three specific propositions:

Proposition 1: Message modality constructs such as interactivity will interact with message content constructs such as threat and efficacy in influencing users' information processing of and engagement with the health message.

Proposition 2: The extent to which users engage with and process the health message will subsequently impact learning and persuasive outcomes, including health beliefs, attitudes, and behaviors.

Proposition 3: Information processing and message engagement will mediate the interaction effects between message content constructs and message modality constructs (i.e., mediated moderation).

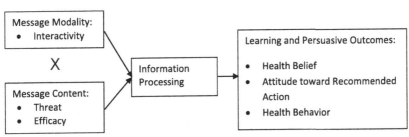

FIGURE 1.1   Theoretical framework of interaction between message modality and message content.

Proposition 2 has been well established in the literature, while proposition 3 builds on the first two propositions. The following section further elaborates on proposition 1 by explicating the possible directions of interaction between interactivity and message content constructs, using threat and efficacy (EPPM; Witte, 1992a) as an example.

Possible directions of interaction and implications

EPPM (Witte, 1992a; 1992b) suggests that threat and efficacy present four combinations of response to a health message. First, high-threat high-efficacy, in which individuals are motivated to protect themselves from the health risk by performing the recommended behavior. Second, high-threat low-efficacy, in which people are less motivated to take self-protective actions due to their low efficacy and tend to avoid information that emphasizes their high-risk health status. Third, low-threat high-efficacy individuals, who perceive strong efficacy beliefs yet do not perceive themselves as at risk. And last, low-threat low-efficacy, in which people do not consider themselves to be vulnerable to the risk, nor do they think they are capable of undertaking the actions to avert the threat. Working from the EPPM, Rimal and Real (2003) advanced the risk perception attitude framework and labeled these four attitudinal groups as responsive (high risk and high efficacy), avoidance (high risk and low efficacy), proactive (low risk and high efficacy), and indifference (low risk and low efficacy). They proposed that these four attitudinal groups would differ in their self-protective motivation and information seeking intention and behavior and found empirical support for their proposition (Rimal & Real, 2003).

EPPM's prediction that high-threat, high-efficacy perception would motivate individuals to protect themselves from the health risk and engage more with the information presented is well established and supported in the literature. The question that remains unanswered is what if the different combinations of threat and efficacy messages are presented on interfaces that vary in the extent to which they are interactive? How, if at all, would message content constructs such as threat and efficacy interact with message modality constructs such as interactivity in influencing communicative, learning, and persuasive outcomes?

The literature suggests that the effects of interactivity may differ depending on whether the messages presented involve high or low threat and efficacy components. Specifically, the interactivity effects literature reviewed earlier proposes that interactivity would be positively associated with message involvement as a result of its ability to help individuals envision and expand the range of things they can do with the interactive interface (i.e., perceptual bandwidth; Reeves & Nass, 2000; Sundar, 2007). For those individuals who read high-threat, high-response efficacy message content, presenting the information in a highly interactive format would help them increase perception of user control and expand perceptual bandwidth, leading to more actively engaged information processing. As a result, individuals' attitudes toward the recommended health behavior would be influenced accordingly; those who are more actively involved in the message would be more likely to think about the information and make judgments based on the message (e.g., Cox & Cox, 1991; Petty & Cacioppo, 1986). Therefore, learning and persuasive outcomes may be enhanced.

In contrast, for those who read high-threat, low-efficacy messages, they perceive the need to take self-protective actions resulting from the high threat. However, they also feel limited due to their low-efficacy perception and may engage in defensive responses such as avoidance, denial, and wishful thinking (Witte, 1992a). While high-efficacy message could strengthen intentions to engage in the information presented and in the use of a rational problem-solving approach to the threat, low-efficacy message could lead to more fatalistic or religious attitudes. That is, when individuals face a dreadful situation but perceive that they have no effective coping response (i.e., low efficacy), they may either resign themselves from the situation or engage in a form of acceptance that is either philosophical (fatalism) or spiritual (religious faith) (Rippetoe & Rogers, 1987). In this case, whether threat and efficacy messages are presented with high, medium, or low interactivity may not influence information processing or learning and persuasive outcomes, due to the lack of motivation among the "avoidance" group (Rimal & Real, 2003). Therefore, interactivity may have little to no impact for those who read high-threat, low-efficacy messages.

However, it is also possible that high-threat, low-efficacy perception could motivate active message scrutiny and involvement and even motivate information seeking (e.g., Block & Keller, 1995; Gleicher & Petty, 1992; Rimal & Real, 2003). For example, in the contexts of sexually transmitted disease and skin cancer, Block and Keller (1995) found that low-efficacy messages motivated more in-depth information processing, which subsequently led to higher information seeking intention. Similarly, Rimal and Real (2003) found that high-threat, low-efficacy messages led to more information seeking intention compared to the control group. If low-efficacy messages can indeed motivate information seeking behavior as a result of heightened uncertainty (as opposed to engage in defensive motivation and initiate fear control process), then presenting the message in a highly interactive format may make a difference in learning and persuasive outcomes. That is, when reading a high-threat, low-efficacy messages, individuals who can utilize enhanced control, speed, range, and mapping of information on a highly interactive medium (Steuer, 1992) would have better coping outcomes in response to the low-efficacy perceptions. In comparison, messages presented in a noninteractive format will limit user experience with the medium, further aggravating the uncertainty and possible anxiety associated with low-efficacy perception, resulting in avoidance and initiation of fear control process.

Along with this line of thinking, those with high-threat, high-efficacy perceptions may initiate danger control process and are ready to take self-protective action to reduce the threat (Witte, 1992a). In this case, presenting the information in either highly interactive or noninteractive presentational format may not influence users' involvement with the message or the learning and persuasive outcomes much, as little or no analysis of the situation is needed (e.g., Block & Keller, 1995). Therefore, interactivity for those who read high-threat, high-efficacy messages may not be as effective.

As can been seen from the discussion above, interactivity as a prominent feature of ICT-based health education and promotion initiatives may generate effects together with health message content in competing and complicated ways. Importantly, health information delivered via highly interactive channels may be especially effective for those with low-efficacy perceptions (e.g., Rimal & Real, 2003) because of its ability to enhance user control (or perceptions of user control) and information seeking. Beyond the threat and efficacy constructs discussed in this chapter, interactivity may also enhance or inhibit the effects of other health message constructs. For example, how may interactivity function together with messages about social norms related to an illness condition? Is health information delivered via interactive channels useful to destigmatize a given condition or does it intensify existing knowledge gaps, because those interested would utilize interactive functions, while those resistant would not? These questions remain unanswered. More research in this area can enhance theoretical understanding about the psychological mechanisms of the interaction between message modality and content. Importantly, findings in this area can provide practical insights about when to use interactive channels to deliver health information, and what information to put on those channels. In addition, future research should examine the effects of interactivity on learning and behavioral outcomes for individuals with high-threat and low-efficacy perceptions. Findings within this area of research could offer insights for practitioners to motivate this group who are at risk but do not have confidence to address the risk issues.

It is also important to note that health is oftentimes contextual and situational. The health conditions individuals find themselves living in (e.g., acute vs. chronic conditions; different levels of uncertainty surrounding a certain condition) can also influence how interactivity interacts with health messages in information processing, message perceptions, and health outcomes. Research has also found that individual differences such as age may affect how people seek and engage with health information and interact with others about health-related topics online (e.g., Macias & McMillan, 2008). So far not much empirical evidence has been obtained to test the potential interaction between message content constructs (e.g., threat and efficacy) and message modality (e.g., interactivity), the conditions under which health information delivered via interactive medium is more or less effective, or how individual differences or specific health conditions may moderate such interactions.

This chapter reviews literature on interactivity with regard to its conceptualizations and operationalizations, together with theory and research that focuses on the effects of interactivity. In synthesizing this line of research and providing an initial theorization of the interaction effect between message content and message modality, this chapter seeks to draw more scholarly attention to the intersection of interactivity and message content constructs. Using two constructs that have been identified as key factors in motivating health behavior change—threat and efficacy—as examples, this chapter illustrates why and how interactivity and health messages may interact in their influences on communicative, learning, and persuasive outcomes. One empirical study tested the interaction effects among interactivity, threat, and efficacy on message involvement, attitude, and behavioral intention and is reviewed in a following chapter (Kuang & Cho, 2016). With the advancements in ICTs and the development of interactive features, health communication delivered via highly interactive interfaces serves as a promising means for effective and efficient health education and promotion initiatives. More research is needed to replicate the findings and to extend the message content constructs beyond the two reviewed (i.e., threat and efficacy) in this chapter.

Conclusion

New technology brings exciting opportunities for health promotion and education and has the potential to be much more influential than traditional formats of health communication (e.g., traditional media–based health campaigns). While much is known about the effects of interactive health interventions, little has been done to understand user experiences considering both *what* message is presented and *how* the message is presented. This chapter represents an initial attempt to theorize potential interaction between message content and message modality, elaborates the possible direction of interaction using threat, efficacy, and interactivity as an example, and calls for more research in this area to further extend theoretical and practical knowledge about new technology and health promotion.

References

Aldrich, F., Rogers, Y., & Scaife, M. (1998). Getting to grips with "interactivity": Helping teachers assess the educational value of CD-ROMs. *British Journal of Educational Technology, 29,* 321–332. https://doi.org/10.1111/1467-8535.00078.

Allen, M. (1991). Meta-analysis comparing the persuasiveness of one-sided and two-sided messages. *Western Journal of Speech Communication, 55,* 390–404. https://doi.org/10.1080/10570319109374395.

Bandura, A. (1994). Self-efficacy. In V. S. Ramachaudran (Ed.), *Encyclopedia of human behavior* (Vol. 4, pp. 71–81). New York: Academic Press.

Bandura, A. (1998). Health promotion from the perspective of social cognitive theory. *Psychology and Health, 13,* 623–649. https://doi.org/10.1080/08870449808407422.

Bennett, G. G., & Glasgow, R. E. (2009). The delivery of public health interventions via the Internet: Actualizing their potential. *Annual Review of Public Health, 30,* 273–292. https://doi.org/10.1146/annurev.publhealth.031308.100235.

Block, L. G., & Keller, P. A. (1995). When to accentuate the negative: The effects of perceived efficacy and message framing on intentions to perform a health-related behavior. *Journal of Marketing Research, 32,* 192–203. https://doi.org/10.2307/3152047.

Block, G., Miller, M., Harnack, L., Kayman, S., Mandel, S., & Cristofar, S. (2000). An interactive CD-ROM for nutrition screening and counseling. *American Journal of Public Health, 90,* 781–785.

Booth, A. O., Nowson, C. A., & Matters, H. (2008). Evaluation of an interactive, Internet-based weight loss program: A pilot study. *Health Education Research, 23,* 371–381. https://doi.org/10.1093/her/cyn007.

Bucy, E. P., & Tao, C. C. (2007). The mediated moderation model of interactivity. *Media Psychology, 9,* 647–672. https://doi.org/10.1080/15213260701283269.

Burger, J., McDermott, M. H., Chess, C., Bochenek, E., Perez-Lugo, M., & Pflugh, K. K. (2003). Evaluating risk communication about fish consumption advisories: Efficacy of a brochure versus a classroom lesson in Spanish and English. *Risk Analysis: An International Journal, 23,* 791–803. https://doi.org/10.1111/1539-6924.00356.

Cairncross, S., & Mannion, M. (2001). Interactive multimedia and learning: Realizing the benefits. *Innovations in Education and Teaching International, 38,* 156–164. https://doi.org/10.1080/14703290110035428.

Carpenter, C. J. (2010). A meta-analysis of the effectiveness of health belief model variables in predicting behavior. *Health Communication, 25,* 661–669. https://doi.org/10.1080/10410236.2010.521906.

Champion, V., Skinner, C. S., Hui, S., Monahan, P., Juliar, B., Daggy, J., & Menon, U. (2007). The effect of telephone versus print tailoring for mammography adherence. *Patient Education and Counseling, 65,* 416–423. https://doi.org/10.1016/j.pec.2006.09.014.

Champion, V. L., Springston, J. K., Zollinger, T. W., Saywell, R. M., Jr., Monahan, P. O., Zhao, Q., & Russell, K. M. (2006). Comparison of three interventions to increase mammography screening in low income African American women. *Cancer Detection and Prevention, 30,* 535–544. https://doi.org/10.1016/j.cdp.2006.10.003.

Cook, D. A., Levinson, A. J., Garside, S., Dupras, D. M., Erwin, P. J., & Montori, V. M. (2008). Internet-based learning in the health professions: A meta-analysis. *Journal of the American Medical Association, 300,* 1181–1196. https://doi.org/10.1001/jama.300.10.1181.

Cox, D., & Cox, A. D. (1991). Communicating the consequences of early detection: The role of evidence and framing. *Journal of Marketing, 65,* 91–103. https://doi.org/10.1509/jmkg.65.3.91.18336.

De Bourdeaudhuij, I., Stevens, V., Vandelanotte, C., & Brug, J. (2007). Evaluation of an interactive computer-tailored nutrition intervention in a real-Life setting. *Annals of Behavioral Medicine, 33,* 39–48. https://doi.org/10.1207/s15324796abm3301_5.

De Vries, H., & Brug, J. (1999). Computer-tailored interventions motivating people to adopt health promoting behaviors: Introduction to a new approach. *Patient Education and Counseling, 36*, 99–105. https://doi.org/10.1016/S0738-3991(98)00127-X.

December, J. (1996). Units of analysis for Internet communication. *Journal of Communication, 46*, 14–38. https://doi.org/10.1111/j.1460-2466.1996.tb01459.x.

Eastin, M. S., & LaRose, R. (2000). Internet self-efficacy and the psychology of the digital divide. *Journal of Computer-Mediated Communication, 6*, JCMC611. https://doi.org/10.1111/j.1083-6101.2000.tb00110.x.

Fischhoff, B., Slovic, P., Lichtenstein, S., Read, S., & Combs, B. (1978). How safe is safe enough? A psychometric study of attitudes towards technological risks and benefits. *Policy Sciences, 9*, 127–152. https://doi.org/10.1007/BF00143739.

Fotheringham, M. J., Owies, D., Leslie, E., & Owen, N. (2000). Interactive health communication in preventive medicine: Internet-based strategies in teaching and research. *American Journal of Preventive Medicine, 19*, 113–120. https://doi.org/10.1016/S0749-3797(00)00188-4.

Foy, R., Hempel, S., Rubenstein, L., Suttorp, M., Seelig, M., Shanman, R., & Shekelle, P. G. (2010). Meta-analysis: Effect of interactive communication between collaborating primary care physicians and specialists. *Annals of Internal Medicine, 152*, 247–258. https://doi.org/10.7326/0003-4819-152-4-201002160-00010.

Free, C., Phillips, G., Galli, L., Watson, L., Felix, L., Edwards, P., … Haines, A. (2013). The effectiveness of mobile-health technology-based health behaviour change or disease management interventions for health care consumers: A systematic review. *PLoS Medicine, 10*, e1001362. https://doi.org/10.1371/journal.pmed.1001362.

Gleicher, F., & Petty, R. E. (1992). Expectations of reassurance influence the nature of fear-stimulated attitude change. *Journal of Experimental Social Psychology, 28*, 86–100. https://doi.org/10.1016/0022-1031(92)90033-G.

Harrison, S., Barlow, J., & Williams, G. (2007). The content and interactivity of health support group websites. *Health Education Journal, 66*, 371–381. https://doi.org/10.1177/0017896907080123.

Heeter, C. (1989). Implications of new interactive technologies for conceptualizing communication. In J. Salvaggio, & J. Bryant (Eds.), *Media in the information age: Emerging patterns of adoption and consumer use* (pp. 217–235). Hillsdale, NJ: Lawrence Erlbaum.

Jankowski, N., & Hanssen, L. (1996). Introduction: Multimedia come of age. In N. Jankowski, & L. Hanssen (Eds.), *The contours of multimedia: Recent technological, theoretical and empirical developments* (pp. 1–20). Luton, UK: University of Luton Press.

Janz, N. K., & Becker, M. H. (1984). The health belief model: A decade later. *Health Education Quarterly, 11*, 1–47. https://doi.org/10.1177/109019818401100101.

Jensen, J. F. (1998). Interactivity: Tracking a new concept in media and communication studies. *Nordicom Review, 19*, 185–204.

Jonassen, D. H. (1999). Designing constructivist learning environments. In C. M. Reigeluth (Ed.), *Instructional design theories and models: A new paradigm of instructional theory* (pp. 215–239). Mahwah, NJ: Lawrence Erlbaum Associates.

Kayany, J. M., Worting, C. E., & Forrest, E. J. (1996). Relational control and interactive media choice in technology-mediated communication situations. *Human Communication Research, 22*, 399–421. https://doi.org/10.1111/j.1468-2958.1996.tb00373.x.

Kim, H., & Stout, P. A. (2010). The effects of interactivity on information processing and attitude change: Implications for mental health stigma. *Health Communication, 25*, 142–154. https://doi.org/10.1080/10410230903544936.

Kiousis, S. (2002). Interactivity: A concept explication. *New Media and Society, 4*, 355–383. https://doi.org/10.1177/146144480200400303.

Kirscht, J. P. (1988). The health belief model and predictions of health actions. In D. S. Gochman (Ed.), *Health behavior* (pp. 27–41). Boston, MA: Springer.

Kreps, G. L. (2017). Online information and communication systems to enhance health outcomes through communication convergence. *Human Communication Research, 43,* 518–530. https://doi.org/10.1111/hcre.12117.

Kreps, G. L., & Neuhauser, L. (2010). New directions in eHealth communication: Opportunities and challenges. *Patient Education and Counseling, 78,* 329–336. https://doi.org/10.1016/j.pec.2010.01.013.

Kreps, G. L., & Neuhauser, L. (2013). Artificial intelligence and immediacy: Designing health communication to personally engage consumers and providers. *Patient Education and Counseling, 92,* 205–210. https://doi.org/10.1016/j.pec.2013.04.014.

Kreuter, M., Farrell, D., Olevitch, L., & Brennam, L. (2000). *Tailoring health messages: Customizing communication with computer technology.* Mahwah, NJ: Lawrence Erlbaum Associates, Inc.

Kroeze, W., Oenema, A., Campbell, M., & Brug, J. (2008). The efficacy of Web-based and print-delivered computer-tailored interventions to reduce fat intake: Results of a randomized, controlled trial. *Journal of Nutrition Education and Behavior, 40,* 226–236. https://doi.org/10.1016/j.jneb.2007.09.008.

Kuang, K., & Cho, H. (2016). Delivering vaccination messages via interactive channels: Examining the interaction among threat, response efficacy, and interactivity in risk communication. *Journal of Risk Research, 19,* 476–495. https://doi.org/10.1080/13669877.2014.988284.

Liu, Y., & Shrum, L. J. (2002). What is interactivity and is it always such a good thing? Implications of definition, person, and situation for the influence of interactivity on advertising effectiveness. *Journal of Advertising, 31,* 53–64. https://doi.org/10.1080/00913367.2002.10673685.

Lustria, M. L. A. (2007). Can interactivity make a difference? Effects of interactivity on the comprehension of and attitudes toward online health content. *Journal of the American Society for Information Science and Technology, 58,* 766–776. https://doi.org/10.1002/asi.20557.

Lustria, M. L. A., Noar, S. M., Cortese, J., Van Stee, S. K., Glueckauf, R. L., & Lee, J. (2013). A meta-analysis of web-delivered tailored health behavior change interventions. *Journal of Health Communication, 18,* 1039–1069. https://doi.org/10.1080/10810730.2013.768727.

Macias, W., & McMillan, S. (2008). The return of the house call: The role of Internet-based interactivity in bringing health information home to older adults. *Health Communication, 23,* 34–44. https://doi.org/10.1080/10410230701805174.

Maloney, E. K., Lapinski, M. K., & Witte, K. (2011). Fear appeals and persuasion: A review and update of the extended parallel process model. *Social and Personality Psychology Compass, 5,* 206–219. https://doi.org/10.1111/j.1751-9004.2011.00341.x.

Massey, B. L., & Levy, M. R. (1999). Interactivity, online journalism and English-language web newspapers in Asia. *Journalism and Mass Communication Quarterly, 76,* 138–151. https://doi.org/10.1177/107769909907600110.

Matzat, U., & Rooks, G. (2014). Styles of moderation in online health and support communities: An experimental comparison of their acceptance and effectiveness. *Computers in Human Behavior, 36,* 65–75. https://doi.org/10.1016/j.chb.2014.03.043.

McMillan, S. J., & Hwang, J. S. (2002). Measures of perceived interactivity: An exploration of the role of direction of communication, user control, and time in shaping perceptions of interactivity. *Journal of Advertising, 31,* 29–42. https://doi.org/10.1080/00913367.2002.10673674.

Narayanan, N. H., & Hegarty, M. (2002). Multimedia design for communication of dynamic information. *International Journal of Human-Computer Studies, 57,* 279–315. https://doi.org/10.1006/ijhc.1019.

Newhagen, J. E., Cordes, J. W., & Levy, M. R. (1995). Nightly@nbc.com: Audience scope and the perception of interactivity in viewer mail on the Internet. *Journal of Communication, 45,* 164–175. https://doi.org/10.1111/j.1460-2466.1995.tb00748.x.

Newhagen, J. E., & Rafaeli, S. (1996). Why communication researchers should study the Internet: A dialogue. *Journal of Computer-Mediated Communication, 1.* https://doi.org/10.1111/j.1083-6101.1996.tb00172.x.

Newman, W. R. (1991). *The future of the mass audience.* Cambridge, MA: Cambridge University Press.

Oenema, A., Tan, F., & Brug, J. (2005). Short-term efficacy of a web-based computer-tailored nutrition intervention: Main effects and mediators. *Annals of Behavioral Medicine, 29,* 54–63. https://doi.org/10.1207/s15324796abm2901_8.

O'Keefe, D. J. (1999). How to handle opposing arguments in persuasive messages: A meta-analytic review of the effects of one-sided and two-sided messages. *Annals of the International Communication Association, 22,* 209–249. https://doi.org/10.1080/23808985.1999.11678963.

O'Keefe, D. J., & Jensen, J. D. (2007). The relative persuasiveness of gain-framed loss-framed messages for encouraging disease prevention behaviors: A meta-analytic review. *Journal of Health Communication, 12,* 623–644. https://doi.org/10.1080/10810730701615198.

Paisley, W. (1983). Computerizing information: Lessons of a videotext trial. *Journal of Communication, 33,* 153–161. https://doi.org/10.1111/j.1460-2466.1983.tb02381.x.

Pavlik, J. (1996). *New media technology: Cultural and commercial perspectives.* Boston: Allyn & Bacon.

Petty, R. E., & Cacioppo, J. T. (1986). *Communication and persuasion.* New York: Springer-Verlag.

Petty, R. E., Wheeler, S. C., & Tormala, Z. L. (2003). Persuasion and attitude change. In T. Millon, & M. J. Lerner (Eds.), *Comprehensive handbook of psychology* (pp. 353–382). New York: John Wiley & Sons.

Prochaska, J. O., DiClemente, C. C., & Norcross, J. C. (1992). In search of how people change: Applications to addictive behaviors. *American Psychologist, 47,* 1102–1114. https://doi.org/10.1037/0003-066X.47.9.1102.

Rafaeli, S. (1988). Interactivity: From new media to communication. In R. Hawkins, J. Weimann, & S. Pingree (Eds.), *Advancing communication science: Merging mass and interpersonal processes* (pp. 110–134). Newbury Park, CA: Sage.

Rafaeli, S., & Ariel, Y. (Eds.). (2007). *Assessing interactivity in computer-mediated research.* New York, NY: Oxford University Press Inc.

Reeves, B., & Nass, C. (2000). Perceptual user interfaces: Perceptual bandwidth. *Communications of the ACM, 43,* 65–70. https://doi.org/10.1145/330534.330542.

Rice, R. E. (2001). The Internet and health communication: A framework of experiences. In R. E. Rice, & J. E. Katz (Eds.), *The Internet and health communication.* Thousand Oaks, CA: Sage.

Rimal, R. N., & Real, K. (2003). Perceived risk and efficacy beliefs as motivators of change. *Human Communication Research, 29,* 370–399. https://doi.org/10.1111/j.1468-2958.2003.tb00844.x.

Rippetoe, P. A., & Rogers, R. W. (1987). Effects of components of protection-motivation theory on adaptive and maladaptive coping with a health threat. *Journal of Personality and Social Psychology, 52,* 596–604. https://doi.org/10.1037/0022-3514.52.3.596.

Rogers, R. W. (1975). A protection motivation theory of fear appeals and attitude change. *Journal of Psychology, 91,* 93–114. https://doi.org/10.1080/00223980.1975.9915803.

Rogers, R. W. (1983). Cognitive and physiological processes in fear appeals and attitude change: A revised theory of protection motivation. In R. E. Petty (Ed.), *Social psychophysiology* (pp. 153–176). New York: Guilford.

Rosenstock, I. M. (1974). Historical origins of the health belief model. *Health Education Monographs, 2,* 328–335. https://doi.org/10.1177/109019817400200403.

Ryan, P., & Lauver, D. R. (2002). The efficacy of tailored interventions. *Journal of Nursing Scholarship, 34,* 331–337. https://doi.org/10.1111/j.1547-5069.2002.00331.x.

Slovic, P. (1987). Perception of risk. *Science, 236,* 280–285. https://doi.org/10.1126/science.3563507.

Slovic, P., Fischhoff, B., & Lichtenstein, S. (1982). Why study risk perception? *Risk Analysis, 2,* 83–93. https://doi.org/10.1111/j.1539-6924.1982.tb01369.x.

Spiro, R., & Jehng, J. (1990). Cognitive flexibility, random access instruction and hypertext: Theory and technology for the nonlinear and multi-dimensional traversal of complex subject matter. In D. Nix, & R. Spiro (Eds.), *Cognition, education, and multimedia: Exploring ideas in high technology* (pp. 163–205). Hillsdale, NJ: Erlbaum.

Steuer, J. (1992). Defining virtual reality: Dimensions determining telepresence. *Journal of Communication, 42,* 73–93. https://doi.org/10.1111/j.1460-2466.1992.tb00812.x.

Stevens, V. J., Glasgow, R. E., Toobert, D. J., Karanja, N., & Smitha, K. S. (2003). One-year results from a brief, computer-assisted intervention to decrease consumption of fat and increase consumption of fruits and vegetables. *Preventive Medicine, 36,* 594–600. https://doi.org/10.1016/S0091-7435(03)00019-7.

Strecher, V. J. (2007). Internet methods for delivering behavioral and health-related interventions (EHealth). *Annual Review of Clinical Psychology, 3,* 53–76. https://doi.org/10.1146/annurev.clinpsy.3.022806.091428.

Strecher, V. J., Greenwood, T., Wang, C., & Dumont, D. (1999). Interactive multimedia and risk communication. *Journal of the National Cancer Institute Monographs, 25,* 134–149. https://doi.org/10.1093/oxfordjournals.jncimonographs.a024188.

Street, R. L., & Rimal, R. N. (1997). Health promotion and interactive technology: A conceptual foundation. In R. L. Street, W. R. Gold, & T. Mannings (Eds.), *Health promotion and interactive technology: Theoretical applications and future directions* (pp. 1–18). Mahwah, NJ: Lawrence Erlbaum Associates.

Struckman-Johnson, C. J., Gilliland, R. C., Struckman-Johnson, D. L., & North, T. C. (1990). The effects of fear of AIDS and gender on responses to fear-arousing condom advertisements. *Journal of Applied Social Psychology, 20,* 1396–1410. https://doi.org/10.1111/j.1559-1816.1990.tb01480.x.

Sundar, S. S. (2007). Social psychology of interactivity in human-website interaction. In A. N. Joinson, K. Y. A. McKenna, T. Postmes, & U.-D. Reips (Eds.), *The Oxford handbook of Internet psychology* (pp. 89–104). Oxford, England: Oxford University Press.

Sundar, S. S., Jia, H., Waddell, T. F., & Huang, Y. (2015). Toward a theory of interactive media effects (TIME): Four models for explaining how interface features affect user psychology. In S. S. Sundar (Ed.), *The handbook of the psychology of communication technology* (pp. 47–86). West Sussex, UK: John Wiley & Sons.

Sundar, S. S., Kalyanaraman, S., & Brown, J. (2003). Explicating web site interactivity: Impression formation effects in political campaign sites. *Communication Research, 30,* 30–59. https://doi.org/10.1177/0093650202239025.

Tanner, J. F., Jr., Hunt, J. B., & Eppright, D. R. (1991). The protection motivation model: A normative model of fear appeals. *Journal of Marketing, 55,* 36–45. https://doi.org/10.2307/1252146.

Tessaro, I., Rye, S., Parker, L., Mangone, C., & McCrone, S. (2007). Effectiveness of a nutrition intervention with rural low-income women. *American Journal of Health Behavior, 31,* 35–43. https://doi.org/10.5993/AJHB.31.1.4.

Tremayne, M., & Dunwoody, S. (2001). Interactivity, information processing, and learning on the World Wide web. *Science Communication, 23,* 111–134. https://doi.org/10.1177/1075547001023002003.

Walther, J. B. (1994). Anticipated ongoing interaction versus channel effects on relational communication in computer-mediated interaction. *Human Communication Research, 20,* 473–501. https://doi.org/10.1111/j.1468-2958.1994.tb00332.x.

Walther, J. B., Pingree, S., Hawkins, R. P., & Buller, D. B. (2005). Attributes of interactive online health information systems. *Journal of Medical Internet Research, 7,* e33. https://doi.org/10.2196/jmir.7.3.e33.

Williams, F., Rice, R., & Rogers, E. (1988). *Research methods and the new media*. New York: Free Press.

Wise, K., Hamman, B., & Thorson, K. (2006). Moderation, response rate, and message interactivity: Features of online communities and their effects on intent to participate. *Journal of Computer-Mediated Communication, 12*, 24–41. https://doi.org/10.1111/j.1083-6101.2006.00313.x.

Witte, K. (1992a). Fear control and danger control: A test of the extended parallel process model (EPPM). *Communication Monographs, 61*, 113–134. https://doi.org/10.1080/03637759409376328.

Witte, K. (1992b). Putting the fear back into fear appeals: The extended parallel process model. *Communication Monographs, 59*, 329–349. https://doi.org/10.1080/03637759209376276.

Witte, K., & Allen, M. (2000). A meta-analysis of fear appeals: Implications for effective public health campaigns. *Health Education and Behavior, 27*, 591–615. https://doi.org/10.1177/109019810002700506.

Xu, Q., & Sundar, S. S. (2014). Lights, camera, music, interaction! Interactive persuasion in e-commerce. *Communication Research, 41*, 282–308. https://doi.org/10.1177/0093650212439062.

Yang, Z. J., Aloe, A. M., & Feeley, T. H. (2014). Risk information seeking and processing model: A meta-analysis. *Journal of Communication, 64*, 20–41. https://doi.org/10.1111/jcom.12071.

2

Digital embodiment and improving health outcomes: Healthy avatars make for healthy people

Jorge Peña[1], Benjamin J. Li[2], Rabindra Ratan[3]

[1] Department of Communication, University of California, Davis, CA, United States; [2] Nanyang Technological University, Wee Kim Wee School of Communication and Information, Nanyang Link, Singapore; [3] Michigan State University, Communication Arts and Sciences, Michigan State University, East Lansing, MI, United States

One of the most fascinating aspects of new technologies is affording users the ability to modify the self and transform sensorial inputs. The ability to embody and control a digital self-representation (avatar, limb, etc.) that is situated within a synthetic environment has profound implications for health scholars and practitioners. For instance, people may change their health behaviors and attitudes after seeing their virtual self as healthy or sick, thin or obese, or old or young (Hershfield et al., 2011). Smokers may regain a sense of control after crushing cigarettes using haptic controllers in a virtual environment (Girard, Turcotte, Bouchard, & Girard, 2009). In addition, participants who played a video game and saw their future face in the game showing the physical consequences of smoking (e.g., wrinkles, spots, grayer skin) showed increased intention to quit smoking and more negative attitudes toward smoking in comparison to those who did not see their future smoker face (Song, Kim, Kwon, & Jung, 2013). In virtual reality (VR), people may learn how to operate a new limb (Won, Bailenson, Lee, & Lanier, 2015), practice pain management strategies (Li, Montaño, Chen, & Gold, 2011), and learn to manage post-traumatic stress disorder (Rothbaum et al., 1999).

The present chapter focuses on the health outcomes of *digital self-representation* and theoretical mechanisms underlying its effects. We use this term broadly to describe the experience of creating, controlling, and interacting with real or synthetic people and objects while personified by a digital limb or a full digital body (i.e., an avatar). The chapter also discusses social processes involving real people interacting with *embodied agents* (e.g., game characters, digital personal assistant, virtual pets) designed to motivate individuals to increase health behaviors. The chapter describes trends, theoretical mechanisms, shortcomings, and future directions in research related to digital self-representation and interaction with embodied agents. Although this chapter is not a comprehensive metaanalysis, the topics covered are representative of current research in the field.

The chapter encompasses a range of options for the visual display of digital self-representations. In some contexts, users' digital bodies are fully visible as when users operate avatars in third-person view. If embodied in first-person view, people may be exposed to their digital appearance by seeing and controlling their digital limbs or when looking at one's avatar reflection in a digital mirror. In other contexts, users' digital bodies are implied as people can move and interact with synthetic objects but do not explicitly see their whole digital body (e.g., point-and-click interface). In this chapter, we reserve the term *avatar* to refer to human-controlled limbs, bodies, and characters that represent the user and allow interactions with real or synthetic partners and objects. In a recent review, Nowak and Fox (2018) define avatars as digital entities that represent users and allow them to interact with other avatars, objects, and characters in a virtual environment. While early forms of digital representations exist as usernames or graphical images and photos, avatars in VR and video games allow users to navigate and interact with digital objects. A key factor here is that the avatar is controlled by the user. Users provide inputs, which traditionally come from button presses in video games or motion detection in VR. Self-representations also experience consequences that come about as a result of the user's decisions and control input. For example, a user's avatar may receive health bonuses, penalties, and/or points as a consequence of user choices.

When a virtual representation is controlled not by the user but through a computer algorithm, it is known as an *agent*. Examples include artificial health assistants, virtual instructors, chatbots, and other characters depicted in anthropomorphic (e.g., human doctor) or non-anthropomorphic forms (e.g., pet or other animals). As such, the concept of human versus machine "agency" sets avatars theoretically apart from agents. Both agents and avatars have their place in health communication, and each contributes in unique ways. Avatars enable users to interact within a shared virtual environment with objects, other avatars, or agents.

Based on theories of social influence and identification, scholars have proposed that interactions with avatars are likely to be more effective than interactions with agents (Blascovich et al., 2002). People's motivations tend to be more easily influenced if they perceive they are in the presence of another individual. In support of this, a metaanalysis of 32 studies showed that avatars produced stronger persuasive responses among users as compared to agents (Fox et al., 2015). Hence, avatar-based manipulations may be ideal for digital health promotion interventions that aim to change attitudes and behavior. That being said, agents have multiple uses and advantages because they are algorithm-controlled and thus do not possess the basic needs of humans, making agents suitable for digital health interventions and services that require a 24/7 availability, such as a virtual health helpdesk. In addition, people engage in parasocial relationships with media characters and synthetic agents, implying that people may perceive agents and mediated characters as sentient anthropomorphic beings and thus build attachment, identification, etc.

Several technologies allow users to control and interact with digital self-representations, including commercial video games, "serious games" meant to educate and raise awareness, apps or smartphone applications, and training simulations. Games, apps, and simulations are displayed in different modalities including traditional two-dimensional (2D) screens (e.g., monitors, smartphones), augmented reality (i.e., AR or sensory information overlaid on the physical world), and VR (experiences taking place within a three-dimensional (3D) computer-generated environment). In health contexts, studies find positive links between embodying avatars and interacting with agents on outcomes such as body image (Kim & Sundar, 2012), attitudes toward sugared beverages (Ahn, Fox, & Hahm, 2014), physical activity (Li & Lwin, 2016), and substance use (Hone-Blanchet, Wensing, & Fecteau, 2014).

In this chapter, we concentrate on the influence of avatar use and interaction with virtual characters on users' health behaviors and attitudes. Avatar and agent-based interactions are becoming increasingly common. For instance, people play video games on phones, consoles, and computer that depict digital characters on a screen and have access to AR apps that overlay such characters on the physical world avatars and agents (e.g., *Pokémon GO*). With the increased accessibility of VR systems, more individuals are equipped to access virtual environments. Research exploring the effects of one's avatar on health attitudes and behaviors helps practitioners and policymakers think about designing virtual worlds or tools that can lead to better health outcomes among the population.

Though using avatar and agent-based interactions to increase health outcomes may at first glance appear to be trivial and inconsequential, there is evidence that people experience virtual experiences as if it was a "real" experience. For example, media equation theorists maintain that people treat technology-mediated experiences and synthetic characters as if they were real places or people (Nass & Moon, 2000; Reeves & Nass, 1996). Individuals apply learned concepts and knowledge structures to their interaction with technology and so avatars and agents that display social cues implying health expertise may be automatically treated as health experts. In addition, new technologies that afford digital self-representation also allow users to experience a sense of presence (Biocca, 1997; Lee, 2004; Lombard, Ditton, & Weinstein, 2009). Games, apps, and simulations provide rich and realistic sensory information via visual, aural, and haptic cues. According to Lombard and Ditton (1997), this may enable users to feel as if they are transported from a physical to a synthetic environment (e.g., "I am there" or spatial presence), perceive conversations with human-controlled avatars or synthetic agents as sociable, warm, or intimate (i.e., "we are together" or social presence), or perceive that an object, avatar, or agent is within reach, as if brought from another place to a user's field of attention (e.g., "It is here," as in AR Pokémon games, in which a synthetic game character is superimposed over the physical world). In addition, self-presence refers to the influence of virtual experiences on perception of body image, physiological and emotional states, traits, and identity (Biocca, 1997; Ratan, 2012). Consider that a sense of presence is vital to conducting exposure therapy, which provides a guided and safe confrontation with the feared stimuli (Parsons & Rizzo, 2008). New technologies that allow users to control avatars, such as VR, facilitate activating learned fear structures for then to be modified through controlled exposure (Rothbaum et al., 1999).

The notion that people experience synthetic events as if it was "real" experience is supported by brain imaging methodologies, which have become popular in communication research (Weber, Mangus, & Huskey, 2015; Weber, Sherry, & Mathiak, 2008), especially to study digital experiences like video games (Klasen, Weber, Kircher, Mathiak, & Mathiak, 2012; Mathiak & Weber, 2006; Weber, Ritterfeld, & Mathiak, 2006). Such studies suggest that brain activity during virtual and physical (nonvirtual) experiences reflects similar neurological processes, such as those involved in spatial navigation (Spiers & Maguire, 2007b), though not necessarily equivalent in magnitude (Baumeister, Reinecke, Cordes, Lerch, & Weiss, 2010; Mikropoulos, 2001). For example, cortical activity associated with attention (frontal theta power) was stronger for participants swinging a physical golf putter than a virtual golf putter, possibly because participants were more familiar with physical putting and better able to attend to the relevant sensory information (Baumeister et al., 2010). Alternatively, in some cases, virtual experiences lead to stronger neurological activity and presence than nonvirtual experiences. For example, participants exhibited less clipping of EEG signals when navigating a simulated virtual environment compared to an equivalent physical space, suggesting that they were paying more attention in the virtual environment (Mikropoulos, 2001). This implies that design elements of virtual experiences may have neurological impact that is smaller, equal, and sometimes even greater in magnitude than real experiences.

Regardless of the differences in magnitude, virtual experiences provide a strong facsimile of real experiences, and thus, VR has been used to study many different neurological correlates of spatial navigation (Hartley, Maguire, Spiers, & Burgess, 2003; Iaria, Petrides, Dagher, Pike, & Bohbot, 2003; Maguire et al., 1998; Nowak, Resnick, Elkins, & Moffat, 2011; Spiers & Maguire, 2006, 2007a) and driving behavior (Calhoun et al., 2002; Carvalho, Pearlson, Astur, & Calhoun, 2006; Spiers & Maguire, 2007c; Walter et al., 2001). For example, skill in spatial navigation of a virtual environment was associated with right anterior/medial temporal engagement, which is consistent with suggestions from research outside of VR (Pine et al., 2002). Below, we review several strands of research investigating how digital self-representations can be leveraged to increase health-related outcomes, such as pain and recovery, physical activity, well-being, and food consumption and body image. We then offer integration, critique, and future directions for this literature.

Pain and recovery

The use of avatars in pain intervention can be broken down into two aspects: acute pain and chronic pain. Pain management of burn injury victims is an example of avatar use in acute pain. Patients embody an avatar in a video game and are tasked to throw snowballs at various targets (Hoffman et al., 2004; Jeffs et al., 2014; Schmitt et al., 2011). Results showed a decrease in perceived pain among participants after the intervention. Jeffs et al. (2014) suggested that the intervention was effective because the VR experience elicited engagement through distraction and enjoyment. The combination of these factors possibly led to the decrease in perceived pain experienced by the participant during the wound care that happened concurrently. Distressing medical procedures such as the insertion of needles is another aspect of acute pain that has received research attention. For instance, Gold et al. (2006) found that while a control group reported increased pain during a needle insertion procedure, participants who went through an embodied VR experience and undertook the needle insertion procedure halfway did not see a significant increase in pain. The authors attributed this to the effectiveness of VR as a tool to distract attention away from pain due to its immersive nature. Indeed, participants in the VR condition were twice as satisfied with their pain management experience as those in the control condition and reported interest in further embodied VR treatments.

Regarding chronic pain, individuals with complex regional pain syndrome were tasked to control virtual limbs to grasp objects in VR with varying levels of difficulty. Findings showed a reduction in pain intensity among participants (Sato et al., 2010). Studies have also examined the effects of translating movements in real life to either larger or smaller magnitudes in an embodied VR experience, with participants showing greater recovery and reduced pain during limb movement rehabilitation (Chen et al., 2017; Won et al., 2015). Several studies employed embodied VR interventions in helping cerebral palsy patients improve reaching kinematics (Chen, Garcia-Vergara, & Howard, 2015; Fluet et al., 2010; Huber et al., 2008). A study recently tasked patients recovering from brain injuries to walk in various embodied VR environments showed an improvement in patients' gross motor abilities, such as standing and walking (Biffi et al., 2017). While the mechanism for the effectiveness of the VR intervention remains unclear, these findings provide initial evidence that VR interventions can potentially help patients in recovery from chronic pain.

The use of embodied experiences for recovery has also been examined in mental health contexts (Freeman et al., 2017). In fear therapy, interventions that place individuals as an avatar in specific scenarios have found positive support in helping patients suffering from phobias such as heights (Emmelkamp, Bruynzeel, Drost, & van der Mast, 2001; Krijn et al., 2004), driving (Wald & Taylor, 2000; Walshe, Lewis, O'Sullivan, & Kim, 2005), insects (Hoffman, Garcia-Palacios, Carlin, Furness, & Botella-Arbona, 2003a), and social interaction (Harris, Kemmerling, & North, 2002; Klinger et al., 2004). Other aspects of mental health where embodied interventions have been developed for include anxiety disorders (Parsons & Rizzo, 2008; Powers & Emmelkamp, 2008) and posttraumatic stress disorder (Beck, Palyo, Winer, Schwagler, & Ang, 2007; Rothbaum, Hodges, Ready, Graap, & Alarcon, 2001). These studies employ embodied experiences to facilitate desensitization effects in which patients are exposed to virtual representations of objects, people, animals, or situations that trigger anxiety, fear, or phobia under controlled clinical conditions to achieve gradual habituation and decreased flight responses. A recent study found that avatars are able to reduce anxiety in individuals if they are asked to design one that represented anxiety and also if they destroyed these creations that represented anxiety (Pimentel, Halan, & Kalyanaraman, 2018). Tapping on self-discrepancy theory, the researchers propose that anxiety forms a part of one's identity as an "anxious self-concept." Individuals who customized avatars that represented their anxious self-concept reported lower anxiety compared to a control group, while those who pressed a button to disintegrate the customized anxiety avatar reported significant decrease in anxiety. Findings suggest that avatar-based health interventions may support anxiety reduction treatment by allowing individuals to project their anxious self-concepts onto avatars through customization and distancing themselves from anxiety through destroying these customized anxiety avatars (Pimentel et al., 2018).

Physical activity

Use of avatars and agents can also enhance attitudes toward physical activity and, more importantly, increase physical activity levels. For instance, playing an exergame with a photorealistic avatar increased physical activity among 12−14 year olds (Thompson et al., 2018). Avatars were constructed from a digital image of the player, and participants then played a pilot exergame. Teens reached vigorous levels of physical activity and kept it up for 74.9% of total game time. Playing with a self-resembling avatar was enjoyable although the exergame was difficult. Teens' perceived autonomy and competence showed small postgame increments relative to baseline (Thompson et al., 2018). In a study in which participants were set on a real treadmill while immersed in VR, participants were randomly assigned to three conditions (Fox & Bailenson, 2009). According to social cognitive theory (SCT), people learn vicariously through modeled behavior (Bandura, 1986). Participants in the vicarious reinforcement condition were assigned to an avatar that donned the participant's face image and gained or lost weight based on participants' concurrent treadmill activity. This was compared to an avatar donning the participant's face which did not change based on the participants' treadmill exercise and also to a control condition in which participants saw no avatar in VR. Participants were then told the study was over but they could stay in the lab and exercise some more if they wanted. Participants in the vicarious reinforcement condition performed more voluntary exercise in the lab as well as in the week following the experiment than those in other two conditions (Fox & Bailenson, 2009). This implies that people are more likely to perform physical activity after seeing an avatar that looks like themselves gain or lose weight, which is congruent with vicarious learning principles and imitation based on perceived similarity.

In addition, embodying avatars with stereotypical physical traits can also influence physical activity. Women were randomly assigned to an obese or thin avatar and then played a tennis exergame while wearing activity monitors with accelerometers (Peña & Kim, 2014). While using either a thin or obese avatar, participants played the game against an onscreen opponent agent that was either obese or thin. Based on accelerometer data, female participants showed increased physical activity when operating thin instead of obese avatars (Peña & Kim, 2014). Similar results were found when replicating these results with a sample of male participants who also showed lower physical activity in a tennis exergame while using obese instead of thin avatars (Peña, Khan, & Alexopoulos, 2016). These results are tied to the Proteus effect, which attempts to explain how avatar appearance (e.g., height, attractiveness, prosocial or antisocial connotations) may influence users' behavior and cognition in VR and video games. The Proteus effect relies on self-perception (i.e., deriving one's attitudes from observation and reflection upon one's own behavior, Yee & Bailenson, 2007) and priming mechanisms (i.e., acting upon subconscious heuristics and schemes initiated by an external influence, Peña, Hancock, & Merola, 2009). These mechanisms can be isolated as operating an avatar has stronger effects than seeing an avatar (Yee & Bailenson, 2009); at the same time, these self-perception and priming may operate simultaneously as controlling an avatar may change how users see themselves, and avatar appearance may also remind them of learned concepts, stereotypes, and behavioral scripts. For example, random assignment to thin or obese avatars activated social stereotypes associated to physical activity, such as thinness and agility, obesity and sluggishness, etc. (Peña et al., 2016). In addition, both men and women assigned to obese avatars playing against thin agents showed decreased physical activity. This points out to upward social comparison mechanisms in which people compare themselves to someone who is more skilled. In this case, men and women showed decreased physical activity while playing a tennis exergame against an agent that looked more in shape in comparison to their own avatar (Peña et al., 2016; Peña & Kim, 2014). Overall, this implies that physical activity can be influenced by common stereotypes related to exercising that are activated by avatar appearance. Social comparison processes may also influence physical activity as self versus opponent judgments help players assess whether they are at advantage or disadvantage (Peña et al., 2016; Peña & Kim, 2014).

Li, Lwin, and Jung (2014) tested the separate effects of embodying an overweight avatar and exposure to stereotype threat. Overweight students were assigned to either overweight or normal weight avatars in a running exergame. Half of the participants were also exposed to a stereotype threat, where they were told that overweight participants tend to perform poorer in the exergame. Participants who were assigned overweight avatars performed poorer than those assigned normal weight avatars, whereas those exposed to the stereotype threat performed poorer than those who did not receive the stereotype threat information. These results lend support to the influence of both the Proteus effect and stereotype threat and show that visual and stereotype salience can influence individuals' physical activity motivations and behavior when they embody a character in virtual environments. A follow-up study (Li & Lwin, 2016) examined the influence of the self-avatar through the lens of SCT (Bandura, 1986). A key factor that influences the impact of learned behavior is similarity between the model and the self. Exergames therefore can offer an enactive learning experience when a player controls his avatar. According to Li and Lwin (2016), there were significant links between presence of a user's avatar and avatar identification, which subsequently increased enjoyment and exercise motivations.

One crucial aspect of digital experiences in general is that people are expected to integrate and match mental models from previous experiences to interactive environments, and vice versa. This may affect their experience with such technology and their willingness to continue using it. In a recent study, participants were assigned to ride the *Expresso HD* bicycle, which features a traditional upright exercise bike with handlebars to steer an onscreen graphical bicycle, while the resistance of the pedals vary depending on the terrain (McGloin & Embacher, 2018). The *Expresso HD* exergame was seen as a more natural experience by participants with higher gaming experience, but real-world road cycling experience was not related to perceiving the exergame riding experience as more natural. Participants who experienced increased immersion also enjoyed the exergame more, and increased enjoyment was associated with more desire to ride the exergame bike again (McGloin & Embacher, 2018). Overall, riding a physical bicycle that displays motion across a virtual landscape may have different effects on people who play video games or bike in the real world more frequently, as people with direct experience may have different mental models when operating exergames with one's own body.

Interacting with synthetic agents playing the role of "pets" may also help promote physical activity (Ahn et al., 2015). This harkens back to handheld digital pets or *Tamagotchi*, which asked users to interact with as small device that presented users with a simulated pet to interact and take care of. Capitalizing on the Youth Physical Activity Promotion (YPAP) model, a study implemented the use of virtual pets to increase children's perceptions of self-efficacy and expected outcomes (e.g., "Am I able to exercise?" "Is it worth it?") to engage in physical activity (Ahn et al., 2015). YPAP describes enabling, predisposing, and reinforcing factors that influence the practice of physical activity. Based on YPAP, Ahn et al. (2015) propose that virtual pets that set activity goals for children and also provide feedback encouraging further exercise may boost physical activity self-efficacy and expected outcomes. Children in a summer camp met a virtual pet dog at kiosks located in the camp. Kiosks were equipped with a screen to render the virtual pet and a Kinect device to detect user voice and gestures. The virtual dog asked children to set physical activity goals and then the child would leave the kiosk and return later. Children wore activity monitors with embedded accelerometers so that they would be congratulated by the virtual dog and allowed to play with it if they had met their physical activity goal. If they had not met their physical activity goal, then the virtual dog would tell the child that the goal was unmet and to continue exercising. Physical activity in the virtual pet group was compared to children in a summer camp with no virtual pets during a 3-day observation period. Children in the virtual pet group engaged in an average 1.09 more hours per day (156% more activity) and had increased intentions to continue engaging in physical activity in the future relative to children in the control group (Ahn et al., 2015). In addition, increased physical activity self-efficacy led to both increased intention for future physical activity and more positive expected outcomes. More positive physical activity expected outcomes were also linked to increased physical activity future intentions (Ahn et al., 2015).

Finally, AR games may also enable users to engage in increased physical activity by leveraging interactions with virtual agents, even if players simply intend to play the game. For example, *Pokémon GO* is an AR game in which users go to different locations to hunt creatures or Pokémon (i.e., agents) to add to their collection. In doing so, players may inadvertently exert themselves more than they would otherwise. To test for this hypothesis, a study combined data from search engine queries ("*Pokémon GO*") with physical activity measurements from wearable devices (Althoff, White, & Horvitz, 2016). Users that made multiple search queries for details about the game increased their activity by an average of 1473 steps a day, which represented an increase of over 25% relative to their baseline physical activity level (Althoff et al., 2016). With over 800 million downloads and counting, this study estimate that *Pokémon GO* added 144 billion steps to physical activity in the United States across a number of inactive populations (Althoff et al., 2016). There is also evidence for *Pokémon GO* increasing self-reported walking and moderate physical activity (Broom & Flint, 2018). These effects lasted after 3 months for those who remained playing (Broom & Flint, 2018). Though it appears that AR games such as *Pokémon GO* are effective health interventions, other studies show no effects and very low rates of continued play over time (Wattanapisit, Saengow, Ng, Thanamee, & Kaewruang, 2018). More research is needed to establish whether AR games are an effective method for increasing physical activity (Wattanapisit et al., 2018).

Psychological well-being

Under specific conditions, embodying avatars and interacting with agents may also boost individuals' subjective well-being. Subjective well-being involves a focus on global well-being factors such as happiness and life satisfaction but also a focus on specific domains, such as job, family, relationships, health, etc (Andrews & Robinson, 1991). Subjective well-being reflects a sum of an individual's life in society, and thus several constructs directly and indirectly tap into subjective well-being. Directly related factors include happiness and satisfaction, whereas indirectly related factors include self-esteem, depression, locus of control, and alienation (Andrews & Robinson, 1991).

Embodying avatars and interacting with other users and agents may influence psychosocial well-being (Slater & Sanchez-Vives, 2016), especially to the degree that users feel immersed in a virtual context (Behm-Morawitz, 2013). For instance, users may psychologically experience self, social, and spatial presence when playing games or using interactive technologies, and these different presence experiences may indirectly influence well-being and health and appearance satisfaction. As noted above, spatial presence is the feeling of being "there" in a mediated environment; social presence refers to perceiving social actors (e.g., avatars, agents) in a game or mediated setting as if it was real human-to-human communication, and self-presence refers to how virtual experiences influence perception of body image, physiological and emotional states, traits, and identity. In particular, self-presence was predicted to be more closely associated with the effects of embodying avatars on individual's identity and well-being as this factor is more linked to individual users than spatial and social presence (Behm-Morawitz, 2013). Confirming this expectation, individuals experiencing more self-presence in *Second Life* reported increased influence of their avatar on their real self in terms of well-being, body management (e.g., dieting and exercise), and satisfactory virtual relationships. One explanation was that heightened presence with one's virtual self may influence users to take more pride in their appearance and increase health consciousness, which in turn may have positive effects on individuals' real self (Behm-Morawitz, 2013). This implies that avatar use can serve as a mirror in which individuals can try on different styles and identities that are impermanent and risk-free (Behm-Morawitz, 2013). Individuals may observe these new identities and stylistic changes applied to one's avatar, and positive changes may be mimicked in real life as inspired by one's virtual self. Avatar use could serve as a source of motivation to take care of one's real body as survey respondents who perceived their avatar to be more attractive than their real self and yet still representative of their ideal appearance were more likely to report avatar influence on their well-being and appearance (Behm-Morawitz, 2013).

In addition, the way in which people customize their avatars may reflect underlying levels of well-being. Participants were asked to choose the features of their avatar for six different game scenarios (Trepte & Reinecke, 2010). Participants with higher life satisfaction created avatars that resembled the users' actual personality factors, whereas users with lower life satisfaction created more dissimilar avatar (Trepte & Reinecke, 2010). Similarly, a sample of World of Warcraft players rated their avatar as possessing more desirable traits compared with their actual self, especially among players with lower psychological well-being (Bessière, Seay, & Kiesler, 2007). These studies imply that avatar customization choices correlate with players' well-being and imply that the ability to create avatars who embody players' ideal selves may have repercussions for psychological well-being (Bessière et al., 2007).

Food consumption and body image

Virtual experiences have been used to examine issues related to health and food consumption. A review of 17 studies suggests that VR-based interventions provide effective treatment for eating disorders and obesity and are particularly well-suited for reducing body image dissatisfaction and increasing self-esteem and self-efficacy (Ferrer-Garcia, Gutiérrez-Maldonado, & Riva, 2013). The success of such approaches derives from the ability for VR technologies to induce similar emotional and behavioral responses as in traditional exposure therapies. However, compared to traditional therapies, VR treatment can be more effective in improving psychological hindrances to healthy eating, increasing motivation for change, and reducing problematic eating behaviors, given the higher level of control and safety afforded by VR (Riva, Bacchetta, Baruffi, & Molinari, 2001).

Supporting the notion that virtual food leads to physiological effects that resemble those of real food, one study found that participants reacted more quickly during interactions with virtual foods compared to virtual ball objects (Schroeder, Lohmann, Butz, & Plewnia, 2016), thus confirming a behavioral bias for food. In another study, obese participants found virtual food presented through an AR interface to be as palatable and arousing as real food (Pallavicini et al., 2016). These studies support the verisimilitude of virtual foods and thus the validity of using virtual experiences to address issues of health and food consumption.

However, the extent of this verisimilitude is dependent of the immersiveness of the technologies being utilized. For example, participants who smelled or touched a physical donut while interacting with a donut in VR ate fewer donuts and felt more satiated compared to participants who only interacted with the virtual donut without smell or touch (Li & Bailenson, 2018). The authors attribute the effects to embodied cognition (Barsalou, 1999). The embodied cognition framework suggests that past experiences can create perceptual symbols of sensory modalities. During a virtual experience of the food item, the individual accesses symbols that are linked to the smell, taste, and touch of the donut. These symbols then allow the individual to experience a simulated food consumption experience, leading to a decrease in the craving for and subsequent consumption of donuts.

Another approach to this research focuses on manipulating avatar features to influence perceptions of and associations with the self in experimental settings (Peña et al., 2009; Yee & Bailenson, 2007, 2009). Multiple studies have found that viewing reduced-weight virtual selves leads to healthier eating behaviors after exposure (Fox, Bailenson, & Binney, 2009; Kuo, Lee, & Chiou, 2016). These studies (Fox et al., 2009; Kuo et al., 2016) suggest that perceiving the self in a virtual environment leads to changes in self-perception that influence subsequent behavior. Another study of college-age students found that health consciousness was correlated with choosing to eat more vegetables at the end of the study for participants who used an avatar to design to reflect the ought self (how others think you ought to be) or the ideal self (how you would ideally like to be; marginally significant), but not for people who designed and used an actual-self avatar (Sah, Ratan, Sandy Tsai, Peng, & Sarinopoulos, 2016). This suggests that the aspects of self-concept made salient during avatar design (see example from this study

FIGURE 2.1 Avatar customization screen from Yoobot vs YooNot (British Health Foundation), used to illustrate self-concept effects on food choices (Sah et al., 2016).

in Fig. 2.1) influence the users' subsequent behaviors. Another study found that participants who participated in an intervention within a 3D avatar in a virtual world compared to those who used a 2D social networking site (no avatar) exhibited greater nutrition and exercise self-efficacy (Behm-Morawitz, Lewallen, & Choi, 2016). Also, children requested larger portions of fruits and vegetables after interacting with a virtual dog whose health improved or deteriorated depending on the user's actual consumption of fruits and vegetables (Ahn et al., 2015). In line with SCT, this finding suggests that self-efficacy with respect to eating fruits and vegetables is an individual-level factor that is influenced by the embodied social (vicarious) experience with the virtual dog within the environmental incentive structure. Altogether, these studies support the notion that self-concept and self-efficacy are malleable and can be influenced by cues embedded within virtual experiences (Wheeler, Demarree, & Petty, 2007).

Discussion and conclusions

Researchers and practitioners have leveraged the ability to embody avatars and interact with embodied agents to foster healthier behaviors and attitudes through games and simulated experiences delivered through tethered or mobile platforms. Simulated experiences can aid in fostering health behaviors as they are perceived as real, and users can experience various facets of presence (e.g., "I am there," "we are together," "it is here"). Simulated experiences and agents may trigger brain activity that is weaker than its real counterpart, but they may also start physiological reactions of an equal or even stronger magnitude. In addition to task familiarity, attention, and task-user mental model matching, more research is needed to clarify which factors predict when a weaker, equal, or stronger physiological reaction is expected.

Virtual experiences have shown promising results for treating acute and chronic pain and pain rehabilitation. Manipulating users' avatar appearance can influence concurrent and subsequent physical activity in exergame and VR contexts. Avatars can bring to mind stereotypes that may influence the performance of physical activity. Interacting with agents embodied as pets or collectible characters may also incentivize physical activity. Avatar selves may allow users to try on different selves and increase control and well-being. VR interventions also show promising results in increasing self-esteem and self-efficacy for individual experiencing food disorders. There is also initial evidence that virtual experiences involving different aspects of the self can influence subsequent food choices.

The studies reviewed rely on various psychological theories (e.g., presence, desensitization, vicarious learning, self-efficacy, modeling, identification, self-perception, priming, self-concept) that are implemented in the design and measurement of virtual experiences. In this sense, the field is translational in nature as it does not generate its own theories as much as it imports tested approaches from related domains, particularly psychology. This has advantages as researchers may implement proven assumptions and methods to test for the effects of avatar and agent-related interventions, but it also limits the field as it does not generate its own specific assumptions and methods. Also, some of the studies reviewed above do not have a strong theoretical grounding and, instead, were more interested in testing whether a given manipulation or intervention effectively influenced a specific health outcome. These trends may be related to the applied nature of investigating how virtual experiences can influence health behaviors and attitudes, and it may change as the field matures and becomes more specialized.

Another noticeable trend is the lack of repeated measures or longitudinal study designs. With a few exceptions, the majority of the studies discussed above are single-exposure laboratory experiments instead of randomized control trials with repeated measures. Establishing lasting health improvements as a result of experimental manipulations of avatar and agents may require more stringent tests that include preregistered studies, randomized controlled trials, use of baseline scales, and longitudinal designs, along with more diverse samples that do not only include college students.

There is also a relative dearth of research utilizing psychophysiological or brain-scanning based techniques. There are huge potential knowledge gains to be developed by connecting health outcomes to the underlying neurological processes involved in using avatars. Such measurement technologies are becoming more accessible to researchers, both financially and technologically. For example, researchers have implemented special VR displays (wide field of view, high resolution, stereographic) within the extremely loud and magnetized environment of fMRI machines that do not interfere with brain scanning and allow participants to experience a sense of presence within the media environment (Hoffman, Richards, Coda, Richards, & Sharar, 2003b; Hoffman, Richards, Magula, et al., 2003c; Ku et al., 2003).

Furthermore, in order to track and render virtual environments, VR systems collect huge amounts of data related to the user. This includes location, voices, product preferences, and physical behavior such as eye gaze, facial expressions, interpersonal distance, gait, and posture. In fact, commercial systems in 2018 are able to collect 18 different kinds of movement. In a typical setup, around 20 million unique data points on nonverbal behavior are collected for a 20 minute VR experience

(Bailenson, 2018). Data derived from these VR setups can be used to optimize the effect of virtual experiences. A VR health intervention that seeks to get people to engage in more physical activity can detect and track user's facial expressions and bodily movements from the base stations and head-mounted displays. Furthermore, patients in clinical settings are often required to put on monitoring devices such as heart rate trackers, physical activity monitors, and pedometers. Data collected from these sources can be analyzed to build predictive models. For example, a recent study showed relationships between head movements in VR experiences and affective responses (Li, Bailenson, Pines, Greenleaf, & Williams, 2017). It is not difficult to see how predictive models built from millions of data points can allow researchers and practitioners to build more effective virtual interventions, not only on an aggregate level but also in tailoring experiences to suit specific individual's preferences and motivations.

Though more research is needed, initial evidence indicates that virtual manipulations and interventions are an effective and engaging tool to instill healthier behaviors and attitudes as these technologies allow for the implementation, manipulation, and expression of basic psychological processes.

References

Ahn, Fox, J., & Hahm, J. M. (2014). Using virtual doppelgängers to increase personal relevance of health risk communication. In *Intelligent virtual agents* (pp. 1–12). Springer International Publishing.

Ahn, S. J. G., Johnsen, K., Robertson, T., Moore, J., Brown, S., Marable, A., & Basu, A. (2015). Using virtual pets to promote physical activity in children: An application of the youth physical activity promotion model. *Journal of Health Communication, 20*(7), 807–815.

Althoff, T., White, R. W., & Horvitz, E. (2016). Influence of Pokémon go on physical activity: Study and implications. *Journal of Medical Internet Research, 18*(12), e315.

Andrews, F. M., & Robinson, J. P. (1991). Measures of subjective well-being. *Measures of Personality and Social Psychological Attitudes, 1*, 61–114.

Bailenson, J. (2018). Protecting nonverbal data tracked in virtual reality. *JAMA Pediatrics, 172*(10), 905–906.

Bandura, A. (1986). The explanatory and predictive scope of self-efficacy theory. *Journal of Social and Clinical Psychology, 4*(3), 359–373.

Barsalou, L. W. (1999). Perceptions of perceptual symbols. *Behavioral and Brain Sciences, 22*(4), 637–660.

Baumeister, J., Reinecke, K., Cordes, M., Lerch, C., & Weiss, M. (2010). Brain activity in goal-directed movements in a real compared to a virtual environment using the Nintendo Wii. *Neuroscience Letters, 481*(1), 47–50.

Beck, J. G., Palyo, S. A., Winer, E. H., Schwagler, B. E., & Ang, E. J. (2007). Virtual reality exposure therapy for PTSD symptoms after a road accident: An uncontrolled case series. *Behavior Therapy, 38*(1), 39–48.

Behm-Morawitz, E. (2013). Mirrored selves: The influence of self-presence in a virtual world on health, appearance, and well-being. *Computers in Human Behavior, 29*(1), 119–128.

Behm-Morawitz, E., Lewallen, J., & Choi, G. (2016). A second chance at health: How a 3D virtual world can improve health self-efficacy for weight loss management among adults. *Cyberpsychology, Behavior and Social Networking, 19*(2), 74–79.

Bessière, K., Seay, A. F., & Kiesler, S. (2007). The ideal elf: Identity exploration in world of Warcraft. *CyberPsychology and Behavior: The Impact of the Internet, Multimedia and Virtual Reality on Behavior and Society, 10*(4), 530–535.

Biffi, E., Beretta, E., Cesareo, A., Maghini, C., Turconi, A. C., Reni, G., & Strazzer, S. (2017). An immersive virtual reality platform to enhance walking ability of children with acquired brain injuries. *Methods of Information in Medicine, 56*(2), 119–126.

Biocca, F. (1997). The cyborg's dilemma: Progressive embodiment in virtual environments. *Journal of Computer-Mediated Communication: JCMC, 3*(2). https://doi.org/10.1111/j.1083-6101.1997.tb00070.x.

Blascovich, J., Loomis, J., Beall, A. C., Swinth, K. R., Hoyt, C. L., & Bailenson, J. N. (2002). Immersive virtual environment technology as a methodological tool for social psychology. *Psychological Inquiry, 13*(2), 103–124.

Broom, D. R., & Flint, S. W. (2018). Gotta catch 'em all: Impact of Pokémon go on physical activity, sitting time, and perceptions of physical activity and health at baseline and three-month follow-up. *Games for Health Journal.* https://doi.org/10.1089/g4h.2018.0002.

Calhoun, V. D., Pekar, J. J., McGinty, V. B., Adali, T., Watson, T. D., & Pearlson, G. D. (2002). Different activation dynamics in multiple neural systems during simulated driving. *Human Brain Mapping, 16*(3), 158–167.

Carvalho, K. N., Pearlson, G. D., Astur, R. S., & Calhoun, V. D. (2006). Simulated driving and brain imaging: Combining behavior, brain activity, and virtual reality. *CNS Spectrums, 11*(1), 52–62.

Chen, Garcia-Vergara, S., & Howard, A. M. (2015). Effect of a home-based virtual reality intervention for children with cerebral palsy using super pop VR evaluation metrics: A feasibility study. *Rehabilitation Research and Practice, 2015*, 812348.

Chen, Sesto, M. E., Ponto, K., Leonard, J., Mason, A., Vanderheiden, G., … Radwin, R. G. (2017). Use of virtual reality feedback for patients with chronic neck pain and kinesiophobia. *IEEE Transactions on Neural Systems and Rehabilitation Engineering: A Publication of the IEEE Engineering in Medicine and Biology Society, 25*(8), 1240–1248.

Emmelkamp, P. M., Bruynzeel, M., Drost, L., & van der Mast, C. A. (2001). Virtual reality treatment in acrophobia: A comparison with exposure in vivo. *CyberPsychology and Behavior: The Impact of the Internet, Multimedia and Virtual Reality on Behavior and Society, 4*(3), 335–339.

Ferrer-Garcia, M., Gutiérrez-Maldonado, J., & Riva, G. (2013). Virtual reality based treatments in eating disorders and obesity: A review. *Journal of Contemporary Psychotherapy, 43*(4), 207–221.

Fluet, G. G., Qiu, Q., Kelly, D., Parikh, H. D., Ramirez, D., Saleh, S., & Adamovich, S. V. (2010). Interfacing a haptic robotic system with complex virtual environments to treat impaired upper extremity motor function in children with cerebral palsy. *Developmental Neurorehabilitation, 13*(5), 335–345.

Fox, J., Ahn, S. J., Janssen, J. H., Yeykelis, L., Segovia, K. Y., & Bailenson, J. N. (2015). Avatars versus agents: A meta-analysis quantifying the effect of agency on social influence. *Human—Computer Interaction, 30*(5), 401–432.

Fox, J., & Bailenson, J. N. (2009). Virtual self-modeling: The effects of vicarious reinforcement and identification on exercise behaviors. *Media Psychology, 12*(1), 1–25.

Fox, J., Bailenson, J., & Binney, J. (2009). Virtual experiences, physical behaviors: The effect of presence on imitation of an eating avatar. *Presence: Teleoperators and Virtual Environments, 18*(4), 294–303.

Freeman, D., Reeve, S., Robinson, A., Ehlers, A., Clark, D., Spanlang, B., & Slater, M. (2017). Virtual reality in the assessment, understanding, and treatment of mental health disorders. *Psychological Medicine*. https://doi.org/10.1017/S003329171700040X.

Girard, B., Turcotte, V., Bouchard, S., & Girard, B. (2009). Crushing virtual cigarettes reduces tobacco addiction and treatment discontinuation. *CyberPsychology and Behavior: The Impact of the Internet, Multimedia and Virtual Reality on Behavior and Society, 12*(5), 477–483.

Gold, J. I., Kim, S. H., Kant, A. J., Joseph, M. H., & Rizzo, A. (2006). Effectiveness of virtual reality for pediatric pain distraction during IV placement. skip *CyberPsychology and Behavior: The Impact of the Internet, Multimedia and Virtual Reality on Behavior and Society, 9*(2), 207–212.

Harris, S. R., Kemmerling, R. L., & North, M. M. (2002). Brief virtual reality therapy for public speaking anxiety. *CyberPsychology and Behavior: The Impact of the Internet, Multimedia and Virtual Reality on Behavior and Society, 5*(6), 543–550.

Hartley, T., Maguire, E. A., Spiers, H. J., & Burgess, N. (2003). The well-worn route and the path less traveled: Distinct neural bases of route following and wayfinding in humans. *Neuron, 37*(5), 877–888.

Hershfield, H. E., Goldstein, D. G., Sharpe, W. F., Fox, J., Yeykelis, L., Carstensen, L. L., & Bailenson, J. N. (2011). Increasing saving behavior through age-progressed renderings of the future self. *Journal of Marketing Research, 48*, S23–S37. https://doi.org/10.1509/jmkr.48.SPL.S23.

Hoffman, H. G., Garcia-Palacios, A., Carlin, A., Furness, T. A., III, & Botella-Arbona, C. (2003a). Interfaces that heal: Coupling real and virtual objects to treat spider phobia. *International Journal of Human–Computer Interaction, 16*(2), 283–300.

Hoffman, H. G., Richards, T. L., Coda, B., Bills, A. R., Blough, D., Richards, A. L., & Sharar, S. R. (2004). Modulation of thermal pain-related brain activity with virtual reality: Evidence from fMRI. *Neuroreport, 15*(8), 1245–1248.

Hoffman, H. G., Richards, T., Coda, B., Richards, A., & Sharar, S. R. (2003b). The illusion of presence in immersive virtual reality during an fMRI brain scan. *CyberPsychology and Behavior: The Impact of the Internet, Multimedia and Virtual Reality on Behavior and Society, 6*(2), 127–131.

Hoffman, H. G., Richards, T. L., Magula, J., Seibel, E. J., Hayes, C., Mathis, M., ... Maravilla, K. (2003c). A magnet-friendly virtual reality fiberoptic image delivery system. *CyberPsychology and Behavior: The Impact of the Internet, Multimedia and Virtual Reality on Behavior and Society, 6*(6), 645–648.

Hone-Blanchet, A., Wensing, T., & Fecteau, S. (2014). The use of virtual reality in craving assessment and cue-exposure therapy in substance use disorders. *Frontiers in Human Neuroscience, 8*, 844.

Huber, M., Rabin, B., Docan, C., Burdea, G., Nwosu, M. E., Abdelbaky, M., & Golomb, M. R. (2008). PlayStation 3-based tele-rehabilitation for children with hemiplegia. In *2008 virtual rehabilitation* (pp. 105–112). ieeexplore.ieee.org.

Iaria, G., Petrides, M., Dagher, A., Pike, B., & Bohbot, V. D. (2003). Cognitive strategies dependent on the hippocampus and caudate nucleus in human navigation: Variability and change with practice. *Journal of Neuroscience: The Official Journal of the Society for Neuroscience, 23*(13), 5945–5952.

Jeffs, D., Dorman, D., Brown, S., Files, A., Graves, T., Kirk, E., ... Swearingen, C. J. (2014). Effect of virtual reality on adolescent pain during burn wound care. *Journal of Burn Care and Research: Official Publication of the American Burn Association, 35*(5), 395–408.

Kim, Y., & Sundar, S. S. (2012). Visualizing ideal self vs. actual self through avatars: Impact on preventive health outcomes. *Computers in Human Behavior, 28*(4), 1356–1364.

Klasen, M., Weber, R., Kircher, T. T. J., Mathiak, K. A., & Mathiak, K. (2012). Neural contributions to flow experience during video game playing. *Social Cognitive and Affective Neuroscience, 7*(4), 485–495.

Klinger, E., Légeron, P., Roy, S., Chemin, I., Lauer, F., & Nugues, P. (2004). Virtual reality exposure in the treatment of social phobia. *Studies in Health Technology and Informatics, 99*, 91–119.

Krijn, M., Emmelkamp, P. M. G., Biemond, R., de Wilde de Ligny, C., Schuemie, M. J., & van der Mast, C. A. P. G. (2004). Treatment of acrophobia in virtual reality: The role of immersion and presence. *Behaviour Research and Therapy, 42*(2), 229–239.

Ku, J., Mraz, R., Baker, N., Zakzanis, K. K., Lee, J. H., Kim, I. Y., … Graham, S. J. (2003). A data glove with tactile feedback for FMRI of virtual reality experiments. *CyberPsychology and Behavior: The Impact of the Internet, Multimedia and Virtual Reality on Behavior and Society, 6*(5), 497–508.

Kuo, H.-C., Lee, C.-C., & Chiou, W.-B. (2016). The power of the virtual ideal self in weight control: Weight-reduced avatars can enhance the tendency to delay gratification and regulate dietary practices. *Cyberpsychology, Behavior and Social Networking, 19*(2), 80–85.

Lee, K. M. (2004). Presence, explicated. Communication theory: CT. *A Journal of the International Communication Association, 14*(1), 27–50.

Li, B. J., & Bailenson, J. N. (2018). Exploring the influence of haptic and olfactory cues of a virtual donut on satiation and eating behavior. *Presence: Teleoperators and Virtual Environments, 26*(3), 337–354.

Li, B. J., Bailenson, J. N., Pines, A., Greenleaf, W. J., & Williams, L. M. (2017). A public database of immersive VR videos with corresponding ratings of arousal, valence, and correlations between head movements and self report measures. *Frontiers in Psychology, 8*, 2116.

Li, B. J., & Lwin, M. O. (2016). Player see, player do: Testing an exergame motivation model based on the influence of the self avatar. *Computers in Human Behavior, 59*, 350–357.

Li, B. J., Lwin, M. O., & Jung, Y. (2014). Wii, myself, and size: The influence of proteus effect and stereotype threat on overweight children's exercise motivation and behavior in exergames. *Games for Health Journal, 3*(1), 40–48.

Li, A., Montaño, Z., Chen, V. J., & Gold, J. I. (2011). Virtual reality and pain management: Current trends and future directions. *Pain Management, 1*(2), 147–157.

Lombard, M., & Ditton, T. (1997). At the heart of it all: The concept of presence. *Journal of Computer-Mediated Communication: JCMC, 3*(2). Retrieved from: https://onlinelibrary.wiley.com/doi/abs/10.1111/j.1083-6101.1997.tb00072.x.

Lombard, M., Ditton, T. B., & Weinstein, L. (2009). Measuring presence: The temple presence inventory. In *Proceedings of the 12th annual international workshop on presence* (pp. 1–15).

Maguire, E. A., Burgess, N., Donnett, J. G., Frackowiak, R. S., Frith, C. D., & O'Keefe, J. (1998). Knowing where and getting there: A human navigation network. *Science, 280*(5365), 921–924.

Mathiak, K., & Weber, R. (2006). Toward brain correlates of natural behavior: fMRI during violent video games. *Human Brain Mapping, 27*(12), 948–956.

McGloin, R., & Embacher, K. (2018). "Just like riding a bike": A model matching approach to predicting the enjoyment of a cycling exergame experience. *Media Psychology, 21*(3), 486–505.

Mikropoulos, T. A. (2001). Brain activity on navigation in virtual environments. *Journal of Educational Computing Research, 24*(1), 1–12.

Nass, C., & Moon, Y. (2000). Machines and mindlessness: Social responses to computers. *Journal of Social Issues, 56*(1), 81–103.

Nowak, K. L., & Fox, J. (2018). Avatars and computer-mediated communication: A review of the definitions, uses, and effects of digital representations. *Review of Communication Research, 6*, 30–53.

Nowak, Resnick, S., Elkins, W., & Moffat, S. (2011). Sex differences in brain activation during virtual navigation: A functional MRI study. In *Proceedings of the annual meeting of the cognitive science society* (Vol. 33). cloudfront.escholarship.org. Retrieved from: https:// cloudfront.escholarship.org/dist/prd/content/qt19054699/qt19054699.pdf.

Pallavicini, F., Serino, S., Cipresso, P., Pedroli, E., Chicchi Giglioli, I. A., Chirico, A., ... Riva, G. (2016). Testing augmented reality for cue exposure in obese patients: An exploratory study. *Cyberpsychology, Behavior and Social Networking, 19*(2), 107–114.

Parsons, T. D., & Rizzo, A. A. (2008). Affective outcomes of virtual reality exposure therapy for anxiety and specific phobias: A meta-analysis. *Journal of Behavior Therapy and Experimental Psychiatry, 39*(3), 250–261.

Peña, J., Hancock, J. T., & Merola, N. A. (2009). The priming effects of avatars in virtual settings. *Communication Research, 36*(6), 838–856.

Peña, J., Khan, S., & Alexopoulos, C. (2016). I am what I see: How avatar and opponent agent body size affects physical activity among men playing exergames. *Journal of Computer-Mediated Communication: JCMC, 21*(3), 195–209.

Peña, J., & Kim, E. (2014). Increasing exergame physical activity through self and opponent avatar appearance. *Computers in Human Behavior, 41*, 262–267.

Pimentel, D., Halan, S., & Kalyanaraman, S. (2018). Customizing your demons: Affective implications of anthropomorphizing the "anxious avatar.". In *Presented at the 68th annual international communication association conference, Prague, Czech Republic.*

Pine, D. S., Grun, J., Maguire, E. A., Burgess, N., Zarahn, E., Koda, V., ... Bilder, R. M. (2002). Neurodevelopmental aspects of spatial navigation: A virtual reality fMRI study. *NeuroImage, 15*(2), 396–406.

Powers, M. B., & Emmelkamp, P. M. G. (2008). Virtual reality exposure therapy for anxiety disorders: A meta-analysis. *Journal of Anxiety Disorders, 22*(3), 561–569.

Ratan, R. (2012). Self-presence, explicated: Body, emotion, and identity. *Handbook of Research on Technoself: Identity in a Technological Society, 322.*

Reeves, B., & Nass, C. I. (1996). *The media equation: How people treat computers, television, and new media like real people and places.* Cambridge university press.

Riva, G., Bacchetta, M., Baruffi, M., & Molinari, E. (2001). Virtual reality–based multidimensional therapy for the treatment of body image disturbances in obesity: A controlled study. *CyberPsychology and Behavior: The Impact of the Internet, Multimedia and Virtual Reality on Behavior and Society, 4*(4), 511–526.

Rothbaum, B. O., Hodges, L., Alarcon, R., Ready, D., Shahar, F., Graap, K., ... Baltzell, D. (1999). Virtual reality exposure therapy for PTSD Vietnam veterans: A case study. *Journal of Traumatic Stress, 12*(2), 263–271.

Rothbaum, B. O., Hodges, L. F., Ready, D., Graap, K., & Alarcon, R. D. (2001). Virtual reality exposure therapy for Vietnam veterans with posttraumatic stress disorder. *Journal of Clinical Psychiatry, 62*(8), 617–622.

Sah, Y. J., Ratan, R., Sandy Tsai, H.-Y., Peng, W., & Sarinopoulos, I. (2016). Are you what your avatar eats? Health-behavior effects of avatar-manifested self-concept. *Media Psychology,* 1–26.

Sato, K., Fukumori, S., Matsusaki, T., Maruo, T., Ishikawa, S., Nishie, H., ... Morita, K. (2010). Nonimmersive virtual reality mirror visual feedback therapy and its application for the treatment of complex regional pain syndrome: An open-label pilot study. *Pain Medicine, 11*(4), 622–629.

Schmitt, Y. S., Hoffman, H. G., Blough, D. K., Patterson, D. R., Jensen, M. P., Soltani, M., ... Sharar, S. R. (2011). A randomized, controlled trial of immersive virtual reality analgesia, during physical therapy for pediatric burns. *Burns: Journal of the International Society for Burn Injuries, 37*(1), 61–68.

Schroeder, P. A., Lohmann, J., Butz, M. V., & Plewnia, C. (2016). Behavioral bias for food reflected in hand movements: A preliminary study with healthy subjects. *Cyberpsychology, Behavior and Social Networking, 19*(2), 120–126.

Slater, M., & Sanchez-Vives, M. V. (2016). Enhancing our lives with immersive virtual reality. *Frontiers in Robotics and AI, 3*(74). https://doi.org/10.3389/frobt.2016.00074.

Song, H., Kim, J., Kwon, R. J., & Jung, Y. (2013). Anti-smoking educational game using avatars as visualized possible selves. *Computers in Human Behavior, 29*(5), 2029–2036. https://doi.org/10.1016/j.chb.2013.04.008sel.

Spiers, H. J., & Maguire, E. A. (2006). Thoughts, behaviour, and brain dynamics during navigation in the real world. *NeuroImage, 31*(4), 1826–1840.

Spiers, H. J., & Maguire, E. A. (2007a). A navigational guidance system in the human brain. *Hippocampus, 17*(8), 618–626.

Spiers, H. J., & Maguire, E. A. (2007b). Decoding human brain activity during real-world experiences. *Trends in Cognitive Sciences, 11*(8), 356–365.

Spiers, H. J., & Maguire, E. A. (2007c). Neural substrates of driving behaviour. *NeuroImage, 36*(1), 245–255.

Thompson, D. I., Cantu, D., Callender, C., Liu, Y., Rajendran, M., Rajendran, M., … Deng, Z. (2018). Photorealistic avatar and teen physical activity: Feasibility and preliminary efficacy. *Games for Health Journal, 7*(2), 143–150.

Trepte, S., & Reinecke, L. (2010). Avatar creation and video game enjoyment. *Journal of Media Psychology, 22*(4), 171–184.

Wald, J., & Taylor, S. (2000). Efficacy of virtual reality exposure therapy to treat driving phobia: A case report. *Journal of Behavior Therapy and Experimental Psychiatry, 31*(3–4), 249–257.

Walshe, D., Lewis, E., O'Sullivan, K., & Kim, S. I. (2005). Virtually driving: Are the driving environments" real enough" for exposure therapy with accident victims? An explorative study. *CyberPsychology and Behavior: The Impact of the Internet, Multimedia and Virtual Reality on Behavior and Society, 8*(6), 532–537.

Walter, H., Vetter, S. C., Grothe, J., Wunderlich, A. P., Hahn, S., & Spitzer, M. (2001). The neural correlates of driving. *NeuroReport, 12*(8), 1763–1767.

Wattanapisit, A., Saengow, U., Ng, C. J., Thanamee, S., & Kaewruang, N. (2018). Gaming behaviour with Pokémon GO and physical activity: A preliminary study with medical students in Thailand. *PLoS One, 13*(6), e0199813.

Weber, Mangus, J. M., & Huskey, R. (2015). Brain imaging in communication research: A practical guide to understanding and evaluating fMRI studies. *Communication Methods and Measures, 9*(1–2), 5–29.

Weber, R., Ritterfeld, U., & Mathiak, K. (2006). Does playing violent video games induce aggression? Empirical evidence of a functional magnetic resonance imaging study. *Media Psychology, 8*(1), 39–60.

Weber, Sherry, J., & Mathiak, K. (2008). The neurophysiological perspective in mass communication research. Biological dimensions of communication: Perspectives. *Methods, and Research,* 41–71.

Wheeler, S. C., Demarree, K. G., & Petty, R. E. (2007). Understanding the role of the self in prime-to-behavior effects: The active-self account. *Personality and Social Psychology Review: An Official Journal of the Society for Personality and Social Psychology, Inc, 11*(3), 234–261.

Won, A. S., Bailenson, J., Lee, J., & Lanier, J. (2015). Homuncular flexibility in virtual reality. *Journal of Computer-Mediated Communication: JCMC, 20*(3), 241–259.

Yee, N., & Bailenson, J. N. (2007). The proteus effect: Self transformations in virtual reality. *Human Communication Research, 33*(3), 271–290.

Yee, N., & Bailenson, J. N. (2009). The difference between being and seeing: The relative contribution of self-perception and priming to behavioral changes via digital self-representation. *Media Psychology, 12*(2), 195–209. https://doi.org/10.1080/15213260902849943.

Avatar embodiment experiences to enhance mental health

Laura Aymerich-Franch

Ramón y Cajal Senior Research Fellow, Pompeu Fabra University, Barcelona, Spain

When users embody a digital or a robot avatar, they may experience the illusion that the body of the avatar temporarily belongs to themselves. Sense of body ownership of avatar bodies has been widely reported in virtual reality (Slater & Sanchez-Vives, 2016) and, more recently, also in humanoid robots (Aymerich-Franch, Petit, Ganesh, & Kheddar, 2016; Aymerich-Franch, Petit, Ganesh, & Kheddar, 2017a, 2017b; Cohen et al., 2012, 2014; Kishore et al., 2014; Kishore, Navarro, Muncunill et al., 2016a; Kishore, Navarro, et al., 2016b).

Avatar embodiment illusions are explained by the high malleability of the *body schema* (Clark, 2007; Slater & Sanchez-Vives, 2016), "a suite of neural settings that implicitly and non-consciously define a body in terms of its capabilities for action" (Clark, 2007). In other words, to understand avatar embodiment illusions, human beings should be regarded as bodily, sensory, and cognitively permeable agents in continuous restructuring of their own boundaries, capable of incorporating external equipment into their beings, rather than as separate entities from the environment (Clark, 2007).

A particularly well-acknowledged empirical demonstration to this high malleability is provided by the rubber hand illusion experiment (Botvinick & Cohen, 1998), which shows how synchronous touch applied to a hidden real hand and a rubber hand visible to the participant leads to sense of ownership over the rubber hand. Previous experiments have shown that people even show a physiological response when an embodied rubber hand is physically threatened (Armel & Ramachandran, 2003). Other experiments have used visuotactile synchronization between a mannequin body and the real body to show that ownership illusions also extend to the full body (Petkova & Ehrsson, 2008).

Technology and Health
https://doi.org/10.1016/B978-0-12-816958-2.00003-4
49

Illusory sense of body ownership of avatar bodies in virtual reality and robots is also created by multisensory correlations. Generally, visuomotor synchronization is used in conjunction with a manipulated visual perspective to generate the illusion of avatar embodiment.

When users embody an avatar, they experience the body of their avatar as if it was their own body, and their sense of self extends to the body of that avatar (Aymerich-Franch, 2018; Aymerich-Franch & Fosch-Villaronga, 2019). This experience is believed to cause important behavioral, attitudinal, and cognitive modifications in embodied users, which can be used to enhance aspects connected to mental health.

The use of avatar embodiment technologies to reduce mental illness and promote psychological well-being is reviewed in this chapter. First, I summarize the technical commonalities used to create the experience of avatar embodiment across the two technologies generally used to create this illusion: virtual reality and, more recently, also humanoid robots. Next, I introduce the phenomenon by which embodying an avatar causes behavioral, attitudinal, and cognitive modifications in users, and I describe the principal theoretical approaches that explain this phenomenon. Then, I review the studies that have used these transformations in connection to health and well-being. I conclude by suggesting potential areas of intervention in which avatar embodiment could contribute to improve mental health in future studies.

Defining avatar embodiment

An *avatar* is the digital representation of the self in a virtual environment (Bailenson & Blascovich, 2004). *Avatar embodiment* (also referred sometimes as *virtual embodiment*, see for instance Spanlang et al., 2014) defines the technologically induced illusion of seeing an avatar in the location where the own physical body is normally experienced and having control over its body movements. The avatar embodiment illusion is generally obtained using a head-mounted display (i.e., a device worn on the head to visualize immersive environments that occludes vision from the physical environment), and body-tracking technologies (Spanlang et al., 2014).

It is important to note that not all experiences with avatars in virtual environments imply embodiment. Indeed, the concept of avatar embodiment is oftentimes misconceived. *Embodiment* refers to the existence in the world through a body (Csordas, 1999). However, this is a polysemic word that is used differently in robotics, philosophy, communication, or psychology and cognitive neuroscience (Kilteni, Groten, & Slater, 2012).

In communication, embodying an avatar is generally related to the process of employing virtual reality hardware and software to temporarily substitute a person's body with a virtual body during an experience in virtual reality (Spanlang et al., 2014). Given recent work with robot avatars in this field (Aymerich-Franch et al., 2017a, 2017b; Cohen et al., 2012; Cohen, Koppel, Malach, & Friedman, 2014; Kishore et al., 2014; Kishore, Navarro Muncunill et al., 2016a), the concept of avatar embodiment can be extended to experiences of humanoid robot embodiment (Aymerich-Franch, 2018; Aymerich-Franch et al., 2017b; Aymerich-Franch & Fosch-Villaronga, 2019). Thus, during avatar embodiment, users can be represented either by a digital or a robotic entity, depending on the nature of the technology used to create the illusion (Aymerich-Franch, 2018; Aymerich-Franch et al., 2017b; Aymerich-Franch & Fosch-Villaronga, 2019). This entity is how the user appears during the experience of avatar embodiment and how other people see them. It is how users see themselves if they were to look in a mirror (or in a digital mirror, in the case of virtual reality). The avatar is also the body through which users interact with other people collocated in the same virtual or physical space as the avatar.

In order for the avatar to be embodied, there are two basic requirements to be met. One is a spatially coincident location between the avatar body and the physical body of the embodied user. In other words, when the embodied user looks down through their head-mounted display, they see the body of their avatar in the location where they would normally experience their physical body (Slater & Sanchez-Vives, 2014). The second requirement is control of the avatar body movements. Embodying an avatar in virtual reality or in robot embodiment implies control over the avatar's movements so that if the embodied user moves, the avatar moves accordingly (Slater & Sanchez-Vives, 2014).

Referring to *avatar embodiment* in the context of mediated experiences should be reserved only for situations in which these criteria are met. An avatar representation on a screen that the user controls with a joystick, for instance, shall not be regarded as an experience of avatar embodiment. Such experience would lack spatial coincidence between the user body and the avatar body. Likewise, not all immersive experiences visualized through a head-mounted display are necessarily avatar embodiment experiences. A user could be immersed in a 360° video and use a head-mounted display to visualize it, but not necessarily have an avatar that is representing them.

To summarize, avatar embodiment requires the following minimum conditions to apply: (a) a digital or physical entity to act as the avatar; (b) a coincident location of the avatar in the space where the user normally experiences their physical body; and (c) control over the avatar movements.

Also, the concept of *avatar embodiment* shall not be confused with *sense of presence*. Being embodied in an avatar generally contributes to feeling present in the virtual environment. However, *presence* defines the sense of "being there," in the virtual environment (Lombard & Ditton, 1997). One can feel present in a virtual environment regardless of being embodied in an avatar or not.

Avatar embodiment and *sense of embodiment* are also connected but different concepts. *Avatar embodiment* refers to the factual aspect of technologically embodying a user to an avatar in a way that satisfies the minimum conditions described above (Spanlang et al., 2014). *Sense of embodiment*, on the other hand, is linked to what the user experiences as a result of embodying an avatar (Kilteni et al., 2012). In particular, *sense of embodiment* refers to "the ensemble of sensations that arise in conjunction with being inside, having, and controlling a body, especially in relation to virtual reality applications" (Kilteni et al., 2012). Someone might wear a head-mounted display, see themselves transformed in an avatar in a virtual mirror, and have control over the avatar. Regardless of that, they might not experience sense of embodiment if they did not feel the illusion that the body of the avatar progressively became their own.

Experiencing sense of embodiment is considered to be defined by three aspects: body ownership, self-location, and agency (Kilteni et al., 2012; Longo, Schüür, Kammers, Tsakiris, & Haggard, 2008). In the context of avatar embodiment, body ownership defines the sense that the body of the avatar belongs to oneself (Aymerich-Franch & Ganesh, 2016; Gallagher, 2000; Tsakiris, 2010). Self-location is the space where one feels to be located (Blanke & Metzinger, 2009). Human beings generally experience their sense of self located within their bodily borders. During experiences of avatar embodiment, the sense of self feels transported and defined by the boundaries of the avatar body. Agency is the capacity to control one's own actions (Haggard, 2017). In avatar embodiment, agency defines the sense of control over the avatar's actions.

Studies with avatars generally use avatars with human-looking appearances. However, sense of embodiment has been also reported in non–human-looking entities such as animals (Ahn et al., 2016) or humanoid robots with highly robotic appearances (Aymerich-Franch, Petit, Ganesh, & Kheddar, 2015; Aymerich-Franch et al., 2016; Aymerich-Franch et al., 2017a, 2017b).

Technical features of avatar embodiment technologies

Virtual reality is the most extended and studied form of avatar embodiment. As mentioned earlier, though, another form of avatar embodiment has been reported, which uses humanoid robots to also provide avatar embodiment experiences (Aymerich-Franch et al., 2015, 2016, 2017a, 2017b; Cohen et al., 2014b, 2012; Kishore et al., 2014, 2016a,b).

In order to experience sense of embodiment in the avatar, first-person visual perspective from the avatar is combined with multisensory correlations between the physical and the avatar body. These two aspects are crucial to experience the body of an avatar as one's own (Lenggenhager, Tadi, Metzinger, & Blanke, 2007).

Regardless of the technology used (i.e., virtual reality or robots), the user is generally equipped with a head-mounted display, which provides first-person visual perspective from the virtual or robotic avatar. The user is able to see the limbs and part of the body of their avatars if they look down, where they would normally see their real limbs and torso. In addition, full-body identification can be achieved by reflecting the avatar's appearance in physical and virtual mirrors or other surfaces (Aymerich-Franch et al., 2016, 2015; Aymerich-Franch, Kizilcec, & Bailenson, 2014; González-Franco, Pérez-Marcos, Spanlang, & Slater, 2010).

While feedback from other senses are not considered a necessary condition to induce the illusion of avatar embodiment, it can contribute to enhance the embodiment experience (Spanlang et al., 2014). Headsets or speakers are used to provide auditory feedback and haptic devices for force feedback, or object controlling is used for haptic feedback (Fox, Arena, & Bailenson, 2009; Stone, 2001). Olfaction and gustation are generally not implemented.

For visuomotor synchronization, head tracking and body movement synchronization are provided. In virtual reality, the movements of the user's head are followed and used to update the user perspective in real time (Spanlang et al., 2014). When the illusion is provided with a robot avatar, head movements are synchronized to the robot's head movements, and the user receives video feedback from cameras mounted on the robot's head in real time (Aymerich-Franch et al., 2015, 2016, 2017a, 2017b, 2019; Kishore et al., 2014, 2016a,b).

User movements can be tracked and synchronized to the avatar's movements for the control of limb and body gestures and to make the avatar walk or move in the space. In virtual reality, user's body movements are generally tracked and synchronized to the avatar body movements, and spaces are rendered according to these movements (Fox et al., 2009; Spanlang et al., 2014). For robot avatars, control of the robot body movement can be obtained with a motion capture suit (Aymerich-Franch, Kishore, & Slater, 2019), a joystick (Aymerich-Franch et al., 2015, 2016), a brain–computer interface (Alimardani et al., 2013; Gergondet et al., 2011), fMRI (Cohen et al., 2012, 2014), or eye-tracking technologies (Kishore et al., 2014).

The effects of avatar embodiment experiences

As I mentioned in the introductory paragraphs, it has been demonstrated that avatar embodiment may lead to important behavioral, attitudinal, and cognitive modifications in embodied users. The resulting effects of embodying an avatar have been broadly studied in the media psychology literature in the last decade. Most studies in this regard have been conducted in the context of virtual reality. Few studies have also examined whether similar consequences also take place when robot avatars are used instead (Aymerich-Franch et al., 2019).

One of the first empirical validations of the behavioral consequences of embodying avatars was provided by Yee and Bailenson (2007). These researchers named *Proteus effect*, the phenomenon by which the appearance of the embodied avatar is able to modify the behavior of the user. The theoretical roots of the Proteus effect are partially founded on self-perception theory (Bem, 1972), which argues that people infer their own attitudes by observing their behaviors as if from a third party (Bem, 1972). More specifically, some experiments provide evidence that observing one's own appearance (e.g., clothing, uniforms) can influence behavior (Frank & Gilovich, 1988; Johnson & Downing, 1979). It is believed that these modifications in behavior are linked to identity cues: observing one's own appearance leads people to make implicit inferences about their disposition, which in turn leads to changes in behavior (Yee & Bailenson, 2009). Similarly, in virtual reality, the Proteus effect is linked to people's association of certain avatar traits to specific behavioral stereotypes and expectations. Embodied users might therefore engage in certain behaviors in response to what they believe is expected from their avatars, based on the appearance that the avatar has (Yee & Bailenson, 2007; Yee, Bailenson, & Ducheneaut, 2009).

The first study on the Proteus effect (Yee & Bailenson, 2007) showed that when participants embodied attractive avatars, they disclosed more personal information and approached another avatar more closely compared to participants embodied in less attractive avatars. Also, they showed that when participants embodied taller avatars, they were more confident in a negotiation task compared to participants embodied in shorter avatars (Yee & Bailenson, 2007). Yee et al. (2009) also demonstrated that the behavioral changes resulting from avatar embodiment experiences persisted after this experience, back to the physical reality. Specifically, these authors found that participants who had taller avatars in virtual reality negotiated more aggressively in subsequent face-to-face interactions than participants given shorter avatars (Yee et al., 2009).

Bailenson and colleagues have further examined the Proteus effect in several contexts, including proenvironmental behavior, prosocial behavior, or savings behaviors, among many others. For instance, a study that looked at the effects of exposure to a digital representation of one's future self found that participants with an avatar that represented an aged-morphed version of their future selves allocated more money to a hypothetical retirement savings account than those who had an avatar that represented their current selves (Hershfield et al., 2011). Another study that examined the capacity of virtual reality to encourage prosocial behavior found that when participants were given the super power of flying as a superhero, they helped the researcher more when she spilled pens after the virtual experience as part of a behavioral measure, as compared with those who experienced a ride as passengers in a helicopter (Rosenberg, Baughman, & Bailenson, 2013). Also, one of their studies, which looked at the effect of embodied experiences on proenvironmental attitude and behavior, found that embodying animal avatars led to greater interconnection between the self and nature compared to a video (Ahn et al., 2016).

The works by Slater and colleagues also provide good empirical support to the fact that avatar embodiment leads to important behavioral modifications. In this regard, Kilteni, Bergstrom, and Slater (2013) found that participants embodied in a dark-skinned casually dressed, "Jimi Hendrix—like" body showed more body movement while drumming than participants in a light-skin body avatar wearing a suit, which suggests a response to the stereotyped expectations of Jimi Hendrix being more bodily expressive (Slater & Sanchez-Vives, 2016). Another study by Banakou, Groten, and Slater (2013) found that embodiment in a virtual child body caused overestimation of object sizes and implicit attitude changes toward becoming childlike. These results were also replicated in Tajadura-Jiménez, Banakou, Bianchi-Berthouze, and Slater (2017).

A related line of studies has looked at the impact of embodiment experiences in attitudinal modifications in a wide range of areas, such as gender and age stereotyping or racial bias. Specifically, Yee and Bailenson (2006) showed how placing participants in avatars of old people contributed more to reduce negative stereotyping of the elderly than placing them in avatars of young people. Another study examined the effects of embodying hypersexualized female avatars in females. The study found that participants who embodied sexualized avatars tended to objectify themselves and reported more body-related thoughts than participants with nonsexualized avatars (Fox, Bailenson, & Tricase, 2013). In the area of racial bias, Groom, Bailenson, and Nass (2009) examined the influence of embodiment on racial bias and found that participants embodied in black avatars showed greater implicit racial bias after the virtual reality experience compared to participants embodied in white avatars. Interestingly, though, Peck, Seinfeld, Aglioti, and Slater (2013) found that implicit racial bias significantly decreased after the embodiment experience for participants who had embodied a black avatar compared to participants embodied in white, purple, or no-body conditions. In a follow-up study to Peck et al. (2013), Banakou, Hanumanthu, and Slater (2016) tested whether the reduction in implicit bias lasted in time and whether it was enhanced by multiple exposures. They found that implicit bias decreased more for those with a black avatar than for those with a white avatar and that it lasted for 1 week after exposure.

The studies by Slater et al. have further demonstrated that avatar embodiment does not only have effects at the attitudinal and behavioral level but also at higher levels of cognitive processing. In a recent paper, Banakou, Kishore, and Slater (2018) showed that embodiment in an avatar that looked like Einstein, strongly associated with high-performing cognitive abilities, resulted in an enhanced cognitive performance. Participants embodied in Einstein, who were young students, also reduced implicit bias against older people.

While not connected to avatar embodiment strictly speaking, another line of studies worth mentioning that has been explored in virtual reality concerning behavioral modifications is the one that uses doppelgängers. Doppelgängers are virtual humans who highly resemble the real self but behave independently. Empirical evidence shows that doppelgängers can influence the behaviors and attitudes of the user that they represent (Aymerich-Franch & Bailenson, 2014; Fox & Bailenson, 2009; Fox, Bailenson, & Binney, 2009; Segovia & Bailenson, 2009). Works with doppelgängers are theoretically based on the assumption of social cognitive theory (Bandura, 1971) sustaining that similarity and identification with a model leads to behavior imitation. According to this theory, rewards and punishments are not necessary for people to learn, as it is possible to learn also through observing models. Due to the high similarity to the self, doppelgängers can be used as powerful models (Bailenson & Segovia, 2010; Fox & Bailenson, 2010).

As mentioned earlier, most studies that demonstrate the capacity of avatar embodiment experiences to modify attitudes, behavior, and cognition have been carried out in the domain of virtual reality. It is worth mentioning, however, the study conducted by Aymerich-Franch et al. (2019), which shows that robot embodiment experiences might also affect behavior. In this study, participants embodied either a rude robot that said offensive words to a confederate or a neutral robot that used neutral words. Participants embodied in the rude robot apologized to the confederate for the bad behavior of their robot avatar. However, more studies are needed to determine whether similar effects in behavioral modifications than those identified in virtual reality also occur when robot avatars are used instead.

Avatar embodiment technologies for mental health

Virtual reality has largely been explored as a useful tool to generate improvement in several areas connected to mental health, principally, for treating anxiety disorders. As a reference, a systematic review of empirical studies recently conducted by Freeman et al. (2017) identified 285 studies that used virtual reality to treat mental health disorders. Of them, 192 dealt with anxiety, 44 with schizophrenia, 22 with substance-related disorders, and 18 with eating disorders. It is important to clarify, however, that these studies used virtual reality to treat mental health disorders, but they did not necessarily use avatar embodiment experiences for that.

It is apparent from the review by Freeman et al. (2017) that anxiety disorders have received the largest attention by scholars. The widest implemented technique to deal with anxieties using virtual reality is virtual reality exposure therapy (VRET). In VRET, virtual simulations of the feared stimuli are recreated so that patients can gradually expose to the stimuli to reduce their fear. Variables that are likely to affect anxiety, such as the closeness, the affability, or the number of perceived threats, are typically manipulated in controlled virtual environments to carry out the therapy (Aymerich-Franch & Bailenson, 2014). VRET can help to treat anxiety disorders, such as specific phobias, social phobia, or posttraumatic stress disorder (Wiederhold & Wiederhold, 2000). However, studies that use VRET are generally limited to variations in the context of the virtual environment, but avatar modifications or doppelgängers are rarely considered (Aymerich-Franch & Bailenson, 2014; Aymerich-Franch et al., 2014).

In one of the few studies that examined the possibility to manipulate avatar appearance to reduce anxiety, Aymerich-Franch et al. (2014) embodied participants either in an avatar with the participant's own face or to a dissimilar avatar. Then, they were asked to deliver a speech in front of a virtual audience. Participants with a dissimilar avatar experienced slightly less social anxiety than those with their own face during the speech. These findings are explained because, according to cognitive models of social phobia, individuals who suffer from social phobia present a negatively distorted self-image, which plays an important role in maintaining this anxiety (Izgiç et al., 2004; Stopa and Jenkins, 2007). The underlying assumption is that if this distorted image can be corrected by providing users with a "new (virtual) self," it is possible that anxiety symptoms can be reduced. The findings of this study suggest that avatar transformations could be useful to treat phobias and other anxiety disorders. As Aymerich-Franch et al. (2014) proposed, avatar transformations might be incorporated in VRET for social phobia in combination with exposure, by progressively increasing patient's avatar resemblance to the real self over the course of several sessions.

Doppelgängers are another useful approach to treating anxiety disorders. Using this technique, Aymerich-Franch and Bailenson (2014) explored the potential of using doppelgängers in conjunction with a visualization technique to reduce public speaking anxiety. Participants were either assigned to a visualization with a doppelgänger or to a visualization through imagination in which they went through a relaxation process before giving a speech. In the doppelgänger condition, participants observed their doppelgänger performing a successful speech. The study found that the doppelgänger technique worked better in males, whereas the imagination technique worked better in females.

Beyond anxiety disorders, avatar embodiment experiences have been explored in other directions that could also greatly contribute to enhance health. In Osimo, Pizarro, Spanlang, and Slater (2015), participants alternately switched between an avatar that resembled themselves where they described a personal problem and an avatar that represented S. Freud, the founder of psychoanalysis, from which they offered themselves counseling. They found that when the counselor resembled Freud, participants improved their mood, compared to the counselor being a self-representation. This experiment connects well with the principles of life coaching, a process oriented to attain life fulfillment and well-being in which the coach acts as a tool to help the client find the solution to their problems by themselves, thus enhancing self-efficacy to resolve personal issues.

Avatar embodiment experiences have also been shown to contribute to treat depression. Falconer et al. (2016) examined the possibilities of avatar embodiment to increase self-compassion in patients with depression. In the study, patients practiced delivering compassion in an avatar and then experienced receiving it from themselves in another avatar. They found that the experience led to a reduction in depression severity and self-criticism, as well as to a significant increase in self-compassion.

A previous study also by Falconer et al. (2014) used avatar embodiment as a technique to reduce self-criticism and increase self-compassion in female participants who scored high in self-criticism. It is interesting to highlight that the authors specifically highlight the added value of the embodiment experience: "while simply rehearsing the delivery and receipt of compassionate behavior leads to a reduction in self-criticism", embodiment "has the additional effect of positively increasing self-compassion."

Another area in which avatar embodiment might make a significant contribution is in increasing empathy to reduce violent behavior. In a recent study, Hamilton-Giachritsis, Banakou, Garcia Quiroga, Giachritsis, and Slater (2018) embodied mothers in the avatars of 4-year-old children.

They interacted with a digital mother who responded either in a positive or a negative way. They found that experiencing negative maternal behavior increased levels of empathy and feelings of fear of violence.

The role of empathy and perspective taking through avatar embodiment was also recently examined in Seinfeld et al. (2018) to prevent aggressive behaviors in domestic violence. In the study, male domestic violence offenders were put in the body of a female victim of domestic abuse. After the experience, offenders were able to recognize fearful female faces more easily, and also their bias to recognize fearful faces as happy was reduced.

Finally, avatar embodiment experiences could also be used to promote healthier lifestyles. In a series of experiments, Fox and Bailenson (2009) addressed the question whether doppelgängers could be used to promote exercise. These authors found that participants who observed a doppelgänger lose weight when they performed physical activity or gain weight when they were physically inactive and exercised more after the virtual experience and also 24 hours afterward compared to participants in various control conditions.

In Fox, Arena, et al. (2009) and Fox, Bailenson, et al. (2009), doppelgängers were explored as potential agents to promote changes in eating habits. The researchers observed a replication of social facilitation effects on eating in their experiment. Provided that participants experienced a high sense of presence, men tended to imitate their doppelgänger and eat candy after the study, whereas women tended to suppress the behavior and not eat candy. These works suggest that doppelgängers might be useful to modify people's health-related behavior by showing the rewards of exercise and proper eating habits (Bailenson & Segovia, 2010).

Future research directions

Avatar embodiment has a unique transformative capacity that can be used to improve psychological well-being. There are several lines of research that could be explored to promote avatar embodiment experiences to improve psychological well-being. These experiences could also be included as part of the treatment for mental illnesses. These studies could be framed from different paradigms that have been explained in this chapter, and they could target different areas of intervention.

A first approach that could be used to frame these interventions is the Proteus Effect. This paradigm has been empirically validated in several studies (Aymerich-Franch et al., 2014; Fox et al., 2013; Yee & Bailenson, 2007, 2009) and offers one of the best approaches for this type of interventions. It has been demonstrated that cues inherent in certain avatars' appearances can ultimately influence the attitudes and behaviors of the embodied user. This effect could be wisely used to design interventions that included avatar embodiment experiences as part of the therapy. This paradigm aligns particularly well with interventions that are rooted on principles from behavioral and cognitive psychology, such as cognitive behavioral therapy (CBT). A main focus of CBT is on modifying unhelpful cognitive distortions and behaviors, which are believed to play a major role in the development and maintenance of psychological disorders (Beck, 2011). Similar to how avatar transformations are effective to reduce social phobia, other works could look at the possibility to embody participants in characters, superheroes, and avatars with appearances that are associated to certain behavioral expectations in the collective imagination or even to specific personality traits (Aymerich-Franch, 2015), which could lead patients to behave in more adaptive manners.

A second useful theoretical approach also covered by the article is that used in the studies with doppelgängers, based on social cognitive theory, which essentially explains how similarity and identification of a model lead to better results in modeling behaviors. Observing a doppelgänger succeeding in anxiety inducing situations might help patients boost their sense of self-efficacy (Fox & Bailenson, 2010). Also, it might allow patients to savor the rewards that they would get if they learned how to effectively manage an anxiety-inducing situation. By observing their doppelgängers succeed in their feared situations, for instance, patients might gain self-confidence and reduce their anxiety.

Another interesting approach develops from perspective taking as a way to increase empathy (Peck et al., 2013; Seinfeld et al., 2018; Yee & Bailenson, 2006) as well as on the fact that the body is central to our understanding of others (Maister, Slater, Sanchez-Vives, & Tsakiris, 2014). Increasing empathy through perspective taking in avatar embodiment experiences might contribute in several of the targeted areas such as problems related to abuse or neglect. Embodying someone else would allow patients to experience situations from the perspective of others, thus potentially increasing the understanding of how that person might be feeling in a given situation.

Regarding areas of intervention, the two main areas in which avatar embodiment experiences could be particularly revealing are the treatment of mental disorders and the improvement of subjective well-being. These two dimensions together constitute a complete model of mental health (Keyes & Lopez, 2002).

The following list can be considered an initial, nonexclusive reference of mental disorders that might potentially benefit of interventions that included avatar embodiment experiences to transform behavior and cognitive distortions:

- Anxiety disorders, including obsessive-compulsive disorder, posttraumatic stress disorder, or specific phobias and social phobia
- Mood disorders, including depression and bipolar disorders
- Substance-related disorders such as dependence and abuse of alcohol or drugs
- Autism
- Body dysmorphic disorder
- Hypochondriasis
- Sexual disorders
- Eating disorders such as anorexia nervosa
- Sleep disorders such as insomnia
- Pathological gambling
- Problems related to abuse or neglect
- Personality disorders such as narcissistic, avoidant, dependent, or antisocial

Psychological well-being, which refers to an optimal psychological functioning and experience (Ryan & Deci, 2001), is another major area that could benefit from interventions that included avatar embodiment experiences as a way to modify attitudes, habits, and behaviors toward a healthier or more fulfilling lifestyle and toward a better quality of life. The potential areas of intervention include, and are not limited to,

- Self-confidence and self-esteem
- Emotional management
- Self-efficacy and goal achievement
- Interpersonal relationships and self-assertion
- Stress management and adaptation to the environment
- Food, nutrition, and health

Conclusion

Despite their huge potential to enhance psychological well-being, very few works have examined avatar embodiment experiences to transform behavior, attitudes, and cognition for the improvement of psychological health and well-being, that is, while the role of avatar embodiment to contribute on the domain of health certainly needs to be further explored, the works already developed in this area present very promising results. These good results suggest that avatar embodiment experiences are indeed a powerful tool to promote attitudinal, behavioral, and cognitive modifications that could contribute to reduce mental illness. Also, these works suggest that avatar embodiment experiences could be used toward boosting healthier lifestyles, ultimately also contributing to enhance physical and psychological well-being.

It should be noted that none of the works that were identified in this theoretical review used robot embodiment experiences to promote mental health. This is explained because the illusion of robot embodiment has only recently been identified as a new form of avatar embodiment (Aymerich-Franch, 2017, 2018), potentially capable of inducing similar effects to those attributed to avatar embodiment in virtual reality (Aymerich-Franch et al., 2016; Aymerich-Franch et al., 2017b; Aymerich-Franch et al., 2019). The capacity of robot embodiment to induce similar changes in users as those identified in virtual reality is an important gap detected in the existing literature of avatar embodiment. Thus, research that provides empirical validation that robot embodiment experiences might also be useful to induce behavioral, attitudinal, and cognitive changes in users to improve health and well-being is particularly encouraged.

Acknowledgments

LAF is supported by Programa de Ayudas Ramón y Cajal (Ref. RYC-2016-19770), Ministerio de Economía, Industria, y Competitividad, Gobierno de España, y Fondo Social Europeo.

References

Ahn, S. J. G., Bostick, J., Ogle, E., Nowak, K. L., McGillicuddy, K. T., & Bailenson, J. N. (2016). Experiencing nature: Embodying animals in immersive virtual environments increases inclusion of nature in self and involvement with nature. *Journal of Computer-Mediated Communication, 21*(6), 399–419. https://doi.org/10.1111/jcc4.12173.

Alimardani, M., Nishio, S., & Ishiguro, H. (2013). Humanlike robot hands controlled by brain activity arouse illusion of ownership in operators. *Scientific reports, 3*, 2396.

Armel, K. C., & Ramachandran, V. S. (2003). Projecting sensations to external objects: Evidence from skin conductance response. *Proceedings Biological Sciences/the Royal Society, 270*(1523), 1499–1506. https://doi.org/10.1098/rspb.2003.2364.

Aymerich-Franch, L. (2015). Exploring avatar personality preferences in virtual worlds. *TIIKM Journal of Film, Media and Communication, 1*(1). https://doi.org/10.17501/jfmc.2448-9328.1.1103.

Aymerich-Franch, L. (2017). Mediated embodiment in new communication technologies. In M. Khosrow-Pour (Ed.), *Encyclopedia of information science and technology* (4th ed.). Hershey, PA: IGI Global.

Aymerich-Franch, L. (2018). Is mediated embodiment the response to embodied cognition? *New Ideas in Psychology, 50*. https://doi.org/10.1016/j.newideapsych.2018.02.003.

Aymerich-Franch, L., & Bailenson, J. (2014). The use of doppelgangers in virtual reality to treat public speaking anxiety: A gender comparison. In *Proceedings of the international society for presence research annual conference. March, 17–19, Vienna, Austria. – Top three paper award.*

Aymerich-Franch, L., & Fosch-Villaronga, E. (2019). What we learned from mediated embodiment experiments and why it should matter to policymakers. *Presence: Teleoperators and Virtual Environments, 27*(1).

Aymerich-Franch, L., & Ganesh, G. (2016). The role of functionality in the body model for self-attribution. *Neuroscience research, 104,* 31–37.

Aymerich-Franch, L., Kishore, S., & Slater, M. (2019). When Your Robot Avatar Misbehaves You Are Likely to Apologize: An Exploration of Guilt During Robot Embodiment. *International Journal of Social Robotics,* 1–10.

Aymerich-Franch, L., Kizilcec, R. F., & Bailenson, J. N. (2014). The relationship between virtual self similarity and social anxiety. *Frontiers in human neuroscience, 8,* 944.

Aymerich-Franch, L., Petit, D., Ganesh, G., & Kheddar, A. (2015). Embodiment of a humanoid robot is preserved during partial and delayed control. In *2015 IEEE international workshop on advanced robotics and its social impacts. Lyon, France.*

Aymerich-Franch, L., Petit, D., Ganesh, G., & Kheddar, A. (2016). The second me: Seeing the real body during humanoid robot embodiment produces an illusion of bi-location. *Consciousness and Cognition, 46.* https://doi.org/10.1016/j.concog.2016.09.017.

Aymerich-Franch, L., Petit, D., Ganesh, G., & Kheddar, A. (2017a). Non-human looking robot arms induce illusion of embodiment. *International Journal of Social Robotics, 9*(4), 479–490. https://doi.org/10.1007/s12369-017-0397-8.

Aymerich-Franch, L., Petit, D., Ganesh, G., & Kheddar, A. (2017b). Object touch by a humanoid robot avatar induces haptic sensation in the real hand. *Journal of Computer-Mediated Communication, 22*(4), 215–230. https://doi.org/10.1111/jcc4.12188.

Bailenson, J. N., & Blascovich, J. (2004). Avatars. In *Encyclopedia of human-computer interaction* (pp. 64–68). Berkshire Publishing Group.

Bailenson, J. N., & Segovia, K. Y. (2010). Virtual doppelgangers: Psychological effects of avatars who ignore their owners. *Online worlds: Convergence of the real and the virtual* (pp. 175–186). London: Springer.

Banakou, D., Groten, R., & Slater, M. (2013). Illusory ownership of a virtual child body causes overestimation of object sizes and implicit attitude changes. *Proceedings of the National Academy of Sciences, 110*(31), 12846–12851. https://doi.org/10.1073/pnas.1306779110.

Banakou, D., Hanumanthu, P. D., & Slater, M. (2016). Virtual embodiment of white people in a black virtual body leads to a sustained reduction in their implicit racial bias. *Frontiers in human neuroscience, 10,* 601.

Banakou, D., Kishore, S., & Slater, M. (2018). Virtually being einstein results in an improvement in cognitive task performance and a decrease in age bias. *Frontiers in psychology, 9,* 917.

Bandura, A. (1971). *Social learning theory. Social learning theory.* https://doi.org/10.1111/j.1460-2466.1978.tb01621.x.

Beck. (2011). *Cognitive behavior therapy: Basics and beyond.* The Guilford Press. https://doi.org/10.1017/CBO9781107415324.004.

Bem, D. J. (1972). *Self-perception theory. Advances in experimental social psychology.* https://doi.org/10.1016/S0065-2601(08)60024-6.

Blanke, O., & Metzinger, T. (2009). Full-body illusions and minimal phenomenal selfhood. *Trends in Cognitive Sciences, 13*(1), 7–13. https://doi.org/10.1016/j.tics.2008.10.003.

Botvinick, M., & Cohen, J. (1998). Rubber hands "feel" touch that eyes see. *Nature, 391*(6669), 756. https://doi.org/10.1038/35784.

Clark, A. (2007). Re-inventing ourselves: The plasticity of embodiment, sensing, and mind. *Journal of Medicine and Philosophy, 32*(3), 263–282. https://doi.org/10.1080/03605310701397024.

Cohen, O., Druon, S., Lengagne, S., Mendelsohn, A., Malach, R., Kheddar, A., & Friedman, D. (2012). fMRI robotic embodiment: A pilot study. In *4th IEEE RAS/EMBS international conference on biomedical robotics and biomechatronics (BioRob)* (pp. 314–319). https://doi.org/10.1109/BioRob.2012.6290866.

Cohen, O., Druon, S., Lengagne, S., Mendelsohn, A., Malach, R., Kheddar, A., & Friedman, D. (2014). fMRI-based robotic embodiment: Controlling a humanoid robot by thought using real-time fMRI. *Presence: Teleoperators and Virtual Environments, 23*(3), 229–241. https://doi.org/10.1162/PRES_a_00191.

Cohen, O., Koppel, M., Malach, R., & Friedman, D. (2014). Controlling an avatar by thought using real-time fMRI. *Journal of Neural Engineering, 11*(3). https://doi.org/10.1088/1741-2560/11/3/035006.

Csordas, T. J. (1999). Embodiment and cultural phenomenology. In *Perspectives on embodiment: The intersections of nature and culture* (pp. 143–162).

Falconer, C. J., Rovira, A., King, J. A., Gilbert, P., Antley, A., Fearon, P.,., & Brewin, C. R. (2016). Embodying self-compassion within virtual reality and its effects on patients with depression. *BJPsych open, 2*(1), 74–80.

Falconer, C. J., Slater, M., Rovira, A., King, J. A., Gilbert, P., Antley, A., & Brewin, C. R. (2014). Embodying compassion: a virtual reality paradigm for overcoming excessive self-criticism. *PloS one, 9*(11). e111933.

Fox, J., Arena, D., & Bailenson, J. N. (2009). Virtual reality: A survival guide for the social scientist. *Journal of Media Psychology, 21*(3), 95–113. https://doi.org/10.1027/1864-1105.21.3.95.

Fox, J., & Bailenson, J. N. (2009). *Virtual self-modeling: The effects of vicarious reinforcement and identification on exercise behaviors.* Media Psychology. https://doi.org/10.1080/15213260802669474.

Fox, J., & Bailenson, J. N. (2010). The use of doppelgängers to promote health behavior change. *CyberTherapy & Rehabilitation, 3*(2), 16–17.

Fox, J., Bailenson, J., & Binney, J. (2009). Virtual experiences, physical behaviors: The effect of presence on imitation of an eating avatar. *Presence: Teleoperators and Virtual Environments, 18*(4), 294–303.

Fox, J., Bailenson, J. N., & Tricase, L. (2013). The embodiment of sexualized virtual selves: The Proteus effect and experiences of self-objectification via avatars. *Computers in Human Behavior, 29*(3), 930–938.

Frank, M. G., & Gilovich, T. (1988). The dark side of self-and social perception: Black uniforms and aggression in professional sports. *Journal of personality and social psychology, 54*(1), 74.

Freeman, D., Reeve, S., Robinson, A., Ehlers, A., Clark, D., Spanlang, B., & Slater, M. (2017). Virtual reality in the assessment, understanding, and treatment of mental health disorders. *Psychological medicine, 47*(14), 2393–2400.

Gallagher, I. (2000). Philosophical conceptions of the self: Implications for cognitive science. *Trends in Cognitive Sciences, 4*(1), 14–21.

Gergondet, P., Druon, S., Kheddar, A., Hintermüller, C., Guger, C., & Slater, M. (2011, December). Using brain-computer interface to steer a humanoid robot. *2011 IEEE International Conference on Robotics and Biomimetics* (pp. 192–197). IEEE.

González-Franco, M., Pérez-Marcos, D., Spanlang, B., & Slater, M. (2010). *The contribution of real-time mirror reflections of motor actions on virtual body ownership in an immersive virtual environment* (Vols. 111–114).

Groom, V., Bailenson, J. N., & Nass, C. (2009). The influence of racial embodiment on racial bias in immersive virtual environments. *Social Influence, 4*(3), 231–248. https://doi.org/10.1080/15534510802643750.

Haggard, P. (2017). Sense of agency in the human brain. *Nature Reviews Neuroscience, 18*(4), 196.

Hamilton-Giachritsis, C., Banakou, D., Quiroga, M. G., Giachritsis, C., & Slater, M. (2018). Reducing risk and improving maternal perspective-taking and empathy using virtual embodiment. *Scientific reports, 8*(1), 2975.

Hershfield, H. E., Goldstein, D. G., Sharpe, W. F., Fox, J., Yeykelis, L., Carstensen, L. L., & Bailenson, J. N. (2011). Increasing saving behavior through age-progressed renderings of the future self. *Journal of Marketing Research, 48*(SPL), S23–S37.

Izgiç, F., Akyüz, G., Doğan, O., & Kuğu, N. (2004). Social Phobia among University Students and its relation to self-esteem and body image. *Canadian Journal of Psychiatry, 49*, 630–634.

Johnson, R. D., & Downing, L. L. (1979). Deindividuation and valence of cues: Effects on prosocial and antisocial behavior. *Journal of Personality and Social Psychology, 37*(9), 1532.

Keyes, C. L. M., & Lopez, S. (2002). Toward a science of mental health: Positive directions in diagnosis and interventions. In *Handbook of positive psychology.* https://doi.org/10.1007/978-94-017-9088-8_16.

Kilteni, K., Groten, R., & Slater, M. (2012). The sense of embodiment in virtual reality. *Presence: Teleoperators and Virtual Environments, 21*(4), 373–387.

Kilteni, K., Bergstrom, I., & Slater, M. (2013). Drumming in immersive virtual reality: The body shapes the way we play. *IEEE Transactions on Visualization and Computer Graphics, 19*(4), 597–605. https://doi.org/10.1109/TVCG.2013.29.

Kishore, S., et al. (November 2016a). Multi-destination beaming: Apparently being in three places at once through robotic and virtual embodiment. *Frontiers in Robotics and AI, 3*, 65. https://doi.org/10.3389/frobt.2016.00065.

Kishore, S., González-Franco, M., Hintemüller, C., Kapeller, C., Guger, C., Slater, M., & Blom, K. J. (2014). Comparison of SSVEP BCI and eye tracking for controlling a humanoid robot in a social environment. *Presence: Teleoperators and Virtual Environments, 23*(3), 242–252. https://doi.org/10.1162/PRES_a_00192.

Kishore, S., Navarro, X., Dominguez, E., de la Peña, N., & Slater, M. (2016b). Beaming into the news: A system for and case study of tele-immersive journalism. *IEEE Computer Graphics and Applications.* https://doi.org/10.1109/MCG.2016.44. In press.

Lenggenhager, B., Tadi, T., Metzinger, T., & Blanke, O. (2007). Video ergo sum: Manipulating bodily self-consciousness. *Science (New York, N.Y.), 317*(5841), 1096–1099. https://doi.org/10.1126/science.1143439.

Lombard, M., & Ditton, T. (1997). At the heart of it all: The concept of presence. *Journal of Computer-Mediated Communication, 3*(2), 20. https://doi.org/10.1111/j.1083-6101.1997.tb00072.x.

Longo, M. R., Schüür, F., Kammers, M. P. M., Tsakiris, M., & Haggard, P. (2008). What is embodiment? A psychometric approach. *Cognition, 107*(3), 978–998. https://doi.org/10.1016/j.cognition.2007.12.004.

Maister, L., Slater, M., Sanchez-Vives, M. V., & Tsakiris, M. (2014). Changing bodies changes minds: Owning another body affects social cognition. *Trends in Cognitive Sciences, 19*(1), 6–12. https://doi.org/10.1016/j.tics.2014.11.001.

Osimo, S. A., Pizarro, R., Spanlang, B., & Slater, M. (2015). Conversations between self and self as Sigmund Freud—A virtual body ownership paradigm for self counselling. *Scientific reports, 5*, 13899.

Peck, T. C., Seinfeld, S., Aglioti, S. M., & Slater, M. (2013). Putting yourself in the skin of a black avatar reduces implicit racial bias. *Consciousness and Cognition, 22*(3), 779–787. https://doi.org/10.1016/j.concog.2013.04.016.

Petkova, V. I., & Ehrsson, H. H. (2008). If I were you: Perceptual illusion of body swapping. *PLoS One, 3*(12), e3832. https://doi.org/10.1371/journal.pone.0003832.

Rosenberg, R. S., Baughman, S. L., & Bailenson, J. N. (2013). Virtual superheroes: Using superpowers in virtual reality to encourage prosocial behavior. *PLoS One, 8*(1), 1–9. https://doi.org/10.1371/journal.pone.0055003.

Ryan, R. M., & Deci, E. L. (2001). On happiness and human potentials: A review of research on hedonic and eudaimonic well-being. *Annual Review of Psychology, 52*(1), 141−166. https://doi.org/10.1146/annurev.psych.52.1.141.

Segovia, K. Y., & Bailenson, J. N. (2009). *Virtually true: Children's acquisition of false memories in virtual reality.* Media Psychology. https://doi.org/10.1080/15213260903287267.

Seinfeld, S., Arroyo-Palacios, J., Iruretagoyena, G., Hortensius, R., Zapata, L. E., Borland, D.,., & Sanchez-Vives, M. V. (2018). Offenders become the victim in virtual reality: impact of changing perspective in domestic violence. *Scientific reports, 8*(1), 2692.

Slater, M., & Sanchez-Vives, M. V. (2014). Transcending the self in immersive virtual reality. *Computer, 47*(7), 24−30.

Slater, M., & Sanchez-Vives, M. V. (2016). Enhancing our lives with immersive virtual reality. *Frontiers in Robotics and AI, 3,* 74.

Spanlang, B., et al. (2014). How to build an embodiment lab: Achieving body representation illusions in virtual reality. *Frontiers in Robotics and AI, 1.* https://doi.org/10.3389/frobt.2014.00009.

Stone, R. J. (2001). Haptic feedback: A brief history from telepresence to virtual reality. *Haptic Human-Computer Interaction,* 1−16. https://doi.org/10.1007/3-540-44589-7_1.

Stopa, L., & Jenkins, A. (2007). Images of the self in social anxiety: Effects on the retrieval of autobiographical memories. *Journal of Behavior Therapy and Experimental Psychiatry, 38*(4), 459−473.

Tajadura-Jiménez, A., Banakou, D., Bianchi-Berthouze, N., & Slater, M. (2017). Embodiment in a child-like talking virtual body influences object size perception, self-identification, and subsequent real speaking. *Scientific reports, 7*(1), 9637.

Tsakiris, M. (2010). My body in the brain: A neurocognitive model of body-ownership. *Neuropsychologia, 48*(3), 703−712. https://doi.org/10.1016/j.neuropsychologia.2009.09.034.

Wiederhold, B. K., & Wiederhold, M. D. (2000). Lessons learned from 600 virtual reality sessions. *CyberPsychology & Behavior, 3*(3), 393−400.

Yee, N., & Bailenson, J. (2006). Walk a mile in digital shoes: The impact of embodied perspective-taking on the reduction of negative stereotyping in immersive virtual environments. In *Proceedings of PRESENCE* (pp. 147−156).

Yee, N., & Bailenson, J. (2007). The proteus effect: The effect of transformed self-representation on behavior. *Human Communication Research, 33*(3), 271−290. https://doi.org/10.1111/j.1468-2958.2007.00299.x.

Yee, N., & Bailenson, J. N. (2009). The difference between being and seeing: The relative contribution of self-perception and priming to behavioral changes via digital self-representation. *Media Psychology, 12*(2), 195−209. https://doi.org/10.1080/15213260902849943.

Yee, N., Bailenson, J. N., & Ducheneaut, N. (2009). The Proteus effect: Implications of transformed digital self-representation on online and offline behavior. *Communication Research, 36*(2), 285−312. https://doi.org/10.1177/0093650208330254.

Age-sensitive well-being support: Design of interactive technologies that modulate internal—external attentional focus for improved cognitive balance and behavioral effectiveness

John A. Waterworth[1], Mark Chignell[2], Henry Moller[2]

[1] Umeå University, Umeå, Sweden; [2] University of Toronto, Toronto, ON, Canada

Introduction

We present an approach to understanding and creating interactive technologies for the support of mental well-being across the life span of the individual. This approach is not only relevant to the familiar cognitive issues that may arise late in life. Rather, we suggest that by taking up insights gained from research on the sense of presence in both the physical and technology-mediated environments, we can better understand a range cognitive issues that tend to arise at different stages of life.

Our perspective on the sense of presence, developed and refined in numerous publications over the last several years (Moller, Barbera, Kayumov, & Shapiro, 2004; Moller & Barbera, 2006; Moller, 2008a,b; Riva, Waterworth, & Waterworth, 2004; Riva, Waterworth, Waterworth, &

67

Mantovani, 2011, 2015; Waterworth & Riva, 2014; Waterworth & Waterworth, 2001, 2003, 2006; Waterworth, Waterworth, Mantovani, & Riva, 2010; Waterworth, Waterworth, Riva, & Mantovani, 2015), is that the degree to which a person feels their own embodied presence in their environment depends on the balance of attention between internal and external information processing. We are primarily concerned with first-person egocentric experiences, in the physical world and through digital technology.

Since many age-specific mental health problems can be related to maladaptive cognitive strategies for engaging with and processing of the external environment in relation to the self, this perspective opens the door to developing technological support for mediating and retraining such cognitive strategies. It provides a rationale for, and approach to, the design of interactive environments in which the level of presence—reflecting the balance of internal/external information processing—can be mediated for therapeutic purposes.

We can identify various suboptimal age-related ways of being in the world that preclude effective functioning and relate them to the habitual levels of presence experienced by the individual. We suggest that, other things being equal, very young children tend to feel highly present in their environment while conscious, whereas the very old generally do not. Because of age-related changes in cognitive strategies, abilities, and habits, the strength of the feeling of presence tends to be a diminishing resource over the course of an individual's lifetime. For example, young children may suffer from attentional problems, where events in the immediate environment are overly distracting. We see this as an overactive presence mechanism, which we term *hyperpresence*. As people become older, more of their waking time is spent in a state of absence—in reminiscence, stories, and daydreaming—predominantly internal information processing that results in generally lower sense of being present in their external, physical environment (Moller et al., 2004; Moller, Devins, Shen, & Shapiro, 2006). At some stage, the ability to be present at the right time—giving timely attention to the environment as needed to carry out their plans—may become lost in what we term *hyperabsence*. Focusing on such developmental changes, we specify several practical strategies for designing interactive technologies to help alleviate cognitive and behavioral problems, by restoring a more balanced relation between individual and environment.

In the next section, we present our well-established framework for understanding presence. In the following sections, we apply this framework to age-related changes in perception and cognition that occur during an individual's lifetime, during both our waking (conscious) and sleeping (unconscious) lives. From this perspective, we outline ways in which developmental changes in mental presence in, and absence from, the external world can help us understand various cognitive and psychological problems as maladaptations of the sense of presence. We then go on to indicate how these problems can be addressed through the design and development of interactive environments.

Presence: the feeling of being in a world

Scientific interest in the experience of presence took off in the early 1990s, when virtual reality (VR) was being intensively developed and applied to a range of application areas. Sheridan (1992) described presence as *"the effect felt when controlling real world objects remotely"* as well as *"the effect people feel when they interact with and immerse themselves in virtual environments"* (pp. 123–124). But, as Biocca (1997) stated, *"the design of virtual reality technology has brought the theoretical issue of presence to the fore, few theorists argue that the experience of presence suddenly emerged with the arrival of virtual reality."*

What is presence and why does it matter?

Many attempts have been made to define presence, and this work continues to this day. Loomis (1992) suggested that presence is a basic state of consciousness and involves the attribution of immediate sensations to distal stimuli, to some other environment that is not in the organism's currently immediate physical space. In this view, the other environment was seen as being either a distant physical one, in which the "operator" feels present, thanks to mediating technology (typically referred to as telepresence), or a virtual 3D environment, in which another (possibly fictional) place is simulated and experienced as (to some extent) real.

Lombard and Jones (2006) point out that *"the first and most basic distinction among definitions of presence concerns the issue of technology"* (p. 25). Some researchers describe the sense of presence only as "mediated presence," a function of our experience of a given medium (e.g., IJsselsteijn, de Ridder, Freeman, & Avons, 2000; Lombard & Ditton, 1997; Loomis, 1992; Marsh, Wright, & Smith, 2001; Sadowski & Stanney, 2002; Schloerb, 1995; Sheridan, 1992, 1996). But as Lee (2004) put it 15 years ago: *"there have been limited attempts to explain the fundamental reason **why** human beings can feel presence when they use media and/or simulation technologies"* (p. 496, emphasis in the original).

The main limitation of viewing presence only as technologically mediated presence is what is not said (Waterworth et al., 2015): what is presence for, and is it a specific cognitive process? Many recent presence researchers have seen the sense of presence as a result of a fundamental cognitive process, one which is not directly linked to the experience of a medium (Baños et al., 2000; Baños, Botella, & Perpiña, 1999; Lee, 2004;

Mantovani & Riva, 1999; Marsh et al., 2001; Moore, Wiederhold, Wiederhold, & Riva, 2002; Riva & Davide, 2001; Riva, Davide, & IJsselsteijn, 2003; Riva & Mantovani, 2012; Schubert, Friedman, & Regenbrecht, 2001; Spagnolli & Gamberini, 2002; Spagnolli, Gamberini, & Gasparini, 2003; Waterworth & Waterworth, 2001, 2003; Zahoric & Jennison, 1998). To feel present in a VR, one must have the capacity to feel present somewhere; this is the sense of presence. The goal of this capacity is the control of the individual in physical space and in social activity. That it can be stimulated by an experience in a virtual environment reflects the extent to which that environment can simulate salient aspects of physical spaces in the real world. Hence, the popular definition of presence as the *"perceptual illusion of non-mediation"* (Lombard & Ditton, 1997).

Adopting the theoretical position of Waterworth et al. (2015), we see presence as a universal animal faculty enabling any sentient organism to distinguish what is part of the organism from what is not—separating the self from the other—and knowing (on some level) which is which. Over the course of evolution, humans and some other animals have acquired the ability, and need, to form mental representations of situations and things that are not currently present in their physical surroundings. When these representations are the main focus of attention, the person is in a state of mental absence (Biocca, 2015; Moller, 2008a,b; Waterworth et al., 2015; Riva et al., 2015).

A well-calibrated sense of presence is needed so that we can identify when and to what extent we are dealing with internal representations of past, possible future, or imaginary events as compared to when we are dealing with current events actually happening in our present environment. When we focus more on the former, we are mentally absent from the world to some extent and experience a low level of presence in our environment, whereas focusing more on the latter—on concrete rather than abstract information—is accompanied by a stronger feeling of presence. Recognition of this absence–presence dichotomy is an important step in understanding of what presence is for, and therefore what it can potentially do, not least because of the immediate link between presence and action in the world.

Concrete external information is realized *as the physical world* or, through digital technology, as *a (virtual) world,* both of which we experience as presently existing outside our minds and bodies and in which our bodies can act. In contrast, internal information, for example, thoughts, memories, or plans, is experienced as, roughly, where it is—inside our heads (Velmans, 1998, 2000). As far as our sense of presence is concerned, there is no difference between a fully compelling immersive VR and the nonsimulated physical world. Thus, mediated presence is no different, from the point of view of the organism and its physical and physiological (re-)actions, from physical presence, precisely because it is the illusion of nonmediation (Lombard & Ditton, 1997).

Following Riva et al. (2004), we distinguish three distinct layers of presence that have emerged over our evolutionary history, inspired by and named after the three evolutionary levels of selfhood as identified by Damasio (e.g., 1999). The most primitive, proto presence, arises basically from movement of the body and operates primarily through proprioception. The next level, core presence, is perceptual in nature and is the principle determinant of the feeling of presence of which we are aware. Finally, extended presence relates to how the significance of events— essentially the reflective meaning of what is currently happening— influences presence. Presence is experienced most strongly when all three layers are integrated and conscious attention is focused on the same external situation, whether this is physical reality, VR, or a mixture of the two. In contrast, we experience maximum mental absence from the external world when conscious attention is focused but the layers are not integrated (see Fig. 4.1).

The experience of an appropriate sense of presence reflects an essential neurological process by which intentions are modeled and subsequently linked to action in the world (Moller & Barbera, 2006; Moller, 2008b; Riva et al., 2011, 2015). In other words, people feel present to the extent that they can, or feel they can, act out intentions in the external world in which they find themselves. This external world may be physical or virtual. In either case *"presence is tantamount to successfully supported action in the environment"* (Zahoric & Jennison, 1998). By viewing presence as more than a media-related phenomenon, we can see not only its importance to the organism but also the potential power of mediated presence.

The feeling of presence that people have in the physical world can be stimulated by the virtual; hence, not only the appeal of immersive computer games but also the potency of VR as a psychotherapeutic tool, used in the treatment of phobias, eating disorders, pain management, and

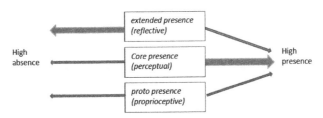

FIGURE 4.1 Strength and focus of attention in high presence and high absence states. *Original figure based on material in Waterworth, J. A., Waterworth, E. L., Mantovani, F., & Riva, G. (2010). On feeling (the) present: An evolutionary account of the sense of presence in physical and electronically-mediated environments.* Journal of Consciousness Studies, 17(1–2), *167–178.*

many other conditions. In a metaanalysis of the literature (Riva, Wiederhold, & Mantovani, 2019), Riva and colleagues found 25 different articles that demonstrated the clinical potential of VR in the diagnosis and the treatment of mental health disorders. They concluded that *"VR compares favorably to existing treatments in anxiety disorders, eating and weight disorders, and pain management, with long-term effects that generalize to the real world"* (page 82). In these cases, virtual realities are being used to retrain the way in which an individual relates to the world around them, to retrain the application of their capacity to feel their own embodiment in the world—which is their capacity to feel present. Viewed through this theoretical lens, many common psychological problems can be seen as arising from an imbalance in the relative levels of presence and absence, which is why VR-based therapy can be so successful. The phenotypic cognitive problems that tend to arise in individuals change over the course of the human life span, as do levels of presence versus absence as people age. The main idea of this chapter is that by identifying, addressing, and mediating these changes with appropriate interactive technologies, we can help alleviate age-related cognitive problems.

Changes in presence across the life span

As mentioned earlier, we suggest that presence can be expected to decline as an individual develops from babyhood to old age. The natural development of the individual is correlated with the gradual and incipient development of absence, not presence, with senescence (Moller et al., 2004, Moller, 2008a,b). Young children sample environmental stimuli frequently, old people less so, as indicated by, for example, a reduced rate and amplitude of saccadic eye movements with age (see, e.g., Dowiasch, Marx, Einhäuser, & Bremmer, 2015). Thus, young people tend to experience high levels of presence; a baby may feel present whenever he or she is conscious. At the other end of life, the very old person experiences relatively little presence; they are mostly psychologically absent from the world, absorbed in an inner world of thoughts, imaginings, and especially memories. An optimal level of presence is required to maximize the efficiency with which intentions can be translated into actions (Riva et al., 2015). As well as shortcomings in their motor competences, we hypothesize that babies may experience too much presence to effectively translate intention into action. Old people, in contrast, may experience too little presence at key times, diminishing their capacity to act effectively on their intentions.

Fig. 4.2 shows a speculative view of how presence tends to vary across the human life span, based on known changes in cognitive performance with age. This pattern of variation will be referred to in the following

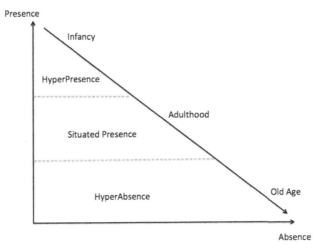

FIGURE 4.2   Hypothetical view of typical changes in presence and absence across the life span.

discussion. In infancy, presence will be high and absence will be low. As a person develops into adulthood and beyond, presence will decrease and absence will grow as the person tends to be more internally- and memory focused. Overall, the ability to feel presence is a diminishing resource over the life of an individual. But while only one decreasing straight line is shown in this simplified figure, there are likely to be many different trajectories (some curved) varying between different types of people, but all tending to move downward over time (to the right).

In the very young, there is a state of high presence ("hyperpresence") where the focus is on observing the surrounding world and learning about it. As the young person learns and grows into adulthood, executive functioning develops and cognitive control can be exerted (see, e.g., Luna, Marek, Larsen, Tervo-Clemmens, & Chahal, 2015). In this zone of "situated presence," the degree of presence varies appropriately from situation to situation (e.g., watching television vs. working on a project). In this zone, the individual is able to adopt the right mix of presence and absence for each given situation. As a person ages, there is an increasing risk of transitioning into a zone of predominant absence ("hyperabsence"), at first temporarily, but eventually more permanently. As we outline in the later section on sleep, wakefulness, and dreaming, these subjective psychological progressions in self-state during the course of human growth, development, and aging correlate with changes in the documented physiologically evolution of sleep-wake consciousness and circadian rhythms across the human life span (Moller et al., 2004; Moller & Barbera, 2006, and see Fig. 4.3 below).

Normal Sleep Cycles in Children

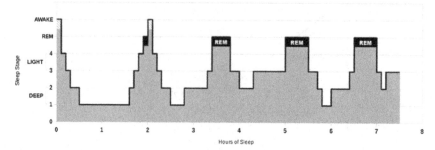

Normal Sleep Cycles in Young Adults

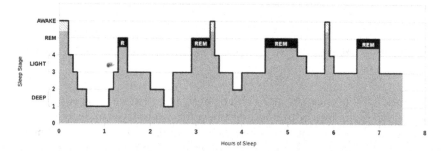

Normal Sleep Cycles in The Elderly

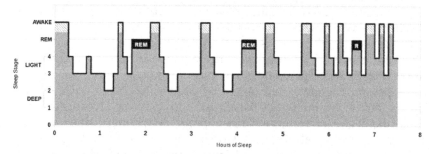

FIGURE 4.3 Sleep architecture changes and aging. *Redrawn from Kales, A., & Kales, J. D. (1974). Sleep disorders: Recent findings in the diagnosis and treatment of disturbed sleep. New England Journal of Medicine, 290(9), 487–499.*

Maladjustments of presence and their remediation

Varying feelings of presence reflect the extent to which attention is focused on the external environment and the experience of an appropriate sense of presence reflects an essential neurological process by which intentions are modeled and subsequently linked to action in the world. Changes in presence are often needed for successful functioning in the world, as a person engages in activities requiring an adaptive balance of reflection and attention to the environment. In some cases, as we have suggested, this balance between internal and external processing is lost; these maladjustments of presence disrupt the link between intentions and actions (Riva et al., 2015). If presence varies over the life span, with young children having very high (and sometimes excessive) levels of presence and elderly people having low (and sometimes suboptimal) levels of presence, how can well-being be improved by modifying presence appropriately with interactive exercises and activities?

Let us look at the mental health implications of the transitions shown in Fig. 4.2. If one considers various psychiatric syndromes, many of them seem to involve a loss of presence and an unhealthy increase in absence. In depression, for instance, the person may ruminate excessively on intrusive negative thoughts. In psychoses such as schizophrenia, the person forms an alternate reality accepting mentally constructed percepts and experiences as if they are real. In delirium (a form of acute brain failure that can occur in the elderly and medically infirm), the person becomes confused and is no longer attending effectively to the outside world (Inouye et al., 1990).

While loss of presence may be maladaptive, there are many times when it is necessary to perform a task. For instance, a mathematician attempting to solve a problem, or a novelist working on her latest book, may get into productive flow states where the outside world is completely forgotten for periods of time. Thus, loss of presence is adaptive when it is voluntary and useful or enjoyable, but maladaptive when it is involuntary and damaging to the person or to nearby people. A person is suffering from hyperabsence when they have frequent and involuntary excursions into absence, with the problem increasing as these excursions become more frequent and prolonged.

How can presence be reestablished when absence becomes maladaptive? One method is to use techniques such as mindfulness training, which can be supported with suitable interactive technology. Parents and educators also use camping, sports, and outdoor activities to increase presence in children and young people, and these too can be simulated and experienced through interactive games, for example, on the Wii and Kinect platforms. Activities such as dancing, exercises, and various games can be used throughout the life span to moderate or promote presence. To the same end, there has also been a renaissance of "reverse Montessori" approaches to engage elders with cognitive slippage in play-oriented therapeutic remediation (e.g., Chiu, Wesson, & Sadavoy, 2013).

Since children play, it is tempting to think that play is inherently associated with presence, but the relationship between play and presence is unlikely to be that simple. A popular view of children's play is that it builds the skills that will be needed when the child becomes an adult (e.g., Piaget, 1962; Vygotsky, 1978). The play of very young children is in some senses purposeless (Rubin, Fein, & Vandenberg, 1983), with the means being more salient than the ends. However, while self-driven play may seem purposeless in young children, in the Internet age the technologically mediated games that older children and teenagers play can be highly purposive, involving goals such as building, conquering, winning, or completing various tasks or levels of proficiency.

As play becomes more purposive and task oriented, attention switches from simple presence in an experienced world to a focus on the task-salient aspects of the game. This involves a shift from engagement of primarily core (and perhaps proto-) presence to incorporate extended (reflective) presence (as illustrated in Fig. 4.1). Thus, in a game like Breath of the Wild, play takes place in a virtual world that is rendered in detail, but the presence is no longer that of a neutral and detached observer, but of an actor who has tasks to perform. Action and interaction have more meaning and require the engagement of more layers of presence (Fig. 4.1). Task-oriented play and visual attention, in general, typically require acquisition of perceptual data using two distinct attentional (focusing) systems (Chica, Bartolomeo, & Lupiáñez, 2013). Endogenous attention is "top-down" and driven by internal goals. Exogenous attention tracks new and potentially relevant information in the environment.

One of the challenges that people face is how to balance the need to pay attention to novel information in the environment (exogenous attention) with the need to focus on attentional information that is relevant to the current task (endogenous attention). High presence states involve primarily exogenous attention, a focus on the surroundings without intruding thoughts and competing goals, the task of "concentration" as practiced in certain religious and philosophical traditions (e.g., Buddhism and yoga). Absence, however cannot be simply equated with overriding endogenous attention; it is maximized when the three layers of presence are not focused on the same content (Fig. 4.1). Absence may be experienced when the individual is mentally drifting, in which case there is no clear focus of attention. This relates to the idea of voluntary (often task-driven) absence versus involuntary (maladaptive) lack of presence.

If, as children, we are naturally playful and immersed in the world around us, what is lost when we lose that presence with age and become more ensconced in our own thoughts and memories? In our view, sustained hyperabsence in the elderly often constitutes a threat to physical, mental, and cognitive health. At the extreme, an elderly person may enter a state of delirium or permanently enter a state of dementia driven by organic changes to the brain.

How can interactive games, exercises, and activities increase presence in the elderly, thereby improving physical, mental, and cognitive health? In order to address this question, it may be useful to reconsider the construct of mindfulness. Mindfulness is a deceptively simple word, but it can be deconstructed into a number of interrelated concepts. For instance, the eight-factor model of mindfulness presented by Bergomi, Tschacher, and Kupper (2014) includes the following individual factors of mindfulness:

- awareness toward inner experiences;
- awareness toward outer experiences;
- acting with awareness (being in the present moment);
- acceptance (accepting, nonjudging, and self-compassionate orientation);
- decentering (nonidentification and nonreactivity);
- openness to experience (nonavoidance);
- relativity of thoughts and beliefs; and
- insightful understanding.

Of these factors, our notion of presence is most closely related to the second and third, i.e., awareness toward outer experiences and acting with awareness (being in the present moment). When awareness toward outer experiences and acting with awareness are combined, this becomes interactive presence. When tasks or goals are added to the experience, this becomes motivated presence; the three layers of presence referred to earlier are integrated (to some extent).

To illustrate the difference between these types of presence, we will use an interactive activity developed in the Centivizer project (see Tong et al., 2017 for an introduction to the project). The activity in this example involves viewing a 360-degree travel video and using a steering wheel to change the viewpoint at different elapsed times in the video. We consider below three conditions applied to this activity, each resulting in a different type of experience that can be related to the three-layer model of presence outlined earlier in the chapter.

Version 1—Passive (perceptual presence): The person watches a 360-degree travel video (e.g., a gondola ride through Venice) where the viewpoint changes as the video plays, but the person has no control over the viewpoint.
Version 2—Interactive (proprioceptive and perceptual presence): The person watches the 360-degree travel video while holding a joystick. As they move the joystick, the viewpoint changes

accordingly so that they create their own personal version of the tour and explore the scenery from different perspectives.

Version 3—Motivated (extended, proprioceptive, and perceptual presence): In this version, the experience is more explicitly gamelike. The person is given a bingo card and told that she will get a prize if she finds all the numbers on the card and clicks on them. Numbers are placed on various viewpoints and different time points in the video. If the person clicks on a number, and it matches a number on the bingo card, then that number is collected. If all the numbers on the card are collected, then the person wins the game and gets the prize. Note that since numbers may only be visible from some viewpoints and only one viewpoint can be seen at a particular point in time, the person may have to go through the video several times in order to collect all the numbers on the bingo card.

In such mediated activities, the type of presence to be experienced can be designed into the system as a setting or choice. For example, the activity could be enjoyed with, or without, a steering wheel to change the viewpoint, and with or without the associated bingo game. One could also create a version of this activity that involved physical exercise. For instance, a heavier steering wheel could be used for selecting the viewpoint, one which would require calibrated physical effort to move. There could also be accelerator and brake pedals to control the speed of playback of the video and even a gear lever which would allow the person to move forward, or back up, through the video. Note that there is also a potentially huge design space of tasks that could be superimposed on 360-degree video. For instance, instead of a bingo task people could do a pathfinding task, where they have to find numbers or letters in a certain order, for example from 1 to 10. There could also be a mystery task where the person has to find clues in the video to then solve the mystery.

Many games and tasks have been proposed for preventing, or slowing, physical and cognitive decline in aging, from existing games such as Guitar Hero, Wii Fit, Sudoko, and Crossword puzzles, to purpose-built activities such as Lumosity (www.lumosity.com). However, we see games that include a strong component of presence or mindfulness as being particularly beneficial. Since our psychological grip on the external world and the immediate moment tends to weaken with age, games should deliberately implement and exercise a significant level of presence.

Presence increases the sense of engagement and is also associated with optical flow, something that the aging brain tends to experience less of, particularly if a person is not driving every day or is sitting down watching television most of the time. The flow in television is no substitute for perceived bodily motion because it tends to be discontinuous, disembodied, and nonimmersive. In contrast, interactive presence applications draw the person in and can then be linked to physical and cognitive exercises so that the experience of engagement and presence amplifies the level of motivation and, we would hypothesize, the benefits of those exercises.

With the recent renewed interest (and some hype) around VR, presence has become integral to a number of applications for audiences of almost all ages (although VR is generally not recommended for use under the age of 13). The most obvious ones are gaming and entertainment, which is where all major HMD (head-mounted display) manufacturers see the biggest potential for growth in the near term, especially for youth and young adult audiences. Another area of rapid growth is education and training where simulations of real-world scenarios help students and trainees prepare for the challenges of their professions.

There are countless use cases for applications that allow users to learn or practice a specific task or workflow and where feeling present is imperative for them to have an impact and be useful. These range from putting firefighters and police officers in simulated dangerous situations to enabling medical students to practice surgeries in a virtual operating room. However, the lack of stimulation of multiple senses still limits this type of application. In the medical sector, VR is used to help children with autism spectrum disorder (Cai, Chiew, Nay, Indhumathi, & Huang, 2017) and teenagers with body image issues (Keizer, Van Elburg, Helms, & Dijkerman, 2016) among many other examples. For elderly patients struggling to cope with dementia, ambient activity technologies are showing promise for both alleviation and remediation of symptoms (Wilkinson, Charoenkitkarn, O'Neill, Kanik, & Chignell, 2017a,b).

Designing for age-specific changes in presence (and its modulation) appears to be a promising route for the development of therapeutic interactive applications. In the following section, we stress the importance of a nuanced and informed understanding of age-related changes in cognition, by considering attendant variations in waking and sleeping patterns—an understanding that opens up further avenues for treatment.

Presence and absence in dreaming and waking life

Neuroscience has established the existence of a fluctuating state of consciousness mediated by oscillations in absence/presence, correlated with oscillations in brain "hardware" functioning, as revealed by, e.g., electroencephalography (EEG), functional MRI (fMRI), or magnetoencephalography, which may be modifiable through external/environmental inputs (Nofzinger, 2005; Moller & Barbera, 2006; Moller, 2008a,b).

The existence of fluctuating states of consciousness (implying also fluctuating levels of presence) has also been well established within the neuroscience of sleeping/waking consciousness research (e.g., Hobson, 2009; Tononi, 2004). It is within unconscious (low-presence) states that offline consolidation of crucial learning and memory cognition is thought to occur, alongside more physiological or nonmental phenomena such as tissue and cellular repair and immunological and endocrine regulation, among others (Moller et al., 2004). Deep (delta), slow-wave sleep (SWS) is thought to be more contributory to physiological restoration and repair of bodily processes, while dreaming (theta) rapid eye movement (REM) sleep contributes mostly to emotional and cognitive integration of perceived novel sensory experiences (Moller & Barbera, 2006; Moller et al., 2004; Tononi, 2004).

A low-presence individual, such as an old person losing faculties due to, for example, dementia or a mood disorder process, may be seen as residing in a parallel consciousness or metaverse state of being, while absenting him or herself to escape from the conventional one that demands performance- and goal-oriented behavior (Moller, 2008a,b). Employing this explanatory model, it is not difficult to see why some attempts to engage an individual affected by neuropsychiatric compromise (irrespective of the cause) in performance task–oriented rehabilitative activities run the risk of setting the individual up for failure (with consequent spikes in anxiety states), due to severe limitations of presence in the world at large. In this sense, procedure and/or protocol-based therapies that disregard the inner life may be limited in their efficacy and therapeutic value. Furthermore, excessive early reliance on task-based rehabilitation may also contravene inclusive design principles, which demand employment of esthetically pleasing interfaces with naturalistic, minimally encumbering affordances and inherent ease-of-use for optimal impact on individuals with handicaps and disabilities (Marti, 2012).

The elderly, especially if institutionalized, are frequently affected by anxiety and depression, and this can accelerate loss of cognitive function. Diminished autonomy and loss of contact with the "real," "natural" world outside institutions lead to a loss of time–place orientation (presence) that is difficult to restore through conventional means in long-term care settings. This results in reduced well-being and quality of life for staff and caregivers, as well as residents. Due to overadministration of tranquilizing drugs, lack of opportunities for exercise and exploration, and a typical institutional focus on stopping, rather than starting behaviors, there is an increased burden of morbidity, mortality, and healthcare costs.

By convention, and in light of more than ample scientific evidence, most neuroscientists currently view human consciousness as consisting of essentially the trinity of wakefulness, nondreaming (unconscious) sleep, and REM sleep, patterns in the cycles of which are known to vary with age (see Fig. 4.3).

In light of our notion of a relatively high level of presence during infancy and early childhood, and the opposite of that during late life, it is worth looking at these patterns of sleep, dreaming, and wakefulness as embodied at the two extremes of age. Infancy and childhood, like old age and senility, exhibit a variation from adult patterns of consciousness (Fig. 4.3). In both, there is a general trend toward a circadian pattern that involves a propensity for polyphasic sleep patterns, which may involve afternoon as well as morning sleep cycles. These cycles include REM, SWS, and "light" sleep.

On the surface, the circadian oscillations of consciousness embodied in infancy and senility could be seen as mirror images of one another with respect to quantitative analysis of sleep need and drive. However, within the gerontologic spectrum, there is a relative paucity of SWS and REM at the expense of light sleep, and light sleep (or "junk sleep") is thought to be, relatively speaking, neither physically nor cognitively regenerative when compared with REM and SWS states of sleep consciousness (Moller et al., 2004).

There is now an extensive evidence-based literature to support the role of cognitive exercise in delaying dementia and other states of neuro-cognitive compromise (e.g., mood disorders), and the idea of "use-it-or-lose-it" has become a staple among clinicians and researchers in the field. However, as a supplement to performance-based views regarding amelioration of cognitive functionality, we propose that access to unconscious processes such as sleep and dreaming may be an undervalued and therefore underemployed modality of therapy (Moller & Barbera, 2006) in relation to changes in presence with aging.

Moller and Barbera (2006) proposed the construct of "dream simulation therapy," where oneiric multisensory stimuli are presented while a person is in REM sleep, with the goal of creating alterations in consciousness (and presence). An alternative approach is to use entrainment of brainwaves, using either sound (e.g., rhythmic oscillations such as binaural frequencies) or visual input (e.g., through stroboscopic presentation of lights or other analogous stimuli), to modify affective or motivational states (Moller, Saynor, Bal, & Sudan, 2016). More recently, the therapeutic paradigm of entraining well-being states for therapeutic purposes via presentation of VR-mediated majestic 3D-naturescapes in technology-mediated mindfulness meditation has been proposed (Moller, Saynor, & Chignell, 2018).

From the perspective of presence versus absence, dreams are typified by a kind of presence within a self-generated VR. Sleep patterns change with aging, and disturbances to sleep are associated with cognitive impairment and risk of dementia (e.g., Cochen et al., 2009). Loss of sleep—related dream presence may be a forerunner of age-related neu-rodegeneration. Evidence for sleep disturbance in aging can be seen in data from the American Time Use Survey as reported by Matulis and Chignell (2019). As can be seen in Fig. 4.4, reported sleeplessness is an increasing problem with age, rising to around 5 minutes a night on average in the early 70s and then increasing to around 10 minutes a night after the age of 85.

As mentioned in the previous section, meditation is an important tool for enhancing attention and presence. Increasingly, meditation is used in general psychiatry, with mindfulness-based stress reduction becoming a broad-spectrum mental health therapy that is now considered main-stream. However, it can be difficult to acquire needed meditation skills, and staffing/care issues are problematic, especially in a frail institution-alized population at risk of, or affected by, not only anxiety and depres-sion but also dementia, which reduces frontal cortical capacity required for active, self-initiated meditation. Protocol-driven technology-enhanced multimodal meditation therapy is a form of broad-spectrum mental health therapy that employs immersive audiovisual displays. It may be a particularly useful therapy for elderly people with cognitive impairment because the meditative state is induced by carefully designed multisen-sory inputs and does not require mind training and self-directed cognitive effort on the part of its recipients.

Key questions for future research include whether or not presence-promoting activities have a beneficial effect on sleep in older people

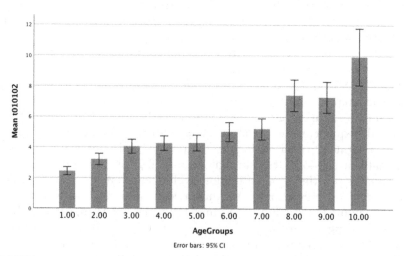

FIGURE 4.4 Increase in Mean reported sleepless (in minutes) with Age as reported in the American Time Use Survey. Age groups are defined as 1 = 40—44; 2 = 45—49; 3 = 50—54; 4 = 55—59; 5 = 60—64; 6 = 65—69; 7 = 70—74; 8 = 75—79; 9 = 80=84; and 10=>85.

and whether techniques such as brain entrainment during REM sleep can improve sleep and thereby have a beneficial impact on cognition, either through improving status or slowing decline.

Conclusions: toward adaptive presence throughout the course of life

In this chapter, we have presented theoretical bases and some practical strategies for designing lifelong well-being support. Well-being, broadly understood as a state of mental and physical health, arises from a pre-dominantly balanced state of being between an individual and their environment. Such states of balance depend on how the individual ex-periences and responds to their embodiment in their environment, and this can be modulated with interactive technologies that promote brain and body training, using virtual and augmented realities.

We have suggested that, other things being equal, presence declines as an individual develops from infancy to old age. New-born babies may always feel present when conscious, since they have not developed the mental capacity for absence, nor do they at first experience themselves to be separate entitles. A young child is mostly present when conscious, whereas a very old person tends to be mostly absent and pays relatively little or infrequent attention to the world around him or her, whether this is a physical or a virtual world, or a blend of the two. This overall diminishment in experienced presence with aging is normal and, in most cases, adaptive—since different habits and skills are called for at different stages of life.

We have also suggested that at least some mental well-being issues can be seen as reflecting maladjustments of presence, suboptimal levels of presence for successful functioning in the world, in relation to the situa-tion and the stage of development of the individual. For example, young children may suffer from attentional problems, typified by a tendency toward distraction by events in the immediate environment. This can be seen as an overactive or too easily engaged presence mechanism. Teen-agers and young adults may tend to focus too much on their developing sense of personal identity, at the expense of a realistic perception of their bodies and place in the world, perhaps currently encouraged by excessive use of social media. This can result in emotional problems, such as body image distortions and eating disorders, panic in public places, depression, and anxiety. These young people have the capacity for presence and ac-tion and yet have become trapped in self-absorbed states of absence. A body of existing evidence suggests that this can be alleviated by experi-encing presence in appropriately designed VRs (e.g., Gutiérrez-

Maldonado, Ferrer-García, Dakanalis, & Riva, 2018). Much work remains to be done in this area.

Successful functioning in any world, whether physical or virtual, centrally involves the smooth execution of intentions as goal-directed and effective actions. This is why some authors have equated mediated presence with the ability—or the feeling of having the ability—to act in a virtual world (e.g., Zahoric & Jennison, 1998). But successfully acting out intentions is not only about presence, which implies paying attention to relevant cues in the environment in a timely fashion. It is also about absence, about forming and holding plans for actions and their completion (Moller, 2008a,b; Riva et al., 2011). As people gradually become older and eventually old, more of their waking time is naturally spent in a state of absence—in reminiscence, stories, and daydreaming. At some stage, the ability to be present at the right time—giving timely attention to the environment as needed to carry out their plans—may become lost. Old people in this state exhibit what can be called intentional problems—difficulties in enacting their plans in the world around them. Although we have discussed presence and its relation to well-being at length in this chapter, we have not attempted to localize presence within functional and mappable brain regions. This is because the neuroscience of presence has yet to be firmly established, and the use of standard neuroscientific tools such as fMRI in this regard has been hampered by methodological challenges (see, e.g., Hoffman, Richards, Coda, Richards, & Sharar, 2003).

Interactive technology can be, and is already being, designed to help with all these problems, and we have presented some suggestions to address further this need and niche. We have outlined how the feeling of presence can be seen as composed of three layers: extended (or reflective), core (perceptual), and proto (proprioceptive) presence. Maximal presence is experienced when all three layers are integrated and conscious attention is focused on the same external situation, whether this is physical reality, VR, or a mixture of the two. Interactive technologies can be designed to stimulate different layers of presence according to the needs of the individual, by varying, for example, perceptual versus problem-solving aspects, or by changing the extent to which a virtual environment engages with the person's sensory—motor capacities. In these ways, individuals can experience controlled levels and types of presence in their external environment, opening up possibilities for a range of therapeutic experiences related to necessary changes in the balance of attention between internal and external worlds.

We see this chapter as a first step in developing a potentially valuable new area of age-calibrated, presence-related well-being research and development. Since little is currently known about age-specific changes in presence this chapter, while founded on evidence-based neuroscientific principles, is necessarily speculative. In spite of this, we expect that managing presence better in targeted populations will lead to major improvements in the status and well-being of those populations. We argue that the future design of age-appropriate presence-modulating interactions could enhance cognitive status and mental wellness, particularly in vulnerable populations with developmental, neurodegenerative, and mental health challenges.

References

Baños, R. M., Botella, C., García-Palacios, A., Villa, H., Perpiñá, C., & Alcañiz, M. (2000). Presence and reality judgment in virtual environments: A unitary construct? *CyberPsychology and Behavior, 3*(3), 327−355.

Baños, R. M., Botella, C., & Perpiña, C. (1999). Virtual reality and psychopathology. *CyberPsychology and Behavior, 2*(4), 283−292.

Bergomi, C., Tschacher, W., & Kupper, Z. (2014). Construction and first validation of the comprehensive inventory of mindfulness experiences. *Diagnostica, 60*(3), 111−125.

Biocca, F. (1997). The Cyborg's Dilemma: Progressive embodiment in virtual environments. *Journal of Computer-Mediated Communication, 3*(2). Online: http://jcmc.indiana.edu/vol3/issue2/biocca2.html.

Biocca, F. (2015). Lighting a path while immersed in presence: A wayward introduction. In M. Lombard, F. Biocca, J. Freeman, W. IJsselsteijn, & R. J. Schaevitz (Eds.), *Immersed in media: Telepresence theory, measurement & technology.* Springer. ISBN: 978-3-319-10189-7.

Cai, Y., Chiew, R., Nay, Z. T., Indhumathi, C., & Huang, L. (2017). Design and development of VR learning environments for children with ASD. *Interactive Learning Environments, 25*(6), 1−12.

Chica, A. B., Bartolomeo, P., & Lupiáñez, J. (2013). Two cognitive and neural systems for endogenous and exogenous spatial attention. *Behavioural Brain Research, 237,* 107−123.

Chiu, M., Wesson, V., & Sadavoy, J. (2013). Improving caregiving competence, stress coping, and mental well-being in informal dementia carers. *World Journal of Psychiatry, 3*(3), 65−73.

Cochen, V., Arbus, C., Soto, M. E., Villars, H., Tiberge, M., Montemayor, T., ... Vellas, B. (2009). Sleep disorders and their impacts on healthy, dependent, and frail older adults. *JNHA-The Journal of Nutrition, Health and Aging, 13*(4), 322−329.

Damasio, A. (1999). *The feeling of what happens: Body, emotion and the making of consciousness.* San Diego, CA: Harcourt Brace and Co, Inc.

Dowiasch, S., Marx, S., Einhäuser, W., & Bremmer, F. (2015). Effects of aging on eye movements in the real world. *Frontiers in Human Neuroscience, 9*(46). https://doi.org/10.3389/fnhum.2015.00046.

Gutiérrez-Maldonado, J., Ferrer-García, M., Dakanalis, A., & Riva, G. (2018). Virtual reality: Applications to eating disorders. In W. S. Agras, & A. H. Robinson (Eds.), *The Oxford handbook of eating disorders* (2nd ed.). Oxford: Oxford University Press.

Hobson, J. A. (2009). REM sleep and dreaming: Towards a theory of proto consciousness. *Nature Reviews Neuroscience, 10*(11), 803−813.

Hoffman, H. G., Richards, T., Coda, B., Richards, A., & Sharar, S. R. (2003). The illusion of presence in immersive virtual reality during an fMRI brain scan. *CyberPsychology and Behavior, 6*(2), 127−131.

IJsselsteijn, W. A., de Ridder, H., Freeman, J., & Avons, S. E. (2000). Presence: Concept, determinants and measurement. In *Paper presented at the human vision and electronic imaging V, San Jose, USA.*

Inouye, S. K., van Dyck, C. H., Alessi, C. A., Balkin, S., Siegal, A. P., & Horwitz, R. I. (1990). Clarifying confusion: The confusion assessment method: A new method for detection of delirium. *Annals of Internal Medicine, 113*(12), 941–948.

Kales, A., & Kales, J. D. (1974). Sleep disorders: Recent findings in the diagnosis and treatment of disturbed sleep. *New England Journal of Medicine, 290*(9), 487–499.

Keizer, A., Van Elburg, A., Helms, R., & Dijkerman, H. C. (2016). A virtual reality full body illusion improves body image disturbance in anorexia nervosa. *PLoS One.* https://doi.org/10.1371/journal.pone.0163921.

Lee, K. M. (2004). Why presence occurs: Evolutionary psychology, media equation, and presence. *Presence, 13*(4), 494–505.

Lombard, M., & Ditton, T. (1997). At the heart of it all: The concept of presence. *Journal of Computer-Mediated Communication, 3*(2). Retrieved February 20, 2018, From: http://onlinelibrary.wiley.com/doi/10.1111/j.1083-6101.1997.tb00072.x/full.

Lombard, M., & Jones, M. T. (2006). Defining presence. In *Proceedings of presence 2006 — the 9th international workshop on presence, Cleveland, OH.* ISBN: 978-0-9792217-0-5 https://ispr.info/presence-conferences/previous-conferences/presence-2006/.

Loomis, J. M. (1992). Distal attribution and presence. *Presence, Teleoperators, and Virtual Environments, 1*(1), 113–118.

Luna, B., Marek, S., Larsen, B., Tervo-Clemmens, B., & Chahal, R. (2015). An integrative model of the maturation of cognitive control. *Annual Review of Neuroscience, 38*, 151–170.

Mantovani, G., & Riva, G. (1999). "Real" presence: How different ontologies generate different criteria for presence, telepresence, and virtual presence. *Presence, Teleoperators, and Virtual Environments, 8*(5), 538–548.

Marsh, T., Wright, P., & Smith, S. (2001). Evaluation for the design of experience in virtual environments: Modeling breakdown of interaction and illusion. *CyberPsychology and Behavior, 4*(2), 225–238.

Marti, P. (2012). *Enabling through design: Exploration of aesthetic and embodied interaction in therapy and care.* Eindhoven Technical University Library. ISBN: 978-90-386-3089-2.

Matulis, H., & Chignell, M. (2019). *Activation of older people.* Submitted for Publication.

Moller, H. J. (2008a). From absence to presence: Blurred consciousness and sleep states. In *Proceedings of PRESENCE 2008. 11th annual international workshop on presence October 16–18, 2008. Padova, Italy.* ISBN: 978-88-6129-287-1 https://ispr.info/presence-conferences/previous-conferences/presence-2008-proceedings/.

Moller, H. J. (2008b). Neural correlates of "absence" in interactive simulator protocols. *CyberPsychology and Behavior, 11*(2), 181–187.

Moller, H. J., & Barbera, J. (2006). Media presence, dreaming and consciousness. Chapter 5, pp 97–123. In G. Riva, M. T. Anguera, B. K. Wiederhold, & F. Mantovani (Eds.), *From communication to presence: The integration of cognition, emotions and culture towards the ultimate communicative experience.* Amsterdam: IOS Press.

Moller, H. J., Barbera, J., Kayumov, L., & Shapiro, C. M. (2004). Psychiatric aspects of late-life insomnia. *Sleep Medicine Reviews, 8*(1), 31–45.

Moller, H. J., Devins, G., Shen, J., & Shapiro, C. M. (2006). Sleepiness is not the inverse of alertness: Evidence from four sleep disorder groups. *Experimental Brain Research, 173*(2), 258–266.

Moller, H. J., Saynor, L., Bal, H., & Sudan, K. (2016). Optimizing non-invasive wellness care for maximum impact: Multisensory meditation environments promote wellbeing. *Universal Journal of Public Health, 4*(2), 70–74.

Moller, H. J., Saynor, L., & Chignell, M. (2018). Towards transformative VR meditation: Synthesizing Nirvana, naturally. In *Proceedings of the 12th ICDVRAT with ITAG, Nottingham, England, 4–6 Sept. 2018. International conference for disability virtual reality and associated therapies.* ISBN 978-0-7049-1548-0.

Moore, K., Wiederhold, B. K., Wiederhold, M. D., & Riva, G. (2002). Panic and agoraphobia in a virtual world. *CyberPsychology and Behavior, 5*(3), 197–202.

Nofzinger, E. A. (2005). Functional neuroimaging of sleep. *Seminars in Neurology, 25*, 9–18.

Piaget, J. (1962). *Play, dreams, and imitation.* New York: Norton.

Riva, G., & Davide, F. (Eds.). (2001). *Communications through virtual technologies: Identity, community and technology in the communication age.* Amsterdam: Ios Press. Online: http://www.emergingcommunication.com/volume1.html.

Riva, G., Davide, F., & IJsselsteijn, W. A. (Eds.). (2003). *Being there: Concepts, effects and measurements of user presence in synthetic environments.* Amsterdam: IOS Press. Online: http://www.emergingcommunication.com/volume5.html.

Riva, G., & Mantovani, F. (2012). From the body to the tools and back: A general framework for presence in mediated interactions. *Interacting with Computers, 24*(4), 203–210.

Riva, G., Waterworth, J. A., & Waterworth, E. L. (2004). The layers of presence: A bio-cultural approach to understanding presence in natural and mediated environments. *CyberPsychology and Behavior, 7*(4), 402–416.

Riva, G., Waterworth, J. A., Waterworth, E. L., & Mantovani, F. (2011). From intention to action: The role of presence. *New Ideas in Psychology, 29*(1), 24–37.

Riva, G., Waterworth, J. A., Waterworth, E. L., & Mantovani, F. (2015). Action, intention and self: An evolutionary model of presence. In M. Lombard, F. Biocca, J. Freeman, W. IJsselsteijn, & R. J. Schaevitz (Eds.), *Immersed in media: Telepresence theory, measurement & technology.* Springer. ISBN: 978-3-319-10189-7.

Riva, G., Wiederhold, B. K., & Mantovani, F. (2019). Neuroscience of virtual reality: From virtual exposure to embodied medicine. *Cyberpsychology, Behavior, and Social Networking, 22*(1), 82–96.

Rubin, K. H., Fein, G., & Vandenberg, B. (1983). Play. In E. M. Hetherington (Ed.), *Handbook of child psychology: Socialization, personality, and social development* (Vol. IV, pp. 693–774). New York: Wiley.

Sadowski, W. J., & Stanney, K. M. (2002). Measuring and managing presence in virtual environments. In K. M. Stanney (Ed.), *Handbook of virtual environments technology.* Mahwah, NJ: Lawrence Erlbaum Associates.

Schloerb, D. (1995). A quantitative measure of telepresence. *Presence: Teleoperators, and Virtual Environments, 4*(1), 64–80.

Schubert, T., Friedman, F., & Regenbrecht, H. (2001). The experience of presence: Factor analytic insights. *Presence: Teleoperators, and Virtual Environments, 10*(3), 266–281.

Sheridan, T. B. (1992). Musing on telepresence and virtual presence. *Presence, Teleoperators, and Virtual Environments, 1*, 120–125.

Sheridan, T. B. (1996). Further musing on the psychophysics of presence. *Presence, Teleoperators, and Virtual Environments, 5*, 241–246.

Spagnolli, A., & Gamberini, L. (2002). Immersion/Emersion: Presence in hybrid environments. In *Paper presented at the presence 2002: Fifth annual international workshop, Porto, Portugal. October 9–11, 2002.* https://ispr.info/presence-conferences/previous-conferences/presence-2002/.

Spagnolli, A., Gamberini, L., & Gasparini, D. (2003). Breakdown analysis in virtual reality usability evaluation. *PsychNology Journal, 1*(1). Online: http://www.psychnology.org/pnj1(1)_spagnolli_gamberini_gasparini_abstract.htm.

Tong, T., Wilkinson, A., Nejatimoharrami, F., He, T., Matilus, H., & Chignell, M. (2017). A system for rewarding physical and cognitive activity in people with dementia. No. 1. In *Proceedings of the international symposium on human factors and ergonomics in health care* (Vol. 6, pp. 44–49). New Delhi, India: SAGE Publications. Sage India.

Tononi, G. (November 2, 2004). An information integration theory of consciousness. *BMC Neuroscience, 5*, 42. Volume 25, 2017 - Issue 8. Retrieved June 26, 2018 from https://doi-org.ocadu.idm.oclc.org/10.1080/10494820.2017.1282877.

Velmans, M. (1998). Physical, psychological and virtual realities. In J. A. Wood (Ed.), *The virtual embodied* (pp. 45–60). London: Routledge.

Velmans, M. (2000). *Understanding consciousness.* London and Philadelphia: Routledge.

Vygotsky, L. (1978). *Mind in society.* Cambridge: Cambridge University Press.

Waterworth, J. A., & Riva, J. (2014). *Feeling present in the physical world and in computer-mediated environments.* Basingstoke, UK: Palgrave Macmillan.

Waterworth, J. A., & Waterworth, E. L. (2001). Focus, locus, and sensus: The three dimensions of virtual experience. *CyberPsychology and Behavior, 4*(2), 203–213.

Waterworth, J. A., & Waterworth, E. L. (2003). The meaning of presence. *Presence-Connect, 3*(2). http://www8.informatik.umu.se/~jwworth/perceotual%20core.html.

Waterworth, J. A., & Waterworth, E. L. (2006). Presence as a dimension of communication: Context of use and the person. In G. Riva, M. T. Anguera, B. K. Wiederhold, & F. Mantovani (Eds.), *From communication to presence: Cognition, emotions and culture towards the ultimate communicative experience* (pp. 80–95). Amsterdam: IOS Press. Online: http://www.emergingcommunication.com/volume88.html.

Waterworth, J. A., Waterworth, E. L., Mantovani, F., & Riva, G. (2010). On feeling (the) present: An evolutionary account of the sense of presence in physical and electronically-mediated environments. *Journal of Consciousness Studies, 17*(1–2), 167–178.

Waterworth, J. A., Waterworth, E. L., Riva, G., & Mantovani, F. (2015). Presence: Form, content and consciousness. In M. Lombard, F. Biocca, J. Freeman, W. IJsselsteijn, & R. J. Schaevitz (Eds.), *Immersed in media: Telepresence theory, measurement & technology.* Springer. ISBN: 978-3-319-10189-7.

Wilkinson, A., Charoenkitkarn, V., O'Neill, J., Kanik, M., & Chignell, M. (2017a). Journeys to engagement: Ambient activity technologies for people living with dementia. In *Proceedings of the 26th international conference on world wide web companion* (pp. 1103–1110). International World Wide Web Conferences Steering Committee.

Wilkinson, A., Kanik, M., O'Neill, J., Charoenkitkarn, V., & Chignell, M. (2017b). Ambient activity technologies for managing responsive behaviours in dementia. No. 1. In , *Vol. 6. Proceedings of the international symposium on human factors and ergonomics in health care* (pp. 28–35). New Delhi, India: SAGE Publications. Sage India.

Zahoric, P., & Jennison, R. L. (1998). Presence as being-in-the-world. *Presence: Teleoperators and Virtual Environments, 7*(1), 78–89.

PART II

VR + AR: Technology for health in virtual world

Virtual reality as a promising tool to promote climate change awareness

*Géraldine Fauville, Anna Carolina Muller Queiroz,
Jeremy N. Bailenson*

Department of Communication, Stanford University, Stanford, CA, United
States

The rapid expansion of the human population and the increasing exploitation of resources are disrupting the functioning of the Earth's systems. Currently, one of the primary disruptions of human activity is the consistently increasing emission of greenhouse gases, such as carbon dioxide and methane, leading to a greater greenhouse effect. The trapping of more heat in the atmosphere subsequently increases the average temperature on Earth, modifying the global climate—an issue commonly known as climate change. Recently, the Intergovernmental Panel on Climate Change (IPCC, 2018) warned that we need to make rapid, far-reaching, and unprecedented changes in all aspects of our societies in order to limit global warming to 1.5°C. The extent and success of mitigation and adaptation strategies will greatly vary across regions and will be strongly influenced by the level of governance, wealth, technology, and infrastructure. In turn, this will result in major discrepancies in how human health will be impacted by the health of our planet (Myers, 2017). Moreover, often, the populations that benefit from human climate change—contributing activities are not the ones suffering from their consequences. These inequalities make it essential for human beings to realize that we are all connected. Individuals need to understand and be able to address the environmental issues. That is, people need to be environmentally literate.

Building on prior work, the environmental literacy framework developed by Hollweg et al. (2011, p. 2–3) defined "an environmentally literate person as someone who, both individually and together with others, makes

91

informed decisions concerning the environment; is willing to act on these decisions to improve the well-being of other individuals, societies, and the global environment; and participates in civic life."

Unfortunately, promoting environmental literacy is a challenging endeavor. First, many environmental issues are partly or completely invisible, for example, greenhouse gases. It is important for citizens to understand how their everyday life actions are responsible for releasing CO_2 and other greenhouse gases. Because these gases are invisible to the naked eye, it is difficult for people to grasp not only the extent of their emission but also the behaviors that are the most damaging for the environment.

Second, much environmental degradation often takes place far away (temporally and spatially) from their cause. The negative consequences of our actions might only be felt by the future generations, or by our contemporaries who live far away from us or belong to another demographic of the local population. This temporal, spatial, and social distance leads to a psychological disconnect, which in turn has led to a lack of personal concern due to the underestimation of the severity of environmental issues (Trope & Liberman, 2010; Weber, 2006).

A third challenge relates to the importance of experiencing nature firsthand in order to develop some connectedness with nature, which is central to proenvironmental behaviors (Bruni, Chance, Schultz, & Nolan, 2012). Experiencing nature is not always an easy task, as some environments that are essential to learn about are often too far away, too expensive to visit, or pose some safety issues.

A final challenge is related to the difficulty of experimenting with the environment. Running experiments to learn about certain environmental issues can require long periods of time to see any effects as well as complex techniques or components that might be dangerous for untrained researchers.

Over the last decades, digital technologies have provided increasing access to information, knowledge, and experiences to individuals around the world. An important characteristic of digital technology is its multimodality—the ability to include texts, images, animations, sound and even haptic feedback to create rich and engaging experiences through a steadily growing supply of interactive applications. Making the invisible visible is a key opportunity offered by digital technologies. By enabling users to visualize something that would otherwise be invisible to them, such as their carbon footprint, digital technologies make it possible to engage with the environmental issues in more specific and engaging ways (Ahn et al., 2016; Fauville, 2017; Fauville, Lantz-Andersson, Mäkitalo, Dupont, & Säljö, 2016). Technologies also allow people to visit places that are inaccessible, far away, do not exist anymore, or even never existed (Jacobson, Militello, & Baveye, 2009; Tarng, Change, Ou, Chang, & Liou, 2008; Tarng, Ou, Tsai, Lin, & Hsu, 2010). Finally, technology can support virtual scientific experiments that otherwise would be out of reach in the real world (Petersson, Lantz-Andersson, & Säljö, 2013).

Immersive virtual reality for environmental literacy

Through the use of a head-mounted display (HMD), hand controllers, stereoscopic sound, and haptic feedback, immersive virtual reality (IVR) provides a vivid first-person experience in a three-dimensional virtual environment augmented with multisensory feedback.

IVR allows users to perceive with multiple senses as if they were actually in the real world. This very unique sense of *being there* is called psychological presence (Heeter, 1992; Slater & Wilbur, 1997). The subjective feeling of presence is what makes the IVR user of an earthquake experience, who is physically in a large empty room, drop to their knees and dive under a virtual table that exists only in the virtual world. The earthquake does not present any physical risk to the user but manages to trigger this reaction of seeking protection (Bailenson, 2018).

As defined by Witmer and Singer (1998, p. 227), "Immersion is a psychological state characterized by perceiving oneself to be enveloped by, included in, and interacting with an environment that provides a continuous stream of stimuli and experiences." Virtual experiences have become more immersive as technological development increases the sensory information provided, allowing users to feel more in touch with the virtual experiences. For example, highly immersive IVR tracks the user's body movements and renders them accurately for the user to feel like their arms and legs are naturally moving in the virtual world, thus creating a sense of presence (Wirth et al., 2007). Another important aspect of IVR is its impact on social behavior triggered by taking the perspective of another person, which is known as virtual reality perspective taking. Becoming someone of a different gender, ethnicity, generation, or species is easy in IVR and has been shown to promote positive prosocial behavior such as inducing helping behavior (Ahn, Le, & Bailenson, 2013), decreasing racial bias (Hasler, Spanlang, & Slater, 2017), and decreasing ageist bias (Oh, Bailenson, Weisz, & Zaki, 2016).

A systematic literature review about the use of various immersive virtual environments (such as augmented, virtual, and mixed reality) identified an increasing number of studies in the last decade focused on the particular environmental issue of climate change (Queiroz, Kamarainen, Preston, & Leme, 2018). In this review, studies were categorized according the three components of engagement necessary to elicit change in the public perspective of climate change, proposed by Ockwell, Whitmarsh, and O'Neill (2009): understanding, emotion, and action. The authors highlighted that although a significant number of studies reported positive outcomes of using IVEs for climate change understanding, few studies investigated more than one component of engagement. They indicated the need for future studies to investigate how virtual experiences could tap into all three dimensions to have a greater understanding of the potential of virtual environmental experiences and climate change engagement. Climate change is just one of many subjects embedded in environmental literacy, and research on the impact of immersive virtual environments for environmental literacy is still in its infancy. Nevertheless, existing studies demonstrate an encouraging sign that immersive virtual environments could be a game changer in promoting environmental literacy and present an avenue for future research. In this chapter, we will describe empirical studies investigating the use of IVR in subjects within environmental literacy dimensions and discuss the implications for future IVR applications and research.

To collect the studies reviewed in this chapter, we searched the following online databases: ERIC, PubMed, IEEE, Scopus, Springer, ACM, and Web of Science. After an exploratory search, the search terms were defined and included a combination of the following: "virtual reality," "immersive technologies," "immersive virtual environments," "virtual environment technologies," "head-mounted display," "environmental education," "climate change," "sustainability," "ecosystem," and "proenvironmental behavior." Only peer-reviewed, empirical studies using head tracking via HMD setup were included in this review. We identified 13 papers (Table 5.1). Then, the papers were categorized based on the four dimensions of environmental literacy. Being environmentally literate is not a binary condition, but instead, it is comprised of a wide range of aspects that are intertwined and therefore influence each other. All of these various aspects can be categorized in the following four multifaceted dimensions of environmental literacy (Cook & Berrenberg, 1981; Hungerford & Volk, 1990; Stern, 2000):

- *Knowledge*: Being environmentally literate requires some degree of knowledge of Earth's science along with physical and ecological systems. Moreover, it is essential to understand the social, political, economic, and cultural influences on the environmental issues and the fact that there are multiple solutions to these issues.
- *Dispositions*: This dimension includes sensitivity, attitude toward the environment, assumption of personal responsibility, self-efficacy, motivation, and intention to act.
- *Competencies*: In this, dimension are skills and abilities such as identifying, analyzing, evaluating, and making personal judgments

TABLE 5.1 Overview of the studies presented in this chapter.

References	Topics addressed	Presented in section	Factors that impacted environmental literacy	Factors that did not impact environmental literacy
Moreno and Mayer (2002)	Botany	1	Speech narration (narration vs. text)	Level of immersion (HMD vs. desktop)
Moreno and Mayer (2004)	Botany	1	Personalization	Level of immersion (HMD vs. desktop)
Ahn, Bailenson, and Park (2014)	Paper consumption	2 and 3	Level of immersion (IVR, video, and print) (D and B)	Level of immersion (HMD vs. print) (D)
Bailey et al. (2015)	Hot water use	3	Level of vividness	Level of personalization
Ahn et al. (2016)	Cattle treatment and ocean acidification	2	Exp 1: Level of immersion (becoming a cow in IVR vs. watching someone else embodying a cow on video) Exp 2: Level of immersion right after the experience	Exp 2: Level of immersion a week after the experience Exp 3: Level of immersion (HMD without haptic feedback vs. video)
Fonseca and Kraus (2016)	Meat consumption	3	Level of emotion	N/A
Knote, Edenhofer, and von Mammen (2016)	Invasive species	4	N/A	N/A
Nim et al. (2016)	Coral reef	4	N/A	N/A
Calvi et al. (2017)	Diving	4	N/A	N/A

Continued

TABLE 5.1 Overview of the studies presented in this chapter.—cont'd

References	Topics addressed	Presented in section	Factors that impacted environmental literacy	Factors that did not impact environmental literacy
Mc Millan et al. (2017)	Virtual ocean exploration	4	N/A	N/A
Soliman, Peetz, and Davydenko (2017)	Nature and built environment	2 and 3	Environment of the experience (nature vs. build) (D)	Level of immersion (D)
Hsu, Tseng, and Kang (2018)	Water conservation	2	Focus of negative impact (resources vs. environment)	N/A
Markowitz, Laha, Perone, Pea, and Bailenson (2018)	Ocean acidification	1 and 2	Visual exploration and engagement (K)	Nature of the avatar (K) Nature of the avatar (D) Level of motion (K) Level of motion (D)

Focus of the four sections: Section 1: proenvironmental knowledge, Section 2: proenvironmental disposition, Section 3: proenvironmental behaviors, and Section 4: descriptive papers. In the two last columns of the table, the factors that did or did not impact the studied dimension of environmental literacy are presented. The letters (B), (D), and (K) indicate that environmental dimension was studied: (B); environmental behavior, (D); environmental disposition, and (K); environmental knowledge.

concerning environmental issues, along with asking relevant questions, argumentation, and creation and evaluation of strategies to resolve these environmental issues.

- *Environmentally responsible behavior:* This dimension includes behaviors people engage in both individually or in a group toward solving current environmental issues and preventing new ones.

The 13 papers included in this review are summarized in four sections. The first three sections present the findings from empirical studies investigating, respectively, three out of the four environmental literacy dimensions: knowledge, dispositions, and behavior. We did not create a section for proenvironmental competencies because we could not find any publications addressing this dimension. The last section summarizes descriptive publications that do not include empirical data.

IVR for promoting the knowledge dimension of environmental literacy

In this section, we describe studies that investigated how different aspects of IVR could promote environmental knowledge, and we discuss how their findings could support future IVR application and research for promoting environmental literacy. The knowledge dimension of environmental literacy encompasses some knowledge of the Earth's physical and ecological systems. It is also crucial to have knowledge concerning the social, political, economic, and cultural influences on the environment. Moreover, it is essential to understand the roles that all these elements play in the health of the environment and how they are interconnected.

Moreno and Mayer (2002) explored the impact on learning of different media and instructional methods in virtual botany learning activity. The goal of this activity was to design a plant that would be able to flourish on an alien planet with specific environmental conditions. The authors conducted two experiments. In the first one, 89 college students were randomly assigned to 1 of the 6 different conditions (modality of verbal information: narration or text combined with level of immersion: desktop, HMD and sitting, or HDM and walking). At the end of the activity, the participants were prompted to answer retention and task-based tests in order to assess learning. The results demonstrated that the students in the speech narration condition outperformed the students in the text condition but that the level of immersion did not have an impact on the knowledge gain.

In their second experiment, 75 college students used the same virtual learning activity and were randomly assigned to six different conditions (modality of verbal information: text, narration or both combined with the level of immersion: desktop or HMD). The findings of this second experiment aligned with the first one, as the students in the text conditions performed significantly worse than the students in the other groups. Moreover, the knowledge gain was not correlated with the level of immersion.

In 2004, Moreno and Mayer used the same virtual botany learning activity to investigate the impact of personalized message on learning. In this activity, a pedagogic agent would offer information to help the students design a plant adapted to the environmental conditions. In the personalized condition, the agent used the first and second person ("I" and "You") as if the student and the agent were sharing the experience. The language used in the nonpersonalized condition was more formal as students received explanations in the third person. The activity was either experienced on a desktop or on an HMD. At the end of the activity, the 48 participants were prompted to answer knowledge tests similar to those in the previous study (Moreno & Mayer, 2002). The students in the personalized conditions significantly outperformed the students in the nonpersonalized conditions. This effect was observed across the two levels of immersion, revealing that the level of immersion of the media did not influence the learning gain.

More recently, Markowitz et al. (2018) explored the efficacy of an IVR for teaching about the consequences of climate change. The IVR activity was first implemented in school as part of a teaching unit running over several weeks. The students embodied a coral avatar and experienced the ill effect of ocean acidification on other species and on their own avatar. The students' knowledge about the topic increased after participating in the IVR activity.

A similar experiment was run, but this time, half of the participants saw themselves as a coral, while the other half embodied a scuba diver. Both groups presented a significant knowledge gain between pre- and posttest, but there was no difference between the two conditions. This indicates that, in this case, the nature of the avatar did not influence the knowledge gain.

A third experiment was focused on the movement in IVR. In this IVR activity, 43 participating college students were randomly assigned to two motion conditions (swimming with remote control or with their physical body). While the motion condition did not influence the knowledge gain, it showed a posthoc correlation between the knowledge gain, the total number of snails found, and the distance traveled underwater. This suggested that visual and physical exploration while in IVR led to a greater knowledge gain.

Although several studies have investigated the effects of desktop-based VR on learning (Dede, 2009; Merchant, Goetz, Cifuentes, Keeney-Kennicutt, & Davis, 2014), research on IVR is in its infancy, and how it affects learning is still unclear (Makransky, Terkildsen, & Mayer, 2017; Suh & Prophet, 2018; Southgate et al., 2019). Even less is known with regard to environmental knowledge.

Findings from the reviewed studies suggest that the effects of design of the virtual environment in learning outcomes may be more relevant than the level of immersion itself. Research comparing different IVR designs is needed to understand how immersive virtual environments can effectively promote the knowledge dimension of environmental literacy.

IVR for promoting the dispositions dimension of environmental literacy

In this section, we present and discuss the studies investigating IVR effects on environmental disposition. The environmental dispositions' dimension of Environmental Literacy encompasses a wide range of psychological attitudes. These dispositions can be seen as environmental sensitivity, attitude or concern, or as assumption of personal responsibility, locus of control/self-efficacy, or intention to act. Five studies investigated environmental dispositions and how they could be influenced by IVR (Ahn et al., 2014, 2016; Hsu et al., 2018; Markowitz et al., 2018; Soliman et al., 2017)

Ahn et al. (2014) investigated the impact of an embodied experience in IVR on environmental behavior and locus of control related to paper consumption. In a first experiment, 47 college students were first informed about paper consumption and its impact on deforestation before being randomly assigned to one of two experimental conditions. Half of the participants put on the HMD and virtually stood in a forest in front of a large tree while holding a chainsaw. They were asked to pay attention to the forest, such as the sound of the birds, before feeling and hearing the chainsaw start-up. They were then prompted to begin moving a haptic joystick to cut the tree down. After 2 minutes of sawing, the tree would fall down, and the forest became suddenly quiet. The rest of the participants simply read a detailed description of the tree-cutting activity and were prompted to create a vivid picture in their minds of this activity. The participants in both conditions demonstrated a significant increase in their belief that their individual actions could be meaningful for the environment, but there was no difference between the two conditions.

The second experiment was similar to the first one, but this time data were collected right after the activity and 1 week later by email. Also there were three conditions for the tree-cutting experience; IVR, video, and print. The participants in the IVR condition showed a significantly higher environmental locus of control compared with the video conditions and marginally higher to the text condition. The findings also revealed that the environmental behavior intention of the participants in the IVR conditions was significantly higher than the participants in the print conditions and marginally higher than the participants in the video condition.

Ahn et al. (2016) conducted a study to investigate how embodying animals in IVR affected inclusion of nature in self (INS; experiencing the connection between nature and self) and involvement with nature. Three experiments were designed to compare the spatial presence, body transfer (the illusion of becoming a virtual body), and INS among individuals embodying a cow in the virtual environment versus those watching a video of the experience. Results suggested that the sensory richness provided by IVRs contributed to greater spatial presence and a more salient experience than watching the same experience in video. Also, only body transfer seemed to consistently drive increased INS, highlighting the importance of IVR in users' feeling of ownership over the embodied animal. In addition, their results suggested that having visual control of the experience seemed sufficient for users to feel this ownership.

Soliman et al. (2017) investigated the impact in nature connectedness, INS, and proenvironmental behavior of watching nature-based video (nature condition) compared to video of a human-built environment (built condition) either on desktop or IVR. After watching the videos, the 230 participants reported their attitude toward nature in two different measures—INS and the connectedness to nature scale (CNS). The participants in the nature conditions reported significantly greater INS and CNS compared with the participants watching the built videos, while the effect of the medium was not significant to nature connectedness, which replicated Ahn et al. findings (2016).

The study of Markowitz et al. (2018; described in the previous section) also paid attention to the environmental disposition. In their first experiment (where school students embodied a coral), the participants did not show an increase in environmental attitude (measured with the NEP scale) after the IVR activity.

In their second experiment, where students embodied either a coral or a scuba diver, there was a significant increase in proenvironmental behavior between pre- and posttest, but no difference between conditions. The CNS also revealed a significant positive attitude change from pre- to posttest, but, again, no difference was found between the two conditions.

The third experiment in this set of studies was conducted at the Tribeca Film Festival. The amount of movement of the 448 participants was recorded. The authors did not find a correlation between the attitude and the amount of movement.

The fourth experiment explored further how movement could correlate to disposition toward the environment (measured with the NEP and CNS scales) and did not reveal any significant effect.

Hsu et al. (2018) investigated the effects of exaggerated feedback to trigger affective response in IVR experience about water conservation. The authors focused on the effect of exaggerated feedback intensifying the negative consequences of water consumption and/or environmental damage in order to emphasize affective responses. 165 student participants played an IVR game simulating water consumption effects. Participants were assigned to one of the four exaggerated feedback conditions: negative impact on the environment (present or absent) and negative impact on resources (present or absent). Participants in the "negative impact on resources" condition demonstrated higher short-term behavior intention to reduce water use than participants in the "negative impact on the environment" condition. Regarding long-term effects of exaggerated feedback, participants in the "negative impact on the environment" condition showed a greater improvement in individual attitude and behavior intention than participants in the other conditions. These results indicated that providing exaggerated feedback of water usage on the environment (i.e., degradation of the environment) elicited the highest levels of affective response and proenvironmental disposition.

IVR for promoting the behavior dimension of environmental literacy

In this section, we discuss the studies focusing on how IVR affects behaviors toward the environment. Environmental literacy includes the ability to engage in service and action to improve the environment. These behaviors can take different forms such as direct conservation and restoration of natural environments, consumer behaviors, and public participation in interpersonal deliberations and debates. Four studies investigated how IVR activities could promote the behavioral dimension of environmental literacy (Ahn et al., 2014; Bailey et al., 2015; Fonseca & Kraus, 2016; Soliman et al., 2017).

Ahn et al. study (2014; described in the previous section) revealed that after experiencing how to cut a tree in the IVR condition, participants used significantly fewer napkins to dry spilled water than participants who read a passage about cutting a tree.

Bailey et al. (2015) investigated the impact of vividness and personalization of feedback on reducing energy consumption related to hot water use. Four versions of an IVR activity where the user took a shower were created, combining two levels of vividness and personal message (vivid, personal; nonvivid, personal; vivid, nonpersonal; nonvivid, nonpersonal). Before and after getting into IVR, the participants were asked to wash their hands for sanitary purposes. The findings revealed that after treatment, the participants in the vivid conditions used significantly colder water than the participants in the nonvivid conditions. As the vivid condition used images of coal, while the nonvivid condition used text, the authors suggested that the vivid condition may require a lower cognitive effort than the nonvivid condition based on text. They argued that the lower cognitive effort might allow participants to better process the impact of hot water on energy consumption, which can contribute to better message processing and ultimately stimulate behavior change.

Fonseca and Kraus (2016) investigated the impact of the degree of immersion and the narrative content on environmental behavior. In this case, they focused on meat consumption. The 64 participants in the two first conditions watched an emotional 360 video about the effects of meat consumption and its relation to climate change either in IVR or on a tablet. The participants in the third condition watched a nonemotional video unrelated to meat consumption in IVR. After watching the video, the participants were offered a buffet of pizza (with or without meat). The participants in the IVR conditions marginally chose more vegetarian pizza than the participants in the nonimmersive condition. In the nonemotional condition, not a single participant chose the vegetarian option. These findings suggested that the level of immersion increased the emotional impact on the viewers and increased proenvironmental attitude.

As previously described, Soliman et al. (2017) studied the impact of watching videos on a desktop or in IVR of natural or human-built environments on proenvironmental behavior. After watching the videos, the participants' proenvironmental behaviors were assessed. They were asked if they wanted a printed or digital copy of the debriefing to subscribe to a monthly newsletter with information about practical tips on sustainability or to get a copy of the sustainability strategic plan of the campus. No significant effect of the type of media, content (nature or urban environment), or interaction was identified between the conditions.

IVR for environmental literacy: descriptive publications

Four publications (Knote et al., 2016; Calvi et al., 2017; Nim et al., 2016; McMillan, Flood, & Glaeser, 2017) described IVR activities that could be used to promote environmental literacy, but without accounting for any empirical data that could support the efficacy of these activities in promoting environmental literacy. While these studies do not provide empirical data concerning the impact of IVR on environmental literacy, they nonetheless provide important information of current IVR activities focusing on the natural environment that could potentially promote environmental literacy. Empirical research is a very long process moving at a slower pace than the technology itself. These kinds of descriptive publications present the advantage of a quick turnover and allow researchers to be kept updated about the latest IVR activities in a timely manner.

Knote et al. (2016) described an IVR activity where the user explored the competition between two species of ants—native and an invasive one. The goal was to help the native species survive the invasion by modifying their environment such as placing a brick on the ants' path, using a water hose, or spraying pheromone or hydrocarbons.

Nim et al. work (2016) focused on the health of the Great Barrier Reef and the indirect impact that the users' water and carbon footprints have on this ecosystem. In this activity, the users started off by answering questions to calculate their footprint. Then, in pairs, participants observed the coral reef bleaching along with an outbreak of a coral predator. Information concerning the indirect impacts of human activities on this ecosystem were also provided to the users. After this activity in dyads, the users were individually immersed through an HMD (Google Cardboard or Oculus DK2) in an environment where the ecosystem's health was correlated with their own water and carbon footprints calculated earlier in the activity (high footprint lead to more sea stars and coral bleaching). During this individual activity, the participants could talk to each other in order to describe and discuss their own ecosystem.

McMillan et al. (2017) described a scuba diving IVR activity that enables users to virtually explore the ocean with Dr. Sylvia Earle—famous ocean explorer—and experience the beauty of the ocean. First intended as an educational tool to fit in the Common Core Curriculum, this activity, available both on desktop and IVR, became a diving simulator.

In 2017, Calvi et al. created an IVR activity to teach about underwater sustainability. In this activity, users experienced the underwater world by virtually driving an underwater vehicle. This activity was implemented at a Science Festival. One hundred participants from primary school age to adults experienced this IVR activity and answered questionnaires. Children up to 10 years old played for almost half of the time compared with other participants and reported the experience as extremely real in comparison with adults. Children also considered the visual effects and control devices to be more distracting than the other groups. These results identified the need for studies investigating if/how feeling high presence in IVR could enhance empathy and increase the engagement with environmental issues, as well as studies targeting different age groups.

Moving forward

This chapter accounts for the current state of research in the field of IVR for environmental literacy as a way to promote climate change awareness. Approximately, a dozen publications over a period of 17 years are presented in this chapter, which illustrates how young this field is and how much more needs to be researched in order to understand how IVR can impact individuals' environmental literacy.

IVR has been evolving rapidly over the course of the last 5 years. Ahn and colleagues in 2014 used an HMD called NVIS SX111 that weighted 1.3 kg and was tethered through a heavy cable to a powerful computer while the interactivity took place through a bulky joystick (Fig. 5.1). The tracking system used with the NVIS SX111 was composed of eight cameras, and the entire IVR system cost about $100,000.

Today, individuals can easily purchase their own IVR systems with hand controllers and an HMD (weighting less than 500 g) for less than $400. This technological evolution has a profound impact on the role that IVR can play in society—specifically on environmental issues and on the research that can be carried out. Research in IVR used to be confined to a handful of advanced research facilities. The physical inaccessibility of the equipment also limited research participants to university students with easier access to these facilities. Now researchers can bring IVR devices to classrooms, supermarkets, or medical centers and study how a wide variety of individuals react to this novel technology. This evolution has tremendously widened the horizons of researchers who can now

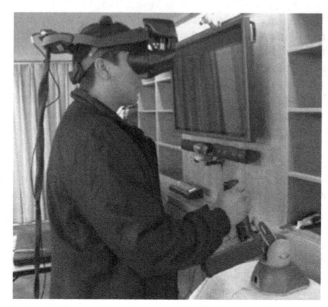

FIGURE 5.1   Experimental setup used by Ahn et al. in 2014.

investigate how individuals with different backgrounds, political views, cultures, or environmental attitudes will react to the use of IVR for environmental literacy (Song & Fiore, 2017).

The fields of research and technology typically have very different timeframes. While technology is frequently replaced by a newer, cheaper, faster, and more sophisticated version within a year, empirical evidence of what a technology can do takes several years to come to fruition, from the design of the experiments to the publications of the results in peer-reviewed journals. Because both the technology and the environmental problems are evolving at a fast pace, it is essential to encourage and maintain a joint effort from the research community to understand what technology can do, in order to promote environmental literacy as soon as possible. The emergence of multidisciplinary research teams working toward understanding how IVR can address one of the most pressing societal issues would be of great benefit for our society.

As described earlier in this chapter, to be considered environmentally literate, a person needs to possess the four dimensions of environmental literacy (knowledge, dispositions, competencies, and environmentally responsible behavior) in various degrees. Moreover, enhancing one of these dimensions might help the individual move forward in the other dimensions, creating a network between all four. It is therefore essential to investigate how VR can promote each of these dimensions in order to have a holistic impact on the development of environmental literacy among the public. As studies on IVR applications are mostly recent, we found that each dimension has only been studied in relation to IVR in a very limited amount. To the best of our knowledge, one of the four dimensions has yet to be investigated. Moreover, no publication has been found, which looks at the impact of IVR on the four dimensions simultaneously. This chapter demonstrates the limited current knowledge in this field and advocates for strengthening the effort from the research community to shed light on the role that IVR could play in promoting the dimensions of environmental literacy—individually or synergistically.

Another challenge is that little is known about what features of the content of learning activities in IVR are key to making these immersive activities effective for environmental literacy. We still need to discover in which conditions IVR constitute an efficient teaching method and what kind of content can be leveraged by this technology.

Another issue resides in the timeframe of the current studies. The 13 studies presented in this chapter present a very short duration of exposure to IVR. Several researchers suggested investigating the impact of multiple exposures (of different lengths) over time (Ahn et al., 2014; Hsu et al., 2018; Song & Fiore, 2017). Another key question is how long the effects of IVR will last on the subject. Most of the studies have measured the outcome variable of interest right after the exposure to IVR. Exploring long-term effect of IVR on ES with longitudinal studies would be valuable.

Besides directly impacting an individual's environmental literacy, IVR also has the potential to help investigate individuals' behaviors in situations that are difficult to create or control in the real world. For example, Verhulst, Lombar, Normand, and Moreau (2017) addressed food waste by studying how consumers would react to misshapen fruits and vegetables by exposing and allowing them to manipulate these foods in IVR. Running this study in IVR instead of in the real world made it possible to overcome experimental challenges that would have made the experiment difficult to run otherwise. The authors argued that "By replacing real fresh products with virtual ones we could ensure the repeatability of user studies as well as easily control different aspects of freshness or appearance (e.g., misshaped products) and evaluate the consumer behavior of participants" (p. 55).

The same technique was used by Khashe, Lucas, Becerik-Gerber, and Gratch (2017) to investigate how building occupants would comply with proenvironmental behavior suggestions delivered in different ways to their computer (gender of the voice, communicators person, delivery styles). Running this study in IVR rather than in real life allowed them to focus on the variable of interest while keeping the other variables constant (e.g., weather condition that might influence compliance with a lighting-related request such as opening the blind rather than turning the light on). Besides being used directly to educate people about environmental issues and reduce the psychological distance between humans and the environment, IVR presents an important potential to mimic real life and investigate how different strategies implemented in real life could make them more environmentally literate.

Importantly, using IVR for environmental literacy should be considered as an addition to other learning activities, not a substitute. Although immersive technology has evolved significantly, its fidelity to the natural setting is still low, and a real experience in nature should be favored over its virtual equivalent. Moreover, adding IVR to the classrooms should be done cautiously, considering the strengths and weakness of IVR for education purpose (Parong & Mayer, 2018). In other words, IVR represents a new learning tool that can potentially be efficient in promoting the various dimensions of environmental literacy among the public as demonstrated by the studies presented in this chapter.

In conclusion, the emergence of IVR as an affordable and increasingly mobile technology opens interesting possibilities to promote environmental literacy. It also requires the attention of the IVR research community in order to make the best use of this novel technology to address environmental problems that threaten our own survival and the health of the planet.

References

Ahn, S. J. G., Bailenson, J. N., & Park, D. (2014). Short-and long-term effects of embodied experiences in immersive virtual environments on environmental locus of control and behavior. *Computers in Human Behavior, 39,* 235–245.

Ahn, S. J., Bostick, J., Ogle, E., Nowak, K. L., McGillicuddy, K. T., & Bailenson, J. N. (2016). Experiencing nature: Embodying animals in immersive virtual environments increases inclusion of nature in self and involvement with nature. *Journal of Computer-Mediated Communication, 21*(6), 399–419.

Ahn, S. J., Le, A. M. T., & Bailenson, J. N. (2013). The effect of embodied experiences on self-other merging, attitude, and helping behavior. *Media Psychology, 16,* 7–38.

Bailenson, J. N. (2018). *Experience on demand: What virtual reality is, how it works, and what it can do.* New York: W.W. Norton.

Bailey, J. O., Bailenson, J. N., Flora, J., Armel, K. C., Voelker, D., & Reeves, B. (2015). The impact of vivid messages on reducing energy consumption related to hot water use. *Environment and Behavior, 47*(5), 570–592.

Bruni, C. M., Chance, R. C., Schultz, P. W., & Nolan, J. M. (2012). Natural connections: Bees sting and snakes bite, but they are still nature. *Environment and Behavior, 44*(2), 197–215.

Calvi, L., Santos, C. P., Relouw, J., Endrovski, B., Rothwell, C., Sara, A., ... Pantaleo, U. (2017). A vr game to teach underwater sustainability while diving. In *Proceedings of the 5th IFIP conference on sustainable internet and ICT for sustainability, SustainIT, 2017* (pp. 1–4).

Cook, S., & Berrenberg, J. L. (1981). Approaches to encouraging conservation behavior: A review and conceptual framework. *Journal of Social Issues, 37*(2), 73–107.

Dede, C. (2009). Immersive interfaces for engagement and learning. *Science, 323,* 66–69.

Fauville, G. (2017). *Digital technologies as support for learning about the marine environment: Steps toward ocean literacy.* Doctoral thesis. Sweden: University of Gothenburg.

Fauville, G., Lantz-Andersson, A., Mäkitalo, Å., Dupont, S., & Säljö, R. (2016). The carbon footprint as a mediating tool in students' online reasoning about climate change. In

O. Erstad, K. Kumpulainen, Å. Mäkitalo, K. C. Schröder, P. Pruulmann-Vengerfeldt, & T. Jóhannsdóttir (Eds.), *Learning across contexts in the knowledge society* (pp. 39—60). Rotterdam, the Netherlands: Sense Publishers.

Fonseca, D., & Kraus, M. (2016). A comparison of head-mounted and hand-held displays for 360° videos with focus on attitude and behavior change. In *Paper presented at AcademicMindtrek '16. Tampere.* New York, NY: ACM.

Hasler, B. S., Spanlang, B., & Slater, M. (2017). Virtual race transformation reverses racial ingroup bias. *PLoS One, 12*(4), 1—20.

Heeter, C. (1992). Being there: The subjective experience of presence. *Presence: Teleoperators and Virtual Environments, 1,* 26—271.

Hollweg, K. S., Taylor, J. R., Bybee, R. W., Marcinkowski, T. J., McBeth, W. C., & Zoido, P. (2011). *Developing a framework for assessing environmental literacy.* Washington, DC: North American Association for Environmental Education.

Hsu, W. C., Tseng, C. M., & Kang, S. C. (2018). Using exaggerated feedback in a virtual reality environment to enhance behavior intention of water-conservation. *Educational Technology and Society, 21*(4), 187—203.

Hungerford, H., & Volk, T. (1990). Changing learner behavior through environmental education. *The Journal of Environmental Education, 21*(3), 8—22.

Intergovernmental Panel On Climate Change (IPCC). (2018). *Summary for policymakers of IPCC special report on global warming of 1.5°C approved by governments.* Retrieved from: https://www.ipcc.ch/sr15/chapter/summary-for-policy-makers/.

Jacobson, A. R., Militello, R., & Baveye, P. C. (2009). Development of computer-assisted virtual field trips to support multidisciplinary learning. *Computers and Education, 52*(3), 571—580.

Khashe, S., Lucas, G., Becerik-Gerber, B., & Gratch, J. (2017). Buildings with persona: Towards effective building-occupant communication. *Computers in Human Behavior, 75,* 607—618.

Knote, A., Edenhofer, S., & von Mammen, S. (2016). Neozoa: An immersive, interactive sandbox for the study of competing. In *Proceedings of the IEEE virtual reality workshop on K-12 embodied learning through virtual and augmented reality* (pp. 5—10).

Makransky, G., Terkildsen, T. S., & Mayer, R. E. (2017). Adding immersive virtual reality to a science lab simulation causes more presence but less learning. *Learning and Instruction, 60,* 225—236.

Markowitz, D. M., Laha, R., Perone, B. R., Pea, R. D., & Bailenson, J. N. (2018). Immersive virtual reality field trips facilitate learning about climate change. *Frontiers in Psychology, 9,* 2364.

McMillan, K., Flood, K., & Glaeser, R. (2017). Virtual reality, augmented reality, mixed reality, and the marine conservation movement. *Aquatic Conservation: Marine and Freshwater Ecosystems, 27,* 162—168.

Merchant, Z., Goetz, E. T., Cifuentes, L., Keeney-Kennicutt, W., & Davis, T. J. (2014). Effectiveness of virtual reality-based instruction on students' learning outcomes in K-12 and higher education: A meta-analysis. *Computers and Education, 70,* 29—40.

Moreno, R., & Mayer, R. E. (2002). Learning science in virtual reality multimedia environments: Role of methods and media. *Journal of Educational Psychology, 94*(3), 598—610.

Moreno, R., & Mayer, R. E. (2004). Personalized messages that promote science learning in virtual environments. *Journal of Educational Psychology, 96*(1), 165—173.

Myers, S. (2017). Planetary health: Protecting human health on a rapidly changing planet. *The Lancet, 390*(10114), 2860—2868.

Nim, H. T., Wang, M., Zhu, Y., Sommer, B., Schreiber, F., Boyd, S. E., & Wang, S. J. (2016). Communicating the effect of human behaviour on the Great Barrier Reef via mixed reality visualisation. *2016 Big Data Visual Analytics (BDVA),* 1—6. IEEE.

Ockwell, D., Whitmarsh, L., & O'Neill, S. (2009). Reorienting climate change communication for effective mitigation: Forcing people to be green or fostering grassroots engagement? *Science Communication, 30*(3), 305–327.

Oh, S. Y., Bailenson, J., Weisz, E., & Zaki, J. (2016). Virtually old: Embodied perspective taking and the reduction of ageism under threat. *Computers in Human Behavior, 60*, 398–410.

Parong, J., & Mayer, R. (2018). Learning science in immersive virtual reality journal of educational psychology. *Journal of Educational Psychology, 110*(6), 785–797.

Petersson, E., Lantz-Andersson, A., & Säljö, R. (2013). Exploring nature through virtual experimentation: Picking up concepts and modes of reasoning in regular classroom practices. *Nordic Journal of Digital Literacy, 3*(8), 139–156.

Queiroz, A. C. M., Kamarainen, A. M., Preston, N. D., & Leme, M. I. S. (2018). Immersive virtual environments and climate change engagement. In *Proceedings of the immersive learning research network* (pp. 153–164).

Slater, M., & Wilbur, S. (1997). A framework for immersive virtual environments (FIVE): Speculations on the role of presence in virtual environments. *Presence, 6*(6), 603–616.

Soliman, M., Peetz, J., & Davydenko, M. (2017). The impact of immersive technology on nature relatedness and pro-environmental behavior. *Journal of Media Psychology, 29*(1), 8–17.

Song, J., & Fiore, S. M. (2017). VR what we eat: Guidelines for designing and assessing virtual environments as a persuasive technology to promote sustainability and health. In *Proceedings of the human factors and ergonomics society* (pp. 1519–1523).

Southgate, E., Smith, S. P., Cividino, C., Saxby, S., Kilham, J., Eather, G., ... Bergin, C. (2019). Embedding immersive virtual reality in classrooms: Ethical, organisational and educational lessons in bridging research and practice. *International Journal of Child-Computer Interaction, 19*, 19–29.

Stern, P. (2000). Toward a coherent theory of environmentally significant behavior. *Journal of Social Issues, 56*(3), 407.

Suh, A., & Prophet, J. (2018). The state of immersive technology research: A literature analysis. *Computers in Human Behavior, 86*, 77–90.

Tarng, W., Change, M. Y., Ou, K. L., Chang, Y. W., & Liou, H. H. (2008). The development of a virtual marine museum for educational applications. *Journal of Educational Technology Systems, 37*(1), 39–59.

Tarng, W., Ou, K. L., Tsai, W. S., Lin, Y. S., & Hsu, C. K. (2010). An instructional design using the virtual ecological pond for science education in elementary schools. *Journal of Educational Technology Systems, 38*(4), 385–406.

Trope, Y., & Liberman, N. (2010). Construal-level theory of psychological distance. *Psychological Review, 117*(2), 440–463.

Verhulst, A., Normand, J. M., Lombard, C., & Moreau, G. (2017). A study on the use of an immersive virtual reality store to investigate consumer perceptions and purchase behavior toward non-standard fruits and vegetables. In *Proceedings of the IEEE virtual reality* (pp. 55–63).

Weber, E. U. (2006). Experience-based and description-based perceptions of long-term risk: Why global warming does not scare us (yet). *Climatic Change, 77*, 103–120.

Wirth, W., Hartmann, T., Böcking, S., Vorderer, P., Klimmt, C., Gouveia, F. R., ... Jäncke, P. (2007). A process model of the formation of spatial presence experiences. *Media Psychology, 9*, 493–525.

Witmer, B. G., & Singer, M. J. (1998). Measuring presence in virtual environments: A presence questionnaire. *Presence, 7*(3), 225–240.

Augmented reality in health and medicine: A review of augmented reality application for health professionals, procedures, and behavioral interventions

Tony Liao¹, Pamara F. Chang¹, SongYi Lee²

¹ Department of Communication, University of Cincinnati, Cincinnati, OH, United States; ² Klein College of Media and Communication, Temple University, Philadelphia, PA, United States

As health and medicine are continually pushing for new ways to improve, they are often at the forefront of technological innovation, design, and communication research. Many studies within these disciplines attempt to explore and design information and communication technologies to improve health outcomes or to function in health contexts, giving rise to research on eHealth topics. Augmented reality (AR) is an emerging and steadily maturing technology that scholars have been applying to study and improve health processes and outcomes. This chapter seeks to explore the intersections between different disciplinary fields in which AR research has explored health questions. The breadth of literature in AR and health suggests that there are many ways to approach this topic, ranging from AR as a medical display, a training mechanism for health professionals (i.e., surgical medical residents), a medical intervention (i.e., treatment of phobias), or a tool for everyday use in various health contexts and conditions (i.e., AR as a component of smarthomes and behavioral interventions). However, the lack of depth of literature in AR and health calls for further research in this interdisciplinary area. This chapter highlights several topics of AR and

109

health with illustrative examples through a review of the literature, identification of emerging trends in research, and suggestions for future research.

AR, defined as three-dimensional (3D), real-time, interactive digital content overlaying physical space (Azuma, 1997; Liao, 2016), has been the subject of computer science and engineering development for several decades (Dey, Billinghurst, Lindeman, & Swan, 2018; Zhou, Duh, & Billinghurst, 2008). Unlike virtual reality technologies, which supplant people's views of reality (Milgram & Kishino, 1994), AR allows for an overlay onto physical space and thus enables different kinds of uses (Fig. 6.1).

The 3D component refers to technologies that render graphics either in 3D space or objects, while the real-time and interactive criteria distinguish AR from technologies that may take images and alter them (e.g., photo editing) or display technologies that are simply visual (e.g., static holograms).

These specific criteria and features of AR give rise to unique possibilities for health interventions. First, it allows for different kinds of visual media to be shown on top of physical space. This enables both specific kinds of visual and interactive interventions, such as those to visualize playmates for children with autism (Bai, Blackwell, & Coulouris, 2013) or for real-time surgical operations (Bichlmeier, Heining, Feuerstein, & Navab, 2009; Hansen, Wieferich, Ritter, Rieder, & Peitgen, 2010; Liao, Inomata, Sakuma, & Dohi, 2010; Navab, Blum, Wang, Okur, & Wendler, 2012). Second, it also allows health practitioners to have complete control over visual interventions, which allows them to improve on existing practices such as exposure therapy because they can minimize any unpredictability that could arise (Botella et al., 2011). Third, the situated and mobile nature of AR can allow practitioners to fundamentally alter their experience of physical space (Graham, Zook, & Boulton, 2013; Liao & Humphreys, 2015). With the rise of AR games and applications for public use, there has been some promise in utilizing AR like Pokémon GO to motivate physical activity and improve overall quality of life (Althoff, White, & Horvitz, 2016; LeBlanc & Chaput, 2017).

Health and medicine are promising settings for AR for a few reasons. For one, it is often the forefront of cutting edge technologies, given the importance of continually improving care and health outcomes. Health contexts are also a way of securing funding for AR hardware, which for a long time was quite expensive and confined to certain laboratories. Additionally, the devices that enable AR can be varied, whether it is through a handheld device (Schmalstieg & Wagner, 2007), a head-

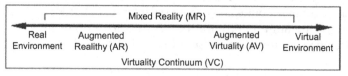

FIGURE 6.1   Mixed reality continuum, Milgram & Kishino, 1994.

mounted display (Liao, 2018; Van Krevelen & Poelman, 2010), or a spacial projection device (Benko, Wilson, & Zannier, 2014). Thus, AR can be employed through small-scale applications or large scale systems and rooms, which lends itself to multiple different health applications and contexts. The visual nature of many health applications in an indoor, confined space makes them well suited to the capabilities of AR.

With growing interest in AR and health, several recent studies have utilized AR in health contexts such as interventions for overcoming phobias, medical training applications as part of health education for health professionals, and behavioral health tools for different demographics. While some of these are clinical studies of interventions, others are more interested in the technology or communication and psychological response mechanisms to AR. Some scholars focus on AR as a medical display, while others see it as an intervention, and still others are thinking about AR as a tool for training medical professionals. Given the different functions of AR, different areas of focus for research, and different starting points for how they are thinking about AR as a technology, this chapter aims to categorize and review the existing AR and health literature. First, there is an examination of some of the research on individual AR interventions, before moving on to field level applications of AR and some of the health contexts where AR is being considered and deployed. Based on an in-depth search of the existing literature on AR and health, there is a discussion on some new possibilities and areas for future research and development focusing on the interplay between AR and health. The goal of this chapter is to help better understand the wide range of possibilities of AR in health, while also mapping current and future developments in an exciting area for future technology and health.

Individual use of AR

AR health interventions

While AR has been the subject of academic research for decades (Dey et al, 2018; Zhou et al., 2008), the earliest publicly available AR applications were accessed through mobile handheld devices (Schmalstieg & Wagner, 2007). Some companies then launched headworn AR devices for consumer use (e.g., Google Glass, Microsoft HoloLens), as a different form factor for AR (Liao, 2018; Van Krevelen & Poelman, 2010). Many of these applications that incorporated AR elements were geared toward an explicit health focus (i.e., Botella et al., 2011; Sielhorst, Obst, Burgkart, Riener, & Navab, 2004). These early studies found that AR applications accessed through both mobile handheld and headworn devices were conducive for various health intervention purposes.

One unique feature that is appealing about AR is its mobility for delivering health interventions. While there are many health interventions that are stationary or tethered to a particular setting, these are limited in their effectiveness due to geographic constraints, the times they are available to patients, and the unnatural environment they are placed. Mobile AR enables certain types of health interventions that can be deployed anywhere the patient is located and at various times (e.g., in-home AR exercises). Mobile technologies are an increasingly promising platform for health interventions because they are attractive and familiar to patients (Guillory et al., 2015; Nacinovich, 2013) and because of their ubiquity. Advantages include widespread adoption of phones with powerful capabilities, daily and continuous possession of mobile technologies, individual attachment to their cellphones, and increased context-aware features enabled through sensing (Klasnja & Pratt, 2012). AR may also be more cost efficient than virtual reality and other comparable mobile emerging technologies because many patients already have these devices (Baus & Bouchard, 2014). All of these factors can increase the adoption of AR applications and the self-efficacy of patients to engage with these interventions.

AR can also enable unique health interventions because of its technical features such as the ability to overlay content over one's physical space resulting in immersion where AR can provide an "uninterrupted and unaltered view of the real world" (Vidal et al., 2006, p. 125). AR technologies can display a wide range of visuals on top of space (e.g., text, video, 2D and 3D images), coupled with audio. These can be triggered by a particular physical object or through geolocational coordinates. This can allow interventions that are designed to interact with existing equipment and spatial settings, as opposed to supplanting the physical space. AR may also enable interventions that rely on increased spatial presence and quality of experience compared to VR because AR utilizes unmediated space that simulates more sensory cues (Oudshoorn, 2012; Tang, Biocca, & Lim, 2004). AR-enabled health interventions in particular can take advantage of the sensing capabilities of mobile technologies that allow designers to track health intervention effects, involve patient's healthcare teams, leverage social influence, increase accessibility of health information, and utilize entertainment such as gamification. These features could add to the effectiveness of the interventions, as well as help AR users accept AR and make it easier to use in a variety of health contexts.

Existing literature has primarily focused on three contexts regarding health interventions and AR: physical and behavioral changes, phobias, and various therapy approaches for autism. Teams of physicians, designers, and scholars have approached these contexts with different AR tools. For example, teams have used serious games (SG) through AR as part of exposure therapy to decrease entomophobia or smile therapy through AR for children with autism. The next section will discuss existing studies that used AR for health interventions, map out implications of these studies, and direct readers to promising directions of using AR for health interventions.

A popular area for health interventions via AR is the focus on physical activity in individuals, ranging from contexts of diet and exercise to prevention of falls for older adults with paralysis. "Exergames," a subgroup of SG, is a term that combines the word exercise and game, and it refers to technologies that promote healthy behaviors by combining video game technologies and exercise (Wright & Bogost, 2007). These games influence players to be physically active to succeed in games, and there is growing evidence that exergames help individuals stay fit and manage their weight (Lieberman, 2006). Because of the mobile features of AR, teams have established exergames in natural urban environments (Frank, Engelke, & Schmid, 2003). For example, a research team at the Technical University of Darmstadt, Germany, created the "Urban Health Games" to promote positive health effects by augmenting various social and cultural dimensions in one's natural environment. AR games that are able to be run on smartphones like *Zombies, Run!* and *Six to Start* have players moving around in their natural environment to deliver the gaming experience with the secondary outcome of exercise. Other games such as *Human PacMan* have been developed at the University of Singapore, where people would use an urban area to chase berries and run away from ghosts (Cheok et al., 2003).

Two commercial location-based AR games are Ingress (Chess, 2014) and Pokémon GO, which have gained widespread popularity and interest due to its potential influence on physical activity for players (LeBlanc & Chaput, 2017). The locational nature of Pokémon GO has been shown to alter player's behaviors and movement patterns in urban areas (Colley et al., 2017). In terms of its effects on physical movement, one study examined a large-scale corpora of wearable sensor data and search engine query logs. They followed 1420 users over a period of 3 months and found that the players increased their daily amount of steps by 1473 a day on average and more than 25% of the participants increased their daily activity level (Althoff et al., 2016). Because the use of AR for health behavior change has been understudied and has been tackled more from a design and usability perspective, there is a need for studies that show how games can motivate players to adopt health behavior changes like eating and exercising through specific mechanisms.

Another area of health interventions via AR is helping individuals overcome phobias, specifically bug phobias. In order to treat bug phobia, studies have utilized the specific mechanism of exposure therapy through AR to decrease the fear of bugs for patients who are clinically diagnosed with phobias (Botella, Breton-Lopez, Quero, Banos, & Garcia-Palacios,

2010; Botella, Juan, Banos, Alcaniz, & Rey, 2005; Wrzesien, Burkhardt, Alcañiz Raya, & Botella, 2011). These studies theorize that AR may actually be an improvement over existing exposure therapy procedures because health providers have total control over the AR stimulus and can categorically guarantee that nothing unexpected can happen to the patient. By using exposure therapy through AR, one study found that there were significant decreases in levels of fear of patients with cockroach phobia after the first treatment, and furthermore, the treatment benefits were maintained at 3, 6, and 12 month follow-up periods (Botella et al., 2010). These studies of utilizing AR to have patients undergo exposure therapy demonstrates that traditional forms of therapy can be translated over to augmented technologies and can be just as effective, with the added advantage of full control over the AR exposure conditions.

Another area of health interventions via AR that is burgeoning is in the context of various disabilities. This context deems appropriate as there is a call for the integration of mobile technologies in behavioral healthcare (Luxton, McCann, Bush, Mishkind, & Reger, 2011). Mobile technologies, like AR, are proven to be effective for assessment and treatment of various conditions; furthermore, AR technologies can enhance emotional engagement and sense of presence for treatment health interventions (Giglioli, Pallavicini, Pedroli, Serino, & Riva, 2015). For example, AR interventions can help adolescents with autism spectrum disorders practice emotional judgments and improve social skills by providing facial modeling to promote emotional expression with AR animation of six basic facial expressions overlaid on participants' faces. Chen, Lee, and Lin (2015) found that AR interventions can improve appropriate recognition and response to facial emotional expressions to improve adolescent's ability to express their own feelings and respond to emotional facial expressions they see in everyday social situations. Another study found that participants evaluated AR interventions for children with autism to be engaging and fun, with an outcome of improved nonverbal communication, increased eye contact, and increased social engagement (Liu, Salisbury, Vahabzadeh, & Sahin, 2017). In particular, AR visualizations could be used to motivate certain developmental practices for children such as engaging in pretend play (Bai et al., 2013). These studies utilizing AR for health interventions are intended to be used in situ and at the patient's convenience, so that individuals can use these therapeutic practices more frequently.

There have been creative implementations for children with different health conditions using AR. One example is a study that used music therapy through AR for children with cerebral palsy to increase motor exercise (Correa, Ficheman, do Nascimento, & de Deus Lopes, 2009). Results from this study showed the potential of AR in the rehabilitation process for music therapy by promoting positive cognitive, physical, mental, and social changes in individuals with cerebral palsy. This type of intervention could serve as an intervention tool for various cognitive, motor, psychological, and social health conditions.

To increase the level of scientific evidence for interventions, it is important to develop and adopt a standardized protocol in terms of interventions, populations, and outcomes. It will help with further comparing between designed experimental studies to translate evidence-based interventions to gaming-based approaches (Fleming et al., 2017). Collaborations between game developers, app designers, and content experts in behavioral health are necessary (Payne, Moxley, & MacDonald, 2015) for effective health interventions via AR for various health conditions. It is also important to explore benefits of AR health interventions in various health contexts like depression, heart disease, type 2 diabetes, etc., while also evaluating these health conditions in different populations like children, older adults, and individuals with disabilities (Althoff et al., 2016; Howe et al., 2016) especially because various demographics have differences in awareness in playing games or using new technologies for favorable health outcomes.

AR health at home

One of the key challenges for healthcare providers is providing outpatient care after patients leave a medical facility. AR offers one technology to remedy this problem, as the "landscape has been transformed recently by the introduction of mass-produced but highly capable devices designed principally for the home entertainment market" (Borghese et al., 2014, p. 290). AR has been utilized as a tool for occupational therapists to walk through a home and visualize modifications that may need to occur to facilitate mobility and prevent falls for stroke patients (Bianco, Pedell, & Renda, 2016). AR has also been considered as a mobile interface for controlling smart home functions and appliances, which may be particularly useful for older adults or individuals with physical disabilities (Tang, Yang, Bateman, Jorge, & Tang, 2015). Each of these applications considers ways that AR can facilitate changes in the home, whether it is by helping therapists improve the spaces where people live or improving a patient's ability to control the functions of their home.

Other applications have considered AR in the home more explicitly as an extension of hospital rehabilitation practices. For victims of stroke, one important element of recovery is exercises for improving range of motion. Researchers have looked into AR systems that can track hand movements and create a virtual interface for performing wrist, elbow, and shoulder exercises (Hondori, Khademi, Dodakian, Cramer, & Lopes, 2013) and help stroke patients to maintain balance and improve gait (Lee, Kim, & Lee, 2014). Other visual applications for AR and motor function include helping children with cerebral palsy perform home-based rehabilitation (Munroe, Meng, Yanco, & Begum, 2016). AR has also been utilized to train and give movement cues to recovering Parkinson's patients to help improve their gait (Espay et al., 2010). These AR systems in patient's homes help improve rehabilitation allowing patients to engage in physiological beneficial practices in their own home at times and locations convenient for patients.

Medical field level

Beyond a focus on individual applications and interventions, there have been many physicians and practitioners who have considered AR to improve the structures in which individuals provide medical care (Barsom, Graafland, & Schijven, 2016; Samset et al., 2008; Sielhorst, Feuerstein, & Navab, 2008; Zhu, Hadadgar, Masiello, & Zary, 2014). In this capacity, AR is not necessarily put directly into the hands of patients but conceptualized as a tool for medical providers and educators to ultimately better serve patients. In this section, there is an outline of several studies that have examined the use of AR to improve medical education, train and simulate medical procedures, and aid in actual surgical operations and remote telemedicine.

AR health education

One of the first areas that scholars considered with AR technologies was how it might improve general education and pedagogy (Dunleavy, Dede, & Mitchell, 2009; Martín-Gutiérrez et al., 2010; Wu, Lee, Chang, & Liang, 2013; Yuen, Yaoyuneyong, & Johnson, 2011). With that research came a subset of scholars interested in adapting AR specifically for education of medical residents and medical schools (Kamphuis, Barson, Schijven & Christoph, 2014; Sherstyuk, Vincent, Berg, & Treskunov, 2011; Zhu et al., 2014). For example, Rolland, Biocca, Hamza-Lup, Ha, and Martins (2005) found that teamwork through the utilization of head-mounted projection displays results in effective collaboration. Medical education can be costly as an upfront investment but is much less costly than the consequences of insufficient training that results in medical errors. Thus, anything that can help medical students learn core competencies such as biology, decision-making, and teamwork more efficiently is worth considering.

Medical education also lends itself to some of the unique capabilities of AR, for example, understanding human body structure. Anatomical training requires dissection of the human body, which enables the students to study the human body structure in 3D. In traditional anatomy, this training requires either a real human cadaver that is costly in price and limited in number or a manikin that is limited in their functions and how they can simulate a real body. AR has specifically been proposed to expand the functionality of manikins, to add visual and tactile AR features to patient simulators (Sherstyuk et al., 2011). AR has also been conceptualized as an alternative way for anatomical education of medical students, using real-time visualization that is integrated in situations with relatively lower cost (Sielhorst et al., 2004). AR has been utilized to help medical students envision the anatomical structure, organ dynamics, surgical procedures, and diagnoses of patients (Barsom et al., 2016; Kamphuis, Barsom, Schijven, & Christoph, 2014; Qu et al., 2014; Thomas, William John, & Delieu, 2010).

Many of the first AR applications were geared toward visualizing medical diagrams and anatomical displays, such as the brain, nervous system, skeletons, and teeth (Blum, Kleeberger, Bichlmeier, & Navab, 2012). Given the ability for AR to depict 3D overlays, some of these applications allowed users to move around a particular object and see it from multiple perspectives, zoom into specific areas, and pull apart displays to see inside a particular system. Early work in this area has examined whether the interactive and 3D nature of AR anatomy displays could help medical students learn and remember more information from their medical training (Chien, Chen, & Jeng, 2010). In particular, some have attempted to pair the visual augmentations with haptic feedback to improve retention of where to place medical objects (Luciano et al., 2011). Across a variety of areas, scholars have been thinking about integrating AR more explicitly into medical education (Kamphuis et al., 2014; Zhu et al., 2014) and supplementing physical tools like cadaver-based education (Thomas et al., 2010).

Much of the literature has stated that AR could be a useful tool for medical education in terms of decreased amounts of practice needed, improved performance accuracy, accelerated learning, and improved attention span and hands-on experience for students (Zhu et al., 2014). However, there are challenges for AR technologies to overcome to be utilized more effectively and efficiently to increase learning outcomes for medical students and health professionals. The challenges are twofold: device and application. As for the device, technological issues challenge the applicability of AR for medical education. Issues with the resolution of images that headworn display projects may not be enough to provide a realistic of an image as it should (Ponce, Menendez, Oladeji, Fryberger, & Dantuluri, 2014), and that lack of quality in image resolution may hamper the effectiveness of AR for medical education. Although there are many applications for medical education in the market, it is hard to say that the validity and effectiveness of these applications are qualified enough for educational material. These findings may also not necessarily be specific to AR, but it may instead reflect the novelty of technology that is contributing to learning and motivation (Noll, Häussermann, von Jan, Raap, & Albrecht, 2014; Thomas et al., 2010). The content itself also needs to be examined through theoretical lenses of pedagogical theories so that the technology becomes able to elicit better learning outcomes (Zhu et al., 2014). Issues with devices and applications remain as challenges to overcome in the future to be able to better provide an effective opportunity for AR medical education for students and health professionals.

AR medical training and simulation

The visual nature of AR also lends itself to training medical professionals for specific operations and procedures. Particularly when it comes to surgery, the situated visualization of AR technologies along with its haptic devices, triggers and simulators have all been considered to improve medical training (Samset et al., 2008; Sielhorst et al., 2004). AR has been found to be an effective tool for training health professionals how to place an injection needle (Yeo et al., 2011) and how to position an intraoral distractor (Qu et al., 2014). Full AR simulations have enabled medical residents to receive more experience in ventriculostomy (Hooten et al., 2014), upper limb prostheses (Lamounier, Lopes, Cardoso, Andrade, & Soares, 2010), and laparoscopic surgery (Botden & Jakimowicz, 2009). AR can also provide useful image training for navigation during heart surgery (Chu et al., 2012) and visualization of blood circulation (Szabó et al., 2013).

This type of training for situational awareness during surgery and adding information to the surgeons' field of vision to reduce mental load can be beneficial. A systematic review of different AR health training systems found that "AR allows trainees to understand the spatial relationships and concepts, and it provides substantial, contextual and situated learning experiences. [...] Moreover, AR helps to create authentic simulated experiences. It is thought to increases trainees' subjective attractiveness, enhancing learning retention and performance" (Barsom, Graafland, & Scijven, 2016, p. 4180). Most of these studies, however, are done on AR systems that are in the pilot or exploratory phase. There needs to be more work on validating and evaluating these systems, similar to studies done assessing how AR can improve doctors' skills in minimally invasive surgery (Lahanas, Loukas, Smailis, & Georgiou, 2015).

AR for remote telemedicine

As a field, one of the key problems in medicine is matching expertise to geographic/local conditions. Specifically, there are well-documented issues of medical staff shortages in rural areas, as well as equipment disparities (Hart, Salsberg, Phillips, & Lishner, 2002). Beyond the broader issue of geographic disparities, there are also certain operations and surgeries where the pool of experts is so small that they are not physically able to travel to all the places where the operation needs to take place. In these cases, telemedicine has been a proposed solution, allowing healthcare professionals to evaluate, diagnose, and treat patients in remote locations using telecommunications technology (Roine, Ohinmaa, & Hailey, 2001; Whitten et al., 2002).

One of the difficulties of telemedicine and teleoperated medical robots is sensory deprivation for the remote operator. With existing technology, it is a challenge to understand what is happening in the remote environment, especially receiving real-time haptic feedback. Given the importance of sensitive response in surgery, researchers from Johns Hopkins University Medical Center have attempted to address these concerns with an AR system comprising force-sensing robotic instruments, a kinematic tool tracker, and a graphic display that overlays a visual representation of force levels on top instruments (Akinbiyi et al., 2006). They found that the system helped reduce the number of broken knots and led to a more consistent application of force (Akinbiyi et al., 2006). Other extant studies have looked at the possibility of using AR to show the real interaction of a tool by haptically painting on objects (Bayart, Diddier, & Kheddar, 2008). Some work on haptics has looked at using a glove for delivering augmented feedback (Kron, Buss, & Schmidt, 2000), while others have opted for a finger-based device for rendering and interacting with AR objects (Scheggi, Salvietti, & Prattichizzo, 2010).

AR for improving health Professional's understanding and empathy for patients

Doctor–patient communication is a key component of healthcare because effective doctor–patient communication enhances patients' motivation, increases overall benefit from the healthcare, and increases perceived levels of support that patients receive (Ha & Longnecker, 2010). Successful communication within medical contexts utilizes two distinctive approaches: instrumental and task-oriented approaches and socioemotional approaches (Ong, De Haes, Hoos, & Lammes, 1995). First, providing explicit health information is central to doctor–patient communication (Garrity, 1981). When patients have dissatisfaction with the healthcare service, it is not primarily about incompetence of the healthcare providers, rather it is more about the communication quality (Ha & Longnecker, 2010). In doctor–patient communication settings, AR can help doctors provide more vivid information through augmentations. Utilizing AR may keep doctors from having divided attention and having to switch contexts from computers to patients, which could enhance the quality of communication from doctors and also patients' perspectives (Monkman & Kushniruk, 2015).

Additionally, several recent studies have explored how AR can potentially evoke empathy (Billinghurst, 2014; Kors, Ferri, Van Der Spek, Ketel, & Schouten, 2016), which is an important factor in family communication and perceived doctor–patient communication (Kim, Kaplowitz, & Johnston, 2004; Squier, 1990). Evoking empathy through AR could have unique applications for understanding patients' situations when they go through an illness. For example, recently, pharmaceutical companies such as Excedrin have attempted to raise awareness and empathy through AR, by offering a visual experience of what it is like to experience a migraine. Through situated visual effects, AR applications in theory could utilize presence and immersion experiences to help people vicariously experience patient symptoms (Baños et al., 2004). Although it has promising potential for health, the use of AR regarding empathy is still in the early stages of research. More research is important to specifically examine the role that AR and specific types of situated experiences can have for empathy and doctor–patient interaction.

Future research and challenges

It is clear that AR has captured the attention of health professionals and technology designers, at both an individual level and at a broader field level. This chapter has covered a wide range of ways that AR has been considered as a tool and an intervention and a technology for training, education, execution, and evaluation. Despite this breadth of literature, there are specific areas that future researchers should tackle. One recommendation is to expand the range of possibilities for AR across health conditions. As AR research becomes more prevalent, merging the technical expertise with local needs and health contexts can lead to new types of interventions and opportunities. Researchers have already called for more work that examines the relationship between AR devices, content, industry, and users (Liao, 2019), and the health field provides unique possibilities and constraints for testing these relationships.

Secondly, there is a need to build theories specific to AR and health. Rather than applying existing health communication theories to the context of AR, scholars should work to develop theories that allow us to look beyond a particular health problem to offer novel insights into the intersections of health and AR technologies. Theories that combine visual processing, attention, and interactivity will help scholars and different health stakeholders better understand AR mechanisms in health communication processes. While much of the current literature is demonstrating the viability of AR, future studies should more explicitly investigate the specific mechanisms of AR health interventions that influence a change in health behavioral outcomes.

It is also important to conduct collaborative projects with researchers from different disciplines and to make an active effort to balance perspectives. Health communication is an applied, interdisciplinary, and practical field of research; AR in health has hailed as a way forward for patient-driven services. Therefore, more research is necessary to fill the gaps in the current state of knowledge and to provide an evidence base for the implementation of AR in health. To maximize benefits while minimizing harm, health and technology researchers should carefully consider and further examine ethical, methodological, theoretical, and technological issues pertaining to health and technology.

At both the individual level and the field level, the main area that future research will need to address is about the adoption, implementation, and scalability of AR as a health and medical solution. The adoption of AR technologies in general has been an ongoing exploration, with recent studies examining why and under what conditions people would choose to buy AR devices (Harborth & Pape, 2017; Rauschnabel, Brem, & Ivens, 2015). Other large-scale surveys of AR users have been primarily around games like Pokémon GO (Colley et al., 2017; Tabacchi, Caci, Cardaci, & Perticone, 2017). Understanding more about how people adopt AR generally as well as how they adopt AR health applications will be an important first step in understanding the relationship between AR and health. Their acceptance may also play a role in the willingness of people within organizations to adopt them, particularly when it comes to head-mounted displays (Schreinemacher, Graafland, & Schijven, 2014). For example, the hope is that with more studies about the effectiveness of in-home improvements via AR and rehabilitation through AR, researchers can make broader claims about the effectiveness and ecological validity of home-based systems.

The implementation of AR technologies in health contexts is another area that needs future research, given that the vast majority of existing studies have been about experimental AR prototypes or pilot studies (Navab et al., 2012; Sielhorst et al., 2008). How to move these from a prototype to full-scale implementation is an area that needs additional study. How to implement and do so at scale is a problem for many industries seeking to implement AR, with many scholars pointing out the comparative lack of studies on applications beyond the proof of concept phase in AR industrial applications (Fite-Georgel, 2011; Liao, 2019). For health organizations, there is a particular need for research in these areas. Scholars in the field note that "in order to implement existent and new augmented reality applications in a training curriculum of medical specialists validly and reliably, uniform assessment strategies and complete validation trajectory are much needed" (Barsom et al., 2016, p. 4181).

This question of external validity and scalability is similarly an issue for the studies about AR for surgical operations and remote telemedicine. Most of the studies are done on individually customized AR systems or are specifically testing novel designs of AR technologies. The degree and ease at which those systems can scale is unknown, given the start-up costs of these systems and the latent knowledge and expertise it takes to create the systems. While off-the-shelf commercial devices may be easier to scale, they may lack the high level of precision tracking, accuracy, and display resolution necessary for particularly sensitive medical operations (Schreinemacher et al., 2014). The health field is also paradoxical in that while it is often testing new technologies and on the forefront of innovation, it can also be slow to adopt and change due to inertia, structure, and regulations. For all the promise that some of this early research in AR and health holds, more work is necessary to integrate and communicate this research to the larger structures and networks of medical providers and policymakers if AR is to break through.

Lastly, almost all of the works found related to AR and health has been cross-sectional or experimental with no follow-up. A systematic review of AR training/education studies came to similar conclusions, observing that "no follow-up studies on retention of skills could be identified, nor could subsequent clinical improvement of trainees be retrieved from studies" (Barsom et al., 2016, p. 4181). Some of the phobia treatment studies followed up on AR users for a period of months, but more longitudinal studies of the interventions are necessary to make claims about the long-term implications of AR tools.

Conclusion

AR is still in the relatively early stages of adoption within all fields, health and medicine included. The early results are positive in terms of improving on key outcomes relevant to health, whether it is individual behavior regarding prevention, intervention, or rehabilitation. Similarly, the early prototypes for medical education, training, and remote telemedicine are also exciting areas of study. Within these diverse areas of AR in medicine, however, there are also important gaps and areas for future research. Much of the literature out there strictly focuses on health outcomes, or comparing AR to non-AR systems. It is important for future studies to further examine how, why, and under what health conditions AR is successful. Rather than focusing on health outcomes utilizing AR, future studies could investigate the specific technical features of AR, the physiological experiences utilizing AR, and affordances of AR that influence health experiences and outcomes.

This gap is particularly important given the next phase of AR and health, which is the adoption, implementation, and scaling of these systems. This chapter helps scholars understand how existing research has been thinking about AR and medicine, what some of the early findings are, and what still needs to be done to further understand an emerging technology for health-related behavioral and cognitive change.

References

Akinbiyi, T., Reiley, C. E., Saha, S., Burschka, D., Hasser, C. J., Yuh, D. D., & Okamura, A. M. (August 2006). Dynamic augmented reality for sensory substitution in robot-assisted surgical systems. In *Engineering in medicine and biology society, 2006. EMBS'06. 28th annual international conference of the IEEE* (pp. 567–570). IEEE.

Althoff, T., White, R. W., & Horvitz, E. (2016). Influence of Pokémon go on physical activity: Study and implications. *Journal of Medical Internet Research, 18*(12).

Azuma, R. T. (1997). A survey of augmented reality. *Presence: Teleoperators and Virtual Environments, 6*(4), 355–385.

Bai, Z., Blackwell, A. F., & Coulouris, G. (October 2013). Through the looking glass: Pretend play for children with autism. In *Mixed and augmented reality (ISMAR), 2013 IEEE international symposium on* (pp. 49–58). IEEE.

Baños, R. M., Botella, C., Alcañiz, M., Liaño, V., Guerrero, B., & Rey, B. (2004). Immersion and emotion: Their impact on the sense of presence. *CyberPsychology and Behavior, 7*(6), 734–741.

Barsom, E. Z., Graafland, M., & Schijven, M. P. (2016). Systematic review on the effectiveness of augmented reality applications in medical training. *Surgical Endoscopy, 30*(10), 4174–4183.

Baus, O., & Bouchard, S. (2014). Moving from virtual reality exposure-based therapy to augmented reality exposure-based therapy: A review. *Frontiers in Human Neuroscience, 8*, 112.

Bayart, B., Diddier, J. Y., & Kheddar, A. (June 2008). Force feedback virtual painting on real objects: A paradigm of augmented reality haptics. In *International conference on human haptic sensing and touch enabled computer applications* (pp. 776–785). Berlin, Heidelberg: Springer.

Benko, H., Wilson, A. D., & Zannier, F. (October 2014). Dyadic projected spatial augmented reality. In *Proceedings of the 27th annual ACM symposium on User interface software and technology* (pp. 645–655). ACM.

Bianco, M. L., Pedell, S., & Renda, G. (November 2016). Augmented reality and home modifications: A tool to empower older adults in fall prevention. In *Proceedings of the 28th Australian conference on computer-human interaction* (pp. 499–507). ACM.

Bichlmeier, C., Heining, S. M., Feuerstein, M., & Navab, N. (2009). The virtual mirror: A new interaction paradigm for augmented reality environments. *IEEE Transactions on Medical Imaging, 28*(9), 1498–1510.

Billinghurst, M. (February 2014). Using augmented reality to create empathic experiences. In *Proceedings of the 19th international conference on intelligent user interfaces* (pp. 5–6). ACM.

Blum, T., Kleeberger, V., Bichlmeier, C., & Navab, N. (March 2012). mirracle: An augmented reality magic mirror system for anatomy education. In *Virtual reality short papers and posters (VRW), 2012 IEEE* (pp. 115–116). IEEE.

Borghese, N. A., Murray, D., Paraschiv-Ionescu, A., de Bruin, E. D., Bulgheroni, M., Steblin, A., … Parra, C. (2014). Rehabilitation at home: A comprehensive technological approach. In *Virtual, augmented reality and serious games for healthcare* (Vol. 1, pp. 289–319). Berlin, Heidelberg: Springer.

Botden, S. M., & Jakimowicz, J. J. (2009). What is going on in augmented reality simulation in laparoscopic surgery? *Surgical Endoscopy, 23*(8), 1693.

Botella, C., Bretón-López, J., Quero, S., Baños, R., & García-Palacios, A. (2010). Treating cockroach phobia with augmented reality. *Behavior Therapy, 41*(3), 401–413.

Botella, C., Breton-Lopez, J., Quero, S., Baños, R. M., Garcia-Palacios, A., Zaragoza, I., & Alcañiz, M. (2011). Treating cockroach phobia using a serious game on a mobile phone and augmented reality exposure: A single case study. *Computers in Human Behavior, 27*(1), 217–227.

Botella, C. M., Juan, M. C., Baños, R. M., Alcañiz, M., Guillén, V., & Rey, B. (2005). Mixing realities? An application of augmented reality for the treatment of cockroach phobia. *CyberPsychology and Behavior, 8*(2), 162–171.

Chen, C. H., Lee, I. J., & Lin, L. Y. (2015). Augmented reality-based self-facial modeling to promote the emotional expression and social skills of adolescents with autism spectrum disorders. *Research in Developmental Disabilities, 36*, 396–403.

Cheok, A. D., Fong, S. W., Goh, K. H., Yang, X., Liu, W., & Farbiz, F. (May 2003). Human Pacman: A sensing-based mobile entertainment system with ubiquitous computing and tangible interaction. In *Proceedings of the 2nd workshop on Network and system support for games* (pp. 106–117). ACM.

Chess, S. (2014). Augmented regionalism: Ingress as geomediated gaming narrative. *Information, Communication and Society, 17*(9), 1105–1117.

Chien, C. H., Chen, C. H., & Jeng, T. S. (March 2010). An interactive augmented reality system for learning anatomy structure. In *Proceedings of the international multiconference of engineers and computer scientists* (Vol. 1, pp. 17–19). Hong Kong, China: International Association of Engineers.

Chu, M. W., Moore, J., Peters, T., Bainbridge, D., McCarty, D., Guiraudon, G. M., … Daly, R. C. (2012). Augmented reality image guidance improves navigation for beating heart mitral valve repair. *Innovations, 7*(4), 274–281.

Colley, A., Thebault-Spieker, J., Lin, A. Y., Degraen, D., Fischman, B., Häkkilä, J., … Wenig, D. (May 2017). The geography of Pokémon GO: Beneficial and problematic effects on places and movement. In *Proceedings of the 2017 CHI conference on human factors in computing systems* (pp. 1179–1192). ACM.

Correa, A. G. D., Ficheman, I. K., do Nascimento, M., & de Deus Lopes, R. (July 2009). Computer assisted music therapy: A case study of an augmented reality musical system for children with cerebral palsy rehabilitation. In *Advanced learning technologies, 2009. ICALT 2009. Ninth IEEE international conference on* (pp. 218–220). IEEE.

Dey, A., Billinghurst, M., Lindeman, R. W., & Swan, J. (2018). A systematic review of 10 Years of augmented reality usability studies: 2005 to 2014. *Frontiers in Robotics and AI, 5*, 37.

Dunleavy, M., Dede, C., & Mitchell, R. (2009). Affordances and limitations of immersive participatory augmented reality simulations for teaching and learning. *Journal of Science Education and Technology, 18*(1), 7–22.

Espay, A. J., Baram, Y., Dwivedi, A. K., Shukla, R., Gartner, M., Gaines, L., ... Revilla, F. J. (2010). At-home training with closed-loop augmented-reality cueing device for improving gait in patients with Parkinson disease. *Journal of Rehabilitation Research and Development, 47*(6).

Fite-Georgel, P. (October 2011). Is there a reality in industrial augmented reality?. In *Mixed and augmented reality (ISMAR), 2011 10th IEEE international symposium on* (pp. 201–210). IEEE.

Fleming, T. M., Bavin, L., Stasiak, K., Hermansson-Webb, E., Merry, S. N., Cheek, C., ... Hetrick, S. (2017). Serious games and gamification for mental health: Current status and promising directions. *Frontiers in Psychiatry, 7*, 215.

Frank, L. D., Engelke, P. I., & Schmid, T. L. (2003). *Health and community design: The impact of the built environment on physical activity.* Washington, DC: Island Press.

Garrity, T. F. (1981). Medical compliance and the clinician-patient relationship: A review. *Social Science and Medicine – Part E: Medical Psychology, 15*(3), 215–222.

Giglioli, C., Pallavicini, F., Pedroli, E., Serino, S., & Riva, G. (2015). Augmented reality: A brand new challenge for the assessment and treatment of psychological disorders. *Computational and Mathematical Methods in Medicine.* https://doi.org/10.1155/2015/862942, 862942-1.

Graham, M., Zook, M., & Boulton, A. (2013). Augmented reality in urban places: Contested content and the duplicity of code. *Transactions of the Institute of British Geographers, 38*(3), 464–479.

Guillory, J., Chang, P., Henderson, C. R., Jr., Shengelia, R., Lama, S., Warmington, M., ... Gay, G. (2015). Piloting a text message-based social support intervention for patients with chronic pain: Establishing feasibility and preliminary efficacy. *The Clinical Journal of Pain, 31*(6), 548.

Ha, J. F., & Longnecker, N. (2010). Doctor-patient communication: A review. *The Ochsner Journal, 10*(1), 38–43.

Hansen, C., Wieferich, J., Ritter, F., Rieder, C., & Peitgen, H. O. (2010). Illustrative visualization of 3D planning models for augmented reality in liver surgery. *International Journal of Computer Assisted Radiology and Surgery, 5*(2), 133–141.

Harborth, D., & Pape, S. (2017). Exploring the hype: Investigating technology acceptance factors of Pokémon go. In *IEEE international symposium on mixed and augmented reality (ISMAR 2017).*

Hart, L. G., Salsberg, E., Phillips, D. M., & Lishner, D. M. (2002). Rural health care providers in the United States. *The Journal of Rural Health, 18*(5), 211–231.

Hondori, H. M., Khademi, M., Dodakian, L., Cramer, S. C., & Lopes, C. V. (2013). A spatial augmented reality rehab system for post-stroke hand rehabilitation. In *MMVR* (Vol. 184, pp. 279–285).

Hooten, K. G., Lister, J. R., Lombard, G., Lizdas, D. E., Lampotang, S., Rajon, D. A., ... Murad, G. J. (2014). Mixed reality ventriculostomy simulation: Experience in neurosurgical residency. *Operative Neurosurgery, 10*(4), 565–576.

Howe, K. B., Suharlim, C., Ueda, P., Howe, D., Kawachi, I., & Rimm, E. B. (2016). Gotta catch'em all! Pokémon GO and physical activity among young adults: Difference in differences study. *BMJ, 355*, i6270.

Kamphuis, C., Barsom, E., Schijven, M., & Christoph, N. (2014). Augmented reality in medical education. *Perspectives on Medical Education, 3*(4), 300–311.

Kim, S. S., Kaplowitz, S., & Johnston, M. V. (2004). The effects of physician empathy on patient satisfaction and compliance. *Evaluation and the Health Professions, 27*(3), 237–251.

Klasnja, P., & Pratt, W. (2012). Healthcare in the pocket: Mapping the space of mobile-phone health interventions. *Journal of Biomedical Informatics, 45*(1), 184–198.

Kors, M. J., Ferri, G., Van Der Spek, E. D., Ketel, C., & Schouten, B. A. (October 2016). A breathtaking journey. On the design of an empathy-arousing mixed-reality game. In

Proceedings of the 2016 annual symposium on computer-human interaction in play (pp. 91–104). ACM.

Kron, A., Buss, M., & Schmidt, G. (2000). Exploration and manipulation of virtual environments using a combined hand and finger force feedback system. In *Intelligent robots and systems, 2000.(IROS 2000). Proceedings. 2000 IEEE/RSJ international conference on* (Vol. 2, pp. 1328–1333). IEEE.

Lahanas, V., Loukas, C., Smailis, N., & Georgiou, E. (2015). A novel augmented reality simulator for skills assessment in minimal invasive surgery. *Surgical Endoscopy, 29*(8), 2224–2234.

Lamounier, E., Lopes, K., Cardoso, A., Andrade, A., & Soares, A. (2010). On the use of virtual and augmented reality for upper limb prostheses training and simulation. In *Conf Proc IEEE Eng Med Biol Soc 2010* (pp. 2451–2454).

LeBlanc, A. G., & Chaput, J. P. (2017). Pokémon go: A game changer for the physical inactivity crisis? *Preventive Medicine, 101*, 235–237.

Lee, C. H., Kim, Y., & Lee, B. H. (2014). Augmented reality-based postural control training improves gait function in patients with stroke: Randomized controlled trial. *Hong Kong Physiotherapy Journal, 32*(2), 51–57.

Liao, T. (2016). Is it 'augmented reality'? Contesting boundary work over the definitions and organizing visions for an emerging technology across field-configuring events. *Information and Organization, 26*(3), 45–62.

Liao, T. (2018). Mobile versus headworn augmented reality: How visions of the future shape, contest, and stabilize an emerging technology. *New Media and Society, 20*(2), 796–814.

Liao, T. (2019). Future directions for mobile augmented reality research: Understanding relationships between augmented reality users, nonusers, content, devices, and industry. *Mobile Media and Communication, 7*(1), 131–149.

Liao, T., & Humphreys, L. (2015). Layar-ed places: Using mobile augmented reality to tactically reengage, reproduce, and reappropriate public space. *New Media and Society, 17*(9), 1418–1435.

Liao, H., Inomata, T., Sakuma, I., & Dohi, T. (2010). Three-dimensional augmented reality for mriguided surgery using integral videography auto stereoscopic-image overlay. *IEEE Transactions on Biomedical Engineering, 57*(6), 1476–1486.

Lieberman, D. A. (2006). *Dance games and other exergames: What the research says.*

Liu, R., Salisbury, J. P., Vahabzadeh, A., & Sahin, N. T. (2017). Feasibility of an autism-focused augmented reality smartglasses system for social communication and behavioral coaching. *Frontiers in Pediatrics, 5*, 145.

Luciano, C. J., Banerjee, P. P., Bellotte, B., Oh, G. M., Lemole, M., Jr., Charbel, F. T., & Roitberg, B. (2011). Learning retention of thoracic pedicle screw placement using a high-resolution augmented reality simulator with haptic feedback. *Operative Neurosurgery, 69*(Suppl_1), ons14–ons19.

Luxton, D. D., McCann, R. A., Bush, N. E., Mishkind, M. C., & Reger, G. M. (2011). mHealth for mental health: Integrating smartphone technology in behavioral healthcare. *Professional Psychology: Research and Practice, 42*(6), 505.

Martín-Gutiérrez, J., Saorín, J. L., Contero, M., Alcañiz, M., Pérez-López, D. C., & Ortega, M. (2010). Design and validation of an augmented book for spatial abilities development in engineering students. *Computers and Graphics, 34*(1), 77–91.

Milgram, P., & Kishino, F. (1994). A taxonomy of mixed reality visual displays. *IEICE — Transactions on Info and Systems, 77*(12), 1321–1329.

Monkman, H., & Kushniruk, A. W. (2015). eHealth literacy issues, constructs, models, and methods for health information technology design and evaluation. *Knowledge Management and E-Learning: International Journal, 7*(4), 541–549.

Munroe, C., Meng, Y., Yanco, H., & Begum, M. (March 2016). Augmented reality eyeglasses for promoting home-based rehabilitation for children with cerebral palsy. In *The Eleventh ACM/IEEE international conference on human robot interaction*. IEEE Press, 565-565.

Nacinovich, M. (2013). Defining mHealth. *Journal of Communication in Healthcare, 4*(1), 1–3. https://doi.org/10.1179/175380611X12950033990296.

Navab, N., Blum, T., Wang, L., Okur, A., & Wendler, T. (2012). First deployments of augmented reality in operating rooms. *Computer, 45*(7), 48–55.

Noll, C., Häussermann, B., von Jan, U., Raap, U., & Albrecht, U. V. (June 2014). Mobile augmented reality in medical education: an application for dermatology. In *Proceedings of the 2014 workshop on Mobile augmented reality and robotic technology-based systems* (pp. 17–18). ACM.

Ong, L. M., De Haes, J. C., Hoos, A. M., & Lammes, F. B. (1995). Doctor-patient communication: A review of the literature. *Social Science and Medicine, 40*(7), 903–918.

Oudshoorn, N. (2012). How places matter: Telecare technologies and the changing spatial dimensions of healthcare. *Social Studies of Science, 42*(1), 121–142.

Payne, H. E., Moxley, V. B., & MacDonald, E. (2015). Health behavior theory in physical activity game apps: A content analysis. *JMIR Serious Games, 3*(2).

Ponce, B. A., Menendez, M. E., Oladeji, L. O., Fryberger, C. T., & Dantuluri, P. K. (2014). Emerging technology in surgical education: Combining real-time augmented reality and wearable computing devices. *Orthopedics, 37*(11), 751–757.

Qu, M., Hou, Y., Xu, Y., Shen, C., Zhu, M., Xie, L., ... Chai, G. (2014). Precise positioning of an intraoral distractor using augmented reality in patients with hemifacial microsomia. *Journal of Cranio-Maxillofacial Surgery, 43*(1), 106–112.

Rauschnabel, P. A., Brem, A., & Ivens, B. S. (2015). Who will buy smart glasses? Empirical results of two pre-market-entry studies on the role of personality in individual awareness and intended adoption of Google glass wearables. *Computers in Human Behavior, 49*, 635–647.

Roine, R., Ohinmaa, A., & Hailey, D. (2001). Assessing telemedicine: A systematic review of the literature. *Canadian Medical Association Journal, 165*(6), 765–771.

Rolland, J. P., Biocca, F., Hamza-Lup, F., Ha, Y., & Martins, R. (2005). Development of head-mounted projection displays for distributed, collaborative, augmented reality applications. *Presence: Teleoperators and Virtual Environments, 14*(5), 528–549.

Samset, E., Schmalstieg, D., Vander Sloten, J., Freudenthal, A., Declerck, J., Casciaro, S., ... Gersak, B. (2008). Augmented reality in surgical procedures. In *Proc. SPIE* (Vol. 68, p. 6).

Scheggi, S., Salvietti, G., & Prattichizzo, D. (September 2010). Shape and weight rendering for haptic augmented reality. In *RO-MAN, 2010 IEEE* (pp. 44–49). IEEE.

Schmalstieg, D., & Wagner, D. (November 2007). Experiences with handheld augmented reality. In *Mixed and augmented reality, 2007. ISMAR 2007. 6th IEEE and ACM international symposium on* (pp. 3–18). IEEE.

Schreinemacher, M. H., Graafland, M., & Schijven, M. P. (2014). Google glass in surgery. *Surgical Innovation, 21*(6), 651–652.

Sherstyuk, A., Vincent, D., Berg, B., & Treskunov, A. (2011). Mixed reality manikins for medical education. In *Handbook of augmented reality* (pp. 479–500). New York, NY: Springer.

Sielhorst, T., Feuerstein, M., & Navab, N. (2008). Advanced medical displays: A literature review of augmented reality. *Journal of Display Technology, 4*(4), 451–467.

Sielhorst, T., Obst, T., Burgkart, R., Riener, R., & Navab, N. (September 2004). An augmented reality delivery simulator for medical training. In *International workshop on augmented environments for medical imaging-MICCAI Satellite Workshop* (Vol. 141, pp. 11–20).

Squier, R. W. (1990). A model of empathic understanding and adherence to treatment regimens in practitioner-patient relationships. *Social Science and Medicine, 30*(3), 325–339.

Szabó, Z., Berg, S., Sjökvist, S., Gustafsson, T., Carleberg, P., Uppsäll, M., ... Smedby, Ö. (2013). Real-time intraoperative visualization of myocardial circulation using augmented reality temperature display. *The International Journal of Cardiovascular Imaging, 29*(2), 521–528.

Tabacchi, M. E., Caci, B., Cardaci, M., & Perticone, V. (2017). Early usage of Pokémon Go and its personality correlates. *Computers in Human Behavior, 72*, 163–169.

Tang, A., Biocca, F., & Lim, L. (2004). Comparing differences in presence during social interaction in augmented reality versus virtual reality environments: An exploratory study. *Proceedings of PRESENCE*, 204–208.

Tang, R., Yang, X. D., Bateman, S., Jorge, J., & Tang, A. (April 2015). Physio@ Home: Exploring visual guidance and feedback techniques for physiotherapy exercises. In *Proceedings of the 33rd annual ACM conference on human factors in computing systems* (pp. 4123–4132). ACM.

Thomas, R. G., William John, N., & Delieu, J. M. (2010). Augmented reality for anatomical education. *Journal of Visual Communication in Medicine, 33*(1), 6–15.

Van Krevelen, D. W. F., & Poelman, R. (2010). A survey of augmented reality technologies, applications and limitations. *International Journal of Virtual Reality, 9*(2), 1.

Vidal, F. P., Bello, F., Brodlie, K. W., John, N. W., Gould, D., Phillips, R., & Avis, N. J. (March 2006). Principles and applications of computer graphics in medicine. No. 1. In *Computer graphics forum* (Vol. 25, pp. 113–137). Oxford, OX4 2DQ, UK: Blackwell Publishing Ltd, 9600 Garsington Road.

Whitten, P. S., Mair, F. S., Haycox, A., May, C. R., Williams, T. L., & Hellmich, S. (2002). Systematic review of cost effectiveness studies of telemedicine interventions. *BMJ, 324*(7351), 1434–1437.

Wright, W., & Bogost, I. (2007). *Persuasive games: The expressive power of videogames.* Mit Press.

Wrzesien, M., Burkhardt, J. M., Alcañiz Raya, M., & Botella, C. (May 2011). Mixing psychology and HCI in evaluation of augmented reality mental health technology. In *CHI'11 extended abstracts on human factors in computing systems* (pp. 2119–2124). ACM.

Wu, H. K., Lee, S. W. Y., Chang, H. Y., & Liang, J. C. (2013). Current status, opportunities and challenges of augmented reality in education. *Computers and Education, 62*, 41–49.

Yeo, C. T., Ungi, T., Thainual, P., Lasso, A., McGraw, R. C., & Fichtinger, G. (2011). The effect of augmented reality training on percutaneous needle placement in spinal facet joint injections. *IEEE Transactions on Biomedical Engineering, 58*(7), 2031–2037.

Yuen, S., Yaoyuneyong, G., & Johnson, E. (2011). Augmented reality: An overview and five directions for AR in education. *Journal of Educational Technology Development and Exchange, 4*(1), 119–140.

Zhou, F., Duh, H. B. L., & Billinghurst, M. (September 2008). Trends in augmented reality tracking, interaction and display: A review of ten years of ISMAR. In *Proceedings of the 7th IEEE/ACM international symposium on mixed and augmented reality* (pp. 193–202). IEEE Computer Society.

Zhu, E., Hadadgar, A., Masiello, I., & Zary, N. (2014). Augmented reality in healthcare education: An integrative review. *PeerJ, 2*, e469.

7

Clinical applications of virtual reality in patient-centered care

Swati Pandita, Andrea Stevenson Won

Department of Communication, Cornell University, Ithaca, NY, United States

Introduction

Research on the clinical applications of virtual reality (VR) has rapidly progressed in the past 20 years. While potential applications range from medical education to surgical visualization, this chapter will focus predominantly on patient-centered care, including the diagnosis and treatment of health conditions. The most common applications of patient-centered VR include mental and physical therapeutic interventions, pain management, and neuropsychological diagnostic and assessment tools (Sutherland et al., 2018). This review is intended to help evaluate VR for the treatment of particular modalities, as well as to manage expectations of what VR can do now and may be able to do in the future. The chapter will begin with a broad definition of VR and its technological requirements, followed by a discussion of current VR interventions. The chapter will conclude with considerations for designing VR patient-centered care interventions and speculation on future applications.

Understanding virtual reality

Defining virtual reality

At its most basic level, VR is an interactive computer-generated experience that users react to as if it were a real, physical, environment. The human brain actively models the world using sensory information. By replacing auditory, visual, and even tactile and olfactory stimuli from the physical world with digital input, researchers can control the representations, or percepts, provided to the brain, creating a "virtual reality."

129

In the physical world, our eyes see different content as we move through the environment. Virtual environments (VEs) mimic this real-world property through real-time rendering, where images are constantly created, updated, and displayed as a response to users' tracked movement through virtual spaces. Real-time rendering, thus, gives users the illusion of being completely surrounded by a visual world.

While VEs frequently focus on representing visual aspects of the environment, they may also include sound, possibly spatialized sound, and sometimes limited haptic or touch feedback, for example, by vibration of the hand controllers or other specialized devices. Rarely, smell may be included.

In any VR experience, the orientation of a user's head must be tracked in order to render the appropriate content. In setups with positional tracking, users can also change their position in the virtual space, by moving horizontally or vertically in the X, Y, and Z axes (e.g., they can walk around rather than just swiveling their head). Sensors also track the movement of hand controllers and any other additional trackable devices (such as the HTC Vive's "puck" that can be attached to any body joint or object, see Fig. 7.1). Popular consumer systems such as the HTC Vive (Vive, 2016) or the Oculus Rift (Oculus, 2018) have 6° of freedom on both head and hands, which include orientation, or rotational tracking, and positional tracking. Thus, a user can interact with a VE by moving around

FIGURE 7.1 An example of a tracker, which can be attached to any object. This image shows HTC Vive's "puck," which can be attached to any body joint or object. *Photos taken and edited by author Swati Pandita.*

the room and potentially moving virtual objects using the hand controllers. Tracked movement is not only helpful for rendering VEs and allowing for interaction but also provides a stream of data, which can be used in conjunction with other data sets, such as self-report, to analyze behavior.

Types of virtual reality setups

VR experiences are supported by a variety of platforms. In its simplest form, mobile VR combines a smartphone with a headset such as Google Cardboard or Gear VR. In these cases, the phone presents content on a split screen to display a VE in which the user can rotate his or her head to look around. The phone's accelerometer tracks head orientation, and virtual content is then updated on the screens in front of the user's eyes. Similar to the Gear VR, but without the need of a smartphone driven computer, the Oculus Go is a standalone headset that serves as an in-between mobile and tethered headsets (Fig. 7.2).

More complex setups can include head-mounted displays (HMDs) with positional tracking and hand controllers, such as consumer systems like the Oculus Rift or Quest, or the HTC Vive. In HMD-based VR, the environment is displayed within the headset, and the view of the physical world is completely obscured. In networked VEs, multiple users can interact within the VE, as long as they each have a headset and the ability to have their movements tracked. In the past 5 years, these types of setups have become widely available on the consumer market, and their portability, ease of use, and low price point mean that their use is rapidly expanding.

Larger institutions may also have setups in which images are projected on three to six walls in a room. These immersive VEs are sometimes referred to as CAVEs (Cruz-Neira, Sandin, DeFanti, Kenyon, & Hart, 1992) In such environments, the user may wear stereoscopic glasses to give the

FIGURE 7.2   The Oculus Go pictured here is an example of a head-mounted display (HMD), that is untethered (not attached to a computer) and also does not rely on a phone. *Photos taken and edited by author Swati Pandita.*

content a 3D appearance, and the correct perspective and stereo projections of the environment are displayed as a function of the user's movement and interactions within the VE. These environments lend themselves well to collaborative work. In such cases, only one user is tracked, but their interactions and the content can be seen by their teammates, who are also in the room. Participants can see one another's actual bodies and respond to each other's gestures. These environments require a permanent, dedicated space installation and are generally expensive.

Creating content in virtual reality

There are two primary methods of creating content to be viewed using an HMD. The first is to create a spherical or 360-degree video. Such videos capture the real-world photo realistically, in such a way that the video creates a "sphere" around the user so that content updates as the user moves his or her head. While such content may be filmed to be stereoscopic, this kind of content only supports orientation—users cannot change their position by moving forward or back in the VE. Viewers also cannot interact with content, as the video is recorded.

In contrast, game engines like Unity or Unreal allow the creation of a virtual world with digital objects that users can interact with. Such environments have video game quality graphics with varying degrees of realism. 3D objects help create an interactive scene for users and are made using 3D modeling programs like Autodesk Maya, 3DS Max, and Blender. Avatars (virtual representations of humans) can also be created using specific software such as Adobe Fuse, Daz3D Studio, or FaceGen.

Often, users can be embodied in these virtual spaces, by controlling an avatar, which responds to their movements in the real world. For example, if a person wearing an HMD and holding a hand tracker holds his or her hand in front of their eyes, they will see their avatar's hand on the screens of their HMD. The illusion of control and realistic interaction of a VE play into the feeling of psychological realness. Having a virtual body can allow a user to feel a greater sense of presence or "being there" within the VE (Heeter, 1992).

VR is not only capable of changing a user's environment but also the way they are embodied. It can change a user's appearance by modifying the appearance of the avatar they control. VR can also change the user's perspective. In VR, users can embody either a first-person perspective, in which a VE is rendered from the avatar's viewpoint (as in the physical world, where only the hands and the front of the torso are visible without the use of a mirror). However, users can also see their virtual body and the actions that are performing from a third person perspective, an out-of-body experience that is not possible in real life.

Patient-centered care

Patient-centered care applications of VR primarily involve diagnostics and assessment and therapeutic uses. VR has been used to diagnose attention deficit hyperactivity disorder (ADHD), Parkinson's disease (PD), Alzheimer's disease (AD), and paranoia. In the case of therapy, VR has been employed in a variety of contexts, including anxiety disorders, body dysmorphia, pain management, and physical therapy.

Diagnostic uses of VR and technological considerations

Diagnosing ADHD with VR: Because of its ability to both manipulate stimuli and track patients' reactions, VR has great potential as a diagnostic tool. An example of this is with ADHD patients. Traditional assessments of neuropsychological function include clinical interviews, psychometrically sound behavior rating scales, and continuous performance tests (CPT). Out of the three, CPTs are the standard and test executive function (issues of goal directed behavior: impulsivity, hyperactivity, and attention in ADHD) most directly by requiring participants to maintain attention and react to specific stimuli in the face of various distractors (Areces, Rodríguez, García, Cueli, & González-Castro, 2018).

CPT often assesses cognitive impairment in traditional laboratory settings that cannot fully emulate the natural conditions in which ADHD symptomology arises. For individuals with ADHD, a more naturalistic setting might be sitting in a classroom with various visual and auditory distractions while being asked to complete a given task. VR can simulate these classroom settings by presenting multiple stimuli, recording response times to assessment tasks, and tracking the amount of movement per given task (Rizzo et al., 2000). Studies using such VR simulations found that children suffering from ADHD were more likely to show signs of restlessness, movement of their head, nondominant arm, and opposite leg. Therefore, VR can readily simulate naturalistic settings in which symptomology may arise and decrease chances of type II error or lack of diagnosis.

Assessing AD and PD with VR: Just as movement data are used to diagnosis individuals with ADHD, the same can be done for identifying individuals with neurodegenerative disorders such as AD and PD. AD is the most common neurodegenerative disorder (Alzheimer's Association, 2015), primarily affecting one's memory and blunting overall cognition. Physical symptoms include impaired executive functioning seen through slowness, rigidity, and tremors (Alzheimer's Association, 2015). In contrast, PD primarily affects one's ability to engage in planned motor action such as walking, writing, grasping, or holding objects.

Early stages of AD and PD can be detected through deficits in visuospatial abilities (Binetti et al., 1996; Levin, Llabre, & Weiner, 1989). Serino, Morganti, Di Stefano, and Riva (2015) created a VR assessment tool that measured differences in spatial encoding, storing, and syncing and found that individuals who suffer from AD have trouble with storing and synching allocentric object views as compared with healthy individuals. Although PD is primarily characterized as a motor disorder, researchers have started to study the role of vision in movement disorders (Davidsdottir, Wagenaar, Young, & Cronin-Golomb, 2008). With this shift in perspective, VR has been particularly helpful in classifying PD subtypes, which are differentiated by side of hemispheric damage onset (Davidsdottir et al., 2008). The characterization of AD and PD symptoms as abnormal changes in spatial bias makes VR an even better fit for assessing PD as it plays to its strength of being a flexible and responsive visual medium. A later section of this chapter will discuss how VR has been used as a *treatment* modality for PD.

Assessing paranoia with VR: Paranoia occurs when an individual falsely believes that others intend to harm him/her. Severe forms of paranoia, such as persecutory delusions, are seen in psychotic disorders like schizophrenia. Paranoia can also occur as a result of a traumatic event, such as physical assault. Paranoia can arise from misinterpreting social cues such as everyday facial expressions.

However, due to the subjective nature of the experience, there is no standardized assessment for paranoia. In order to create an assessment, Freeman et al. (2014) ran participants through a 4-minute VR train ride populated by computer agents (humanoid avatars controlled by the computer) with neutral expressions that could facilitate paranoia. In this study, all computer agents were programmed to have naturalistic gaze, but some were programmed to respond to the participant's gaze by looking in their direction. The study was interested in predicting the frequency of paranoid thought up to 6 months after the VR intervention. Participants were individuals who had suffered from physical assault a month prior and thereby susceptible to paranoid thought. Upon completing the virtual experience, participants answered surveys that measured paranoid thought and PTSD symptoms, which were used as predictors for the recurrence of a paranoid event. Thus, the VE served as an assessment method for the severity of paranoia and PTSD symptoms.

Technological considerations for diagnostic uses: There are several aspects of VR that make it an ecologically valid tool for neuropsychological assessment. HMDs can improve a user's attentional focus on their assessment task by occluding distracting stimuli from the physical world (e.g., movement and noise). Attention assessments may be more reliably measured in VR due to more consistent stimulus presentation and more reliable scoring. Tracked movement can detect behaviors that may not be easily perceptible to the human eye, which, in turn, can improve neuropsychological assessment.

For effective use, VEs for diagnostic use must be easy to use, avoiding complex controls (e.g., use of multiple buttons). Nonverbal behavior such as eye gaze and body movement must be tracked in order to assess behaviors associated with disorders. Similarly, since VEs are often used in conjunction with other assessment apparatus (e.g., a treadmill for PD), it is important that the headset is compatible with other gear. It may also be important that headsets and sensors are wireless if connections might compromise patient safety by restricting movement.

Treating anxiety disorders and phobias with VR and technological considerations

Generalized anxiety disorder (GAD) is characterized by consistent and excessive daily worrying for a period of 6 months or greater. Experiencing constant anxiety can impair one's ability to take care of their personal health, social interactions, work, and everyday activities. Individuals suffering from anxiety typically feel restless, easily fatigued, and irritable (NIMH, 2018). Phobias share a similar etiology to anxiety disorders; however, phobias are specific to an object or situation. Treatment for GAD and phobias typically includes psychotherapy or talk therapy, cognitive behavioral therapy (CBT), exposure therapy, and pharmacological interventions in the form of antidepressants or antianxiety medication.

VR can induce powerful perceptual cues that can recreate an anxiety-inducing moment. These cues can recreate an anxiety-inducing moment that a patient can relive through and reappraise with a therapist. The reality of the experience is shown through patient reports of anxiety symptoms such as "sweating, the butterflies, and weakness" while in the virtual worlds, which serve as evidence to the "realness" and immersion of the experience (Anderson, Rothbaum, & Hodges, 2003). By allowing individuals to interact with the fear memory, in conjunction with traditional CBT techniques such as extinction and habituation, the fear structure is slowly modified to a less aversive memory.

The treatment of phobias requires an extensive recreation of the environment in which graded versions of the phobia exist, making VR the perfect platform for administering CBTs. The most well-known forms of VR CBTs are exposure therapies (Powers & Emmelkamp, 2008). A nonexhaustive list of VR therapies includes some designed for flight anxiety (Rus-Calafell, Gutiérrez-Maldonado, Botella, & Baños, 2013), arachnophobia (Bouchard, Côté, St-Jacques, Robillard, & Renaud, 2006; Hoffman, Garcia-Palacios, Carlin, Furness, & Botella-Arbona, 2003; Shiban et al., 2016), claustrophobia (Botella, Baños, Villa, Perpiñá, & García-Palacios, 2000; Malbos, Mestre, Note, & Gellato, 2008), acrophobia or fear of heights (Emmelkamp et al., 2002; Rothbaum et al., 1995), and kinesiophobia of the back and neck (Bolte, de Lussanet, & Lappe, 2014; Chen et al., 2014).

A high level of stimulus control in virtual experiences is also advantageous. For example, in VEs designed to address the fear of public speaking, therapists can control the audience's reactions such as how interested, bored, or neutral they look and whether or not they applaud upon speech completion (Anderson, Zimand, Hodges, & Rothbaum, 2005).

VR is also a treatment medium that is capable of recreating once in a lifetime events (e.g., 9/11, Vietnam War) that patients can relive and reappraise with the help of a therapist. Experience recreation in VR is often utilized in the treatment of posttraumatic stress disorder or PTSD (Difede et al., 2007; Rizzo, Reger, Gahm, Difede, & Rothbaum, 2009; Rothbaum, Hodges, Ready, Graap, & Alarcon, 2001).

Before a VR intervention, patient's needs are discussed and evaluated by the therapist in a series of imaginal therapy (describing the fear-inducing situation) and reflective questions. These fear-inducing scenarios can then be typically recreated in a VE. Scenarios are graded from least to most fear inducing, where patients begin with the former situation and gradually work their way to the next scenario until their anxiety has decreased. In VE, the therapist can communicate with the patient via microphone, helping guide the patient throughout the exposure session (Anderson et al., 2003).

While each phobia is unique in its magnitude and fear-inducing stimuli, certain considerations need to be taken into account when designing VEs for phobia treatment: (1) Therapists need control of the scene, ranging from what a patient sees, feels (tactile), and hears, in the environment to modify the magnitude of the fearful stimulus. (2) Patients will ideally be embodied in an avatar to induce a sense of presence and realness within the VE. However, early therapies did not include an avatar body and were still successful in treating phobias (Difede & Hoffman, 2002), possibly due to patient's limited experiences and expectations of VR at the time (e.g., not expecting an avatar body). (3) Patients need agency or the ability to leave the scene whenever it becomes too frightening or overwhelming. This allows a patient to feel safe and more receptive toward starting or continuing treatment. (4) Therapists need a way to communicate with patients while they are in VR in order to guide them through appraising fearful situations in a less harmful way. (5) The VE should allow patients to change between perspectives (first to third) in order to get an alternative interpretation of the situation.

Body rescripting for body dysmorphia and technological considerations

The concept of negative body image, or high levels of dissatisfaction with one's body, is prevalent in body image disorders. Perceived body image can affect the likelihood of an individual engaging with and adhering to health-related behaviors (Manzoni et al., 2016). Individuals with negative body image are thought to be less adherent to weight maintenance treatments and efforts (Riva, 2011). The use of positively appraised virtual avatars for individuals with high body image dissatisfaction can decrease social physique anxiety and improve exergame experience (Song, Kim, & Lee 2014). Thus, some researchers think individuals with body dysmorphia perseverate or are stuck on a negative body image.

The allocentric lock theory posits that individuals are locked into an allocentric (third person view) of their past self, such as a negative memory of body image, which is no longer updated with egocentric (first person) sensory input of strenuous diet changes and change in body shape. If initial feelings of body dissatisfaction are not updated, people may give up on their weight maintenance efforts or try extreme diets that can lead to worse outcomes such as disordered (binge) eating. VR CBT in conjunction with a standard behavioral inpatient program, which provides individuals with weight maintenance guidelines, a low-calorie diet, and physical training, was used to update the allocentric memory or stored objective representation of oneself, in individuals seeking treatment for morbid obesity over a 6-week period (Manzoni et al., 2016). Upon 1 year of completing the VR CBT therapy and inpatient program, individuals in VR CBT as compared to traditional CBT maintained their weight loss (Manzoni et al., 2016). Thus, individuals were able to improve their level of body dissatisfaction through body rescripting and changing from allocentric and egocentric views of the self by using VR CBT (Riva, 2011).

Clinicians need to provide patients with various scenarios in which they would engage in behavior affected by their body dissatisfaction. The treatment should take place in a setting where the patient feels safe, and the patient should be able to leave the VE at her/his own discretion. VEs for body rescripting must include the ability to switch between allocentric and egocentric perspectives of the body (allow the patient to see themselves from the first and third person). Similarly to exposure therapies, the therapist must be able to talk to the patient while they are in the VE. Communication in VE is imperative to guiding patients through reappraisal of previously negative situations through body rescripting.

Lastly, custom avatars should be given careful consideration. Patients are more likely to identify with avatars that share physical similarity with them, such as age and race (Fox, 2012). The ability to identify with an avatar can increase a patient's level of presence within a VE, thereby affecting therapeutic VR outcomes. Avatars can also accurately portray a patient's health condition, which can further increase avatar adoption and presence. In light of individuals suffering from body dysmorphia, who are already hyperaware of their own bodies and may be hypercritical of bodies that are assigned to them, researchers should carefully consider avatar design and how it may affect a patient's avatar adoption, subsequent presence levels, and treatment outcomes.

Depression and technological considerations

Individuals with depression often engage in overly self-critical behavior that can maintain a negative mood state. Clinical researchers are addressing this behavior through self-compassion eliciting VEs, which encourage patients to engage in perspective taking (Falconer et al, 2014, 2016). Falconer et al. (2016) created an 8-minute scenario in which 15 patients practiced delivering compassion to a child. Their movements and speech were recorded, and then they were switched to experience receiving compassion as a child themselves. Their previously recorded compassionate response was then played to them, as a child, so they could see their own comforting words and gestures. The intervention proved successful, in that three repetitions of the scenario led to reductions in depression severity and self-criticism. The authors also found a significant increase in self-compassion after a 4-week follow-up, with four patients showing significant clinical improvement.

Self-compassion therapy in VR hinges on the ability to track, record, and rerender movement. The ability to track movement data in VR is important for instilling a sense of presence in the virtual world and connection with the virtual body, but most importantly, it allows for the ability to record virtual experiences and replay them back to an individual from the perspective of another virtual body. This also leads to the ability to easily switch virtual bodies in order to experience multiple perspectives. Other requirements, previously discussed, include ensuringthat the patient feels safe in the VE, can leave the environment at their discretion, and that the environment is easy to use. Lastly, depressed individuals have difficulty in actively seeking treatment, thus when designing interventions, one must consider the portability of the VR intervention and ease of access. With the increased interest of serious games and accessibility of consumer-grade VR technology, mental health in VR is soon becoming a greater possibility.

Pain management and technological considerations

Pain is an adaptive sensation that helps us avoid damage to ourselves and promote one's health and safety (Melzack & Katz, 2014; Scholz & Woolf, 2002; Woolf, 2010). Thus, people naturally attend to pain as it signals that there is something wrong, requiring immediate attention. However, pain management is necessary for the successful outcome of medical procedures and adherence to treatment.

Pain management varies by pain type, which is classified by several factors: (1) its chronicity, or the length of time one endures pain for, (2) its frequency, or how often it occurs, and (3) cause for onset. Acute pain is classified as pain that lasts no more than 6 months, with less frequency, and has a known cause for onset. Conversely, chronic pain lasts for more than 6 months, occurs more frequently, and the direct cause for onset is often unknown. VR works as a noninvasive and nonpharmacological treatment for acute pain (Li, Montaño, Chen, & Gold, 2011).

Many VR pain management interventions work on the underlying assumption that our attentional capacity for any perceptual event is limited. Therefore, distraction, or reorienting attention away from pain sensation during painful medical treatments such as wound care, dental pain (Hoffman et al., 2001), and IV placement (Gold, Kim, Kant, Joseph, & Rizzo, 2006), is key to pain management with VR. Various VR environments have been designed to distract individuals from burn wound pain (Hoffman et al., 2000, 2008), phantom limb pain (Murray et al., 2007), cold pressor pain (Dahlquist et al., 2008), dental pain (Hoffman et al., 2001), cystoscopy (Walker et al., 2014), and palliative care for terminal cancer patients (Niki et al., 2019). An early example of a distraction task was Snow World, where patients aimed snowballs at snowmen in a fantastical winter environment (Hoffman, 2004). At its best, VR interventions can lessen perceived pain intensity during treatment and reduce treatment times as compared to standard distractions provided by TV, stories, music, and caregivers (Gold, Belmont, & Thomas, 2007).

Acute pain treatment often occurs in a hospital setting, thus equipment must be easy to clean, or sterilize, transport, and set up. Due to pain's attention-orienting abilities, VEs must be attentionally engaging. Like any other treatment, medical professionals need to see what the patient is viewing in their headset to ensure that the experience is working properly. The tasks in the environment must be easy to understand and be hands-free or require limited mobility (interactivity) in the event of medical procedures (e.g., reduced movement or flinching while cleaning deep wounds is preferred). The equipment must also be able to withstand specialized environments, such as hydrotanks in the case of burn wound pain (Hoffman et al., 2004; 2008).

Pain management and rehabilitation in chronic pain and physical therapy and technological considerations

VR and chronic pain management: While there is considerable evidence to suggest VR's effectiveness as a pain distractor in acute pain management, less is known about VR and chronic pain management. VR interventions in this domain have included studies on chronic neck pain (Harvie et al., 2015; Sarig-Bahat et al., 2015), back pain (Bolte et al., 2014), walking-related pain (Gromala et al., 2011), complex regional pain syndrome (Sato et al., 2010), and phantom limb pain (Chan et al., 2007).

Chronic regional pain syndrome (CRPS) and phantom limb pain typically occur after a physically traumatic event, such as stroke or an amputation. In these conditions, the traumatic event is thought to trigger maladaptive cortical rewiring, which leads to chronic pain patients reporting heightened pain sensitivity and lowered pain tolerance. One popular form of therapy, known as mirror visual feedback (MVF) therapy, aims to modify this maladaptive wiring through providing visual feedback of the injured limb moving naturally (Ramachandran & Altschuler, 2009; Ramachandran & Rogers-Ramachandran, 1996). In traditional MVF, patients view a mirrored image of their intact limb positioned to appear in the same place as their affected limb, while their injured limb is kept out of sight. Moving the intact limb thus gives the appearance of two healthy limbs (Mercier & Sirigu, 2009). Multiple MVF sessions in conjunction with routine physical therapy may relieve pain.

Like traditional MVF, nonimmersive VRMVF works by a similar principle, with the use of a virtual mirror and sensor tracking instead of a physical mirror. Some early studies in phantom limb pain and CRPS mirrored movement from the intact to injured sides (Chan et al., 2007; Yavuzer et al., 2008). A well-cited study by Sato et al. (2010) illustrated one complex setup: the researchers tracked movement in both limbs (e.g., hands) by different devices. The intact hand was precisely measured through a data glove that tracked finer gestures such as grasping an object. In addition, a sensor was attached to the forearm, above the affected hand, and this sensor tracked global movement, such as moving an arm up and down. The hand on the computer screen moved along with the patient's hand and arm movement. Thus, the hand's position was controlled by the affected side, whereas the ability to grasp an object was controlled by the intact (glove wearing) side. Similar treatments with different configurations of hardware have been used to treat individuals with idiopathic facial pain (Won & Collins, 2012) and phantom limb pain (Fukumori, Gofuku, Isatake, & Sato, 2014).

PD: Patients suffering from PD can also benefit from VR rehabilitation environments that improve coordinated movement. PD patients typically present with gait disturbances, which make them more prone to swaying

and falling. Complex gait tasks, which involve multiple and simultaneously coordinated movements, such as walking and talking, are
particularly difficult for PD patients. A common treatment for gait
instability is treadmill training (TT), but this does little to help with
complex gait disturbances. Mirelman et al. (2011) created a PD treatment
to help improve both cognitive and motor skills in PD patients by
combining TT with multistimuli decision-making tasks in VR, known as
obstacle negotiation. The VE demanded participant's attention, calling for
multiple object tracking and heightened perceptual processing in order to
avoid obstacles while walking in VR. Upon 6 weeks of completing the
intervention, patients not only improved in walking speed but also stride
length in the dual task conditions.

Physical therapy: Strokes are a major cause of motor impairment,
affecting one's ability to conduct everyday activities. After a serious
stroke episode, sufferers can report paresis, or loss of limb control and
movement (Pollock, Baer, Pomeroy, & Langhorne, 2007), along with difficulty in thinking and sensing. This can lead to underutilization of the
affected limb, which results in overuse, increasing wear and tear, of the
intact limb (Pollock et al., 2007). Typical interventions for stroke patients
include repetitive muscle movement, which can be boring, decreasing
patient motivation and adherence to prescribed rehabilitation treatments.
Virtual games provide a solution to this problem, motivating patients to
move for the purposes of fun and engagement. Similar to the aforementioned posture training in PD patients, VR interventions can also improve
"dynamic balance" (postural stability) in stroke patients (Cho, Lee, &
Song, 2012), who suffer from postural imbalances and uneven weight
distribution and also have to engage in repetitive muscle movement
training to improve postural stability.

Technological considerations: Treatment should be cheap, ideally
portable, and easy to use for the long term. Portability and ease of use are
essential for supporting treatment adherence, allowing for continuity of
care at home. Patients may not need to be embodied in a full body avatar,
but their affected body part should at least be present in the VE. A sense of
presence should be established through synchronous limb movement in
real time, and the task may require the use of both the affected and intact
limb to be tracked.

Many of these therapies require extensive patient movement and
detailed sensory feedback on these movements. In such therapies,
movement tracking to follow patient progress can be particularly useful.
While VR may allow for more engaging tasks (Won et al., 2017), equipment
may be heavy or get sweaty. If participants are moving around the VE,
they must be protected from accidently falling and injuring themselves or
others. Thus, the actual hardware used must be assessed for compatibility
with the patient, and guardian systems of some kinds are necessary.

General considerations and accessibility

Decisions about what needs to be represented in the VE to achieve specific clinical goals are imperative to a successful (virtual) experience. Designers must also decide what type of sensory stimuli is needed for a given level of interactivity and responsivity in an environment. For example, is it necessary to incorporate spatialized sound? Do users require the ability to pick up or otherwise interact with objects and do they need haptic feedback when they do so?

While designers must make decisions about how to represent objects in the environment, they must also decide how to represent individual users. Questions about representation include, but are not limited to, how a person views their self in a VE. Do they have an avatar body? If so, does the appearance of the avatar indicate gender, race, or ethnicity? In addition to self-avatars, the appearance and capabilities of other social actors, whether these are avatars controlled by other, real people, or agents controlled by the computer, should be considered if they are to be included in the experience.

Treatments occurring in VR are often time consuming. VR interventions may require many appointments because individuals are not advised to be in VEs for extended periods due to reports of dizziness, disorientation, or motion sickness. While immersed, a user might lose spatial awareness of the room, which can cause the user to bump into objects, putting the patient at risk for injury. Thus, participants in a clinical setting must be protected from their environment to an extent, and participants in a home setting will need to have safeguards in place to prevent injury.

Researchers and clinicians must be considerate of those who are at an increased risk of in VR. Examples of such cases include those with epilepsy or seizure disorders or people who have recently undergone concussions. Other groups that can undergo deleterious VR experiences are elderly adults, who suffer vision impairment as lens flexibility and visual acuity slowly decrease as we age. VR experiences can induce greater amounts of eyestrain in individuals, which is a problem for both individuals with normal and poor eyesight. Children also have special needs associated with VR (Won et al., 2017).

Another known issue in VR is eyestrain due to issues with the technology. One example is the vergence-accommodation problem, which can also affect healthy individuals. When an individual looks at an object in the physical world, two perceptual processes occur concurrently at the same point: accommodation and vergence. However, in VR, the accommodation point (the surface of the HMD screen) is much closer than the vergence point, which is simulated to look much further away in order to provide depth perception. Thus, the person's lens is accommodating to a screen that is a few inches away from the face, and the brain thinks the point of convergence (where eyes meet to view the object) is further away. This discrepancy can cause eye fatigue and discomfort (e.g., headaches).

Along with issues of eyestrain come problems of fit with those who have smaller heads or nose bridges, as well as individuals wearing glasses. While this problem may be solved by future iterations of the technology, it must be kept in mind that currently, VR is not equally comfortable or useable for all potential patients.

While the majority of this chapter was spent discussing the technical needs for designing virtual reality treatment (VRT) interventions, another aspect of VRTs is perceived accessibility. This is especially important for individuals suffering from mental health disorders. Concerns for safety and ability to leave the environment made patients more likely and willing to try VRTs over conventional CBTs with in vivo exposure (Garcia-Palacios et al., 2007). In a similar vein, clinicians must consider individuals who need help but have little motivation to go to a clinic and receive treatment. This is a reality for depressed individuals, who often are aware of their need for treatment, but cannot be tasked with seeking it. Thus, making treatments more easily accessible through consumer-grade VR technology would be helpful for individuals seeking at home treatment.

Earlier in this chapter, various methods of self-referential perspective taking in VR were introduced as treatments for self-critical behavior in depression, extinguishing phobias, and unlocking negative body images in body dysmorphic disorders. The ability to switch between perspectives allows individuals to reappraise how patients think about themselves. Given VR's ability to help with mental health conditions that bring about negative affect, it comes as no surprise that VR could be leveraged as an emotional feedback mechanism. Such that, if individuals with mood disorders saw their virtual selves present with positive affective emotions, such as joy, this would reflect in an actual mood change. Seeing a joyful self could show a depressed person that feeling joy is possible, even if they cannot simulate the feeling themselves. Thus, with the combination of perspective taking and 3D visualizations, VR can continue to pave the way for innovative treatments for mood disorders.

The future of VR and technical improvements

To review, immersive media for patient care offers the following advantages:

(1) *Ecological validity*: Enhanced ability to provide realistic experiences
(2) *Flexibility*: Potential to offer greater variety of test or therapeutic stimuli to subjects
(3) *Tracking*: Improved means of monitoring the effect of stimuli

(4) *Interactivity*: Increased ability of the subject to interact with and respond to stimuli
(5) *Standardization* of tests/treatments
(6) *Control*: Improved ability to calibrate the treatment experience

Potential improvements that could broaden the reach of VR in patient care in specific areas are listed below. For example, VR is becoming untethered. Standalone wireless headsets, such as the Oculus Quest, which was released in May 2019, use cameras positioned on the headset to detect the scene around the user and use this information to track the user's movement in the actual, physical space. Researchers and clinicians may expect at least some of the following improvements as well:

(1) As the visual quality of headsets improves, light field displays and eye tracking may allow for better depth perception and less fatigue when wearing headsets.
(2) Headsets will continue to become lighter and more customized to allow them to be comfortable for a wider range of users.
(3) Tracking facial expressions and eye movements will allow for more realistic social presence.
(4) Tracking of hands and the rest of the body without requiring users to hold sensors will allow more naturalistic gestures or gestures from users with injuries and will also reduce the need for sterilizing these controllers in a hospital environment.

The present chapter reviewed the clinical applications of VR within the realm of patient-centered care. Currently, applications include VR interventions that serve diagnostic, mental health improvement, pain management, and rehabilitation purposes. These factors can be influenced by the technological aspects of a VR experience such as visual display type and quality, which in turn are affected by computer processing power. As VR hardware and software continue to improve upon their technical aspects, the applications of patient-centered VR will only grow.

References

Alzheimer's, A. (2015). 2015 Alzheimer's disease facts and figures. *Alzheimer's and Dementia: The Journal of the Alzheimer's Association, 11*(3), 332.

Anderson, P., Rothbaum, B. O., & Hodges, L. F. (2003). Virtual reality exposure in the treatment of social anxiety. *Cognitive and Behavioral Practice, 10*(3), 240–247.

Anderson, P. L., Zimand, E., Hodges, L. F., & Rothbaum, B. O. (2005). Cognitive behavioral therapy for public-speaking anxiety using virtual reality for exposure. *Depression and Anxiety, 22*(3), 156–158.

Areces, D., Rodríguez, C., García, T., Cueli, M., & González-Castro, P. (2018). Efficacy of a continuous performance test based on virtual reality in the diagnosis of ADHD and its clinical presentations. *Journal of Attention Disorders, 22*(11), 1081–1091.

Binetti, G., Cappa, S. F., Magni, E., Padovani, A., Bianchetti, A., & Trabucchi, M. (1996). Disorders of visual and spatial perception in the early stage of Alzheimer's disease. *Annals of the New York Academy of Sciences, 777*(1), 221–225.

Bolte, B., de Lussanet, M., & Lappe, M. (2014). Virtual reality system for the enhancement of mobility in patients with chronic back pain. In *Proc. 10th Intl Conf. disability, virtual reality & associated technologies.*

Botella, C., Baños, R. M., Villa, H., Perpiñá, C., & García-Palacios, A. (2000). Virtual reality in the treatment of claustrophobic fear: A controlled, multiple-baseline design. *Behavior Therapy, 31*(3), 583–595.

Bouchard, S., Côté, S., St-Jacques, J., Robillard, G., & Renaud, P. (2006). Effectiveness of virtual reality exposure in the treatment of arachnophobia using 3D games. *Technology and Health Care, 14*(1), 19–27.

Chan, B. L., Witt, R., Charrow, A. P., Magee, A., Howard, R., Pasquina, P. F., … Tsao, J. W. (2007). Mirror therapy for phantom limb pain. *New England Journal of Medicine, 357*(21), 2206–2207.

Chen, K. B., Ponto, K., Sesto, M. E., & Radwin, R. G. (September 2014). Influence of altered visual feedback on neck movement for a virtual reality rehabilitative system. *Proceedings of the Human Factors and Ergonomics Society Annual Meeting* (Vol. 58,(1), 693–697.

Cho, K. H., Lee, K. J., & Song, C. H. (2012). Virtual-reality balance training with a video-game system improves dynamic balance in chronic stroke patients. *Tohoku Journal of Experimental Medicine, 228*(1), 69–74.

Cruz-Neira, C., Sandin, D. J., DeFanti, T. A., Kenyon, R. V., & Hart, J. C. (1992). The CAVE: Audio visual experience automatic virtual environment. *Communications of the ACM, 35*(6), 64–73.

Dahlquist, L. M., Weiss, K. E., Dillinger Clendaniel, L., Law, E. F., Ackerman, C. S., & McKenna, K. D. (2008). Effects of videogame distraction using a virtual reality type head-mounted display helmet on cold pressor pain in children. *Journal of Pediatric Psychology, 34*(5), 574–584.

Davidsdottir, S., Wagenaar, R., Young, D., & Cronin-Golomb, A. (2008). Impact of optic flow perception and egocentric coordinates on veering in Parkinson's disease. *Brain, 131*(11), 2882–2893.

Difede, J., Cukor, J., Jayasinghe, N., Patt, I., Jedel, S., Spielman, L., … Hoffman, H. G. (2007). Virtual reality exposure therapy for the treatment of posttraumatic stress disorder following September 11, 2001. *Journal of Clinical Psychiatry, 68*(11), 1639.

Difede, J., & Hoffman, H. G. (2002). Virtual reality exposure therapy for world trade center post-traumatic stress disorder: A case report. *CyberPsychology and Behavior, 5*(6), 529–535.

Emmelkamp, P. M. G., et al. (2002). Virtual reality treatment versus exposure in vivo: A comparative evaluation in acrophobia. *Behaviour Research and Therapy, 40*(5), 509–516.

Falconer, C. J., Rovira, A., King, J. A., Gilbert, P., Antley, A., Fearon, P., … Brewin, C. R. (2016). Embodying self-compassion within virtual reality and its effects on patients with depression. *BJPsych Open, 2*(1), 74–80.

Falconer, C. J., Slater, M., Rovira, A., King, J. A., Gilbert, P., Antley, A., & Brewin, C. R. (2014). Embodying compassion: A virtual reality paradigm for overcoming excessive self-criticism. *PLoS One, 9*(11).

Fox, J. (2012). Avatars for health behavior change. In *eHealth Applications* (pp. 109–122).

Freeman, D., Antley, A., Ehlers, A., Dunn, G., Thompson, C., Vorontsova, N., … Slater, M. (2014). The use of immersive virtual reality (VR) to predict the occurrence 6 months later of paranoid thinking and posttraumatic stress symptoms assessed by self-report and interviewer methods: A study of individuals who have been physically assaulted. *Psychological Assessment, 26*(3), 841.

Fukumori, S., Gofuku, A., Isatake, K., & Sato, K. (October 2014). Mirror therapy system based virtual reality for chronic pain in home use. In *Industrial electronics society, IECON 2014-40th annual conference of the IEEE* (pp. 4034–4039).

Garcia-Palacios, A., Botella, C., Hoffman, H., & Fabregat, S. (2007). Comparing acceptance and refusal rates of virtual reality exposure vs. in vivo exposure by patients with specific phobias. *Cyberpsychology & Behavior, 10*(5), 722–724.

Gold, J. I., Belmont, K. A., & Thomas, D. A. (2007). The neurobiology of virtual reality pain attenuation. *CyberPsychology and Behavior, 10*(4), 536–544.

Gold, J. I., Kim, S. H., Kant, A. J., Joseph, M. H., & Rizzo, A. S. (2006). Effectiveness of virtual reality for pediatric pain distraction during IV placement. *CyberPsychology and Behavior, 9*(2), 207–212.

Gromala, D., Song, M., Yim, J., Fox, T., Barnes, S. J., Nazemi, M., … Squire, P. (2011). Immersive VR: A non-pharmacological analgesic for chronic pain. In *Proceedings of the 2011 annual conference extended abstracts on Human factors in computing systems* (pp. 1171–1176).

Harvie, D. S., Broecker, M., Smith, R. T., Meulders, A., Madden, V. J., & Moseley, G. L. (April 2015). Bogus visual feedback alters onset of movement-evoked pain in people with neck pain. *Psychological Science, 26*(4), 385–392. https://doi.org/10.1177/0956797614563339.

Heeter, C. (1992). Being there: The subjective experience of presence. *Presence: Teleoperators and Virtual Environments, 1*(2), 262–271.

Hoffman, H. G. (2004). Virtual-reality therapy. *Scientific American, 291*(2), 58–65.

Hoffman, H. G., Garcia-Palacios, A., Carlin, A., Furness, T. A., III, & Botella-Arbona, C. (2003). Interfaces that heal: Coupling real and virtual objects to treat spider phobia. *International Journal of Human-Computer Interaction, 16*(2), 283–300.

Hoffman, H. G., Garcia-Palacios, A., Patterson, D. R., Jensen, M., Furness, T., III, & Ammons, W. F., Jr. (2001). The effectiveness of virtual reality for dental pain control: A case study. *CyberPsychology and Behavior, 4*(4), 527–535.

Hoffman, H. G., Patterson, D. R., & Carrougher, G. J. (2000). Use of virtual reality for adjunctive treatment of adult burn pain during physical therapy: A controlled study. *The Clinical Journal of Pain, 16*(3), 244–250.

Hoffman, H. G., Patterson, D. R., Magula, J., Carrougher, G. J., Zeltzer, K., Dagadakis, S., & Sharar, S. R. (2004). Water-friendly virtual reality pain control during wound care. *Journal of Clinical Psychology, 60*(2), 189–195.

Hoffman, H. G., Patterson, D. R., Seibel, E., Soltani, M., Jewett-Leahy, L., & Sharar, S. R. (2008). Virtual reality pain control during burn wound debridement in the hydrotank. *The Clinical Journal of Pain, 24*, 299–304.

Levin, B. E., Llabre, M. M., & Weiner, W. J. (1989). Cognitive impairments associated with early Parkinson's disease. *Neurology, 39*(4), 557-557.

Li, A., Montaño, Z., Chen, V. J., & Gold, J. I. (2011). Virtual reality and pain management: Current trends and future directions. *Pain Management, 1*(2), 147–157.

Malbos, E., Mestre, D. R., Note, I. D., & Gellato, C. (2008). Virtual reality and claustrophobia: Multiple components therapy involving game editor virtual environments exposure. *CyberPsychology and Behavior, 11*(6), 695–697.

Manzoni, G. M., Cesa, G. L., Bacchetta, M., Castelnuovo, G., Conti, S., Gaggioli, A., … Riva, G. (2016). Virtual reality—enhanced cognitive—behavioral therapy for morbid obesity: A randomized controlled study with 1 year follow-up. *Cyberpsychology, Behavior, and Social Networking, 19*(2), 134–140.

Melzack, R., & Katz, J. (2014). The neuromatrix in behavioral medicine. *The Handbook of Behavioral Medicine*, 759–774.

Mercier, C., & Sirigu, A. (2009). Training with virtual visual feedback to alleviate phantom limb pain. *Neurorehabilitation and Neural Repair, 23*(6), 587–594.

Mirelman, A., Maidan, I., Herman, T., Deutsch, J. E., Giladi, N., & Hausdorff, J. M. (2011). Virtual reality for gait training: Can it induce motor learning to enhance complex walking and reduce fall risk in patients with Parkinson's disease? *Journal of Gerontology: Series A, 66*(2), 234–240.

Murray, C. D., Pettifer, S., Howard, T., Patchick, E. L., Caillette, F., Kulkarni, J., & Bamford, C. (2007). The treatment of phantom limb pain using immersive virtual reality: Three case studies. *Disability and Rehabilitation, 29*(18), 1465–1469.

National Institute of Mental Health. (2018). *Anxiety Disorders*. Retrieved September 20, 2018, from: https://www.nimh.nih.gov/health/topics/anxiety-disorders/index.shtml.

Niki, K., Okamoto, Y., Maeda, I., Mori, I., Ishii, R., Matsuda, Y., & Uejima, E. (2019). A novel palliative care approach using virtual reality for improving various symptoms of terminal cancer patients: A preliminary prospective, multicenter study. *Journal of Palliative Medicine, 22*(6), 702–707.

Oculus Homepage. (2018). Retrieved October 13, 2018, from: http://www.oculus.com/.

Pollock, A., Baer, G., Pomeroy, V. M., & Langhorne, P. (2007). Physiotherapy treatment approaches for the recovery of postural control and lower limb function following stroke. *Cochrane Database of Systematic Reviews*, (1).

Powers, M. B., & Emmelkamp, P. M. (2008). Virtual reality exposure therapy for anxiety disorders: A meta-analysis. *Journal of Anxiety Disorders, 22*(3), 561–569.

Ramachandran, V. S., & Altschuler, E. L. (2009). The use of visual feedback, in particular mirror visual feedback, in restoring brain function. *Brain, 132*(7), 1693–1710.

Ramachandran, V. S., & Rogers-Ramachandran, D. (1996). Synaesthesia in phantom limbs induced with mirrors. *Proceedings of the Royal Society London Part B* (Vol. 263,(1369), 377–386.

Riva, G. (2011). *The key to unlocking the virtual body: Virtual reality in the treatment of obesity and eating disorders.*

Rizzo, A. A., Buckwalter, J. G., Bowerly, T., Van Der Zaag, C., Humphrey, L., Neumann, U., ... Sisemore, D. (2000). The virtual classroom: A virtual reality environment for the assessment and rehabilitation of attention deficits. *CyberPsychology and Behavior, 3*(3), 483–499.

Rizzo, A., Reger, G., Gahm, G., Difede, J., & Rothbaum, B. O. (2009). Virtual reality exposure therapy for combat-related PTSD. *Post-Traumatic Stress Disorder*, 375–399.

Rothbaum, B. O., Hodges, L. F., Kooper, R., Opdyke, D., Williford, J. S., & North, M. (1995). Virtual reality graded exposure in the treatment of acrophobia: A case report. *Behavior Therapy, 26*(3), 547–554.

Rothbaum, B. O., Hodges, L. F., Ready, D., Graap, K., & Alarcon, R. D. (2001). Virtual reality exposure therapy for Vietnam veterans with posttraumatic stress disorder. *Journal of Clinical Psychiatry, 62*, 617–622.

Rus-Calafell, M., Gutiérrez-Maldonado, J., Botella, C., & Baños, R. M. (2013). Virtual reality exposure and imaginal exposure in the treatment of fear of flying: A pilot study. *Behavior Modification, 37*(4), 568–590.

Sarig, B. H., Takasaki, H., Chen, X., Bet-Or, Y., & Treleaven, J. (2015). Cervical kinematic training with and without interactive VR training for chronic neck pain – a randomized clinical trial. *Manual Therapy, 20*(1), 68–78.

Sato, K., Fukumori, S., Matsusaki, T., et al. (2010). Nonimmersive virtual reality mirror visual feedback therapy and its application for the treatment of complex regional pain syndrome: An open-label pilot study. *Pain Medicine, 11*(4), 622–629.

Scholz, J., & Woolf, C. J. (2002). Can we conquer pain? *Nature Neuroscience, 5*, 1062.

Serino, S., Morganti, F., Di Stefano, F., & Riva, G. (2015). Detecting early egocentric and allocentric impairments deficits in Alzheimer's disease: An experimental study with virtual reality. *Frontiers in Aging Neuroscience, 7*, 88.

Shiban, Y., Fruth, M. B., Pauli, P., Kinateder, M., Reichenberger, J., & Mühlberger, A. (2016). Treatment effect on biases in size estimation in spider phobia. *Biological Psychology, 121*, 146–152.

Song, H., Kim, J., & Lee, K. M. (2014). Virtual vs. real body in exergames: Reducing social physique anxiety in exercise experiences. *Computers in Human Behavior, 36,* 282–285.

Sutherland, J., Belec, J., Sheikh, A., Chepelev, L., Althobaity, W., Chow, B. J., ... La Russa, D. J. (2018). Applying modern virtual and augmented reality technologies to medical images and models. *Journal of Digital Imaging,* 1–16.

VIVE. (2016). Retrieved October 13, 2018, from: https://www.vive.com/us/.

Walker, M. R., Kallingal, G. J., Musser, J. E., Folen, R., Stetz, M. C., & Clark, J. Y. (2014). Treatment efficacy of virtual reality distraction in the reduction of pain and anxiety during cystoscopy. *Military Medicine, 179*(8), 891–896.

Won, A., Bailey, J., Bailenson, J., Tataru, C., Yoon, I., & Golianu, B. (2017). Immersive virtual reality for pediatric pain. *Children, 4*(7), 52.

Won, A. S., & Collins, T. A. (2012). Non-immersive, virtual reality mirror visual feedback for treatment of persistent idiopathic facial pain. *Pain Medicine, 13*(9), 1257–1258.

Woolf, C. J. (2010). What is this thing called pain? *Journal of Clinical Investigation, 120*(11), 3742–3744.

Yavuzer, G., Selles, R., Sezer, N., Sütbeyaz, S., Bussmann, J. B., Köseoğlu, F., ... Stam, H. J. (2008). Mirror therapy improves hand function in subacute stroke: A randomized controlled trial. *Archives of Physical Medicine and Rehabilitation, 89*(3), 393–398.

PART III

MHealth: Mobile technology for health

8

Theoretical advances in mobile health communication research: An empowerment approach to self-management

Nicola Brew-Sam[1], Arul Chib[2]

[1] Department of Media and Communication Studies, University of Erfurt, Erfurt, Germany; [2] Wee Kim Wee School of Communication and Information, Nanyang Technological University, Singapore

Introduction

Chronic lifestyle—related diseases like diabetes are developing into a major health burden worldwide, changing primarily from developed country problems to global health concerns. Prevalence numbers are increasing drastically not only in developed countries but rising in developing countries as well (International Diabetes Federation, 2010, 2014). With forecasts of widespread incidence of chronic diseases due to a range of factors — including improved standards of living, aging societies, and increased obesity — limited healthcare resources (manpower and facilities) are ill-equipped to face the impending crisis (Halter, 2012; Miller, 2018). With healthcare costs skyrocketing for chronic disease care, the focus has shifted away from medical system approaches toward strengthening self-management with much stronger responsibility given to the patient (Snoek, 2007). Patient self-management is defined as "the conscious use of strategies to manipulate situations to reduce the impact of disease on daily life" (Clark & Houle, 2009, p. 27). Self-management includes all behaviors that are related to the active management of chronic diseases by the patients themselves, like blood sugar testing or physical activity.

151

Research has shown that self-management approaches as well as preventive[1] approaches are more cost-effective than mere symptom treatment at a late disease stage and reduce mortality as well (e.g., Diabetes Prevention Program Research Group, 2012).

New technology, such as mobile smart device tools, is being harnessed to support chronic disease self-management strategies. These mobile solutions are frequently subsumed under the term *mHealth*, defined as the use of mobile communications for health information and services (Nacinovich, 2011). mHealth for chronic diseases can include diverse mobile tools, ranging from text message interventions (Fortmann et al., 2017; Nelson et al., 2016) to apps for disease self-management (Chavez et al., 2017; Holtz et al., 2017). Diabetes apps are designed to support daily disease self-management, for example, by providing diary apps to monitor blood sugar developments, food content databases, or insulin calculators (Drincic, Prahalad, Greenwood, & Klonoff, 2016; Veazie et al., 2018).

However, the effectiveness of mHealth for disease self-management is still unclear, with previous studies showing weak effects of mHealth use on self-management outcomes. Buhi et al. (2013) reported that only 6 out of 17 studies published statistically significant improvements in blood glucose concentrations due to the use of mHealth solutions for diabetes management. Additionally, in most studies displaying significant positive effects, effect sizes are very small and of limited clinical importance (Free et al., 2013). In line with these results, recent reviews increasingly take a critical position toward mHealth effectiveness (e.g., Fu, McMahon, Gross, Adam, & Wyman, 2017). Further, most reviews do not deliver explanations for the lack of proven usage effects, apart from pointing toward study weaknesses (Buhi et al., 2013; Jones, Lekhak, & Kaewluang, 2014).

We argue that there is a research gap in understanding, and examination, of antecedents influencing mHealth adoption and usage processes. This gap might account for poor mHealth designs leading to weak or absent usage effects. This relationship can be explained by using the *input–mechanisms–output* pathway, which is a tool to categorize mHealth studies proposed by Chib, van Velthoven, and Car (2015). The *input–mechanism–output* heuristic offers a framework to determine the focus of prior mHealth research and subsumes the main foci of previous studies under the three categories *mHealth inputs*, *mechanisms behind mHealth use*, and *mHealth usage outputs*. According to the authors, *input* factors include technology access and use factors (e.g., research on access to or usability

[1] Prevention in terms of prevention of the development of chronic diseases, or prevention of worsening of an existing condition.

of diabetes apps, Arnhold, Quade, and Kirch, 2014). With smart technology (apps) established in the market, a large number of studies have already examined access, usability, and usage potential (Fu et al., 2017; Zapata, Fernandez-Aleman, Idri, & Toval, 2015). Following Chib et al. (2015), *output* factors of mHealth have been investigated in terms of healthcare process factors, including efficiency measures within the health system and effectiveness measures of patient healthcare factors (Ryan et al., 2017; Wang, Xue, Huang, Huang, & Zhang, 2017). In contrast to both available research on *inputs* and *outputs*, there is still insufficient research on underlying *mechanisms* of mHealth adoption and use, like psychosocial influences (Chib et al., 2015). Relevant underlying factors influencing technology adoption and usage mechanisms are still not identified and examined comprehensively in studies of mobile health technology (Jones et al., 2014). We argue that a lack in understanding mechanisms behind mHealth adoption and use is a potential explanation for poor mHealth designs leading to weak or absent provable usage effects.

As part of mechanisms research, some studies have specifically looked into antecedents of mHealth adoption and use (e.g., Deng, 2013; Dwivedi, Shareef, Simintiras, Lal, & Weerakkody, 2016; Hoque & Sorwar, 2017; Lin, 2011; Rai, Chen, Pye, & Baird, 2013; Woldeyohannes & Ngwenyama, 2017) and a small number specifically focused on antecedents of mHealth adoption and use for self-management (Azhar & Dhillon, 2016; Zhu, Liu, Che, & Chen, 2017). However, a much more comprehensive theoretical and systematic understanding of antecedents of mHealth adoption and use specifically related to chronic disease self-management is still necessary to account for special characteristics in this context (e.g., specific mHealth use barriers like psychological pressure, compare Glasgow, Toobert, & Gillette, 2001). Appropriate theory is required as a foundation, with theory providing the opportunity to enhance mHealth effectiveness (Riley et al., 2011).

In this chapter, we introduce empowerment as a theoretical approach to address shortcomings of previous research on underlying mechanisms (antecedents) of mHealth use. We aim at contributing to theoretical advancement of mHealth research in the context of disease self-management, by shedding light on empowerment as a fundamental antecedent of disease self-management behaviors. First, we explain shortcomings of previous theory used to study antecedents of technology use. Second, empowerment is introduced as a unique multidimensional approach that is of fundamental relevance for disease self-management, and that addresses theoretical shortcomings in the context of mHealth for self-management. We present the benefits of using a theoretical empowerment approach for understanding antecedents of mHealth use. Based on previous research on empowerment as an outcome of mHealth use, we deliver arguments as to why empowerment should be connected to mHealth research more broadly, examining empowerment as an antecedent factor of mHealth use, to understand the overall process of mHealth use for self-management in more detail. This logic forms a first step toward promoting improved mHealth designs, which could result in more convincing outcomes of effects research.

Addressing theoretical shortcomings in mHealth research

Theories examining factors influencing mHealth effectiveness are mainly limited to either (1) health behavior change theories or (2) technology adoption theories applied to an mHealth context. These perspectives are markedly different, since the former views mHealth use as an independent variable, the latter positions use of mHealth technology as the dependent variable.

(1) mHealth studies based on theory mainly used traditional behavior change theories (Jones et al., 2014). Research has shown that the use of strategies based on behavior change theory and addressing behavioral determinants is related to effectiveness (Middelweerd, Mollee, van der Wal, Brug, & te Velde, 2014). Yet, in their systematic mHealth review, Free et al. (2013) found that out of 26 mHealth studies, only 7 used different behavior change theories as a theoretical foundation, including social cognitive and learning theory, elaboration likelihood theory, protection motivation theory, and the transtheoretical model. These theories include a number of antecedent factors used to explain behavioral outcomes (Table 8.1). However, some authors attribute a mainly static and linear nature to behavior change theories used to study between-person differences that do not account for the intraindividual dynamics of mHealth and within-person developments. According to Riley et al. (2011), "the development of time-intensive, interactive, and adaptive health behavior interventions via mobile technologies demands more intra-individual dynamic regulatory processes than represented in our current health behavior theories" (p. 66).

(2) Technology adoption models provide theoretical explanations for antecedent factors of technology use. A recent technology adoption theory, increasingly used as a foundation for mHealth studies (e.g., Hoque & Sorwar, 2017; Woldeyohannes & Ngwenyama, 2017) and considering antecedent factors, is the Unified Theory of Acceptance and Use of Technology (UTAUT, Venkatesh, Morris, Davis, & Davis, 2003). The UTAUT is one of the

TABLE 8.1 Factors included in health behavior change theories.

Factor	Examples	Theory
Attitude and belief	Stigma/stereotype/ health belief	Self-regulatory model (SRM)[b], integrative model (IM)[a], health belief model (HBM)[h], health decision model[k, d]
Barriers to change	Costs, barriers on personal/social/ environmental level	Social cognitive theory (SCT)[i], HBM[h, c]
Control expectations	Self-efficacy	IM[a], transtheoretical model of behavior change[e], protection motivation theory (PMT)[o]
Coping	Healthy coping	Coping theories[l], SRM[b]
Culture and environmental factors	Migration background, underserved population/minorities	IM[a], SRM[b]
Demography	Gender, socioeconomic status, age	IM[a, g]
Emotion and mood	Depression, anxiety, anger, fear	IM[a, c, f]
Experience and past behavior	Experiences with diabetes	IM[a], SRM[b]
Intervention, information, and media exposure/usage	Smartphone experience, information exposure	IM[a], elaboration likelihood model (ELM)[n]
Knowledge	Health/media literacy[j], education	HBM [h, c], SRM[b]
Motivation	Motivation caused by social pressure or fear	IM[a], ELM[n]
Norms and values	Values	Theory of reasoned action (TRA)[m], IM[a]
Outcome evaluation	Response efficacy, benefits, response costs, extrinsic and intrinsic rewards	IM[a], HBM[h, c, g], PMT[o]
Personality	Risk behavior	IM[a], SRM[b]
Risk perception	Perceived severity/ seriousness, susceptibility/ vulnerability	IM[a], HBM[h], PMT[o]

Continued

TABLE 8.1   Factors included in health behavior change theories.—cont'd

Factor	Examples	Theory
Skills and learning	Learning, ability to process information	Theory of planned behavior (TPB)[m], IM[a], social learning theory[i], ELM[n]
Social networks and contacts	Social networks, social pressure, gatekeepers	IM[a], HBM[h, c], SRM[b]
Well-being and quality of life and physical condition	Well-being based on illness (cues to action), complications, interference (everyday life)	HBM[h, c, f, g]

Selected popular behavior change models included.

[a]Fishbein and Cappella (2006).
[b]Leventhal, Diefenbach, and Leventhal (1992).
[c]Harvey and Lawson (2009).
[d]Whittemore, Bak, Melkus, and Gray (2003).
[e]Prochaska, Johnson, and Lee (2009).
[f]Fisher, Thorpe, DeVellis, and DeVellis (2007).
[g]Eiser, Riazi, Eiser, Hammersley, and Tooke (2001).
[h]Rosenstock, Strecher, and Becker (1994).
[i]Bandura (1977b).
[j]Parker and Gazmararian (2010).
[k]Eraker, Becker, Strecher, and Kirscht (1985).
[l]Martz, Livneh, and Wright (2007).
[m]Fishbein and Ajzen (1975).
[n]Petty and Cacioppo (1986).
[o]Rogers (1975).

most recognized and validated theoretical models for explaining technology use based on eight previous models (Lee & Rho, 2013), including the frequently used technology acceptance model (TAM). The UTAUT is a further development of the TAM and seven other models and thus has a comprehensive focus. The UTAUT mentions four factors — performance expectancy, effort expectancy, social influence, and facilitating conditions — as influencing user acceptance and technology usage behaviors, and four factors — gender, age, experience, and voluntariness of use — as key moderating variables (Venkatesh et al., 2003).

However, the UTAUT (and similar models) has been criticized for a number of limitations. According to Al-Mamary, Al-Nashmi, Hassan, and Shamsuddin (2016), research has shown that the variables included in these models might be insufficient predictors of technology acceptance and usage. The UTAUT does not comprehensively include intrinsic and extrinsic motivational factors in the final model to explain the intention to adopt and to use technology.[2] Extrinsic motivation is represented only as part of the UTAUT factor *performance expectancy,* while intrinsic motivation is only represented as part of *attitude toward technology use.* Attitude is excluded from the final model, not having a significant influence on intention to use technology (supported hypothesis 5c in Venkatesh et al., 2003). As analyzed by Venkatesh, Thong, and Xu (2016), a number of studies have suggested UTAUT extensions, including new exogenous and endogenous mechanisms, new moderation mechanisms, and new outcome mechanisms. Further criticisms arise from the fact that the UTAUT factors contribute to behavioral intention but not necessarily to the behavior itself (Chang, 2012). Previous studies demonstrated that there is a gap between intention and actual behavior (e.g., James, Perry, Gallagher, & Lowe, 2016), particularly given high barriers toward usage.

With the outlined existing shortcomings of behaviour change and technology adoption theory for investigating underlying antecedents of smart mobile health technology use (e.g., apps), and a general lack of theory in mHealth research (Riley et al., 2011), the scope has to be extended by additional theoretical foundation to examine and to understand antecedents of mobile smart health technology use.

In the following, we introduce a multi-dimensional empowerment approach as a relatively new theoretical perspective that offers potential for complementing behavior change and technology adoption theories. Empowerment is — in contrast to behavior change theories — characterized by an intraindividual process perspective and thus is suitable to address an intraindividual dynamic processes in (mobile smart technology-supported) self-management. Moreover, it includes — in contrast to technology adoption models — both an intrinsic and extrinsic motivational perspective. As a motivational approach (Menon, 2001; Schulz & Nakamoto, 2013; Spreitzer, 1995; Thomas & Velthouse, 1990), empowerment delivers useful perspectives for modern participatory self-care approaches. The approach is appropriate for explaining the self-determined and self-motivated use of smart mobile health tools, for example apps for disease self-management. In contrast to short message interventions, which automatically deliver SMS to the mobile patient device (so called *push* media), health apps require a higher level of user initiative and engagement (active search for

---

[2] In the UTAUT2 as a further development of the UTAUT hedonic motivation appears as an additional influencing factor (Venkatesh, Thong, & Xu, 2012). However, other types of motivation are still lacking in UTAUT2.

apps, download, content management; so-called *pull* media, compare Kingsley, 1987). Thus, patient empowerment is needed.

Multidimensional empowerment approach

Psychological empowerment

Most commonly, in health (communication) research, empowerment is referred to as *patient empowerment* which is defined "as the patient's participation as an autonomous actor taking increased responsibility for and a more active role in decision making regarding his or her health" (Schulz & Nakamoto, 2013, p. 5). Patient empowerment indicates that a patient participates in health decisions with a feeling of control and self-esteem (Schulz & Nakamoto, 2013), is able to make autonomous decisions based on informed choice, and manages a (chronic) condition with professional support herself. The feeling of being empowered is called *psychological* empowerment in previous research (Schulz & Nakamoto, 2013).

Early approaches in management research comprehended psychological empowerment as synonymous to the motivational concept of self-efficacy (Conger & Kanungo, 1988). Self-efficacy refers to expectations of personal efficacy (Bandura, 1977a) or the "belief in one's agentive capabilities, that one can produce given levels of attainment" (Bandura, 1997, p. 382), which could be described as perceived competence to perform an action. Thomas and Velthouse (1990) commented critically on the perception of empowerment as self-efficacy, with self-efficacy not going far enough to define (psychological) empowerment. According to them, psychological empowerment includes other psychological aspects in addition to self-efficacy. Thus, they suggested a cognitive model of psychological empowerment including the four psychological indicators *perceived relevance/meaningfulness, perceived competence, self-determination,* and *perceived impact*instead. Spreitzer (1995) developed an operationalization for these four psychological indicators. This was later adapted for the health communication context by Schulz and Nakamoto (2013), and to the general health context by Menon (2002) (the latter uses three indicators).

Translated to health communication by Schulz and Nakamoto (2013), the indicator *perceived relevance* (or *meaningfulness*) relates to the patient's experience that the health activities she performs are relevant and worth investing energy in, potentially leading to higher involvement or commitment. *Perceived competence* (which is used synonymously for *self-efficacy* by the authors) has been shown to have positive effects on health behaviors and outcomes, due to confidence about the ability to manage one's own health. If a patient feels competent to deal with a (chronic) disease, her interest in self-management behaviors is likely to be higher. *Self-determination* comprises the possibility of actions initiated by the patients themselves. *Perceived impact* is the feeling about making a difference in health outcomes, for example, exercises that result in weight loss.

Empowerment by others — social influence

Psychological empowerment comprises human's inner feelings on an individual level. But the uniqueness of the empowerment concept derives from empowerment not only comprising an individual feeling but also additionally including empowerment of a subordinate (e.g., patient) by a superordinate (e.g., physician) on an interpersonal level (Asimakopoulou, Gilbert, Newton, & Scambler, 2012; Lee & Koh, 2001). Empowerment therefore comprises an individual intrinsic feeling of being empowered, as well as an extrinsic influence by others who empower, because people are actors but also acted upon (Hewson, 2010). Logan and Ganster (2007) also termed this as *role empowerment*, with the role a subordinate takes in her relation to the ordinate, and in contrast to psychological empowerment. Because of this social influence component, empowerment cannot happen only within the individual ("I empower myself").

The term *em*-power-ment itself states the extrinsic influence by literally meaning that someone is given the power to do something (Oxford Dictionaries, 2016). Empowering support by others has been shown to influence the feeling of psychological empowerment (Logan & Ganster, 2007; Spreitzer, 1996). Lee and Koh (2001) provided an empowerment definition that includes both a psychological dimension and a social influence dimension, stating that "a proper definition of empowerment has to integrate aspects of both behavior and perception. Thus, we define empowerment as the psychological state of a subordinate (...), which is affected by empowering behaviors of the supervisor (Lee & Koh, 2001, p. 686)."

This definition shows why the overall empowerment concept — including a psychological dimension and a social influence dimension — cannot be replaced or be used synonymously with self-efficacy only. Social influence is a fundamental dimension of the empowerment concept, while self-efficacy can be increased without influence by others (Lee & Koh, 2001).

Indicators of social influence, for example, include behaviors by the healthcare professional (e.g., physician), like the style of decision-making used by the healthcare professional (HCP), or aspects of HCP-patient communication. Decision-making is "defined as the propensity of physicians to involve patients in treatment decisions" (Heisler, Bouknight, Hayward, Smith, & Kerr, 2002, p. 246). Looking at physician-patient interaction, Emanuel and Emanuel (1992) suggested four models of a physician-patient relationship with more or less participatory decision-making styles of the physician (paternalistic, informative, interpretive, and deliberative). They pleaded for a deliberative model as the preferable one, reflecting the idea of shared decision-making. An empowering physician-patient relationship comprises neither exclusive control by the physician ("paternalistic" model) nor absolute autonomy by the patient ("informative" model), but rather a collaborative process of shared decision-making with an active contribution of both parties (deliberative model, Emanuel & Emanuel, 1992). The more the physician shows a participatory or shared decision-making style, the more the behavior can be called empowering. Additionally, communication can reflect decision-making styles, for example, during medical consultations. Thus, communication styles can also be considered an indicator of the social influence dimension of empowerment. Heisler et al. (2002), for example, developed scales for measuring participatory decision-making and provider-patient communication.

Empowerment as a unique motivational concept

There is agreement in the scientific literature that psychological empowerment is a motivational construct. For example, Schulz and Nakamoto (2013) stated that patient empowerment can be clearly labeled a motivational construct because there has to be willingness to participate in health decision-making. Despite the fact that the authors suggest a relation between empowerment and motivation, it is unclear *how* they are related. Previous literature describes empowerment as motivational (Menon, 2001; Schulz & Nakamoto, 2013; Spreitzer, 1995; Thomas & Velthouse, 1990) but does not clarify this relationship further, or uses both concepts synonymously (e.g., Kamphoff, Hutson, Amundsen, & Atwood, 2016). The distinction between empowerment and motivation is needed to avoid the criticism that empowerment is just a different term for existing motivational concepts ("old wine in new bottles", Lincoln, Travers, Ackers, & Wilkinson, 2002). Lee and Koh (2001) argued that motivation and empowerment are not synonymous concepts, with empowerment being one method of motivation (however, the term *method* is problematic when talking about psychological empowerment, because a feeling of being empowered cannot be called a method).

Relationships between empowerment and motivation are discussed in previous studies, hinting toward empowerment being an antecedent of motivation. There is a certain similarity of the two empowerment dimensions (psychological empowerment and social influence) to the concepts of intrinsic and extrinsic motivation, respectively. Regarding psychological empowerment, Gagné, Senécal, and Koestner (1997) reported that "aspects of empowerment differentially affected intrinsic motivation" (p. 1222) and that intrinsic motivation is "the resulting will and energy that drives behavior, whereas the feelings of competence and the like that precede it are cognitive evaluations of the context and of oneself" (p. 1224). Similarly, Thomas and Velthouse (1990) called psychological empowerment a cause of intrinsic task motivation. Regarding the social influence dimension of empowerment, other studies found that social support could not just be a source of extrinsic motivation (similar to, e.g., rewards) but also influence intrinsic motivation (Vatankhah & Tanbakooei, 2014). Despite the plausible conclusion that motivation is the result of empowerment, it is insufficient to consider motivation merely an outcome of empowerment. Lee and Koh (2001) argued that the relationship cannot be simplified, and that empowerment has to be considered a new paradigm instead of being considered part of traditional motivation theory. Similarly, Bainbridge Frymier (1994) described empowerment as an expanded and more inclusive conceptualization of motivation. Empowerment is unique by incorporating intrinsic and extrinsic motivational aspects in one approach and thus adding value to existing motivational theories.

Relevance of empowerment for self-management

Empowerment as a motivational approach is essential for disease self-management. As argued in literature, empowerment is able to improve (the capacity for) self-management and to promote lifestyle changes (Gutschoven & van den Bulck, 2006), due to stronger perceptions of self-management relevance, competence for self-management, self-determination, and impact on health outcomes. Moreover, studies reported that empowered people have shown to be healthier (Gutschoven & van den Bulck, 2006).

A significant body of contemporary literature explains the relevance of empowerment for chronic disease self-management, for example for diabetes self-management (Asimakopoulou et al., 2012; Cinar & Schou, 2014; Di Iorio, Carinci, & Massi, 2015; Funnell & Anderson, 2004; Graffy, 2013; Meer, 2015; Scambler, Newton, & Asimakopoulou, 2014; Sigurdardottir & Jonsdottir, 2008; Yang, Hsue, & Lou, 2015). A cross-sectional study by Yang et al. (2015) with 885 diabetics in China proved that psychological empowerment was a predictor of self-care behavior and HbA1c in type 2 diabetes patients. Eyuboglu and Schulz (2016) reported that the psychological empowerment indicators of impact and self-determination predicted the frequency of self-reported self-care behaviors in 167 Turkish diabetes patients. Tol, Alhani, Shojaeazadeh, Sharifirad, and Moazam (2015) argued that self-efficacy is one of the main key concepts in psychological empowerment, going along with the previous explanation that self-efficacy is understood as one out of four indicators of psychological empowerment here. Self-efficacy has been shown to be an important precondition of behavior change (Tol et al., 2015).

Similarly, plenty of studies prove the impact of empowerment in terms of social influence by HCPs, peers, and family on behavioral and health outcomes, for example in research on diabetes (Bennich et al., 2017; Grant & Schmittdiel, 2013; Rosland et al., 2008; Shao, Liang, Shi, Wan, & Yu, 2017; Strom & Egede, 2012; van Dam et al., 2005). Evidence suggests that higher levels of social support influence more positive clinical and psychosocial outcomes, as well as positive behavior change outcomes, in study participants (Strom & Egede, 2012).

To summarize, studies have shown that both the psychological and the social influence dimensions of empowerment have predictive value for health behaviors (Anderson, Funnell, Fitzgerald, & Marrero, 2000; Yang et al., 2015), that empowerment can lead to successful self-management (Tol et al., 2015), and thus is an antecedent factor of self-management, for example diabetes self-management (Funnell & Anderson, 2003; Tol et al., 2015).

As a result, both a psychological empowerment dimension and a social influence dimension need to be considered when looking into antecedents or predictors of (technology-supported) disease self-management because on the one hand empowerment needs to be defined as a multi-level construct that comprises both a psychological sense of control and actual social influence (Rappaport, 1987) and on the other hand self-management operates on both an internal level in terms of patient psychology and an external level in terms of HCP-patient interaction (Gomersall, Madill, & Summers, 2011).

Previous research on empowerment and mHealth use

Previous research on the combination of a theoretical empowerment approach and mHealth research is rare (Anshari & Almunawar, 2015), and empowerment is not often explained sufficiently in this context (Bradway, Arsand, & Grottland, 2015; Cumming, Strnadová, Knox, & Parmenter, 2014). Most self-management- and empowerment-related mHealth projects are applied and do not explain theoretical background related to their understanding of *empowerment* (e.g., Park, Burford, Lee, & Toy, 2016). Park et al. (2016), for example, developed an "exploratory" mHealth program for diabetics that used participatory approaches and aimed at patient empowerment. Even though they gave hints about their understanding of empowerment in their study report, they did not provide a specific definition or explanation of their underlying empowerment concept.

To overcome this lack of a combination of theoretical empowerment approaches with mHealth research, Brew-Sam and Chib (2019) used a theoretical empowerment concept for examining diabetes apps for self-management. However, this study did not look into mHealth use, but rather into technological app features corresponding with theoretical indicators of empowerment. They found that diabetes app features only supported patient empowerment to a limited extent, and that quality partly was low in diabetes apps (measured with an adapted version of the Mobile App Rating Scale by Stoyanov et al., 2015).

Previous research looking into empowerment in context of mHealth use mostly focused on empowerment as an outcome of mHealth use (Bradway et al., 2015; Chib & Jiang, 2014; Cumming et al., 2014; Mantwill, Fiordelli, Ludolph, & Schulz, 2015; Park, Burford, Hanlen et al., 2016). In the following paragraphs, we introduce studies examining empowerment as an outcome of mHealth use and then argue why the focus should be extended from an outcome perspective, also looking into empowerment as an antecedent of mHealth use.

Krošel, Švegl, Vidmar, and Dinevski (2016) were one of the few researchers addressing empowerment with mobile health technologies from a theoretical point of view. The authors explained empowerment as a result of (technology-supported) self-management with mHealth offering technological means for empowerment in patients' everyday lives. According to the authors, by the use of mHealth tools for education, self-management, and shared decision-making, empowerment can be promoted by active involvement of the patient. Unfortunately, the authors did not explain relationships between their concepts in detail. A more detailed look into relationships between mHealth use, empowerment, and self-management processes is therefore necessary. Describing empowerment as an outcome of mHealth use in more detail, Park, Burford, Hanlen et al. (2016) explored how mobile devices can be tools both for compelled self-management and for (psychological) patient empowerment for type 2 diabetes patients. They found that empowerment could occur when people with diabetes shared information or received social support using the mobile devices, when patients realized the outcomes of their mHealth supported activities (perceived impact as an indicator of psychological empowerment) or when the mobile devices were used for better activity or support planning. In a different study, Mantwill et al. (2015) used a psychological empowerment scale (including the four indicators relevance, competence, self-determination, and impact) to study the effects of the use of a web- and mobile-based platform on psychological patient empowerment in diabetics. Similarly, Li, Owen,

Thimbleby, Sun, and Rau (2013) examined if the use of mHealth features affected empowerment and health outcomes. A study by Signorelli et al. (2018) investigated the feasibility of a nurse-led eHealth intervention for engaging cancer survivors in cancer-related follow-ups. The examined outcome was health-related self-efficacy (described as one indicator of psychological empowerment here) measured at several points in time. Study results have not been published yet for the mentioned three studies. Other research studies looked into psychological empowerment as an outcome of eHealth systems in healthcare organizations (Anshari, Almunawar, Low, & Al-Mudimigh, 2012). It seems that on-going research on psychological empowerment outcomes after mHealth use has yet to provide a conclusive answer.

Only occasionally papers added aspects of social influence to psychological empowerment aspects when examining empowerment as an outcome of mHealth use (e.g., Chib & Jiang, 2014). Mostly, studies focusing on aspects of social support (or social influence) in relation to mHealth use did not examine social support as an outcome of mHealth use, but looked at the influence of social support delivered through mHealth or eHealth channels (e.g., online support groups, mobile chats) on health and self-management outcomes (e.g., Burner et al., 2018). For example, Burner et al. (2018) reported that patients who received support from their family and friends network in an mHealth program showed improved HbA1c, glucose self-monitoring, and physical activity compared to control groups.

After briefly introducing previous research looking into psychological empowerment and social influence related to mHealth use, it is argued in the following why empowerment has to be understood as a process, including both a perspective of empowerment as an outcome and as an antecedent factor of mHealth use.

Extending the focus toward a process perspective

Apart from investigating empowerment as an outcome of mHealth use, and thus considering it a state that emerges after app use, empowerment has been proven an antecedent of self-management behaviors (Funnell & Anderson, 2003; Tol et al., 2015). Thus, empowerment has to be acknowledged a process rather than a state (Rappaport, 1987). Following a process perspective, there is a preexisting level of psychological empowerment in the patient that is dynamic, and that psychological empowerment develops in the course of a patient's self-management process. Spreitzer (1995) as well as Lee and Koh (2001) referred to empowerment as a continuous variable: "subordinates will be considered more or less empowered, rather than empowered or not empowered" (Lee & Koh, 2001, p. 687). If the patient receives basic education and has necessary skills and knowledge (Funnell & Anderson, 2003), the feeling of psychological empowerment is able to develop if there is ongoing psychosocial self-management support (Anderson & Funnell, 2010). Transferred to mHealth use for self-management, this means that a preexisting level of psychological empowerment can influence mHealth adoption and use (as an antecedent factor), and then can change in the course of the mHealth use, and in combination with social support by others (outcome of mHealth use). For example, looking at indicators of psychological empowerment, after the use of a diabetes app that provides features for structured self-care behaviors (e.g., regular blood glucose testing and recording), the app user could feel more competent for self-management than before the app use, might perceive the self-care relevance as higher, or might perceive his or her impact on diabetes outcomes as higher, e.g., more structured and regular blood glucose recording might lead to higher awareness for fluctuating blood glucose values, and to improved insulin-food regulation in return. In addition, diabetes apps can provide direct contact to HCPs, and thus an opportunity for more frequent HCP feedback, which can support the feeling of empowerment to a larger extent than without an app use. Thus, adopting a process perspective means to include both an understanding of empowerment as an antecedent factor and as an outcome of mHealth use.

Very few publications focused on the *process* of empowerment in relation to eHealth or mHealth by using pretest-posttest and/or longitudinal designs. Camerini and Schulz (2012) examined whether psychological empowerment mediated a possible relationship between the use of interactive eHealth features and fibromyalgia syndrome health outcomes. They used a pretest-posttest design to measure empowerment before and after the use of different versions of an eHealth application (posttest after 5 months of eHealth use). With this study design, they did not only measure empowerment at one point in time, but rather compared empowerment before and after an eHealth use. Despite hypothesizing that knowledge and empowerment mediated the effect of interactivity on health outcomes, they did not find any significant impact of functional interactivity on empowerment or on knowledge. Generally, they found that the relevance and impact of empowerment indicators positively affected health outcomes.

In a different study, Miller et al. (2017) used a pretest—posttest design to examine the effects of training on perceptions of psychological empowerment, comparing healthful food-choice empowerment before and after eHealth label-reading sessions. They found statistically significant improvements in empowerment after the web-based label-reading training.

Fortuna et al. (2018) investigated preliminary effects of a peer-delivered technology-supported self-management intervention for elderly in a pretest–posttest study (data collected at baseline, 1 month, and 3 months). They measured empowerment at several points in time and found nonsignificant improvements in psychological empowerment when the peer-delivered technology was used. Their findings offered preliminary evidence that the peer-delivered technological intervention was feasible, acceptable, and associated with enhanced self-management and empowerment.

Overall, longitudinal study designs with an assessment of empowerment at several points in time and over a longer period of time are needed to investigate the influence of psychological empowerment and social influence on mHealth use, as well as changes in psychological empowerment and social support/influence throughout and after an mHealth use. The mentioned studies did not include a focus on empowerment as a factor influencing mHealth or eHealth use (antecedent factor).

Only focusing on empowerment as an outcome of mHealth use neglects that empowerment is a process. Thus, it is necessary to take one step back from mere outcome research and look into empowerment as an antecedent of mHealth use to understand the overall empowerment process in relation to mHealth use. It has to be investigated if preexisting psychological empowerment levels and social influence are affecting mHealth adoption and use before successful use can even influence empowerment levels or health outcomes in return.

Empowerment as an antecedent of mHealth adoption and use

We suggest empowerment as a theoretical approach that can close research gaps when investigating antecedents of (smart mobile health) technology adoption and usage. A patient has preexisting levels of empowerment before adopting and using mHealth for self-management (e.g., Camerini & Schulz, 2012). A low psychological empowerment level and low social support for self-management might result in insufficient patient initiative for self-management behaviors (Bennich et al., 2017), including a lack of motivation for the use of mHealth tools. It was previously argued that empowerment could deliver intrinsic or extrinsic motivation for self-management behavior.

Research on psychological empowerment as an antecedent of mHealth use is still lacking. The four indicators of psychological empowerment can be expected to influence mHealth use in a similar way as they influence other self-management behaviors (Tol et al., 2015). For example, the patient has to perceive the mHealth use as *relevant* for her self-management to start and maintain the use of mHealth tools. If a patient feels *competent* to use mHealth for self-management (e.g., perceived technological competence), the use is more likely than when there is a lack in perceived competence. Regarding *self-determination*, mHealth use is more likely if the technology (e.g., app) use is voluntary rather than obligatory — following literature on intrinsic motivation with voluntary actions being more efficient than forced action (Deci, 1975; Leasure & Jones, 2008). Concerning the indicator *impact*, use is more likely if the patient feels that she can influence self-management or health outcomes by using mHealth tools.

Social influence, as a dimension of empowerment, can also be considered an antecedent of mHealth use. *Perceived social influence* is included as influencing factor in the UTAUT model. However, the UTAUT only includes perceptions of the individual about others believing that she should use the technology, which differs from actual social influence in form of behaviors. Davis (1985) and Davis, Bagozzi, and Warshaw (1989) "observed that it is difficult to distinguish if usage behavior is caused by the influence of referents on one's intent or by one's own attitude" (Malhotra & Galletta, 1999, abstract).

More recently, and in relation to this question, Talukder and Quazi (2011) studied peer and social network influences on technology attitudes and resulting adoption behaviors and found that social influences significantly affected attitudes toward innovation, which influenced actual innovation adoption behaviors in return. Brew-Sam (2019) found that the support by the private patient network (as an indicator of the social influence dimension of empowerment) significantly predicted the use of diabetes apps for self-management, with less support by family and friends increasing the chance of diabetes app use. The empowerment indicator *family/friend support* complemented other factors predicting diabetes app use, including a higher chance of app use in patients with supervision by diabetes specialists (in contrast to general practitioners) and in patients with a better perceived health status.

Looking into specific patient groups, Bozan, Davey, and Parker (2015) examined social influence on patient portal use among elderly. Their findings suggested that the elderly followed advice from their HCPs, as well as advice from respected higher-status peers. Thus, the study was able to confirm that social influence had effects on eHealth or mHealth use in elderly. In a different study, Hao, Padman, Sun, and Telang (2014) examined effects of social influence on sustained health technology use and found psychological changes in users caused by social influence at different stages of technology adoption and use.

Apart from these, other studies did not examine how social support influenced mHealth adoption or use, but how social support delivered through mHealth influenced health outcomes and self-management. Omboni, Caserini, and Coronetti (2016) showed that most benefits with the technological devices were achieved under supervision of HCPs. Generally, most studies looking into social support influencing mHealth or technology adoption and use did not refer to empowerment. We conclude that more research is still required on aspects of empowerment affecting mHealth use.

Summarizing model

Fig. 8.1 summarizes the outlined processes between empowerment, mHealth use, other self-management behaviors, and health outcomes. The main focus is put on empowerment as an antecedent factor while acknowledging empowerment as an outcome of mHealth use in addition.

We have argued that both psychological empowerment and social influences have been shown to be antecedents of self-management behaviors (Tol et al., 2015) (Fig. 8.1, arrow 1). Similarly, psychological empowerment in the patient and social influence by others (e.g., HCPs) can be expected to serve as antecedents of mHealth use (Fig. 8.1, arrow 1). mHealth use is a behavior (because *use* is a behavior) and thus can be part of behaviors executed in the overall disease self-management. mHealth use is likely related to other self-management behaviors, for example, when overall self-management is poor, the likelihood for self-management—related technology use is also likely to decrease. Or reverse, the use of a blood glucose diary app for example increases the likelihood of improved blood glucose monitoring due to structured assistance by the app.

We argue that higher empowerment can make mHealth use more likely (Fig. 8.1, arrow 1), if no other anteceding factors hinder the use (Azhar & Dhillon, 2016) (Fig. 8.1, arrow 2), like characteristics of mHealth tools

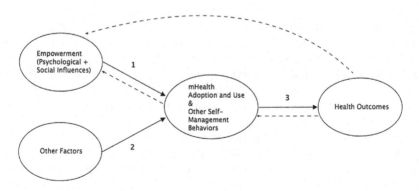

FIGURE 8.1   The process of empowerment and mHealth use.

(quality was shown to influence usage intentions and usage behaviors, e.g., Dutta, Pfister, & Kosmoski, 2010; Inukollu, Keshamon, Kang, & Inukollu, 2014). Following a process perspective, successful mHealth use and other improved self-management behaviors potentially improve health outcomes (Fig. 8.1, arrow 3). For example improved technology-supported blood glucose monitoring along with improved awareness of behaviors could lead to lower blood glucose values.

With perceived improvements of self-management and health outcomes, psychological empowerment might improve in return. This is because the positive outcomes might influence perceptions (positively), like the perceived impact of behaviors on health outcomes, or the perceived competence for dealing with the health condition. Moreover, social support might be influenced by self-management and health outcomes as well. For example, a physician noticing improved self-management outcomes might react in certain more or less supportive ways toward the patient. The overall process is expected to be circular.

Conclusion

Based on theoretical implications, and on previous findings of research on mHealth effects, this chapter proposes that mHealth tools such as diabetes smart device apps, and related chronic disease self-management strategies, could be designed more effectively if knowledge on antecedents for mHealth adoption and use was considered more comprehensively. For example, diabetes apps for self-management could support empowerment processes to a larger extent if knowledge on empowerment as an antecedent of mHealth adoption and use was taken into account when designing these apps (e.g., tailoring for diabetics with low empowerment). Antecedents for mHealth adoption and use have to be investigated before designing self-management apps, and before conducting effect studies based on the app use. The empowerment approach is one step toward understanding underlying processes of mHealth use in context of self-management. Previous research on empowerment as an outcome of mHealth use for self-management has to be complemented by research on empowerment as an antecedent of mHealth use to understand overall processes.

The suggested empowerment approach combines research that previously either examined psychological empowerment or investigated single indicators of social influence (without referral to empowerment). Thus, by using a multidimensional empowerment approach with a psychological dimension and a social influence dimension as a theoretical framework, knowledge from different research directions is brought together and connected to a theoretical concept. The result is a more robust theoretical and empirical foundation for an explanation of self-management outcomes, as well as of mHealth use as part of disease self-management — as compared to previous studies focusing on single aspects of empowerment only.

Apart from empowerment, other antecedents of mHealth use have to be understood, and further research is required to predict and increase the success of mHealth applications for specific target audiences. Practice has to be instructed to use knowledge from research on mHealth antecedents in their mHealth designs. These actions will allow researchers and practitioners to step out of the never ending circle of inadequately designed mHealth interventions and weak effect studies showing minimal outcomes of mHealth use in self-management processes.

References

Al-Mamary, Y. H., Al-Nashmi, M., Hassan, Y. A. G., & Shamsuddin, A. (2016). A critical review of models and theories in field of individual acceptance of technology. *International Journal of Hospitality Information Technology, 9*(6), 143–158. https://doi.org/10.14257/ijhit.2016.9.6.13.

Anderson, R. M., & Funnell, M. M. (2010). Patient empowerment: Myths and misconceptions. *Patient Education and Counseling, 79*(3), 277–282. https://doi.org/10.1016/j.pec.2009.07.025.

Anderson, R. M., Funnell, M. M., Fitzgerald, J. T., & Marrero, D. G. (2000). The diabetes empowerment scale: A measure of psychosocial self-efficacy. *Diabetes Care, 23*(6), 739–743. https://doi.org/10.2337/diacare.23.6.739.

Anshari, M., & Almunawar, M. N. (2015). mHealth technology implication: Shifting the role of patients from recipients to partners of care. In S. Adibi (Ed.), *mHealth multidisciplinary verticals*. Boca Raton, London, New York: CRC Press, Taylor & Francis Group.

Anshari, M., Almunawar, M. N., Low, P. K., & Al-Mudimigh, A. S. (2012). Empowering clients through e-health in healthcare services: Case Brunei. *The International Quarterly of Community Health Education, 33*(2), 189–219. https://doi.org/10.2190/IQ.33.2.g.

Arnhold, M., Quade, M., & Kirch, W. (2014). Mobile applications for diabetics: A systematic review and expert-based usability evaluation considering the special requirements of diabetes patients age 50 years or older. *Journal of Medical Internet Research, 16*(4), e104. https://doi.org/10.2196/jmir.2968.

Asimakopoulou, K., Gilbert, D., Newton, P., & Scambler, S. (2012). Back to basics: Re-examining the role of patient empowerment in diabetes. *Patient Education and Counseling, 86*(3), 281–283. https://doi.org/10.1016/j.pec.2011.03.017.

Azhar, F. A. B., & Dhillon, J. S. (2016). A systematic review of factors influencing the effective use of mhealth apps for self-care. In *Paper presented at the 3rd International Conference on Computer and Information Sciences (ICCOINS), Kuala Lumpur*.

Bainbridge Frymier, A. (1994). A model of immediacy in the classroom. *Communication Quarterly, 42*(2), 133–144. https://doi.org/10.1080/01463379409369922.

Bandura, A. (1977a). Self-efficacy: Toward a unifying theory of behavioral change. *Psychological Review, 84*(2), 191–215.

Bandura, A. (1977b). *Social learning theory.* Englewood Cliffs; N.J: Prentice Hall.

Bandura, A. (1997). *Self-efficacy: The exercise of control.* New York, NY: Freeman.

Bennich, B. B., Roder, M. E., Overgaard, D., Egerod, I., Munch, L., Knop, F. K., ... Konradsen, H. (2017). Supportive and non-supportive interactions in families with a type 2 diabetes patient: An integrative review. *Diabetology and Metabolic Syndrome, 9*, 57. https://doi.org/10.1186/s13098-017-0256-7.

Bozan, K., Davey, B., & Parker, K. (2015). Social influence on health it adoption patterns of the elderly: An institutional theory based use behavior approach. *Procedia Computer Science, 63*, 517–523. https://doi.org/10.1016/j.procs.2015.08.378.

Bradway, M., Arsand, E., & Grottland, A. (2015). Mobile health: Empowering patients and driving change. *Trends in Endocrinology and Metabolism, 26*(3), 114–117. https://doi.org/10.1016/j.tem.2015.01.001.

Brew-Sam, N. (2019). *Advancing theory-guided mHealth research: Empowerment as an antecedent of app use for diabetes self-management.* PhD thesis. Erfurt, Germany: University of Erfurt.

Brew-Sam, N., & Chib, A. (2019). How do smart device apps for diabetes self-management correspond with theoretical indicators of empowerment? An analysis of app features. *International Journal of Technology Assessment in Health Care*, 1–10. https://doi.org/10.1017/S0266462319000163.

Buhi, E. R., Trudnak, T. E., Martinasek, M. P., Oberne, A. B., Fuhrmann, H. J., & McDermott, R. J. (2013). Mobile phone-based behavioural interventions for health: A systematic review. *Health Education Journal, 72*(5), 564–583. https://doi.org/10.1177/0017896912452071.

Burner, E., Lam, C. N., DeRoss, R., Kagawa-Singer, M., Menchine, M., & Arora, S. (2018). Using mobile health to improve social support for low-income latino patients with diabetes: A mixed-methods analysis of the feasibility trial of text-med + fans. *Diabetes Technology and Therapeutics, 20*(1), 39–48. https://doi.org/10.1089/dia.2017.0198.

Camerini, L., & Schulz, P. J. (2012). Effects of functional interactivity on patients' knowledge, empowerment, and health outcomes: An experimental model-driven evaluation of a web-based intervention. *Journal of Medical Internet Research, 14*(4), e105. https://doi.org/10.2196/jmir.1953.

Chang, A. (2012). UTAUT and UTAUT 2: A review and agenda for future research. *The Winners, 13*(2), 10. https://doi.org/10.21512/tw.v13i2.656.

Chavez, S., Fedele, D., Guo, Y., Bernier, A., Smith, M., Warnick, J., & Modave, F. (2017). Mobile apps for the management of diabetes. *Diabetes Care, 40*(10), e145–e146. https://doi.org/10.2337/dc17-0853.

Chib, A., & Jiang, Q. (2014). Investigating modern-day talaria: Mobile phones and the mobility-impaired in Singapore. *Journal of Computer-Mediated Communication, 19*(3), 695–711. https://doi.org/10.1111/jcc4.12070.

Chib, A., van Velthoven, M. H., & Car, J. (2015). mHealth adoption in low-resource environments: A review of the use of mobile healthcare in developing countries. *Journal of Health Communication, 20*(1), 4–34. https://doi.org/10.1080/10810730.2013.864735.

Cinar, A. B., & Schou, L. (2014). Impact of empowerment on toothbrushing and diabetes management. *Oral Health and Preventive Dentistry, 12*(4), 337–344. https://doi.org/10.3290/j.ohpd.a32130.

Clark, N. M., & Houle, C. R. (2009). Theoretical models and strategies for improving disease management by patients. In S. A. Shumaker, J. K. Ockene, & K. A. Riekert (Eds.), *The handbook of health behavior change* (3 ed., pp. 19–38). New York: Springer Pub. Co.

Conger, J. A., & Kanungo, R. N. (1988). The empowerment process: Integrating theory and practice. *Academy of Management Review, 13*(3), 471–482.

Cumming, T. M., Strnadová, I., Knox, M., & Parmenter, T. (2014). Mobile technology in inclusive research: Tools of empowerment. *Disability and Society, 29*(7), 999–1012. https://doi.org/10.1080/09687599.2014.886556.

van Dam, H. A., van der Horst, F. G., Knoops, L., Ryckman, R. M., Crebolder, H. F., & van den Borne, B. H. (2005). Social support in diabetes: A systematic review of controlled intervention studies. *Patient Education and Counseling, 59*(1), 1—12. https://doi.org/10.1016/j.pec.2004.11.001.

Davis, F. D. (1985). *A technology acceptance model for empirically testing new end-user information systems — theory and results.* PhD thesis. Massachusetts: Massachusetts Inst. of Technology.

Davis, F. D., Bagozzi, R. P., & Warshaw, P. R. (1989). User acceptance of computer technology: A comparison of two theoretical models. *Management Science, 35*(8), 982—1003. https://doi.org/10.1287/mnsc.35.8.982.

Deci, E. L. (1975). *Intrinsic motivation.* New York: Plenum Press.

Deng, Z. (2013). Understanding public users' adoption of mobile health service. *International Journal of Mobile Communications, 11*(4), 351—373. https://doi.org/10.1504/IJMC.2013.055748.

Di Iorio, C. T., Carinci, F., & Massi, B. M. (2015). The diabetes challenge: From human and social rights to the empowerment of people with diabetes. In R. A. DeFronzo, E. Ferrannini, K. Alberti, P. Zimmet, & G. Alberti (Eds.), *International textbook of diabetes mellitus* (4 ed., Vol. 1, pp. 1103—1112). Oxford: Wiley.

Diabetes Prevention Program Research Group. (2012). The 10-year cost-effectiveness of life-style intervention or metformin for diabetes prevention: An intent-to-treat analysis of the dpp/dppos. *Diabetes Care, 35*(4), 723—730. https://doi.org/10.2337/dc11-1468.

Drincic, A., Prahalad, P., Greenwood, D., & Klonoff, D. C. (2016). Evidence-based mobile medical applications in diabetes. *Endocrinology and Metabolism Clinics of North America, 45*(4), 943—965. https://doi.org/10.1016/j.ecl.2016.06.001.

Dutta, M. J., Pfister, R., & Kosmoski, C. (2010). Consumer evaluation of genetic information online: The role of quality on attitude and behavioral intentions. *Journal of Computer-Mediated Communication, 15*(4), 592—605. https://doi.org/10.1111/j.1083-6101.2009.01504.x.

Dwivedi, Y. K., Shareef, M. A., Simintiras, A. C., Lal, B., & Weerakkody, V. (2016). A generalised adoption model for services: A cross-country comparison of mobile health (m-health). *Government Information Quarterly, 33*(1), 174—187. https://doi.org/10.1016/j.giq.2015.06.003.

Eiser, J. R., Riazi, A., Eiser, C., Hammersley, S., & Tooke, J. E. (2001). Predictors of psycholog-ical well-being in types 1 and 2 diabetes. *Psychology and Health, 16*(1), 99—110. https://doi.org/10.1080/08870440108405492.

Emanuel, E. J., & Emanuel, L. L. (1992). Four models of the physician-patient relationship. *The Journal of the American Medical Association, 267*(16), 2221. https://doi.org/10.1001/jama.1992.03480160079038.

Eraker, S. A., Becker, M. H., Strecher, V. J., & Kirscht, J. P. (1985). Smoking behavior, cessation techniques, and the health decision model. *The American Journal of Medicine, 78*, 817—825.

Eyuboglu, E., & Schulz, P. J. (2016). Do health literacy and patient empowerment affect self-care behaviour? A survey study among Turkish patients with diabetes. *BMJ Open, 6*(3), e010186. https://doi.org/10.1136/bmjopen-2015-010186.

Fishbein, M., & Ajzen, I. (1975). *Belief, attitude, intention, and behavior: An introduction to theory and research.* Reading, MA: Addison-Wesley.

Fishbein, M., & Cappella, J. N. (2006). The role of theory in developing effective health communications. *Journal of Communication, 56*(s1), 1—17. https://doi.org/10.1111/j.1460-2466.2006.00280.x.

Fisher, E. B., Thorpe, C. T., DeVellis, B. M., & DeVellis, R. F. (2007). Healthy coping, negative emotions, and diabetes management: A systematic review and appraisal. *The Diabetes Educator, 33*(6), 1080—1103. https://doi.org/10.1177/0145721707309808.

Fortmann, A. L., Gallo, L. C., Garcia, M. I., Taleb, M., Euyoque, J. A., Clark, T., ... Philis-Tsimikas, A. (2017). Dulce digital: An mHealth sms-based intervention improves glyce-mic control in Hispanics with type 2 diabetes. *Diabetes Care.* https://doi.org/10.2337/dc17-0230. dc170230.

Fortuna, K. L., DiMilia, P. R., Lohman, M. C., Bruce, M. L., Zubritsky, C. D., Halaby, M. R., … Bartels, S. J. (2018). Feasibility, acceptability, and preliminary effectiveness of a peer-delivered and technology supported self-management intervention for older adults with serious mental illness. *Psychiatric Quarterly, 89*(2), 293–305. https://doi.org/10.1007/s11126-017-9534-7.

Free, C., Phillips, G., Galli, L., Watson, L., Felix, L., Edwards, P., … Cornford, T. (2013). The effectiveness of mobile-health technology-based health behaviour change or disease management interventions for health care consumers: A systematic review. *PLoS Medicine, 10*(1), e1001362. https://doi.org/10.1371/journal.pmed.1001362.

Fu, H., McMahon, S. K., Gross, C. R., Adam, T. J., & Wyman, J. F. (2017). Usability and clinical efficacy of diabetes mobile applications for adults with type 2 diabetes: A systematic review. *Diabetes Research and Clinical Practice, 131*, 70–81. https://doi.org/10.1016/j.diabres.2017.06.016.

Funnell, M. M., & Anderson, R. M. (2003). Patient empowerment: A look back, a look ahead. *The Diabetes Educator, 29*(3), 454–464. https://doi.org/10.1177/014572170302900310.

Funnell, M. M., & Anderson, R. M. (2004). Empowerment and self-management of diabetes. *Clinical Diabetes, 22*(3), 123–127. https://doi.org/10.2337/diaclin.22.3.123.

Gagné, M., Senécal, C. B., & Koestner, R. (1997). Proximal job characteristics, feelings of empowerment, and intrinsic motivation: A multidimensional model. *Journal of Applied Social Psychology, 27*(14), 1222–1240. https://doi.org/10.1111/j.1559-1816.1997.tb01803.x.

Glasgow, R. E., Toobert, D. J., & Gillette, C. D. (2001). Psychosocial barriers to diabetes self-management and quality of life. *Diabetes Spectrum, 14*(1), 33–41. https://doi.org/10.2337/diaspect.14.1.33.

Gomersall, T., Madill, A., & Summers, L. K. M. (2011). A metasynthesis of the self-management of type 2 diabetes. *Qualitative Health Research, 21*(6), 853–871. https://doi.org/10.1177/1049732311402096.

Graffy, J. (2013). Approaches to diabetes: Empowerment, control or both? *Primary Health Care Research and Development, 14*(3), 221–223. https://doi.org/10.1017/S1463423613000236.

Grant, R. W., & Schmittdiel, J. A. (2013). Adults with diabetes who perceive family members' behaviour as unsupportive are less adherent to their medication regimen. *Evidence-Based Nursing, 16*(1), 15–16. https://doi.org/10.1136/eb-2012-100947.

Gutschoven, K., & van den Bulck, J. (2006). Towards the measurement of psychological health empowerment in the general public. In *Paper presented at the annual conference of the international comm. association, Dresden, Germany.*

Halter, J. B. (2012). Diabetes mellitus in an aging population: The challenge ahead. *The Journals of Gerontology. Series A, Biological Sciences and Medical Sciences, 67*(12), 1297–1299. https://doi.org/10.1093/gerona/gls201.

Hao, H., Padman, R., Sun, B., & Telang, R. (2014). Examining the social influence on information technology sustained use in a community health system: A hierarchical bayesian learning method analysis. In *Paper presented at the 47th Hawaii international conference on system science, Hawaii.*

Harvey, J. N., & Lawson, V. L. (2009). The importance of health belief models in determining self-care behaviour in diabetes. *Diabetic Medicine, 26*(1), 5–13. https://doi.org/10.1111/j.1464-5491.2008.02628.x.

Heisler, M., Bouknight, R. R., Hayward, R. A., Smith, D. M., & Kerr, E. A. (2002). The relative importance of physician communication, participatory decision making, and patient understanding in diabetes self-management. *Journal of General Internal Medicine, 17*(4), 243–252. https://doi.org/10.1046/j.1525-1497.2002.10905.x.

Hewson, M. (2010). Agency. In A. Mills, G. Durepos, & E. Wiebe (Eds.), *Encyclopedia of case study research* (pp. 13–17). Thousand Oaks, CA: SAGE Publications, Inc.

Holtz, B. E., Murray, K. M., Hershey, D. D., Dunneback, J. K., Cotten, S. R., Holmstrom, A. J., … Wood, M. A. (2017). Developing a patient-centered mHealth app: A tool for adolescents with type 1 diabetes and their parents. *JMIR mHealth and uHealth, 5*(4), e53. https://doi.org/10.2196/mhealth.6654.

Hoque, R., & Sorwar, G. (2017). Understanding factors influencing the adoption of mHealth by the elderly: An extension of the UTAUT model. *International Journal of Medical Informatics, 101,* 75–84. https://doi.org/10.1016/j.ijmedinf.2017.02.002.

International Diabetes Federation, IDF. (2010). *Diabetes burden shifting to developing countries.* Retrieved from http://www.idf.org/diabetes-burden-shifting-developing-countries.

International Diabetes Federation, IDF. (2014). *IDF diabetes atlas. Key findings 2014.* Retrieved from http://www.idf.org/diabetesatlas/update-2014.

Inukollu, V. N., Keshamon, D. D., Kang, T., & Inukollu, M. (2014). Factors influencing quality of mobile apps: Role of mobile app development life cycle. *International Journal of Science and Engineering Applications, 5*(5), 15–34. https://doi.org/10.5121/ijsea.2014.5502.

James, S., Perry, L., Gallagher, R., & Lowe, J. (2016). Diabetes educators' intended and reported use of common diabetes-related technologies: Discrepancies and dissonance. *Journal of Diabetes Science and Technology, 10*(6), 1277–1286. https://doi.org/10.1177/1932296816646798.

Jones, K. R., Lekhak, N., & Kaewluang, N. (2014). Using mobile phones and short message service to deliver self-management interventions for chronic conditions: A meta-review. *Worldviews on Evidence-Based Nursing, 11*(2), 81–88. https://doi.org/10.1111/wvn.12030.

Kamphoff, C. S., Hutson, B. L., Amundsen, S. A., & Atwood, J. A. (2016). A motivational/empowerment model applied to students on academic probation. *Journal of College Student Retention: Research, Theory and Practice, 8*(4), 397–412. https://doi.org/10.2190/9652-8543-3428-1j06.

Kingsley, B. R. (1987). Push and pull strategies: Applications for health care marketing. *Health Care Strategic Management, 5*(8), 13–15.

Krošel, M., Švegl, L., Vidmar, L., & Dinevski, D. (2016). Empowering diabetes patients with mobile health technologies. In W. Bonney (Ed.), *Mobile health technologies - theories and applications: InTech.*

Leasure, J. L., & Jones, M. (2008). Forced and voluntary exercise differentially affect brain and behavior. *Neuroscience, 156*(3), 456–465. https://doi.org/10.1016/j.neuroscience.2008.07.041.

Lee, M., & Koh, J. (2001). Is empowerment really a new concept? *The International Journal of Human Resource Management, 12*(4), 684–695. https://doi.org/10.1080/713769649.

Lee, J., & Rho, M. J. (2013). Perception of influencing factors on acceptance of mobile health monitoring service: A comparison between users and non-users. *Healthcare Informatics Research, 19*(3), 167–176. https://doi.org/10.4258/hir.2013.19.3.167.

Leventhal, H., Diefenbach, M., & Leventhal, E. A. (1992). Illness cognition: Using common sense to understand treatment adherence and affect cognition interactions. *Cognitive Therapy and Research, 16*(2), 143–163. https://doi.org/10.1007/bf01173486.

Lin, S.-P. (2011). Determinants of adoption of mobile healthcare service. *International Journal of Mobile Communications, 9*(3). https://doi.org/10.1504/IJMC.2011.040608.

Lincoln, N. D., Travers, C., Ackers, P., & Wilkinson, A. (2002). The meaning of empowerment: The interdisciplinary etymology of a new management concept. *International Journal of Management Reviews, 4*(3), 271–290. https://doi.org/10.1111/1468-2370.00087.

Li, Y., Owen, T., Thimbleby, H., Sun, N., & Rau, P.-L. P. (2013). A design to empower patients in long term wellbeing monitoring and chronic disease management in mHealth. In M.-C. Beuscart-Zéphir, M. Jaspers, C. Kuziemsky, C. Nøhr, & J. Aarts (Eds.), *Context sensitive health informatics: Human and sociotechnical approaches* (Vol. 194, pp. 82–87). Amsterdam et al: IOS Press.

Logan, M. S., & Ganster, D. C. (2007). The effects of empowerment on attitudes and performance: The role of social support and empowerment beliefs. *Journal of Management Studies, 44*(8), 1523–1550. https://doi.org/10.1111/j.1467-6486.2007.00711.x.

Malhotra, Y., & Galletta, D. F. (1999). Extending the technology acceptance model to account for social influence: Theoretical bases and empirical validation. In *Paper presented at the 32nd annual Hawaii international conference on systems Sciences, Hawaii*.

Mantwill, S., Fiordelli, M., Ludolph, R., & Schulz, P. J. (2015). Empower – support of patient empowerment by an intelligent self-management pathway for patients: Study protocol. *BMC Medical Informatics and Decision Making, 15*, 18. https://doi.org/10.1186/s12911-015-0142-x.

Martz, E., Livneh, H., & Wright, B. A. (2007). *Coping with chronic illness and disability*. Boston, MA: Springer US.

Meer, M. (2015). Empowering patients with diabetes. *British Journal of Nursing, 24*(16), 828. https://doi.org/10.12968/bjon.2015.24.16.828.

Menon, S. T. (2001). Employee empowerment: An integrative psychological approach. *Applied Psychology, 50*(1), 153–180. https://doi.org/10.1111/1464-0597.00052.

Menon, S. T. (2002). Toward a model of psychological health empowerment: Implications for health care in multicultural communities. *Nurse Education Today, 22*(1), 28–43. https://doi.org/10.1054/nedt.2001.0721.

Middelweerd, A., Mollee, J. S., van der Wal, C. N., Brug, J., & te Velde, S. J. (2014). Apps to promote physical activity among adults: A review and content analysis. *International Journal of Behavioral Nutrition and Physical Activity, 11*(1). https://doi.org/10.1186/s12966-014-0097-9.

Miller, J. A. (2018). *Facing the diabetes crisis*. Retrieved from https://http://www.aacc.org/publications/cln/articles/2018/september/facing-the-diabetes-crisis.

Miller, L. M. S., Sutter, C. A., Wilson, M. D., Bergman, J. J., Beckett, L. A., & Gibson, T. N. (2017). An evaluation of an eHealth tool designed to improve college students' label-reading skills and feelings of empowerment to choose healthful foods. *Front Public Health, 5*, 359. https://doi.org/10.3389/fpubh.2017.00359.

Nacinovich, M. (2011). Defining mHealth. *Journal of Communication in Healthcare, 4*(1), 1–3. https://doi.org/10.1179/175380611x12950033990296.

Nelson, L. A., Mayberry, L. S., Wallston, K., Kripalani, S., Bergner, E. M., & Osborn, C. Y. (2016). Development and usability of reach: A tailored theory-based text messaging intervention for disadvantaged adults with type 2 diabetes. *JMIR Human Factors, 3*(2), e23. https://doi.org/10.2196/humanfactors.6029.

Omboni, S., Caserini, M., & Coronetti, C. (2016). Telemedicine and m-health in hypertension management: Technologies, applications and clinical evidence. *High Blood Pressure and Cardiovascular Prevention, 23*(3), 187–196. https://doi.org/10.1007/s40292-016-0143-6.

Oxford Dictionaries. (2016). *Definition of empower in English*. Retrieved from http://www.oxforddictionaries.com/definition/english/empower.

Park, S., Burford, S., Hanlen, L., Dawda, P., Dugdale, P., Nolan, C., & Burns, J. (2016). An integrated mHealth model for type 2 diabetes patients using mobile tablet devices. *Journal of Mobile Technology in Medicine, 5*(2), 24–32. https://doi.org/10.7309/jmtm.5.2.4.

Park, S., Burford, S., Lee, J. Y., & Toy, L. (2016). *Mobile health: Empowering people with type 2 diabetes using digital tools*. Canberra: News & Media Research Centre, University of Canberra.

Parker, R. M., & Gazmararian, J. A. (2010). Health literacy: Essential for health communication. In G. L. Kreps (Ed.), *Health communication* (Vol. I, pp. 153–156). Los Angeles; Calif: SAGE.

Petty, R. E., & Cacioppo, J. T. (1986). The elaboration likelihood model of persuasion. In L. Berkowitz (Ed.), *Advances in experimental social psychology* (Vol. 19, pp. 123–205). New York: Academic Press.

Prochaska, J. O., Johnson, S., & Lee, P. (2009). The transtheoretical model of behavior change. In S. A. Shumaker, J. K. Ockene, & K. A. Riekert (Eds.), *The handbook of health behavior change* (Vol. 3, pp. 59–84). New York: Springer.

Rai, A., Chen, L., Pye, J., & Baird, A. (2013). Understanding determinants of consumer mobile health usage intentions, assimilation, and channel preferences. *Journal of Medical Internet Research, 15*(8), e149. https://doi.org/10.2196/jmir.2635.

Rappaport, J. (1987). Terms of empowerment/exemplars of prevention: Toward a theory for community psychology. *American Journal of Community Psychology, 15*(2), 121–148.

Riley, W. T., Rivera, D. E., Atienza, A. A., Nilsen, W., Allison, S. M., & Mermelstein, R. (2011). Health behavior models in the age of mobile interventions: Are our theories up to the task? *Translational Behavioral Medicine, 1*(1), 53–71. https://doi.org/10.1007/s13142-011-0021-7.

Rogers, R. W. (1975). A protection motivation theory of fear appeals and attitude change. *The Journal of Psychology, 91*(1), 93–114. https://doi.org/10.1080/00223980.1975.9915803.

Rosenstock, I. M., Strecher, V. J., & Becker, M. H. (1994). The health belief model and HIV risk behavior change. In R. J. DiClemente, & J. L. Peterson (Eds.), *Preventing Aids* (pp. 5–24). Boston, MA: Springer.

Rosland, A. M., Kieffer, E., Israel, B., Cofield, M., Palmisano, G., Sinco, B., … Heisler, M. (2008). When is social support important? The association of family support and professional support with specific diabetes self-management behaviors. *Journal of General Internal Medicine, 23*(12), 1992–1999. https://doi.org/10.1007/s11606-008-0814-7.

Ryan, E. A., Holland, J., Stroulia, E., Bazelli, B., Babwik, S. A., Li, H., … Greiner, R. (2017). Improved A1C levels in type 1 diabetes with smartphone app use. *Canadian Journal of Diabetes, 41*(1), 33–40. https://doi.org/10.1016/j.jcjd.2016.06.001.

Scambler, S., Newton, P., & Asimakopoulou, K. (2014). The context of empowerment and self-care within the field of diabetes. *Health (London), 18*(6), 545–560. https://doi.org/10.1177/1363459314524801.

Schulz, P. J., & Nakamoto, K. (2013). Health literacy and patient empowerment in health communication: The importance of separating conjoined twins. *Patient Education and Counseling, 90*(1), 4–11. https://doi.org/10.1016/j.pec.2012.09.006.

Shao, Y., Liang, L., Shi, L., Wan, C., & Yu, S. (2017). The effect of social support on glycemic control in patients with type 2 diabetes mellitus: The mediating roles of self-efficacy and adherence. *Journal of Diabetes Research, 2017*, 2804178. https://doi.org/10.1155/2017/2804178.

Signorelli, C., Wakefield, C. E., Johnston, K. A., Fardell, J. E., Brierley, M. E., Thornton-Benko, E., … Cohn, R. J. (2018). 'Re-engage' pilot study protocol: A nurse-led eHealth intervention to re-engage, educate and empower childhood cancer survivors. *BMJ Open, 8*(4), e022269. https://doi.org/10.1136/bmjopen-2018-022269.

Sigurdardottir, A. K., & Jonsdottir, H. (2008). Empowerment in diabetes care: Towards measuring empowerment. *Scandinavian Journal of Caring Sciences, 22*(2), 284–291. https://doi.org/10.1111/j.1471-6712.2007.00506.x.

Snoek, F. J. (2007). Self management of type 2 diabetes. *BMJ, 335*(7618), 458–459. https://doi.org/10.1136/bmj.39315.443160.BE.

Spreitzer, G. M. (1995). Psychological empowerment in the workplace: Dimensions, measurement, and validation. *Academy of Management Journal, 38*(5), 1442–1465. https://doi.org/10.2307/256865.

Spreitzer, G. M. (1996). Social structural characteristics of psychological empowerment. *Academy of Management Journal, 35*, 483–504.

Stoyanov, S. R., Hides, L., Kavanagh, D. J., Zelenko, O., Tjondronegoro, D., & Mani, M. (2015). Mobile app rating scale: A new tool for assessing the quality of health mobile apps. *JMIR Mhealth Uhealth, 3*(1), e27. https://doi.org/10.2196/mhealth.3422.

Strom, J. L., & Egede, L. E. (2012). The impact of social support on outcomes in adult patients with type 2 diabetes: A systematic review. *Current Diabetes Reports, 12*(6), 769–781. https://doi.org/10.1007/s11892-012-0317-0.

Talukder, M., & Quazi, A. (2011). The impact of social influence on individuals' adoption of innovation. *Journal of Organizational Computing and Electronic Commerce, 21*(2), 111–135. https://doi.org/10.1080/10919392.2011.564483.

Thomas, K. W., & Velthouse, B. A. (1990). Cognitive elements of empowerment: An "interpretive" model of intrinsic task motivation. *Academy of Management Review, 15*(4), 666–681.

Tol, A., Alhani, F., Shojaeazadeh, D., Sharifirad, G., & Moazam, N. (2015). An empowering approach to promote the quality of life and self-management among type 2 diabetic patients. *Journal of Education and Health Promotion, 4*, 13. https://doi.org/10.4103/2277-9531.154022.

Vatankhah, M., & Tanbakooei, N. (2014). The role of social support on intrinsic and extrinsic motivation among Iranian EFL learners. *Procedia – Social and Behavioral Sciences, 98*, 1912–1918. https://doi.org/10.1016/j.sbspro.2014.03.622.

Veazie, S., Winchell, K., Gilbert, J., Paynter, R., Ivlev, I., Eden, K. B., … Helfand, M. (2018). Rapid evidence review of mobile applications for self-management of diabetes. *Journal of General Internal Medicine.* https://doi.org/10.1007/s11606-018-4410-1.

Venkatesh, V., Morris, M. G., Davis, G. B., & Davis, F. D. (2003). User acceptance of information technology: Toward a unified view. *MIS Quarterly, 27*(3), 425–478.

Venkatesh, V., Thong, J., & Xu, X. (2012). Consumer acceptance and use of information technology: Extending the unified theory of acceptance and use of technology. *MIS Quarterly, 36*(1), 157–178.

Venkatesh, V., Thong, J., & Xu, X. (2016). Unified theory of acceptance and use of technology: A synthesis and the road ahead. *Journal of the Association for Information Systems, 17*(5), 328–376. https://doi.org/10.17705/1jais.00428.

Wang, Y., Xue, H., Huang, Y., Huang, L., & Zhang, D. (2017). A systematic review of application and effectiveness of mHealth interventions for obesity and diabetes treatment and self-management. *Advances in Nutrition: An International Review Journal, 8*(3), 449–462. https://doi.org/10.3945/an.116.014100.

Whittemore, R., Bak, P. S., Melkus, G., & Grey, M. (2003). Promoting lifestyle change in the prevention and management of type 2 diabetes. *Journal of the American Academy of Nurse Practitioners, 15*(8), 341–349.

Woldeyohannes, H. O., & Ngwenyama, O. K. (2017). Factors influencing acceptance and continued use of mHealth apps. In *Paper presented at the HCI in business, government and organizations. Interacting with information systems: 4th international conference, Vancouver, BC, Canada.*

Yang, S., Hsue, C., & Lou, Q. (2015). Does patient empowerment predict self-care behavior and glycosylated hemoglobin in Chinese patients with type 2 diabetes? *Diabetes Technology and Therapeutics, 17*(5), 343–348. https://doi.org/10.1089/dia.2014.0345.

Zapata, B. C., Fernandez-Aleman, J. L., Idri, A., & Toval, A. (2015). Empirical studies on usability of mHealth apps: A systematic literature review. *Journal of Medical Systems, 39*(2), 1. https://doi.org/10.1007/s10916-014-0182-2.

Zhu, Z., Liu, Y., Che, X., & Chen, X. (2017). Moderating factors influencing adoption of a mobile chronic disease management system in China. *Informatics for Health and Social Care*, 1–20. https://doi.org/10.1080/17538157.2016.1255631.

Health goes mobile: State-of-the art and future research agenda

Isabell Koinig, Sandra Diehl

Department of Media and Communication Studies, University of Klagenfurt, Klagenfurt, Austria

Introduction

Coined by Istepanian, Laxminarayan, Pattichis, and Constantinos (2006, p. xxiii), mHealth describes "emerging mobile communications and network technologies for healthcare." A few years later, the mHealth summit, hosted by the Foundation for the National Institute of Health, agreed on a first definition, referring to mHealth as "the delivery of healthcare services via mobile communication devices" (Torgan, 2009, p. 75). Following the WHO, mHealth is part of electronic health (eHealth) and refers to "the use of mobile and wireless technologies to support the achievement of health objectives" (WHO, 2011). The WHO issued an mHealth report, which is based on the findings produced by the second global survey on eHealth (WHO, 2011). This report serves as a basis for one of the United Nations' Sustainable Development Goals—the objective to "ensure health lives and promote well-being for all at all ages" (UN, 2017). In consequence, not only is there an increasing concern with health throughout the world but also two other developments have led the health arena to grow in relevance: first, the scope of what health is has been broadened considerably, also integrating aspects of diet, fitness, and wellness among others (Banos et al., 2016; Schiavo, 2014), and second, new technologies have altered how people perceive health, opening up new opportunities for individuals to take an active part in their health (care and management) (Bhavnani, Narula, & Sengupta, 2016) as well as empowering them (Koinig, 2016; Koinig, Diehl, & Mueller, 2017).

Listed as a fundamental human right by the World Health Organization (WHO, 2013), health has become a matter of global relevance—even more so in recent years. The WHO (1946) conceptualizes health as "a state of complete physical, mental and social well-being and not merely the absence of disease or infirmity." Even though it is not implicitly mentioned at this point, it later also started to take environmental and cultural parameters into account (Ewles & Simnett, 2003). Moreover, it is worth mentioning that the influence of lifestyle factors and social aspects is not only emphasized by the WHO but also by a variety of other authors (Berry, 2007; Schiavo, 2007; Tones & Tilford, 2001). A group of authors explicitly referring to social factors are Stokes, Noren, and Shindell (1982, p. 34), who perceive health as "a state characterized by anatomic, physiologic, and psychological integrity; ability to perform personally valued family, work, and community roles; ability to deal with physical, biological, psychological, and social stress."

According to a contemporary view, health—if maintained properly—makes for a good quality of life (Rod & Saunders, 2004; Buchanan, 2000) and is claimed to consist of three essential qualities: (1) wholeness, as it is linked to a person's immediate environment and subjective experiences, (2) pragmatism, which pays tribute to health's relative nature in terms of experience and is closely linked to the third quality, namely (3), individualism, according to which health is highly personal (Svalastog et al., 2017), especially in the digital age, in which the use of health applications and services via private devices enabled through digitalization and digital technologies is on the rise (Bhavnani et al., 2016).

In the advent of eHealth (Eysenbach, 2001) and mHealth (mobile health; Abidi, 2015), health has emerged as "a field in the intersection of medical informatics, public health and business, referring to health services and information delivered or enhanced through the Internet and related technologies" (Eysenbach, 2001, p. 20). Coined in the first years of the new century (Bashshur, Shannon, Krupinski, & Grigsby, 2011), mHealth has been the center of the debate in the health context for some time. Following the WHO's (2011) call to discover "new horizons for health through mobile technologies," one area that warrants further research is mHealth.

Taking these assumptions as a starting point, the present investigation will start out by analyzing the changing health (communication) landscape. It will look at studies dealing with mHealth in both developed and developing countries to carve out the potential for stakeholders with diverse interests. As such, it pays attention to existing and previously identified research gaps stating that it is essential to improve the knowledge about the usability, design, and acceptance of mHealth services (Hether et al., 2016; Wu et al., 2017). For this purpose, also links to selected theories that intend to describe respectively explain health-related behaviors as well as bring about behavioral changes are established. The contribution will close by highlighting future research agendas in the mHealth context.

Current developments in digital health (communication)

Researchers agree that the Internet holds the potential for transforming conventional notions of both personal and public health (Eng & Gustafson, 1999; Sonnenberg, 1997). The Internet is growing in importance as a source of drug and health-related information (Friedman & Gould, 2007; Menon et al., 2002), responsible for extending "the scope of health care beyond its traditional boundaries" (Eysenbach, 2001, p. 20; Viswanath, 2005). To marketers and governmental parties, it has not only widened their scopes of reaching prospective customers (Buckley, 2004) but also allowed them to accommodate their audience's needs for specific information offered via different, interactive channels (Friedman & Gould, 2007). Extending the functionalities of traditional media vehicles, the Internet offers several benefits to consumers, such as enabling them to actively participate in their healthcare and delivering a vast range of health-related information (Bischoff & Kelley, 1999; Spain et al., 2001).

Health Information Technology (HIT, Buntin et al., 2010) has significantly altered individuals' health seeking behaviors. Due to the variety of online and mobile services, such as wireless and mobile services, online doctor review portals, self-diagnosing websites, or rating sites amongst others, information channels have multiplied and have led digital health information to be available in abundance. In consequence, former patients are turned into consumers, who are enabled to be or become more strongly involved in their healthcare (Hall et al., 2012; Martin, 2012). Demand for digital health information is also increasingly requested by consumers and was already of interest in the early 2000s (Rice & Katz, 2001). Past surveys have indicated that of the people inquired, almost two-thirds browsed the Internet for health-related information (Twibell & Anzalone, 2001), making it the sixth most research issue online (Henkel, 2002). Recent surveys have produced further evidence of the Internet's growing importance as a source of information for people's healthcare decisions and drug choices (Fox, 2005; Rice, 2004; Fox & Rainie, 2002; Cassil, 2008)—it is even attributed higher degrees of credibility and reliability than other sources (family, friends, and/or health professionals; Atkinson et al., 2009). In 2013, 77% of Americans reportedly went online to look for health information—equaling 8 in 10 search inquiries (Pew, 2013). In 2015, 70% of Americans used the Internet as a first point of reference when looking up health information; the same year, 1 out of 20 Google searches was also reported to be concerned with health-related information (President's Cancer Panel, 2016). Digital health technologies are driving change toward a more individually centered, self-responsible, and empowered healthcare (Banos et al., 2016), enhancing not only the accessibility of health information but also making health delivery more efficient and precise (Bhavnani et al., 2016).

Advantages and disadvantages of digital health information

Due to the convergence of technologies, digital and genomic content is increasingly digitized, leading to the development of digital health. There are many advantages associated to online health information: on the one hand, "digital health is empowering us to better track, manage, and improve our own and our family's health" (Morolla, 2019, p. 101), involving users more deeply in their healthcare (Laugesen et al., 2015). This is especially facilitated by better and easier access to (public) health information (Huntington et al., 2004). In addition, it is the interactive nature of new technologies that allows for increased user engagement (e.g., email consultations with doctors or other medical personnel, online appointments, or patient support groups on social media; Huntington et al., 2004). Online support groups are of immense relevance in today's interconnected health environment, as they award patients with numerous advantages, including access to information around the clock, anonymity, no potential for discrimination, mutual support by people similar to them, as well as the opportunity of getting a second opinion (Cline & Haynes, 2001; White & Dorman, 2001). For instance, in the case of dietary support groups, participants of online fora were more motivated to change their unhealthy styles of living, further expressing a higher willingness to stick to and maintain their new dietary routine. This willingness mostly stemmed from the increased monitoring and frequent exchange with peers online who were going through a similar situation and only shared their experiences with one another (Ba & Wang, 2013). Hence, allowing for consumer anonymity when debating illnesses as well as their treatment options respectively, this aspect is listed as one of the most frequent mHealth advantages (Bischoff & Kelley, 1999; Spain et al., 2001). Moreover, in the age of data monitoring, epidemic outbreaks and disease processes can be tracked and monitored through big data analyses (Lupton, 2014)—a facet that might be beneficial to several parties (e.g., the government and NGOs). eHealth and mHealth, however, do not only benefit individuals; there are also benefits for the healthcare system, as both forms hold the potential to reduce doctor consultations, examinations, as well as the length of hospital stays (Statista, 2017e).

Yet, despite the many advantages, there is also a significant number of downsides to online and digital health information. First, users do not have any control as to which data is published online (Williams et al., 2003), which might lead to false and misleading data to be spread (Ferguson, 1997). However, one study even found that if users come across incorrect information, they have a tendency to correct it (White & Dorman, 2001). Second, comprehension among online message recipients might be limited due to their low health literacy levels (Adams et al., 2009), leading to insecurity among recipients. Third, the present-day health information landscape is still characterized by information asymmetry, since selected population groups are disadvantaged in either their comprehension of or access to health-enabling information (Williams et al., 2003). This inability to access or comprehend information has further implications, negatively affecting patient compliance with doctor recommendations or medication adherence (Laugesen et al., 2015). Fourth, data security is one additional concern, especially in a time when "data harvesting" has become a buzz-word. Getting insights into personal preferences and usage patterns is crucial for commercial success nowadays and proves to be useful to (pharmaceutical) companies, governmental and healthcare institutions, as well as insurance companies among others. Following a recent study, there are some barriers that prevent providers from literally prescribing mHealth solutions. These predominantly concern devices' limited connectivity, reimbursement challenges, problems with regard to privacy and data se-curity, missing scientific proof regarding app efficiency, as well as their inability to reach vulnerable and minority groups (IQIVA, 2017). Hence, the necessity to conduct more critical digital health studies is repeatedly put forward (Lupton, 2014; Lupton, 2016).

In 2015, the concept of the wired patient has been identified as one of the core health topics (Makovsky, 2015), suggesting that through inter-active as well as mobile health technologies, consumers can become more involved (and empowered) in their healthcare. Yet, while the availability of online services should allow for a faster delivery of care and increased participation (Street, 2003), consumers are also asked to agree to the disclosure of their online health records to receive more tailored treat-ments, which has led to much criticism (Makovsky, 2015). Surveys found that albeit being burdened by already high healthcare costs, Americans would still leverage technology, even expressing a high willingness to pay for those innovative services (Makovsky, 2015). This then proposes that new tools "have the potential to improve communication with clinicians, access to personal health information, and health education with the goal of preparing patients to take a more active role in their care" (Franklin et al., 2009, p. 169f.).

The 2019 Global Health Care Outlook further revealed that the use of technologies constitutes an essential element of a "smart health commu-nity" (Deloitte, 2019, p. 5), where these "technologies can improve engagement, enable convenience-driven access to care, and nurture a two-way relationship for the long term" (Deloitte, 2019, p. 19). Healthcare systems around the world have started to prioritize the implementation, respectively advancement of new digital technology, in the healthcare sector, among them Australia, China, Japan, Brazil, and the Netherlands. With changing healthcare environments, the different media channels involved in present-day medical encounters might be worth studying, too.

Toward mHealth: Categories and reach

mHealth categories

The broadening scope of health is also reflected in the number of app categories that qualify as mHealth. In a 2015 study, the majority of apps were classified as "wellness management apps," concerning aspects such as fitness (36%), lifestyle, and stress management (17%), as well as diet and nutrition (12%; IMS Health, 2017). On the other hand, there are disease-related apps, which assist individuals in preventing and reducing the risk of disease as well as maintaining their health. The number of purposes apps fulfill are numerous, ranging from information, instruction, and recording, over data display and guidance, to reminders and enablers of patient-provider communication (IMS Health, 2015). According to another 2015 study, consumers utilized three of these functions more frequently than all other functions combined: information, instruction, and recording—a logical consequence since most apps only featured one functionality (IMS Health, 2015). A more extensive framework classifying mHealth interventions was developed by Free et al. (2010), who included a total of 13 interventions into their framework while assigning them to four different groups of stakeholders (note: interventions often affect more than one group): health researchers (1 intervention), healthcare professionals (6 interventions), patients (9 interventions), and the general population (3 interventions). The authors came up with the following interventions: data collection, education, medical record, test result notification, disease monitoring, clinical decision support systems, appointment reminders, treatment programs, chronic disease management, medication adherence, health behavior change, acute disease management (first aid and emergency care), and untargeted mass health promotion campaigns. Moreover, the interventions' scope also varied significantly, ranging from facilitating health research, over improving health services, to improving health outcomes. A study by Fiordelli, Diviani, and Schulz (2013) also found that most studies on mHealth focused on selected aspects and were predominantly concerned with health promotion (38%), self-management (22%), remote monitoring (21%), data collection (21%), medication adherence (20%), and education (13%). The scope of mHealth apps is constantly expanding, now even comprising areas such as biofeedback, which help with the management of conditions like insomnia (Taylor & Roane, 2010), headaches (Nestoriuc, Martin, Rief, & Andrasic, 2008), and chronic pain (Palermo, Eccleston, Lewandowski, Williams, & Morley, 2010). While smartphones have been used in conventional medicine, they are transforming healthcare lastingly, where they have become "keeper[s] of an expanding array of health care apps" (Deloitte, 2012, p. 5). They have already been increasingly utilized in specialized areas, including mental health (Luxton, McCann, Bush, Mishkind, & Reger, 2011), diabetes management (Ciemins, Coon, & Sorli, 2010), infectious disease management (Focosi, 2008), and immunization management among others (Kaewkungwal et al., 2010).

mHealth reach

mHealth apps and services were already used by more than one-third of Americans in 2014 (39%; Statista, 2017a). By 2018, almost half of all US respondents claimed to utilize mHealth apps (46%; Accenture, 2018a). Already in 2012, numbers suggested that consumers—on grounds of their high acceptance rates—are driving mHealth growth (Deloitte, 2012). While they do trust online health information, they also rely on online resources for recommendations on treatment options (63%; Deloitte, 2012). Hence, they are also responsible for the high demand in health apps. In 2012, the value of mHealth services was expected to reach almost 60 billion by 2020 (58.8%; Statista, 2017b). In early 2014, there were already more than 100,000 health apps available for download (Research2Guidance, 2014). According to IQVIA (2017), there are more than 300,000 mHealth apps available for download in 2017. In the last year, more than 75,000 apps had been added to major app stores (Research2Guidance, 2017). Following a 2018 mHealth market snapshot, there are almost 320,000 health-related apps available for download; when compared with 2015, the number almost doubled (Liquid State, 2018). In terms of market value, the mHealth sector was worth approximately USD 28 billion in 2018 but is expected to hit the USD 100 billion mark by 2023 (Liquid State, 2018), respectively USD 112 billion by 2025 (Grand View Research, 2017).

Following a 2018 Accenture survey, 75% of US respondents rate new technology as either very important or important to their health. Thereby, the most commonly eHealth managing tools concern websites (56%) as well as mobile phones (46%) (Accenture, 2018b). Acceptance among older patients is on the rise as well, with 16% of US consumers over 65 years of age reporting positive experiences with health-related technology (PWC, 2017). Drivers of mHealth popularity are multiple and concern its potential for cost reductions (Statista, 2017c) and its vast array of applicability, ranging from remote monitoring, diagnosing symptoms, consulting doctors, and complying with treatment or dietary regimes (Statista, 2017d). The benefits of new technology are also reflected in consumers' choices of general practitioners, with 79% of respondents claiming to prefer a doctor who can be contacted online or via a mobile device (Medical Economics, 2015), allowing not only for timely care but also accommodating patients' individual schedules (Accenture, 2018a, b). Almost 50% of consumers even indicate a willingness to change their providers for doctors who are more technologically savvy (Business Wire, 2018). Overall, doctors themselves believe that new technology can enhance patient's health experiences (93%; Health Works Collective, 2018).

The applicability of mHealth services is constantly growing on grounds of their numerous potentials, warranting increasing investments of 5.4 billion in 2016 (Research2Guidance, 2017). For instance, social networking sites award individuals (online) social assistance, offering both informational and emotional support to several parties, like patients, survivors, and family members (Hether et al., 2016; Murthy & Eldredge, 2016).

mHealth in developed and developing countries: State-of-the-art research

The tremendous growth of mobile devices does not only affect health in the developed world but also offers hope to vulnerable populations in resource-poor environments (United Nations Foundation, 2011). In the following, selected studies investigating apps that benefit both doctors and patients will be presented, whereby the authors purposely decided to capture the width of the field instead of focusing on a specific topic.

Developed countries

There is a plethora of fields in which mHealth technologies and solutions can be applied, which have also found their way to academic research. For instance, Singh, Wilkinson, and Braganza (2014) placed their study in the context of medical homes, respectively urban pediatric clinics, in the Bronx, New York, scrutinizing inasmuch mobile devices and services were used by urban pediatric clinics. Their cross-sectional study among teenagers and caregivers found that both groups did not only own multiple apps (on average 15) but also expressed an interest in utilizing these apps for medical purposes. Caregivers were, however, almost three times as likely as teenagers to utilize these apps or the Internet in general for health information retrieval.

In the nursing context, mHealth is attributed the potential to engage patients even outside the hospital setting, not only involving patients more into their healthcare but also enhancing their day-to-day healthcare and illness prevention activities (Samples, Ni, & Shaw, 2014). Likewise, Doswell, Braxter, DeVito Dabbs, Nilsen, and Klem (2013) attest mHealth a broader applicability in the nursing field, proposing to utilize mHealth in both nursing education and practice to improve the care of distantly located patients. Thus, mHealth could pave the way toward achieving consumer-centric nursing.

Mental health patients have also been found to rely on smartphones, respectively mobile apps. In their content of relevant articles published after conferences in the field, East and Harvard (2015) were able to demonstrate that counselors are key actors to promote health apps to affected patients, as—by providing engaging, stimulating, and interactive content—these can assist them in building up their cognitive capacities, while also advancing personal growth and improving mental health.

Smartphones and related apps also turned out to be promising tools for individuals completing substance use treatment, as suggested by Dahhne and Lejuez (2015). The authors concluded that owning devices and installing apps can benefit users to follow through with their treatment and continue to foster the development of treatment skills.

mHealth tools have also prominently been used in cardiovascular care (Chow, Ariyarathna, Islam, Thiagalingam, & Redfern, 2016). As exemplified by Australia, the diverse services of mHealth (such as apps, GPS, and Bluetooth) hold enormous potential; however, their use is not without risk. Therefore, the authors call for the repeated testing and evaluation of apps to ensure the safety and robustness of mHealth solutions.

Developing countries and rural areas

Following the WHO (2011, p. 1), mobile technology has the potential to "transform the face of health service delivery across the globe." Being characterized as the fastest growing sector in low-income countries (Pew, 2015), mHealth benefits from rapid advancements, more seamless solutions, and an ever-expanding availability of cellular services. This is also seen to put developing countries in general and remote areas in particular back on the map, which are claimed to see a redefinition of healthcare due to the introduction of mHealth solutions (Gurman, Rubin, & Roess, 2012). This is crucial as 70% of wireless subscribers can be found in low- respectively middle-income countries (WHO, 2011), where mHealth activity is very restricted. Moreover, the population in these countries falls victim to the national healthcare system, which does not prioritize mHealth development in most instances (WHO, 2011). Nonetheless, research has started to explore mHealth capacities and potentials for the developing part of the world in quite some depth.

In its mHealth for Development paper, the United Nations (2009, p. 5) attest mobile technologies enormous potential for improving healthcare in the developing world. The organization stresses the core benefits mHealth brings to rural areas, including "increased access to healthcare and health-related information, particularly for hard-to-reach populations, improved ability to diagnose and track diseases, timelier, more actionable public health information, [and] expanded access to ongoing medical education and training for health workers." While mHealth has improved over the years, most services are still in their trial stages, but appear to be promising future solutions. The report takes a look at more than 50 projects pursuing different health-related goals, such as (1) achieve education and raise awareness, (2) enable remote data collection, (3) enable remote monitoring, (4) facilitate communication and training for healthcare workers, (5) offer disease and epidemic outbreak tracking, and (6) provide diagnostic and treatment support.

In the case of medical doctors in Zimbabwe, however, mHealth was revealed to both benefit and hinder healthcare delivery at the same time. In the rural African setting, it was specifically doctors who felt overwhelmed with the use of mobile devices, citing their lack of knowledge and unawareness of mHealth use as a main hindrance to the implementation of these solutions. While they were convinced that mHealth had its benefits, they also stated that they were in desperate need for further education and advanced training before employing mHealth themselves (Marufu & Maboe, 2017).

With regard to diabetes treatment, which is the most important driver of mHealth as well as the leading mHealth therapy field (Research2-Guidance, 2017), mobile apps are meant to complement disease management besides diet optimization and regular exercise. Peng, Yuan, and Holtz (2016) discovered that through the utilization of mobile apps, self-management and compliance could be improved significantly in rural community settings. Yet, there are some barriers that need to be addressed when developing future apps for chronic disease management. Chronic disease management via mHealth solutions is also discussed by Anstey Watkins et al. (2018). In their "realistic review," the authors suggest that interventions can be indeed successful, especially if they are based on existing frameworks and theories. They go about identifying several main components that determine mHealth's positive outcomes in low-resource settings (Kenya, Pakistan, Honduras, Mexico, and South Africa), such as reminders, patient observation, or advice among others. Similar results were obtained by Mburu and Oboko (2018). Locating their study in a low-resource setting in sub-Saharan Africa, the authors examined whether mHealth is a suitable intervention tool for an environment that is characterized not only by a lack of suitable medical facilities and health workers but also by a predominantly illiterate and culturally diverse audience. Despite a high mobile penetration (90%), apps can only be effective if the design caters to the users' needs and requirements, making usability a key aspect of interventions. mHealth services are also able to appeal to the interests of cancer survivors in less developed areas. According to McCarthy, Matthews, Battaglia, and Meek (2018), a nurse-led telemedicine-based intervention was able to improve sleep results by breast cancer survivors in rural Western US territories, positively affecting sleep latency and sleep efficiency.

When assisting community workers in underdeveloped areas, mobile apps present a fruitful approach as well. Related to maternal and infant death in rural India, community workers have turned to mHealth to improve their performance—an advantage, from a societal perspective. Nonetheless, the cost-saving potential of these solutions benefits society and a replication in other low-resource settings as recommended by the authors (Prinja et al., 2018). Likewise, Hegde et al. (2018) discuss the implementation of a toll-free service line in rural India, assisting community workers in catering to their clients in an improved manner. A study with a similar scope was conducted in Guatemala, which found that in the case of the indigenous Maya population, the reliance of a birth attendant via mHealth was shown to be reflected in higher referral rates to facility-level care (Martinez et al., 2018).

In addition, it is absolutely crucial to foster mHealth development for conditions that affect vulnerable populations to the largest extent. One example is cardiovascular disease, which accounts for one-third of all deaths in low- or middle-income countries (Nilsen et al., 2012). Finally, one of the biggest issues affecting developing countries is that health initiatives utilizing mHealth services are short-lived. For instance, in Uganda alone, 23 out of 36 mHealth projects did not go beyond the trial phase (Tomlinson, Rotheram-Borus, Swartz, & Tsai, 2013), leading governments, care providers, as well as industry representatives to utter calls to scale these projects.

mHealth—usability and design aspects

Chomutare, Fernandez-Luque, Arsand, and Hartvigsen (2011) conducted a literature review on mobile diabetes app features and contrasted their findings with evidence-based guidelines on app design. Their sample consisted of roughly 140 apps, whose primary functions concerned insulin, respectively medication monitoring, data recording and communication with primary care providers, diet recording, and weight management. The authors stress the existence of gaps between evidence-based recommendations and actual app functionality. Arnhold, Quade, and Kirch (2014) carried out a systematic review of available diabetic apps, paying special attention to app functions, languages, available interfaces, etc. Furthermore, they determined the apps' suitability for a specific target group, namely patients 50 years and older. Out of more than 650 apps, slightly more than half offered one function of the functions mentioned before; the same number of apps also allowed for documentation. Apps were predominantly free of charge, directed at patients, and specifically targeted to the English-speaking population. In terms of usability, the authors rated the apps as comprehensible, allowing for text to be read aloud, catering to the interests, respectively needs, of an aging population. In a study on the same subject, Williams and Schroeder (2015) proposed to grasp the potential of minorities as potential target groups and highlight the necessity to include not only different language interfaces but also basic (educational) features, reminder functions, and connective buttons in future diabetes apps.

Both tailoring and customization have become buzz words in recent years. For mHealth solutions, this implies that user needs and preferences already need to be borne in mind during the development and/or design phase. Following Schnall et al. (2016), the Information Systems Research (ISR) framework presents a fruitful approach to ensure mHealth user centricity. Consisting of needs assessment, functional requirement identification and user interface design, the ISR can be understood as a holistic and comprehensive model to turn to in the course of the individual development stages, which are nourished by both end-user feedback (as collected via different research methods) and expert guidance, ultimately enriching the end product. However, this requires continuous testing and feedback loops (Heath, 2015). A guideline for app developers is often also offered by related parties; for instance, it is issued by the Swiss Government's Health Suisse initiative.[1]

mHealth—acceptance, use, and promotion

mHealth can only be fruitful and present beneficial solutions, if usage rates and acceptance are high. Davies, Kotadia, Mughal, Hannan, and

---

[1] For further information, please see https://www.e-health-suisse.ch/fileadmin/user_upload/Dokumente/2018/E/180731_Leitfaden_fuer_App_Entwickler_def_EN.pdf.

Algarni (2015), for instance, inquired the attitudes of three important stakeholder groups toward mHealth apps, namely those of pharmacists, pharmacy students, and the general public. Their study found low usage of mHealth apps among the general public (1.5%) as well as among pharmacists and the student population. Age was found to be an important determinant of use, with younger respondents being more likely to employing apps. Training was found to be an important variable as well, with pharmacists being willing to assist the public (82%), which would be responsive to receiving such guidance (84%). Apart from educational input, also design aspects and promotion of mHealth solutions are regarded as necessary components for success by the authors. Another study from England looking at how mobile apps are used by diverse stakeholders revealed that while half of the pharmacists inquired were aware of mHealth apps' existence, only slightly more than a half recommended these apps to their patients. Among the general population, apps were used not that frequently, whereby especially low usage rates were reported for diabetic patients. While users enjoyed the apps, low awareness and usage rates still need to be overcome (Kayyali et al., 2017). Among Latinos, who are more prone to incur diabetes and more likely to suffer from complications, Spanish language apps were reported to allow for blood glucose reporting, medication diaries, and activity logs. The prior two functionalities were reportedly most commonly used among the 1600 respondents. Yet, as the affected population lacks awareness of the existence of such apps, benefits are only moderately pronounced (Williams & Schroeder, 2015). Thus, a stronger promotion of health-related apps seems to be advantageous.

With regard to both physical and mental health treatment, mHealth applications were shown to benefit self-guided care tremendously. The authors conducted a literature review consisting of 27 studies, according to which mHealth services were able to improve healthcare efficacy, while reducing stress, anxiety, and related conditions (Rathbone & Prescott, 2017). Rubanovich, Mohr, and Schueller (2017) scrutinized the use of health apps by individuals suffering from depression and anxiety. Roughly, one quarter of their study population made use of an app treating mental health; but those deploying apps did so on a daily basis and showed a high acceptance. Functionalities that were most appealing to users were their access to health-related data, training, and habit building.

For adolescents, chronic health conditions continue to pose serious health threats. As this population is especially prone to using new technologies, mHealth interventions are encouraged. Following a study by Badawy et al. (2017), mobile services (including text messaging and applications) hold the potential to lastingly improve medication adherence among young adults, enjoying high levels of acceptability.

Yet, their study review hinted at some important research gaps, including the long-term effects and cost-effectiveness of these solutions. A more modest efficiency of mHealth apps was attested by Badawy and Kuhns (2017), who call for a uniform design to compare results in the future.

mHealth also serves as a potential companion for pregnant women. Overdijkink et al. (2018) determined in their review of 29 studies that when app acceptance is moderate to high, positive effects can be noted, including a decreased gestational weight gain, increased vegetable and fruit consumption, and decreased infection potentials among others. Tamony, Holt, and Barnard (2015) determined that use among this particular population suffering from diabetes was very limited; consequently, awareness could be improved through direct communication possibilities with an immediate healthcare team. Nonetheless, the majority of participants still favored direct communication over mobile-enhanced interaction; the preference for direct communication should then be elaborated on in future research projects.

In the case of bipolar disorder, a review of mHealth solutions on the Australian continent was conducted. With regard to app content, slightly more than one-third was found to provide information, while approximately two-thirds of the apps assisted individuals in managing their conditions. Privacy concerns were only addressed by about one quarter. In terms of app usefulness, the authors identified some shortcomings, as critical information (e.g., medication or sleep) was not recorded. Hence, the authors advised to use these tools with caution (Nicholas, Larsen, Proudfoot, & Christensen, 2015).

Anderson, Burford, and Emmerton (2016) considered mHealth an essential facilitator of self-care, conducting a qualitative study to inquire user experiences. Utilizing the technology acceptance model (TAM) and the mobile application rating scale as a theoretical foundation, they identified four thematic themes as indicated by the study participants: usage engagement, technical functionality, ease of use and design appeal, and data management. Overall, users were convinced of the apps' benefits and informed the research team that usability and functionality were core aspects that fostered their adoption processes.

mHealth and theory development

Following Kasl and Cobb (1966), health (communication) can be broadly classified into health behavior theories, illness behavior theories, and sick behavior theories. In recent years, the first class has been redefined by Glanz, Rimer, and Lewis (2002) into theories of "health promotion and preventive behavior," while the third category has become known as "disease management" theories (Clark, Gong, & Kaciroti, 2001). The most prominent theories include the health belief model (HBM), theory of reasoned action (TRA), theory of planned behavior, the process of behavioral change, or the behavioral change wheel (BCW) among others (for an overview, please see Clark & Houle, 2009 and Cocoran, 2007).

Among the wide range of health theories available, behavioral research theories have dominated the discussion. In Morrison's (2015) study, the author herself discovered a lot of conceptual frameworks and models to exist, which can guide intervention planning and development, such as the elaboration likelihood model or social cognitive theory; however, insufficient attention has been given to existing theories and these psychological concepts' potentials to inform the optimal implementation and delivery of the design features commonly used in digital health behavior change interventions. She thus urges researchers in this area to formulate additional theory-based guidance to optimize mHealth solutions.

Presuming that mHealth discussions cannot do without a solid theoretical foundation, some authors managed to bridge the gap between theory and practice. For instance, Wozney et al. (2017) set out to test how the highly effective eMental healthcare could be implemented into healthcare systems. Turning to BCW, the authors were able to demonstrate that three core conditions characteristic for the BCW could be improved through mHealth interventions, namely individual capabilities (e.g., by acquiring necessary knowledge and skills to implement eMental health services), motivations (e.g., by reducing waiting times), and opportunities (e.g., by bringing about improvements through improvements through collaboration between academics, end users, and professional health providers).

Another theory that has been useful in describing mHealth phenomena is the Uses and Gratification Approach. This model regards individuals as active information seekers who select, out of the many sources available, the most appropriate information source to fulfill their individually unfulfilled needs. For the digital age, the authors posit that people turn to the Internet as a competing source of information to look for the information they need since doctors do not provide them with satisfying health information. Time constraints during provider–patient consultations are cited as a main reason for turning to online health information (Faith, Thorburn, & Smit, 2015).

TAM has also been given more consideration in the healthcare context. A study by Becker (2016) looked into the acceptance of mobile mental health applications by young adults in Germany to identify factors that positively impacted app use. They start out by describing people's intentions to use mobile treatment applications, extending the traditional TAM which has been used in the past to access the acceptance and adaption of new medical applications. His findings suggest that knowledge about the existence and clinical effectiveness of mobile mental health applications is considerably low. And while mobile apps are generally considered to be easy to use, young adults question their effectiveness in treating mental problems alongside data privacy issues, inhibiting their acceptance of such tools and services. The author highlights the necessity to improve the acceptance and increase future usage and recommends that mobile mental health applications should be promoted as a supporting tool which is always available to everyone and can facilitate mental treatment.

In the mHealth context, Zhang, Gou, Lai, Guo, and Li (2014) turned to the TRA to explain gender differences in mHealth adoption in China. By use of a slightly modified TRA (i.e., by integrating nonlinearities between attitude and subjective norms as well as the moderating effect of gender), the authors identified adoption intention of mHealth services to be subject to facilitating conditions (e.g., resources, time, knowledge), attitudes toward new technologies, as well as subjective norms. Also, the nonlinearity between respondents' attitudes and subjective norms toward mHealth adoption intention was found to offer greater insights into explaining adoption behavior than the linear model. Overall, men were uncovered to be more likely to adapt health-related mHealth technology than women. The model was also found to explain the proposed relations better for the male population than the female population, highlighting that technology acceptance as well as adoption must not neglect the influence of gender.

Both the influence of age and gender in the context of mHealth acceptance was also analyzed by using protection motivation theory (PMT). Guo, Han, Zhang, Dang, and Chen (2015) presume mHealth adoption to be subjected not only to technology-related aspects but also—first and foremost—to health-related aspects. For this reason, they link adoption of mHealth to the PMT's core variables of threat appraisal and coping appraisal. The authors discovered that, besides gender and age, both threat appraisal and coping appraisal influence mHealth adoption intention through attitude toward mHealth technology. In detail, the effect of perceived vulnerability and perceived severity (threat appraisal factors) on attitude toward mHealth was reported to be stronger for women and older respondents than for men and younger respondents. Interestingly, reverse results are reported for coping appraisal factors (response efficacy and self-efficacy), which were found to be more pronounced for men and younger respondents. While gender and age can be claimed to play moderating roles with threat appraisal and coping appraisal, they play different roles in the acceptance of mHealth.

Another more tailored model to investigate the usability of mHealth offerings is the Health IT Usability Evaluation Model (Health-ITUEM). Brown, Yen, Rojas, & Schnall (2013) called for a more elaborate understanding as to assessing mHealth usability, which is seen as crucial since the use of mHealth technology rapidly increases. By use of focus groups, they initially determined consumers' health information needs, while in a second step tested consumers responses to an existing mHealth app. While the first study identified important categories that can be used to assess mHealth usability (error prevention, completeness, memorability, information needs, flexibility/customizability, learnability, performance speed, competency, and other outcomes), the second study found performance speed (i.e., efficient use; 21%), other outcomes (35%; integration of offline services), and information needs (29%; information needed for task performance) to be the most frequently occurring codes, while memorability of the task (2.5%) and error prevention (0.5%) were the least frequently listed categories. Nevertheless, the study was able to demonstrate the usefulness of the Health-ITUEM in evaluating mobile health technology usability.

There are quite a high number of scientific articles that discuss eHealth, paying particular attention to its behavioral change potentials (e.g., Faith et al., 2015; Vandelanotte et al., 2016; Wozney et al., 2017). In line with her colleagues, Vandelanotte et al. (2016) observe that eHealth interventions—if tailored to the target audience's needs—can lead to positive short-term changes in individual behaviors. Little, however, is known about the long-term effects of such apps and services. This might also be grounded in the fact that most apps are developed without the help of behavioral experts, suggesting that evidence-based theories are seen as secondary in mHealth intervention planning and development and, thus, also missing from the academic discourse. The authors hence plead for the inclusion of behavior theories into the mHealth research agenda to make apps profitable and successful (Vandelanotte et al., 2016).

It is without question that the emergence of mHealth also calls for the development of new measurement instruments. For instance, for the purpose of testing consumers' motivation to engage with new technology in a healthcare context, Dewar, Bull, Malvey, and Szalma (2016) introduced the mHealth Technology Engagement Index, an innovative measure that links motivation to accept new technology to autonomy, competence, relatedness, goal attainment, and goal setting. The index was found to be reliable across interface and device type and was further found to be valid across time. Future studies are recommended to take up this measure in order to account for the ongoing technological developments affecting the medical sector.

The examples given above illustrate that some studies have started to link eHealth and mHealth to existing theories in an attempt to bridge the boundaries between theory and practice. However, there is still room for improvement, as hardly any studies take up HBM, PMT, or the extended parallel process model as their theoretical foundation. As such, these topics definitely invite future research.

Future outlook and research agenda

The present contribution looked at how mHealth has changed and—in part—even revolutionized traditional notions of health and healthcare. Conditioned by technological advancements, mHealth has started to rise in relevance, assisting in the attainment of the United Nation's Sustainable Development Goal of "health for all." Over the years, the scope of mHealth applicability has been broadened, comprising not only health but also fitness and wellness. In consequence, usage is on the rise globally, allowing individuals to become more engaged in their healthcare. Besides individuals, also healthcare workers and practitioners benefit from mobile services, which are able to bring care to vulnerable populations and rural areas. Yet, improvement in health app design is desirable and missing from most recent publications, as are links to established health communication models and theories.

Thus, future research on mHealth should try to overcome the disadvantages and research gaps identified before. Most studies to date have inquired the use, usability, acceptance, and effectiveness of selected smart phone features (e.g., text messages or apps), while the overall impact of selected initiatives have been left to scrutiny (Fiordelli et al., 2013). In their review, the authors uncovered that almost half of the studies dealt with the potentials of text messaging, while voice assistance (12%), video (6%), and multimedia delivery methods (3%) received rather limited attention (Fiordelli et al., 2013). Moreover, studies addressing mHealth's long-term effects are missing from the debate (Gurman et al., 2012). In order to raise awareness for mHealth solutions, communication campaigns might be useful in familiarizing the general public, respectively selected target audiences, with the services, highlighting individual benefits and health-related gains. One form that is also increasingly utilized by journalists and advertisers is storytelling, defined as telling messages as emotional stories. To date, it has been tested and deemed suitable for raising breast cancer awareness among women, whereby recipients of such messages have been found to be more willing to initiate discussions on the topic as well as share their experiences with other peer group members (Cueva et al., 2015). mHealth has been suggested to bring about innovations; however, little is known as to whether mHealth applications have grasped technology's innovative potential to date. Hence, future studies should address this aspect following the example of Ali, Chew, and Yap (2015). Moreover, gamification might offer an enormous potential to promote and stimulate health-supportive behaviors (Papastergiou, 2009). This might also be facilitated by apps, which are more consumer-centric and tailored to individual interests and needs (Schnall et al., 2016; Williams & Schroeder, 2015). In addition, industry guidelines listing relevant design components are recommended.

The ethical aspects of app design are addressed by Sharp and O'Sullivan (2017). Their literature review revealed that while privacy and security are commonly taken up in academic research, ethical issues receive only limited attention. The authors encourage to do more in-depth studies on selected ethical aspects in mHealth, as these are likely to impact individual app usage. Likewise, the authors emphasize that ethical issues already need to be thematized in the app design process, suggesting that the development of guidelines might assist developers in taking up the most important issues at an early stage. Selected aspects warranting further research also concern data protection or data encryption, as suggested by Silva, Rodrigues, Canelo, Lopes, and Zhou (2013) or Gurman et al. (2012) (also see on Advantages and Disadvantages of Digital Health Information section).

Yet, the use of mHealth applications is not without problems, as the extent to which such services or tools are successful in enabling the adoption of new and desired behaviors can vary drastically. Some apps are more effective than others, some are free to download, while others require a nominal or substantial charge, contradicting the WHO's and UN's desperate call to ensure "health for all." It is important to note that costs alone are not indicative of app quality or service effectiveness. This is important because the use of health apps by the public is likely to increase in the future, for healthcare professionals have started to realize the potential of mHealth in personalized healthcare (Fitzgerald & McClelland, 2017). Therefore, practitioners need to be better informed regarding what makes a health app appealing to users and successful as an intervention to facilitate behavior change—not temporarily, but in the long run. Future investigations should also investigate the increasing role of virtual reality, augmented reality, and digital reality in the healthcare sector (Deloitte, 2019), which is expected to amount to USD 1.5 billion by 2025 (Medical Simulation Training, 2017). Summarizing, there are a lot of interesting research areas in the mHealth sector, which warrant further research.

References

Abidi, S. (Ed.). (2015). *Mobile health: A technology road map*. Wiesbaden: Springer.

Accenture. (2018a). *Accenture 2018 consumer survey on digital health*. Retrieved from: https://www.accenture.com/us-en/insight-new-2018-consumer-survey-digital-health?utm_source=newsletter&utm_medium=email&utm_campaign=newsletter_axiosvitals&stream=top-stories.

Accenture. (2018b). *2018 consumer survey on digital health: US results*. Retrieved from: https://www.accenture.com/t20180306T103559Z__w__/us-en/_acnmedia/PDF-71/accenture-health-2018-consumer-survey-digital-health.pdf.

Adams, R. J., Stocks, N. P., Wilson, D. H., Hill, C. L., Gravier, S., Kickbusch, I., & Beilby, J. J. (2009). Health literacy. A new concept for general practice? *Australian Family Physician, 38*(3), 144−147.

Ali, E. E., Chew, L., & Yap, K. Y.-L. (2015). *Evolution and current status of mHealth research: A systematic review. BMJ of innovation*. Online first: 05 January 2016. https://doi.org/10.1136/bmjinnov-2015-000096.

Anderson, K., Burford, O., & Emmerton, L. (2016). Mobile health apps to facilitate self-care: A qualitative study of user experiences. *PLoS One, 11*(5). https://doi.org/10.1371/journal.pone.0156164.

Anstey Watkins, J., Goudge, J., Gómez-Olivé, F. X., Huxley, C., Dodd, K., & Griffiths, F. (2018). mHealth text and voice communication for monitoring people with chronic diseases in low-resource settings: a realist review. *BMJ of Global Health, 3*(2), 1—15.

Arnhold, M., Quade, M., & Kirch, W. (2014). Mobile applications for diabetics: A systematic review and expert-based usability evaluation considering the special requirements of diabetes patients age 50 years or older. *Journal of Medical Internet Research, 16*(4), 104.

Atkinson, N. L., Saperstein, S. L., & Pleis, J. (2009). Using the internet for health-related activities: Findings from a national probability sample. *Journal of Medical Internet Research, 11*(1), e4.

Ba, S., & Wang, L. (2013). Digital health communities: The effect of their motivation mechanisms. *Decision Support Systems, 55*(4), 941—947.

Badawy, S. M., Barrera, L., Sinno, M. G., Kaviany, S., O'Dwyer, L. C., & Kuhns, L. M. (2017). Text messaging and mobile phone apps as interventions to improve adherence in adolescents with chronic health conditions: A systematic review. *Journal of mHealth and uHealth, 5*(5), 66.

Badawy, S. M., & Kuhns, L. M. (2017). Texting and mobile phone app interventions for improving adherence to preventive behavior in adolescents: A systematic review. *Journal of mHealth and uHealth, 5*(4), 50.

Banos, O., Amin, M. B., Khan, W. A., Afzal, M., Hussain, M., Kang, B. H., & Lee, S. (2016). The mining minds digital health and wellness framework. *BioMedical Engineering Online, 15*, 76.

Bashshur, R., Shannon, G., Krupinski, E., & Grigsby, J. (2011). The taxonomy of telemedicine. *Telemedical Journal of Electronic Health, 17*(6), 484—494.

Becker, D. (2016). Acceptance of mobile mental health treatment applications. *Procedia Computer Science, 98*, 220—227.

Berry, D. (2007). *Health communication. Theory and practice.* New York: Open University Press.

Bhavnani, S. P., Narula, J., & Sengupta, P. P. (2016). Mobile technology and the digitization of healthcare. *European Heart Journal, 37*(18), 1428—1438.

Bischoff, W. R., & Kelley, S. J. (1999). 21st century house calls: The internet and the world wide web. *Holistic Nursing Practices, 13*(4), 42—50.

Brown, W., Yen, P.-Y., Rojas, M., & Schnall, R. (2013). Assessment of the health IT usability evaluation model (Health-ITUEM) for evaluating mobile health (mHealth) technology. *Journal of Biomedical Informatics, 46*(6), 1080—1087.

Buchanan, D. R. (2000). *An ethic for health promotion: Rethinking the sources of human well-being.* New York: Oxford University Press.

Buckley, J. (2004). Pharmaceutical marketing — time for change. *Electronic Journal of Business Ethics and Organization Studies, 9*(2), 4—11.

Buntin, M. B., Jain, S. H., & Blumenthal, D. (2010). Health information technology: Laying the infrastructure for national health reform. *Health Affairs, 29*, 1214—1219.

Business Wire. (2018). *NTT DATA study finds nearly two-thirds of consumers expect their healthcare digital experience to be more like retail.* Retrieved from: https://www.businesswire.com/news/home/20180305005288/en/NTT-DATA-Study-Finds-Two-Thirds-Consumers-Expect.

Cassil, A. (2008). *Rising rates of chronic health conditions: What can be done? Issue Brief No. 125.* Retrieved from: http://www.hschange.com/CONTENT/1027/.

Chomutare, T., Fernandez-Luque, L., Arsand, E., & Hartvigsen, G. (2011). Features of mobile diabetes applications: Review of the literature and analysis of current applications compared against evidence-based guidelines. *Journal of Medical Internet Research, 13*(3), 65.

Chow, C. K., Ariyarathna, N., Islam, S. M., Thiagalingam, A., & Redfern, J. (2016). *Heart Lung and Circulation, 25*(8), 802—807.

Ciemins, E., Coon, P., & Sorli, C. (2010). An analysis of data management for diabetes self-management: Can smart phone technology keep up? *Journal of Diabetes Science and Technology, 4*, 958—960.

Clark, N. M., Gong, M., & Kaciroti, N. (2001). A model of self-regulation of control for chronic disease. *Health Education and Behavior, 28*(6), 769–782.

Clark, N. M., & Houle, C. R. (2009). Theoretical models and strategies for improving disease management by patients. In S. A. Shumaker, J. K. Ockene, & K. A. Riekert (Eds.), *The handbook of health behavior change* (3rd ed., pp. 19–37). New York: Springer.

Cline, R. J., & Haynes, K. M. (2001). Consumer health information seeking on the Internet: The state of the art. *Health Education Research, 16*(6), 671–692.

Cocoran, N. (2007). Theories and models in communicating health messages. In N. Cocoran (Ed.), *Communicating health: Strategies for health promotion* (pp. 5–31). London: Sage.

Cueva, M., Kuhnley, R., Revels, L., Schoenberg, N. E., & Dignan, M. (2015). Digital storytelling: A tool for health promotion and cancer awareness in rural Alaskan communities. *International Journal of Circumpolar Health, 74*(1). https://doi.org/10.3402/ijch.v74.28781.

Dahhne, J., & Lejuez, C. W. (November 2015). Smartphone and mobile application utilization prior to and following treatment among individuals enrolled in residential substance use treatment. *Journal of Substance Abuse Treatment, 58*, 95–99.

Davies, M. J., Kotadia, A., Mughal, H., Hannan, A., & Algarni, H. (2015). The attitudes of pharmacists, students and the general public on mHealth applications for medication adherence. *Pharmacy Practice (Grenada), 13*(4), 644.

Deloitte. (2012). *mHealth in an mWorld: How mobile technology is transforming health care.* Retrieved from: https://www2.deloitte.com/us/en/pages/life-sciences-and-health-care/articles/center-for-health-solutions-mhealth-in-an-mworld.html.

Deloitte. (2019). *2019 global health care outlook.* Retrieved from: https://www2.deloitte.com/global/en/pages/life-sciences-and-healthcare/articles/global-health-care-sector-outlook.html.

Dewar, A. R., Bull, T. P., Malvey, D. M., & Szalma, J. L. (2016). Testing the reliability of a measure of motivation to engage with telehealth technology. *Journal of Telemedicine and Telecare, 23*(2), 248–255.

Doswell, W. M., Braxter, B., DeVito Dabbs, A., Nilsen, W., & Klem, M. L. (2013). mHealth: Technology for nursing practice, education, and research. *Journal of Nursing Education and Practice, 3*(10), 99–109.

East, M. L., & Harvard, B. C. (2015). Mental health mobile apps: From infusion to diffusion in the mental health social system. *Journal of Mental Health, 31*(2/1), 10.

Eng, T. R., & Gustafson, D. H. (1999). *Wired for health and well-being the emergence of interactive health communication. Science panel on interactive communication and health.* Washington, DC: Office of Disease Prevention and Health Promotion US Department of Health and Human Services.

Ewles, L., & Simnett, I. (2003). *Promoting health: A practical guide* (5th ed.). Edinburgh: Bailliere Tindall.

Eysenbach, G. (2001). What is eHealth? *Journal of Medical Internet Research, 3*(2), e20.

Faith, J., Thorburn, S., & Smit, E. (2015). Body mass index and the use of the Internet for health information. *Health Education Journal, 75*(1), 94–104.

Fiordelli, M., Diviani, N., & Schulz, P. J. (2013). Mapping mHealth research: A decade of evolution. *Journal of Medical Internet Research, 15*(5), 95.

Fitzgerald, M., & McClelland, T. (2017). What makes a mobile app successful in supporting health behaviour change? *Health Education Journal, 76*(3), 373–381.

Ferguson, T. (1997). Health online and the empowered medical consumer. *Journal of Quality Improvement, 23*(5), 251–257.

Focosi, D. (2008). Smartphone utilities for infectious dieses specialists. *Clinical Infectious Diseases, 47*, 1234–1235.

Fox, S. (2005). *Health information online* (pp. 1–16). Washington, DC: Pew Internet and American Life Project.

Fox, S., & Rainie, L. (2002). *The online health care revolution: How the Web helps Americans take better care of themselves.* Washington, DC: Pew Internet and American Life Project.

Franklin, P. D., Farzanfar, R., & Thompson, D. (2009). E-health strategies to support adherence. In S. A. Shumaker, J. K. Ockene, & K. A. Riekert (Eds.), *The handbook of health behavior change* (pp. 169–190). New York: Springer.

Free, C., Phillips, G., Lambert, F., Galli, L., Patel, V., & Edwards, P. (2010). The effectiveness of M-health technologies for improving health and health services: A systematic review protocol. *BMC Research Notes, 3,* 250.

Friedman, M., & Gould, J. (2007). Consumer attitudes and behaviours associated with direct-to-consumer prescription drug marketing. *Journal of Consumer Marketing, 24*(2), 100–109.

Glanz, K., Rimer, K. B., & Lewis, F. M. (2002). The scope of health behavior and health education. In K. Glanz, B. K. Rimer, & F. M. Lewis (Eds.), *Health behavior and health education: Theory, research, and practice* (3rd ed., pp. 3–21). San Francisco: Jossey-Bass.

Grand View Research. (2017). *mHealth apps market size worth $111.8 billion by 2025 | CAGR: 44.2%.* Retrieved from: https://www.grandviewresearch.com/press-release/global-mhealth-app-market.

Guo, X., Han, X., Zhang, X., Dang, Y., & Chen, C. (2015). Investigating m-health acceptance from a protection motivation theory perspective: Gender and age differences. *Telemedicine and eHealth, 21*(8), 661–669.

Gurman, T. A., Rubin, S. E., & Roess, A. A. (2012). Effectiveness of mHealth behavior change communication interventions in developing countries: A systematic review of the literature. *Journal of Health Communication, 17*(1), 82–104.

Hall, A. K., Stellefson, M., & Bernhardt, J. M. (2012). Healthy aging 2.0: The potential of new media and technology. *Preventing Chronic Disease, 9,* E67.

Health Works Collective. (2018). *Mobile medical apps: A game changing healthcare innovation.* Retrieved from: https://www.healthworkscollective.com/mobile-medical-apps-a-game-changing-healthcare-innovation/.

Heath, S. (2015). *How mHealth technology supports patient engagement strategies.* Retrieved from: https://patientengagementhit.com/features/how-mhealth-technology-supports-patient-engagement-strategies.

Hegde, S. K. B., Saride, S. P., Kuruganty, S., Banker, N., Patil, C., & Phanse, V. (2018). Large-scale mHealth professional support for health workers in rural Maharashtra, India. *WHO South Eastern Asian Journal of Public Health, 7*(1), 51–57.

Henkel, J. (2002). *Buying drugs on-line: It's convenient and private, but beware of 'rouge sites'.* FDA Consumer Magazine. Retrieved from: http://www.fda.gov/Drugs/EmergencyPreparedness/BioterrorismandDrugPreparedness/ucm137269.htm.

Hether, H. J., Murphy, S. T., & Valente, T. W. (2016). A social network analysis of supportive interactions on prenatal sites. *Digital Health, 0,* 2–12.

Huntington, P., Nicholas, D., Homewood, J., Polydoratou, P., Gunter, B., & Russell, C. (2004). The general's public use of (and attitudes towards) interactive, personal digital health information and advisory services. *Journal of Documentation, 60*(3), 245–265.

IMS Health. (2015). *IMS Health Marktbericht Entwicklung des deutschen Pharmamarktes im Juli 2015.* Retrieved from: http://www.imshealth.com/files/web/Germany/Marktbericht/IMS_Pharmamarktbericht_Juli_2015.pdf.

IMS Health. (2017). *Patient adoption of mHealth: Use, evidence and remaining barriers to mainstream acceptance.* Retrieved from: https://www.iqvia.com/-/media/iqvia/pdfs/institute-reports/patient-adoption-of-mhealth.pdf?la=en&hash=B3ACFA8ADDB143F29EAC0C33D533BC5D7AABD689.

IQVIA. (2017). *The growing value of digital health: Evidence and impact on human health and the healthcare system.* Retrieved from: https://www.iqvia.com/institute/reports/the-growing-value-of-digital-health.

Istepanian, R. S. H., Laxminarayan, S., Pattichis, & Constantinos, S. (2006). *M-Health: Emerging mobile health systems. Topics in biomedical engineering.* Boston, MA: Springer.

Kaewkungwal, J., Singhasivanon, P., Khamsiriwatchara, A., Sawang, S., Meankaew, P., & Wechsart, A. (2010). Applicating of smart phone in "better border healthcare program": A module for mother and child care. *Medical Information and Decision Making, 10,* 69.

Kasl, S. V., & Cobb, S. (1966). Health behavior, illness behavior, and sick-role behavior. *Archives of Environmental Health, 12*(4), 531–541.

Kayyali, R., Peletidi, A., Ismail, M., Hashim, Z., Bandeira, P., & Bonnah, J. (2017). Awareness and use of mHealth apps: A study from England. *Pharmacy: Journal of Pharmacy, Education and Practice, 5*(2), 33. https://doi.org/10.3390/pharmacy5020033.

Koinig, I. (2016). *Pharmaceutical advertising as a source of consumer self-empowerment. Evidence from four countries.* Wiesbaden: Springer.

Koinig, I., Diehl, S., & Mueller, B. (2017). Are pharmaceutical ads affording consumers a greater say in their health care? The evaluation and self-empowerment effects of different ad appeals in Brazil. *International Journal of Advertising, 36*(6), 945–974.

Laugesen, J., Hassanein, K., & Yuan, Y. (2015). The impact of internet health information on patient compliance: A research model and an empirical study. *Journal of Medical Internet Research, 17*(6), e143. https://doi.org/10.2196/jmir.4333.

Liquid State. (2018). *The rise of mHealth apps: A market snapshot.* Retrieved from: https://liquid-state.com/mhealth-apps-market-snapshot/.

Lupton, D. (2014). Self-tracking modes: reflexive self-monitoring and data practices. *Social Science Research Network. SSRN Electronic Journal.* https://doi.org/10.2139/ssrn.2483549.

Lupton, D. (2016). Digitized health promotion: Risk and personal responsibility for health in the Web 2.0 era. In J. Davis, & A. M. Gonzalez (Eds.), *To fix or to heal: Patient care, public health, and the limits of biomedicine* (pp. 152–176). New York: New York University Press.

Luxton, D. D., McCann, R. A., Bush, N. E., Mishkind, M. C., & Reger, G. M. (2011). mHealth for mental health: Integrating smartphone technology in behavioral healthcare. *Professional Psychology: Research and Practice, 42*(6), 505–512.

Makovsky. (2015). *Fifth annual "Pulse of Online Health" survey finds 66% of Americans eager to leverage digital tools To manage personal health.* Retrieved from: http://www.makovsky.com/insights/articles/733.

Martin, T. (2012). Assessing mHealth: Opportunities and barriers to patient engagement. *Journal of Health Care for the Poor and Underserved, 23,* 935–941.

Martinez, B., Ixen, E. C., Hall-Clifford, R., Juarez, M., Miller, A. C., Francis, A., … Rohloff, P. (2018). mHealth intervention to improve the continuum of maternal and perinatal care in rural Guatemala: a pragmatic, randomized controlled feasibility trial. *Reproductional Health, 15*(1), 120.

Marufu, C., & Maboe, K. A. (2017). Utilisation of mobile health by medical doctors in a Zimbabwean health care facility. *Health SA Gesondheid, 22,* 228–234.

Mburu, S., & Oboko, R. (2018). A model for predicting utilization of mHealth interventions in low-resource settings: Case of maternal and newborn care in Kenya. *BMC for Medical Information Decision Making, 18*(1), 67.

McCarthy, M. S., Matthews, E. E., Battaglia, C., & Meek, P. M. (2018). Feasibility of a telemedicine-delivered cognitive behavioral therapy for insomnia in rural breast cancer survivors. *Oncology Nursing Forum, 45*(5), 607–618.

Medical Economics. (2015). *Engaging patients to decrease costs and improve outcomes.* Retrieved from: https://www.medicaleconomics.com/medical-economics/news/engaging-patients-decrease-costs-and-improve-outcomes.

Medical Simulation Training. (2017). *The future of medical training potentially lives in virtual reality.* Retrieved from: https://medicalsimulation.training/technology/future-medical-training-vr-technology/.

Menon, A. M., Deshpande, A. D., Perry, M., & Zinkhan, G. M. (2002). Trust in on-line prescription drug information among internet users: The impact on information search behavior after exposure to direct-to-consumer advertising. *Health Marketing Quarterly, 20*(1), 17–35.

Morolla, C. (2019). *Information and communication technology for sustainable development.* Boca Raton, FL: Taylor and Francis.

Morrison, L. G. (2015). Theory-based strategies for enhancing the impact and usage of digital health behaviour change interventions: A review. *Digital Health, 1,* 1–10.

Murthy, D., & Eldredge, M. (2016). Who tweets about cancer? An analysis of cancer-related tweets in the USA. *Digital Health, 2*, 1–16.

Nestoriuc, Y., Martin, A., Rief, W., & Andrasic, F. (2008). Biofeedback treatment for headache disorders: A comprehensive efficacy review. *Applied Psychophysiology and Biofeedback, 33*, 125–140.

Nicholas, J., Larsen, M. E., Proudfoot, J., & Christensen, H. (2015). Mobile apps for bipolar disorder: A systematic review of features and content quality. *Journal of Medical Internet Research, 17*(8), 198.

Nilsen, W., Kumar, S., Shar, A., Varoquiers, C., Wiley, T., Riley, W. T., ... Atienza, A. A. (2012). Advancing the science of mHealth. *Journal of Health Communication, 17*, 5–10.

Overdijkink, S. B., Velu, A. V., Rosman, A. N., van Beukering, M. D., Kok, M., & Steegers-Theunissen, R. P. (2018). The usability and effectiveness of mobile health technology-based lifestyle and medical intervention apps supporting health care during pregnancy: Systematic review. *Journal of mHealth and uHealth, 6*(4), 109.

Palermo, T. M., Eccleston, C., Lewandowski, A. S., Williams, A. C., & Morley, S. (2010). Randomized controlled trials of psychological therapies for management of chronic pain in children and adolescents: An updated meta-analytic review. *Pain, 148*, 387–397.

Papastergiou, M. (2009). Exploring the potential of computer and video games for health and physical education: A literature review. *Computers and Education, 53*, 603–622.

Peng, W., Yuan, S., & Holtz, B. E. (2016). Exploring the challenges and opportunities of health mobile apps for individuals with type 2 diabetes living in rural communities. *Telemed Journal of Electronic Health, 22*(9), 733–738.

Pew. (2013). *Health online 2013*. Retrieved from: http://www.pewinternet.org/2013/01/15/health-online-2013/.

Pew. (2015). *Internet seen as positive influence on education but negative on morality in emerging and developing nations*. Retrieved from: http://assets.pewresearch.org/wp-content/uploads/sites/2/2015/03/Pew-Research-Center-Technology-Report-FINAL-March-19-20151.pdf.

President's Cancer Panel. (2016). *Improving cancer-related outcomes with connected health — Part 1: Growing role of technology in society and health*. Retrieved from: https://prescancerpanel.cancer.gov/report/connectedhealth/Part1.html.

Prinja, S., Bahuguna, P., Gupta, A., Nimesh, R., Gupta, M., & Thakur, J. S. (2018). Cost effectiveness of mHealth intervention by community health workers for reducing maternal and newborn mortality in rural Uttar Pradesh, India. *Cost Effectiveness and Resource Allocation, 16*, 25.

PWC. (2017). *Top health industry issues of 2018: A year for resilience amid uncertainty*. Retrieved from: https://www.pwc.com/us/en/health-industries/assets/pwc-health-research-institute-top-health-industry-issues-of-2018-report.pdf.

Rathbone, A. L., & Prescott, J. (2017). The use of mobile apps and SMS messaging as physical and mental health interventions: Systematic review. *Journal of Medical Internet Research, 19*(8), 295.

Research2Guidance. (2014). *mHealth app developer economics 2014: the state of the art of mHealth app publishing*. Retrieved from: https://www.fer.unizg.hr/_download/repository/research2guidance-mHealth-App-Developer-Economics-2014.pdf.

Research2Guidance. (2017). *mHealth app economics 2017: Current status and future trends in mobile health*. Retrieved from: http://www.uzelf.org/wp-content/uploads/2017/12/R2G-mHealth-Developer-Economics-2017-Status-And-Trends.pdf.

Rice, R. (2004). *Influences, usage, and outcomes of Internet health information searching: Multivariate results from selected Pew surveys*. Retrieved from: http://www.escholarship.org/uc/item/0m10f3x5.

Rice, R. E., & Katz, J. E. (2001). *The Internet and health communication: Experiences and expectations*. Thousand Oaks: SAGE.

Rod, M., & Saunders, S. (2004). The informative and persuasive components of pharmaceutical promotion: An argument for why the two can coexist. *International Journal of Advertising, 28*(2), 313–349.

Rubanovich, C. K., Mohr, D. C., & Schueller, S. M. (2017). Health app use among individuals with symptoms of depression and anxiety: A survey study with thematic coding. *Journal of Mental Health, 4*(2), 22. https://doi.org/10.2196/mental.7603.

Samples, C., Ni, Z., & Shaw, R. J. (2014). Nursing and mHealth. *International Journal of Nursing Sciences, 1*(4), 330—333.

Schiavo, R. (2007). *Health communication: From theory to practice.* San Francisco: Wiley and Sons.

Schiavo, R. (2014). *Health communication: From theory to practice* (2nd ed.). San Francisco: Jossey-Bass.

Schnall, R., Rojas, M., Bakken, S., Brown, W., Carballo-Dieguez, A., Carry, M., ... Travers, J. (2016). A user-centered model for designing consumer mobile health (mHealth) applications (apps). *Journal of Biomedical Informatics, 60,* 243—251.

Sharp, M., & O'Sullivan, D. (2017). Mobile medical apps and mHealth devices: A framework to build medical apps and mHealth devices in an ethical manner to promote safer use — a literature review. *Studies in Health Technology and Informatics, 235,* 363—367.

Silva, B. M., Rodrigues, J. J., Canelo, F., Lopes, I. C., & Zhou, L. (2013). A data encryption solution for mobile health apps in cooperation environments. *Journal of Medical Internet Research, 15*(4), 66.

Singh, A., Wilkinson, S., & Braganza, S. (2014). Smartphones and pediatric apps to mobilize the medical home. *Journal of Pediatrician, 165*(3), 606—610.

Sonnenberg, F. A. (1997). Health information on the Internet: Opportunities and pitfalls. *Archives of Internal Medicine, 157,* 151—152.

Spain, J. W., Siegel, C. F., & Ramsey, R. P. (2001). Selling drugs online: Distribution-related legal/regulatory issues. *International Marketing Review, 18*(4), 432—449.

Statista. (2017a). *Availability of selected telemedicine practices to U.S. patients as of 2014.* Available via Statista. Retrieved from: https://www.statista.com/statistics/419533/availability-of-selected-telemedicine-practices-to-us-patients/.

Statista. (2017b). *mHealth (mobile health) industry market size projection from 2012 to 2020 (in billion U.S. dollars)*.* Available via Statista. Retrieved from: https://www.statista.com/statistics/295771/mhealth-global-market-size/.

Statista. (2017c). *Cost drivers where mobile health will have the highest positive impact worldwide in the next five years, as of 2016*.* Available via Statista. Retrieved from: https://www.statista.com/statistics/625219/mobile-health-global-healthcare-cost-reductions/.

Statista. (2017d). *Mobile health app categories that will offer the highest global market potential in the next five years, as of 2016*.* Available via Statista. Retrieved from https://www.statista.com/statistics/625181/mobile-health-app-category-market-potential-worldwide/.

Statista. (2017e). *Potential cost savings in health care by mHealth in 2014.* Available via Statista. Retrieved from: https://www.statista.com/statistics/449430/potential-mhealth-cost-savings-in-health-care/.

Stokes, J., Noren, J., & Shindell, S. (1982). Definition of terms and concepts applicable to clinical preventive medicine. *Journal of Community Health, 8*(1), 33—41.

Street, R. (2003). Communication in medical encounters. An ecological perspective. In T. L. Thompson, A. M. Dorsey, K. I. Miller, & R. Parrott (Eds.), *Handbook of health communication* (pp. 63—93). Mahwah, NJ: Erlbaum.

Svalastog, A. L., Donev, D., Jahren Kristoffersen, N., & Gajović, S. (2017). Concepts and definitions of health and health-related values in the knowledge landscapes of the digital society. *Croation Medical Journal, 58*(6), 431—435.

Tamony, P., Holt, R., & Barnard, K. (2015). The role of mobile applications in improving alcohol health literacy in young adults with type 1 diabetes: Help or hindrance? *Journal of Diabetes Science and Technology, 9*(6), 1313—1320.

Taylor, D. J., & Roane, B. M. (2010). Treatment of insomnia in adults and children: A practice-friendly review of research. *Journal of Clinical Psychology, 66,* 1137—1147.

Tomlinson, M., Rotheram-Borus, M. J., Swartz, L., & Tsai, A. C. (2013). Scaling up mHealth: Where is the evidence? *PLoS Medicine, 10*(2). https://doi.org/10.1371/journal.pmed.1001382.

Tones, K., & Tilford, S. (2001). *Health promotion: Effectiveness, efficiency and equity* (3rd ed.). Cheltenham: Nelson Thornes.

Torgan, C. (2009). *The mHealth summit: Local and global converge.* Retrieved from: http://caroltorgan.com/mhealth-summit/.

Twibell, D., & Anzalone, M. (2001). *DTC on the web: Fad or fundamental?* DTC Perspectives (pp. 28–29). May/June(2001).

UN. (2017a). *Goal 3: Ensure healthy lives and promote well-being for all at all ages.* Retrieved from: http://www.un.org/sustainabledevelopment/health/.

United Nations. (2009). *mHealth for development: The opportunity of mobile technology for healthcare in the developing world. UN foundation-vodafone foundation partnership.* Retrieved from: http://www.globalproblems-globalsolutions-files.org/unf_website/assets/publications/technology/mhealth/mHealth_for_Development_full.pdf.

United Nations Foundation. (2011). *mHealth for development. The opportunity of mobile technology for healthcare in the developing world.* Available via United Nations Foundation. Retrieved from: https://web.archive.org/web/20121203014521/http://vitalwaveconsulting.com/pdf/2011/mHealth.pdf.

Vandelanotte, C., Müller, A. M., Short, C. E., Hingle, M., Nathan, N., Williams, S. L., ... Maher, C. A. (2016). Past, present, and future of eHealth and mHealth research to improve physical activity and dietary behaviors. *Journal of Nutrition Education and Behavior, 48*(3), 219–228.

Viswanath, K. (2005). Science and society: The communications revolution and cancer control. *National Review of Cancer, 5*(10), 828–835.

WHO. (1946). *Preamble to the constitution of WHO as adopted by the international health conference.* New York, 19 June - 22 July 1946. Retrieved from: http://www.who.int/suggestions/faq/en/.

WHO. (2011). *mHealth new horizons for health through mobile technologies.* Retrieved from: http://www.who.int/goe/publications/goe_mhealth_web.pdf.

WHO. (2013). The right to health. Available via WHO. Retrieved from http://www.who.int/mediacentre/factsheets/fs323/en/.

White, M., & Dorman, S. M. (2001). Receiving social support online: Implications for health education. *Health Education Research, 16*(6), 693–707.

Williams, J. P., & Schroeder, D. (2015). Popular glucose tracking apps and use of mHealth by latinos with diabetes: Review. *Journal of mHealth and uHealth, 3*(3), 84.

Williams, P., Huntington, P., & Nicholas, D. (2003). Health information on the Internet: A qualitative study of NHS direct online users. *Aslib Proceedings, 55*(5/6), 304–312.

Wozney, L., Newton, A. S., Gehring, N. D., Bennett, K., Huguet, A., Hartling, L., ... McGrath, P. (2017). Implementation of eMental health care: Viewpoints from key informants from organizations and agencies with eHealth mandates. *BMC Medical Informatics and Decision Making, 17*(1), 1–15.

Wu, J., Tombor, I., Shahab, L., & West, R. (2017). Usability testing of a smoking cessation smartphone application ('SmokeFree Baby'): A think-aloud study with pregnant smokers. *Digital Health, 3*, 1–9.

Zhang, X., Gou, X., Lai, K. H., Guo, F., & Li, C. (2014). Understanding gender differences in m-health adoption: A modified theory of reasoned action model. *Telemedicine and eHealth, 20*(1), 39–46.

10

At the nexus of participatory design and action research: Use of a public online forum in designing text messages for dads

Emily M. Cramer[1], Alexis K. Marsh[2]

[1] Howard University, Washington, DC, United States; [2] Washington University in St. Louis, St. Louis, MO, United States

The deadbeat or doofus dad envisioned through the lens of popular media—lazy (Homer from *The Simpsons*), oblivious (Daddy Pig from *Peppa Pig*), incompetent (Ray from *Everybody Loves Raymond*), even a bit deranged (Hal from *Malcolm in the Middle*; Peterson, 2013)—belies what the literature purports to be true: that fathers are a vital presence in the life of a child. In fact, extant research continues to show us the detrimental effects of father absence. Children living without the presence of a dad are at greater risk for alcohol and substance abuse (Mandara & Murray, 2006; Mandara, Rogers, & Zinbarg, 2011; Patock-Peckham, & Morgan-Lopez, 2007), physical abuse and maltreatment (Alexandre, Nadanovsky, Moraes, & Reichenheim, 2010; Bendheim-Thomas Center for Research on Child Wellbeing and Social Indicators Survey Center, 2010; Hilton, Harris, & Rice, 2015), criminal activity (Allen & Lo, 2012; Cobb-Clark & Tekin, 2014; Coley & Medeiros, 2007), decreased educational attainment (Gillette & Gudmunson, 2014), emotional and behavioral problems (Bocknek, Brophy-Herb, Fitzgerald, Schiffman, & Vogel, 2014; Hofferth, 2006), poverty (Nepomnyaschy, Miller, Garasky, & Nanda, 2014), risky sexual activity and teenage pregnancy (Antecol & Bedard, 2007; Burn, 2008; Ellis et al., 2003; Hendricks et al., 2005; Lang et al., 2013), and suicidal ideation (Reed, Bell, & Edwards, 2011; Vaszari, Bradford, Callahan O'Leary, Ben Abdallah, & Cottler, 2011).

Technology and Health
https://doi.org/10.1016/B978-0-12-816958-2.00010-1

Despite the crucial role of their presence and involvement, fathers generally feel they need to spend more time with their children (Pew Research Center, 2017a), and 48% of working fathers would like to be home with their kids but work obligations—and the need for income—pull them away (Parker & Wang, 2013). Fathers continue to spend just over half the time as mothers on childcare and are somewhat less likely to rate themselves as doing an excellent or very good job parenting, compared with mothers. Fifty-three percent of Americans, and 56% of men, feel that mothers do a better job than fathers caring for a new baby (Pew Research Center, 2017b). Additionally, 63% of fathers feel it is harder to be a dad today than it was a generation ago (Taylor, Parker, Livingston, Wang, & Dockterman, 2011).

Dads may need more help in boosting confidence and developing parenting skills. Hence, the overarching focus of the Text4Dads project, launched in 2015, was to use mobile messaging (mHealth) as a source of empowerment for fathers. Equipped with the aim to promote a father's sense of self-efficacy (see Bandura & Adams, 1977) by sharing informative and validating text messages, we turned to the individuals who we believed would know the most about supporting fathers: dads themselves, along with stakeholders invested in fatherhood work. Thus, this chapter describes the first phase of the Text4Dads project, the use of a public online forum to acquire feedback on a series of mobile messages for expectant/recent fathers.

During this phase, we used a methodological approach blending principles of participatory action and participatory design research (PDR) in the development of message content. Drawing from a public health methodology, participatory action research (PAR) engages both researchers and participants in reflective and collaborative inquiry and, subsequently, action to improve health conditions and experiences (Baum, MacDougall, & Smith, 2006). PDR—rooted in technological development and usability disciplines—engages participants through an interactive and iterative process of designing artifacts and systems to be used by the participants themselves (Spinuzzi, 2005).

We employed principles from PAR/PDR in engaging fatherhood stakeholders to review and comment on a set of father-focused messages that would ultimately be disseminated via mobile phone. By visiting an online, public forum, participants rated 67 messages—to be sent during a partner's pregnancy as well as after birth—on a range of criteria having to do with the content of the messages as well as the features of the technology itself. This chapter demonstrates ways PAR and PDR can be used via an online public forum to inform health research design, specifically the development of mobile messages.

Mobile health

According to Hall, Cole-Lewis, and Bernhardt (2015), mobile health (mHealth) is the "application of mobile technologies, including phones, tablets, telemonitoring, and tracking devices, to support and enhance the performance of health care and public health practice" (p. 394). A growing base of research exists on the topic of mHealth, specifically mobile messaging as a conduit for health behavior change. Hall et al. (2015) examined 15 systematic reviews and meta-analyses of mobile text-messaging, distilling outcomes associated with 89 unique mHealth intervention studies focused on health promotion, disease prevention, and chronic disease self-management. The researchers concluded that nearly all reviews and meta-analyses reported positive behavioral and health outcomes across the domains under study, demonstrating that mHealth may be a viable option in improving and managing health. At the same time, authors of the original 15 studies reported several limitations (e.g. lack of rigorous study designs, small sample sizes, short intervention durations, and lack of representative study populations and environments). Hall and colleagues conclude the review by recommending that future studies in mHealth should (a) focus on specific health behaviors and outcomes, populations, setting, and text-messaging intervention characteristics; (b) include multimedia messaging service components; and (c) evaluate the cost-effectiveness of specific mHealth programs.

The current study responds to recommendations from previous work (Hall et al., 2015) by reaching out to a new population—expectant/recent fathers, as well as fatherhood stakeholders—and by aiming to increase specific health outcomes: paternal efficacy and father engagement.

Perinatal education and tech-based interventions

Researchers have found both success and challenges in the development and implementation of mHealth interventions for expectant/recent parents. mHealth information services such as Text4Baby, a free service of the nonprofit National Healthy Mothers, Healthy Babies Coalition, deliver pertinent information to expectant/recent mothers (Text4Baby, 2017). The Health Resources and Services Administration (Health Resources and Services Administration, 2015) of the U.S. Department of Health and Human Services completed a mixed-method evaluation of Text4Baby and found that 90% of participant mothers read the messages and found them easy to understand, and 64% thought the messages were useful. Moreover, Text4Baby participants demonstrated a significantly higher level of knowledge on four critical topics—safe sleep, infant feeding, best time to deliver in a healthy pregnancy, and the meaning of full term—when compared to participants who did not receive the Text4Baby messages. As of 2017, Text4Baby sends three messages to fathers with the goal of providing critical information about supporting the mother, fatherhood engagement, and health and safety tips for the baby (Dads Matter, 2017). The mobile messages used in the Text4Baby served as an exemplar for the current study, as the father-focused messages we designed were intended to be engaging and educational.

With the rising interest in mHealth interventions for pregnant women and new mothers, some studies have measured the development and implementation of mobile technology, and mobile messages geared toward expectant/recent fathers so that they too benefit from gains in knowledge and parental efficacy. Lee and Walsh (2015), offering seminal work in this area, developed mobile messages for the mDad (Mobile Device Assisted Dad) smartphone application with the intent to focus on father-friendly content for expectant/recent fathers. Preliminary focus groups carried out by the researchers found that fathers had multiple parenting-support needs including finding ways to engage with young children and infants, learning about children's growth and development, and gaining effective coparenting and communication skills. Once content was developed around these needs by social workers and psychologists, Lee and Walsh (2015) conducted usability and acceptability interviews with fathers from diverse backgrounds, including African American fathers and military fathers. Overall, fathers in the study found the smartphone application interesting and reported appreciating suggestions for activities with infants, the ability to track their child's development, and the opportunity to allow shared participation with a coparent (Lee & Walsh, 2015).

A key step in delivering mobile messages to expectant/recent fathers involves ensuring that mobile message content includes credible and relevant information regarding the needs of the father. Lee and Walsh (2015) point out that the process requires substantial investment: for example, the development, revision, and tailoring of mobile message content takes considerable time and resources to (a) conduct multiple rounds of acceptability and usability testing by perinatal and fatherhood experts, (b) gather feedback at multiple time points through focus groups comprising fathers from diverse backgrounds, and (c) test the application and messages with the population in a beta setting. For these reasons, along with goals to streamline the message review process and provide transparency among mobile message reviewers, the current study highlights the use of a public online forum to share mobile message content with fatherhood and perinatal professionals. To date, no study we have found uses an online forum in developing the content and design of an mHealth intervention. However, we believe such a method is aligned with the PAR/PDR approaches in that it increases community engagement within research and design processes.

Participatory action research

PAR is a theoretical and methodological research paradigm involving both researcher(s) and communities under study as collaborative participants in generating knowledge that ultimately informs action (Coghlan & Brydon-Miller, 2014). Inherent to PAR is an agenda of social change borne through empowering local participants to take an active role in identifying and solving problems in their communities. What differentiates this process of inquiry from conventional forms of research is its (a) focus on enabling action rather than expanding a theoretical corpus, (b) attention to structures of power and advocating for equality among researcher and researched, and (c) contextualization of information gathered within the lived experience of community members (Baum et al., 2006).

The work of PAR often is described as cyclical, moving through stages of constructing the study and diagnosing the issue, planning for action, taking action, and then evaluating the action (Coghlan & Brannick, 2014). The methodology blends critical theory and constructivism and can involve both qualitative methods and quantitative methods as research collaborators cycle through the PAR process (Baum et al., 2006). For example, a community needs assessment—helpful to diagnosing the issue—may be constructed through surveys as well as interviews and focus groups with community stakeholders.

In the realm of health, PAR has been used to uncover processes and discover solutions in a range of health domains such as cerebral palsy (Gross et al., 2018), end-of-life care (Marsh, Gartrell, Egg, Nolan, & Cross, 2017), epilepsy (Varley, Power, Saris, & Fitzsimons, 2017), and pediatric cancer (Wikman et al. 2018). In the realm of maternal and child health, a number of PAR studies across various countries demonstrate successful outcomes in using the approach (in 2018, see, for example, Esienumoh, Allotey, & Waterman, 2018; Jones et al., 2018).

At the time of this writing, however, few studies have been identified that use PAR in conjunction with fathers. Daly, Ashbourne, and Brown (2009) drew from PAR in a qualitative study on Canadian fathers' perceptions of how their children influenced their identities and personal development. In the study, fatherhood researchers, practitioners, family members, and the fathers themselves developed a research agenda leading to policy recommendations to support fathers' well-being. In the

United Kingdom, Meek (2007) used a form of PAR in offering parenting education for a group of 75 fathers in prison. Participants reported appreciating the flexible, needs-based approach to the course. A group of Danish fathers, mothers, and health professionals were engaged via PAR to develop principles for a father-friendly neonatal unit (Noergaard, Johannessen, Fenger-Gron, Kofoed, & Ammentorp, 2016).

Participatory design research

Coming out of the Scandinavian Design Movement of the late 1970 and 1980s (see, for example, Ehn, 1990; Nygard, 1979), PDR examines technical communication—oftentimes referred to as human-computer interaction—by "establishing mutual learning situations between users and designers" (Simonsen & Hertzum, 2012, p. 10). Both participant users and research designers work together to construct and interpret an emerging technological design (Spinuzzi, 2005). PDR involves engaging all stakeholders as active participants with roles and responsibilities integral to the process of design (Participate in Design, 2018). The result—ideally—is an artifact, system of work, or work environment that grows out of and is reflective of a collaborative user-designer effort (Spinuzzi, 2005).

Not surprisingly, PDR also can be situated historically in notions of action research (Spinuzzi, 2005) and therefore shares several characteristics with PAR. First, like PAR, PDR aims to produce designs that lead to individual, organizational, and technological change (Simonsen & Hertzum, 2012; Vines, Clarke, Wright, McCarthy, & Olivier, 2013). The notion of "transcendence" often accompanies this work, in that stakeholders are challenged to let go of current practices and imagine unaccounted-for possibilities, with the goal to improve peoples' lives. Second, PDR and PAR share the attempt to emancipate power structures inherent to conventional research (Vines et al., 2013). Both user and designer are perceived to be stakeholders of equal value in the design process. Third, PDR as a sustained practice is iterative, moving in a cycle quite similar to PAR, from problem identification to design to trial to evaluation, circling back to previous steps based on outcomes (Simonsen & Hertzum, 2012).

Halskov and Hansen (2015), in a review of PDR literature from 2002 to 2012, note that, although PDR was originally deployed primarily in the workplace context, a relatively new domain for PDR is the healthcare sector. Kelly and Matthews (2010), for example, engaged with preusers of insulin-injection devices and hearing aids to forecast potential benefits and barriers of technologies they may need to use in the future. Björgvinsson and Hillgren (2004) discovered, through PDR, that an on-the-spot experiment in the form of self-produced videos by intensive care unit nurses could be a helpful learning tool.

Two recent PDR studies offer insight into our work with fatherhood stakeholders in designing a corpus of mobile messages for expectant/ recent fathers. Owens et al. (2011) engaged users and clinicians in a text message program to reduce repetition of self-harm. Study participants reported a preference for individualized rather than generic, one-size-fits-all messages, which ultimately led users to author their own self-efficacy messages to store and then review during times of crises. Another study (Hess et al., 2008), albeit with a media software company, employed the principles of PDR with an online community looking to design a new software. The researchers argued that virtual communities can overcome spatial limitations and reflect a shared interest in a project. Both participant users and researcher designers reported shared learning, a high level of motivation to engage with the online community, and a willingness to engage with the community again in future development.

Methods

As stated earlier, the first phase of the Text4Dads mHealth initiative was to gather fathers and fatherhood stakeholders on a public online forum to review a series of mobile messages that ultimately would be sent to expectant/recent fathers. The goal was to develop a corpus of messages containing informative, supportive, stakeholder-generated information delivered to fathers during pregnancy and infancy milestones. Armed with information deemed useful by forum participants, fathers receiving the messages would perceive an increased sense of self-efficacy in preparing or caring for their child.

Investigators aimed to adopt PAR and PDR approaches in our engagement of fatherhood stakeholders for this phase. The researchers advocated for equality in posting the messages publicly on the forum and welcoming all thoughts and feedback (i.e., ratings and comments) from the fatherhood stakeholder community as to the content of messages and the outreach design. We felt the online forum could minimize a sense of status that oftentimes characterizes offline research (see Suler, 2004).

Message development

Message development began with an assessment of the information needs of fathers. Previous research with expectant/recent fathers (Cramer, 2018) found dads' information needs to be diverse, ranging from responsible parenting and childcare to government and community resources, employment, and birth control, particularly among low-income groups. Additional high-impact areas were identified based on compiling and analyzing existing literature and scholarly work. We searched article databases with current related-research and also health and government websites such as Mayo Clinic. All articles identified were housed in a shared folder.

Once we had a solid database of literature, we began drafting messages—oftentimes translating a 20+ page research article into a 160-character text message. For example, an article by Leerkes and Burney (2007) revealed that a strong network of social support for a new father increased his sense of efficacy after the birth of the child. The finding was then parsed down to the following message: "A confident dad has a solid support system. Be sure to talk with your partner, family & friends about your experiences with baby."

A drafted message was then added to an Excel spreadsheet containing the following information: week/day to send, message number, message itself, character amount, scholarly source, and action required (e.g. an action would be a link to another website for additional information). Messages were then reviewed for style, structure, relevance to the target audience, diversity of topics, order of content, and foundation in the literature.

Sample and procedures

The study was approved by the Institutional Review Board of a small, independent private college located in the suburbs of a large Midwest urban area. Participants, representing government, academic, community, health, and volunteer/lay organizations across the United States and abroad, agreed to review father-focused pregnancy and infancy text messages posted to a public online forum (www.muut.com/text4dads). Recruitment began in June 2015, with participants responding to a mailed letter sent by the researchers, an e-mail sent via Mailchimp by the researchers, or a request posted to the Fatherhood Research & Practice Network listserv (900 contacts). In total, 59 individuals participated in reviewing the text messages (59/986 = 6% response rate). No compensation was provided beyond the opportunity to add a logo to our research website.

In July 2015, participants were invited to log onto a public forum (muut.com/text4dads) to provide feedback on 67 text messages to be sent to expectant/recent fathers depending on stage of child development (see Appendices 10.1 and 10.2 for both pregnancy and infancy messages). Before posting, participants had to create an account on the forum, which enabled them to choose a display name and/or photo that would accompany posts in the forum. In this way, participants could manage their own degree of anonymity on the site.

Response length ranged from simply providing a number evaluating the messages (see Evaluation Criteria and Analysis below) or in-depth feedback offering critique, suggestions, or additional resources to enhance message content. When the forum closed on August 21, 2015, participants had logged 194 suggestions to improve the texts messages—suggestions identifying concerns and issues inherent to fatherhood work and to the technology to be designed.

Evaluation criteria and analysis

After logging onto the forum, participants were asked to review pregnancy and infancy messages posted in a PDF format on the site. Then, they were encouraged to provide feedback in six areas: breadth/depth of content, connectivity, accessibility, relevance, and rigor of the messages. The six evaluation criteria, developed by the researchers, were featured as "channels" in the forum. By clicking on the "Breadth of Content" channel, for example, the participant could respond to the following prompt: "Please rate the breadth of content ($1 = $ poor, $2 = $ fair, $3 = $ good, $4 = $ excellent) of the text messages and share your thoughts and suggestions. Breadth of content refers to the quantity of the topic areas covered by the text messages" (see Figs. 10.1 and 10.2 for examples):

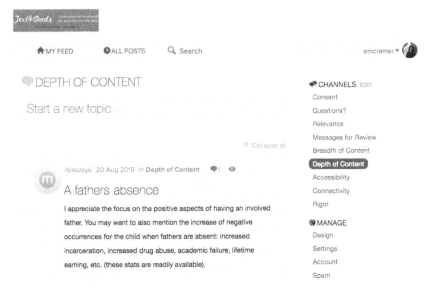

FIGURE 10.1 Depth of Content comments on Text4Dads muut public forum (www. muut.com/text4dads).

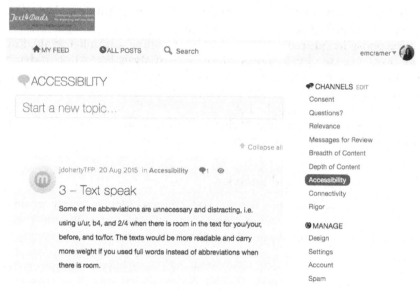

FIGURE 10.2 Accessibility comments on Text4Dads muut public forum (www.muut.com/text4dads).

- As stated above, *breadth of content* referred to the quantity of the topic areas covered by the text messages. 24 individuals commented on the channel, with 9 ($n = 9$) offering ratings on the messages on a scale from 1 to 4 ($M = 3.44$; $SD = 0.53$).
- *Depth of content* referred to the quality of the topic areas covered by the text messages and the extent participants felt certain topics should be covered more comprehensively. 32 individuals commented on the messages' depth of content, and 11 ($n = 11$) rated the messages on a scale from 1 to 4 ($M = 3.55$; $SD = 0.52$).
- *Relevance* referred to the extent participants felt the messages were helpful to fathers. 11 ($n = 11$) out of 18 participants on this channel rated the messages on a scale from 1 to 4 ($M = 3.23$; $SD = 0.68$).
- *Accessibility* indicated the extent to which messages were easily read and understood. Out of 18 participants who posted on this channel, 11 ($n = 11$) rated the messages on a scale from 1 to 4 ($M = 3.27$; $SD = 0.47$).
- *Connectivity* referred to the extent to which messages linked out to other resources that may be helpful to fathers. 17 out of 20 participants ($n = 17$) rated the message on the scale from 1 to 4 ($M = 3.65$, $SD = 0.50$).
- *Rigor* had to do with the extent messages were grounded in evidence. 14 individuals commented on the rigor of the messages

and 14 ($n = 14$) rated the messages on the scale from 1 to 4 ($M = 4.0$, $SD = 0$).

- *General*—49 additional suggestions, comments, or questions were posted in the forum.

After the forum closed, 194 suggestions were analyzed deductively, using a directed content analysis approach conceptualized by Hsieh and Shannon (2005). Directed content analysis involves the development of initial coding categories derived from existing theoretical frameworks. Researchers can either choose to (a) identify concepts or variables and then define them using theory as a guide or (b) use predetermined codes derived from the theory. In the case of this study, we opted to identify concepts inherently related to the six evaluation criteria and then define those concepts using PAR or PDR approaches.

In reviewing fatherhood stakeholder feedback on the forum, comments related to the content of the messages and any other issues that may influence how fathers connect with and react to the messages at a demographic and psychographic level were considered the realm of PAR. Issues raised by stakeholders such as the father's relationship with the mother of the child, residence status, education and reading level, mental health, and employment situation were identified as reflective of the lived experience of participants and requiring action in the form of changing the number, order, and content of the messages themselves. PDR, with its emphasis on "technochange" (see Markus, 2004) driving individual and organizational change, was conceptualized as addressing issues inherent to the use of the technology in connecting with fathers. We invited participants not only to reflect on the topics communicated in the messages but also connectivity and accessibility issues accompanying the use of mobile messaging. Thus, we engaged both participant users and designer researchers in the process of cooperative design, with an aim to improve the self-efficacy of expectant/recent fathers via information delivered through mobile messaging.

First, the researchers made several global passes through the content—reading the suggestions in their entirety to get a sense of their scope. We initially identified PAR concepts as associated with comments made in the breadth and depth of content and relevance channels as well as some general comments. These comments had to do with the experience of being a father (lived experience) as well as actions fathers can take to improve confidence or skills (action for change). Subthemes found under these conceptual headers were identified and defined (see Results section).

The researchers then conducted another pass through the data for PDR principles by zeroing in on accessibility, connectivity, and general comments about the technology. We found these comments to be associated with PDR concepts of connectivity and accessibility—issues inherent to product design. Subthemes found within these concepts were identified, defined, and are reported in the Results section.

Following the directed coding process, a final pass was made across the suggestions to ensure data were captured within the themes identified. We agreed the themes functioned well in representing the suggestions made by forum visitors.

Results

The following themes were identified by research paradigm: *PAR*: staying safe and attention to emotional health and efficacy; *PDR*: reformatting for relationship type; deleting text speak; and increasing linkage, apps, and interactivity.

Staying safe

Within the realm of PAR, many forum participants felt more could be covered with regard to the safety of the child. Safe sleep was a substantial theme, with many stakeholders advocating for more text messages encouraging safe sleeping habits at nighttime. Stakeholders also suggested text messages about testing for lead poisoning, smoking/guns in the home, never leaving a baby unattended in a car, and getting the child immunized.

Two additional safety issues emerged in the forum: a focus on assisting dads with a crying baby and observing a child's cognitive development. One participant suggested a statement about "not shaking babies," while another offered a lengthy tip about supporting dads when babies cry:

> I think there could be some added information for Dads on what to do, or what to expect when baby cries, and they get frustrated. Unfortunately, the data tells us that fathers (or mothers boyfriends) are most often the perpetrators in the abuse deaths of infants. And in most cases - the perpetrators are young, between the ages of 20–24 years of age. [These dads] ... probably have low threshold or tolerance for meeting the demands of a crying or cranky infant. I think some messaging and links to strategies for developing coping skills and referring to Dads specific parenting groups might be helpful.

The participant states that young fathers may not be mentally able to manage a fussy or crying baby and shares research suggesting a father's role in infant-related abuse deaths. Coping skills and support groups are cited as ways to ensure dads and children stay safe.

Several participants also stressed the importance of focusing on a child's cognitive development: "the scope of the text messages would benefit   from   additional   information   focusing   on   language comprehension, language expression, and general cognition." In support of the effectiveness of early intervention, another emphasized being mindful of signs of autism.

Attending to emotional health and efficacy

Father stakeholders posting in the forum felt the text messages could be inclusive of the social and emotional health of fathers and mothers. Several focused on the toll postpartum depression (PPD) can take on the mother as well as her relationship with the father. One participant stressed:

> At a bare minimum, validation of emotional challenges during pregnancy and first year of birth for both mother and father seems to be required.

Finding support for both the mother and the father during pregnancy and infancy was emphasized. One participant suggested directly asking text message recipients "Are you feeling worried, depressed or anxious? Do you have someone to talk to?" Another mentioned data that states paternal PPD increases when the mother experiences PPD. Another group of participants requested more information about how a father's health impacted the health of the baby.

In addition to addressing emotional health, many stakeholders focused on ways a father's efficacy during pregnancy and after birth could be addressed. Accompanying the child's mother on visits to the doctor and asking questions was widely supported across participants. Many mentioned the effectiveness of skin-to-skin contact with baby (i.e., kangaroo care). Reading to baby was stressed as a way to ensure involvement and offer support. And—with a nod to PAR—one participant wrote "I think dads will really like the actionable texts—where they are given ideas of things they can do to help their babies develop." The participant felt that fathers would benefit from concrete suggestions that could translate into action steps to take with their child.

Reformatting for relationship type

Within the PRD paradigm, a primary concern of participants was that the content of the messages excluded fathers not in relationship with the mother of the child. A considerable number of suggestions posted in the forum had to do with the text messages being more mindful of the many iterations of a father's relationship with the mother of the child. Some participants felt the initial messages were irrelevant or "inappropriate" for fathers who were not in a relationship with the child's mother. To remedy this issue, one participant chose a technological solution: the development of a minimum of two sets of messages based on the user's relationship to the mother of the child.

> ... consider having two separate bodies of texts (and possibly more) to accommodate very different populations. Dads cohabiting with pregnant partners are very different than dads living apart from a pregnant partner. (Further, there are even differences between married dads and dads who are cohabiting but unmarried.) 90 percent of the messages would be the same, but slight nuances could make the recipients much more comfortable remaining involved with the long-term period of messaging in order to keep coming back and reading these texts.

The suggestion calls for a substantial change in the formatting of the messages, in that users would essentially be "tracked" based on relationship status. Another participant also supported a similar "segmentation:"

> In general it feels like the tone of the messages targets a father that is involved in a relationship with the mom and will be living with the baby—I'm concerned that this will leave out fathers in other situations: adoptive fathers, single fathers, fathers in military, unmarried fathers that will care for baby in their own home, unmarried fathers that can't see baby due to incarceration or conflict with mother, etc. Can you ask ... about the situation and then segment messages based upon response?

Another participant shared a similar sentiment:

> ... especially with young fathers ... in marginalized communities where infant mortality is an especially large problem, the mother's parents might view the dad as an undesirable and try to stifle his involvement. Perhaps Text4Dads could ask at the outset, right after asking the due date or date of birth, whether the dad's situation is warm or cold in relationship to the mother's family, and then tailor at least some of the subsequent messages for fathers who need help, advice, suggestions and encouragement.

The participants both envision a technology whereby the user would be routed to a specific set of messages aligning with his unique relationship with the mother of the child.

Deleting text speak

Conventional forms of SNS messaging limit the number of characters available in a text message to 160. Therefore, the features of the technology may impact the content of the messages. The initial text messages posted to the forum contained several forms of text speak or a shorthand form of communication used in mobile messaging. Vowel, words, and punctuation were deleted or truncated in some instances to meet the 160-character requirement (Drouin & Davis, 2009). An example from the infancy messages to be sent to dads at Week 31: "Help baby explore safely. Remove items known 2 b poisonous, cause choking, or r sharp (Baby-proofing tips: 1.usa.gov/1nfhF36" [link to US Consumer Product Safety Commission]).

Many participants found the text speak to be distracting, difficult, and unprofessional. Three participants felt the use of "u" and "ur" to be distracting: one shared that she/he found it unnecessary and another deemed it condescending as well. Others spoke to the difficulty in grasping content delivered in text speak:

> From a health literacy perspective, I found that the messages were a bit difficult to read due to the texting shorthand. While I know the shorthand saves on space, [it de-creases] the readability of the messages especially for fathers who may not be familiar with texting shorthand.

Another participant argued that credible language enforced responsiveness:

> ... low-income, disadvantaged, and ... "at-risk" [parents] ... respond well to a credible authority on matters of health and well-being .... Clarity is more important than "hip" [language] or brevity in my personal and professional opinion.

The individual felt text speak devalued the content of the messages and potentially risked fathers' feeling patronized, confused, or concerned about the quality of the source.

Increasing linkages, apps, and interactivity

A feature of text message technology is its ability to link out to other sources. The researchers attempted to offer a number of links after each message so the user could go to a website for more information. Overall, participants posting to the "Connectivity" channel welcomed the use of links and felt more could be provided. Comments included the following: "More links—numerous resources out there to pull from" "More links would be beneficial as resources [sic] for fathers" "The linking is great. Some will use it, others wont [sic]. I would love to see links in more of the texts for the dads that really want to know more." One participant suggested adding more phone numbers as well in addition to links. Another participant felt the use of links were a good way to remedy problems with depth of content. Another participant noted an issue in linking to content designed for a maternal audience:

> ... you could link to custom-made, Dad-friendly Text4Dad pages. I note, for instance, that some of the current linked pages are specifically addressed to women.

Even if all you did was to essentially re-package or re-purpose the current linked content on new pages with male-friendly pictures and pronouns …

The suggestion calls for more user-specific content in taking the father to pages designed especially with him in mind.

Two participants also suggested connecting the user to Bump or What to Expect, popular applications whereby the user can track the pregnancy, even compare the size of the baby to a fruit. In a similar vein, another participant felt it was important for the user to learn a bit more about what the baby looks like. While the use of an app does not constitute a linkage per se, the participants seemed to feel that the app could be used in conjunction with receiving the text messages.

Finally, participants in the forum felt that interactivity could be improved, supporting a transition from HCI to computer-mediated communication between humans. One participant stated that "true interactivity" would increase his/her score from a 3 to a 4. Another participant stated

> … it could be helpful for dads to be given a hotline number to ask questions that may arise during both pregnancy and the first year of parenting. I suppose the ideal would be that they could text you back with questions or problems as they arose, but that seems beyond the scope of your current effort. Two-way communication is obviously much more challenging than just sending messages out, but a meaningful and credible relationship usually involves the opportunity to respond and interact.

The participant identified HCI as a problematic component of the messages arguing that two-way communication would be more effective in engaging fathers' responses.

Discussion

The broader contribution of the chapter is threefold: (a) to share how PAR and PDR can be used to inform mHealth-related interventions and design, (b) to introduce the benefit an online public forum in carrying out PAR/PDR, and (c) to offer more evidence of the importance of tailoring messages for effective mHealth applications.

First, PAR themes emerging in the Text4Dads forum included staying safe and attending to emotional health and efficacy. These themes were grounded in the lived experiences of fatherhood stakeholders, elicited in a context emancipated from conventional research formats, and aimed at increasing an overall sense of efficacy among expectant/recent fathers. The forum also challenged participants to think through the technological design and deployment of the messages. Resultant PDR themes included deleting text speak; increasing linkage, apps, and interactivity; and reformatting for relationship types.

We support the approach of Lee and Walsh (2015), believing mHealth research to require considerable investment—a cyclical process of feedback and review. This interactive approach resonates with both PAR (Coghlan & Brannick, 2014) and PDR (Simonsen & Hertzum, 2012) approaches, highlighting the process of change as slow-going but comprehensive and the working and reworking as crucial steps in the process of carrying out the research. Obtaining feedback in an online forum is one phase of many in ensuring that the content and design of the final mHealth initiative is reflective of the concerns of multiple stakeholders.

Second, we find the public online forum may be especially suited to conducting PAR and PDR research, as an affordance of communicating online is that power structures can be minimized (Suler, 2004). The lay father, the nonprofit CEO, the tenured researcher, the local community worker, the neonatal nurse are all welcome to contribute as much or as little as they would like, even to disagree. The process also emancipates the researchers (Vines et al., 2013) from conventional, empirically driven content and design, moving toward concepts and modes of communication that otherwise would not have been considered. For example, suggestions to provide tailored messaging to fathers depending upon their paternity status or relationship with the mother were only identified by several direct-practice professionals, not the researchers. Diversity of opinion is harnessed in the online public forum approach to developing mobile messages, allowing for more accessible and father-friendly content moving forward.

Notably, in providing support to expectant/recent fathers, the use of a public online forum in the context of PAR/PDR encourages a healthy conversation about the needs of this population and also offers a sense of community. By crowdsourcing feedback for mobile message content, fatherhood professionals and community members viewing the forum can look to the forum's comments to guide their own program content and delivery mechanisms, as well as provide new topics and ideas to investigate for practice and professional development. Furthermore, a natural sense of community develops among those participating in the online space—the shared sense that others are similarly invested in increasing paternal efficacy and engagement.

Finally, we began this work believing that the use of an mHealth intervention with expectant/recent fathers holds great potential for providing pertinent health information to a population prepared to make strides in efficacy and engagement. Stakeholder feedback gathered on the online forum supports the advice proffered by Hall et al. (2015) that mHealth initiatives be tailored to the population they are meant to engage. A "one-size-fits-all" approach to mHealth is not sufficient, rather a thorough understanding of the unique experiences of a population—in this case, expectant/recent fathers—must be at the forefront of mHealth intervention technology. To ensure that the mHealth intervention supports expectant/recent fathers holistically, an interactive technology must be deployed and modified by fathers and fatherhood professionals who understand the needs of their community and can provide direct services and mobile interactivity in tandem. Results also suggest that mHealth interventions must contain accurate, comprehensive health information about expectant/recent fathers' ability to care for themselves and their children, while also being relatable, timely, and organized. Therefore, a balance must be struck between the breadth and depth of content areas covered and the accessibility of mobile messages within the mHealth intervention.

Limitations

The limitations of this phase of mHealth research can guide future work in this area. First, the public online forum is a new tool for health researchers and therefore best practices do not exist for the process of obtaining consent in this space. On one hand, individuals logging on to the forum must comply with its terms and conditions, specifically agreeing to publishing their comments publicly. On muut.com, individuals can choose their own username—effectively managing their own level of anonymity. On the other hand, we felt consent should have been obtained earlier in the process, before individuals logged on to the forum and posted comments. We ended up obtaining consent after comments had been posted using an opt-out process. Only one individual indicated that their comments posted to the forum could not be used for research.

Another limitation of the study could be the deductive approach to data analysis. A deductive approach may bias the researcher to see only the themes relevant to the theory, thereby obscuring a fuller picture of the data obtained. We attempted to address this issue by making several passes through the data to ensure all voices and concepts were encapsulated by the themes generated. However, an inductive, grounded theory approach (Glaser & Strauss, 1967) may be more suitable for identifying categories that resonate more fully with the data.

Finally, the affordances of the online space are tempered by challenges as well. The online public forum may reduce the sense of social presence (Short, Williams, & Christie, 1976) that can be so vital for qualitative research—the sense of intimacy that develops between researcher and participant (Argyle & Dean, 1965), the immediacy that accompanies the gesture, facial expressions, and tone of voice of individuals conversing face to face (Wiener & Mehrabian, 1968). Some may argue that the online forum simply shortchanges the interview or the focus group. At the same time, we find the quantity and diversity of voices represented in our forum participants to outweigh the challenges of reduced social presence. More research should be conducted using this tool to ascertain more fully its benefits and limitations.

Conclusion

An online public forum engaging invested stakeholders in participatory action and design research emerges as a viable step in developing a comprehensive mHealth intervention. Following PAR and PDR cyclical approaches, the themes reported in this chapter will inform next steps in the reconceptualization of the message format, the content of the messages contained in the design, and the implementation of this program among expectant/recent fathers. Our aim is to work with this community hand-in-hand to increase a father's sense of efficacy in preparing for a baby or caring for a child.

Appendix 10.1

See Table 10.1.

TABLE 10.1   Pregnancy messages.

Wk	#	Message	Character	Source	Action
Start-up					
S	1	Welcome to Text4Dads! If u are receiving this message, ur baby is on the way or has been born already.	102		None
S	2	If you have received this message in error, reply STOP to this message. Or call (630) 637-5380 with questions.	110		Respond to STOP requests

Continued

TABLE 10.1   Pregnancy messages.—cont'd

Wk	#	Message	Character	Source	Action
S	3	Over the next weeks, u will be getting lots of helpful info. 4 info that's right for u, please text us ur baby's due date or date of birth.	139		Send 4a or 4b
S	4a	Thanks! Based on the date u texted, u will get info about preparing for baby and caring for baby after birth.	109		Put on Pregnancy track
S	4b	Thanks! Based on the date u texted, u will get info about caring for baby.	75		Put on Infant track
1 trimester					
2	1	The first trimester means the 0-13 weeks of pregnancy. Ur baby grows and develops rapidly during this time.	107	UCSF Medical Center. (2015). Pregnancy: The three trimesters. Retrieved from: http://www.ucsfhealth.org/conditions/pregnancy/trimesters.html	
	2	Ur baby's brain, spinal cord and organs begin to form, and heart begins to beat. Fingers and toes start to take shape too.	122	Mayo Clinic. (2015). Pregnancy week by week: First trimester. Retrieved from: http://www.mayoclinic.org/healthy-lifestyle/pregnancy-week-by-week/basics/first-trimester/hlv-20049471	

TABLE 10.1   Pregnancy messages.—cont'd

Wk	#	Message	Character	Source	Action
4	1	Even tho u can't see baby, Dad, u can bcome attached by thinking happy thoughts about baby and dreaming about the future.	120	Condon, J. T., & Corkindale, C. (1997). The correlates of antenatal attachment in pregnant women. British Journal of Medical Psychology, 70(4), 359–372.	
6	1	Dad, odds are ur involvement in pregnancy means a better chance Mom will quit smoking. Help her quit now, visit smokefree.gov 4 support.	136	Martin, L. T., McNamara, M. J., Milot, A. S., Halle, T., & Hair, E. C. (2007). The effects of father involvement during pregnancy on receipt of prenatal care and maternal smoking. Maternal and child health journal, 11(6), 595–602.	Link to Smokefree.gov (DHHS, NCI, NIH)
8	1	Expecting dads may feel out of the loop. Hear heartbeats & touch Mom's belly 2 feel more involved. Join Mom on prenatal visits too.	131	Finnbogadottir, H., Crang Svalenius, E., Persson E. (2003). Expectant first-time fathers' experiences of pregnancy. Midwifery, 19, 96–105.	
10	1	Believe it or not, dads' hormones also can change during pregnancy. Watch 4 weight gain, nausea & fatigue. More info: bit.ly/ 1e0xr07	132	Wynn-Edwards, K. (2004, June 28). Why do some men experience pregnancy symptoms such as vomiting and nausea when their wives are pregnant? Scientific American. Retrieved from http://www. scientificamerican. com/article/why- do-some-men- experienc/	Link to Scientific American article

Continued

TABLE 10.1 Pregnancy messages.—cont'd

Wk	#	Message	Character	Source	Action
12	1	Dad, u matter! Ur involvement in pregnancy means better health for baby at birth and less complications for Mom too.	116	Alio, A. P., Salihu, H. M., Kornosky, J. L., Richman, A. M., & Marty, P. J. (2010). Feto-infant health and survival: does paternal involvement matter? Maternal and child health journal, 14(6), 931–937.	
13	1	Moms with involved partners are 1.5X more likely to receive prenatal care. Dad, ur support matters 4 a healthy baby!	116	Martin, L. T., McNamara, M. J., Milot, A. S., Halle, T., & Hair, E. C. (2007). The effects of father involvement during pregnancy on receipt of prenatal care and maternal smoking. Maternal and child health journal, 11(6), 595–602.	
2 trimester					
14	1	Welcome to the second trimester! The second trimester means the 14-26 weeks of pregnancy.	95	UCSF Medical Center. (2015). Pregnancy: The three trimesters. Retrieved from: http://www.ucsfhealth.org/conditions/pregnancy/trimesters.html	
	2	Ur baby will be developing bones, starting to hear, growing hair. U can learn your baby's sex during this time too.	116	Mayo Clinic. (2015). Fetal development: The second trimester. Retrieved from: http://www.mayoclinic.org/healthy-lifestyle/pregnancy-week-by-week/in-depth/fetal-development/art-20046151?pg=1	

TABLE 10.1   Pregnancy messages.—cont'd

Wk	#	Message	Character	Source	Action
17	1	Supporting Mom & baby may mean looking for employment and training. For assistance, go to: http://www.doleta.gov/	113	Alio, A. P., Bond, M. J., Padilla, Y. C., Heidelbaugh, J. J., Lu, M., & Parker, W. J. (2011). Addressing Policy Barriers to Paternal Involvement During Pregnancy. Maternal & Child Health Journal, 15(4), 425–430. https://doi.org/10.1007/s10995-011-0781-1	Link to United States Department of Labor Employment and training Administration
20	1	Ur halfway there, Dad! Mom might feel baby move around. Baby will gain weight quicker, start to swallow & form fingerprints & footprints.	137	Mayo Clinic. (2015). Fetal development: The second trimester. Retrieved from: http://www.mayoclinic.org/healthy-lifestyle/pregnancy-week-by-week/in-depth/fetal-development/art-20046151?pg=2	
23	1	Choosing 2 breastfeed? Dad support helps Mom's decision. Breast milk is best 4 baby! Talk 2 MD/follow link: 1.usa.gov/PG6T8V	124	Wolfberg, A., Michels, K., Shields, W., O'Campo, P., Bronner, Y., & Bienstock, J. (2004). Dads as breastfeeding advocates: results from a randomized controlled trial of an educational intervention. American Journal Of Obstetrics & Gynecology, 191(3), 708–712.	Link to United States Office of Women's Health/Breastfeeding

Continued

TABLE 10.1   Pregnancy messages.—cont'd

Wk	#	Message	Character	Source	Action
24	1	Dads who r committed & care 4 baby during pregnancy (in utero) feel more attached to baby & connected to baby's future.	119	Vreeswijk, C. M., Maas, A. J., Rijk, C. H., & van Bakel, H. J. (2014). Fathers' experiences during pregnancy: Paternal prenatal attachment and representations of the fetus. Psychology of Men & Masculinity, 15(2), 129.	
26	1	Dad, ur baby might be able to respond to familiar voices, such as yours. Hearing ur sounds might make ur baby move around.	122	Mayo Clinic. (2015). Fetal development: The second trimester. Retrieved from: http://www. mayoclinic.org/ healthy-lifestyle/ pregnancy-week-by-week/in-depth/ fetal-development/ art-20046151?pg=2	
3 trimester					
27	1	Ur in the third trimester now, meaning weeks 27-40, or whenever baby comes. U will see the MD with ur partner more regularly.	125	UCSF Medical Center. (2015). Pregnancy: The three trimesters. Retrieved from: http:// www.ucsfhealth.org/ conditions/ pregnancy/ trimesters.html; Office on Women's Health, U.S. Department of Health and Human Services. (2012). Prenatal care fact sheet. Retrieved from: http://www. womenshealth.gov/ publications/our-publications/fact-sheet/prenatal-care. html#f	

TABLE 10.1 Pregnancy messages.—cont'd

Wk	#	Message	Character	Source	Action
	2	Ur baby will open eyes, practice breathing, detect light, grow fingernails, fully develop bones, & gain weight fast!	116	Mayo Clinic. (2015). Fetal development: The third trimester. Retrieved from: http://www.mayoclinic.org/healthy-lifestyle/pregnancy-week-by-week/in-depth/fetal-development/art-20045997?pg=2	
29	1	Help Mom 2 relax during final weeks of pregnancy w favorite things. Extra stress now can harm Mom & baby in the long run.	122	Gerhardt, S. (2015). Why love matters (2nd ed.). New York: Routledge.	
31	1	Nervous about relationship w Mom after baby arrives? Changes are normal. Talk 2 MD about what to expect & possible counseling services.	136	Yu, C., Hung, C., Chan, T., Yeh, C., & Lai, C. (2012). Prenatal predictors for father-infant attachment after childbirth. Journal of Clinical Nursing, 21(11/12), 1577–1583. https://doi.org/10.1111/j.1365-2702.2011.04003.x	
33	1	B4 baby is here plan w Mom ur household goals and chores that suit each of u. Having a plan & teamwork helps w post-birth timing & stress.	139	Raeburn, P. (2014). Do Father's Matter? What Science is Telling us about the Parent We've Overlooked. New York: Scientific American.	

Continued

IV. MHealth: Mobile technology for health

TABLE 10.1 Pregnancy messages.—cont'd

Wk	#	Message	Character	Source	Action
35	1	Ur mental health matters! Dads who r depressed/anxious feel less attached to baby. Learn more about mental health here: 1.usa.gov/1FaG66s	137	Vreeswijk, C. M., Maas, A. J., Rijk, C. H., & van Bakel, H. J. (2014). Fathers' experiences during pregnancy: Paternal prenatal attachment and representations of the fetus. Psychology of Men & Masculinity, 15(2), 129.	Link to DHHS Mental Health
37	1	Questions about car seats? Find a location 2 get it inspected & learn driving w baby safety tips @ safercar.gov	111	How to Find the Right Car Seat. (n.d.). Retrieved July 14, 2015.	Link to United States Department of transportation
39	1	An involved dad tends 2 read to, play with, care 4 baby in the future, and find employment if out of work.	106	Cabrera, N. J., Fagan, J., & Farrie, D. (2008). Explaining the long reach of fathers' prenatal involvement on later paternal engagement. Journal of Marriage and Family, 70(5), 1094–1107; Raeburn, P. (2014). Do Father's Matter? What Science is Telling us about the Parent We've Overlooked. New York: Scientific American.	
40	1	40 weeks = full term. Baby coming any day! Studies show supporting Mom thru labor & delivery means a better experience with u by her side.	138	Gungor, I., & Beji, N. K. (2007). Effects of fathers' attendance to labor and delivery on the experience of childbirth in Turkey. Western journal of nursing research, 29(2), 213–231.	

TABLE 10.1 Pregnancy messages.—cont'd

Wk	#	Message	Character	Source	Action
	2	Plan 2 b in delivery room? Dad support during birth helps Mom have positive experience overall & gr8 bonding time w new baby.	116	Condon, J. T., & Corkindale, C. (1997). The correlates of antenatal attachment in pregnant women. British Journal of Medical Psychology, 70(4), 359–372.	

Appendix 10.2

See Table 10.2.

TABLE 10.2 Infancy messages.

Mo	Wk	#	Message	Char	Source	Action
	1	1	Congrats, new dad! Ur presence in baby's life is important, especially in 1st year. Ur support helps Mom & helps baby grow healthy/strong.	138		
	2	1	Baby tears = baby needs something: feeding, diaper change, warm contact. Responding 2 baby's crying builds bond & settles baby.	128	Mayo Clinic. (2014). Infant development: Birth to 3 months. Retrieved from http://www.mayoclinic.org/healthy-lifestyle/infant-and-toddler-health/in-depth/infant-development/art-20048012	

Continued

TABLE 10.2   Infancy messages.—cont'd

Mo	Wk	#	Message	Char	Source	Action
		2	Going 2 well-child visits can tell u a lot about baby! Talk w/Mom about scheduling appts convenient 4 u so u can learn about baby's health.	135	Garfield, C. F., & Isacco, A. (2006). Fathers and the well-child visit. Pediatrics, 117(4), e637–e645.	
		3	Dads help prevent SIDS! Baby needs 2 sleep on backside & firm surface, avoid exposure 2 smoke/ alcohol/drugs & overheating. www.cdc.gov/ sids	139	American Academy of Pediatrics. (2011). SIDS and other sleep-related infant deaths: Expansion of recommendations for a safe infant sleeping environment. Pediatrics, 128(5), 1030–1039. https://doi.org/ 10.1542/peds. 2011-2284	Link to CDC SIDS
	3	1	A newborn's head is wobbly! Support neck when u hold baby, but don't hesitate 2 try new holding positions, such as facing baby outward.	136	Mayo Clinic. (2014). Infant development: Birth to 3 months. Retrieved from http://www. mayoclinic.org/ healthy-lifestyle/ infant-and-toddler-health/ in-depth/infant-development/art-20048012	

TABLE 10.2 Infancy messages.—cont'd

Mo	Wk	#	Message	Char	Source	Action
1						
	4	1	Begin tracking baby development right away 2 share w MD as baby gets older. U will be asked ?s at MD visits about baby's growth & movement.	139	Well-child visits: MedlinePlus Medical Encyclopedia. (2015, July 1). Retrieved July 15, 2015.	
	5	1	Tummy time = putting baby on his/her tummy 4 brief moments 2 help baby's neck get stronger. Baby might not like it, so watch baby closely.	139	Mayo Clinic. (2014). Infant development: Birth to 3 months. Retrieved from http://www.mayoclinic.org/healthy-lifestyle/infant-and-toddler-health/in-depth/infant-development/art-20048012	
	6	1	Hard truth: 40% of unmarried dads move in & out of being involved in baby's life. U matter even if u don't live with baby, Dad!	127	Coley, R. L., & hase–Lansdale, P. L. (1999). Stability and change in paternal involvement among urban African American fathers. Journal of Family Psychology, 13(3), 416.	
	7	1	Make sure 2 add dad-baby bonding time 2 ur new routine! Spend time w baby while mom relaxes. Smile & hold baby close 2 increase bond.	134	Gerhardt, S. (2015). Why love matters (2nd ed.). New York: Routledge.	

Continued

TABLE 10.2   Infancy messages.—cont'd

Mo	Wk	#	Message	Char	Source	Action
2						
	9	1	Ur baby will start 2 respond 2 ur voice. Speak 2 baby w/simple words: ask ?s, describe sights, smells, sounds 2 help develop language.	135	Mayo Clinic. (2014). Infant development: Birth to 3 months. Retrieved from http://www.mayoclinic.org/healthy-lifestyle/infant-and-toddler-health/in-depth/infant-development/art-20048012	
	11	1	Need help finding childcare in ur area? 4 qualified programs close 2 u, visit http://families.naeyc.org/	105	Phillips, D., & Adams, G. (2001). Child care and our youngest children. The Future of Children/Center for the Future of Children, the David and Lucile Packard Foundation, 11(1), 34–51.	Link to National Association for the Education of Young Children
		2	When looking 4 out-of-home childcare, focus on a low child-caregiver ratio & well trained, responsive staff. Check references!	126	Phillips, D., & Adams, G. (2001). Child care and our youngest children. The Future of Children/Center for the Future of Children, the David and Lucile Packard Foundation, 11(1), 34–51.	

TABLE 10.2   Infancy messages.—cont'd

Mo	Wk	#	Message	Char	Source	Action
3						
	12	1	U have a 3-month-old, Dad! Talk to MD if baby can't hold head up by now or baby doesn't smile, follow objects w/ eyes or respond 2 sounds.	138	Mayo Clinic. (2014). Infant development: Birth to 3 months. Retrieved from http://www.mayoclinic.org/healthy-lifestyle/infant-and-toddler-health/in-depth/infant-development/art-20048012	
	14	1	Reading books, singing songs, running errands w/baby: Dad, studies show ur time w/baby helps baby's mind develop & be able 2 solve problems.	140	Bronte-Tinkew, J., Carrano, A., Horowitz, A., & Kinukawa, A. (2008). Involvement among resident fathers and links to infant cognitive outcomes. Journal of Family Issues, 29(9). 1211–1244.	
4						
	17	1	4-6 month old babies begin to grasp things, move w/purpose, see more clearly, turn head, & make babbling & other sounds.	121	Mayo Clinic. (2014). Infant development: Milestones from 4 to 6 months. Retrieved from http://www.mayoclinic.org/healthy-lifestyle/infant-and-toddler-health/in-depth/infant-development/art-20048178	

Continued

TABLE 10.2   Infancy messages.—cont'd

Mo	Wk	#	Message	Char	Source	Action
5	19	1	Tummy time = Use toy or noise 2 help baby roll over & hold up head. Hold baby in standing position 2 make legs strong.	118	Mayo Clinic. (2014). Infant development: Milestones from 4 to 6 months. Retrieved from http://www.mayoclinic.org/healthy-lifestyle/infant-and-toddler-health/in-depth/infant-development/art-20048178	
	21	1	Baby waking @ night? Take turns w Mom caring 4 baby during day/ night if not feeding & help baby (& Mom) get better sleep!	121	Tikotzky, L., Sadeh, A., Volkovich, E., Manber, R., Meiri, G., & Shahar, G. (2015). VII. Infant Sleep Development from 3 to 6 Months Postpartum: Links with Maternal Sleep and Paternal Involvement. Monographs of the Society for Research in Child Development, 80(1), 107–124. https://doi.org/10.1111/mono.12147	
	25	1	Offer baby simple toys, 1 or 2 at a time, at a small distance 2 help baby stretch & reach. Use music 2 sooth baby. Be sure 2 cuddle.	132	Mayo Clinic. (2014). Infant development: Milestones from 4 to 6 months. Retrieved from http://www.mayoclinic.org/healthy-lifestyle/infant-and-toddler-health/in-depth/infant-development/art 20048178	

TABLE 10.2   Infancy messages.—cont'd

Mo	Wk	#	Message	Char	Source	Action
6						
	27	1	Talk 2 your MD if ur 6-month-old seems floppy/stiff, or doesn't laugh, try to sit/roll over, respond 2 light/loud noises or reach 4 things.	138	Mayo Clinic. (2014). Infant development: Milestones from 4 to 6 months. Retrieved from http://www. mayoclinic.org/ healthy-lifestyle/ infant-and-toddler-health/ in-depth/infant-development/art-20048178	
	29	1	Postpartum depression (PPD) 4 moms/ dads = anxiety/ guilt, disconnected from baby, unable 2 care 4 self/baby, changed sleep & eating.	132	MedlinePlus. (2014). Postpartum depression. Retrieved from http://www.nlm. nih.gov/ medlineplus/ ency/article/ 007215.htm	
		2	Need to talk w some1 about PPD? Helpline: 1.800.944.4773 or visit http:// bit.ly/ 1gL0NKh.	88	MedlinePlus. (2014). Postpartum depression. Retrieved from http://www.nlm. nih.gov/ medlineplus/ ency/article/ 007215.htm	Link to postpartum Support International
7						
	31	1	Baby on the move! 7-9 month olds roll over & start to scoot, sit up, rock, or pull up 2 standing. 1st tooth means	137	Mayo Clinic. (2014). Infant development: Milestones from 7 to 9 months. Retrieved from http://www. mayoclinic.org/	

Continued

IV. MHealth: Mobile technology for health

TABLE 10.2   Infancy messages.—cont'd

Mo	Wk	#	Message	Char	Source	Action
			drooling & chewing too.		healthy-lifestyle/ infant-and-toddler-health/ in-depth/infant-development/art-20047086	
		2	Help baby explore safely. Remove items known 2 b poisonous, cause choking, or r sharp. Babyproofing tips: 1.usa.gov/ 1nfhF36	123	Mayo Clinic. (2014). Infant development: Milestones from 7 to 9 months. Retrieved from http://www. mayoclinic.org/ healthy-lifestyle/ infant-and-toddler-health/ in-depth/infant-development/art-20047086	Link to U.S. Consumer Product Safety commission

Acknowledgments

This work emerged from a summer research program funded by the Faculty Professional Development Committee at North Central College, where the authors met and began to collaborate. We also are grateful for the Fatherhood Research and Practice Network for connecting us to fathers and fatherhood stakeholders as well as James Rodriguez and the Fathers and Families Coalition of America for receiving our work at the organization's national conference.

References

Alexandre, G. C., Nadanovsky, P., Moraes, C. L., & Reichenheim, M. (2010). The presence of a stepfather and child physical abuse, as reported by a sample of Brazilian mothers in Rio de Janeiro. *Child Abuse and Neglect, 34*, 959–966. https://doi.org/10.1016/j.chiabu.2010.06.005.

Allen, A. N., & Lo, C. C. (2012). Drugs, guns, and disadvantaged youths: Co-occurring behavior and the code of the street. *Crime and Delinquency, 58*(6), 932–953. https://doi.org/10.1177/0011128709359652.

Antecol, H., & Bedard, K. (2007). Does single parenthood increase the probability of teenage promiscuity, substance use, and crime? *Journal of Popular Economics, 20*, 55–71. https://doi.org/10.1007/s00148-005-0019-x.

Argyle, M., & Dean, J. (1965). Eye contact and distance affiliation. *Sociometry, 28*(3), 289–304. https://doi.org/10.2307/2786027.

Bandura, A., & Adams, N. E. (1977). Analysis of self-efficacy theory of behavioral change. *Cognitive Therapy and Research, 1*(4), 287–310. https://doi.org/10.1007/BF01663995.

Baum, F., MacDougall, C., & Smith, D. (2006). Participatory action research. *Journal of Epidemiol Community Health, 60*, 854–857. https://doi.org/10.1136/jech.2004.028662.

Bendheim-Thomas Center for Research on Child Wellbeing and Social Indicators Survey Center. (2010). CPS involvement in families with social fathers. *Fragile Families Research Brief, 46*. https://fragilefamilies.princeton.edu/briefsBBT.

Björgvinsson, E., & Hillgren, P. A. (July 2004). On the spot experiments within healthcare. In , *Materials and practices: Vol. 1. Proceedings of the eighth conference on participatory design: Artful integration* (pp. 93–101). Interweaving Media. https://doi.org/10.1145/1011870.1011882.

Bocknek, E. L., Brophy-Herb, H. E., Fitzgerald, H. E., Schiffman, R. F., & Vogel, C. (2014). Stability of biological father presence as a proxy for family stability: Cross-racial associations with the longitudinal development of emotion regulation in toddlerhood. *Infant Mental Health Journal, 35*(4), 309–321. https://doi.org/10.1002/imhj.21454.

Burn, V. E. (2008). Living without a strong father figure: A context for teen mothers' experience of having become sexually active. *Issues in Mental Health Nursing, 29*, 279–297. https://doi.org/10.1080/01612840701869692.

Cobb-Clark, D. A., & Tekin, E. (2014). Fathers and youths' delinquent behavior. *Review of Economics of the Household, 12*(2), 327–358. https://doi.org/10.1007/s11150-013-9194-9.

Coghlan, D., & Brannick, T. (2014). *Doing action research in your own organization*. Sage.

Coghlan, D., & Brydon-Miller, M. (2014). Participatory action research. In *The SAGE encyclopedia of action research* (Vols. 1–2).London: SAGE Publications Ltd. https://doi.org/10.4135/9781446294406.

Coley, R. L., & Medeiros, B. L. (2007). Reciprocal longitudinal relations between nonresident father involvement and adolescent delinquency. *Child Development, 78*, 132–147. https://doi.org/10.1111/j.1467-8624.2007.00989.x.

Cramer, E. M. (2018). Health information behavior of expectant and recent fathers. *American Journal of Men's Health, 12*(2), 313–325. https://doi.org/10.1177/1557988316637576.

Daly, K. J., Ashbourne, L., & Brown, J. L. (2009). Fathers' perceptions of children's influence: Implications for involvement. *The Annals of the American Academy of Political and Social Science, 624*(1), 61–77. https://doi.org/10.1177/0002716209334695.

Drouin, M., & Davis, C. (2009). R u txting? Is the use of text speak hurting your literacy? *Journal of Literacy Research, 41*(1), 46–67. https://doi.org/10.1080/10862960802695131.

Ehn, P. (1990). *Work-oriented design of computer artifacts*. Hillsdale, NJ: L. Erlbaum Associates, Inc.

Ellis, B. J., Bates, J. E., Dodge, K. A., Fergusson, D. M., Horwood, L. J., Pettit, G. S., & Woodward, L. (2003). Does father absence place daughters at special risk for early sexual activity and teenage pregnancy? *Child Development, 74*, 801–821. https://doi.org/10.1111/1467-8624.00569.

Esienumoh, E. E., Allotey, J., & Waterman, H. (2018). Empowering members of a rural southern community in Nigeria to plan to take action to prevent maternal mortality: A participatory action research project. *Journal of Clinical Nursing, 27*(7–8), e1600–e1611. https://doi.org/10.1111/jocn.14244.

Gillette, M. T., & Gudmunson, C. G. (2014). Processes linking father absence to educational attainment among African American females. *Journal of Research on Adolescence, 24*(2), 309–321. https://doi.org/10.1111/jora.12066.

Glaser, B. G., & Strauss, A. L. (1967). *The discovery of grounded theory: Strategies for qualitative research*. Chicago: Aldine Publishing Company.

Gross, P. H., Bailes, A. F., Horn, S. D., Hurvitz, E. A., Kean, J., & Shusterman, M. (2018). *Cerebral Palsy Research Network Setting a patient-centered research agenda for cerebral palsy: A participatory action research initiative. Developmental medicine & child neurology* (e-pub ahead of print) https://onlinelibrary.wiley.com/journal/14698749.

Hall, A., Cole-Lewis, H., & Bernhardt, J. (2015). Mobile text messaging for health: A systematic review of reviews. *The Annual Review of Public Health, 36,* 393–415. https://doi.org/10.1146/annurev-publhealth-031914-122855.

Halskov, K., & Hansen, N. B. (2015). The diversity of participatory design research practice at PDC 2002–2012. *International Journal of Human-Computer Studies, 74,* 81–92. https://doi.org/10.1016/j.ijhcs.2014.09.003.

Health Resources and Services Administration. (2015). *Promoting maternal and child health through health text messaging: An evaluation of the Text4baby program—final report. U.S. Department of Health and Human Services.* Retrieved from https://www.hrsa.gov/sites/default/files/archive/healthit/.../text4babyfinalreport.pdf.

Hess, J., Offenberg, S., & Pipek, V. (October, 2008). Community driven development as participation?: Involving user communities in a software design process. In *Proceedings of the tenth anniversary conference on participatory design 2008* (pp. 31–40). Indiana University.

Hendricks, C. S., Cesario, S. K., Murdaugh, C., Gibbons, M. E., Servonsky, E. J., Bobadilla, R. V., ... Tavakoli, A. (2005). The influence of father absence on the self-esteem and self-reported sexual activity of rural Southern adolescents. *ABNF Journal, 16,* 124–131. http://tuckerpub.com/abnf.htm.

Hilton, N. Z., Harris, G. T., & Rice, M. E. (2015). The step-father effect in child abuse: Comparing discriminative parental solicitude and antisociality. *Psychology of Violence, 5*(1), 8–15. https://doi.org/10.1037/a0035189.

Hofferth, S. L. (2006). Residential father family type and child well-being: Investment versus selection. *Demography, 43,* 53–78. https://doi.org/10.1353/dem.2006.0006.

Hsieh, H. F., & Shannon, S. E. (2005). Three approaches to qualitative content analysis. *Qualitative Health Research, 15*(9), 1277–1288. https://doi.org/10.1177/1049732305276687.

Jones, T., Ho, L., Kun, K. K., Milsom, P., Shakpeh, J., Ratnayake, R., & Loewenson, R. (2018). Rebuilding people-centred maternal health services in post-Ebola Liberia through participatory action research. *Global Public Health,* 1–20. https://doi.org/10.1080/17441692.2018.1427772.

Kelly, J., & Matthews, B. (2010). Taking transition into account: Designing with pre-users of medical devices. In *Proceedings of the 11th biennial participatory design conference* (pp. 71–80). https://doi.org/10.1145/1900441.1900452. ACM.

Lang, D. L., Rieckmann, T., DiClemente, R. J., Crosby, R. A., Brown, L. K., & Donenberg, G. R. (2013). Multi-level factors associated with pregnancy among urban adolescent women seeking psychological services. *Journal of Urban Health, 90,* 212–223. https://doi.org/10.1007/s11524-012-9768-5.

Leerkes, E. M., & Burney, R. V. (2007). The development of parenting efficacy among new mothers and fathers. *Infancy, 12*(1), 45–67. https://doi.org/10.1111/j.1532-7078.2007.tb00233.x.

Lee, S., & Walsh, T. (2015). Using technology in social work practice: The mDad (Mobile Device Assisted Dad) case study. *Advances in Social Work, 16*(1), 107–124. http://journals.iupui.edu/index.php/advancesinsocialwork.

Mandara, J., & Murray, C. B. (2006). Father's absence and African American adolescent drug use. *Journal of Divorce and Remarriage, 46,* 1–12. https://doi.org/10.1300/J087v46n01_01.

Mandara, J., Rogers, S. Y., & Zinbarg, R. E. (2011). The effects of family structure on African American adolescents' marijuana use. *Journal of Marriage and Family, 73*(3), 557–569. https://doi.org/10.1111/j.1741-3737.2011.00832.x.

Markus, M. L. (2004). Technochange management: Using IT to drive organizational change. *Journal of Information Technology, 19*(1), 4–20. https://doi.org/10.1057/palgrave.jit.2000002.

Marsh, P., Gartrell, G., Egg, G., Nolan, A., & Cross, M. (2017). End-of-life care in a community garden: Findings from a Participatory Action Research project in regional Australia. *Health and Place, 45*, 110–116. https://www.journals.elsevier.com/health-and-place.

Meek, R. (2007). Parenting education for young fathers in prison. *Child and Family Social Work, 12*(3), 239–247. https://doi.org/10.1111/j.1365-2206.2007.00456.x.

Dads Matter. (2017). January 17, 2019, Retrieved from https://partners.text4baby.org/index. php/miscellaneous/374-dads-matter.

Nepomnyaschy, L., Miller, D. P., Garasky, S., & Nanda, N. (2014). Nonresident fathers and child food insecurity: Evidence from longitudinal data. *Social Service Review, 88*(1), 92–133. https://doi.org/10.1086/674970.

Noergaard, B., Johannessen, H., Fenger-Gron, J., Kofoed, P. E., & Ammentorp, J. (2016). Participatory action research in the field of neonatal intensive care: Developing an intervention to meet the fathers' needs. A case study. *Journal of Public Health Research, 5*(3). https://doi.org/10.4081/jphr.2016.744.

Nygaard, K. (1979). The iron and metal project: Trade union participation. In A. Sandberg (Ed.), *Computers dividing man and work* (Vol. 12, pp. 94–107). Malmo, Sweden: I Utbildningsproduktion.

Owens, C., Farrand, P., Darvill, R., Emmens, T., Hewis, E., & Aitken, P. (2011). Involving service users in intervention design: A participatory approach to developing a text-messaging intervention to reduce repetition of self-harm. *Health Expectations, 14*(3), 285–295. https://doi.org/10.1111/j.1369-7625.2010.00623.x.

Parker, K., & Wang, W. (2013). *Modern parenthood: Roles of moms and dads converge as they balance work and family. Pew Research Center.* Retrieved from http://www.pewsocialtrends. org/2013/03/14/modern-parenthood-roles-of-moms-and-dads-converge-as-they-balance-work-and-family/.

Patock-Peckham, J. A., & Morgan-Lopez, A. A. (2007). College drinking behaviors: Mediational links between parenting styles, parental bonds, depression, and alcohol problems. *Psychology of Addictive Behaviors, 21*, 297–306. https://doi.org/10.1037/0893-164X.21.3.297.

Participate in Design. (2018). *What is participatory design?.* Retrieved from http:// participateindesign.org/approach/what/.

Peterson, S. (February 27, 2013). *Dumbing down Dad: How media present husbands, fathers as useless.* Deseret News. Retrieved from https://www.deseretnews.com/article/ 865574236/Dumbing-down-Dad-How-media-present-husbands-fathers-as-useless.html.

Pew Research Center. (2017a). *Wide partisan gaps in U.S. over how far the country has come on gender equality.* Retrieved from http://www.pewsocialtrends.org/2017/10/18/wide-partisan-gaps-in-u-s-over-how-far-the-country-has-come-on-gender-equality/.

Pew Research Center. (2017b). *Americans widely support paid family and medical leave, but differ over specific policies.* Retrieved from http://www.pewsocialtrends.org/2017/03/23/ americans-widely-support-paid-family-and-medical-leave-but-differ-over-specific-policies/.

Reed, S., Bell, J., & Edwards, T. (2011). Adolescent well-being in Washington State military families. *American Journal of Public Health, 101*, 1676–1682. https://doi.org/10.2105/ AJPH.2011.300165.

Short, J., Williams, E., & Christie, B. (1976). *The social psychology of telecommunications.* London: John Wiley & Sons.

Simonsen, J., & Hertzum, M. (2012). Sustained participatory design: Extending the iterative approach. *Design Issues, 28*(3), 10–21. https://doi.org/10.1162/DESI_a_00158.

Spinuzzi, C. (2005). The methodology of participatory design. *Technical Communication, 52*(2), 163–174. https://www.stc.org/techcomm/.

Suler, J. (2004). The online disinhibition effect. *Cyberpsychology and Behavior, 7*(3), 321–326. https://doi.org/10.1089/1094931041291295.

Taylor, P., Parker, K., Livingston, G., Wang, W., & Dockterman, D. (2011). *A tale of two fathers: More are active, but more are absent*. Washington, D.C.: Pew Research Center.

Text4Baby. (2017). Retrieved from https://partners.text4baby.org/index.php.

Varley, J., Power, R., Saris, J., & Fitzsimons, M. (2017). ISQUA17-2402 Co-designing patient-centered care using participatory action research (PAR): The Epilepsy Partnership in Care (EPIC) project. *International Journal for Quality in Health Care, 29*(Suppl. 1_1), 8–9. https://doi.org/10.1093/intqhc/mzx125.8.

Vaszari, J. M., Bradford, S., Callahan O'Leary, C., Ben Abdallah, A., & Cottler, L. B. (2011). Risk factors for suicidal ideation in a population of community-recruited female cocaine users. *Comprehensive Psychiatry, 52*, 238–246. https://doi.org/10.1016/j.comppsych.2010.07.003.

Vines, J., Clarke, R., Wright, P., McCarthy, J., & Olivier, P. (2013). Configuring participation: On how we involve people in design. In *Proceedings of the SIGCHI conference on human factors in computing systems* (pp. 429–438). https://doi.org/10.1145/2470654.2470716. ACM.

Wiener, M., & Mehrabian, A. (1968). *Language within language: Immediacy, a channel in verbal communication*. New York: Appleton-Century-Crofts.

Wikman, A., Kukkola, L., Börjesson, H., Cernvall, M., Woodford, J., Grönqvist, H., & von Essen, L. (2018). Development of an internet-administered cognitive behavior therapy program (ENGAGE) for parents of children previously treated for cancer: Participatory action research approach. *Journal of Medical Internet Research, 20*(4). https://doi.org/10.2196/jmir.9457.

11

The effectiveness and moderators of mobile applications for health behavior change

Stephanie K. Van Stee[1], Qinghua Yang[2]

[1] Department of Communication, University of Missouri - St. Louis, United States; [2] Department of Communication Studies, Texas Christian University, United States

Introduction

The widespread adoption of mobile devices, including smartphones, has allowed for increased access to and use of health-related mobile apps on the part of consumers. As of 2015, 58% of US mobile phone owners have downloaded at least one of the thousands of health-related mobile apps available (Krebs & Duncan, 2015). Many researchers have begun investigating the effectiveness of health-related mobile apps, with some examining the effectiveness of preexisting apps developed by nonprofit, governmental, or other organizations (e.g., Fitbit; Wang et al., 2015) and others developing their own health-related mobile apps for dissemination and evaluation (e.g., ALICE app; Mira et al., 2014). Although mobile application—based interventions offer a variety of advantages and innovative features, the effectiveness of health-related mobile apps has yet to be evaluated using metaanalytic techniques. Although some meta-analyses of health-related mobile apps exist, they are limited to particular health topics and/or do not evaluate potential moderators (e.g., weight loss and physical activity; Mateo, Granado-Font, Ferré-Grau, & Montaña-Carreras, 2015). To fill a gap in the literature, this metaanalysis evaluates health-related mobile apps across health topics and explores potential moderators of their effectiveness.

Technology and Health
https://doi.org/10.1016/B978-0-12-816958-2.00011-3

243

Advantages of health-related mobile apps

Increased mobile phone ownership, and smartphone ownership in particular (Pew Research Center, 2018), allows for delivery of innovative health interventions to a variety of target populations. Health-related mobile apps are one form of mHealth, or mobile health, interventions. There are thousands of health-related mobile apps available to the public (Krebs & Duncan, 2015), which range widely in terms of their foci from diabetes management (e.g., Glucose Buddy) to family planning (Ovia). For some of the health conditions with the greatest global burden, there is a wealth of mobile apps available (e.g., diabetes), whereas fewer mobile apps are available for other highly prevalent conditions (e.g., iron deficiency anemia; Martínez-Pérez, de la Torre-Díez, & López-Coronado, 2013).

The delivery of health interventions via mobile apps offers a variety of advantages including just-in-time resources and social support, wide reach, cost effectiveness, and monitoring capabilities. Perhaps one of the greatest advantages of using mobile apps to deliver health interventions is the ability to provide users with just-in-time resources and social support. This advantage is particularly important for certain health behaviors. Take, for instance, smoking cessation. Although it can be helpful to provide cessation resources and social support through other channels, mobile apps allow for smokers to access cessation resources and social support when they need it most (i.e., when they experience cravings). Mobile application—based health interventions also benefit from a wide reach, since smartphone ownership has become more ubiquitous, particularly in the United States and other developed countries (Pew Research Center, 2018). This is further underscored by the finding that 58% of adult mobile phone users in the United States have downloaded at least one mobile health app (Krebs & Duncan, 2015). Mobile apps are also a cost-effective means to engage target audiences in disease management and prevention behaviors and to enhance health outcomes. A systematic review found that 74.3% ($k = 24$) of studies found that mHealth interventions were "cost-effective, economically beneficial, or cost saving at base case" (Iribarren, Cato, Falzon, & Stone, 2017, Abstract). Although the review included mHealth interventions more broadly (e.g., mobile health apps, SMS, etc.), not solely mobile health apps, the findings do provide some support for the cost effectiveness of health-related mobile apps.

A rather unique advantage of mobile apps for encouraging healthy behaviors and enhancing health outcomes is that they can harness the capabilities of mobile technology, such as devices' "accelerometer, Global Positioning System, camera, diary, microphone, and speaker" (Higgins, 2016, Basics of Health and Fitness Applications). The aforementioned capabilities of mobile apps allow for easy monitoring and recording of users' health behaviors. One mobile app that used the camera function in an innovative way allowed participants to take before and after photos of their meals to determine fruit, vegetable, and junk food consumption (Kerr et al., 2016). Other mobile apps, such as commercial fitness-related apps, monitor and record behaviors related to physical activity (e.g., step count), using the accelerometer function of mobile technology.

Considering the many advantages of mobile apps for delivering health interventions, this channel presents a potentially powerful means for reaching and engaging target audiences to improve their health and prevent or manage disease. Apps have the potential for far-reaching, cost-effective monitoring of health behaviors and provision of resources and social support. There are many ways in which health-related mobile apps have leveraged the benefits of mobile technology to enhance individuals' health.

Features of health-related mobile apps

Health-related mobile apps provide a range of opportunities for engagement among users. Types of engagement can be classified into the following categories: changing personal environment, facilitating social support, goal setting, progress tracking, reinforcement tracking, self-monitoring, social presentation/announcement, and social referencing (Sama, Eapen, Weinfurt, Shah, & Schulman, 2014). Changing personal environment allows users to alter their environment, such as calming music for stress relief. Social support provides a means by which users can connect to others via groups for encouragement, problem solving, etc. Social presentation/announcement allows users to share their accomplishments with others in-app or via social media. Social referencing provides a reference point to users so that they can see how their accomplishments compare to those of similar others. While goal setting feature allows users to set a goal (e.g., a desired weight), the progress tracking feature provides secondary goals to assist users in achieving their ultimate goals, and the reinforcement tracking gives some form of feedback to users based on the health data recorded in the app. Self-monitoring is a type of engagement in which users are able to track their health behavior(s), such as step count. A review of health-related apps in the Apple iTunes store found that self-monitoring was by far the most common form of engagement (299 out of 400 apps; 74.8%; Sama et al., 2014).

Despite the possibility for health-related mobile apps to use multiple engagement features to assist users in disease management and health promotion, many of these apps may not be fully realizing their potential. Sama et al.'s (2014) review of commercially available health apps indicated that only one-fifth of apps in the sample used more than one type of engagement. It is worth noting, however, that engagement features were coded based on descriptions of the apps provided in the Apple iTunes store. This may have limited the authors' ability to identify all engagement features of the sampled apps, as the descriptions may not have reflected all of the engagement features of the apps. The current metaanalysis investigates the engagement features of health-related apps tested in research studies to determine whether/how these features may moderate effects on health behaviors.

Effectiveness of health-related mobile apps

Although health-related mobile apps have the potential to be a powerful tool for health behavior change, the extent of their effectiveness across health behaviors has yet to be determined. Studies of the effectiveness of health-related mobile apps have found that some were quite successful. In one study, Glynn et al. (2014) found that a physical activity app was effective at increasing the mean daily step count of adults in Ireland ($d = 0.57$). In other studies, however, health-related apps have failed to achieve significantly greater effects compared to control/comparison groups. A study of a mobile application tested among US adults found that it was less effective at enhancing physical activity and decreasing stress relative to a comparison condition ($d = -0.80$; Du, Venkatakrishnan, Youngblood, Ram, & Pirolli, 2016). Due to the inconsistent results across studies of health-related mobile apps, metaanalytic work is needed to closely examine the overall effectiveness of health-related mobile apps and investigate potential moderators of such effects, which may help explain differences across studies.

Research questions

The primary purpose of the current study is to elucidate the effectiveness of health interventions via mobile apps relative to other channels or control conditions. Due to mixed results among studies of the effectiveness of health-related mobile apps (e.g., Du et al., 2016; Glynn et al., 2014) relative to control/comparison conditions, the following research question was posed:

RQ1: Are health-related mobile apps more effective than comparison conditions at improving health behaviors?

The secondary purpose of our study is to determine which participant, methodological, theoretical, and other factors, may moderate the effects of health-related mobile apps relative to comparison conditions. Previous research has found that participant characteristics and methodological factors moderate the relative effects of health interventions (e.g., Yang, 2017).

Theoretical framework is included as a potential moderator because use of a theoretical framework has been found to enhance effects of health interventions (Glanz & Bishop, 2010). Health topic is also considered as a potential moderator, as research has found that some health intervention strategies may be more useful for certain health topics. For example, a metaanalysis found that gain-framed messages are more persuasive than loss-framed messages for disease prevention, but an analysis by health topic indicated that the health topic of dental hygiene was the only one with a statistically significant difference in persuasion based on framing (O'Keefe & Jensen, 2007). Similarly, another metaanalysis found that type of health behavior moderated framing effects, such that gain-framed messages were most effective (compared to loss-framed messages) for smoking, skin cancer prevention, and physical activity (Gallagher & Updegraff, 2012).

A variety of design/features, particularly engagement types such as changing personal environment, social support, goal setting, and progress tracking, which are afforded by mHealth interventions and aim to engage users, may impact intervention effectiveness. For example, progress-tracking interventions have statistically significant effects on goal attainment, such that progress-tracking interventions increased goal attainment (Harkin et al., 2016). Other engagement types, such as changing personal environment and reinforcement tracking, may enhance relative effectiveness of mobile application—based interventions by providing timely functionality/information that decreases perceived barriers to health behavior change.

Mobile use type was included as a potential moderator to determine whether intervention effects are strengthened by combining text/SMS messaging with a mobile application—based health intervention. Text/SMS messages could complement the in-app messages and/or features. In a similar vein, including other channels in addition to mobile phone may strengthen intervention effects by providing complementary messages and/or features and increasing exposure to intervention content. A previous metaanalysis of text message interventions for preventive health behavior found that using additional components increased the ES of text message interventions, with authors indicating that additional components may have functioned to reinforce text messages (Armanasco, Miller, Fjeldsoe, & Marshall, 2017). Other methodological and participant characteristics may moderate relative effectiveness as well; both methodological and participant characteristics have significantly moderated intervention effects in previous research (e.g., Noar, Benac, & Harris, 2007; Yang, 2017). Considering evidence from previous research related to potential moderators of health intervention effects, the following research question was posed:

RQ2: Are the relative effects of health-related mobile apps on health behavior moderated by theoretical paradigm; health topic; types of engagement; mobile use type (mobile app only vs. mobile app + SMS); intervention channels (mobile phone only vs. mobile phone + other channels); message frequency; type of comparison condition; length of intervention and follow-up; and participant characteristics?

Method

Literature search

To understand the effectiveness of mobile application–based interventions in improving health behaviors, comprehensive searches of the *Communication & Mass Media Complete, PsycINFO, Web of Knowledge, Academic Search Premier, PubMed* and *Medline* databases were conducted to identify potentially eligible studies in peer-reviewed journals, conference proceedings, dissertations, and master theses. Search queries were formulated using a combination of search terms in either title or abstract, including intervention, health, *phone*, black-berr*, mHealth, application*, app*, mobile, cellular, short messag*, palm*, iPhone*, MP3*, MP4*, and iPod*. Truncation technique using the asterisk (*) was applied to enable retrieving studies including variations of the keywords with the stem. The abstracts (and full text, as necessary) of each retrieved study were reviewed for relevance. Studies were screened in multiple stages using explicit inclusion and exclusion criteria, and citations were evaluated for inclusion of qualified studies.

Overview of metaanalysis

Cohen's *d* was computed as the basic unit of analysis for the meta-analytic review (Hunter & Schmidt, 2004; Rosenthal, 1991). The statistical analyses were based on methods proposed by Hedges and Olkin (1985), which were also described in Cooper, Hedges, and Valentine (2009). The current metaanalysis used the variance-weighted analysis (Hedges & Olkin, 1985): the overall weighted ES was computed by weighting the unbiased ES (*d*) by the inverse of its associated variance ($W_i = 1/V_i$). A positive ES indicates that the mobile app produced greater behavior change in the desired direction, whereas a negative ES indicates that the mobile app produced less behavior change in the desired direction. The overall homogeneity of ESs was tested using *Q* statistics to determine whether all effects were from the same population. When the *Q* statistic is significant, the ESs are not from the same population, and the overall ES should be computed under the random effects models (REM), which incorporates between-studies uncertainty in the computation (Raudenbush, 2009). Otherwise, a fixed-effect model (FEM) would be used.

In the moderator analysis, ANOVA-like categorical models were conducted to analyze categorical moderators (e.g., health topic, engagement feature). The $Q_{between}$ statistics were applied to explore if study features explained between-group variations in ESs. If $Q_{between}$ was not significant under FEM, the moderator was not significant. If $Q_{between}$ was significant while Q_{within} was not, then this moderator explained the total variance, and the FEM was retained. When both $Q_{between}$ and Q_{within} were significant, there was still unexplained variance remaining, so mixed-effect models (MEM) were performed. A FEM with a categorical moderator assumes that all studies in one subgroup share a common ES, while the MEM allows true variation of effects within the subgroups of studies (Borenstein, Hedges, Higgins, & Rothstein, 2009). The same logic was applied when using metaregression modeling to analyze continuous moderators (e.g., duration of the intervention, participants' age). In the cases where moderator analyses were statistically significant (i.e., $Q_{between}$ statistics were significant under the MEM), posthoc analysis using Tukey contrasts with adjusted P-value was conducted for pairwise comparison.

Besides the overall and moderator analyses, since publication bias may exist when the publication status depends on the statistical significance of study results (Sutton, 2009), multiple analytic approaches were used to check for a potential publication bias problem. First, a funnel plot was used to examine whether ESs from smaller studies show more variability than those from larger studies. Given that the funnel plot interpretation was open to subjectivity, Rosenthal's fail-safe N (1979) and Duval and Tweedie's (2000) trim and fill method were also applied to provide statistical evidence of publication bias. All the analyses were conducted using *Metafor* and *Multcomp* package in R software.

Moderator coding

A variety of moderators were coded, including theoretical, methodological, and participant characteristics of mobile application–based health interventions. Theoretical paradigm, health topic, engagement type, mobile use type, intervention channels, message frequency, control/comparison group design, participants' health condition, participants' mean age, percentage of female participants (to examine the influence of gender), length of the intervention, and length of follow-up were coded as potential moderators.

Theoretical paradigm was coded into four categories (1 = no theory, 2 = behavioral theory, 3 = cognitive theory, 4 = behavioral and cognitive theories combined). Health topic was also coded into four categories (1 = mental health, 2 = nutrition and weight status, 3 = physical activity, 4 = chronic disease management). There were eight types of engagement (Sama et al., 2014), which were each coded as present (1) or absent (0). Mobile use type was coded into two categories as to whether the intervention only used a mobile application or used a mobile application and SMS. Intervention channel was coded into four categories to indicate whether only a mobile phone was used, a mobile phone was used with other types of media, a mobile phone was used with face-to-face communication, or a mobile phone was used with face-to-face communication and additional media. Intervention message frequency was coded based on how often messages were sent to participants, either through a mobile app or SMS (1 = once, 2 = monthly, 3 = weekly, 4 = daily, 5 = continuous access or undefined). The control/comparison group design was coded into five categories (1 = no intervention, 2 = intervention based on interpersonal communication [no media], 3 = intervention using other type of media than mobile phone, 4 = intervention using mobile phone, 5 = intervention with multiple features).

Several participant characteristics were also coded as potential moderators. Participants' health condition was coded for each sample as either general healthy adults or a vulnerable population. Vulnerable populations included those with a short-term or chronic illness (e.g., back pain, diabetes) and/or those at heightened risk of disease (e.g., high BMI, prehypertension). Participants' mean age was coded as the arithmetic average of ages in the sample. Percentage of female participants was coded as the proportion of females in the sample. Length of the intervention and length of follow-up were coded at the ratio level using number of weeks. Length of follow-up was coded as the number of weeks after the end of the intervention at which data were collected.

Results

Study description

After excluding duplicated studies or protocols without results ($n = 2153$), studies that are not empirical quantitative and/or not RCT interventions ($n = 672$), studies not using mobile apps ($n = 484$), and studies without health behavior—related outcome or enough statistical information to for ES calculation ($n = 92$), a total of 25 studies were included in the current metaanalysis (Table 11.1). Following Schmidt and Hunter's (1999) approach, 76 ESs were computed.

TABLE 11.1 Effect sizes (d), variances (V), sample size (N), and characteristics of metaanalyzed studies.

	Study	ES	V	N	Participants	Theory	Topic	Engage	Media	Freq	Ctrl	Outcome	Length	Age	Female %
1	Biddle et al. (2015)	0.14	0.05	87	Overweight/obese individuals	SCT, behavioral choice theory, CMS	Diabetes risk—sedentary behavior	(6)	Workshop and phone call	5	3	Sedentary behavior	48/0	32.8	68.5
2	Buller et al. (2015)	0.10	0.02	195	Adult mobile phone users	SCT	Sun safety	(5), (6)	App	5	1	Sun protection behaviors	8/0	33.3	73.5
		-0.21	0.02												
		0.12	0.02												
3	DeVito Dabbs et al. (2016)	1.20	0.03	186	Lung transplant recipients	Orem's theory	Self-management	(4), (5), (6)	Discharge session, handout	4	5	Self-monitoring	48/0	62	44.8
4	Direito et al. (2015)	0.01	0.12	34	Insufficiently active healthy adults	SRBCT	PA	(1), (4), (6)		3	1	PA	8/0	15.7	57
		0.00	0.13												
5	Du et al. (2016)	0.80	0.04	124	Adults	TPB, SCT	NutriWalking, StressBusting	(2), (3), (4), (6), (7), (8)		4	3	Healthy eating	8/0	36	64.5
6	Duncan et al. (2014)	0.09	0.03	148	Adults	SCT, social regulation	PA	(2), (3), (4), (5), (6), (8)	Website/app	5	3	PA	36/0	44.1	0
		0.17													
		0.07													
7	Frederix et al. (2015)	0.44	0.03	139	CVD patients	NA	Cardio disease	(5), (6)	Telemon, text, text/email	3	2	PA	24/0	61	12.5
8	Glynn et al. (2014)	0.57	0.05	78	Adults (over 16)	NA	Physical activity	(3), (4), (6)	App + brochure	5	3	PA-steps	8/0	44	64

Continued

TABLE 11.1 Effect sizes (*d*), variances (*V*), sample size (*N*), and characteristics of metaanalyzed studies.—cont'd

	Study	ES	V	N	Participants	Theory	Topic	Engage	Media	Freq	Ctrl	Outcome	Length	Age	Female %
9	Hebden et al. (2014)	0.19	0.08	51	Young adults (18–35)	TTM	Eating habits and PA, sedentary behavior	(5), (6)	Emails, internet forums, printed booklet, meeting dietician	5	5	PA	12/1	22.8	80.4
		0.02	0.08												
		0.12	0.08												
		0.01	0.08												
		0.02	0.08												
		0.06	0.12												
10	Holmen et al. (2014)	0.09	0.05	81	Diabetics with elevated HbA1C	TTM	Diabetes self-management	(3), (6)	App + phone counseling + texts + usual care	5	2	Self-management	48/0	57	41
		0.12	0.05												
		0.45	0.05												
		0.25	0.05												
		0.21	0.05												
		0.07	0.05												
		0.00	0.05												
		0.46	0.05												
		0.02	0.05												
		0.10	0.05												
		0.06	0.05												
		0.08	0.05												
		0.08	0.05												
		0.48	0.05												
		0.28	0.05												
		0.06	0.05												

#	Study	ES	SE	N	Population	Theory	Behavior	BCTs	Delivery			Outcome	Ratio	%	%
11	Hurling et al. (2007)	0.37	0.06	77	Healthy adults	Social comparison, decisional balance, ELM	PA	(3), (5), (6), (8)	App/website, email/text	5	2	PA	9/0	40.4	66.3
12	Hutcheson (2013)	0.18 −0.09	0.13 0.13	31	Ethnic minority female children/adolescents	SCT	Diet	(3), (5), (6)		5	3	Fruit intake	4/4	11.3	100
13	Irvine et al. (2015)	0.35 0.67 0.30 0.79	0.01 0.01 0.01 0.01	398	Adults with nonspecific back pain	SCT, TPB	Nonspecific low back pain	(4), (6)	App/website, email reminders	3 3 3 3	3 1 3 1	Prevention-helping behaviors	8/0 8/0 8/8 8/8		58.5 60.6 58.5 60.6
14	Johnson et al. (2016)	0.65	0.7	87	Adolescents taking asthma medications	NA	Medication adherence	(5), (6)	App/website	3	3	Medication adherence	3/0	14.1	49.4
15	Kerr et al. (2016)	0.00 0.23 0.00 0.18 0.12 0.00 0.12 0.18	0.03 0.03 0.03 0.03 0.03 0.03 0.03 0.03	147	Adults 18–30 years old	SDT	Diet/nutrition	(5), (6)		3	1	Fruit servings Vegetable servings SSCS EDNPS Fruit servings Vegetable servings SSCS ENDS	24/0	24.6	65.2

Continued

TABLE 11.1 Effect sizes (*d*), variances (*V*), sample size (*N*), and characteristics of metaanalyzed studies.—cont'd

	Study	ES	V	N	Participants	Theory	Topic	Engage	Media	Freq	Ctrl	Outcome	Length	Age	Female %
16	Maher et al. (2015)	0.36 0.72 0.06 0.11 0.09 0.16	0.04 0.04 0.04 0.04 0.04 0.04	98	Insufficiently active adults	TPB, fun theory	PA	(2), (3), (4), (5), (6), (7), (8)	Emails, social media (FB)	5	1	Self-reported total weekly MVPA	8/0	35.6	70.9
17	Mauriello et al. (2016)	0.57 0.44	0.02 0.02	219	Women with at least one risk	TTM	Risk management during pregnancy	(2), (3), (4), (5)	Behavior change guide	3	3	Fruit and vegetable consumption	24/4 24/16	26.9	100
18	McGillicuddy et al. (2013)	1.57	0.28	19	Recipients of kidney transplant	SDT	Medical adherence and blood pressure	(4), (5), (6)	Email	3	5	Adherence	12/0	50.4	42.1
19	Mira et al. (2014)	0.78	0.04	99	65 yrs or older multimorbid patients	N/A	Adherence	(4), (6)	N/A	4	1	Adherence	12/0	71.9	44.4
20	Mummah et al. (2016)	1.26	0.28	17	Overweight adults	Behavioral theory	Vegetable consumption	(1), (3), (4), (5), (6), (7), (8)	Class	5	2	Vegetable consumption	12/0	42	64.7
21	Oh et al. (2015)	0.28	0.01	334	Obese patients with metabolic syndrome	N/A	Weight control	(2), (4), (5), (6)	Mobile intervention and treatment	4	2	Diet habit	24/0	48.4	49.1

#	Author			N	Population	Theory	Engage	Target	Delivery			Outcome	Int/Ctrl	%	%
22	Petrella et al. (2014)	0.10	0.03	127	Adults with at least two metabolic syndrome risk factors	N/A	(6)	Diabetes management	Training session, pedometer	4	2	Physical exercise	12/0	56.7	74.5
		0.04	0.03									Exercise compliance			
23	Voth et al. (2016)	2.15	0.15	39	Randomly selected	SCT, behavior change theory	(4), (5), (6)	Exercise behavior	Mobile phone	4	1	Self-monitoring of exercise	8/0	40	57
		0.72	0.11									Self-reported exercise			
24	Wang et al. (2015)	0.32	0.06	67	Obese/overweight	N/A	(2), (3), (4), (6)	PA	FitBit one	4	4	Steps	6/0	48.2	91
		0.24	0.06									MVPA			
		0.37	0.06									All intensity			
		0.19	0.06									Steps			
		0.09	0.06									MVPA			
		0.41	0.06									All intensity			
25	Whittaker et al. (2012)	0.18	0.00	835	Depressive symptoms	CBT	(3)	Depression	Mobile phone	4	4	Functioning	9/0	14	68.3
		0.16	0.00												
		0.12	0.00												

Ctrl = control/comparison group design: 1 = no intervention, 2 = intervention using interpersonal communication (no media), 3 = intervention based on interpersonal communication, 4 = intervention using mobile phone, 5 = intervention with multiple features. Engage = engagement type: (1) changing personal environment, (2) facilitating social support, (3) goal setting, (4) progress tracking, (5) reinforcement tracking, (6) self-monitoring, (7) social presentation or announcement, (8) social referencing. *CBT*, cognitive behavioral therapy; *CMS*, common sense model; *EDNPS*, energy-dense nutrient-poor servings; *ELM*, elaboration likelihood model; *Freq*, message frequency; *Length*, Length of the intervention/length of follow-up; *PA*, physical activity; *SCT*, social cognitive theory; *SDT*, self-determination theory; *SRBCT*, self-regulatory behavior change techniques; *SSBS*, Sugar sweetened beverage servings; *TPB*, theory of planned behavior, and *TTM*, transtheoretical model.

Among the 25 studies, 18 were based on at least one theory, including SCT (e.g., Biddle et al., 2015), transtheoretical model (e.g., Hebden et al., 2014), self-determination theory (e.g., Kerr et al., 2016), and theory of planned behavior (e.g., Du et al., 2016). The metaanalyzed mHealth interventions focused on four topics, namely mental health (Whittaker et al., 2012), nutrition and weight status (e.g., Oh et al., 2015), physical activity (e.g., Wang et al., 2015), and chronic disease management (e.g., McGilli-cuddy et al., 2013)[1]. In total, 3717 ($N = 3717$) participants were included.

Overall analysis

The Q statistic was significant (Q_{total} ($df = 75$) = 234.01, $P < .001$) and estimated under the FEM, indicating that the ESs were not homogeneous, and this mean ES should be estimated under the REM using restricted maximum likelihood estimation method. Under the REM, the sample weighted mean for standardized mean difference was 0.19 (95% CIs [0.12, 0.27]), which is a small (Cohen, 1988) but statistically significant ES ($P < .001$). In other words, there was a statistically significant mean difference between the mobile application–based health intervention and comparison groups according to the overall analysis. Moreover, I^2, an index representing the ratio of true heterogeneity to total variance across observed ESs, is 71.01%, indicating large between-study variance according to the benchmarks suggested by Higgins, Thompson, Deeks, and Altman (2003). Similarly, Birge's ratio, another index to quantify the magnitude of heterogeneity (computed as $Q/df = 234.01/75 = 3.12$), is larger than one (the ratio when all the variance comes from sampling error), indicating large between-study heterogeneity. Sampling error variance ($S_e^2 = 0.0187$) only accounted for 25.48% of the total variance ($S^2 = 0.0734$), suggesting the presence of moderator(s). Therefore, the moderators proposed in RQ2 were analyzed.

Moderator analyses

Moderator analyses were conducted by analyzing theoretical paradigm, health topic, engagement type, mobile use type, intervention channel, intervention message frequency, control/comparison group design, and

---

[1] The categorization of health topics was based on Healthy People 2020 (2015) at http://www.healthypeople.gov/2020/topicsobjectives2020/default. There were originally eight categories in the code book (i.e., 1 = tobacco use, 2 = mental health, 3 = nutrition and weight status, 4 = physical activity, 5 = sexual health, 6 = health-related quality of life and well-being, 7 = HIV/AIDS, 8 = chronic disease management). However, since no study focused in tobacco use, sexual health, health-related quality of life and well-being, and HIV/AIDS, these four categories were excluded from analyses.

participants' health condition as categorical moderators respectively. Moreover, participants' mean age, percentage of female participants (to examine the influence of gender), length of the intervention, and length of follow-up were analyzed as continuous moderators.

Theoretical paradigm: The theoretical paradigm was marginally significant as a moderator (MEM, $Q_{between}$ ($df = 3$) = 7.55, $P = .056$) (Fig. 11.1). Mobile application—based health interventions applying both cognitive and behavioral theories ($d = 0.34$, $P < .05$) had the highest weighted mean ES among the four categories and was significantly higher at 0.05 level ($z = 2.16$) than the interventions applying cognitive theories only, which showed the lowest mean ES ($d = 0.03$, $P = .53$).

Health topic: Under MEM, the health topic was not a significant moderator ($Q_{between}$ ($df = 3$) = 3.31, $P = .35$). The weighted mean ES of interventions targeting on mental health ($d = 0.15$, $P < .001$), physical activity ($d = 0.24$, $P < .001$), and chronic disease management ($d = 0.23$, $P < .01$) was significant, while the ES of interventions on nutrition and weight status was not ($d = 0.08$, $P = .27$). There was no significant difference between the mean ESs across topics.

Engagement types: Among the eight types of engagement proposed by Sama et al. (2014), only progress tracking (MEM, $Q_{between}$ ($df = 1$) = 16.98, $P < .001$) was a significant moderator. Specifically, the weighted mean ES of the mobile app—based health interventions that can create subsidiary tasks based on the user-defined goal and log the users' progress ($d = 0.38$, $P < .001$) was significantly higher than that of the mobile app—based

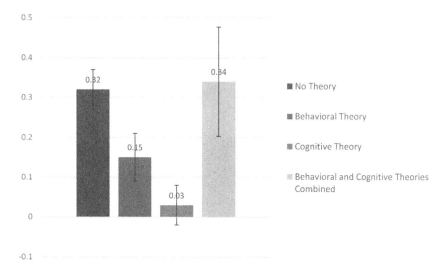

FIGURE 11.1 Theoretical paradigm as the moderator and the weighted mean ES for each category.

health interventions without this feature ($d = 0.09, P < .001$) at 0.001 level ($z = 4.11$).

Mobile use type: Whether the health intervention applied mobile apps only or combined mobile apps with SMS was not a significant moderator (MEM, $Q_{between}$ ($df = 1$) $= 0.07, P = .79$). Health interventions using mobile apps only ($d = 0.19$, $P < .001$) yielded similar weighted mean ES with interventions combining SMS and mobile apps ($d = 0.16, P < .001$).

Intervention channel: The channels through which the mobile application–*based* health interventions were implemented turned out to be another significant moderator (MEM, $Q_{between}$ ($df = 3$) $= 14.55, P < .01$) (Fig. 11.2). Pairwise comparison indicated that the weighted mean ES of interventions combining mobile phone with another type of media ($d = 0.35, P < .001$) was significantly higher than that of the interventions using mobile apps only ($d = 0.12, P = .14$) at 0.01 level ($z = 2.81$) and higher than that of the interventions combining mobile phone with face-to-face communication ($d = -0.09, P = .23$) at 0.001 level ($z = 3.37$).

Intervention message frequency: The frequency of the intervention's message delivery was found as a significant moderator (MEM, $Q_{between}$ ($df = 2$) $= 9.99, P < .01$) (Fig. 11.3). No intervention in the current sample delivered the intervention message only once or on a monthly basis. In regard to the other three categories, the interventions without a clearly defined frequency (or enabling participants to access the apps continuously; $d = 0.08, P < .05$) had significantly lower weighted mean ES than those delivering weekly ($d = 0.35, P < .001$) and daily messages ($d = 0.34$, $P < .01$) at $0.001(z = 2.75)$ and 0.01 levels ($z = 2.29$), respectively.

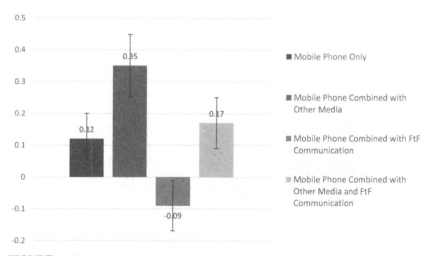

FIGURE 11.2 Intervention channel as the moderator and the weighted mean ES for each category.

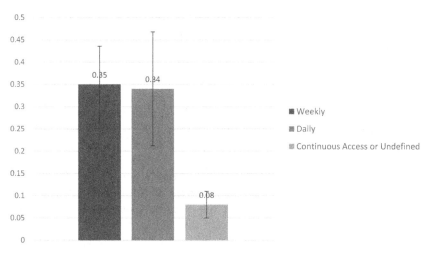

FIGURE 11.3   Message frequency as the moderator and the weighted mean ES for each category.

Control/comparison group design: According to the nonsignificant between-study variance under MEM ($Q_{between}$ ($df = 4$) = 3.02, $P = .56$), the control/comparison group design did not show a significant difference in the comparative effectiveness of the mobile application—based interventions. The lowest weighted mean ES was produced by the interventions with control group based on interpersonal communication without media ($d = 0.10$, $P = .06$), while the highest ES was by those with control groups using multiple features ($d = 0.30$, $P = .14$), which, however, are not significantly different from each other.

Participants' age, gender, and health condition: The majority of the interventions in the current sample were conducted with at-risk populations, except for eight studies (Buller et al., 2015; Du et al., 2016; Duncan et al., 2014; Glynn et al., 2014; Hebden et al., 2014; Hurling et al., 2007; Kerr et al., 2016; Voth, Oelke, & Jung, 2016). Whether the participants were healthy or at-risk populations was found as a significant moderator of the ESs (MEM, $Q_{between}$ ($df = 1$) = 4.85, $P < .05$). Specifically, interventions conducted with at-risk populations has significantly higher weighted mean ES ($d = 0.25$, $P < .001$) than those with healthy populations ($d = 0.08$, $P = .26$) at 0.05 level ($z = 2.24$). Neither participants' age (FEM, $Q_{between}$ ($df = 1$) = 1.94, $P = 0.16$) nor gender (FEM, $Q_{between}$ ($df = 1$) = 1.00, $P = .32$) was a significant moderator.

Length of intervention and follow-up: How long the interventions lasted was a marginally significant moderator (MEM, $Q_{between}$ ($df = 1$) = 3.58, $P = .06$), with one additional week reducing the mean ES by 0.005. The length of the follow-up ranged from 3 weeks (Johnson et al., 2016) to

2 years later (Holmen et al., 2014), with an average follow-up period being 16.92 weeks ($SD = 13.78$). However, the length of the follow-up measure did not moderate the ESs (MEM, $Q_{between}$ ($df = 1$) = 0.82, $P = .37$).

Publication bias

Publication bias may exist when the publication status depends on the statistical significance of study results (Sutton, 2009). Multiple techniques were applied to the data to check for a potential publication bias problem. First, a funnel plot can be used to examine whether ESs from smaller studies show more variability than those from larger studies. The funnel plot of ESs seems to be generally symmetric, but three ESs were located at the bottom right. To further analyze the potential existence of publication bias, the regression test for funnel plot asymmetry ($z = 1.63$, $P = .10$) was implemented and not significant, which provides evidence for the absence of publication bias. In addition, Rosenthal's fail-safe N was 2,340, which is much larger than the tolerance level ($5k + 10 = 390$), and no study was found missing for symmetry using Duval and Tweedie's (2000) trim and fill method, which further confirmed the absence of publication bias in the current sample.

Discussion

In examining the effectiveness of mobile application—based health interventions, the current metaanalysis found that health interventions delivered via mobile apps were significantly more effective than comparison conditions, with an ES of $d = 0.19$ (95% CI [0.12, 0.27]). Support for the efficacy of mobile application—based interventions in the current study is consistent with findings of previous metaanalyses of mHealth interventions in several areas, including physical activity (SMS; Fanning, Mullen, & McAuley, 2012), medication adherence, (SMS; Thakkar et al., 2016), and diabetes management (mobile apps; Bonoto et al., 2017). Furthermore, results indicated that several factors significantly moderated the relative effects of mobile application—based health interventions. Specifically, there were significant differences based on theoretical paradigm, engagement type, channel, message frequency, participants' health condition, and intervention length.

Moderators

Scholars have emphasized the importance of grounding health interventions and campaigns in theory, with several reviews finding that interventions based on theory were more effective than those without a theoretical basis (as described by Glanz & Bishop, 2010). In the current metaanalysis, it is not the presence or absence of theory but, rather, the types of theories that moderated the relative effects of health-related mobile apps. When mobile application–based health interventions included cognitive and behavioral theories, their relative effects were significantly higher than when they included only cognitive theories. This finding does not serve to undermine the importance of cognitive theory but highlights the greater effects that such health interventions may achieve through the combination of cognitive and behavioral theories. Cappella (2006) has argued that behavior change and information processing theories are complementary as each type of theory answers questions that the other type does not, both of which are important for informing message design. Based on results of the current metaanalysis, it may be prudent for scholars to combine different types of theories, such as cognitive/information processing and behavioral theories, to inform design of mobile application–based health interventions.

Type of engagement also moderated the relative effects of mobile application–based health interventions, such that effects were significantly greater for interventions in which progress tracking was incorporated. Of the eight types of engagement, only progress tracking served as a significant moderator. Progress tracking may more directly serve as a map to reaching one's goals than other types of engagement, thereby facilitating goal achievement. Unlike self-monitoring, which is simply tracking one's behaviors, progress tracking is a means of not only tracking one's behavior but also comparing it to a goal(s). As such, progress tracking provides a reference for users to see how far they have come. The self-reflection or self-appraisal that progress tracking initiates may enhance perceived self-efficacy, resulting in further improvements in health behaviors. Perceived self-efficacy can determine motivation and accomplishments, as described by Bandura (1993). Metaanalytic findings support the importance of progress tracking in the process of turning intentions into behaviors, with results indicating that "monitoring goal progress is an effective self-regulation strategy, and that interventions that increase the frequency of progress monitoring are likely to promote behavior change" (Harkin et al., 2016, p. 198). Therefore, the current findings related to progress tracking are consistent with previous findings and suggest that mobile application–based health interventions should incorporate progress tracking when it is feasible and appropriate.

The channels (in addition to the mobile app) that were used in health interventions influenced intervention effects. Mobile application–based interventions that incorporated another form of media had significantly greater relative effects than mobile application–based interventions that did not use any additional media channels or combined a health-related app with face-to-face channel. Integrating additional media and mobile application–based interventions may be more effective than app-only interventions because the use of multiple mediums increase users' exposure to health-related messaging and resources. Alternatively, or additionally, using multiple types of media may allow for different but complementary messages to be delivered via particular mediums. In a previous metaanalysis, authors found that combining additional intervention components with text messages increased intervention effects and argued that the additional components helped to reinforce text messages (Armanasco et al., 2017), which may also be the case with mobile application–based health interventions in the current meta-analysis. There may also be different functionalities/interactivity available through the various media that work together to enhance interventions. Therefore, distinct media may serve different functions for users, in keeping with media complementarity theory, which has been supported in the realm of health information (Ruppel & Rains, 2012; Tian & Robinson, 2008).

The frequency of messages within the health intervention influenced the size of the relative effects of mobile application–based interventions, such that interventions with daily and weekly messages exhibited significantly greater relative effects than interventions with continuous or undefined access. Due to the way in which messaging was operationalized, the continuous/undefined category represented health interventions in which participants had continuous access to the app, but were not necessarily provided with in-app/out-of-app intervention messages or messages reminding them to use the app. Therefore, this finding is rather intuitive in that more content or reminders sent to participants in the form of daily or weekly messages resulted in greater effects of mobile application–based interventions relative to comparison conditions. It may be that it was the content of messages themselves that enhanced intervention effects and/or it could be that reminders to use the app led to greater engagement with intervention content within the app. Previous research has found that reminders can be effective techniques in and of themselves for encouraging positive health behaviors, such as clinic attendance (Guy et al., 2012) and adherence to antiretroviral therapy (Pop-Eleches et al., 2011). Messages may also have prompted participants to engage with intervention components within the app, thereby leading to greater effectiveness via greater exposure to intervention content. Additional research is needed to further investigate the theoretical processes by which messages in mobile application–based health interventions enhance effectiveness.

The effects of mobile application–based interventions became significantly smaller for each week of the intervention, with the greatest effects exhibited by one-time interventions. This finding may reflect the difficulty that health interventions generally face in keeping people interested and engaged, particularly considering that they must compete with so many other media. For mobile application–based health interventions, in particular, they have an extreme amount of competition from other health-related apps as well as apps that serve other purposes (e.g., entertainment, education, etc.). With limited time available, people must choose which apps and other forms of media to attend to in any given time period. It may be that current mobile application–based health interventions do not adequately sustain users' interest and engagement. However, our findings related to intervention length are inconsistent with previous mHealth research. For example, Armanasco et al. (2017) found that text message interventions lasting 6–12 months had the largest effects. There may still be some explanation for shorter interventions having greater relative effects, as one study found that 45.7% of participant stopped using health apps that they had downloaded; 40.5% of those who stopped using health apps did so because they lost interest in them (Krebs & Duncan, 2015). It may be beneficial to incorporate app notifications/messages to maintain interest considering that the current findings indicated greater relative effectiveness of mobile application–based health interventions using daily or weekly messaging.

One participant characteristic served as a significant moderator, which was the health condition of participants. Mobile application–based interventions used by at-risk groups (e.g., overweight/obese) produced higher relative effects than those used by generally healthy groups, which is consistent with a metaanalysis of interventions via social networking services (Yang, 2017). The explanation for this may lie in differences in the need to make health behavior changes. Since at-risk groups require behavior change to a greater extent than generally healthy groups, people who are part of at-risk groups may be more motivated to make behavior changes than those who are not; similarly, there may be a ceiling effect for generally healthy populations, who have smaller changes to make (Yang, 2017). Perceived threat, a construct included in cognitive and behavioral health models (e.g., extended parallel process model, Witte, 1992; health belief model, Rosenstock, 1974), may be relevant here, as it contributes to health message acceptance and behavior change. If at-risk groups realize that they are at risk, those perceptions could have contributed to their greater behavior change.

Limitations

As with all empirical research, the current study has some limitations. Some studies that otherwise qualified could not be included in the metaanalysis due to a lack of necessary information for calculating ESs. Attempts were made to gain the necessary information by contacting authors, but many authors did not respond to the inquiries or no longer had access to the data that were needed for ES calculation. Another limitation is that the search for qualified studies included conference papers, theses, and dissertations, which may not be of the same quality as peer-reviewed journal articles. However, this limitation is not likely to be a serious concern considering that the majority of the studies that met inclusion criteria were peer-reviewed articles published in first tier journals ($k = 22/25\%$; 88%).

Implications and future research

This metaanalysis provides implications for health communication researchers as well as health practitioners. Mobile application–based health interventions were significantly more effective at improving health behavior than comparison conditions/interventions. These findings suggest that mobile application–based health interventions can be an effective tool for health behavior change. Healthcare organizations may be able to complement in-person care with health behavior monitoring and consultations via mobile apps. For example, mobile apps for medication adherence (e.g., MyMedSchedule) could allow health professionals to monitor patients' medication taking, which could improve health outcomes and reduce costs (Dayer, Heldenbrand, Anderson, Gubbins, & Martin, 2013).

Mobile application–based interventions were relatively more effective when they used cognitive and behavioral theories, incorporated progress tracking, combined an app with other media, and included daily or weekly messaging. Health communication professionals and healthcare practitioners should consider these findings when designing and/or implementing mobile application–based interventions for patients/target groups. Perhaps the first thing to address in developing/implementing mobile application–based interventions is how cognitive and behavioral theories can be used together to guide app development. It may also be beneficial to include multiple media to interact with and engage users in a health behavior intervention. Such a strategy would allow for greater exposure to intervention content and complementary messages/functions that work well with each medium. Furthermore, including daily or weekly messaging and progress tracking within the app may help users to stay engaged with the app and move forward toward their health behavior goals.

Additional studies are needed to further our understanding of the effectiveness of mobile application—based health interventions and the mechanisms behind their effectiveness. Although the current metaanalysis included studies of mobile application—based health interventions across health topics, some topics (e.g., sexual health, smoking cessation) were addressed in only a few studies or not at all. Future research should expand the literature on mobile health apps by conducting randomized controlled trials of mobile application—based health interventions for important health topics that are underrepresented in the literature. Another avenue for future research relates to the usefulness of various features for engaging users in mobile health apps. Progress tracking was the only engagement type that moderated the relative effectiveness of mobile application—based health interventions. However, some engagement types were used in few of the studies included in the metaanalysis (e.g., changing personal environment), so additional research could help further our knowledge of the extent to which different engagement types function independently and in combination to more effectively change health behavior.

Conclusion

This metaanalysis found that mobile application—based health interventions were relatively more effective than comparison conditions at influencing positive health behavior change. Mobile health apps had the greatest relative effects when they combined cognitive and behavioral theory; incorporated progress tracking; used media channels in addition to the app; included daily or weekly messaging; targeted at-risk groups; and were implemented as one-time interventions. Health professionals should consider using cognitive and behavioral theories to inform interventions, including progress tracking, using engaging features to keep users interested throughout the duration of the intervention, incorporating additional media channels, and providing daily or weekly messages. Future research should investigate the effectiveness of mobile health apps for health topics that are underrepresented in the literature and determine how engagement features can be used to optimize positive health behavior change.

References

References marked with an asterisk indicate studies included in the meta-analysis.
Armanasco, A. A., Miller, Y. D., Fjeldsoe, B. S., & Marshall, A. L. (2017). Preventive health behavior change text message interventions: A meta-analysis. *American Journal of Preventive Medicine, 52*(3), 391—402. https://doi.org/10.1016/j.amepre.2016.10.042.

Bandura, A. (1993). Perceived self-efficacy in cognitive development and functioning. *Educational Psychologist, 28*(2), 117–148. https://doi.org/10.1207/s15326985ep2802_3.

* Biddle, S. J., Edwardson, C. L., Wilmot, E. G., Yates, T., Gorely, T., Bodicoat, D. H., … Davies, M. J. (2015). A randomised controlled trial to reduce sedentary time in young adults at risk of type 2 diabetes mellitus: Project STAND (sedentary time and diabetes). *PLoS One, 10*(12), e0143398, 10.137/journal.pone.0143398.

Bonoto, B. C., de Araújo, V. E., Godói, I. P., de Lemos, L. L. P., Godman, B., Bennie, M., … Guerra, A. A., Jr. (2017). Efficacy of mobile apps to support the care of patients with diabetes mellitus: A systematic review and meta-analysis of randomized controlled trials. *JMIR mHealth and uHealth, 5*(3), e4. https://doi.org/10.2196/mhealth.6309.

Borenstein, M., Hedges, L. V., Higgins, J. P. T., & Rothstein, H. R. (2009). *Introduction to meta-analysis.* UK: John Wiley & Sons.

Buller, D. B., Berwick, M., Lantz, K., Buller, M. K., Shane, J., Kane, I., & Liu, X. (2015). Evaluation of immediate and 12-week effects of a smartphone sun-safety mobile application: A randomized clinical trial. *JAMA Dermatology, 151*(5), 505–512. https://doi.org/10.1001/jamadermatol.2014.3894.

Cappella, J. N. (2006). Integrating message effects and behavior change theories: Organizing comments and unanswered questions. *Journal of Communication, 56*(S1), S265–S279. https://doi.org/10.1111/j.1460-2466.2006.00293.x.

Cohen, J. (1988). *Statistical power analysis for the behavioral sciences* (2nd ed.). Hillsdale, NJ: Lawrence Erlbaum.

Guy, R., Hocking, J., Wand, H., Stott, S., Ali, H., & Kaldor, J. (2012). How effective are short message service reminders at increasing clinic attendance? A meta-analysis and systematic review. *Health Services Research, 47*(2), 614–632. https://doi.org/10.1111/j.1475-6773.2011.01342.x.

Cooper, H. M., Hedges, L. V., & Valentine, J. C. (Eds.). (2009). *The handbook of research synthesis and meta-analysis* (2nd ed.). New York, NY: Russell Sage Foundation.

Dayer, L., Heldenbrand, S., Anderson, P., Gubbins, P. O., & Martin, B. C. (2013). Smartphone medication adherence apps: Potential benefits to patients and providers. *Journal of the American Pharmacists Association, 53*(2), 172–181. https://doi.org/10.1331/JAPhA.2013.12202.

* DeVito Dabbs, A., Song, M. K., Myers, B. A., Li, R., Hawkins, R. P., Pilewski, J. M., … Dew, M. A. (2016). A randomized controlled trial of a mobile health intervention to promote self-management after lung transplantation. *American Journal of Transplantation, 16*(7), 2172–2180. https://doi.org/10.1111/ajt.13701.

* Direito, A., Jiang, Y., Whittaker, R., & Maddison, R. (2015). Apps for IMproving FITness and increasing physical activity among young people: The AIMFIT pragmatic randomized controlled trial. *Journal of Medical Internet Research, 17*(8), e210. https://doi.org/10.2196/jmir.4568.

* Du, H., Venkatakrishnan, A., Youngblood, G. M., Ram, A., & Pirolli, P. (2016). A group-based mobile application to increase adherence in exercise and nutrition programs: A factorial design feasibility study. *JMIR mHealth and uHealth, 4*(1), e4. https://doi.org/10.2196/mhealth.4900.

* Duncan, M., Vandelanotte, C., Kolt, G. S., Rosenkranz, R. R., Caperchione, C. M., George, E. S., … Mummery, W. K. (2014). Effectiveness of a web- and mobile phone-based intervention to promote physical activity and healthy eating in middle-aged males: Randomized controlled trial of the ManUp study. *Journal of Medical Internet Research, 16*(6), e136. https://doi.org/10.2196/jmir.3107.

Duval, S., & Tweedie, R. (2000). A nonparametric "trim and fill" method of accounting for publication bias in meta-analysis. *Journal of the American Statistical Association, 95*(449), 89–98. https://doi.org/10.1080/01621459.2000.10473905.

Fanning, J., Mullen, S. P., & McAuley, E. (2012). Increasing physical activity with mobile devices: A meta-analysis. *Journal of Medical Internet Research, 14*(6), e161. https://doi.org/10.2196/jmir.2171.

* Frederix, I., Hansen, D., Coninx, K., Vandervoort, P., Vandijck, D., Hens, N., ... Dendale, P. (2015). Medium-term effectiveness of a comprehensive internet-based and patient-specific telerehabilitation program with text messaging support for cardiac patients: Randomized controlled trial. *Journal of Medical Internet Research, 17*(7). https://doi.org/10.2196/jmir.4799. e185−e185.

Gallagher, K. M., & Updegraff, J. A. (2012). Health message framing effects on attitudes, intentions, and behavior: A meta-analytic review. *Annals of Behavioral Medicine, 43*, 101−116. https://doi.org/10.1007/s12160-011-9308-7.

Glanz, K., & Bishop, D. B. (2010). The role of behavioral science theory in development and implementation of public health interventions. *Annual Review of Public Health, 31*, 399−418. https://doi.org/10.1146/annurev.publhealth.012809.103604.

* Glynn, L. G., Hayes, P. S., Casey, M., Glynn, F., Alvarez-Iglesias, A., Newell, J., ... Murphy, A. W. (2014). Effectiveness of a smartphone application to promote physical activity in primary care: The SMART MOVE randomised controlled trial. *British Journal of General Practice, 64*(624), e384−e391. https://doi.org/10.3399/bjgp14X680461.

Harkin, B., Webb, T. L., Chang, B. P. I., Prestwich, A., Conner, M., Kellar, I., ... Sheeran, P. (2016). Does monitoring goal progress promote goal attainment? A meta-analysis of the experimental evidence. *Psychological Bulletin, 142*(2), 198−229. https://doi.org/10.1037/bul0000025.

* Hebden, L., Cook, A., Ploeg, H. P., King, L., Bauman, A., & Allman-Farinelli, M. (2014). A mobile health intervention for weight management among young adults: A pilot randomised controlled trial. *Journal of Human Nutrition and Dietetics, 27*(4), 322−332. https://doi.org/10.1111/jhn.12155.

Hedges, L. V., & Olkin, I. (1985). *Statistical methods for meta-analysis.* Orlando, FL: Academic.

Higgins, J. P. (2016). Smartphone applications for patients' health and fitness. *The American Journal of Medicine, 129*(1), 11−19. https://doi.org/10.1016/j.amjmed.2015.05.038.

Higgins, J. P., Thompson, S. G., Deeks, J. J., & Altman, D. G. (2003). Measuring inconsistency in meta-analyses. *British Medical Journal, 327*(7414), 557−560. https://doi.org/10.1136/bmj.327.7414.557.

* Holmen, H., Torbjornsen, A., Wahl, A. K., Jenum, A. K., Smastuen, M. C., Arsand, E., & Ribu, L. (2014). A mobile health intervention for self-management and lifestyle change for persons with type 2 diabetes, part 2: One-year results from the Norwegian randomized controlled trial RENEWING HEALTH. *Journal of Medical Internet Research mHealth and uHealth, 2*(4), e57. https://doi.org/10.2196/mhealth.3882.

Hunter, J. E., & Schmidt, F. L. (2004). *Methods of meta-analysis: Correcting error and bias in research findings* (2nd ed.). Thousand Oaks, CA: Sage.

* Hurling, R., Catt, M., Boni, M. D., Fairley, B. W., Hurst, T., Murray, P., ... Sodhi, J. S. (2007). Using internet and mobile phone technology to deliver an automated physical activity program: Randomized controlled trial. *Journal of Medical Internet Research, 9*(2), e7. https://doi.org/10.2196/jmir.9.2.e7.

* Hutcheson, T. D. (2013). *Using mobile technology to impact fruit and vegetable consumption in low-income youth.* Doctoral dissertation. Retrieved from https://kuscholarworks.ku.edu/bitstream/handle/1808/10817/Hutcheson_ku_0099D_12535_DATA_1.pdf. sequence=1.

Iribarren, S. J., Cato, K., Falzon, L., & Stone, P. W. (2017). What is the economic evidence for mHealth? A systematic review of economic evaluations of mHealth solutions. *PLoS One, 12*(2), e0170581. https://doi.org/10.1371/journal.pone.0170581.

* Irvine, A. B., Russell, H., Manocchia, M., Mino, D. E., Cox Glassen, T., Morgan, R., ... Ary, D. V. (2015). Mobile-web app to self-manage low back pain: Randomized controlled trial. *Journal of Medical Internet Research, 17*(1), e1. https://doi.org/10.2196/jmir.3130.

* Johnson, K. B., Patterson, B. L., Ho, Y. X., Chen, Q., Nian, H., Davison, C. L., ... Mulvaney, S. A. (2016). The feasibility of text reminders to improve medication adherence in adolescents with asthma. *Journal of the American Medical Informatics Association, 23*(3), 449–455. https://doi.org/10.1093/jamia/ocv158.

* Kerr, D. A., Harray, A. J., Pollard, C. M., Dhaliwal, S. S., Delp, E. J., Howat, P. A., ... Boushey, C. J. (2016). The connecting health and technology study: A 6-month randomized controlled trial to improve nutrition behaviours using a mobile food record and text messaging support in young adults. *International Journal of Behavioral Nutrition and Physical Activity, 13*(1). https://doi.org/10.1186/s12966-016-0376-8.

Krebs, P., & Duncan, D. T. (2015). Health app use among US mobile phone owners: A national survey. *Journal of Medical Internet Research mHealth and uHealth, 3*(4), e101. https://doi.org/10.2196/mhealth.4924.

* Maher, C., Ferguson, M., Vandelanotte, C., Plotnikoff, R., De Bourdeaudhuij, I., Thomas, S., ... Olds, T. (2015). A web-based, social networking physical activity intervention for insufficiently active adults delivered via Facebook app: Randomized controlled trial. *Journal of Medical Internet Research, 17*(7), e174. https://doi.org/10.2196/jmir.4086.

Martínez-Pérez, B., de la Torre-Díez, I., & López-Coronado, M. (2013). Mobile health applications for the most prevalent conditions by the World Health Organization: Review and analysis. *Journal of Medical Internet Research, 15*(6), e120. https://doi.org/10.2196/jmir.2600.

Mateo, G. F., Granado-Font, E., Ferré-Grau, C., & Montaña-Carreras, X. (2015). Mobile phone apps to promote weight loss and increase physical activity: A systematic review and meta-analysis. *Journal of Medical Internet Research, 17*(11), e253. https://doi.org/10.2196/jmir.4836.

* Mauriello, L. M., Van Marter, D. F., Umanzor, C. D., Castle, P. H., & de Aguiar, E. L. (2016). Using mHealth to deliver behavior change interventions within prenatal care at community health centers. *American Journal of Health Promotion, 30*(7), 554–562. https://doi.org/10.4278/ajhp.140530-QUAN-248.

* McGillicuddy, J. W., Gregoski, M. J., Weiland, A. K., Rock, R. A., Brunner-Jackson, B. M., Patel, S. K., ... Treiber, F. A. (2013). Mobile health medication adherence and blood pressure control in renal transplant recipients: A proof-of-concept randomized controlled trial. *Journal of Medical Internet Research Research Protocols, 2*(2). https://doi.org/10.2196/resprot.2633.

* Mira, J. J., Navarro, I., Botella, F., Borras, F., Nuno-Solinis, R., Orozco, D., ... Toro, N. (2014). A Spanish pillbox app for elderly patients taking multiple medications: Randomized controlled trial. *Journal of Medical Internet Research, 16*(4), e99. https://doi.org/10.2196/jmir.3269.

* Mummah, S. A., Mathur, M., King, A. C., Gardner, C. D., & Sutton, S. (2016). Mobile technology for vegetable consumption: A randomized controlled pilot study in overweight adults. *Journal of Medical Internet Research mHealth and uHealth, 4*(2), e51. https://doi.org/10.2196/mhealth.5146.

Noar, S. M., Benac, C. N., & Harris, M. S. (2007). Does tailoring matter? Meta-analytic review of tailored print health behavior change interventions. *Psychological Bulletin, 133*(4), 673–693. https://doi.org/10.1037/0033-2909.133.4.673.

* Oh, B., Cho, B., Han, M. K., Choi, H., Lee, M. N., Kang, H. C., ... Kim, Y. (2015). The effectiveness of mobile phone-based care for weight control in metabolic syndrome patients: Randomized controlled trial. *Journal of Medical Internet Research mHealth and uHealth, 3*(3). https://doi.org/10.2196/mhealth.4222.

O'Keefe, D. J., & Jensen, J. D. (2007). The relative persuasiveness of gain-framed and loss-framed messages for encouraging disease prevention behaviors: A meta-analytic review. *Journal of Health Communication, 12*(7), 623–644. https://doi.org/10.1080/10810730701615198.

* Petrella, R. J., Stuckey, M. I., Shapiro, S., & Gill, D. P. (2014). Mobile health, exercise and metabolic risk: A randomized controlled trial. *BioMed Central Public Health, 14*(1082). https://doi.org/10.1186/1471-2458-14-1082.

Pew Center Research. (2018, June)). *Social media use continues to rise in developing countries, but plateaus across developed ones.* Retrieved from http://www.pewglobal.org/2018/06/19/2-smartphone-ownership-on-the-rise-in-emerging-economies/.

Pop-Eleches, C., Thirumurthy, H., Habyarimana, J. P., Zivin, J. G., Goldstein, M. P., … Bangsberg, D. R. (2011). Mobile phone technologies improve adherence to antiretroviral treatment in a resource-limited setting: A randomized controlled trial of text message reminders. *AIDS, 25*(6), 825–834. https://doi.org/10.1097/QAD.0b013e32834380c1.

Raudenbush, S. W. (2009). Analyzing effect sizes: Random-effects models. In B. S. Cooper, L. V. Hedges, & J. C. Valentine (Eds.), *The handbook of research synthesis and meta-analysis* (pp. 295–316). New York, NY: Russell Sage Foundation.

Rosenstock, I. M. (1974). The health belief model and preventive health behavior. *Health Education Monographs, 2*(4), 354–386. https://doi.org/10.1177/109019817400200405.

Rosenthal, R. (1991). In *Meta-analytic procedures for social research* (Rev. ed.). Newbury Park, CA: Sage.

Rosenthal, R. (1979). The file drawer problem and tolerance for null results. *Psychological Bulletin, 86*(3), 638–641. https://doi.org/10.1037/0033-2909.86.3.638.

Ruppel, E. K., & Rains, S. A. (2012). Information sources and the health information-seeking process: An application and extension of channel complementarity theory. *Communication Monographs, 79*(3), 385–405. https://doi.org/10.1080/03637751.2012.697627.

Sama, P. R., Eapen, Z. J., Weinfurt, K. P., Shah, B. R., & Schulman, K. A. (2014). An evaluation of mobile health application tools. *Journal of Medical Internet Research mHealth and uHealth, 2*(2), e19. https://doi.org/10.2196/mhealth.3088.

Schmidt, F. L., & Hunter, J. E. (1999). Comparison of three meta-analysis methods revisited: An analysis of Johnson, Mullen, and Salas (1995). *Journal of Applied Psychology, 84*(1), 144–148. https://doi.org/10.1037/0021-9010.84.1.144.

Sutton, A. J. (2009). Publication bias. In B. S. Cooper, L. V. Hedges, & J. C. Valentine (Eds.), *The handbook of research synthesis and meta-analysis* (pp. 435–452). New York, NY: Russell Sage Foundation.

Thakkar, J., Kurup, R., Laba, T. L., Santo, K., Thiagalingam, A., Rodgers, A., … Chow, C. K. (2016). Mobile telephone text messaging for medication adherence in chronic disease: A meta-analysis. *Journal of the American Medical Association Internal Medicine, 176*(3), 340–349. https://doi.org/10.1001/jamainternmed.2015.7667.

Tian, Y., & Robinson, J. D. (2008). Media use and health information seeking: An empirical test of media complementarity theory. *Health Communication, 23*(2), 184–190. https://doi.org/10.1080/10410230801968260.

* Voth, E. C., Oelke, N. D., & Jung, M. E. (2016). A theory-based exercise app to enhance exercise adherence: A pilot study. *Journal of Medical Internet Research mHealth and uHealth, 4*(2), e62. https://doi.org/10.2196/mhealth.4997.

* Wang, J. B., Cadmus-Bertram, L. A., Natarajan, L., White, M. M., Madanat, H., Nichols, J. F., … Pierce, J. P. (2015). Wearable sensor/device (Fitbit one) and SMS text-messaging prompts to increase physical activity in overweight and obese adults: A randomized controlled trial. *Telemedicine Journal and e-Health, 21*(10), 782–792. https://doi.org/10.1089/tmj.2014.0176.

* Whittaker, R., Merry, S., Stasiak, K., McDowell, H., Doherty, I., Shepherd, M.,., & Rodgers, A. (2012). MEMO—a mobile phone depression prevention intervention for adolescents: Development process and postprogram findings on acceptability from a randomized controlled trial. *Journal of Medical Internet Research, 14*(1). https://doi.org/10.2196/jmir.1857.

Witte, K. (1992). Putting the fear back into fear appeals: The extended parallel process model. *Communication Monographs*, *59*(4), 329–349. https://doi.org/10.1080/03637759209376276.

Yang, Q. (2017). Are social networking sites making health behavior change interventions more effective? A meta-analytic review. *Journal of Health Communication*, *22*(3), 223–233. https://doi.org/10.1080/10810730.2016.1271065.

The impact of mHealth interventions: Improving health outcomes through narratives, mixed methods, and data mining strategies

Rebecca K. Britt[1], Jessica Maddox[1], Shaheen Kanthawala[1], Jameson L. Hayes[2]

[1] Department of Journalism and Creative Media, The University of Alabama, Tuscaloosa, AL, United States; [2] Department of Advertising and Public Relations, College of Communication & Information Sciences, The University of Alabama, Tuscaloosa, AL, United States

Mobile media have the capacity to more easily and frequently connect with individuals and adapt depending on the context, activity, and specific health behavior in question (Setyono, 2015; Thinnukool, Khuwuthyakorn, & Wietong, 2017; Ziden, Rosli, Gunasegaren, & Azizan, 2017). Increasingly, researchers partner with professional organizations and build interventions to take advantage of mobile technologies to determine how to mitigate affordances with the user behaviors in order to provide dynamic experiences (Ziden et al., 2017). Presently, studies on mobile health (mHealth) have integrated theoretical models as the foundation for their development, underscoring the need to explore factors such as social influence (Wang & Chou, 2016), attitude, and user intent (Seol & Lee, 2016). Likewise, researchers have articulated an increased need for mHealth interventions to utilize theory-based underpinnings an evaluation (Thinnukool et al., 2017). mHealth interventions have been informed by behavior change theories (e.g., those that measure user attitudes and intent; e.g., Ajzen & Fishbein, 1980; Glanz, Rimer, & Vaswanath, 2008), which are beneficial to mHealth development, evaluation, and assessment. Against these preexisting frameworks, scholars and practitioners seek to push at the margins of these strategies by focusing on ways to harness the power and potential of mHealth to target specific nuances within mHealth interventions for particular diseases, conditions, or social problems. This chapter focuses primarily on mixed methods to thoroughly capture the potential of mHealth interventions to be highly targeted to individuals: qualitative interviewing and focus groups and data mining. Because mHealth has the potential to be highly tailored, this chapter explores how specific, highly tailored research on the front end of these interventions can help yield strategies even more specific and beneficial to an in individual.

Within the context of this chapter, mHealth interventions are defined as those by researchers or developers that use mobile devices to bring about health behavior change (Conn, Hafdahl, & Mehr, 2011; Dobson et al., 2016; Holtz & Lauckner, 2012; Middelweerd, Mollee, van der Wal, Brug & Te Velde, 2014). This chapter presents preexisting literature on the subjects of mHealth, narrative strategies, and data mining for more effective mHealth interventions. As mHealth itself continues to be crucial in the development of technological health advances, the synthesis of narratives and data science methods can improve future outcomes. These approaches can improve the development and outcomes in mHealth interventions. There are several ways where mHealth interventions will benefit from mixed methods: for instance, narratives have been used in many stages within healthcare interventions and provide an avenue for greater engagement within an mHealth context (Lyons et al., 2016). The power of narratives in mHealth interventions today can result in improved patient compliance and positive behavior change (Tong & Laranjo, 2018). Narratives can emerge through qualitative interviews and focus groups (Lindlof & Taylor, 2017) and can be used to better help refine keywords, searches, and topical themes in big data practices.

Likewise, the intersection of mHealth and big data has been called rapid technological advancements in healthcare, especially in the ways it can benefit patients (Bates, Saria, Ohno-Machado, Shah, & Escobar, 2014; Nash, 2014; Weiler, 2016), machine learning, and data analytics (Istepanian & Al-Anzi, 2018) and in development (Lv, Chirivella, & Gagliardo, 2016). However, there remain a myriad ways in which the nexus of mHealth and big data is underexplored. As such, this chapter proposes research strategies for mHealth interventions that utilize the role of narratives and data science. These approaches can help create better interventions that meet the needs of varied communities, especially those that are traditionally designated as medically underserviced (e.g., Malvey & Slovensky, 2014), as well as those that may be generalizable. As these technologies and strategies are increasingly incorporated into scholarly work, it is necessary to include theories to empirically test the adoption and maintenance of health behaviors.

In response to an ever-changing media landscape, directions are offered for methodological approaches to mHealth, both in developing and implementing appropriate interventions. As part of the strategies set forth by the World Health Organization, this chapter investigates mHealth interventions and directions with a focus on the role of narrative, coupled with strategies in data mining. Traditional research approaches may benefit from employing the use of narrative structures in conjunction with other research practices (e.g., social media analyses, typically, in the role of larger scale data analyses to better understand a population, or in the role of qualitative data analysis paired with large-scale data mining). This chapter suggests that qualitative methods should be coupled with emerging quantitative practices as part of the "big data revolution" to aid in the development of mHealth interventions. Such strategies can be used in a variety of projects, in varied contexts, and for many purposes. This plan of mixed-method approaches is offered with a conclusion for future research strategies in mHealth interventions.

mHealth interventions

Among the greater advantages of mHealth include the efficiency and precision of delivery, the ability to reach communities, and empowering users through tracking, managing, and helping to improve health (Wallis et al. , 2017). mHealth can likewise provide structure in an individual's management of their respective condition, such as checklists and calendars, which have been shown to dramatically improve adherence to protocol, specifically in low-income populations (Bryce et al., 2005). Similarly, text messaging reminders can be used for similar structural affordances and improving behavioral outcomes (Jordan, Ray, Johnson, & Evans, 2011). For example, mHealth programs like Text4baby and Text2Quit (Abroms et al., 2012; Evans, Abroms, Poropatich, Nielson, & Wallace, 2012) offer text messaging services that deliver messages on prenatal news, conditions, and updates for pregnant women and new mothers. Readership of the texts was high and was sustained over time versus that of emails, demonstrating the success text messaging had when emails did not. Even for individuals not facing chronic health issues, mHealth has benefits for acute instances, for example, in cases of wound care (Sikka et al., 2012). In some cases when an individual experiences laceration symptoms, the use of a mobile phone to submit an image to a remote physician can review and help provide medical care decisions (Sikka et al., 2012). All of these interventions were just-in-time programs (Sikka et al., 2012), with the use of theory as informing the content and design of the interventions.

Likewise, pilot interventions have been conducted on hard-to-reach populations, (Chang et al., 2011) such as middle-aged men, to assess their opinions and needs on the use of mobile phones to improve physical activity and nutrition (Vandelanotte et al., 2013). There can be challenges in reaching and working with hard-to-reach or medically underserved populations, which make it a struggle to develop and evaluate the success of mobile app usage and the challenges associated with harnessing the increased presence of mobile devices among these groups (Chang et al., 2011; Kallender et al., 2013). Often, these challenges stem from a lack of transportation access, access to healthcare resources, and access to technologies, for both the community and researcher. For researchers and intervention designers, such structural devices are useful for evaluation and further design in helping to serve a given population (Thinnukool et al., 2017; Whittaker, Merry, Dorey, & Maddison, 2012). Although the results of these programs are promising, the long-term effects of mHealth interventions, however, remain a limitation.

mHealth intervention opportunities and challenges

mHealth opportunities and challenges are diverse, though a prominent opportunity is that they offer the capacity for greater user engagement through tailored healthcare and easier ways to manage data associated with a health condition. As previously discussed, text message has been found to be an effective tool in providing organization and structure to a patient's care, and, furthermore, studies have found that exposure to health and risk messages in texts can improve adherence to a program (Willoughby, 2017). Smartphone applications also benefit that can be harnessed in mHealth interventions. Apps can assist with features such as goal setting, rapid intention formation, performance measurement, self-monitoring, individually tailored feedback, goal reviewing, and progression (Conn et al., 2011; Middelweerd et al., 2014). These features in mHealth apps have been found to be more effective than apps without these abilities (Conn et al., 2011; Middelweerd et al., 2014).

Another advantage of mHealth is that it can serve as a cost-effective solution to healthcare. Successful and cost-effective mHealth interventions have efficiently managed interventions, data collection, and analysis (e.g., Tate et al., 2013). Similarly, mHealth interventions are able to widely reach various age groups and populations. For instance, mHealth interventions have been conducted to monitor childhood obesity (Tate et al., 2013), which have been successful in providing evidence of self-management of healthcare. Additionally, diabetes interventions have been carried out through the use of text messages and mobile phone applications (Dobson et al., 2016; Holtz & Lauckner, 2012). mHealth interventions have also been successful in bringing about behavior change in eating habits and physical activity for both younger (Ashrafian et al., 2014; Wohlers, Sirard, Barden, & Moon, 2009) and older (Recio-Rodríguez, et al., 2014) adults. Notably, among those interventions conducted in low-income populations, evidence suggests that mHealth offers improved communication with physicians and cost-effective clinical outcomes. This means that two key areas are needed in future mHealth interventions: serving low-income populations and countries and conducting longitudinal studies or long-term work.

While mHealth offers many opportunities, there are also numerous challenges that persist. Chief among these are technology adoption and implementation. Moreover, the healthcare industry remains one of the most highly regulated fields (Balch Samora, Blazar, Lifchez, Bal, & Drolet, 2018), which means that for mobile devices to be used as part of an intervention strategy in a clinical practice, rules, and requirements must be met. These hurdles, while they can be overcome, certainly pose a burden on both researchers and developers. Usability is key to helping technological adoption and implementation, as any type of mHealth intervention needs ease of use and ease of engagement with materials. Typically, the core components of usability include learnability, efficiency, memorability, errors, and satisfaction (Nielsen, 2012). These attributes assess how easy user interfaces are to use and are structural guidelines to keep in mind when designing a mHealth project. By keeping such components in mind, designers and implementers of mHealth interventions can make sure that their designs are user-friendly. These are challenges as mHealth interventions continue to develop, particularly since tailoring and improving usability is not a one-time process, but a continual one (e.g., Gurupur & Gutierrez, 2016).

Additional mHealth challenges include the physical features and interactive components of the intervention technologies, such as the size of the device, available screen space on a user's mobile device, and other related visual components. Effectiveness is also a key challenge to grapple with, and much scholarship has explored the assessment of mHealth impacts (Marcolino et al., 2018). A systematic review of mHealth interventions found that the evidence for efficacy is low, given that no long-term studies have been conducted and that most interventions are performed in high-income countries (Marcolino et al., 2018). These findings are not unexpected, given that prior reviews have noted similar limitations (Riley et al., 2011).

Other challenges associated with mHealth design and interventions, particularly as scholars and practitioners look to the future of mHealth, include data security. Data security challenges are twofold: on data access, the use of cloud computing and applications means that there are often unknown locations used for storage, which could pose risks for data storage in unsecured locations. Second, there are challenges with accessing data depending on the user's location, such as in public locations in nonsecured wireless networks. Users choose to willingly provide access to their personal information to health apps in exchange for free usage of apps or services the health app might provide, but this information is often sold to third parties and can cause issues in security

(Grace, Zhou, Jiang, & Sadeghi, 2012; Meng, Ding, Chung, Han, & Lee, 2016; Prince, 2018; Vickery, 2015). While there are information systems that specialize in storing healthcare data, this cannot account for the user's personal use of mHealth and where they choose to access their data, which could result in using unsecured access (Atienza et al., 2015; Gurupur & Wan, 2017; Joeckel, Dogruel, & Bowman, 2016; Kelley, Cranor, & Sadeh, 2013; Park & Jang, 2014).

Despite these challenges, the advantages of mHealth outweigh the potential disadvantages, if mitigated appropriately and effectively. Therefore, in choosing a methodology for research that will ultimately lead to the development of future mHealth interventions, strategy is key in helping to attenuating the foregoing challenges. A strategy to assist in navigating these benefits and challenges involves mixed methods, specifically those of narrative interviewing and data science. Specifically, this chapter offers data mining strategies and how those apply to narrative structures, as the role of patient-centered experience and messages is critical in future intervention designs.

Narratives and data mining in mHealth

Despite this prevalence of the use of narratives in intervention studies, and the popularity of mobile phones and platforms, the application of narratives on mobile platforms is still in very early stages (Willoughby & Liu, 2018). Using participant narratives from qualitative approaches and applying them to big data techniques such as data mining provides an amalgamation of methodological approaches and allows for a new way to approach mHealth interventions.

Narrative-based research approaches

Traditional research approaches in mHealth interventions have often relied on mixed-method approaches to better tailor campaign strategies to best fit the needs of a particular demographic (Finucane & Mercer, 2006; Johnson & Schoonenboom, 2016; Moffatt, White, Mackintosh, & Howel, 2006; Nelson et al., 2014; Reisner, Perkovich, & Mimiaga, 2010; Young & Jaganath, 2013). Herein, future research should explore the mixed-method approach of converging qualitative interviewing and data mining, and the bridge this chapter builds between these methodologies is narrative. Narratives have often been used in health campaign design, implementation, and mHealth interventions (Baezconde-Garbanati et al., 2014; Parsons, Walsemann, Jones, Knopft, & Blake, 2016). Frequently, narratives in these contexts appear as narratives messages, which are those that consist of characters that are identifiable with the audience of the message

(Slater, 2002). Regarding health, these messages would allow individuals to relate to the people in a message and process the health information embedded in the narrative (Moyer-Gusé, 2008). Such narrative messages have often been used in persuasive communication (Willoughby & Liu, 2018), including health topics such as promotion of physical activity (Falzon, Radel, Cantor, & d'Arripe-Longueville, 2015), health-promoting behaviors (Perrier & Martin Ginis, 2016), breast cancer detection (McQueen & Kreuter, 2010), healthy snacking (Oh & Larose, 2015), and sexual health (Moyer-Gusé, Chung, & Jain, 2011).

However, narratives can also be key on the front end of mHealth interventions, even before the design work begins. By adopting a mixed-method approach early on in the mHealth research and planning, researchers and designs open up the possibilities for targeting interventions to specific issues, topical themes, and user needs at the outset, as opposed to just in the design phase. This allows for a specific tailoring of issues and themes throughout the entire research process, which could become an apt benefit for the individual tailoring of a mHealth intervention later on. Future research should explore such mixed-method approaches in the design phase of such interventions to make sure they are addressing the needs of a given population by listening to the needs of individuals in that population. Two such ways of listening are through qualitative interviewing and focus groups and data mining, and narrative is the bridge built between these methodologies. Narratives have long been invoked in health communication to better tailor interventions, explore their function in efficacy, and assist in behavior change (Falzon et al., 2015; McQueen & Kreuter, 2010; Moyer-Gusé et al., 2011; Oh & Larose, 2015; Perrier & Martin Ginis, 2016; Willoughby & Liu, 2018). As more and more focus turns to mHealth (Lyons et al., 2016; Willoughby, Niu, & Liu, 2018), avenues open up for researchers and practitioners to assess how narratives may be used in these mobile environments. Qualitative research, particularly in this context of interviews and focused groups, can use narrative to fine-tune searches of large data sets. Similarly, qualitative research, with its emphasis on the often tension-filled dialectic of performance and practices (Lindlof & Taylor, 2017), provides ample opportunities to use, and learn from, narratives.

Narratives help individuals make sense of their lives and lived experiences. This is helpful for the health researcher and practitioner, who must often meet individuals where they are at in order to strive to change behavior (Holtz et al., 2018, pp. 1–8; Mitchell, Holtz, & McCarroll, 2018; Occa & Suggs, 2016). Using qualitative interviews or focus groups allows for individuals, ideally in the target population, to shine a spotlight on their own experiences. In these qualitative methodologies, individuals invite the researcher into their world, invite them to listen to their narrative, and invite them to watch as they actively make sense of their world (Lindlof & Taylor, 2017). The stories people tell are always already imbricated with issues of race, class, gender, sexuality, and other politicized identities (Lindlof & Taylor, 2017), and this can help researchers really address access, power, behavior, or political discrepancies that may currently be present and tailor campaigns to bridge those chasms. Because many of the low-income and underserved populations that can most benefit from mHealth struggle with the realities of these politicized identities and power discrepancies, allowing these characteristics to come through in narratives can help better tailor interventions.

Previously, narratives have been used in all stages of the research process to inform health interventions. For instance, Baezconde-Garbanati et al. (2014) employed narratives within a mixed-method study to create a narrative video that aimed to change attitudes and behavior on cervical cancer and vaccination. They found that narrative was indeed effective in their intervention in increasing knowledge, attitudes, and behaviors (Baezconde-Garbanati et al., 2014). Other researchers, such as Parsons et al. (2016), used prevailing cultural narratives as the starting point for their mixed-method research and set out to design an intervention that challenged macro-level discourses regarding childhood obesity. Because these dominant narratives can often be internalized and have detrimental effects on decisions individuals make regarding their health (Parsons et al., 2016), they are worth considering at the starting point of research in order to best assess how to problematize them and examine the ways prevailing common sense takes certain issues for granted (Lindlof & Taylor, 2017). As scholars and practitioners explore ways to bridge the gap in health research, in terms of theory, method, and approach, one might also consider a text mining approach to be employed for narratives on the front end of mHealth interventions, as part of the evaluative process, or in data gathering, among other creative ways. Text mining approaches use techniques from natural language processing and data mining to efficiently process large data to support information extraction, which can be useful in an mHealth initiative. Text mining approaches have been used in narrative-based research, such as injury surveillance (McKenzie, Scott, Campbell, & McClure, 2009) and analyzing discourse about posttraumatic stress disorder as an evaluation (He, Veldkamp, & de Vries, 2012).

Narratives also have functions within the research process, including the write-up stage (Lindlof & Taylor, 2017). Within the research process, Wiederhold (2014) uses narrative as her mechanism for research dissemination and employed tenets of autoethnography in order to write up her research on escorts and protesters at abortion clinics. Wiederhold (2014) uses narrative as a bridge in her publication, not only to bridge the ideological divides of protesters and clinic escorts but also to invite the reader to serve as a unifier. Wiederhold (2014) extolls future researchers to find ways to bridge gaps in health research, whether those gaps are between those with ideological divides, power imbalances, or physical issues of access that needed to be connected.

As mHealth evolves, scholars and practitioners have examined how narratives may be used in mobile contexts. Willoughby et al. (2018) used narrative in an entertainment—education format via text messages to test attitudes on women, alcohol, and sex. Lyons et al. (2016) adopted a narrative gaming strategy to encourage breast cancer survivors to be physically active. These studies relate to the examples outlined above, which address the benefits and challenges of mHealth interventions, and they further help us define the field in moving narrative and emerging technologies forward in mHealth. While it is important to note both studies did acknowledge certain drawbacks, they also did note their success with potential benefits of narrative in mHealth intervention.

As Wiederhold (2014) notes, narratives can function as bridges, and narratives are used as a convergence point in a mixed methodology of qualitative interviews and data mining. Data mining allows individuals to examine large data sets in order to obtain new information. But given the size, scope, and depth of these data sets, it behooves researchers to make sure they are guided when setting out to discover the patterns that may emerge. Narratives that emerge from qualitative interviews and focus groups can help be such guides. To be sure, narratives are not the final answer to this type of research and should be used strategically; one does not want narrative in conjunction with data to be the proverbial putting of the cart before the horse. Narratives that emerge from qualitative interviews or focus groups should always *inform* data mining and not solely dictate the process. But narratives can serve as guides when utilizing programs such as Crimson Hexagon (2018) or computational text analytics tools like Leximancer (2018) because they can inform the terms that should be searched for in conjunction with a particular demographic population. When data mining is considered, one could simply search broad terms to arrive at broad outcomes. By examining the narratives that come from qualitative interviews and focus groups, search terms can be much more tailored to the specific group in question. Because everything people say in an interview typically comes from the purview of their own life experiences (Lindlof & Taylor, 2017), narratives in a mixed-method approach using qualitative data and large-scale data mining function like zooms on a lens: researchers can zoom in to the specific lived experiences of research participants' lives, zoom out with specific terms to guide the data mining, and then zoom back in to use the information gleaned in order to tailor an intervention to the specific needs of a particular demographic population. It is with these affordances in mind that this chapter now turns to a discussion of how such an approach can be used specifically in the context of mHealth interventions.

Narratives inform data mining strategies for mHealth interventions

It is no longer surprising that the use of large-scale data analysis can be useful to inform an intervention, whether in isolation (e.g., focusing on a single segment of a population) or on a much larger level. However, the use of large-scale data, data mining, and related practices (e.g., the use of object-oriented programming to collect and analyze public data around a given phenomena) remains an area where researchers can more strategically employ strategies to build more effective mHealth programs. Narratives can inform data mining on a large scale, can inform the design of interventions, and be a useful tool in analyzing intervention effectiveness. The objective of collecting and analyzing big data, data mining, and related practices to data science for mHealth is different here than how it is normally described. Big data typically refers to large data sets that are complex in nature or otherwise have more observations than traditional data processing software can run. In an mHealth context, this could be used for electronic data sets for patient records, pharmacy, insurance, or health data in the "background" (Lv et al., 2016). However, in this social science—based context, it is within the context of this chapter referred to big data as it relates to the context of mHealth interventions by researchers and developers. This can provide a particularly promising opportunity to leverage technology to improve health outcomes by accessing public online conversations (e.g., Crimson Hexagon) via social media to help inform the design of tailored mHealth interventions. For instance, AI-based software like these allow users to gather large data sets from social networks using data from historical to current points in time. User-friendly approaches like these (which draw upon graphical user interfaces) could allow for tailored data gathering that could be used to both inform interventions and be used in tandem with an mHealth intervention. Notably, such data sets are large, yet result in timely information that can assist with mHealth solutions.

Notably, as the development and methods applied to research in mHealth evolve, the practical efficiency of the "big data revolution" (Walker, 2014) offers one opportunity for new analytic approaches to shape, develop, and analyze mHealth research. For instance, scholars argue that for mHealth interventions to be optimal, the user must have customized experiences through existing algorithms, which are highlighted in existing computer-enhanced applications (Shipley & Chakraborty, 2019) and social media. Likewise, data stored on secure servers can help to combat issues associated with security (Balch Samora et al., 2018). However, these approaches should not be used in isolation. Instead, the use of optimized experiences, spurred by working with appropriate data, can be used concurrently with narrative approaches to build a more complete assessment that squarely focuses on the end user. This chapter suggests the use of narratives and qualitative research should be paired with these approaches, looking to the future to develop mHealth projects and interventions that can push the boundaries of better science and better work that serves populations of interest. For example, the current research team is conducting a series of mHealth intervention studies that begin with narrative accounts of patient experiences that are key for several reasons. First, narrative accounts allow the researchers to first understand the lived experiences of patients, their needs ,and understanding of technologies as they relate to the given topic. Second, those accounts and information help to inform highly tailored strategies in data mining, text mining as another approach. Finally, narrative accounts help the researchers to ensure that tailored mHealth applications are developed with user input; as such, narratives are key throughout the intervention process, from the beginning of the design process to the end-stage evaluation phase.

In January 2013, the Center for US Health Reform reported that the big data revolution had reached the healthcare industry, noting that stakeholders, researchers, and practitioners would benefit from big data initiatives. Through the use of working with narrative approaches that prioritize the individual user, and using data mining approaches to develop and analyze all data available, rather than subsamples, scholars can address user behavior, conduct advanced predictive analytics and social network analysis, and build improved interventions. In a relevant report, it is noted that the "potential for value creation is still unclaimed" (Center for U.S. Health Reform, 2013, p. 3), meaning that there are analytical and design capabilities offered by big data that are yet unexplored. A goal of the big data revolution and healthcare, then, is to offer the "right living, care, provider, value, and innovation" (p.9), meaning that big data can provide more personalized healthcare experiences, deliver more tailored interventions, and do a better job of automating app design according to user preferences. With this in mind, future mHealth research can play a significant role in helping to assess the effectiveness of outcomes—largely through interventions that reach the public—through assessing the patient experience, determining the effectiveness of the app, and properly evaluating all components of user experience and evaluation. The future of mHealth and developing interventions is exciting, and numerous opportunities exist through research and development.

Future directions

The present chapter explored how mHealth interventions provide substantial opportunities and challenges spurred by technological revolutions to date. As existing theoretical models are used to inform the design of mHealth apps, and as the role of user engagement is increasingly applied to mHealth apps and subsequent interventions, the role of narrative immersion often prompts benefits in improved outcomes relating to health-based decision-making. These are likewise informed by strategies often informed by data mining and analytics to develop mHealth solutions to serve populations of interest, healthcare practitioners, scholars, and educators, accordingly. These approaches can provide accurate and real-time data collection, allowing for improved updates made to mHealth as they apply to short- and long-term projects. With this in mind, mHealth interventions that employ narratives will be increasingly important as these programs increasingly emphasize user and patient experiences to improve behavior change (Baezconde-Garbanati et al., 2014; Willoughby et al., 2018). Narratives can assist in patient acceptance and work in tandem with the user experience of an app and likewise be critical in the development and assessment of an app. Perhaps most importantly, narratives can function as a bridge in mHealth research, especially as data mining approaches encourage researchers to use computational methods and resources to serve such projects.

Future mHealth research that explores the role of pairing narrative approaches and data mining in design and practice should consider the existing challenges in mHealth interventions, especially the need for serving low-income populations and building longitudinal interventions. For instance, addressing chronic illness through mHealth solutions could be beneficial to users for self-management of care. There are numerous opportunities for the future of mHealth interventions that employ a variety of methods: applying data mining strategies with social media data, the use of predictive analyses, using big data as part of longitudinal design, and so forth. Current examples of this have addressed national health priorities, such as cardiovascular disease (CVD), by data mining the social media activity of state health departments related to CVD to inform an mHealth intervention (Musaev et al., 2019).This approach also demonstrates the way that social media usage by public health departments to the broader public can be used to help facilitate conversations that can inform patient communication (e.g., narrative guides), user activity, and the social structure of conversations on a state-by-state level and help mHealth interventions be developed in a tailored and meaningful way. Notably, future studies should continue to be tailored to populations of interest and must always consider the end user with continued tailoring and ensuring that patient needs are met (Nielsen, 2012; Shipley & Chakraborty, 2019).

Likewise, it remains important to address the availability of technological access in mHealth. The availability of Internet access in populations of interest through which an intervention is applied, particularly in grassroots projects or those in low-income areas, remains an important area to be studied, be they guidelines developed that assist researchers and practitioners as they develop their intervention so that populations are accordingly reached. Likewise, mHealth interventions, the use of narratives, and data science are not without their own struggles. Ethical and security considerations in the development of any mHealth program must be considered, if not explicitly addressed during the design and evaluation process (Grace et al., 2012), and mHealth interventions should consider the unique value that their app and solution provides compared to comparable ones (Tate et al., 2013; Willoughby, 2017). These approaches can be done in many ways: through the use of partnerships with health practitioners and through understanding their public communication (e.g., Musaev et al., 2019), the necessary servicing of a particular region or area, or pilot testing and significance that a prior tool has already established, among other necessary factors. As health apps increase in proliferation and in the potential for positive benefits, there is potential for improved behavioral outcomes. There are many exciting opportunities in mHealth that can serve underexplored populations and emphasizing user-centric apps to facilitate tailored experiences. As such, this chapter asks readers to consider the use of mHealth interventions and designs to invoke the role of narratives and data science in future exploration in areas outlined within this chapter.

References

Abroms, L. C., Ahuja, M., Kodl, Y., Thaweethai, L., Sims, J., Winickoff, J. P., & Windsor, R. A. (2012). Text2Quit: Results from a pilot test of a personalized, interactive mobile health smoking cessation program. *Journal of Health Communication, 17*(1), 44–53. https://doi.org/10.1080/10810730.2011.649159.

Ajzen, I., & Fishbein, M. (1980). *Understanding attitudes and predicting social behavior.* New Jersey: Prentice-Hall.

Ashrafian, H., Toma, T., Harling, L., Kerr, K., Athanasiou, T., & Darzi, A. (2014). Social networking strategies that aim to reduce obesity have achieved significant although modest results. *Health Affairs, 33*(9), 1641–1647. https://doi.org/10.1377/hlthaff.2014.0370.

Atienza, A. A., Zarcadoolas, C., Vaughon, W., Hughes, P., Patel, V., Chou, W.-Y. S., & Pritts, J. (2015). Consumer attitudes and perceptions on mHealth privacy and security: Findings from a mixed-methods study. *Journal of Health Communication, 20*(6), 673–679. https://doi.org/10.1080/10810730.2015.1018560.

Baezconde-Garbanati, L. A., Chatterjee, J. S., Frank, L. B., Murphy, S. T., Moran, M. B., Werth, L. N., ... O'Brien, D. (2014). Tamale lesson: A case study of a narrative health communication intervention. *Journal of Communication in Healthcare, 7*(2), 82–92. https://doi.org/10.1179/1753807614Y.00000000055.

Balch Samora, J., Blazar, P. E., Lifchez, S. D., Bal, B. S., & Drolet, B. C. (2018). Mobile messaging communication in health care: Rules, regulations, penalties, and safety of provider use. *Joural of Bone and Joint Surgery Reviews, 6*(3), e4. https://doi.org/10.2106/JBJS.RVW.17.00070.

Bates, D. W., Saria, S., Ohno-Machado, L., Shah, A., & Escobar, G. (2014). Big data in health care: Using analytics to identify and manage high-risk and high-cost patients. *Health Affairs, 33*(7). https://doi.org/10.1377/hlthaff.2014.0041.

Bryce, J., Gouws, E., Adam, T., Black, R. E., Schellenberg, J. A., Manzi, F., ... Habicht, J. P. (2005). Improving quality and efficiency of facility-based child health care through Integrated Management of Childhood Illness in Tanzania. *Health Policy and Planning, 20*(Suppl. 1), i69–i76.

Center for U.S. Health System Reform. (2013). *The "big data" revolution in healthcare: Accelerating value and innovation.* Retrieved from: https://www.mckinsey.com/industries/healthcare-systems-and-services/our-insights/the-big-data-revolution-in-us-health-care.

Chang, L. W., Kagaayi, J., Arem, H., Nakigozi, G., Ssempijja, V., Serwadda, D., ... Reynolds, S. J. (2011). Impact of a mHealth intervention for peer health workers on AIDS care in rural Uganda: A mixed methods evaluation of a cluster-randomized trial. *AIDS and Behavior, 15*(8), 1776. https://doi.org/10.1007/s10461-011-9995-x.

Conn, V. S., Hafdahl, A. R., & Mehr, D. R. (2011). Interventions to increase physical activity among healthy adults: meta-analysis of outcomes. *American Journal of Public Health, 101*(4), 751–758. https://doi.org/10.2105/AJPH.2010.194381.

Crimson Hexagon. (2018). *Crimson hexagon: AI powered consumer insights.* Retrieved from: https://www.crimsonhexagon.com.

Dobson, R., Whittaker, R., Jiang, Y., Shepherd, M., Maddison, R., Carter, K., ... Murphy, R. (2016). Text message-based diabetes self-management support (SMS4BG): Study protocol for a randomised controlled trial. *Trials, 17*, 179. https://doi.org/10.1186/s13063-016-1305-5.

Evans, W. D., Abrons, L. C., Poropatich, R., Nielsen, P. E., & Wallace, J. L. (2012). Mobile health evaluation methods: The Text4baby case study. *Journal of Health Communication, 17*, 22–29. https://doi.org/10.1080/10810730.2011.649157.

Falzon, C., Radel, R., Cantor, A., & d'Arripe-Longueville, F. (2015). Understanding narrative effects in physical activity promotion: The influence of breast cancer survivor testimony on exercise beliefs, self-efficacy, and intention in breast cancer patients. *Supportive Care in Cancer, 23*, 761e768. https://doi.org/10.1007/s00520-014-2422-x.

Finucane, A., & Mercer, S. W. (2006). An exploratory mixed methods study of the acceptability and effectiveness of mindfulness-based cognitive therapy for patients with active depression and anxiety in primary care. *BMC Psychiatry, 6*(1), 14. https://doi.org/10.1186/1471-244X-6-14.

Glanz, K., Rimer, B. K., & Viswanath, K. (2008). *Health behavior and health education: Theory, research, and practice.* San Francisco, CA: Wiley.

Grace, M. C., Zhou, W., Jiang, X., & Sadeghi, A.-R. (2012). Unsafe exposure analysis of mobile in-app advertisements. In *Proceedings of the fifth ACM conference on security and privacy in wireless and mobile networks* (pp. 101–112). New York, NY, USA: ACM. https://doi.org/10.1145/2185448.2185464.

Gurupur, V. P., & Gutierrez, R. (2016). Designing the right framework for healthcare decision support. *Journal of Integrated Design and Process Science, 20*(1), 7–32. https://doi.org/10.3233/jid-2016-0001.

Gurupur, V. P., & Wan, T. T. H. (2017). Challenges in implementing mHealth interventions: A technical perspective. *mHealth, 3*. https://doi.org/10.21037/mhealth.2017.07.05.

He, Q., Veldkamp, B. P., & de Vries, T. (2012). Screening for posttraumatic stress disorder using verbal features in self narratives: A text mining approach. *Psychiatry Research, 198*, 441–447. https://doi.org/10.1016/j.psychres.2012.01.032.

Holtz, B., & Lauckner, C. (2012). Diabetes management via mobile phones: A systematic review. *Telemedicine and E-Health, 18*(3), 175–184. https://doi.org/10.1089/tmj.2011.0119.

Holtz, B. E., Mitchell, K. M., Nuttall, A. K., Cotten, S. R., Hershey, D. D., Dunneback, J. K., & Wood, M. A. (2018). *Using user-feedback to develop a website: MyT1DHope, for parents of children with T1D* (pp. 1–8). Health Communication. https://doi.org/10.1080/10410236.2018.1560579.

Istepanian, R. S., & Al-Anzi, T. (2018). m-Health 2.0: New perspectives on mobile health, machine learning and big data analytics. *Methods, 151*, 34–40. https://doi.org/10.1016/j.ymeth.2018.05.015.

Joeckel, S., Dogruel, L., & Bowman, N. D. (2016). The reliance on recognition and majority vote heuristics over privacy concerns when selecting smartphone apps among German and US consumers. *Information, Communication and Society, 20*(4), 1–16. https://doi.org/10.1080/1369118X.2016.1202299.

Johnson, R. B., & Schoonenboom, J. (2016). Adding qualitative and mixed methods research to health intervention studies: Interacting with differences. *Qualitative Health Research, 26*(5), 587–602. https://doi.org/10.1177/1049732315617479.

Jordan, E. T., Ray, E. M., Johnson, P., & Evans, W. D. (2011). Early results: Text4baby program reaches the intended audience. *Nursing for Women's Health, 15,* 206–212.

Kallender, K., Tibenderana, J. K., Akpogheneta, O. J., Strachan, D. L., Hill, Z., Asbroek, T., … Meek, S. R. (2013). Mobile health (mHealth) approaches and lessons for increased performance and retention of community health workers in low- and middle-income countries: A review. *Journal of Medical Internet Research, 15*(1). https://doi.org/10.2196/jmir.2130.

Kelley, P. G., Cranor, L. F., & Sadeh, N. (2013). Privacy as part of the app decision-making process. In *Proceedings of the SIGCHI conference on human factors in computing systems* (pp. 3393–3402). New York, NY, USA: ACM. https://doi.org/10.1145/2470654.2466466.

Leximancer. (2018). *Leximancer academic products.* Retrieved from: https://info.leximancer.com/products-academic/.

Lindlof, T. R., & Taylor, B. C. (2017). *Qualitative communication research methods* (4th ed.). Newbury Park, CA: SAGE Publications.

Lv, Z., Chirivella, J., & Gagliardo, P. (2016). Big data oriented multimedia mobile health applications. *Journal of Medical Systems, 40,* 120. https://doi.org/10.1007/s10916-016-0475-8.

Lyons, E. J., Baranowski, T., Basen-Engquist, K. M., Lewis, Z. H., Swartz, M. C., Jennings, K., & Volpi, E. (2016). Testing the effects of narrative and play on physical activity among breast cancer survivors using mobile apps: Study protocol for a randomized controlled trial. *BMC Cancer, 16*(202), 1–18. https://doi.org/10.1186/s12885-016-2244-y.

Malvey, D., & Slovensky, D. J. (2014). From telemedicine to telehealth to eHealth: Where does mHealth fit? In D. Malvey, & D. J. Slovensky (Eds.), *mHealth: Transforming healthcare* (pp. 19–43). Springer.

Marcolino, M. S., Oliveira, J. A. Q., D'Agostino, M., Ribeiro, A. L., Alkmim, M. B. M., & Novillo-Ortiz, D. (2018). The impact of mHealth interventions: Systematic review of systematic reviews. *JMIR mHealth uHealth, 6*(1), e23. https://doi.org/10.2196/mhealth.8873.

McKenzie, K., Scott, D. A., Campbell, M., & McClure, R. J. (2009). The use of narrative text for injury surveillance research: A systematic review. *Accident Analysis and Prevention, 42*(2), 354–363. https://doi.org/10.1016/j.aap.2009.09.020.

McQueen, A., & Kreuter, M. W. (2010). Women's cognitive and affective reactions to breast cancer survivor stories: A structural equation analysis. *Patient Education and Counseling, 81*(Suppl. 1), S15–S21. https://doi.org/10.1016/j.pec.2010.08.015.

Meng, W., Ding, R., Chung, S. P., Han, S., & Lee, W. (2016). *The price of free: Privacy leakage in personalized mobile in-app ads.* Retrieved from: http://wenkewww.gtisc.gatech.edu/papers/ndss16_mobile_ad.pdf.

Middelweerd, A., Mollee, J. S., van der Wal, C. N., Brug, J., & Te Velde, S. J. (2014). Apps to promote physical activity among adults: A review and content analysis. *International Journal of Behavioral Nutrition and Physical Activity, 11*(1), 97. https://doi.org/10.1186/s12966-014-0097-9.

Mitchell, K. M., Holtz, B. E., & McCarroll, A. (2018). Patient-centered methods for designing and developing health information communication technologies: A systematic review. *Telemedicine and e-Health.* https://doi.org/10.1089/tmj.2018.0236.

Moffatt, S., White, M., Mackintosh, J., & Howel, D. (2006). Using quantitative and qualitative data in health services research—what happens when mixed method findings conflict? *BMC Health Services Research, 6*(1), 28. https://doi.org/10.1186/1472-6963-6-28.

Moyer-Gusé, E. (2008). Toward a theory of entertainment persuasion: Explaining the persuasive effects of entertainment-education messages. *Communication Theory, 18*, 407–425. https://doi.org/10.1111/j.1468-2885.2008.00328.x.

Moyer-Gusé, E., Chung, A. H., & Jain, P. (2011). Identification with characters and discussion of taboo topics after exposure to an entertainment narrative about sexual health. *Journal of Communication, 61*, 387–406. https://doi.org/10.1111/j.1460-2466.2011.01551.x.

Musaev, A., Britt, R. K., Hayes, J., Britt, B. C., Maddox, J., & Sheindashtegol, P. (2019). *Study of Twitter communications on cardiovascular disease by state health departments.* Manuscript accepted at the 2019 International Conference on Web Services.

Nash, D. B. (2014). Harnessing the power of big data in healthcare. *American Health Drug Benefits, 7*(2), 69–70.

Nelson, G., Stefancic, A., Rae, J., Townley, G., Tsemberis, S., Macnaughton, E., … Stergiopoulos, V. (2014). Early implementation evaluation of a multi-site housing first intervention for homeless people with mental illness: A mixed methods approach. *Evaluation and Program Planning, 43*, 16–26. https://doi.org/10.1016/j.evalprogplan.2013.10.004.

Nielsen, J. (2012). *Usability 101: Introduction to usability.* Retrieved from https://www.nngroup.com/articles/usability-101-introduction-to-usability/U+0020.

Occa, A., & Suggs, L. S. (2016). Communicating breast cancer screening with young women: An experimental test of didactic and narrative messages using video and infographics. *Journal of Health Communication, 21*(1), 1–11. https://doi.org/10.1080/10810730.2015.1018611.

Oh, H. J., & Larose, R. (2015). Tell me a story about healthy snacking and I will follow: Comparing the effectiveness of self-generated versus message-aided implementation intentions on promoting healthy snacking habits among college students. *Health Communication, 30*, 962–974. https://doi.org/10.1080/10410236.2014.910289.

Park, Y. J., & Jang, S. M. (2014). Understanding privacy knowledge and skill in mobile communication. *Computers in Human Behavior, 38*, 296–303.

Parsons, A. A., Walsemann, K. M., Jones, S. J., Knopf, H., & Blake, C. E. (2016). The influence of dominant obesity discourses on child health narratives: A qualitative study. *Critical Public Health, 26*(5), 602–614. https://doi.org/10.1080/10410236.2013.769661.

Perrier, M.-J., & Martin Ginis, K. A. (2016). Changing health-promoting behaviours through narrative interventions: A systematic review. *Journal of Health Psychology, 11*, 1499–1517. https://doi.org/10.1177/1359105316656243.

Prince, C. (2018). Do consumers want to control their personal data? Empirical evidence. *International Journal of Human-Computer Studies, 110*, 21–32. https://doi.org/10.1016/j.ijhcs.2017.10.003.

Recio-Rodríguez, J. I., Martín-Cantera, C., González-Viejo, N., Gómez-Arranz, A., Arietaleanizbeascoa, M. S., Schmolling-Guinovart, Y., … García-Ortiz, L. (2014). Effectiveness of a smartphone application for improving healthy lifestyles, a randomized clinical trial (EVIDENT II): Study protocol. *BMC Public Health, 14*(1), 254. https://doi.org/10.1186/1471-2458-14-254.

Reisner, S. L., Perkovich, B., & Mimiaga, M. J. (2010). A mixed methods study of the sexual health needs of New England transmen who have sex with nontransgender men. *AIDS patient care and STDs, 24*(8), 501–513. https://doi.org/10.1089/apc.2010.0059.

Riley, W. T., Rivera, D. E., Atienza, A. A., Nilsen, W., Allison, S. M., & Mermelstein, R. (2011). Health behavior models in the age of mobile interventions: Are our theories up to the task? *Translational Behavioral Medicine, 1*, 53–71. https://doi.org/10.1007/s13142-011-0021-7.

Seol, S., & Lee, H. (2016). Exploring factors affecting the adoption of mobile office in business: An integration of TPB with perceived value. *International Journal of Mobile Communications, 14*(1), 1–25.

Setyono, A. (2015). An adaptive multimedia messaging framework for mobile telemedicine. *International Journal of Interactive Mobile Technologies, 9*(4), 34–41.

Shipley, N., & Chakraborty, J. (2019). Big data and mHealth: Increasing the usability of healthcare through the customization of Pinterest-literary perspective. In M. Khosrow-Pour (Ed.), *Consumer-driven technologies in healthcare: Breakthroughs in research and practice* (pp. 34−54). Hershey, PA: IGI Global.

Sikka, N., Carlin, K. N., Pines, J., Pirri, M., Strauss, R., & Rahimi, F. (2012). The use of mobile phones for acute wound care: Attitudes and opinions of emergency department patients. *Journal of Health Communication, 17*, 37−42. https://doi.org/10.1080/10810730.2011.649161.

Slater, M. D., & Rouner, D. (2002). Entertainment education and elaboration likelihood: Understanding the processing of narrative persuasion. *Communication Theory, 12*, 173−191. https://doi.org/10.1111/j.1468-2885.2002.tb00265.x.

Tate, E. B., Spruijt-Metz, D., O'Reilly, G., Jordan-Marsh, M., Gotsis, M., Pentz, M. A., & Dunton, G. F. (2013). mHealth approaches to child obesity prevention: Successes, unique challenges, and next directions. *Translational Behavioral Medicine, 3*(4), 406−415. https://doi.org/10.1007/s13142-013-0222-3.

Thinnukool, O., Khuwuthyakorn, P., & Wietong, P. (2017). Non-prescription medicine mobile healthcare application: Smartphone-based software design and development review. *International Journal of Interactive Mobile Technologies, 11*(5), 130−146.

Tong, H. L., & Laranjo, L. (2018). The use of social features in mobile health interventions to promote physical activity: A systematic review. *Nature Digital Medicine, 43*. https://doi.org/10.1038/s41746-018-0051-3.

Vandelanotte, C., Caperchione, C. M., Ellison, M., George, E. S., Maeder, A., Kolt, G. S., … Mummery, W. K. (2013). What kinds of website and mobile phone-delivered physical activity and nutrition interventions do middle-aged men want? *Journal of Health Communication, 18*(9), 1070−1083. https://doi.org/10.1080/10810730.2013.768731.

Vickery, J. R. (2015). "I don't have anything to hide, but … ": The challenges and negotiations of social and mobile media privacy for non-dominant youth. *Information, Communication and Society, 18*(3), 281−294. https://doi.org/10.1080/1369118X.2014.989251.

Walker, S. J. (2014). Big data: A revolution that will transform how we live, work, and think. *International Journal of Advertising, 33*(1), 181−183. https://doi.org/10.2501/IJA-33-1-181-183.

Wang, E. S., & Chou, N. P. (2016). Examining social influence factors affecting consumer continuous usage intention for mobile social networking applications. *International Journal of Mobile Communications, 14*(1), 43−55.

Wallis, L., Blessing, P., Dalwai, M., & Shin, S. D. (2017). Integrating mHealth at point of care in low and middle-income settings: The system perspective. *Global Health Action, 10*(3). https://doi.org/10.1080/16549716.2017.1327686.

Weiler, A. (2016). mHealth and big data will bring meaning and value to patient- reported outcomes. *mHealth, 31*(2), 2. https://doi.org/10.3978/j.issn.2306.9740.2016.01.02.

Whittaker, R., Merry, S., Dorey, E., & Maddison, R. (2012). A development and evaluation process for mHealth interventions: Examples from New Zealand. *Journal of Health Communication, 17*, 11−21. https://doi.org/10.1070/10810730.2011.649103.

Wiederhold, A. M. (2014). Narrative spaces between intractability outside the clinic. *Health Communication, 29*(7), 741−744. https://doi.org/10.1080/10410236.2013.769661.

Willoughby, J. F. (2017). Mobile health and exposures to health and risk messages. In *Oxford research encyclopedia of communication.* https://doi.org/10.1093/acrefore/9780190228613.013.333. Online publication date: July, 2017.

Willoughby, J. F., & Liu, S. (2018). Do pictures help tell the story? An experimental test of narrative and emojis in a health text message intervention. *Computers in Human Behavior, 79*, 75−82. https://doi.org/10.1016/j.chb.2017.10.031.

Willoughby, J. F., Niu, Z., & Liu, S. (2018). Assessing the potential use of narrative and the entertainment education strategy in an mHealth text-message intervention. *Journal of Health Communication, 23*(1), 20−27. https://doi.org/10.1080/10810730.2017.1396628.

Wohlers, E. M., Sirard, J. R., Barden, C. M., & Moon, J. K. (September 2009). Smart phones are useful for food intake and physical activity surveys. In *Engineering in medicine and biology society, 2009* (pp. 5183–5186). Annual International Conference of the IEEE. https://doi.org/10.1109/IEMBS.2009.5333721. EMBC 2009.

Young, S. D., & Jaganath, D. (2013). Online social networking for HIV education and prevention: A mixed methods analysis. *Sexually Transmitted Diseases, 40*(2). https://doi.org/10.1097/OLQ.0b013e318278bd12.

Ziden, A. A., Rosli, M., Gunasegaren, T., & Azizan, S. N. (2017). Perceptions and experience in mobile learning via SMS: A case study of distance education students in a Malaysian university. *International Journal of Interactive Mobile Technologies, 11*(1), 116–132.

PART IV

Social media: Networked technology for health

Beyond liking: Inspiring user-generated content for health promotion

Heather J. Hether[1], Christopher Calabrese[1]

[1] Department of Communication, University of California, Davis, CA, United States

Social media offer unprecedented opportunities for health promotion campaigns. More than simply new tools for campaign planners, social media support a level of campaign reach and engagement previously unimagined. Social media are distinct from mass media with their promise of interaction: they are, after all, *social* media. Thus, social media are leveraged fully when organizations tap into their capacity to facilitate user interaction, rather than rely on them for one-way messaging. For organizations, however, inspiring interaction and engagement on social media is not easy. Health organizations must apply innovative social media strategies if they want to break through the online clutter and competition and facilitate a higher level of user engagement, which is essential for health promotion campaigns to achieve their goals.

Inspiring social media users to create and post their own content on social media, known as user-generated content (UGC), is a strategy that health organizations can apply to facilitate a higher level of engagement with their audiences. UGC, such as posted comments, tweets, and uploaded photos or videos, can strengthen a campaign's impact by supporting user involvement and simultaneously extending and amplifying the campaign's reach. While UGC is a promising strategy for online health promotion campaigns, few health organizations have had success capitalizing on its potential.

The current chapter is oriented around the achievement of three goals. Firstly, the chapter synthesizes social media research related to engagement, health promotion, and audience participation. This synthesis

291

provides a broad perspective of current knowledge and understanding of the challenges and opportunities of social media for health promotion. Secondly, a comparative case study analysis of three innovative health-related social media campaigns identifies trends across these campaigns and provides insight into the tactics of highly engaging campaigns. While case studies do not provide generalizable data, these qualitative data provide an opportunity to "describe an intervention and the real-life context in which it occurred" (Yin, 2009, p. 20). Thus, the case studies provide rich, detailed descriptions of effective social media campaigns. Lastly, by examining scholarship and practice side by side, this chapter bridges these two domains and identifies new directions for both research and application.

Literature review

Social media, engagement, and influence

In recent years, the social media environment has shifted toward an even greater emphasis on UGC and user participation. Ellison and Boyd (2013) describe social network sites as a "communication networked platform in which participants have uniquely identifiable profiles ..., can publicly articulate connections ..., and can consume, produce, and/or interact with user-generated content" (Ellison & Boyd, 2013, p. 158). Though referring to social network sites, this definition applies to all types of social media, such as microblogging sites (i.e., Twitter), photo sharing websites (i.e., Instagram), and video sharing websites (i.e., YouTube). Thus, by design, social media are more than consumption sites— they facilitate interaction and production, as well.

Unlike legacy media, such as newspaper (print), radio, or television, which are recognized for their ability to reach a wide audience with one-way messaging (i.e., sender-to-receiver), social media are designed to be interactive and facilitate two-way, or multiway, communication among all users (Ellison & Boyd, 2013; Heldman, Schindelar, & Weaver, 2013). Therefore, organizations leverage these platforms fully when they use them to facilitate interaction and engagement with users, as opposed to broadcasting one-way messages.

Interaction and engagement are terms used extensively in social media research and practice; however, there is no clear agreement on their definitions. Interaction most often refers to a discrete behavior, such as an interaction between users or between users and content (Khan, 2017; Shao, 2009). Every time a user does something with social media content, such as liking or sharing it, they are interacting with it. Perhaps more commonly, though, interaction refers to an exchange between users. Thus, on social media, users can have a content interaction or a social interaction (e.g., Veale et al., 2015).

Engagement is a broader concept that not only includes interaction but also extends beyond it (York, 2017). Scholars have identified engagement as a multidimensional relational construct that includes emotional, cognitive, and behavioral aspects (Brodie, Hollebeek, Juric, & Ilic, 2011; Brodie, Ilic, Juric, & Hollebeek, 2013; Sashi, 2012). Thus, engagement typically reflects dimensions of trust, commitment, and participation, whereas interaction does not. Interaction is often identified as the physical or behavioral manifestation of engagement (Sashi, 2012).

Social media engagement can be parsed further into a continuum of user behaviors that reflect different levels of commitment and involvement with an organization. Researchers have proposed a hierarchy of engagement that consists of low, medium, and high levels (Neiger et al., 2012; Neiger, Thackeray, Burton, Giraud-Carrier, & Fagen, 2013). In this hierarchy, low engagement reflects discrete interactions such as liking and following; medium engagement reflects the start of dialogic communication; and high engagement is conceived of as "online or off-line audience member involvement with a health promotion program either as a partner or as a participant" (Neiger et al., 2013, p. 161). These three distinctions are similarly reflected in Muntinga, Moorman, and Smit's (2011) typology of online brand engagement in which they suggest that a low level of engagement includes content consumption, such as reading, listening, or watching brand-related content; a medium level of engagement includes contributing content, such as comments; and a high level of engagement consists of more extensive UGC, such as blog or video development.

From these typologies, it is clear that UGC reflects a medium or high level of engagement, depending on the commitment, time, and involvement of the user. Moreover, a long history of communication research has established how important engagement, or involvement, is as a mediating variable for message impacts. Research suggests the more engaged or involved an audience member is, the more likely they are to be impacted by their media exposure. For example, McGuire's hierarchy of effects model (1984, 2012) proposes that audience involvement with a message is necessary for higher level effects to occur. Information processing theories, such as the elaboration likelihood model, also indicate that message elaboration, or cognitive engagement, is essential as a means of facilitating message impacts that are more durable over time (Cacioppo & Petty, 1984). Similarly, the uses and gratifications paradigm also postulates that active media users are more involved with their chosen media and "involvement suggests a state of readiness to select, interpret, and respond to messages" (Rubin, 2002, p. 536). In fact, across a variety of media effects research, cognitive, and emotional involvement are frequently identified as important mediators of effects (e.g., Perse, 1990; Sood, 2002).

On social media, UGC is important not only for the effects it may facilitate on the content creator but also because UGC supports message diffusion across social networks. Diffusion of innovations theory (Rogers, 2003) describes how innovations, or new ideas, move through communities. While people adopt new innovations at varying speeds depending on a variety of factors, one group of people essential to the diffusion process is opinion leaders (Rogers, 2003). Opinion leaders, also known as influentials, are helpful for diffusing innovations to people in their network who may look to them for guidance on novel ideas or behaviors. Opinion leaders are also an important part of the classic media effects theory, the two-step flow of communication (Katz, Lazarsfeld, & Roper, 2006), which hypothesized that opinion leaders mediate the influence of mass media on the general audience. Subsequent to the two-step flow model, other scholars have suggested a multistep flow of communication in which influence is postulated to flow in multiple directions, including both horizontally and reciprocally between opinion leaders and others (Robinson, 1976; Weimann, 1982).

Research has identified the important role interpersonal influence plays in the diffusion of new phenomenon. For example, Rogers (2003) suggests that interpersonal influence is more important for persuading an individual to adopt a new idea than are media. Katz et al. (2006) also highlight the role of personal influence in "determining the way people made up their minds" (p. 32). In fact, health communication scholars have found that interpersonal influence is more strongly associated with behavior change than are mass media (Cassell, Jackson, & Cheuvront, 1998; Valente, 2002). Consequently, in the context of social media and UGC, research suggests if users, particularly inattentive users, see others in their network engaging with a campaign, they are likely to be more influenced by these individuals than they would be from an organizational message source. The precise dynamics of this influence are beyond the scope of the current chapter; however, theoretical mechanisms related to social cognitive theory (Bandura, 1986), norms (e.g., Lapinski & Rimal, 2005), social influence (Christakis & Fowler, 2007; Valente, 2010), and social support (Berkman, 1984; Berkman, Glass, Brissette, & Seeman, 2000) provide some plausible explanations.

Social media use and content creation

The number of social media sites and users has exploded in recent years. Research suggests that at least 64% of US adults aged 18−64 use social media, and the percentage is higher for younger adult audiences (Smith & Anderson, 2018). Social media have become thoroughly integrated into people's lives: users connect with their friends and acquaintances, read and share news, and even make charitable donations through these media (Facebook, 2018). As technology continues to evolve, social media are increasingly a staple in people's lives. YouTube and Facebook are used by the majority of adults, followed by Instagram, Pinterest, and Snapchat (Smith & Anderson, 2018). These platforms all involve creating and uploading text, photos, or videos.

The prevalence of social media use among adults triggers the question as to why users are motivated to create content. Motivations for using social media and creating content reflect the participation dimension of engagement (Sashi, 2012). Matikainen (2015) conducted qualitative interviews and an Internet panel survey in Finland and found self-development, self-expression, and community engagement are the primary motivations for creating content online. Similarly, other related research suggests that content creation is mainly driven by three dominant motivations including users' needs for belonging; self-presentation and expression; and entertainment.

One of the primary motivations for social media use is connecting with peers (Barker, 2009; Quan-Haase & Young, 2010; Stern, 2008). Not surprisingly, many Facebook users stay engaged with the platform because they feel a sense of belonging (Nadkarni & Hofmann, 2012). A study examining the motivations of social media use found that social interaction was a reason for college students to use Facebook, Twitter, Instagram, and Snapchat (Alhabash & Ma, 2017).

Furthermore, people may also participate on social media because it enables them to engage in a desired self-presentation and expression. Some youth develop their own personal websites to project a well-polished image of themselves to others (Stern, 2008). This type of self-presentation allows users to portray themselves in a light that is favorable to their friend groups. The need for self-presentation was also identified as a primary motivation for Facebook use among adults (Nadkarni & Hofmann, 2012). Similar to self-presentation, people may create content online for self-expression (Davies, 2007). Some of the primary uses of Instagram were to document events and to express creativity (Sheldon & Bryant, 2016). Moreover, people tend to use Instagram and Snapchat more for self-expression in comparison to Facebook and Twitter (Alhabash & Ma, 2017). Similar to how artists create to express themselves or their feelings, people may develop content to communicate their thoughts and emotions in a constructive way.

The entertainment value of social media is also a driving force for social media use and content creation. Sheldon and Bryant (2016) found that Instagram is mainly used to create content, to gain knowledge about others, for entertainment, and for perceived "coolness." Similarly, people tend to use Facebook, Instagram, Twitter, and Snapchat for entertainment (Alhabash & Ma, 2017). Quan-Haase and Young (2010) also found that college students use social media because it is fun and can provide information about their peers. Those who create online videos are primarily motivated by entertainment, and they view video content creation as fun, whereas web bloggers' main goal is to disseminate information (Stoeckl, Rohrmeier, & Hess, 2007).

Understanding the motivations for creating original content online brings up the question of why certain people do not engage online, while others actively do. Stoeckl et al. (2007) found that the main reasons "lurkers" do not produce content online is because of time consumption, concerns about privacy, and their perceived inability to produce interesting content. Similarly, Sun, Rau, and Ma (2014) found that people lurk rather than participate online due to external factors, personal preferences, the relationship between the user and the online group, and security and privacy reasons. Moreover, people's primary motivations to use social media, such as their need to belong and their need for self-presentation, may dictate what content they engage in (Nadkarni & Hofmann, 2012; Stern, 2008). Younger users may not create content on certain health topics because it may not seem personally relevant or ideal for how they want to shape their online identity (Evers, Albury, Byron, & Crawford, 2013). These studies suggest that one underlying factor for not engaging with or creating content is self-protection and the fear of negative consequences from putting oneself out for criticism and visibility.

Social media for health promotion campaigns

Similar to how people negotiate the challenges and opportunities of social media, so, too, do health organizations. While health organizations appreciate the benefits of social media and realize social media are an important part of their outreach (Hackworth & Kunz, 2011; Hether, 2014), social media also present unique challenges for health promotion. Thus, health organizations manage their online presence by negotiating both the benefits and challenges that come with these media.

Among the benefits that public health practitioners value are the opportunity to engage directly with an audience of unprecedented size at an unprecedented price; the ability to create targeted communication directed toward niche communities; and the ability to cultivate dialog with stakeholders (Chou, Prestin, Lyons, & Wen, 2013). Thus, social media offer both the reach of mass media and the persuasiveness of interpersonal communication (Flanagin, 2017; Fogg, 2008). Moreover, by engaging with opinion leaders, health promotion messages can be diffused more rapidly and persuasively across the network (Rogers, 2003). In the context of health communication, research suggests that horizontal, peer-to-peer communication may be perceived as more reliable, trustworthy, and credible than vertical messages that come from experts (Bernhardt, 2010;

Goodman, Wennerstrom, & Springgate, 2011). Peer-to-peer communication can also be tailored better to its audience of connected users (Abroms & Craig Lefebvre, 2009). This may help explain why these peer inter-actions are less obtrusive to users because they are part of their regular, desired social media activity (Goodman et al., 2011).

For health organizations, interacting with stakeholders on social media and fostering a community around a health issue are key benefits of using social media for health promotion. However, these interactions also present the greatest challenge for health promotion specialists. When audience members, or social media users, participate with a campaign at medium and high levels, the sponsoring health organization cannot control how its campaign messaging may evolve or become distorted. Thus, using social media for outreach "requires a shift from the traditional command-and-control approach to a more participatory approach" (Ramanadhan, Mendez, Rao, & Viswanath, 2013, p. 2), wherein users may be more accurately regarded as cocreators of an organization's brand (Kamboj, Sarmah, Gupta, & Dwivedi, 2018), rather than passive recipients.

This also suggests that on social media, the boundaries between the experts and the consumers, or the producers and the consumers, are blurred (Ramanadhan et al., 2013). On social media, producers are consumers and consumers are producers (Shirky, 2008). Communication flows across networks in a myriad of directions (Robinson, 1976; Weimann, 1982), aided by technological affordances that make content easily shareable. This is challenging for public health practitioners who are committed to delivering accurate, evidence-based information and behavioral recommendations (Levine, 2011). The consequences of message distortion in public health can be serious, with adverse impacts on the very population that is the target of the health promotion campaign. However, participating on social media requires accepting a certain loss of control over these interactions (Ramanadhan et al., 2013), as well as the implementation of other safeguards for contingency planning.

Unfortunately, studies indicate that health organizations tend to rely on social media more for information dissemination than for other more engaging activity with their stakeholders (Hether, 2014; Park, Reber, & Chon, 2016). However, researchers (Guo & Saxton, 2014; Lovejoy & Saxton, 2012) have also suggested that rather than reflecting a lack of initiative, the preponderance of information dissemination may, instead, reflect a hierarchy of engagement in which information dissemination forms the base of online communication, followed by dialogic commu-nication, and culminating in mobilization and action. These studies complement other research on audience engagement (Neiger et al., 2012, 2013), with both lines of work suggesting online engagement between organizations and their stakeholders moves through a series of steps in which engagement—reflecting an emotional, cognitive, and behavioral investment (Brodie et al., 2011, 2013; Sashi, 2012)—gradually increases. However, for behavior change to occur, information dissemination is not enough to produce change (McGuire, 1984, 2012), and organizations must ensure there are sufficient opportunities for audience members to engage at higher levels.

Beyond a lack of message control and the difficulty in facilitating audience engagement, other challenges confront social media campaigns. These include a cluttered stream of content competing for users' attention, as well as competition from both individuals and businesses promoting unhealthy behaviors. Companies, such as those selling alcohol, soda, or unhealthy foods (Dunlop, Freeman, & Jones, 2016), have access to more financial resources that support the development of sophisticated campaigns, and they are tough competition for health organizations operating on more modest budgets, with limited human resources (Dunlop et al., 2016). Similarly, peer glamorization or promotion of unhealthy behaviors on platforms also presents a challenge to health promotion (Griffiths & Casswell, 2010). This competition is yet another reason why health organizations need to develop more dynamic outreach efforts, particularly for younger audiences who are avid social media users and often the target of unhealthy product marketing. Despite the challenges of facilitating engagement on social media, researchers and public health professionals have encouraged organizations to utilize social media for campaigns designed to promote positive health behaviors (Korda & Itani, 2013; Shi, Poorisat, & Salmon, 2018; Wong, Merchant, & Moreno, 2014).

As the previous discussion illustrates, health organizations face several challenges with inspiring audiences to create UGC. In fact, a search for exemplar health-related social media campaigns resulted in few campaigns that had risen above the noise to achieve popular appeal, as suggested by search results through both Google and popular academic databases. However, three successful social media campaigns were identified and are analyzed below with a comparative case study analysis.

Methodology

Sample

Case study analysis—a detailed, in-depth examination of a specific phenomenon—provides an opportunity to examine social media campaigns in context, and it may be an especially valuable methodology because this area of research is still relatively nascent (Yin, 2009). Thus, three campaigns that met the following criteria were selected: (1) they were identified in the literature and/or press as successful and innovative—as evidenced by novel strategies and/or campaign metrics; (2) they were health-related; (3) their success relied on UGC; and (4) they were "genuine" outreach campaigns designed to achieve health-related objectives, not research interventions. While the campaigns are different, when examined together they provide further insight into leveraging social media to facilitate UGC and high engagement.

Analysis

Information was gathered about each social media campaign and included articles published in academic journals, popular press, and/or the Internet (websites and social media). Together, these materials were analyzed to identify the primary outreach strategies and tactics used by each campaign as well as to collect more information regarding the audience, reception, and context of each campaign. The campaigns were individually analyzed and then a comparative analysis sought to identify the commonalities and major differences across the campaigns. While these data are not generalizable, they provide an in-depth examination of the factors that contributed to campaign success and they suggest strategies for future campaigns to consider.

Findings

Case 1: The ice bucket challenge

The Ice Bucket Challenge (IBC) stands as one of the most successful social media campaigns that inspired an unprecedented amount of UGC. This campaign was designed to raise awareness and research funds for amyotrophic lateral sclerosis (ALS), also known commonly as "Lou Gehrig's disease." ALS is a progressive neurodegenerative disease that affects the nerves in the brain and spinal cord and for which there is no cure (ALS Association, 2019).

While there is some discrepancy as to the origins of the IBC, most accounts suggest that a version of this challenge had existed in the sporting world and had been used previously with other causes. On July 15, 2014, however, a golfer named Chris Kennedy was the first person to link the IBC to ALS (Sifferlin, 2014). He posted a video of himself doing the challenge and then he nominated three others to complete the challenge—which is to dump a bucket of ice water on their heads and upload the video of themselves doing so or donate $100 to ALS within 24 hours. From there, the challenge reached a few other opinion leaders and influencers, including Pat Quinn and, later, Pete Frates. Both Quinn and Frates had been diagnosed with ALS at young ages (30 and 27, respectively), and they are typically identified as the cofounders of IBC for their roles in connecting the movement with their large online networks and facilitating its momentum (Sifferlin, 2014).

During the summer of 2014, the IBC became a social media phenomenon that was very successful in engaging people and raising donations. The ALS Association reported that during an 8-week period in 2014, 17 million Challenge videos were uploaded to Facebook, which were watched by 440 million people more than 10 billion times (ALS Association, n.d.). Moreover, during this period, $115 million dollars was donated to the ALS Association, with an additional $13 million donated to regional branches (Wolf-Mann, 2015).

This campaign's success has been attributed to several integral elements, including its (1) tailored design specific to social media; (2) positive, lighthearted tone; and (3) accessibility. Moreover, the campaign relied on opinion leaders and the social network to diffuse its message. The campaign flowed across social networks in multiple directions, from opinion leaders to their followers (e.g., celebrities to fans), horizontally (peer-to-peer), and even reciprocally (e.g., fans to celebrities). The sharing of these videos facilitated both a user and content interaction, and, in fact, the campaign encouraged participant engagement on multiple dimensions—behaviorally, emotionally, cognitively, and socially.

The sharing of these user videos connected people and supported the development of an online community that facilitated a sense of belonging in a worldwide movement among those who participated, thus strengthening the online network (Phing & Yazdanifard, 2014; Sutherland, 2016). This campaign successfully leveraged the affordances of social media for both interpersonal communication and the broad diffusion of content. Asynchronous interpersonal communication was seen through individuals specifically tagging other people in their videos and personally calling them out to participate. Moreover, the creation of videos that were circulated for public viewing leveraged qualities that traditionally have been more characteristic of mass media (Flanagin, 2017).

This campaign's popularity was also attributed to videos that were emotionally appealing because they were fun to watch and highly shareable (Gualano et al. 2016). Participating in the challenge was easy to do and timely: in the United States, the campaign ran in the summertime when cold water was more appealing than at another time of year (Phing & Yazdanifard, 2014).

While the campaign was immensely successful, it had some detractors. Some critics suggested that it was a form of slacktivism, "a way for people to feel good without doing much" (Surowiecki, 2016, para. 2). Others suggested many participants did not mention ALS or donating (Conner, 2014), while some also criticized it for wasting water during a drought

(Stevens, 2014). Perhaps more importantly, since the campaign required a one time only response, its audience impacts were short-lived. When the campaign was relaunched the following summer, it failed to replicate (van der Linden, 2017). Despite these limitations, all evidence indicates the campaign was a huge success in inspiring UGC around a health issue and raising donations for research and patient services (Rogers, 2016).

Case 2: Movember

Similar to the IBC, the Movember campaign is a health campaign that has garnered a noteworthy amount of engagement and popular appeal. In 2016, the campaign generated more than 900,000 social media mentions (Rajsekar, 2017), and in 2017, it raised AUD $88 million globally and more than 300,000 participants registered to participate (Movember, 2018). This campaign shares several characteristics with the IBC, yet it also has a few noteworthy differences. While the campaign started before the IBC, it has not peaked as the IBC did; instead, it has managed to sustain steady engagement for nearly 15 years.

The campaign idea was hatched in 2003 when two male friends in Australia were discussing the ebb and flow of various trends, including facial hair. Inspired by a friend's mother who was fundraising for breast cancer, these men decided to start a campaign for men's health. The next year, in 2004, Movember launched as an official charity and fundraiser for prostate cancer (Movember, 2015). As the Movember website reports (Movember, 2015), gradually the campaign has spread to 21 countries and has raised more than AUD $550M globally since its launch, and it has funded more than 1000 men's health programs.

Currently, the campaign, and foundation of the same name, focuses its attention on raising awareness of men's health issues and fundraising for research and health service projects. The organization focuses not only on prostate cancer but also on testicular cancer and mental health and suicide prevention among men. The premise of the Movember campaign is to encourage men to grow a mustache during November to raise awareness and donations. Movember's slogan is "changing the face of men's health." During November, men can register on their website and they are encouraged to share their progress and to fundraise on social media. Movember is primarily an online campaign and participants rely on social media to "build community, interact with, and talk about Movember" (Jacobson & Mascaro, 2016, p. 2).

The similarities between this campaign and the IBC include its tailored design for social media, widespread appeal (including celebrity involvement), lighthearted tone, and accessibility. Similar to the IBC, Jacobson and Mascaro (2016) have likened this campaign to a social movement, wherein people are joined together and form a sense of collective identity in pursuit of a common goal. As a social media campaign, it relies on opinion leaders to get involved in the campaign and post about their participation. Like the IBC, it requires an offline action (facial hair growth) to drive online participation; thus, it encourages engagement at multiple levels.

Yet, Movember differs from the IBC in a few significant ways. As a campaign, Movember has cultivated institutional support, both in the form of corporate sponsorships and an organizational infrastructure that is completely intertwined with the campaign. The campaign also has some other strategic advantages over the IBC, which primarily include the 30-day peak activity of the campaign and its basic premise: the growth of men's facial hair.

By asking men to grow a mustache and share their progress online, the campaign leverages a man's physical appearance to support campaign goals. Thus, the campaign encourages men to define their identity in relation to this cause and campaign (Jacobson & Mascaro, 2016; van der Linden, 2017) for at least a 1-month period. Consequently, participants may be more intrinsically motivated to help support this cause because they are so personally, and publicly, committed to it. Moreover, growing a mustache links an online campaign to the offline world as men become walking billboards (Jacobson & Mascaro, 2016) for the campaign. Therefore, this campaign has potential for a gradual, deeper engagement from its participants and those people in their lives as it inspires conversation about the campaign and men's health for at least a 30-day period every year (van der Linden, 2017).

As with other campaigns, there are critiques of Movember, too. Most importantly for campaign planners, research suggests that, despite high online engagement with the campaign, few tweets actually contained actionable health information (Bravo & Hoffman-Goetz, 2017). In addition, there have been critiques of the campaign's health information (McCartney, 2012), and others have suggested there may be a misalignment between the campaign channel, health issue, and audience with more young men discussing prostate cancer when they are at greater risk for testicular cancer (Bravo & Hoffman-Goetz, 2016).

Despite these criticisms, there is no mistaking the tremendous popularity of the Movember campaign. Consequently, it has raised a large amount of money for men's health issues and has engaged millions of people. Both the IBC and the Movember campaigns were successful at inspiring UGC on grand scale. While other campaigns may not attract broad public attention as these have, they can inspire UGC that is purposeful, supports campaign goals, and provides opportunities to reach niche communities.

Case 3: The it gets better project

The It Gets Better Project is a social media campaign about mental health and suicide prevention directed toward youth who identify as lesbian, gay, bisexual, transgender, or another sexual minority (LGBTQ+). Adolescents who identify as a sexual minority have higher levels of depression, hopelessness, and suicidal tendencies than heterosexual adolescents (Safren & Heimberg, 1999). It Gets Better aims to address these disparities, empower LGBTQ + youth, and prevent these tragic events from occurring.

This campaign is noteworthy because it addresses a sensitive topic on social media and it has been successful at inspiring UGC. This campaign supports the development of an online community that offers its members a sense of belonging and social support, and it relays campaign messages that were created and developed by participants themselves. This powerful youth-oriented campaign encourages people to create and share their own compelling stories through online videos or website posts. The content then engages and empowers others who have dealt with hate or discrimination and motivates them to share their own stories, thus furthering the campaign.

The It Gets Better Project, founded on September 21, 2010, by Dan Savage and his husband Terry Miller, was initiated in response to the suicide of Billy Lucas, a teenage boy who was bullied for being perceived as gay (LGBTQ Nation, 2010). Savage, a gay rights activist and sex columnist, decided to upload a video discussing his experiences growing up and how his life had drastically improved since the hate and bullying he faced as a teen. With his video, he also encouraged others to share their own stories. After response videos started to pour in, Savage and Miller launched the nonprofit organization, also of the same name.

The concept of the campaign is to provide LGBTQ + youth with a support system and a sense of hope for the future. Two primary strategies that rely on UGC help this campaign achieve its goals. These strategies focus on storytelling and building community (It Gets Better Project). The campaign's storytelling strategy encourages people within the LGBTQ + community to post their own stories through videos or online posts discussing how their lives have improved after high school. The goal of these videos is to inspire and provide hope to LGBTQ + youth by offering role models who have gone through similar experiences. The campaign encourages storytellers to discuss their personal experiences of feeling alone or isolated; how they found resources and support; and to emphasize positivity and a sense of community. These videos offer youth in these marginalized communities a sense of belonging, and they create an online support network, which youth may not have offline.

Consequently, youth may also feel encouraged to upload their own stories to help others as well.

The campaign has also gained traction with supporters of LGBTQ + youth, mobilizing allies of the community and growing the movement beyond those that identify as LGBTQ+. Supporters of the campaign, including politicians and celebrities, have also created their own response videos to voice their support. These videos build and extend the support network so that its members are not only those in the community, but LGBTQ + allies as well.

All evidence indicate that the campaign has been effective at reaching out to its targeted audience, inspiring them to create original content. More than 60,000 individuals have shared their own stories through online videos or post submissions, and more than 625,000 have signed the pledge through the It Gets Better website to support LGBTQ + youth (It Gets Better Project). Currently, the YouTube channel has more than 56,000 subscribers and almost 5 million views, and the campaign has launched branch channels for other countries, such as Australia, Greece, and Mexico (It Gets Better Project - YouTube).

As with the other campaigns, The It Gets Better Project has faced some criticism, primarily around its messaging. Critics have suggested the campaign's message focuses too strongly on "waiting it out"—that is, telling LGBTQ + youth that things will get better—as opposed to tackling the larger issue of discrimination itself (Avery, 2017; Majkowski, 2011). Savage (2011) has responded by emphasizing that the ultimate goal of the campaign is to provide hope and support for struggling youth, not try to tackle the whole culture of discrimination.

Despite the criticism of the It Gets Better Project, the campaign has been successful and has reached LGBTQ + youth globally. Attempting to measure the direct behavioral effects of this campaign is difficult; however, the success of the campaign is evident through its main campaign element of user-generated, peer-to-peer storytelling videos. By focusing on the trust aspect of storytelling and community building and the participation of peers and opinion leaders, this campaign exemplifies the several dimensions of engagement. Together, the three campaigns highlighted here provide evidence that campaign planners can use social media to inspire higher levels of audience engagement, if they are willing to also take the risks.

Discussion and implications

Social media have revolutionized public communication, yet health organizations have received low grades for their participation on these platforms. While health organizations may hesitate to engage in this new world, audiences are increasingly growing up in this context, native to these tools (Thomas, 2011). Hence, social media campaigns must adapt their outreach strategies to better connect with an experienced community of users.

There is an extensive and growing area of multidisciplinary research that explores social media processes and impacts. The proliferation of this research has resulted in the development of new theoretical approaches and research findings that provide insight into the impacts of social media participation on a host of outcomes. However, this burst of research also has resulted in some inconsistency in how key terms are used. For example, across both academic research and practitioner publications, there is no clear, agreed-upon definition of engagement and interaction. Hence, there is a need for clearer definition of key terms that would make research studies more easily comparable and build more cohesion across the disparate research trajectories.

This review of current research also suggests several potential directions for new areas to explore related to social media strategy. While communication theories like diffusion of innovations (Rogers, 2003) and the two-step flow model (Katz et al., 2006) predict how information will flow through a population, research is less clear on the mechanisms that would encourage the opinion leaders (or influencers) to engage with novel social media messaging, particularly related to health issues. While the case studies presented herein have identified some key "levers" that seemed to help diffuse campaign messaging, quantitative studies with rigorous sampling methods are needed to produce generalizable findings.

The current context is health promotion; thus, future research is also needed to compare the similarities and differences of inspiring UGC across other contexts. Since social media is used to support a range of organizational goals, it is worthwhile to identify which strategies translate well across disciplines and desired outcomes and whether there are some strategies that are more effective for specific contexts and outcomes.

Another important area of needed research is one that explores how the institutional barriers that prevent health-related organizations from pursuing high engagement social media strategies can be overcome. Studies are fairly unanimous in suggesting that health organizations can do more on social media, but adopting new models of outreach does not come easy to organizations with traditional approaches for interacting with media, such as government agencies. This may be the reason as to why the most innovative social media health campaigns were initiated by individuals rather than health organizations themselves. Thus, identifying how public health agencies can be encouraged to innovate from the inside is needed.

The three case studies presented here each describe innovative social media campaigns that were launched outside of any formal organization.

Instead, each campaign was initiated by individuals who were personally motivated and engaged in the issue. Thus, these campaigns originated from the margins, not from a mainstream organization. In some ways, this is not surprising as innovative ideas have more freedom to develop outside the constraints of an organization. While there are certainly examples of creative campaigns focused on UGC developed from within an organizational context, research is needed to better understand how more agencies can be motivated to change their approach to social media.

The three brief case studies presented here—IBC, Movember, and the It Gets Better Project—worked with different health issues and deployed different strategies, yet similarities can be identified across all of them that provide insight into generating UGC. The common themes across all three case studies included (1) a sense of community; (2) positive emotional affect; (3) celebrity involvement; and (4) the opportunity for creative expression. While case study analysis does not provide generalizable findings, these themes suggest avenues for future research to validate the current findings.

Each of these campaigns applied various strategies to support and facilitate the building of online community. These campaigns leveraged social media to bring people together and provide opportunities for people to interact and be *social*. The IBC did this most explicitly by tagging people in each video, but the Movember campaign also encouraged participants to garner support both online and offline and build community around this issue and campaign. Similarly, the It Gets Better Project called on people to participate in storytelling through their creation of online videos; thus, building and mobilizing an online support community of LGBTQ + individuals and allies.

Building peer communities is important for the success of an online campaign because these communities reflect user engagement with the issue. Previous research has identified engagement as a multidimensional construct that includes trust, commitment, and participation (Brodie et al., 2011, 2013; Sashi, 2012), each of which are supported in online community. In addition, these peer communities are important because Internet users may perceive peer-to-peer health promotion content as more reliable and credible than content developed by experts in the field (Goodman et al., 2011). In addition, this peer-to-peer content is also perceived as more trustworthy (Bernhardt, 2010). For example, from the It Gets Better Project, user-generated videos featuring other people's stories within the same community are seen as more trustworthy to another person in the community because of their shared experiences and commonalities. These communities are especially important for youth audiences who are motivated to engage in social media to fulfill belonging needs (Boyd, 2007).

Each of these campaigns also encouraged positive, "fun" UGC. While this was most apparent in the IBC and Movember campaigns, even the It Gets Better Project encouraged participants to be optimistic and positive in their videos. Indeed, research suggests that enjoyable content associated with pleasant emotions is more likely to be shared than content that highlights unpleasant emotions (Kilgo, Lough, & Riedl, 2017; Phing & Yazdanifard, 2014). Moreover, research indicates that people are motivated to engage with social media for entertainment (Alhabash & Ma, 2017; Sheldon & Bryant, 2016; Stoeckl et al., 2007). Thus, to the extent that it is possible, integrating positive emotion and entertaining content into a social media campaign can support its impact.

The entertainment value of all three campaigns was also heightened through celebrity involvement. While the celebrities may not have been involved formally, celebrity involvement may indicate the campaign has achieved a tipping point (Gladwell, 2006). Moreover, this involvement may signify to others that the campaign is effective (Li & Wen, 2017). Celebrity involvement offers benefits including more diffusion to other users, as well as more offline attention to the campaign. For example, the IBC received tremendous coverage from journalists who were drawn to the campaign because of the celebrity participation (Kilgo et al., 2017).

Finally, as is the nature of UGC, each campaign offered its participants room to interact with the content as they liked. Participants could get creative and participate in a way that felt unique and personal to them. The IBC saw a variety of creative iterations, while Movember was truly personal as each man grew and groomed his mustache as a means of self-expression. The It Gets Better Project, too, encouraged creativity and personal expression through individual storytelling. These creative opportunities also reflect motivations for creative self-expression and self-presentation (Davies, 2007; Sheldon & Bryant, 2016; Stern, 2008). With both being primary motivations for social media use among youth, the ability to create interesting and expressive content that peers would approve further propagates the reach and spread of campaigns.

Though health organizations are encouraged to leverage social media, social media campaigns are not without limitations. While public health is drawn to social media due to its widespread popularity, affordability, and opportunity for interaction, the impacts of social media campaigns are difficult to assess (Korda & Itani, 2013). Few studies have data demonstrating positive health impacts of a social media campaign, particularly as they relate to health behaviors. However, others suggest that despite these limitations, the overall net impact of a strategic social media campaign, with widespread participation, is good for health promotion.

Conclusion

Increasingly, social media have become an important tool for public communication, yet health promotion campaigns have not fully leveraged the interactive affordances of these platforms. Facilitating audience engagement is an important step in leveraging social media more effectively, and the three case studies presented herein illustrate how this can be done. While UGC may not be a panacea for health promotion, it provides campaigns with additional opportunities to be more impactful with their outreach. Despite the challenges of social media for health promotion, a resource of outstanding campaigns is slowly being built, which illustrates that the potential rewards are worth it.

References

Abroms, L. C., & Craig Lefebvre, R. (2009). Obama's wired campaign: Lessons for public health communication. *Journal of Health Communication, 14*(5), 415–423.

Alhabash, S., & Ma, M. (2017). A tale of four platforms: Motivations and uses of Facebook, Twitter, Instagram, and Snapchat among college students? *Social Media + Society, 3*(1), 2056305117691544.

ALS (n.d.) ALS Ice Bucket Challenge Returning this August. Retrieved from. http://www.alsa.org/news/media/press-releases/als-ice-bucket-challenge.html.

ALS Association. Who gets ALS?, May 2019, Retrieved from. http://www.alsa.org/about-als/facts-you-should-know.html.

Avery, D. (2017). *"It gets better" is bad advice for gay kids, study claims.* NewNowNext. Retrieved from http://www.newnownext.com/it-gets-better-study/05/2017/.

Bandura, A. (1986). *Social foundations of thought and action: A social cognitive theory.* New Jersey: Prentice-Hall.

Barker, V. (2009). Older adolescents' motivations for social network site use: The influence of gender, group identity, and collective self-esteem. *CyberPsychology and Behavior, 12*(2), 209–213. https://doi.org/10.1089/cpb.2008.0228.

Berkman, L. F. (1984). Assessing the physical effects of social networks and social support. *Annual Review of Public Health, 5*, 413–432.

Berkman, L. F., Glass, T., Brissette, I., & Seeman, T. E. (2000). From social integration to health: Durkeim in the new millennium. *Social Science and Medicine, 51*, 843–857.

Bernhardt, J. (January 22, 2010). *Public health 2.0: New media for advancing health and advancing your career.* Retrieved from https://www.slideshare.net/jaybernhardt/public-health-20.

Boyd, D. (2007). Why youth (heart) social networking sites: The role of networked publics in teenage social life. In *MacArthur foundation series on digital learning – Youth, identity, and digital media* (Vol. 119, p. 142).

Bravo, C. A., & Hoffman-Goetz, L. (2016). Tweeting about prostate and testicular cancers: Do twitter conversations and the 2013 movember Canada campaign objectives align? *Journal of Cancer Education, 31*(2), 236–243.

Bravo, C. A., & Hoffman-Goetz, L. (2017). Social media and men's health: A content analysis of twitter conversations during the 2013 movember campaigns in the United States, Canada, and the United Kingdom. *American Journal of Men's Health, 11*(6), 1627–1641.

Brodie, R. J., Hollebeek, L. D., Jurić, B., & Ilić, A. (2011). Customer engagement: Conceptual domain, fundamental propositions, and implications for research. *Journal of Service Research, 14*(3), 252–271.

Brodie, R. J., Ilic, A., Juric, B., & Hollebeek, L. (2013). Consumer engagement in a virtual brand community: An exploratory analysis. *Journal of Business Research, 66*(1), 105–114.

Cacioppo, J. T., & Petty, R. E. (1984). The elaboration likelihood model of persuasion. *ACR North American Advances, 11*, 673–675.

Cassell, M., Jackson, C., & Cheuvront, B. (1998). Health communication on the internet: An effective channel for health behavior change? *Journal of Health Communication, 3*(1), 71–79.

Chou, W. Y. S., Prestin, A., Lyons, C., & Wen, K. Y. (2013). Web 2.0 for health promotion: Reviewing the current evidence. *American Journal of Public Health, 103*(1), e9–e18.

Christakis, N. A., & Fowler, J. H. (2007). The spread of obesity in a large social network over 32 years. *New England Journal of Medicine, 357*, 370–379.

Conner, C. (March 9, 2014). *"Were the ice buckets worth it? New and deeper analytics say 'yes.'" forbes.* Retrieved from https://www.forbes.com/sites/cherylsnappconner/2014/09/03/were-the-ice-buckets-worth-it-new-and-deeper-analytics-say-yes/.

Davies, J. (2007). Display, identity and the everyday: Self-presentation through online image sharing. *Discourse: Studies in the Cultural Politics of Education, 28*(4), 549–564.

Dunlop, S., Freeman, B., & Jones, S. C. (2016). Marketing to youth in the digital age: The promotion of unhealthy products and health promoting behaviours on social media. *Media and Communication, 4*(3), 35–49.

Ellison, N. B., & Boyd, D. M. (2013). Sociality through social network sites. In *The Oxford handbook of internet studies.*

Evers, C. W., Albury, K., Byron, P., & Crawford, K. (2013). *Young people, social media, social network sites and sexual health communication in Australia: This is funny, you should watch it.?* (Vol. 7).

Facebook. (2018). *Charitable giving tools.* Retrieved from https://donations.fb.com/.

Flanagin, A. J. (2017). Online social influence and the convergence of mass and interpersonal communication. *Human Communication Research, 43*(4), 450–463.

Fogg, B. J. (June 2008). Mass interpersonal persuasion: An early view of a new phenomenon. In *International conference on persuasive technology* (pp. 23–34). Berlin, Heidelberg: Springer.

Gladwell, M. (2006). *The tipping point: How little things can make a big difference.* Boston: Little, Brown.

Goodman, J., Wennerstrom, A., & Springgate, B. F. (2011). Participatory and social media to engage youth: From the Obama campaign to public health practice. *Ethnicity and Disease, 21*(3 Suppl. 1). S1-94-99.

Griffiths, R., & Casswell, S. (2010). Intoxigenic digital spaces? Youth, social networking sites and alcohol marketing. *Drug and Alcohol Review, 29*(5), 525–530.

Gualano, M. R., Bert, F., Gili, R., Andriolo, V., Scaioli, G., & Siliquini, R. (2016). *New ways to promote public health: Lessons from the international ice bucket challenge* (pp. 1–2). Public Health.

Guo, C., & Saxton, G. D. (2014). Tweeting social change: How social media are changing nonprofit advocacy. *Nonprofit and Voluntary Sector Quarterly, 43*(1), 57–79.

Hackworth, B. A., & Kunz, M. B. (2011). Health care and social media: Building relationships via social networks. *Academy of Health Care Management Journal, 7*(2), 55–68.

Heldman, A. B., Schindelar, J., & Weaver, J. B. (2013). Social media engagement and public health communication: Implications for public health organizations being truly "social". *Public Health Reviews, 35*(1), 1–18.

Hether, H. J. (2014). Dialogic communication in the health care context: A case study of Kaiser Permanente's social media practices. *Public Relations Review, 40*(5), 856–858.

It Gets Better Project, About - It gets better, Retrieved from. https://itgetsbetter.org/about/.

It Gets Better Project - YouTube, It gets better project, Retrieved from http://www.youtube.com/itgetsbetterproject.

It Gets Better Project, Our Vision/Mission/People - It gets better, Retrieved from https://itgetsbetter.org/initiatives/mission-vision-people/.

Jacobson, J., & Mascaro, C. (2016). Movember: Twitter conversations of a hairy social movement. *Social Media + Society, 2*(2), 2056305116637103.

Kamboj, S., Sarmah, B., Gupta, S., & Dwivedi, Y. (2018). Examining branding co-creation in brand communities on social media: Applying the paradigm of Stimulus-Organism-Response. *International Journal of Information Management, 39*, 169–185. https://doi.org/10.1016/j.ijinfomgt.2017.12.001.

Katz, E., Lazarsfeld, P. F., & Roper, E. (2006). *Personal influence.* New Brunswick: Transaction Publishers.

Khan, M. L. (2017). Social media engagement: What motivates user participation and consumption on YouTube? *Computers in Human Behavior, 66*, 236–247.

Kilgo, D. K., Lough, K., & Riedl, M. J. (2017). Emotional appeals and news values as factors of shareworthiness in ice bucket challenge coverage. *Digital Journalism*, 1–20.

Korda, H., & Itani, Z. (2013). Harnessing social media for health promotion and behavior change. *Health Promotion Practice, 14*(1), 15–23.

Lapinski, M. K., & Rimal, R. N. (2005). An explication of social norms. *Communication Theory, 15*(2), 127–147.

Levine, D. (2011). Using technology, new media, and mobile for sexual and reproductive health. *Sexuality Research and Social Policy, 8*(1), 18–26.

LGBTQ Nation. (2010). *Dan savage has a message for gay teens facing adversity: 'It gets better'.* LGBTQ Nation. Retrieved from https://www.lgbtqnation.com/2010/09/dan-savage-has-a-message-for-gay-teens-facing-adversity-it-gets-better/.

van der Linden, S. (2017). The nature of viral altruism and how to make it stick. *Nature Human Behaviour, 1*(41), 1–3.

Li, J. Y., & Wen, J. (2017). Motivations behind donations for health-related organizations: Threat appraisal and coping appraisal—the case of the ALS ice bucket challenge. *Health Marketing Quarterly, 34*(3), 217–231.

Lovejoy, K., & Saxton, G. D. (2012). Information, community, and action: How nonprofit organizations use social media. *Journal of Computer-Mediated Communication, 17*(3), 337–353.

Majkowski, T. (2011). The "It Gets Better Campaign": An unfortunate use of queer futurity. Women & Performance. *A Journal of Feminist Theory, 21*(1), 163–165. https://doi.org/10.1080/0740770X.2011.563048.

Matikainen, J. T. (2015). Motivations for content generation in social media. *Participations: Journal of Audience and Reception Studies, 12*(1), 41–58.

McCartney, M. (2012). Is Movember misleading men? *BMJ, 345*, e8046.

McGuire, W. J. (1984). Public communication as a strategy for inducing health-promoting behavioral change. *Preventive Medicine, 13*, 299–319.

McGuire, W. J. (2012). McGuire's classic input-output framework for constructing persuasive messages. In R. E. Rice, & C. Atkin (Eds.), *Public communication campaigns* (pp. 133–145). Thousand Oaks, CA: Sage.

Movember. (2015). *A hairy tale- the history of Movember's early years.* Retrieved from https://us.movember.com/news/11213/.

Movember. (2018). *Movember foundation: Annual report 2018.* Retrieved from https://us.movember.com/about/annual-report.

Muntinga, D. G., Moorman, M., & Smit, E. G. (2011). Introducing COBRAs: Exploring motivations for brand-related social media use. *International Journal of Advertising, 30*(1), 13–46.

Nadkarni, A., & Hofmann, S. G. (2012). Why do people use Facebook? *Personality and Individual Differences, 52*(3), 243–249. https://doi.org/10.1016/j.paid.2011.11.007.

Neiger, B. L., Thackeray, R., Burton, S. H., Giraud-Carrier, C. G., & Fagen, M. C. (2013). Evaluating social media's capacity to develop engaged audiences in health promotion settings: Use of twitter metrics as a case study. *Health Promotion Practice, 14*(2), 157–162.

Neiger, B. L., Thackeray, R., Van Wagenen, S. A., Hanson, C. L., West, J. H., Barnes, M. D., & Fagen, M. C. (2012). Use of social media in health promotion: Purposes, key performance indicators, and evaluation metrics. *Health Promotion Practice, 13*(2), 159–164.

Park, H., Reber, B. H., & Chon, M. (2016). Tweeting as health communication: Health organizations' use of twitter for health promotion and public engagement. *Journal of Health Communication, 21*(2), 188–198. https://doi.org/10.1080/10810730.2015.1058435.

Perse, E. M. (1990). *Media involvement and local news effects.*

Phing, A. N. M., & Yazdanifard, R. (2014). How does ALS ice bucket challenge achieve its viral outcome through marketing via social media? *Global Journal of Management and Business Research, 14*(7).

Quan-Haase, A., & Young, A. L. (2010). Uses and gratifications of social media: A comparison of Facebook and instant messaging. *Bulletin of Science, Technology and Society, 30*(5), 350–361. https://doi.org/10.1177/0270467610380009.

Rajsekar, S. (2017). *How movember is changing social media.* Retrieved at http://scion-social.com/blog/how-movember-is-changing-social-media/.

Ramanadhan, S., Mendez, S. R., Rao, M., & Viswanath, K. (2013). Social media use by community-based organizations conducting health promotion: A content analysis. *BMC Public Health, 13*(1), 1129.

Robinson, J. P. (1976). Interpersonal influence in election campaigns: Two step-flow hypotheses. *Public Opinion Quarterly, 40*(3), 304–319.

Rogers, E. M. (2003). *Diffusion of innovations.* New York: Free Press.

Rogers, K. (July 27, 2016). *The ice bucket challenge helped scientists discover a new gene tied to A.LS. The New York Times.* Retrieved online https://www.nytimes.com/2016/07/28/health/the-ice-bucket-challenge-helped-scientists-discover-a-new-gene-tied-to-als.html.

Rubin, A. M. (2002). The uses-and-gratification perspective of media effects. In J. Bryant, & D. Zillman's (Eds.), *Media effects* (pp. 525–548). Mahwah, NJ: Lawrence Erlbaum Associates Publishers.

Safren, S. A., & Heimberg, R. G. (1999). Depression, hopelessness, suicidality, and related factors in sexual minority and heterosexual adolescents. *Journal of Consulting and Clinical Psychology, 67*(6), 859–866.

Sashi, C. M. (2012). Customer engagement, buyer-seller relationships, and social media. *Management Decision, 50*(2), 253–272.

Savage, D. (2011). *It gets better: A programming note. theStranger.*

Shao, G. (2009). Understanding the appeal of user-generated media: A uses and gratification perspective. *Internet Research, 19*(1), 7–25.

Sheldon, P., & Bryant, K. (2016). Instagram: Motives for its use and relationship to narcissism and contextual age. *Computers in Human Behavior, 58*, 89–97. https://doi.org/10.1016/j.chb.2015.12.059.

Shi, J., Poorisat, T., & Salmon, C. T. (2018). The use of social networking sites (SNSs) in health communication campaigns: Review and recommendations. *Health Communication, 33*(1), 49–56. https://doi.org/10.1080/10410236.2016.1242035.

Shirky, C. (2008). *Here comes everybody: The power of organizing without organizations.* New York: Penguin.

Sifferlin, A. (August 18, 2014). *Here's how the ALS ice bucket challenge actually started.* Retrieved from http://time.com/3136507/als-ice-bucket-challenge-started/.

Smith, A., & Anderson, M. (2018). *Social media use in 2018.* Washington, DC: Pew Internet & American Life Project.

Sood, S. (2002). Audience involvement and entertainment-education. *Communication Theory, 12*(2), 153–172.

Stern, S. (2008). Producing sites, exploring identities: Youth online authorship. *Youth, Identity, and Digital Media, 6*, 95–117.

Stevens, M. (2014). *Ice bucket challenge stirs controversy in drought-plagued California.* Los Angeles Times. Retrieved from https://www.latimes.com/local/lanow/la-me-ln-ice-bucket-challenge-water-drought-20140819-story.html.

Stoeckl, R., Rohrmeier, P., & Hess, T. (2007). Motivations to produce user generated content: Differences between webloggers and videobloggers. *BLED 2007 Proceedings, 30.* http://aisel.aisnet.org/bled2007/30.

Sun, N., Rau, P. P.-L., & Ma, L. (2014). Understanding lurkers in online communities: A literature review. *Computers in Human Behavior, 38*, 110–117. https://doi.org/10.1016/j.chb.2014.05.022.

Surowiecki, J. (July 25, 2016). *What happened to the ice bucket challenge?* The new yorker. Retrieved from https://www.newyorker.com/magazine/2016/07/25/als-and-the-ice-bucket-challenge.

Sutherland, K. E. (2016). Using propinquital loops to blend social media and offline spaces: A case study of the ALS ice-bucket challenge. *Media International Australia, 160*(1), 78–88.

Thomas, M. (2011). *Deconstructing digital natives: Young people, technology, and the new literacies.* Taylor & Francis.

Valente, T. W. (2002). *Evaluating health promotion programs.* Oxford University Press.

Valente, T. W. (2010). *Social networks and health: Models, methods, and applications.* Oxford University Press.

Veale, H. J., Sacks-Davis, R., Weaver, E. R., Pedrana, A. E., Stoové, M. A., & Hellard, M. E. (2015). The use of social networking platforms for sexual health promotion: Identifying key strategies for successful user engagement. *BMC Public Health, 15*(1), 85.

Weimann, G. (1982). On the importance of marginality: One more step into the two-step flow of communication. *American Sociological Review,* 764–773.

Wolf-Mann, E. (August 21, 2015). *Remember the ice bucket challenge? Here's what happened to the money.* TIME.

Wong, C. A., Merchant, R. M., & Moreno, M. A. (2014). Using social media to engage adolescents and young adults with their health. *Healthcare (Amsterdam, Netherlands), 2*(4), 220–224. https://doi.org/10.1016/j.hjdsi.2014.10.005.

Yin, R. K. (2009). *Case study research: Design and methods (4th ed.).* Los Angeles: SAGE Publications.

York, A. (2017). *What is social media engagement and why should I care?* Retrieved from https://sproutsocial.com/insights/what-is-social-media-engagement/.

Revisiting the social enhancement and social compensation hypotheses in the social media era: Evidence from a two-wave panel study

Chul-joo Lee[1]*, Jeong-woo Jang*[2]*,
Macarena Pena-y-Lillo*[3]*, Ningxin Wang*[4]

[1] Department of Communication, Seoul National University, Seoul, South Korea; [2] School of Humanities and Social Sciences, Korea Advanced Institute of Science and Technology, Daejeon, South Korea; [3] School of Journalism Universidad Diego Portales, Santiago, Chile; [4] Department of Communication Studies, University of Pennsylvania, Bloomsburg, PA, United States

The remarkable increase in the number of academic papers on subjective well-being reflects escalating interest in managing a good life (Diener, 2013; Diener, Lucas, & Oishi, 2002). Social interactions are a major source of well-being, as they enable people to have a sense of belonging and to build intimacy with others (Ryan & Deci, 2001; Vaillant, 2012). Given this, many studies have examined whether Internet use for social interactions is associated with well-being. These studies have differed in how they conceptualize Internet use. Early studies in this area have treated it as a unidimensional concept and simply examined how daily or weekly time spent on the Internet predicts well-being (e.g., Kraut et al., 1998, 2002); however, recent research has focused on particular online activities, such as editing one's profile or engaging in different types of self-presentation on social networking sites (SNS), to see how each of

Technology and Health
https://doi.org/10.1016/B978-0-12-816958-2.00014-9 313

these activities affects well-being (e.g., Gonzales & Hancock, 2011; Kim & Lee, 2011; Liu, Tov, Kosinski, Stillwell, & Qiu, 2015; Toma, 2010).

This study aims to join these recent endeavors and posits that it is through various types of activities that determine how Internet use is related to subjective well-being (Valkenburg & Peter, 2007a). Considering that people engage in multiple activities on the Internet, we aim to test if different socially oriented online activities—instant messaging (IM), checking or updating one's profile on SNS, accessing to and posting on Twitter, sharing photos or videos, and posting messages on discussion or message boards—affect users' well-being and if so how. Moreover, we examine the roles of extraversion and social support as moderators of these effects, assuming that a person's level of sociability may influence the degree to which individuals reap benefits from their Internet use. Lastly, by employing a longitudinal survey, we aim to establish a causal order between online activities and well-being.

Literature review

Online activities and subjective well-being

Subjective well-being is a widely used indicator of psychological and physical health. Well-being refers to people's evaluations of their lives as the absence of negative psychological states (e.g., loneliness, stress, depression) and a person's sense of fullness and satisfaction with life (Diener, 2013; Diener et al., 2002). Having close connections with others contributes to a person's well-being (Ryan & Deci, 2001; Vaillant, 2012). A few early studies showed that the Internet is harmful to its users' well-being by decreasing time spent with offline social ties (e.g., Kraut et al., 1998; Nie, Hillygus, & Erbring, 2002). Moreover, it was recently reported that frequent socially oriented online activities, such as IM use and SNS use, decrease life satisfaction and increase depression (e.g., Goodman-Deane, Mieczabkowski, Johnson, Goldhaber, & Clarkson, 2016; van den Eijnden, Meerkerk, Vermulst, Spijkerman, & Engels, 2008). On the other hand, another group of studies demonstrated that online communication does not necessarily discourage face-to-face interactions (e.g., Kraut et al., 2002; Valkenburg & Peter, 2007a) and that a large portion of social interactions on the Internet occur among offline social network members (Lampe, Ellison, & Steinfield, 2006). In this vein, some studies (Bessière, Kiesler, Kraut, & Boneva, 2008; Ellison, Steinfield, & Lampe, 2007; Valkenburg & Peter, 2007a) found that socially oriented online activities increases well-being.

The inconsistent findings may be due to the fact that previous studies conceptualize and operationalize Internet use in different manners. Previous studies suggest that some online activities are beneficial to well-being, whereas others are detrimental (Valkenburg & Peter, 2007a). In order to consider particularities of different types of online communication, we try to theorize and empirically test the differential effects of five socially oriented online activities on well-being.

Instant messaging and well-being

IM has become one of the most popular and prevalent forms of online communication, especially among young populations (Fox, Rosen, & Crawford, 2008). Prior studies point out that IM is mostly useful for maintaining existing relationships and thus has positive effects on subjective well-being (Ramirez & Broneck, 2009; Valkenburg & Peter, 2007a). Specifically, Valkenburg & Peter (2007a) found that by increasing the time spent with existing friends and the quality of these friendships, IM use strengthened relationships among adolescents and enhanced their well-being. These prior findings lead us to propose the following hypothesis:

H1: IM use will be positively associated with subjective well-being over time.

Checking or updating profiles on SNS and well-being

Prior studies suggest that checking or updating profiles on SNS increases subjective well-being. Specifically, simply viewing or editing one's own Facebook profile enhanced self-esteem and self-worth because Facebook profiles, which encapsulate desired and positive self-image, satisfy users' ego needs and boost their self-worth (Gonzales & Hancock, 2011; Toma & Hancock, 2013). Moreover, a variety of SNS functions (e.g., a friends list, comments sections) allow its users to shape or change their SNS friends' profiles and to provide casual and lightweight comments on their SNS friends' profiles (Ellison & boyd, 2013). That is, SNS profiles have become a dynamic and public space for social interactions. Therefore, we expect the following:

H2: Checking or updating one's profile on SNS will be positively associated with subjective well-being over time.

Sharing photos or videos and well-being[1]

Sharing images is considered to be an important act of self-expression and a relationship maintenance practice. Prior research indicates that online photo sharing positively relates to certain domains of self-worth, such as self-evaluations of physical appearance and approval from generalized others (Stefanone, Lackaff, & Rosen, 2011). Moreover, photo sharing has a positive association with the size of a social support

---

[1] Recent IM applications include such features as file transfer, clickable hyperlinks, voice over IP, video chat, and many more other than text transmission. Thus, IM use and sharing photos and videos sometimes occur at the same time. However, considering that the bivariate association between these two online activities is 0.25 ($p < 0.001$) and that only IM use (not sharing photos and videos) emerged as a statistically significant predictor of well-being, we believe they should be treated as separate variables.

network, such that those with more close friends tend to share more photos online (Stefanone & Lackaff, 2009). Therefore, we posit the following hypothesis:

H3: Sharing photos or videos will be positively associated with subjective well-being over time.

Twitter and well-being

Twitter is a special kind of SNS, which allows users to post short messages of 140 characters or less. Unlike most SNS that foster reciprocal relationships and associations with acquaintances from the offline world (Valenzuela, Park, & Kee, 2009), Twitter is characterized by asymmetrical relationships in that Twitter lets people follow others without requiring them to follow back (Kwak, Lee, Park, & Moon, 2010). Therefore, whereas most SNS (e.g., Facebook) are likely to foster social interactions due to the symmetrical nature of the network, Twitter users may tweet without getting a response or a comment from their followers. Given this fundamental difference, one might expect the effect of Twitter to be not as beneficial as other SNS use, or even negative to well-being. The opposite prediction is also plausible. Some empirical evidence suggests that Twitter use is positively associated with the degree to which individuals gratify their needs to connect with others (e.g., Chen, 2011). Thus, we pose the following research question:

RQ1: How will accessing to and posting on Twitter affect subjective well-being over time?

Discussion boards and well-being

Discussion or message boards provide platforms for users to express their opinions about a topic or engage in conversations with others by commenting on others' posts. Similar to Twitter, however, discussion or message boards often lack relational features, as they are geared mainly toward hosting transient discussions on issues of interest rather than building or maintaining durable social networks. A dearth of prior studies on the associations of using discussion boards with well-being leads us to propose the following research question:

RQ2: How will posting messages on discussion or message boards affect subjective well-being over time?

Moderating roles of extraversion and social support

As outlined earlier, we also investigate whether the effects of socially oriented online activities on subjective well-being are moderated by a person's level of sociability, thereby revisiting two competing hypotheses: "social enhancement" and "social compensation" hypotheses. The "social enhancement" hypothesis posits that if communicating with others through Internet activities increases a person's subjective well-being, those benefits may be greater for those with higher levels of sociability. Consistent with this hypothesis, Kraut et al. (2002) found that extraverted Internet users were less lonely than introverted Internet users. Chen (2014) also found that extraverted college students made more Facebook friends when using SNS than did their nonextraverted counterparts. Plausibly, extraverts' inherent social skills facilitated broadening online social networks.

In sharp contrast, the "social compensation" hypothesis suggests that socially anxious individuals perceive the Internet as a more useful medium to express their thoughts and feelings than do nonsocially anxious ones, and thus the former are more inclined to use the Internet for social interactions than are the latter (Kraut et al., 2002; Orr et al., 2009; Valkenburg & Peter, 2007b). This could be due to the Internet's characteristics of high user control and reduced nonverbal cues, which make those with lower levels of sociability feel more comfortable communicating with others (McKenna, Green, & Gleason, 2002).

In revisiting these two competing predictions, we focus on social support and extraversion as potential moderators of the associations between socially oriented online activities and subjective well-being. Social support speaks to the actual resources embedded in one's social network, which consists of emotional aid, informational support, positive social interaction, and instrumental support (Sherbourne & Stewart, 1991). Extraversion, on the other hand, is a personality trait that describes an individual who is potentially adept at accessing and mobilizing social resources, though this trait is no guarantee the individual actually has those resources. According to the "social enhancement" hypothesis, the effects of socially oriented online activities on well-being may be bigger for individuals with higher levels of extraversion and social support than those with lower levels of extraversion and social support. Conversely, the "social compensation" perspective suggests that those with lower extraversion and social support experience increases in well-being from their Internet use to a greater extent than do their counterparts. Thus, the present study proposes the following research questions:

RQ3: Will extraversion moderate the effects of (a) IM use, (b) updating or checking one's SNS profile, (c) sharing photos or videos, (d) accessing to and posting on Twitter, and (e) posting messages on discussion or message boards on subjective well-being?

RQ4: Will social support moderate the effects of (a) IM use, (b) updating or checking one's SNS profile, (c) sharing photos or videos, (d) accessing to and posting on Twitter, and (e) posting messages on discussion or message boards on subjective well-being?

Method

Participants

Undergraduates from a large university in the US Midwest attending four communication courses were invited to participate in the study in exchange for course credit. We visited each classroom and explained the purpose of the study. Interested students accessed the online survey website, provided informed consent, and completed the Wave 1 online survey questionnaire in January 2014. Out of a total of 778 students enrolled in the courses, 521 students participated at Wave 1. Of these, 41 cases were excluded because of incomplete survey responses, resulting in a sample of 480 cases at Wave 1 (62% participation rate). We invited participants after 3 months to complete the Wave 2 online survey. Of the cases from Wave 1, 67 did not participate at Wave 2, resulting in 413 cases at follow-up (retention rate of 86%). Participants from Wave 1 were offered double extra credits to encourage them to complete the Wave 2 survey. The study protocol was approved by Institutional Review Board of the university. Table 14.1 summarizes the demographic information from both waves.

TABLE 14.1 Descriptive characteristics of the sample.

	Wave 1		Wave 2	
	N	Percent	N	Percent
Age				
18–20	285	59	260	63
21–23	156	33	136	33
24+	14	3	11	3
Gender				
Male	145	30.2	121	29.3
Female	312	65.0	288	69.7
Race/ethnicity				
Hispanic	47	9.8	38	9.2
White	311	64.8	283	68.5
Asian	90	18.8	77	18.6
African American	47	9.8	40	9.7
Other	11	2.3	10	2.4
Household income				
<$50,000	111	23	98	24
≥$50,000	342	71	308	75

Measures

Dependent variable: Subjective well-being

The satisfaction with life scale (Diener, Emmons, Larsen, & Griffin, 1985) was used to assess subjective well-being ("In most ways my life is close to my ideal," "So far I have gotten the important things I want in life," "The conditions of my life are excellent," "I am satisfied with my life," and "If I could live my life over, I would change almost nothing") on a seven-point scale ($1 = strongly\ disagree$, $7 = strongly\ agree$). We averaged the five items to create the score for subjective well-being, which achieved excellent reliability ($\alpha_{wave\ 1} = 0.88$, $M_{wave\ 1} = 5.17$, $SD_{wave\ 1} = 1.26$; $\alpha_{wave\ 2} = 0.90$, $M_{wave\ 2} = 5.23$, $SD_{wave\ 2} = 1.32$).[2]

Independent variables: Socially oriented online activities

Participants were asked on a six-point scale ($1 = never$, $2 = less\ than\ monthly$, $3 = monthly$, $4 = weekly$, $5 = daily$, $6 = several\ times\ a\ day$) how frequently they performed each of the five socially oriented online activities: IM use ($M_{wave\ 1} = 4.72$, $SD_{wave\ 1} = 1.54$; $M_{wave\ 2} = 4.68$, $SD_{wave\ 2} = 1.54$), checking or updating one's profile on SNS including Facebook, MySpace, or LinkedIn ($M_{wave\ 1} = 4.97$, $SD_{wave\ 1} = 1.36$; $M_{wave\ 2} = 4.95$, $SD_{wave\ 2} = 1.37$), sharing photos or videos ($M_{wave\ 1} = 4.38$, $SD_{wave\ 1} = 1.25$; $M_{wave\ 2} = 4.40$, $SD_{wave\ 2} = 1.18$), accessing to and posting on Twitter ($M_{wave\ 1} = 4.12$, $SD_{wave\ 1} = 1.98$; $M_{wave\ 2} = 4.05$, $SD_{wave\ 2} = 1.85$), and posting messages on discussion or message boards ($M_{wave\ 1} = 2.62$, $SD_{wave\ 1} = 1.57$; $M_{wave\ 2} = 2.73$, $SD_{wave\ 2} = 1.56$).[3]

---

[2] Although our dependent variable, subjective well-being, was slightly nonnormal (skewness $= -1.03$, kurtosis $= 0.72$), we decided not to transform the dependent variable for the following reasons. First, it is better to use the original scale unless the data drastically violate the statistical assumption. Transformed variables are sometimes harder to interpret (Tabachnick & Fidell, 2007). The absolute value of well-being's skewness is smaller than 2 and that of its kurtosis is smaller than 7. According to Curran, West, and Finch (1996), a moderately nonnormal distribution is characterized by skewness between 2 and 3, and by kurtosis between 7 and 21; and a severely nonnormal distribution should have skewness of 3 or higher and kurtosis of 21 or higher. Similarly, George and Mallery (2016) contended that the values for skewness and kurtosis between -2 and $+2$ are considered acceptable in order to prove normal univariate distribution. Second, the substantive pattern of results was highly consistent when we transformed the dependent variable by taking its square for the analyses.

[3] We tested the correlation of each socially oriented online activity between Wave 1 and Wave 2. These were 0.48 ($p < 0.001$) for IM use, 0.39 ($p < 0.001$) for posting messages on discussion or message boards, 0.49 ($p < 0.001$) for checking or updating one's profile on SNS, 0.51 ($p < 0.001$) for sharing photos or videos, and 0.78 ($p < 0.001$) for accessing to and posting on Twitter, respectively. Therefore, one can conclude that socially oriented online activities did change between Wave 1 and Wave 2 to some extent.

Moderating variables: Extraversion and social support

The first moderating variable is extraversion. We used Laverdière, Morin, and St-Hilaire's (2013) a four-item measure to assess extraversion at Wave 1 ("I am the life of the party," "I talk to a lot of different people at parties," "I don't talk a lot," and "I keep in the background "; the latter two were reverse coded) on a five-point scale (1 = *strongly disagree*, 5 = *strongly agree*). We averaged the four items to create a scale ($\alpha = 0.85$, $M = 3.70$, $SD = 1.05$).

The second moderating variable is social support. We used Sherbourne and Stewart's (1991) 15-item measure to assess social support at Wave 1. Participants were asked "People sometimes look to others for companionship, assistance, or other types of support. How often is each of the following kinds of support available to you if you need it?: response categories 0 = *none of the time*, 1 = *a little of the time*, 2 = *some of the time*, 3 = *most of the time*, 4 = *all of the time*." Sample items included "someone you can count on to listen to you when you need to talk," "someone to take you to the doctor if you need it," and "someone to give you information to help you understand a situation." A scale was constructed by averaging these 15 items ($\alpha = 0.96$, $M = 3.24$, $SD = 0.77$).

Control variables: Sociodemographics

All models controlled for demographics and healthcare coverage (*yes/ no*). Demographic variables included age, gender, race (white, black, Asian, other), ethnicity (Hispanic/Latino vs. non-Hispanic), and household income (1 = *$0 to $9999* to 9 = *$200,000 or more*).

Analytic procedures

We conducted a series of ordinary least squares (OLS) lagged dependent variable regression analyses to account for causal ordering.[4] We tested H1-3 and answered RQ1-2 by examining the lagged associations between socially oriented online activities at Wave 1 and well-being at Wave 2, controlling for well-being at Wave 1 and measured potential confounding factors. The effect of socially oriented online activities at Wave 1 on well-being at Wave 2, controlling for well-being at Wave 1, can

---

[4] In this chapter, we propose that Internet use is a predictor of well-being, but it could be argued that the association goes in the opposite direction. We tested five regression models, one for each of the examined socially oriented online activities, in order to evaluate whether well-being at Wave 1 predicted Internet use at Wave 2, after controlling for all potential confounders and socially oriented online activities at Wave 1. We found that neither of the examined socially oriented online activities at Wave 2 was predicted by well-being at Wave 1.

be interpreted as an effect of socially oriented online activities on the *change* of well-being over time.

To address RQ3-4, we constructed two hierarchical OLS regressions, which included all the aforementioned control variables, the main effects (i.e., socially oriented online activities), followed by the interaction terms between online activities and extraversion for RQ3, and the interaction terms between online activities and social support for RQ4. In order to mitigate multicollinearity, we obtained z-scores for each variable involved in the interactions before forming the multiplicative terms and tested the interactive effects of extraversion and social support in different models. We predicted well-being at Wave 2 as a function of well-being at Wave 1, Wave 1 independent and control variables, and Wave 1 interaction terms. When a statistically significant interaction was observed, we conducted a simple slope analysis to interpret the pattern of the interaction.

Results

We regressed Wave 2 subjective well-being on subjective well-being, social support, extraversion, the five socially oriented online activities, and potential confounds at Wave 1 (see Table 14.2, Model 1). As expected, the strongest predictor of well-being at Wave 2 was well-being at Wave 1. H1 was not supported, as IM use did not predict well-being at Wave 2 ($\beta = 0.02, p > 0.05$). Supporting H2, updating or checking one's profile on SNS significantly predicted an increase in well-being over time ($\beta = 0.09$, $p < 0.05$). H3 received no support as sharing images online did not predict a change in well-being over time ($\beta = -0.06, p > 0.05$). Similarly, no main effect was found for accessing to and posting on Twitter ($\beta = -0.02$, $p > 0.05$). Finally, we found that posting messages on discussion or messaging boards predicted a decrease in well-being over time ($\beta = -0.10, p < 0.01$).

Next, we tested whether extraversion moderated the effect of each of the five socially oriented online activities on subjective well-being (see Table 14.2, Model 2). We found a significant interaction between extraversion and IM use (interaction term $\beta = 0.08, p < 0.05$). To gain a clearer understanding of the interaction, the effects of Wave 1 IM use ($M - 1SD$, $M + 1SD$) were examined at two levels of extraversion ($M - 1SD$, $M + 1SD$). Simple slope tests showed that the more people used IM, the greater well-being those with higher levels of extraversion reported ($b = 0.15, t = 3.24, p < 0.001$). In contrast, for those with lower levels of extraversion, IM use did not predict subjective well-being ($b = -0.06$, $t = -1.41, p = 0.16$) (Fig. 14.1).

TABLE 14.2 Testing the effects of socially oriented online activities, extraversion, and social support at Wave 1 on subjective well-being at Wave 2.

Predictors	Zero-order correlation	Model 1: Main effect	Model 2: Extraversion x online activities	Model 3: Social support x online activities
Step 1				
Age	−0.13**	−0.06	−0.06	−0.05
Gender (female = 1)	0.04	−0.05	−0.05	−0.04
Income	0.16***	−0.02	−0.03	−0.02
Hispanic (vs. Non-Hispanic)	−0.05	−0.04	−0.04	−0.03
Asian (vs. white)	−0.12**	0.00	0.01	0.01
African American (vs. white)	−0.19***	−0.06	−0.07	−0.07
Other (vs. white)	0.04	0.01	0.01	0.01
Well-being (Wave 1)	0.70***	0.61***	0.62***	0.62***
Extraversion	0.27***	0.04	0.05	0.03
Social support	0.46***	0.13**	0.13**	0.14**
Step 2				
Using IM	0.08*	0.02	0.03	0.02
Posting on discussion boards	−0.10*	−0.10**	−0.10**	−0.10**
Checking or updating SNS	0.18***	0.09*	0.08*	0.08*
Sharing photos or videos	0.05	−0.06	−0.05	−0.07
Posting on twitter	0.11*	−0.02	−0.02	−0.01

TABLE 14.2 Testing the effects of socially oriented online activities, extraversion, and social support at Wave 1 on subjective well-being at Wave 2.—cont'd

Predictors	Zero-order correlation	Model 1: Main effect	Model 2: Extraversion x online activities	Model 3: Social support x online activities
Step 3				
Using IM	—	—	0.08*	0.07*
Posting on discussion boards	—	—	0.03	0.00
Checking or updating SNS	—		0.02	0.04
Sharing photos or videos	—	—	0.04	0.04
Posting on twitter	—	—	0.01	0.07*
Total R^2 (%)	—	53.4***	54.2***	54.3***
N	—	413	413	413

Displayed are standardized regression coefficients and explained variances. For the interaction terms, before entry betas are shown (see Step 3 in Models 2 and 3). *$p < 0.05$; **$p < 0.01$; ***$p < 0.001$ (two-tailed); *IM*, instant messaging; *SNS*, social networking sites.

The interaction between IM use and social support was statistically significant ($\beta = 0.07$, $p < 0.05$). According to simple slope analyses, only respondents with higher social support benefited from IM use ($b = 0.11$, $t = 2.48$, $p < 0.01$). IM use was not significantly related to subjective well-being among those with lower social support ($b = -0.07$, $t = -1.63$, $p = 0.10$) (Fig. 14.2).

Moreover, the interaction between Twitter use and social support was statistically significant ($\beta = 0.07$, $p < 0.05$). For those who receive lower social support, Twitter use predicted a decrease in subjective well-being over time ($b = -0.11$, $t = -2.48$, $p < 0.01$). The opposite pattern was detected for those with higher social support, although marginally significant ($b = 0.08$, $t = 1.86$, $p = 0.06$) (Fig. 14.3).

Discussion

Using the Internet to establish and maintain social connections is becoming more and more prevalent among young adults. The present study examined (a) the effects of each Internet social activity on well-being after controlling for those of other activities and (b) the moderating roles of individuals' sociability in these associations. When the effects of multiple activities were tested simultaneously, only certain activities appeared to be beneficial above and beyond the effects of other activities. Moreover, aligning with the "social enhancement" hypothesis, the findings are consistent with the proposition that benefits of socially oriented online activities depend, to some extent, on users' sociability.

In this context, a few interesting findings should be highlighted. First, the effect of connecting with others through the Internet differs from one activity to another. Notably, there is no evidence that this result occurred because people with higher or lower levels of well-being at Wave 1 preferred or used certain online activities more frequently than others (see footnote 1). While checking or updating profiles on SNS significantly increased subjective well-being after adjustment for the effects of other online activities, sharing photos or videos had no effect. The absence of the effect of sharing photos or videos on well-being may be explained by the fact that people utilize specific online platforms to share photos or

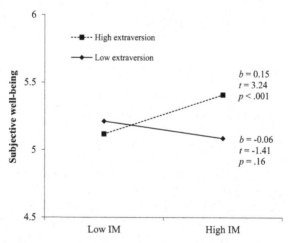

FIGURE 14.1   Relationship between instant messaging and extraversion at Wave 1 and well-being at Wave 2. *Notes:* Well-being was measured on a seven-point scale (1 = *strongly disagree* to 7 = *strongly agree*).

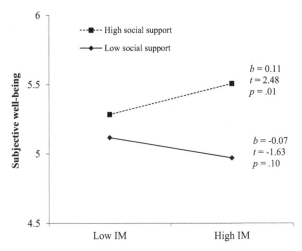

FIGURE 14.2 Relationship between instant messaging and social support at Wave 1 and well-being at Wave 2. *Notes*: Well-being was measured on a seven-point scale (1 = *strongly disagree*, 7 = *strongly agree*).

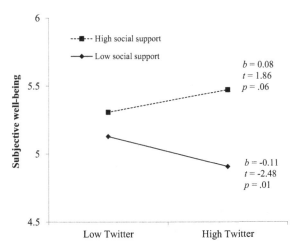

FIGURE 14.3 Relationship between Twitter use and social support at Wave 1 and well-being at Wave 2. *Notes*: Well-being was measured on a seven-point scale (1 = *strongly disagree* to 7 = *strongly agree*).

videos, such as SNS. That is, any significant effect of sharing photos or videos reported in previous studies (Stefanone et al., 2011; Stefanone & Lackaff, 2009) may be spurious, resulting from other socially oriented online activities that may take place along with sharing photos or videos. For instance, SNS users may check or update their profiles while sharing their photos or videos. Or, people may use IM as a venue to share their image files. Based on this finding, one cannot overemphasize the importance of considering various online activities all together in examining the effects of a specific type of online communication.

Moreover, extraversion and social support moderate the extent to which IM use is related to subjective well-being over time, and social support conditions the degree to which accessing to and posting on Twitter influences subjective well-being. In the case of IM, it appears that only those with higher levels of extraversion cultivated intimate relationships through such activity (Valkenburg & Peter, 2007b) and consequently increased subjective well-being over time. Similarly, IM use predicted increases in subjective well-being only for respondents with higher social support possibly by making them experience more instances of actually receiving social support through IM use, for example, by gaining information or encouragement from important people they contact. These findings are in line with the social enhancement hypothesis, which argues that benefits of the Internet are greater for more sociable users than for the less sociable.

However, we should also acknowledge that a group of studies (e.g., Ellison et al., 2007; Steinfield, Ellison, & Lampe, 2008) reported that those with lower self-esteem gain disproportionately more from their Facebook use than do their higher self-esteem counterparts. Because self-esteem is positively related to extraversion, involvement in social interactions, and propensity to form relationships (Ellison et al., 2007; Steinfield et al., 2008), these studies suggest that introverted and socially incompetent individuals may sometimes garner more benefits from SNS use, which renders evidence supporting the social compensation hypothesis. These differential patterns of interaction lead us to argue that scholars should theorize the interaction between Internet use and a third variable, such as personality, social anxiety, and self-esteem, depending on the type of benefit and platform.

In addition, the effect of accessing to and posting on Twitter depends on social support. Interestingly, Twitter use decreased subjective well-being for respondents with lower levels of social support. As discussed earlier, due to the asymmetrical nature of relationships among users, Twitter users are likely to receive no responses or comments from other users (Kwak et al., 2010). In this case, Twitter users with higher social support may better deal with these asymmetrical interactions than their lower social support counterparts. For instance, if a person is able to find alternative support in his or her social networks, asymmetrical interactions on Twitter may be less frustrating. The different findings of SNS and Twitter underscore the importance of taking into account the nature of the relationship individuals can establish and maintain through such platforms.

In this vein, this study has wide-ranging implications for research on the effects of new communication technologies on mental health in general and well-being in particular. It should be noted that we were interested in the technical affordances of each of the five online activities rather than each specific platform per se (Walther, 2011). That is, our main focus was on the degree to which each platform enables its users to interact with others. Among the online activities we examined, (1) IM, (2) SNS, and (3) online services designed to share photos and videos are more suited to creating and maintaining networks of relationships among users than are (4) Twitter and (5) discussion or message boards. Overall, this study suggests that the former are likely to increase well-being especially among those with social competence and outgoing personality than are the latter. Therefore, when a new online platform appears and researchers try to figure out outcomes of its use, we should assess the extent to which it provides cheap and easy tools to facilitate social exchanges among users.

Finally, regardless of levels of sociability, posting messages on discussion or message boards decreased well-being over time. Because interactions on discussion or message boards occur primarily among strangers, users are less likely to form long-term relationships with others. Although through this online activity people may be able to exchange useful information with one another, their relationship with other users may be transient. Our speculation is supported by the previous studies reporting that frequent social interactions that are not tuned to facilitate stable social ties may threaten well-being (e.g., Sum, Mathews, Pourghasem, & Hughes, 2008).

However, we should note a few limitations of the present study. First, we used a convenience sample of undergraduate students; therefore, our findings are not generalizable to other populations. For instance, our sample reported very high frequencies of SNS and IM use, which is not likely the case among the elderly and the less educated (van Deursen & van Dijk, 2014). Second, our data are limited in that the averages of extraversion and social support are high (3.70 on a 1–5 scale and 3.24 on a 0–4 scale, respectively). However, we made use of some variations in these two moderators in the sample to test the moderating roles of sociability in the associations between online activities and well-being. The third limitation stems from our measure of socially oriented online activities. Our measure was more comprehensive than those employed in prior research that considered only general Internet use (e.g., Kraut et al., 1988, 2002), particular types of online communication (e.g., IM or chat;

Valkenburg & Peter, 2007a), or activities on one specific site (e.g., Facebook; Ellison et al., 2007). However, it is still limited in that only one item was employed to assess activities on each platform. For instance, people often use SNS for a number of purposes (e.g., on Facebook one can use private messaging, all posts and status updates to send messages to one or multiple friends) other than updating or checking one's profile. Future studies thus should use a more comprehensive measure of socially orientated Internet activities to deepen our understanding of the associations between social media use and well-being.

In conclusion, the major contribution of this study is to demonstrate how various socially oriented online activities play a role in predicting subjective well-being. More interestingly, individuals' sociability, captured by extraversion and social support, determines the effects of certain socially oriented online activities on subjective well-being. Altogether, our findings suggest that using the Internet for social activities cannot be considered a monolithic behavior and that individuals' sociability has to be taken into account when examining the effects of online interactions on subjective well-being.

References

Bessière, K., Kiesler, S., Kraut, R., & Boneva, B. S. (2008). Effects of internet use and social resources on changes in depression. *Information, Communication, and Society, 11*, 47–70. https://doi.org/10.1080/13691180701858851.

Chen, G. M. (2011). Tweet this: A uses and gratifications perspective on how active twitter use gratifies a need to connect with others. *Computers in Human Behavior, 27*, 755–762. https://doi.org/10.1016/j.chb.2010.10.023.

Chen, G. M. (2014). Revisiting the social enhancement hypothesis: Extroversion indirectly predicts number of Facebook friends operating through Facebook usage. *Computers in Human Behavior, 39*, 263–269. https://doi.org/10.1016/j.chb.2014.07.015.

Curran, P. J., West, S. G., & Finch, J. F. (1996). The robustness of test statistics to nonnormality and specification error in confirmatory factor analysis. *Psychological Methods, 1*, 16–29. https://doi.org/10.1037/1082-989X.1.1.16.

van Deursen, A. J., & van Dijk, J. A. (2014). The digital divide shifts to differences in usage. *New Media and Society, 16*, 507–526. https://doi.org/10.1177/1461444813487959.

Diener, E. (2013). The remarkable changes in the science of subjective well-being. *Perspectives on Psychological Science, 8*, 663–666. https://doi.org/10.1177/1745691613507583.

Diener, E., Emmons, R. A., Larsen, R. J., & Griffin, S. (1985). The satisfaction with life scale. *Journal of Personality Assessment, 49*, 71–75. https://doi.org/10.1207/s15327752jpa4901_13.

Diener, E., Lucas, R. E., & Oishi, S. (2002). Subjective well-being: The science of happiness and life satisfaction. In S. J. Lopez, & C. R. Snyder (Eds.), *The Oxford handbook of positive psychology* (pp. 63–73). Oxford, UK: Oxford University Press.

van den Eijnden, R., Meerkerk, G.-J., Vermulst, A. A., Spijkerman, R., & Engels, R. (2008). Online communication, compulsive internet use, and psychological well-being among adolescents: A longitudinal study. *Developmental Psychology, 44*, 655–665. https://doi.org/10.1037/0012-1649.44.3.655.

Ellison, N. B., & Boyd, D. (2013). Sociality through social network sites. In W. H. Dutton (Ed.), *The Oxford Handbook of internet studies*. Oxford, UK: Oxford University press.

Ellison, N. B., Steinfield, C., & Lampe, C. (2007). The benefits of Facebook "friends": Social capital and college students' use of online social network sites. *Journal of Computer-Mediated Communication, 12*, 1143−1168. https://doi.org/10.1111/j.1083-6101.2007.00367.x.

Fox, A. B., Rosen, J., & Crawford, M. (2008). Distractions, distractions: Does instant messaging affect college students' performance on a concurrent reading comprehension task? *CyberPsychology and Behavior, 12*, 51−53. https://doi.org/10.1089/cpb.2008.0107.

George, D., & Mallery, M. (2016). *IBM SPSS statistics 23 step by step: A simple guide and reference* (14th ed.). New York: Routledge.

Gonzales, A. L., & Hancock, J. T. (2011). Mirror, mirror on my Facebook wall: Effects of exposure to Facebook on self-esteem. *Cyberpsychology, Behavior, and Social Networking, 14*, 79−83. https://doi.org/10.1089/cyber.2009.0411.

Goodman-Deane, J., Mieczakowski, A., Johnson, D., Goldhaber, T., & Clarkson, P. J. (2016). The impact of communication technologies on life and relationship satisfaction. *Computers in Human Behavior, 57*, 219−229. https://doi.org/10.1016/j.chb.2015.11.053.

Kim, J., & Lee, J. R. (2011). The Facebook paths to happiness: Effects of the number of Facebook friends and self-presentation on subjective well-being. *Cyberpsychology, Behavior, and Social Networking, 14*, 359−364. https://doi.org/10.1089/cyber.2010.0374.

Kraut, R., Kiesler, S., Boneva, B., Cummings, J., Helgeson, V., & Crawford, A. (2002). Internet paradox revisited. *Journal of Social Issues, 58*, 49−74. https://doi.org/10.1111/1540-4560.00248.

Kraut, R., Patterson, M., Lundmark, V., Kiesler, S., Mukophadhyay, T., & Scherlis, W. (1998). Internet paradox: A social technology that reduces social involvement and psychological well-being? *American Psychologist, 53*, 1017−1031. https://doi.org/10.1037/0003-066X.53.9.1017.

Kwak, H., Lee, C., Park, H., & Moon, S. (2010). What is Twitter, a social network or a news media?. In *Proceedings of the 19th international conference on World wide web* (pp. 591−600). https://doi.org/10.1145/1772690.1772751.

Lampe, C., Ellison, N., & Steinfield, C. (2006). A Face(book) in the crowd: Social searching vs. social browsing. In *Proceedings of the CSCW conference on computer supported cooperative work, USA* (pp. 167−170). https://doi.org/10.1145/1180875.1180901.

Laverdière, O., Morin, A. J. S., & St-Hilaire, F. (2013). Factor structure and measurement invariance of a short measure of the Big Five personality traits. *Personality and Individual Differences, 55*, 739−743. https://doi.org/10.1016/j.paid.2013.06.008.

Liu, P., Tov, W., Kosinski, M., Stillwell, D. J., & Qiu, L. (2015). Do Facebook status updates reflect subjective well-being? *Cyberpsychology, Behavior, and Social Networking, 18*, 373−379. https://doi.org/10.1089/cyber.2015.0022.

McKenna, K. Y., Green, A. S., & Gleason, M. E. (2002). Relationship formation on the internet: What's the big attraction? *Journal of Social Issues, 58*, 9−31. https://doi.org/10.1111/1540-4560.00246.

Nie, N. H., Hillygus, D. S., & Erbring, L. (2002). Internet use, interpersonal relations, and sociability: A time diary study. In B. Wellman, & C. Haythornthwaite (Eds.), *The Internet in everyday life* (pp. 215−243). Oxford, UK: Blackwell.

Orr, E. S., Sisic, M., Ross, C., Simmering, M. G., Arseneault, J. M., & Orr, R. R. (2009). The influence of shyness on the use of Facebook in an undergraduate sample. *CyberPsychology and Behavior, 12*, 337−340. https://doi.org/10.1089/cpb.2008.0214.

Ramirez, A., & Broneck, K. (2009). 'IM me': Instant messaging as relational maintenance and everyday communication. *Journal of Social and Personal Relationships, 26*, 291−314. https://doi.org/10.1177/0265407509106719.

Ryan, R. M., & Deci, E. L. (2001). On happiness and human potentials: A review of research on hedonic and eudaimonic well-being. *Annual Review of Psychology, 52,* 141−166. https://doi.org/10.1146/annurev.psych.52.1.141.

Sherbourne, C. D., & Stewart, A. L. (1991). The MOS social support survey. *Social Science and Medicine, 32,* 705−714. https://doi.org/10.1016/0277-9536(91)90150-B.

Stefanone, M. A., & Lackaff, D. (2009). Reality television as a model for online behavior: Blogging, photo, and video sharing. *Journal of Computer-Mediated Communication, 14,* 964−987. https://doi.org/10.1111/j.1083-6101.2009.01477.x.

Stefanone, M. A., Lackaff, D., & Rosen, D. (2011). Contingencies of self-worth and social-networking-site behavior. *Cyberpsychology, Behavior, and Social Networking, 14,* 41−49. https://doi.org/10.1089/cyber.2010.0049.

Steinfield, C., Ellison, N. B., & Lampe, C. (2008). Social capital, self-esteem, and use of online social network sites: A longitudinal analysis. *Journal of Applied Developmental Psychology, 29,* 434−445. https://doi.org/10.1016/j.appdev.2008.07.002.

Sum, S., Mathews, M. R., Pourghasem, M., & Hughes, I. (2008). Internet technology and social capital: How the Internet affects seniors' social capital and well-being. *Journal of Computer-Mediated Communication, 14,* 202−220. https://doi.org/10.1111/j.1083-6101.2008.01437.x.

Tabachnick, B. G., & Fidell, L. S. (2007). *Using multivariate statistics* (5th ed.). Boston: Allyn and Bacon.

Toma, C. L. (2010). Affirming the self through online profiles: Beneficial effects of social networking sites. *Proceedings of the SIGCHI Conference on Human Factors in Computing Systems,* 1749−1752. https://doi.org/10.1145/1753326.1753588.

Toma, C. L., & Hancock, J. T. (2013). Self-affirmation underlies Facebook use. *Personality and Social Psychology Bulletin, 39,* 321−331. https://doi.org/10.1177/0146167212474694.

Vaillant, G. E. (2012). *Triumphs of experience: The men of the harvard grant study.* Cambridge, MA: Belknap Press of Harvard University Press.

Valenzuela, S., Park, N., & Kee, K. F. (2009). Is there social capital in a social network site? Facebook use and college students' life satisfaction, trust, and participation. *Journal of Computer-Mediated Communication, 14,* 875−890. https://doi.org/10.1111/j.1083-6101.2009.01474.x.

Valkenburg, P. M., & Peter, J. (2007a). Online communication and adolescent well-being: Testing the stimulation versus the displacement hypothesis. *Journal of Computer-Mediated Communication, 12,* 1169−1182. https://doi.org/10.1111/j.1083-6101.2007.00368.x.

Valkenburg, P. M., & Peter, J. (2007b). Preadolescents' and adolescents' online communication and their closeness to friends. *Developmental Psychology, 43,* 267−277. https://doi.org/10.1037/0012-1649.43.2.267.

Walther, J. B. (2011). Theories of computer-mediated communication and interpersonal relations. In M. L. Knapp, & J. A. Daly (Eds.), *The handbook of interpersonal communication* (pp. 443−479). Thousand Oaks, CA: Sage.

PART V

How technology changes
our mind and behavior

Innovative health interventions at the intersection of neuroimaging and multimedia design

Jacob T. Fisher, René Weber

Media Neuroscience Lab, Department of Communication, The University of California Santa Barbara, Santa Barbara, CA, United States

Functional magnetic resonance imaging (fMRI) has significantly contributed to the scientific understanding of the brain (Mather, Cacioppo, & Kanwisher, 2013; Smith, 2012). Neuroimaging approaches are used to build and constrain theory (Coltheart, 2013; Weber, Fisher, Hopp, & Lonergan, 2017) as well as to construct predictive models of human behavior (Berkman & Falk, 2013; Falk, Berkman, Whalen, & Lieberman, 2011; Gabrieli, Ghosh, & Whitfield-Gabrieli, 2015). In recent years, this research has been aided by theoretical and methodological advancements on multiple fronts (Turner, Huskey, & Weber, 2018; Weber et al., 2017). Most notably, brain imaging methods are more accessible than they have ever been, with many research universities electing to develop their own research centers dedicated to neuroimaging and other physiological measures. In addition, advancements in computational architectures and mathematical models allow for novel forms of analysis that consider the brain as a dynamic network of regions interacting throughout a task (Bassett & Sporns, 2017). This has allowed researchers to build more refined models of how the brain enables human behavior.

A burgeoning area of recent research seeks to leverage the predictive and explanatory power of neuroimaging to design multimedia messages to promote positive health changes. This work has revealed that activity in key brain regions can be used to build predictive models of human behavior that are much more accurate than those built on behavioral or self-report data (Berkman & Falk, 2013; Falk et al., 2011; Huskey, Mangus, Turner, & Weber, 2017; Weber, Huskey, Mangus, Westcott-Baker, & Turner, 2015). By characterizing how a message activates specific brain regions, how brain regions connect to one another during message processing (Cooper et al., 2018; Huskey et al., 2017), and how the neural dynamics of message processing covary between individuals, researchers can increase the accuracy of predictions as to how effective a health message will be at eliciting cognitive and behavioral change—even months later.

Additionally, neuroimaging is assisting researchers in making headway toward designing digital interventions for cognitive processing disorders (Mishra, Anguera, & Gazzaley, 2016; Mishra & Gazzaley, 2014). Research in this area uses video games, movies, and other tools in combination with brain imaging methods (Mathiak & Weber, 2006; Weber, Ritterfeld, & Mathiak, 2006). Combining naturalistic stimuli with brain imaging has allowed researchers to develop promising research programs aimed at understanding, diagnosing, and treating attention deficit hyperactivity disorder (ADHD) (Alegria et al., 2017; Johnstone, Roodenrys, Johnson, Bonfield, & Bennett, 2017; Mishra, Sagar, Joseph, Gazzaley, & Merzenich, 2016), autism (Kouijzer, de Moor, Gerrits, Congedo, & van Schie, 2009), schizophrenia (Kühn, Gleich, Lorenz, Lindenberger, & Gallinat, 2014), age-related cognitive decline (Anguera et al., 2013), impulsivity/aggressiveness (Klasen et al., 2013; Wolf et al., 2018), and many other health issues. The combination of neuroscience and multimedia design makes these areas particularly promising for communication scholars who are familiar with brain imaging tools and analysis techniques, especially in developing more informed and effective interventions and treatments for improving human health.

In this chapter, we review extant literature relating to the interacting roles of brain imaging technology and multimedia design. We focus this review in two primary areas: first, we discuss the use of neuroimaging as an individualized predictive tool for health-related outcomes of interest. Next, we review the promise of neuroimaging and media design for the diagnosis and treatment of cognitive disorders such as ADHD and autism.

Promoting positive health changes

The study of persuasive health messages enjoys a long and productive history within communication science (for an overview see; Fishbein & Cappella, 2006). Health communication scholars are often interested in the design of successful message campaigns that (a) increase public awareness of negative consequences associated with certain risky behaviors; (b) promote positive health behaviors; and (c) provide information regarding the detection or treatment of certain illnesses (Kaye, White, & Lewis, 2016). In a typical research approach in this area, audiences are exposed to messages of interest—such as public service announcements or drug advertisements—and are asked a series of questions regarding their attentiveness, their perceptions of argument strength, and their intent to follow the recommendations of the message. In many studies, follow-up measures are also collected to index actual behavioral change.

Unfortunately, despite a wealth of research in this area, it has become clear that self-reported measures of message persuasiveness, although they predict some variation in future beliefs and behaviors, frequently do not predict nearly as well as expected (Falk, Berkman, Mann, Harrison, & Lieberman, 2010). This is especially problematic for large-scale health campaigns that rely on message pretesting of this sort to determine which messages are worth the expense of large-scale broadcasting. The dearth of predictive ability afforded by self-report measures has often been attributed to the possibility that actual behavior change is influenced by unconscious processes that are not able to be accurately reported following message exposure (Lang, Bradley, Chung, & Lee, 2003).

The introduction of psychophysiological measures (Potter & Bolls, 2012) into message processing research gave researchers additional tools to assess conscious and unconscious reactions to messages in real time. By using physiological indicators of the brain and body's responses during a message, researchers can more accurately index the arousingness and valence of messages as well as the extent to which they capture audience attention. This knowledge can be used to create more accurate models to predict when messages will be remembered and when they will be tuned out or argued against (see e.g., Clayton, Lang, Leshner, & Quick, 2018). Psychophysiological measures have also contributed to our understanding of how complex emotional appeals in messages can lead to conflicting feelings and how those feelings contribute to memory and persuasion (Keene & Lang, 2016; Liu & Bailey, 2018).

Brain as predictor

An additional leap forward in the study of persuasive health messages came with the discovery that brain activity can be monitored in specific regions to determine how individuals are processing health messages (for review of this research area, see Kaye et al., 2016; Weber, Eden, Huskey, Mangus, & Falk, 2015; Weber, Mangus, & Huskey, 2015). The first and arguably the most productive finding in this area is that activity in the medial prefrontal cortex (mPFC)—a small region in the front of the brain—can be used as an index of how valuable or rewarding an individual finds a message (Falk et al., 2010). The mPFC is a part of a large-scale network of brain regions common to almost all higher-order organisms that work to predict the reward that may result from particular actions and to update these predictions in light of real-world outcomes (Berridge & Robinson, 1998). This network is also involved in taking the perspective of others (also called mentalizing; Amodio & Frith, 2006; Barrett & Satpute, 2013). These evaluations serve to bias behavioral choices toward those that will be the most efficacious at any given point in time. Thus, activation in these reward and mentalizing regions are a likely indicator of how persuasive an individual finds a message, even if they are unable or unwilling to report its persuasiveness in a self-report measure. In a series of foundational studies, Falk and colleagues used activity in the mPFC (and other areas associated with persuasion) during persuasive messages to predict health-related outcomes of interest such as using sunscreen (Falk et al., 2010), reducing smoking and drug use (Chua et al., 2011; Cooper, Tompson, O'Donnell, & Falk, 2015; Falk et al., 2011; Falk, O'Donnell, Tompson, et al., 2015; Huskey et al., 2017; Weber, Huskey, et al., 2015), and becoming more active (Cooper, Bassett, & Falk, 2017; Falk, O'Donnell, Cascio, et al., 2015; Kang et al., 2018).

This approach has been shown to increase the predictive accuracy of persuasion models by over 20% (Falk et al., 2010) and to predict media effects at the population level when self-report data do not (Falk, Berkman, & Lieberman, 2012; Falk, O'Donnell, Tompson, et al., 2015). This means that message designers can potentially use brain imaging analyses to pretest messages using small groups of individuals for optimal effectiveness in larger populations. Increasingly, these approaches combine content analysis of messages with neural measures to understand what sorts of individual message features activate brain regions and networks associated with persuasion (O'Donnell & Falk, 2015) and how variations of message features and activation patterns can lead to message-level outcomes of interest such as virality (Falk, O'Donnell, & Lieberman, 2012). In combining analyses of message content with analyses of message processing, researchers can build tighter models for what sorts of structural/content features will be expected to elicit which responses in which individuals. This provides message designers with additional data that can be used to create more persuasive health messages and to understand when and why these messages lead to behavioral change.

More recent work in this area has incorporated methodological tools from network science to investigate how collections of brain regions act in concert with one another in the persuasion process. This allows researchers to parse apart more fine-grained processes, such as self-reflection, social cognition, and information valuation (Cooper et al., 2017; Scholz et al., 2017), and to understand how these processes are modulated by health-related individual differences such as drug use risk (Huskey et al., 2017). Networked connections between brain regions can also be examined over time, providing information as to how often and how robustly nodes within these networks connect with one another during message processing (Cooper et al., 2018). This research shows that the predictive accuracy of neural models of message persuasion can be improved when considering not only activity in the mPFC and other regions but also how these regions are connected to one another over time during message processing. As an example, smokers whose mPFC was highly active *and* highly flexible in its connection patterns were more likely to reduce their smoking in response to a strong health message (Cooper et al., 2018).

Synchrony and message processing

Work at the intersection of message design and neuroscience has shown that activity in the brain can be used to predict outcomes of interest like persuasion and memory. As mentioned in the previous section, connectivity or synchronous patterns of activation across brain networks *within* an individual brain may become an especially significant predictor in future studies. Increasingly, communication scholars and neuroscientists are also beginning to consider how synchronous patterns of activity in specific brain regions can predict message effectiveness *between* individuals. In other words, in this research paradigm, brain activity within specific regions is compared between subjects over time. The extent to which activity in one brain resembles activity in another brain (in the location or time course of neural activity) is recorded as a measure of *intersubject synchrony.*

Intersubject synchrony (or lack thereof) of brain activity has been investigated in the context of movies (Hasson, Furman, Clark, Dudai, & Davachi, 2008), political speeches (Schmälzle, Häcker, Honey, & Hasson, 2015), narrated short stories (Brennan et al., 2012), and even interpersonal conversations (Dikker, Silbert, Hasson, & Zevin, 2014).

Synchronous responses between individuals have been shown to predict shared perceptions of risk (Schmalzle, Hacker, Renner, Honey, & Schupp, 2013), interpersonal communication success (Hasson & Frith, 2016), and friendship (Parkinson, Kleinbaum, & Wheatley, 2018). Intersubject synchrony of neural activity patterns can also predict how well a person remembers a video clip (Chen et al., 2016) and can be used to parse apart attitude differences between groups (Yeshurun et al., 2017). For health messages, brain responses between individuals have been shown to be more synchronous for more effective antismoking messages, suggesting that more effective messages engage the brains of different people in similar ways (Imhof, Schmälzle, Renner, & Schupp, 2017).

Brain and social networks

Over the last 10 years, the landscape of message spread has changed dramatically. Individuals spend less time engaging with traditional mass communication platforms such as television and radio and more time on personal digital devices such as smartphones, personal computers, and tablets (Lee, 2017). This creates new challenges for health-related message campaigns. In a traditional mass media model, message spread is unidirectional and highly controlled. Thus, extra message factors such as ad spend, television viewer demographics, and message placement largely determine the size of an audience for a health message. In the modern media landscape, message spread is multidirectional—messages are spread by both the message producer and the message consumer. Thus, propagation of a message is dependent on the actions of the message producer and also on factors within the message itself that drive message consumers to share the message—usually with their connections on a social network. In this landscape, message creators must understand the message factors that contribute to the persuasiveness of the health message and also those that contribute to its "virality" or "sharability."

Emerging research at the intersection of brain and social networks aims to elucidate the neural underpinnings of message sharing (see, e.g., Baek, Scholz, & O'Donnell, 2017; Scholz et al., 2017). This research has shown that intentions to share a message are processed in a network of brain regions that include those important for information valuation and self-referential processing—such as the mPFC—and also other regions related to mentalizing and perspective taking. These regions include the temporoparietal junction, the precuneus, and the dorsomedial prefrontal cortex (Baek et al., 2017; Dufour et al., 2013). Activation in these regions is associated with receiving social feedback (Welborn et al., 2015), viewing pictures that others have "liked" on social media (Sherman, Payton, Hernandez, Greenfield, & Dapretto, 2016), and with incorporating peer feedback into one's own perceptions of the value of a product (Cascio, O'Donnell, Bayer, Tinney Jr, & Falk, 2015). Activity in this network predicts intentions to share news articles (Scholz et al., 2017) and is related to the effectiveness of antismoking and antidrug PSAs (Imhof et al., 2017; Weber, Huskey, et al., 2015).

Importantly, a person's social network position also influences the neural underpinnings of information propagation. As a particularly salient example, adolescents who are considered *information brokers* (i.e., highly central in a social network, bridging gaps between large groups) show greater activity in mentalizing networks when making product recommendations to their peers (O'Donnell, Bayer, Cascio, & Falk, 2017). This research is a part of a large and rapidly growing research area investigating the numerous linkages between brain activity and social network structure (for an overview see; Falk & Bassett, 2017). This research has also shown that an individual's ability to judge the virality of a news article depends on how frequently they read the news—those who were infrequent readers exhibited more selective activation of sharing networks in the brain than did those who were more frequent news readers (Doré et al., 2018). Although this research area is still in its beginning stages, it stands to increase understanding of the message variables and individual difference variables that influence the virality of health messages. An important future step for this research is to begin constructing strong theory as to when and why brain regions, intrabrain networks, interbrain networks, and social networks predict health outcomes of interest, constraining and refining predictions.

Diagnosing and treating health problems

Neuroimaging has significantly contributed to our understanding of the neural underpinnings of many psychosocial disorders, including schizophrenia, autism, ADHD, depression, impulsivity, aggression disorders, and many others. This has resulted in marked progress toward the development of diagnosis and treatment tools for many of these disorders. An especially promising subdomain within this area is in the combined use of neuroimaging approaches and specially developed video games that activate brain regions of interest in certain ways.

These approaches allow researchers to better understand how the brain responds to naturalistic tasks and how these responses vary in healthy and in disordered individuals (Mathiak & Weber, 2006). This then allows for the development of targeted treatments and interventions that are individualized based on a person's brain responses. In this section, we discuss emerging research that combines neuroimaging and multimedia design to better understand and treat psychological disorders and to improve cognitive function in the general population.

Identifying and diagnosing cognitive disorders

One of the most promising recent applications of neuroimaging methods is in the development of machine learning algorithms that can help identify potential markers of cognitive and neural disorders (Craddock, Holtzheimer III, Hu, & Mayberg, 2009; Deshpande, Libero, Sreenivasan, Deshpande, & Kana, 2013; Guo et al., 2012; Rosenberg, Finn, Scheinost, Constable, & Chun, 2017). Although neuroimaging is not (yet) capable of replacing traditional diagnostic tools, an emerging synergy between multivariate machine learning, data sharing initiatives, and large-scale diagnostic validation efforts has rapidly improved the accuracy of these models in recent years (Woo, Chang, Lindquist, & Wager, 2017). In addition, these approaches have given researchers and medical professionals an additional tool to understand how differences in the structure and function of the brain lead to health-related outcomes of interest.

In order to understand health-relevant differences within and between brains, researchers can compare (a) structure/anatomy of specific brain regions or pathways, (b) activity in the brain while the participant is at rest (e.g., laying quietly in the brain imaging scanner), (c) activity in the brain under some external intervention with a known or presumed cognitive effect (e.g., taking a typical antipsychotic drug prior to scanning compared to a placebo), (d) behavioral responses after manipulating neural activity in specific regions (e.g., temporarily impeding activity in specific brain regions via an external strong magnetic pulse), and (e) activity in the brain while the participant is engaged in a particular activity of interest (e.g., responding to an attention task or playing a video game). Although all of these methods hold great promise for understanding and treating health-related cognitive issues, it is the final approach (e) that holds particular promise for multimedia researchers interested in designing novel treatments and brain training applications. Recent work has outlined how carefully designed tasks can either emphasize or deemphasize the differences between brains (Finn et al., 2017). A recent turn in the psychological and brain sciences toward more naturalistic stimuli has led to the development of fMRI tasks based on multimedia processing. These include watching movies (Hasson et al., 2008), playing video games (Huskey, Craighead, Miller, & Weber, 2018), or interacting with others via digital media (Dikker et al., 2014).

Brain imaging research using naturalistic tasks is vital for understanding how individual differences in brain function contribute to differences in real-world outcomes of interest (Mathiak & Weber, 2006; Weber et al., 2017). Communication scholars are uniquely situated to guide the creation of these sorts of tasks in that they require a deep understanding of the role of structural and content features of messages in guiding processing toward specific outcomes. Combining brain imaging with rigorous manual (Weber, 2008; Weber et al., 2006) or computational (Huskey, Craighead, et al., 2018; O'Donnell & Falk, 2015) content analysis can help brain researchers to more quickly understand what sorts of message features or interactive tasks lead to highly differentiable neural activation in groups of interest and what features/tasks produce highly similar patterns of activation. These approaches help researchers answer the question "When does the disordered brain look different from the normal brain and when does it look similar?"

Understanding health-related individual differences

In addition to diagnosing neurological, cognitive, and behavioral problems, brain imaging is increasingly used to understand health-related individual differences that are not necessarily pathological. One of the most notable examples of this approach is the use of brain imaging to understand neural changes across the life span and how these changes contribute to cognitive and behavioral outcomes (Dosenbach et al., 2010; Meier et al., 2012). In addition, extant work has sought to characterize how the brains of drug users respond differently than those of nonusers to persuasive messaging (Huskey et al., 2017) or drug cues (Goldstein et al., 2007; McBride, Barrett, Kelly, Aw, & Dagher, 2006). Other work has used machine learning classifiers to identify cognitive states—such as attention or distraction—that are relevant for understanding individual differences in cognitive function (Mourao-Miranda, Bokde, Born, Hampel, & Stetter, 2005; Shirer, Ryali, Rykhlevskaia, Menon, & Greicius, 2012).

Age-related neural differences are especially salient for understanding cognitive decline in senior adults. Individuals over 65 currently comprise about 13% of the population, and this number is expected to double in the next 30 years (US Census Bureau, 2010). For many, the onset of age-related cognitive decline is a source of a large amount of stress and negative affect (Hasher & Zacks, 1988). Many competing hypotheses have been proposed for the nature of this seemingly domain-general decline in cognitive functioning during normal aging (Gazzaley & D'esposito, 2007). Brain imaging approaches have allowed for novel forms of investigation into this problem, finding that these age-related differences in cognitive processing can be attributed to reduced activity in inhibitory circuits (Gazzaley & D'esposito, 2007), slower neural responses (Zanto, Toy, & Gazzaley, 2010), and reduced activation and synchrony in cortical networks (Ho et al., 2012). In contrast, increased activation and synchrony in these networks is associated with successful cognitive aging (Eyler, Sherzai, Kaup, & Jeste, 2011).

Another area in which brain imaging has been especially helpful is in understanding individual differences in cognitive control and executive functioning. Cognitive control is a domain-general process involving active maintenance of goals and inhibition of potential distractors (Botvinick, Braver, Barch, Carter, & Cohen, 2001; Miller & Cohen, 2001). Cognitive control can take two primary forms: proactive control—involving active maintenance of goal-relevant information in working memory—and reactive control—involving noticing goal-relevant information in the environment and updating behavior as a result (Braver, 2012). Individual differences in cognitive control ability are associated with individual differences in activation in specific brain regions (Braver, Cole, & Yarkoni, 2010), and in large-scale dynamic networks (Bressler &

Menon, 2010; Seeley et al., 2007). Recent work has sought to describe the behavior of cognitive control networks during a naturalistic task (Weber, Alicea, Huskey, & Mathiak, 2018), finding that networks underlying successful attentional performance exhibit a curvilinear pattern of robustness to distractions. Further research has shown that intrinsic motivation can increase activation in cognitive control networks (Huskey, Craighead, et al., 2018) and can also increase network connectivity measures in these networks (Huskey, Wilcox, & Weber, 2018).

Brain training

These research areas point to a central question: can we design multimedia stimuli that improve cognitive functioning? For more than a decade now "brain training" applications (sometimes referred to as "brain games") have purported to do just this.

Initially, brain training programs held promise for improving cognitive functioning, but recent work reveals that evidence of their utility is limited at best (Simons et al., 2016). Most importantly, skills that are gained when using brain training applications do not seem to *transfer*, rather these improvements are circumscribed within the narrow bounds of the brain training task itself (e.g., people improve their memory training task performance, but not their real-life memory performance). For this reason, much of the initial enthusiasm surrounding brain training applications has cooled in recent years (Owen et al., 2010).

In order to improve the effectiveness of these games, researchers have called for the development of approaches that take into account individual cognitive differences (Jaeggi, Buschkuehl, Shah, & Jonides, 2014) as well as the neural underpinnings of desired cognitive improvements (Owen et al., 2010) in order to build a stronger science of human neuroplasticity and performance (Lindenberger, Wenger, & Lövdén, 2017; Lövdén, Bäckman, Lindenberger, Schaefer, & Schmiedek, 2010). In this framework, a brain training application would be developed not to train a particular skill per se but to activate brain regions found to be critical for the performance of a skill in a domain-general fashion. To do this, researchers aim to advance knowledge on three primary fronts: (a) how structure and content features of digital media influence cognitive processes; (b) the neural underpinnings of these cognitive processes (such as working memory, attentional control, or learning); and (c) salient individual differences that may influence training or transfer of cognitive improvements (such as age, prevalence of disorders, or socioeconomic environments).

Research has already shown that more naturalistic and interactive tasks (such as action video games) seem to hold promise for the improvement of cognitive functioning in certain groups (Green &

Bavelier, 2012). Furthermore, improvements in cognitive functioning observed following interactive video game play seem to transfer to a variety of different tasks (Cardoso-Leite & Bavelier, 2014; Green & Bavelier, 2006, 2008). In this sense, engaging video games seem to be remarkably useful tools for "removing brakes on human plasticity" (Bavelier, Levi, Li, Dan, & Hensch, 2010) in order to train and improve cognitive skills—although these effects may be constrained to certain groups (Ritterfeld, Weber, Fernando, & Vorderer, 2004).

The unique effectiveness of action video games for catalyzing neuroplastic changes is thought to be due to two primary factors. First, interactive video games often match the difficulty of the game to the ability of the player (Sherry, 2004). This balance of difficulty and ability has been shown to elicit *flow*, a state in which attentional and reward networks in the brain are highly active and synchronized with one another (Huskey, Wilcox, et al., 2018; Weber et al., 2018; Weber, Tamborini, Westcott-Baker, & Kantor, 2009).

Importantly, the activation of reward networks is crucial in the learning of new behavioral patterns (Bassett & Mattar, 2017; Bavelier, Green, Pouget, & Schrater, 2012). Thus, flow states frequently observed during action video game play may pose a unique opportunity for improving the effectiveness of cognitive interventions through activating and synchronizing brain networks that are important for learning domain-general cognitive skills.

Second, interactive and action-packed video games involve the rapid performance of numerous and interacting subskills (locating objects, enacting complex motor programs, making spatial/temporal judgments, etc.) in an environment that often resembles the "real world" (Green & Bavelier, 2008). In contrast, traditional brain training games tend to focus on one skill in isolation, limiting their utility in even closely related skills (Owen et al., 2010). For this reason, neuroscientifically informed brain training games should look to design tasks that are as naturalistic as possible while recruiting neural substrates of interest.

Neurofeedback

Thus far, we have discussed emerging research approaches at the intersection of neuroimaging and multimedia design that take into account the neural underpinnings of health-related outcomes of interest, individual neural differences, and relevant structure/content of media. A final research frontier in this area is in the development of fMRI and EEG interfaces that allow individuals to view indices of their brain activity in real time and train them to activate certain brain regions at certain times. These tools are collectively referred to as *neurofeedback* (Weiskopf et al., 2004). Neurofeedback tools, although not currently widely used within communication science, are an exciting frontier for communication questions of interest (Hopp & Weber, 2019).

In a neurofeedback paradigm, individuals are presented with a graphical readout of their brain activity throughout the task. This readout is typically shown via a digital display and can take numerous forms. For example, a participant could be presented with a simple dial or bar chart depicting their brain activity in a particular region and asked to modulate their brain activity to keep the dial within a certain range (Caria et al., 2007; Weiskopf, 2012; Weiskopf et al., 2004; Zotev et al., 2011). Other paradigms—especially those designed for children—present a more abstract index of neural activity, such as a rocket launching into space (Alegria et al., 2017) or a wizard broomstick in flight (Johnstone et al., 2017). Neurofeedback affords a unique tool to gamify neural activity. Because the graphical readout is directly manipulated by brain activity, these programs are often called "closed-loop systems." In contrast, open-loop systems respond to other inputs (such as researcher manipulation, etc.) rather than or in addition to neural activity (Sitaram et al., 2017). Both closed-loop and open-loop neurofeedback systems stand as an exciting new frontier in medical treatment and cognitive optimization (Mishra, Anguera, et al., 2016).

EEG and fMRI neurofeedback treatment has been shown to be effective in reducing symptoms of ADHD (Alegria et al., 2017; Baumeister et al., 2016; Johnstone et al., 2017), helping individuals downregulate inappropriate emotional responses (Brühl et al., 2013; Zotev et al., 2011), increasing cognitive control (Mathiak et al., 2015), attenuating nicotine cravings in recovering smokers (Hartwell et al., 2016), improving symptoms of depression (Linden, 2014) and PTSD (Zweerings et al., 2018), improving motor function after a stroke (Liew et al., 2015), and many others. Neurofeedback approaches have also been developed for neurocognitive optimization (Mishra, Anguera, et al., 2016) and for reducing the symptoms of cognitive decline in senior adults (Anguera et al., 2013; Mishra & Gazzaley, 2014).

Conclusion

In this chapter, we have reviewed a collection of exciting tools and methodologies at the intersection of neuroimaging and multimedia design that are especially useful for developing health-related interventions. The brain-as-predictor approach (Berkman & Falk, 2013) has provided communication scientists with more useful tools for more accurate predictions of when health messages will lead to positive behavioral change. New advancements in this area have extended the brain-as-predictor approach, allowing for more precise predictions regarding how activation and synchrony within and between brain regions predicts outcomes related to message effectiveness and message sharing. The development of multimedia tools informed by a neuroscientific understanding of message processing has also contributed to the diagnosis and treatment of various cognitive processing disorders like ADHD, aggression, PTSD, and depression. New efforts in real-time fMRI and neurofeedback have led to more effective interventions to treat disorders and optimize cognitive function.

In humans—as well as almost all complex organisms—the brain is the ringmaster of essentially all behaviors. By necessity, a greater understanding of the brain will lead to a greater understanding of how to design messages for desired health-related change. For this reason, the development of tools aimed at facilitating cognitive and behavioral change has been greatly assisted by rapid increases in the availability of and access to neuroscience methods. Neuroimaging allows communication researchers and message designers to isolate the core processes underlying communication phenomena of interest, constraining theories, and facilitating more optimal outcomes (Weber et al., 2017). Neuroimaging holds potential for developing individualized predictive, persuasive, therapeutic, and optimization tools for the advancement of both practical and humanitarian goals (Gabrieli et al., 2015). The research outlined in this chapter has just begun to scratch the surface of what is possible.

References

Alegria, A. A., Wulff, M., Brinson, H., Barker, G. J., Norman, L. J., Brandeis, D., … Rubia, K. (2017). Real-time fMRI neurofeedback in adolescents with attention deficit hyperactivity disorder. *Human Brain Mapping, 17*, 379–20.

Amodio, D. M., & Frith, C. D. (2006). Meeting of minds: The medial frontal cortex and social cognition. *Nature Reviews Neuroscience, 7*(4), 268.

Anguera, J. A., Boccanfuso, J., Rintoul, J. L., Al-Hashimi, O., Faraji, F., Janowich, J., … Gazzaley, A. (2013). Video game training enhances cognitive control in older adults. *Nature, 501*(7465), 97–101.

Baek, E. C., Scholz, C., & O'Donnell, M. B. (2017). The value of sharing information: A neural account of information transmission. *Psychological Science, 2*(3), 1–11.

Barrett, L. F., & Satpute, A. B. (2013). Large-scale brain networks in affective and social neuroscience: Towards an integrative functional architecture of the brain. *Current Opinion in Neurobiology, 23*(3), 361–372.

Bassett, D. S., & Mattar, M. G. (2017). A network neuroscience of human learning: Potential to inform quantitative theories of brain and behavior. *Trends in Cognitive Sciences, 21*(4), 250–264.

Bassett, D. S., & Sporns, O. (2017). Network neuroscience. *Nature Neuroscience, 20*(3), 353–364.

Baumeister, S., Wolf, I., Holz, N., Boecker, R., Adamo, N., Holtmann, M., … Brandeis, D. (2016). Neurofeedback training effects on inhibitory brain activation in ADHD: A matter of learning? *Neuroscience, 378*, 89–99.

Bavelier, D., Green, C. S., Pouget, A., & Schrater, P. (2012). Brain plasticity through the life span: Learning to learn and action video games. *Annual Review of Neuroscience, 35,* 391–416.

Bavelier, D., Levi, D. M., Li, R. W., Dan, Y., & Hensch, T. K. (2010). Removing brakes on adult brain plasticity: From molecular to behavioral interventions. *Journal of Neuroscience, 30*(45), 14964–14971.

Berkman, E. T., & Falk, E. B. (2013). Beyond brain mapping: Using neural measures to predict real-world outcomes. *Current Directions in Psychological Science, 22*(1), 45–50.

Berridge, K. C., & Robinson, T. E. (1998). What is the role of dopamine in reward: Hedonic impact, reward learning, or incentive salience? *Brain Research Reviews, 28,* 309–369.

Botvinick, M. M., Braver, T. S., Barch, D. M., Carter, C. S., & Cohen, J. D. (2001). Conflict monitoring and cognitive control. *Psychological Review, 108*(3), 624–652.

Braver, T. S. (2012). The variable nature of cognitive control: A dual mechanisms framework. *Trends in Cognitive Sciences, 16*(2), 106–113.

Braver, T. S., Cole, M. W., & Yarkoni, T. (2010). Vive les differences! Individual variation in neural mechanisms of executive control. *Current Opinion in Neurobiology, 20*(2), 242–250.

Brennan, J., Nir, Y., Hasson, U., Malach, R., Heeger, D. J., & Pylkkänen, L. (2012). Syntactic structure building in the anterior temporal lobe during natural story listening. *Brain and Language, 120*(2), 163–173.

Bressler, S. L., & Menon, V. (2010). Large-scale brain networks in cognition: Emerging methods and principles. *Trends in Cognitive Sciences, 14*(6), 277–290.

Brühl, A. B., Scherpiet, S., Sulzer, J., Stämpfli, P., Seifritz, E., & Herwig, U. (2013). Real-time neurofeedback using functional MRI could improve down-regulation of amygdala activity during emotional stimulation: A proof-of-concept study. *Brain Topography, 27*(1), 138–148.

Cardoso-Leite, P., & Bavelier, D. (2014). Video game play, attention, and learning: How to shape the development of attention and influence learning. *Current Opinion in Neurology, 27*(2), 185–191.

Caria, A., Veit, R., Sitaram, R., Lotze, M., Weiskopf, N., Grodd, W., & Birbaumer, N. (2007). Regulation of anterior insular cortex activity using real-time fMRI. *NeuroImage, 35*(3), 1238–1246.

Cascio, C. N., O'Donnell, M. B., Bayer, J., Tinney, F. J., Jr., & Falk, E. B. (2015). Neural correlates of susceptibility to group opinions in online word-of-mouth recommendations. *Journal of Marketing Research, 52*(4), 559–575.

Chen, J., Leong, Y. C., Honey, C. J., Yong, C. H., Norman, K. A., & Hasson, U. (2016). Shared memories reveal shared structure in neural activity across individuals. *Nature Neuroscience, 20*(1), 115–125.

Chua, H. F., Ho, S. S., Jasinska, A. J., Polk, T. A., Welsh, R. C., Liberzon, I., & Strecher, I. J. (2011). Self-related neural response to tailored smoking-cessation messages predicts quitting. *Nature Scientific Reports, 14*(4), 426–427.

Clayton, R. B., Lang, A., Leshner, G., & Quick, B. L. (2018). *Who fights, who flees? An integration of the LC4MP and psychological reactance theory.* Media Psychology (Published online ahead of print).

Coltheart, M. (2013). How can functional neuroimaging inform cognitive theories? *Perspectives on Psychological Science, 8*(1), 98–103.

Cooper, N., Bassett, D. S., & Falk, E. B. (2017). Coherent activity between brain regions that code for value is linked to the malleability of human behavior. *Nature Scientific Reports, 7*(43250), 43250.

Cooper, N., Garcia, J. O., Tompson, S., O'Donnell, M. B., Falk, E. B., & Vettel, J. M. (2018). Time-evolving dynamics in brain networks forecast responses to health messaging. *Network Neuroscience, 27,* 1–19.

Cooper, N., Tompson, S., O'Donnell, M. B., & Falk, E. B. (2015). Brain activity in self- and value-related regions in response to online antismoking messages predicts behavior change. *Journal of Media Psychology, 27*(3), 93–109.

Craddock, R. C., Holtzheimer, P. E., III, Hu, X. P., & Mayberg, H. S. (2009). Disease state prediction from resting state functional connectivity. *Magnetic Resonance in Medicine, 62*(6), 1619–1628.

Deshpande, G., Libero, L., Sreenivasan, K. R., Deshpande, H., & Kana, R. K. (2013). Identification of neural connectivity signatures of autism using machine learning. *Frontiers in Human Neuroscience, 7*, 670.

Dikker, S., Silbert, L. J., Hasson, U., & Zevin, J. D. (2014). On the same wavelength: Predictable language enhances speaker-listener brain-to-brain synchrony in posterior superior temporal gyrus. *Journal of Neuroscience, 34*(18), 6267–6272.

Doré, B. P., Scholz, C., Baek, E. C., Garcia, J. O., O'Donnell, M. B., Bassett, D. S., … Falk, E. B. (2018). Brain activity tracks population information sharing by capturing consensus judgments of value. *Cerebral Cortex, 8*, 1–9.

Dosenbach, N. U., Nardos, B., Cohen, A. L., Fair, D. A., Power, J. D., Church, J. A., … Schlaggar, B. L. (2010). Prediction of individual brain maturity using fMRI. *Science, 329*(5997), 1358–1361.

Dufour, N., Redcay, E., Young, L., Mavros, P. L., Moran, J. M., Triantafyllou, C., … Saxe, R. (2013). Similar brain activation during false belief tasks in a large sample of adults with and without autism. *PLoS One, 8*(9), e75468.

Eyler, L. T., Sherzai, A., Kaup, A. R., & Jeste, D. V. (2011). A review of functional brain imaging correlates of successful cognitive aging. *Biological Psychiatry, 70*(2), 115–122.

Falk, E. B., & Bassett, D. S. (2017). Brain and social networks: Fundamental building blocks of human experience. *Trends in Cognitive Sciences, 21*(9), 674–690.

Falk, E. B., Berkman, E. T., & Lieberman, M. D. (2012). From neural responses to population behavior: Neural focus group predicts population-level media effects. *Psychological Science, 23*(5), 439–445.

Falk, E. B., Berkman, E. T., Mann, T., Harrison, B., & Lieberman, M. D. (2010). Predicting persuasion-induced behavior change from the brain. *Journal of Neuroscience, 30*(25), 8421–8424.

Falk, E. B., Berkman, E. T., Whalen, D., & Lieberman, M. D. (2011). Neural activity during health messaging predicts reductions in smoking above and beyond self-report. *Helath Psychology, 30*(2), 177–185.

Falk, E. B., O'Donnell, M. B., Cascio, C. N., Tinney, F., Kang, Y., Lieberman, M. D., … Strecher, V. J. (2015). Self-affirmation alters the brain's response to health messages and subsequent behavior change. *Proceedings of the National Academy of Sciences, 112*(7), 1977–1982.

Falk, E. B., O'Donnell, M. B., & Lieberman, M. D. (2012). Getting the word out: Neural correlates of enthusiastic message propagation. *Frontiers in Human Neuroscience, 6*(313), 1–14.

Falk, E. B., O'Donnell, M. B., Tompson, S., Gonzalez, R., Dal Cin, S. D., Strecher, V., … An, L. (2015). Functional brain imaging predicts public health campaign success. *Social Cognitive and Affective Neuroscience, 11*, 204–214.

Finn, E. S., Scheinost, D., Finn, D. M., Shen, X., Papademetris, X., & Constable, R. T. (2017). Can brain state be manipulated to emphasize individual differences in functional connectivity? *NeuroImage, 160*, 1–12.

Fishbein, M., & Cappella, J. N. (2006). The role of theory in developing effective health communications. *Journal of Communication, 56*, S1–S17.

Gabrieli, J. D. E., Ghosh, S. S., & Whitfield-Gabrieli, S. (2015). Prediction as a humanitarian and pragmatic contribution from human cognitive neuroscience. *Neuron, 85*(1), 11–26.

Gazzaley, A., & D'esposito, M. (2007). Top-down modulation and normal aging. *Annals of the New York Academy of Sciences, 1097*(1), 67–83.

Goldstein, R. Z., Tomasi, D., Rajaram, S., Cottone, L. A., Zhang, L., Maloney, T.e. a., ... Volkow, N. D. (2007). Role of the anterior cingulate and medial orbitofrontal cortex in processing drug cues in cocaine addiction. *Neuroscience, 144*(4), 1153–1159.

Green, C. S., & Bavelier, D. (2006). Effect of action video games on the spatial distribution of visuospatial attention. *Journal of Experimental Psychology: Human Perception and Performance, 32*(6), 1465.

Green, C. S., & Bavelier, D. (2008). Exercising your brain: A review of human brain plasticity and training-induced learning. *Psychology and Aging, 23*(4), 692.

Green, C. S., & Bavelier, D. (2012). Learning, attentional control, and action video games. *Current Biology, 22*(6), R197–R206.

Guo, H., Cao, X., Liu, Z., Li, H., Chen, J., & Zhang, K. (2012). Machine learning classifier using abnormal brain network topological metrics in major depressive disorder. *NeuroReport, 23*(17), 1006–1011.

Hartwell, K. J., Hanlon, C. A., Li, X., Borckardt, J. J., Canterberry, M., Prisciandaro, J. J., ... Brady, K. T. (2016). Individualized real-time fMRI neurofeedback to attenuate craving in nicotine-dependent smokers. *Journal of Psychiatry and Neuroscience, 41*(1), 48–55.

Hasher, L., & Zacks, R. T. (1988). Working memory, comprehension, and aging: A review and a new view. In *Psychology of learning and motivation* (Vol. 22, pp. 193–225). Elsevier.

Hasson, U., & Frith, C. D. (2016). Mirroring and beyond: Coupled dynamics as a generalized framework for modelling social interactions. *Philosophical Transactions of the Royal Society B, 371*, 20150366.

Hasson, U., Furman, O., Clark, D., Dudai, Y., & Davachi, L. (2008). Enhanced intersubject correlations during movie viewing correlate with successful episodic encoding. *Neuron, 57*(3), 452–462.

Ho, M.-C., Chou, C.-Y., Huang, C.-F., Lin, Y.-T., Shih, C.-S., Han, S.-Y., ... Liu, C.-J. (2012). Age-related changes of task-specific brain activity in normal aging. *Neuroscience Letters, 507*(1), 78–83.

Hopp, F. R., & Weber, R. (2019). The state-of-the-art and the future of brain imaging methodology in communication research. In K. Floyd, & R. Weber (Eds.), *Handbook of communication science and biology*. Routledge.

Huskey, R., Craighead, B., Miller, M. B., & Weber, R. (2018). Does intrinsic reward motivate cognitive control? A naturalistic-fMRI study based on the synchronization theory of flow. *Cognitive, Affective, and Behavioral Neuroscience, 18*, 902–924.

Huskey, R., Mangus, J. M., Turner, B. O., & Weber, R. (2017). The persuasion network is modulated by drug-use risk and predicts anti-drug message effectiveness. *Social Cognitive and Affective Neuroscience, 12*(12), 1902–1915.

Huskey, R., Wilcox, S., & Weber, R. (2018). Network neuroscience reveals distinct neuromarkers of flow during media use. *Journal of Communication, 68*(5), 872–895.

Imhof, M. A., Schmälzle, R., Renner, B., & Schupp, H. T. (2017). How real-life health messages engage our brains: Shared processing of effective anti-alcohol videos. *Social Cognitive and Affective Neuroscience, 12*(7), 1188–1196.

Jaeggi, S. M., Buschkuehl, M., Shah, P., & Jonides, J. (2014). The role of individual differences in cognitive training and transfer. *Memory and Cognition, 42*(3), 464–480.

Johnstone, S. J., Roodenrys, S. J., Johnson, K., Bonfield, R., & Bennett, S. J. (2017). Game-based combined cognitive and neurofeedback training using Focus Pocus reduces symptom severity in children with diagnosed AD/HD and subclinical AD/HD. *International Journal of Psychophysiology, 116*, 32–44.

Kang, Y., Cooper, N., Pandey, P., Scholz, C., O'Donnell, M. B., Lieberman, M. D., ... Falk, E. B. (2018). Effects of self-transcendence on neural responses to persuasive messages and health behavior change. *Proceedings of the National Academy of Sciences United States of America, 115*(40), 9974−9979.

Kaye, S.-A., White, M. J., & Lewis, I. (2016). The use of neurocognitive methods in assessing health communication messages: A systematic review. *Journal of Health Psychology, 22*(12), 1534−1551.

Keene, J. R., & Lang, A. (2016). Dynamic motivated processing of emotional trajectories in public service announcements. *Communication Monographs, 83*(4), 468−485.

Klasen, M., Zvyagintsev, M., Schwenzer, M., Mathiak, K. A., Sarkheil, P., Weber, R., & Mathiak, K. (2013). Quetiapine modulates functional connectivity in brain aggression networks. *NeuroImage, 75*, 20−26.

Kouijzer, M. E., de Moor, J. M., Gerrits, B. J., Congedo, M., & van Schie, H. T. (2009). Neurofeedback improves executive functioning in children with autism spectrum disorders. *Research in Autism Spectrum Disorders, 3*(1), 145−162.

Kühn, S., Gleich, T., Lorenz, R. C., Lindenberger, U., & Gallinat, J. (2014). Playing super mario induces structural brain plasticity: Gray matter changes resulting from training with a commercial video game. *Molecular Psychiatry, 19*(2), 265.

Lang, A., Bradley, S. D., Chung, Y., & Lee, S. (2003). Where the mind meets the message: Reflections on ten years of measuring psychological responses to media. *Journal of Broadcasting and Electronic Media, 47*(4), 650−655.

Lee, A. M. (2017). Media use: United States. In *The international encyclopedia of media effects*. Hoboken, NJ, USA: John Wiley & Sons, Inc.

Liew, S.-L., Rana, M., Cornelsen, S., Fortunato de Barros Filho, M., Birbaumer, N., Sitaram, R., ... Soekadar, S. R. (2015). Improving motor corticothalamic communication after stroke using real-time fMRI connectivity-based neurofeedback. *Neurorehabilitation and Neural Repair, 30*(7), 671−675.

Linden, D. E. (2014). Neurofeedback and networks of depression. *Dialogues in Clinical Neuroscience, 16*(1), 103.

Lindenberger, U., Wenger, E., & Lövdén, M. (2017). Towards a stronger science of human plasticity. *Nature Reviews Neuroscience, 18*(5), 261.

Liu, J., & Bailey, R. L. (2018). *Effects of substance cues in negative public service announcements on cognitive processing*. Health Communication (Published online ahead of print).

Lövdén, M., Bäckman, L., Lindenberger, U., Schaefer, S., & Schmiedek, F. (2010). A theoretical framework for the study of adult cognitive plasticity. *Psychological Bulletin, 136*(4), 659.

Mather, M., Cacioppo, J. T., & Kanwisher, N. (2013). How fMRI can inform cognitive theories. *Perspectives on Psychological Science, 8*(1), 108−113.

Mathiak, K. A., Alawi, E. M., Koush, Y., Dyck, M., Cordes, J. S., Gaber, T. J., ... Mathiak, K. (2015). Social reward improves the voluntary control over localized brain activity in fMRI-based neurofeedback training. *Frontiers in Behavioral Neuroscience, 9*, 136.

Mathiak, K., & Weber, R. (2006). Toward brain correlates of natural behavior: fMRI during violent video games. *Human Brain Mapping, 27*(12), 948−956.

McBride, D., Barrett, S. P., Kelly, J. T., Aw, A., & Dagher, A. (2006). Effects of expectancy and abstinence on the neural response to smoking cues in cigarette smokers: An fMRI study. *Neuropsychopharmacology, 31*(12), 2728.

Meier, T. B., Desphande, A. S., Vergun, S., Nair, V. A., Song, J., Biswal, B. B., ... Prabhakaran, V. (2012). Support vector machine classification and characterization of age-related reorganization of functional brain networks. *NeuroImage, 60*(1), 601−613.

Miller, E. K., & Cohen, J. D. (2001). An integrative theory of prefrontal cortex function. *Annual Review of Neuroscience, 24*(1), 167−202.

Mishra, J., Anguera, J. A., & Gazzaley, A. (2016). Video games for neuro-cognitive optimization. *Neuron, 90*(2), 214−218.

Mishra, J., & Gazzaley, A. (2014). Harnessing the neuroplastic potential of the human brain & the future of cognitive rehabilitation. *Frontiers in Human Neuroscience, 8*(218), 1−4.

Mishra, J., Sagar, R., Joseph, A. A., Gazzaley, A., & Merzenich, M. M. (2016). Training sensory signal-to-noise resolution in children with ADHD in a global mental health setting. *Translational Psychiatry, 6*(e781).

Mourao-Miranda, J., Bokde, A. L., Born, C., Hampel, H., & Stetter, M. (2005). Classifying brain states and determining the discriminating activation patterns: Support vector machine on functional MRI data. *NeuroImage, 28*(4), 980–995.

Owen, A. M., Hampshire, A., Grahn, J. A., Stenton, R., Dajani, S., Burns, A. S., ... Ballard, C. G. (2010). Putting brain training to the test. *Nature, 465*(7299), 775.

O'Donnell, M. B., Bayer, J. B., Cascio, C. N., & Falk, E. B. (2017). Neural bases of recommendations differ according to social network structure. *Social Cognitive and Affective Neuroscience, 12*, 61–69.

O'Donnell, M. B., & Falk, E. B. (2015). Big data under the microscope and brains in social context: Integrating methods from computational social science and neuroscience. *The Annals of the American Academy of Political and Social Science, 659*(1), 274–289.

Parkinson, C., Kleinbaum, A. M., & Wheatley, T. (2018). Similar neural responses predict friendship. *Nature Communications, 9*(332), 1–14.

Potter, R. F., & Bolls, P. (2012). *Psychophysiological measurement and meaning: Cognitive and emotional processing of media.* New York, NY: Routledge.

Ritterfeld, U., Weber, R., Fernando, S., & Vorderer, P. (2004). Think science! entertainment education in interactive theaters. *Computer Entertainment, 2*, 1–58.

Rosenberg, M. D., Finn, E. S., Scheinost, D., Constable, R. T., & Chun, M. M. (2017). Characterizing attention with predictive network models. *Trends in Cognitive Sciences, 21*(4), 1–13.

Schmälzle, R., Häcker, F. E. K., Honey, C. J., & Hasson, U. (2015). Engaged listeners: Shared neural processing of powerful political speeches. *Social Cognitive and Affective Neuroscience, 10*(8), 1137–1143.

Schmalzle, R., Hacker, F., Renner, B., Honey, C. J., & Schupp, H. T. (2013). Neural correlates of risk perception during real-life risk communication. *Journal of Neuroscience, 33*(25), 10340–10347.

Scholz, C., Baek, E. C., O'Donnell, M. B., Kim, H. S., Cappella, J. N., & Falk, E. B. (2017). A neural model of valuation and information virality. *Proceedings of the National Academy of Sciences of the United States of America, 114*(11), 2881–2886.

Seeley, W. W., Menon, V., Schatzberg, A. F., Keller, J., Glover, G. H., Kenna, H., ... Greicius, M. D. (2007). Dissociable intrinsic connectivity networks for salience processing and executive control. *Journal of Neuroscience, 27*(9), 2349–2356.

Sherman, L. E., Payton, A. A., Hernandez, L. M., Greenfield, P. M., & Dapretto, M. (2016). The power of the like in adolescence: Effects of peer influence on neural and behavioral responses to social media. *Psychological Science, 27*(7), 1027–1035.

Sherry, J. L. (2004). Flow and media enjoyment. *Communication Theory, 14*(4), 328–347.

Shirer, W., Ryali, S., Rykhlevskaia, E., Menon, V., & Greicius, M. D. (2012). Decoding subject-driven cognitive states with whole-brain connectivity patterns. *Cerebral Cortex, 22*(1), 158–165.

Simons, D. J., Boot, W. R., Charness, N., Gathercole, S. E., Chabris, C. F., Hambrick, D. Z., & Stine-Morrow, E. A. (2016). Do "brain-training" programs work? *Psychological Science in the Public Interest, 17*(3), 103–186.

Sitaram, R., Ros, T., Stoeckel, L., Haller, S., Scharnowski, F., Lewis-Peacock, J., ... Sulzer, J. (2017). Closed-loop brain training: The science of neurofeedback. *Nature Reviews Neuroscience, 18*(2), 86.

Smith, K. (2012). fMRI 2.0: Functional magnetic resonance imaging is growing from showy adolescence into a workhorse of brain imaging. *Nature Communications, 484*, 24–26.

Turner, B. O., Huskey, R., & Weber, R. (2018). Charting a future for fMRI in communication science. *Communication Methods and Measures, 13*(1), 1–18.

U.S. Census Bureau. (2010). *Decennial Census Data and Population Projections*. Retrieved from https://www.census.gov/programs-surveys/popproj.html.

Weber, R. (2008). *Connectivity of brain regions during social interactions. theory-based, event-related content analysis of continuous, semi-natural stimuli as paradigm in functional magnetic resonance imaging*. Aachen, Germany: RWTH Library.

Weber, R., Alicea, B., Huskey, R., & Mathiak, K. (2018). Network dynamics of attention during a naturalistic behavioral paradigm. *Frontiers in Human Neuroscience, 12*.

Weber, R., Eden, A., Huskey, R., Mangus, J. M., & Falk, E. (2015). Bridging media psychology and cognitive neuroscience. *Journal of Media Psychology, 27*, 146–156.

Weber, R., Fisher, J. T., Hopp, F. R., & Lonergan, C. (2017). Taking messages into the magnet: Method–theory synergy in communication neuroscience. *Communication Monographs, 85*(1), 81–102.

Weber, R., Huskey, R., Mangus, J. M., Westcott-Baker, A., & Turner, B. O. (2015). Neural predictors of message effectiveness during counterarguing in antidrug campaigns. *Communication Monographs, 82*(1), 4–30.

Weber, R., Mangus, J. M., & Huskey, R. (2015). Brain imaging in communication research: A practical guide to understanding and evaluating fMRI studies. *Communication Methods and Measures, 9*(1–2), 5–29.

Weber, R., Ritterfeld, U., & Mathiak, K. (2006). Does playing violent video games induce aggression? Empirical evidence of a functional magnetic resonance imaging study. *Media Psychology, 8*(1), 39–60.

Weber, R., Tamborini, R., Westcott-Baker, A., & Kantor, B. (2009). Theorizing flow and media enjoyment as cognitive synchronization of attentional and reward networks. *Communication Theory, 19*(4), 397–422.

Weiskopf, N. (2012). Real-time fMRI and its application to neurofeedback. *NeuroImage, 62*(2), 682–692.

Weiskopf, N., Mathiak, K., Bock, S. W., Scharnowski, F., Veit, R., Grodd, W., … Birbaumer, N. (2004). Principles of a brain-computer interface (BCI) based on real-time functional magnetic resonance imaging (fMRI). *IEEE Transactions on Biomedical Engineering, 51*(6), 966–970.

Welborn, B. L., Lieberman, M. D., Goldenberg, D., Fuligni, A. J., Galván, A., & Telzer, E. H. (2015). Neural mechanisms of social influence in adolescence. *Social Cognitive and Affective Neuroscience, 11*(1), 100–109.

Wolf, D., Klasen, M., Eisner, P., Zepf, F. D., Zvyagintsev, M., Palomero-Gallagher, N., … Mathiak, K. (2018). Central serotonin modulates neural responses to virtual violent actions in emotion regulation networks. *Brain Structure and Function, 223*(7), 3327–3345.

Woo, C.-W., Chang, L. J., Lindquist, M. A., & Wager, T. D. (2017). Building better biomarkers: Brain models in translational neuroimaging. *Nature Neuroscience, 20*(3), 365.

Yeshurun, Y., Swanson, S., Simony, E., Chen, J., Lazaridi, C., Honey, C. J., & Hasson, U. (2017). Same story, different story: The neural representation of interpretive frameworks. *Psychological Science, 57*, 1–13.

Zanto, T. P., Toy, B., & Gazzaley, A. (2010). Delays in neural processing during working memory encoding in normal aging. *Neuropsychologia, 48*(1), 13–25.

Zotev, V., Krueger, F., Phillips, R., Alvarez, R. P., Simmons, W. K., Bellgowan, P., … Bodurka, J. (2011). Self-Regulation of amygdala activation using real-time fMRI neurofeedback. *PLoS One, 6*(9). e24522–17.

Zweerings, J., Pflieger, E., Mathiak, K. A., Zvyagintsev, M., Kacela, A., Flatten, G., & Mathiak, K. (2018). Impaired voluntary control in PTSD: Probing self-regulation of the acc with real-time fMRI. *Frontiers in Psychiatry, 9*, 219.

Using persuasive messages to increase engagement with mental health video game apps

Subuhi Khan[1], Jorge Peña[2]

[1] Global Marketing, VSP Global, Rancho Cordova, CA, United States;
[2] Department of Communication, University of California, Davis, CA, United States

Video games are becoming increasingly common to treat physical or psychological conditions (Wilkinson, Ang, & Goh, 2008). Psychological conditions, commonly known as mental health disorders, comprise of a group of symptoms that interfere with an individual's ability to function normally as a productive member of society (World Health Organization, 2019). An emerging field of study suggests that playing video games can induce positive structural changes in brain regions associated with mental health disorders (Kühn, Gleich, Lorenz, Lindenberger, & Gallinat, 2014). For instance, playing Super Mario can induce changes in brain regions associated with posttraumatic stress disorder, neurodegenerative disease, and schizophrenia (Kuhn et al., 2014). Additionally, functional brain changes produced through commercial video games are being harnessed to treat mental health conditions such as schizophrenia (Suenderhauf, Walter, Lenz, Lang, & Borgwardt, 2016). Owing to the specific symptomology of mood disorders (e.g., loss of interest in daily activities, lack of motivation), interventions that provide motivational incentives to change attitude or behavior are considered effective for treating them (Westra, Arkowitz, & Dozois, 2009). Video games are characterized by fun, optimal challenge, and immersion and thus have the potential of increasing patient motivation to initiate and continue behavior change (Mohr, Burns, Schueller, Clarke, & Klinkman, 2013). Given the potential of video games to engage patients, games designed for changing health outcomes, also

Technology and Health
https://doi.org/10.1016/B978-0-12-816958-2.00016-2

known as game interventions, are available both online and offline (Wilkinson et al., 2008). Hundreds of mobile apps for mental health, featuring video games for cognitive control, have become available for smart devices (Donker et al., 2013). Empirical evidence exists supporting effectiveness of mental health mobile phone apps (Arean et al., 2016). In a fully remote randomized clinical field trial of a cognitive control mobile phone app for depression, positive mood changes were observed for participants with moderate depression compared with a control group in the first 2 weeks of use (Arean et al., 2016). Most participants stopped using the app or used it infrequently over the course of the field trial (Arean et al., 2016). In another randomized controlled trial of a smartphone-based self-help mobile app, SuperBetter, participants' self-reported depression symptoms reduced on using the app. However, high attrition rates render the study's results partially valid (Roepke et al., 2015). Field trials and experiments with mental health video game apps repeatedly show a pattern of high attrition (Arean et al., 2016; Kühn et al., 2014; Roepke et al., 2015).

It is now well established that mental health video game apps have a high attrition rate, where attrition is described as premature discontinuation, nonusage, and nonadherence to the app (Doherty, Coyle, & Sharry, 2012; Swift & Greenberg, 2012). In other words, attrition indicates dropout and discontinuation of technology-enabled interventions. Practitioners and researchers have recommended several approaches to manage attrition when implementing behavioral technology interventions (Mohr et al., 2013). These recommendations include improving usability, increasing incentives, and augmenting adherence via the use of reminders (Mohr et al., 2013).

In order to reduce attrition, reduce noncompliance, and increase adoption of health recommendations, persuasive messages aimed at prompting individuals to regularly perform some health-related behavior are presented to users through telephone calls, text messages, multimedia messages, emails, and automated calls (Alkhaldi et al., 2016). Message prompts are effective in promoting health behavior. For instance, message prompts delivered through mobile phones and SMS for self-management interventions (e.g., information, reminders, monitoring) can lead to short-term smoking cessation rates and increased adherence to appointments (Jones, Lekhak, & Kaewluang, 2014). In particular, studies have looked at the frequency of message prompts on health outcomes, type of content in the prompts (e.g., generic or personalized), and different types of health outcomes that can be affected through message prompts (Alkhaldi et al., 2016; Kannisto, Koivunen, & Välimäki, 2014).

The studies discussed above provide knowledge on the effects of messages seeking to increase treatment adherence; however, there are fewer studies examining the persuasive effects of message prompts in the context of video game health applications. For instance, a review of message prompts for increasing adherence to digital programs providing information and support for physical and mental problems found that none of the 14 studies used any theory to design the message prompts (Alkhaldi et al., 2016). Considering this, the present chapter examines the effect of theoretically designed persuasive message prompts embedded in a mental health app on participants' subsequent game behaviors and attitudes. Based on the successful application of linguistic agency and causality attribution in persuasive health messages (Khan & Peña, 2017), linguistic agency and locus of causality are discussed in this chapter in the context of messages embedded within mental health apps.

In addition to message prompts, features such as the game interface affect engagement with health video games (Tolentino, Battaglini, Pereira, De Oliveria, & De Paula, 2011). The interface itself is composed of software as well as the device or media that allows a user to communicate with the computer (Breitfelder & Messina, 2000). In particular, there is extensive research on screen size as a formal media feature affecting engagement with media content. Empirical studies have shown that screen size influences audience's viewing experience through arousal and enjoyment of the media (Grabe, Lombard, Reich, Bracken, & Ditton, 1999; Lombard & Ditton, 1997). Large screen size is expected to improve evaluation of content on television screens (Lombard & Ditton, 1997) or enhance players' subjective experience of immersion in a video game on mobile devices (Thompson, Nordin, & Cairns, 2012). Despite its influence on engagement with mediated content (Reeves, Lang, Kim, & Tatar, 1999), there is scant research on the influence of screen size as a media feature in the context of health video games. To address this gap, the present chapter examines how screen size interacts with persuasive messages in influencing engagement with a mental health video game application. Two studies, Khan and Peña (2017) and a follow-up to it, will be discussed throughout this chapter to highlight the use of theoretically driven persuasive message features for increasing engagement with mental health games apps and the interaction of these features with screen size.

Linguistic agency effects

Assigning linguistic agency refers to the act of ascribing action, change, or potential for change of an event to an event-related entity (McGlone & Pfiester, 2009). According to Dowty (1989), the syntactic structure of a sentence can be conceptualized in terms of only two role types for verbal predicates: protoagent and protopatient. Simply put, protoagent is the subject in a sentence, such that the meaning of the verb in the sentence specifies the subject as causing or doing something, e.g., *Jack hits the ball*, here Jack is the protoagent, and protopatient is the object in a sentence such that the verb characterizes the object as having something happen to, for example, in *Jack hits the ball*, the ball is the protopatient. Volition (e.g., *John meets Jane*), sentience (e.g., *Jack likes Jane*), causes of events (e.g., *John kicked the ball*), and movement (e.g., *the boat sailed down the river*) characterize protoagent roles. Change of state, incremental theme, and causal effects of events characterize protopatient roles (Dowty, 1989). The definition of protoagent implies ascription of agency to someone or something, automatically suggesting that other entities in the sentence are passive (Dowty, 1989). For example, in the sentence *he caught a virus* agency is being ascribed to the person who is sick, while in the sentence *the virus got him*, agency is being ascribed to the virus causing the sickness. Given these linguistic characteristics, the agent in a sentence is perceived as having most control in an event or situation. If a message conveying threat ascribes agency to a health threat (e.g., a virus, chemical, or substance), then the threat should be perceived as more active and uncontrollable. Also, threats conveying human passivity are perceived as more severe than those conveying human agency (McGlone, Bell, Zaitchik, & McGlynn, 2013). Overall, linguistic agency is an intrinsic syntactical element of language that is processed subconsciously and ascribes control to inanimate entities (e.g., *cancer is coming to get you*) and to events that are abstract (e.g., *sickness can occur in many forms*) (Bell, McGlone, & Dragojevic, 2014a).

When designing messages to induce health behavior change, assigning agency to threats may imply greater conscious intent and potency to the threat over people, thus enhancing perceptions of perceived severity and personal susceptibility toward the threat (Bell et al., 2014a; McGlone et al., 2013). High perceived threat should also motivate individuals to pay attention to the message and result in increased message processing (Witte, 1994). Studies have demonstrated the effectiveness of linguistic agency in increasing perceived threat in health messages related to virus, bacteria, and radon gas (Bell et al., 2014a; Bell, McGlone, & Dragojevic, 2014b; McGlone et al., 2013). Intentions to adopt protective measures against the health threat increase when agency is assigned to the health threat such as bacteria or radon gas (Bell et al., 2014a; Dragojevic Bell & McGlone, 2014). It is also possible to increase adoption of protective measures when agency is assigned to the protective measure (e.g., *vaccines can effectively protect people from HPV*) than to humans (e.g., *people can effectively protect themselves against HPV with vaccines*, see Bell et al., 2014b). Agency assignment to the recommended behavior increases its adoption through an increase in perceived response efficacy suggesting that the agency assignment to medical interventions may enhance the perceived potency of the intervention.

Linguistic causality effects

Locus of causality or attributions of internal or external causes of health issues is another variable that can be manipulated linguistically to change perception of control said health condition (Kirkwood & Brown, 1995). In a study on linguistic agency assignment to colon cancer, participants perceived themselves to be more susceptible to colon cancer when agency was assigned to individuals instead of cancer. The authors propose that these unexpected findings can be attributed to the locus of causality of colon cancer (Chen, McGlone, & Bell, 2015). Since colon cancer is located internally, the disease may be perceived as being under an individual's control owing to its internal location (Chen et al., 2015). Locus of causality derives from Weiner's attribution theory and is in relation to threat attributions within specific situations (Roesch & Weiner, 2001). According to attribution theory, locus, stability, and controllability are the three main dimensions of causality attributions. In a given a situation, individuals can assess their expected success or failure in the situation based on how controllable the situation is, in terms of whether the situation is changeable or not through individual effort (Weiner, 1985). In health communication, locus of causality is associated with individual's mental schema for a health threat (Lau & Hartman, 1983). A threat or illness can be located within an individual or considered externally located. The causal location of a health threat imparts responsibility of the threat to either the individual who faces the threat or to the environment (Lau & Hartman, 1983). Causality can be attributed to one's self or something within the person, other people, environment, or chance. Causes such as those located within oneself are endogenous, while those coming from other people, environment, or chance are exogenous.

Exogenous causes, such as the belief that a polluted environment produces cancer, bestow responsibility to the environment and may reduce expectancy that personal behavior can avoid the illness. Attributing an illness or condition to exogenous causes would result in low probability of engaging in corrective or preventive behavior because of their uncontrollability, while endogenous causes would lead to higher probability of engaging in corrective or preventive behavior (Ducette & Keane, 1984; Lau & Hartman, 1983).

For mental health conditions such as depression, people understand causality in terms of external and internal loci (Abrahamson, Seligman, &

Teasdale, 1978). Examples of external or exogenous causes of depression are life events such as a stress at work, ending a relationship, death in family, physical trauma, etc. In comparison to this, internal or endogenous causes of depression locate the cause within the individual (e.g., *"chemical imbalance in your brain can trigger depression"*). Since endogenous causes are perceived as more controllable than exogenous causes (Roesch & Weiner, 2001), exposure to messages attributing depression causality to endogenous causes may make people feel more in control of taking action to control depression, which should increase perceived usability of interventions such as mental health apps.

At the same time, exogenous causes, by nature of existing outside the individual, are usually perceived less controllable. Uncontrollable situations, when the outcome of the situation is perceived as not related to the individual's response or actions, trigger learned helplessness (Abrahamson et al., 1978). Learned helplessness is the difficulty experienced in acquiring adaptive behavior when a stressor is perceived as uncontrollable (Maier & Watkins, 2005; Seligman, 1972). When learned helplessness kicks in people, stop trying to engage in actions that mitigate the negative outcome (Abrahamson et al., 1978). However, learned helplessness may also temporarily facilitate performance in an attempt to gain control over the stressor (Roth & Bootzin, 1974). Considering this, it is possible that reading a message conveying exogenous causality to a health threat may increase adherence to a recommended treatment as a short-lived knee-jerk reaction to control the threat.

Comparing linguistic agency and linguistic causality effects

In a study using theoretically designed messages embedded within a video game application for depression, the authors manipulated linguistic agency and causality to increase engagement with the app (Khan & Peña, 2017). The author designed an experimental health app, ReFocus, that featured six games and persuasive messages, designed using linguistic agency and causality language, and embedded within the app. The messages appeared right after the app loaded on the screen and before the games menu appeared. The messages stayed on the screen for 40 seconds after which the games menu appeared. Each game was 3 minutes long. The games comprised neurophysiological training tasks associated with improved cognitive control among people experiencing depression, namely the Simon task, emotional go/no go, emotional face Stroop task, and flanker task (Millner, Jaroszewski, Chamarthi, & Pizzagalli, 2012) (Figs. 16.1–16.5).

In each game, participants scored a point every time they pressed the button according to the instructions (Khan & Peña, 2017). The total

FIGURE 16.1   Screenshot of Menu Screen.

number of responses and the incorrect responses were recorded. Score feedback was not provided to avoid confounding the results (Fogg & Nass, 1997).

Before playing with the games in ReFocus app, participants read the persuasive messages assigning agency to depression (e.g., *depression is taking over your life*), agency to humans (e.g., *you are letting yourself become depressed*), or assigned no agency (e.g., *depression is known to occur in people*) (Khan & Peña, 2017) (Fig. 16.6).

160 participants were randomly assigned to read 1 of the 6 messages assigning agency to depression or human and depicting causality as exogenous or endogenous—and then engaged with ReFocus app (Khan & Peña, 2017). Participants were asked to self-report their intention to use the app and usability of the app using Likert scales. Behavioral engagement of participants was captured by the app in the form of time spent with the app and game performance. Participants in this study had mild depression as indicated in their scores on the depression scale, PHQ-9 (Kroenke & Spitzer, 2002).

After controlling for preexisting depression scores, the results showed that participants exposed to messages portraying depression

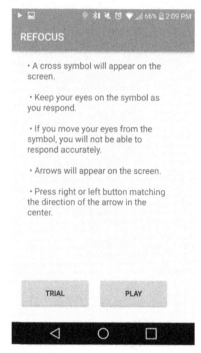

FIGURE 16.2   Instructions for Flanker Task.

as an endogenous causal factor perceived the game app to be more useable and reported higher intentions of using the app compared with participants exposed to messages depicting depression as an exogenous factor (Khan & Peña, 2017). Taken together, these findings support the notion that participants felt that they could do something about mitigating their chances of being depressed when depression was portrayed as located internally due to brain chemical imbalance, and consequently, they reported the app to be more useable and also intended to use the app more frequently (Khan & Peña, 2017). This finding can be explained with the help of message causality in attribution theory (Roesch & Weiner, 2001). According to the attribution theory, assigning health threat causality to an internal cause imparts responsibility of the threat to the individual who faces it (Lau & Hartman, 1983). Being responsible for a health threat imparts control over the threat to the individual; hence, endogenous causes are expected to lead to higher probability of engaging in corrective behavior (Roesch & Weiner, 2001). Previous studies applying endogenous causality attribution to health threats have found that preference for corrective behavior is related to the treatment type (Deacon & Baird, 2009; Goldstein & Rosselli, 2003). For example, Deacon and Baird (2009) found

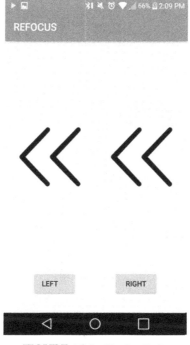

FIGURE 16.3   Flanker Task.

attributing endogenous causality to mental health conditions produced low preference for psychosocial interventions compared with preference for medication. In another study of causality attribution to mental health conditions, participants assigned to endogenous causality condition felt more empowered to seek help and preferred psychotherapy (Goldstein & Rosselli, 2003). Findings from this study show that exposure to endogenous causality language, particularly to brain chemical imbalance, at the outset of self-help cognitive training games increases intention to use and usability of such games. There was also an interaction effect in Khan and Peña (2017), showing that participants who read the human agency messages simultaneously depicting exogenous causality of depression spent more time with the app compared with participants exposed to messages stressing endogenous causality of depression. While exogenous causality might have increased the helplessness because of the uncontrollability of depression (Abrahamson et al., 1978), human agency likely gave participants a sense of control (Dowty, 1991), and consequently, they perceived more efficacy in using the app to control the threat of depression, and, thus, they spent more time with the app.

FIGURE 16.4　Simon Task (sample screenshot 1).

However, for self-reported intentions to use the app and its usability in protecting them from depression, participants considered the app more useable in protecting them against depression when they read an endogenous causality message relative to participants who read an exogenous causality message. One possibility is that while immediate behavior was more automatic, participants gave more careful thought to self-reports regarding the game app experience. Since self-reports have been identified as introspective tools which facilitate meaning making (Baumeister, Vohs, & Funder, 2007), it makes sense that participants exposed to messages implying endogenous causes for depression felt that they could make more use of the experimental app because it involved brain training, which would relate directly to endogenous causes. While this finding and evidence from previous studies support endogenous causality attribution to influence self-reported depression treatment preferences, the most important finding from Khan and Peña (2017) relates to showing that immediate behavioral outcomes are affected by manipulating causality in depression messages. In terms of actual behavior, participants exposed to exogenous causality messages spent more time with ReFocus app

FIGURE 16.5   Simon Task (sample screenshot 2).

and performed better in the games compared with participants exposed to endogenous causality message.

One departure for Khan and Peña (2017) from the literature is not finding any linguistic agency effects for boosting app usage. Previous research on linguistic agency manipulation has shown that assignment of agency to threat is an effective tool to increase interest in recommended responses for an illness through increased threat (Bell et al., 2014b, 2014a; Dragojevic, Bell, & McGlone, 2014). However, in Khan and Peña (2017), linguistic agency assignment did not affect perceptions of intervention usability or engagement with the health intervention. This study was the first in the series of linguistic agency manipulation research to assign agency to a mental health threat, in this case depression. It is also possible that causality assignment was more dominant compared to agency assignment in attribution perceptions for mental health conditions, which are largely understood in terms of endogenous–exogenous etiology (Deacon & Baird, 2009; Goldstein & Rosselli, 2003). Overall, the results encouraged further exploration of linguistic causality in health messages in the context of apps aiming to alleviate depression. In the next section, we increase the theoretical depth of this concept by outlining how internal

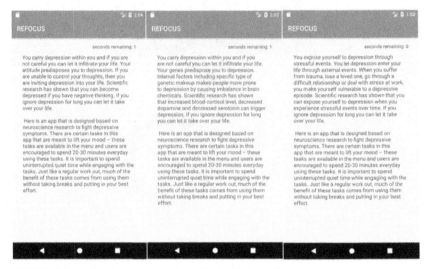

FIGURE 16.6   Screenshot of Messages (left to right: Endogenous unstable cause; endogenous stable cause; exogenous cause).

and internal causality can also be stable or unstable and how the formal features of the medium in which the app is played, such as screen size, can influence health app engagement.

Causality stability effects

In addition to attributions of locus of control, causality can be attributed to stable or unstable causes, where stability refers to changeability of the cause over time (Roesch & Weiner, 2001). Unstable causes are expected to be changeable over time, which evokes approach-centered coping, whereas stable causes evoke a sense of irreversibility, which triggers avoidance (Roesch & Weiner, 2001). Mental health conditions are susceptible to causal attributions that vary along the stable—unstable dimension because of the biogenetic and attitudinal causal explanations associated with mood disorders (Calhoun, Johnson, & Boardman, 1975; Deacon & Baird, 2009; Goldstein & Rosselli, 2003). Both biogenetic and mood-related causes are endogenous causes but differ on the dimension of stability, where attitudinal cause (e.g., negative thinking) is unstable as it is malleable, while biological cause (e.g., brain chemical imbalance) is perceived as stable (Calhoun et al., 1975; Lebowitz, Ahn, & Nolen-Hoeksema, 2013). The perception of controllability that endogenous causes evoke could be further enhanced when coupled with an unstable cause due to the malleability assigned to unstable causes. Consequently, endogenous-unstable cause of a mood disorder such as depression should trigger behavioral- and cognitive approach—oriented coping compared with endogenous-stable cause or exogenous cause.

Findings discussed so far examine how message features affect persuasive outcomes in engagement with the mental health games app, ReFocus. Given that such apps are delivered and used through devices that vary in their own features, it is important to explore how some of these channel features would affect the persuasive outcome (Oinas-Kukkonen & Harjumaa, 2018). The next section in this chapter discusses channel features, specifically screen size, in influencing engagement with the mental health app.

Channel features

The objective features of the channel of communication through which health game apps are delivered may affect cognitive processes and persuasive outcomes (Chae & Kim, 2004; Kim & Sundar, 2016). Several studies have documented the relation between large screens and attention (Kim & Kim, 2012; Maniar, Bennett, Hand, & Allan, 2008). Large screen nontouch mobile phones can increase video-based learning and subjective opinion of screen quality (Maniar et al., 2008). Text-only vocabulary learning is enhanced in self-instruction programs on large screen (600 × 800 pixels; e.g., Kindle) compared with a small computer screen (320 × 240 pixels; e.g., iPod) (Kim & Kim, 2012). Kim and Kim (2012) speculated that the decrease in learning on the small screen occurred due to increased cognitive load that affected students' attention and visual perception. Raptis, Tselios, Kjeldskov, and Skov (2013) showed a gain in efficiency in browsing tasks when using a large screen (5.3 inches) compared with small screen (3.5 inches) Android touch phones. Large screens also enhance perceived trust in information (Kim & Sundar, 2016). In comparison with smaller screens, larger screens also increase performance on cognitive tasks (Cherni, Kadri, Taruella, Joseph, & Roy, 2011). The advantage of large screens in terms of increased attention and information processing has been documented for video and text information (Cherni et al., 2011; Kim & Sundar, 2013, 2016; Reeves et al., 1999). For video game content, effect of screen size on engagement with game content is limited (Hou, Nam, Peng, & Lee, 2012). Large screen enhanced engagement with video games by increasing self-presence or feeling of "being there" inside the game due to increased immersion (Hou et al., 2012). Overall, it is expected that depression-themed health apps rendered on large screens (e.g., large monitor) will be more effective than the same app rendered on smaller screens (e.g., mobile phone) due to decreased cognitive load and an increase in information processing of message content.

Based on these two concepts discussed in the section above, a follow-up study to Khan and Peña (2017) was designed to specifically test the effects of message causality and channel features. The primary aim of this next study was to examine self-report and behavioral data of engagement with a depression-themed video game app, ReFocus, as an outcome of causality attribution to stable—unstable, exogenous—endogenous causes, and screen size manipulation. Using the same material and scales as in the first study, 223 participants were randomly assigned to engage with the video games app after reading one of the three messages assigning causality to endogenous—exogenous causes which varied on the dimension of stability. This second study teases apart stable—unstable dimension of attribution on engagement with the depression-themed health games app, Refocus.

Additionally, this study also tests the ReFocus app on two different screen size. Considering the advantages of larger screens compared with small screens, the second study examines how message feature manipulations interact with experimental manipulations of medium features, such as ReFocus, being rendered on a PC or on a smartphone (for detailed hypotheses, method and results see online supplementary material https://osf.io/9uqg8/?view_only=f7590a31482f4247a7a1fb1e1d5b0bfe).

This study followed the same procedure as discussed for the Khan and Peña (2017). Participants came to the lab and were randomly assigned to one of the six experimental conditions. Each participant saw one of the randomly assigned messages (i.e., endogenous-unstable causality to negative thinking, endogenous-stable causality to chemical imbalance, exogenous causality to environmental stress) on a PC (large screen) or smartphone (small screen), before accessing the games in ReFocus. In order to keep the experiment simple and to tease apart influence of stability one step at a time, stability was varied only on endogenous causes. All messages carried recommendations for using the health games app designed to help people cope with depression symptoms. ReFocus was adapted for an android phone as well as a PC and was identical on both platforms.

Intention to use the health game app was higher when depression was depicted as caused by endogenous-stable (chemical imbalance) instead of an endogenous-unstable (negative attitude) factor prior to playing with the app, and app usability was rated higher when depression was depicted as caused by endogenous-stable (chemical imbalance) cause instead of exogenous (environmental stress) or endogenous-unstable cause, but only in the large screen (PC) condition. See Tables 16.1 and 16.2. In both cases, self-reported intention to use the app and app usability was higher for endogenous-stable cause. This finding replicates findings from Khan and Peña (2017), in which endogenous cause (chemical imbalance) increased intentions and usability of the app compared with exposure to exogenous causality messages. In the Khan and Peña (2017), the mechanism underlying endogenous causality effect was explained in terms of controllability over depression, such that endogenous causes when attributed to a mental health threat impart a greater sense of controllability over the threat compared with exogenous causes, therefore enhancing the perception of an intervention's usefulness. In addition to supporting the controllability hypothesis, the follow-up study also points to endogenous-stable causality compared with endogenous-unstable causality as more effective at increasing self-reported intention to use a mental health app. Although not examined in any of the studies discussed in this chapter, it is possible that chemical imbalance causality was perceived in terms of onset uncontrollable but offset controllable. In health causality attribution, onset controllability is related to how much control an individual has on controlling the initiation of the health issue, and offset controllability conveys how much control the individual has on mitigating the health problem (Corrigan, 2000; Weiner, 1985). According to Weiner (1995), if the cause of an outcome is onset uncontrollable but offset controllable, then people engage in behavior that may change the outcome. In the two studies discussed in this chapter, brain chemical imbalance causality was endogenous-stable, but the stability could have been perceived in terms of the onset of depression. In order words, participants could have perceived that they had no control over getting depressed if depression is caused by brain chemical imbalance; however, they could still have perceived the app as a viable solution to alleviate depression. By nature of being directly related to the brain, endogenous-stable causality was perceived as more responsive to a brain training games app compared with endogenous-unstable causes (Dunlop et al., 2012). Taken together, self-report findings from this study help tease out the effect of endogenous—exogenous and stable—unstable dimensions of attribution in causality messages for depression to promote engagement with a cognitive training games app.

In addition to message causality effects, the follow-up study to Khan and Peña (2017) also showed how technological features overpower persuasive effects of linguistic causality manipulations implemented in mental health game apps. After statistically controlling for viewing angle and controller responsiveness between a PC and a

TABLE 16.1 MANCOVA results for self-report and behavioral data for follow-up study.

Effect	Intention to use the app			App usability			Game performance			Time spent with the app		
	F	p	η^2	F	p	η^2	F	p	η^2	F	p	η^2
Intercept												
Causality	0.47	0.63	0.01	0.49	0.62	0.01	2.28	0.11	0.03	1.11	0.33	0.02
Screen size	0.89	0.35	0.00	0.65	0.42	0.00	4.19	0.04	0.03	45.40	0.00*	0.22
Causality × screen size	4.42	0.01*	0.04	5.30	0.01*	0.05						
Viewing angle	0.03	0.86	0.00	0.29	0.59	0.00	0.16	0.69	0.00	0.49	0.48	0.00
Controller responsiveness	3.55	0.06	0.02	41.08	0.001*	0.17	1.44	0.23	0.01	0.77	0.38	0.01
Depression scores	1.10	0.30	0.01	0.03	0.86	0.00	0.29	0.59	0.00	1.24	0.27	0.01

*statistically significant.

TABLE 16.2 Mean and Standard Deviations (SD) From Multivariate Analysis of Covariance for follow-up study.

Condition	Usability	Intention to use	Time spent	Game performance
Endogenous-unstable causality	4.26(0.10)	3.61(1.43)	562.44(219.08)	0.15(0.01)
Endogenous-stable causality	4.48(1.07)	3.68(1.35)	628.16(230.35)	0.15(0.01)
Exogenous causality	4.38(0.98)	3.69(1.56)	555.81(218.88)	0.14(0.12)
PC	4.30(1.01)	3.50(1.45)	701.18(191.78)*	0.15(0.01*)*
Phone	4.44(1.01)	3.71(1.41)	486.45(201.44)*	0.14(0.01*)*
PC × exogenous causality	4.08(0.81)	3.33(1.51)	689.13(186.07)	0.14(0.01)
PC × endogenous-stable causality	4.66(1.08)*	3.95(1.28)*	722.07(218.09)	0.15(0.01)
PC × endogenous-unstable causality	4.13(1.04)	3.17(1.50)	689.33(171.53)	0.15(0.01)

*significantly different at $P < 0.05$.

smartphone, screen size emerged as the main variable influencing both behavioral and self-reported outcomes. Time participants spent using the app was higher for the PC compared with the smartphone condition. Neither device type nor causality messages had an effect on game performance. We regard time spent with the app to be a more direct measure of engagement than game performance as the games themselves were rather difficult (Boyle, Connolly, Hainey, & Boyle, 2012). Considering this, using self-help mental health apps on PC may contribute in alleviating attrition. In addition, assigning endogenous causality (brain chemical imbalance) to depression increased usability and intention to use the app targeting depression, but only in the PC condition. If mental health practitioners or researchers want to increase engagement with mental health video games in the long term, then they can design and embed messages in the app that assign depression causality to endogenous causes. Also, such games should be designed for large screen devices (e.g., laptops and desktops) to reduce dropout or premature discontinuation from the games.

Although, on comparing app use on PC and smartphone, screen size emerged as the technological feature affecting engagement with the mental health app, future research needs to test the mental health games app on identical devices with different screen sizes. Additionally, this study did not measure attention or heuristic-systematic processing that might have mediated the effect of screen size on the outcomes of interest. Previous studies have shown that large screen size increases attention to content and has also been associated with more detailed processing of digital content compared with small screens (Reeves et al., 1999; Kim & Sundar, 2016). Future studies should measure psychophysiological mechanisms in order to build models and develop theory that can explain how technological features interact with message features to effect engagement with health technology.

Discussion

The two studies discussed in this chapter provide evidence for how persuasive messages using linguistic causality and larger screens enhance engagement with a mental health game app, ReFocus. The first study findings show that attributing causality to endogenous causes for depression increases self-reported intentions and usability of ReFocus; the second study replicates this finding and also shows that using the app on a PC compared with a smartphone results in increased engagement with the app due to the bigger screen size of a PC.

In addition, the second study shows that engagement with a mental health cognitive training game is affected by the device on which it is used, specifically by screen size of the device. Moreover, the persuasive effect of messages is also overpowered by the screen size, showing that screen size influences health persuasive message effects. While previous studies have shown that engagement with serious games differs across devices (Hookham, Nesbitt, & Kay-Lambkin, 2016; Li & Wang, 2015), no study on mental health game apps has shown screen size to be the specific technological feature influencing game engagement. The fact that perceived controller responsiveness did not differ across the two devices and controller responsiveness along with viewing angle was statistically controlled in the analysis provides increased rigor to the screen size finding on game engagement as participants did not frequently move or manipulate their smartphones once in position. This finding is important because medium features have to be considered in tandem with message content for determining the success of any persuasive context (Oinas-Kukkonen & Harjumaa, 2018). Since persuasion involves information processing (McGuire, 1973; Petty & Cacioppo, 1988) and information processing is a function of features that affect attention, cognitive capacity, and emotion, medium and message features have to be considered together in health persuasive contexts (Lang, 2006; Reeves et al., 1999; Sundar & Kim, 2005). In particular, large screen size is associated with increased physiological arousal and increased attention to persuasive content (Reeves et al., 1999). Additionally, reading a persuasive message on a PC versus reading the same on another device may induce cognitive load and hence influence persuasive effects (Zambarbieri & Carniglia, 2012). This implies that message and medium effects should be examined together since message effects can be overpowered by screen size of the device, while we formally expected that message and medium would yield interaction effects.

Together, these two studies confirm that portraying depression as located internally because of biological causes makes participants feel that they could do something to control their likelihood of becoming depressed by spending time with a suitable game app rendered in a large screen. This finding resonates with other studies that attribute increased engagement to increased attention to large screens (Maniar et al., 2008). Future studies need to measure attention in real time (e.g., eye tracking) as the interaction effect between message and large screen could be indicative of screen size influence on information processing (Kim & Sundar, 2016). For instance, large screens facilitate heuristic processing and can lower cognitive load (Kim & Sundar, 2016), thereby increasing attention. Eye tracking studies can also reveal ocular fixation and regressions patterns for the persuasive message which could further inform which part of the message content is processed easily or requires greater cognitive effort (Zambarbieri & Carniglia, 2012).

Overall, findings from these two studies provide support for designing persuasive messages and embedding them within mental health games apps to affect behavioral engagement and self-reported intentions and usability. Messages framing how to use a health app should depict depression causality as endogenous if self-reported intentions and usability have to be increased, which are indicators of increased usage in the long run. However, if interventions want to affect immediate behavior in terms of app engagement, then messages framing how to use a health app should portray depression as externally caused since behavioral performance was better for exogenous threat.

The messages increase engagement by enhancing functional benefits of using the mental health app (Yardley et al., 2016). Users may engage with the app, even if they do not find it intrinsically enjoyable because the message features produce a knee-jerk reaction or increase the perceived value of using the app.

Future studies should also test for longitudinal effects of causality messages by exposing participants to the messages in more than one in-lab session. If the effect produced due to exogenous causality message is due to learned helplessness, then the boost in performance should fade over time. In addition, a third follow-up study is underway to test whether linguistic causality message and health app use can, besides increasing engagement, also help alleviate depression among participants.

Conclusion

Persuasive messages designed to change people's attributions of causality and the screen size in which these messages are shown can influence behavioral and self-reported engagement with a mental health game app. Messages targeting depression causality beliefs can be used to enhance user engagement with self-help video game apps for depression. Features of the channel of communication such as screen size should also be taken into account when designing self-help game apps for depression. The two studies in this dissertation chart new ways for increasing engagement with mental health apps by showing that we have the capacity to increase mental health app engagement and reduce attrition with self-help mental health apps.

References

Abrahamson, L. Y., Seligman, M. E., & Teasdale, J. D. (1978). Learned helplessness in humans: Critique and reformulation. *Journal of Abnormal Psychology, 87*(1), 49–74. https://doi.org/10.1037/0021-843X.87.1.49.

Alkhaldi, G., Hamilton, F. L., Lau, R., Webster, R., Michie, S., & Murray, E. (2016). The effectiveness of prompts to promote engagement with digital interventions: A systematic review. *Journal of Medical Internet Research, 18*(1). https://doi.org/10.2196/jmir.4790.

Arean, P. A., Hallgren, K. A., Jordan, J. T., Gazzaley, A., Atkins, D. C., Heagerty, P. J., & Anguera, J. A. (2016). The use and effectiveness of mobile apps for depression: Results from a fully remote clinical trial. *Journal of Medical Internet Research, 18*(12). https://doi.org/10.2196/jmir.6482.

Baumeister, R. F., Vohs, K. D., & Funder, D. C. (2007). Psychology as the science of self-reports and finger movements: Whatever happened to actual behavior? *Perspectives on Psychological Science, 2*(4), 396–403. https://doi.org/10.1111/j.1745-6916.2007.00051.x.

Bell, R. A., McGlone, M. S., & Dragojevic, M. (2014a). Bacteria as bullies: Effects of linguistic agency assignment in health message. *Journal of Health Communication, 19*(3), 340–358. https://doi.org/10.1080/10810730.2013.798383.

Bell, R. A., McGlone, M. S., & Dragojevic, M. (2014b). Vicious viruses and vigilant vaccines: Effects of linguistic agency assignment in health policy advocacy. *Journal of Health Communication, 19*(10), 1178–1195. https://doi.org/10.1080/10810730.2013.811330.

Boyle, E. A., Connolly, T. M., Hainey, T., & Boyle, J. M. (2012). Engagement in digital entertainment games: A systematic review. *Computers in Human Behavior, 28*(3), 771–780. https://doi.org/10.1016/j.chb.2011.11.020.

Breitfelder, K., & Messina, D. (2000). *IEEE 100: The authoritative dictionary of IEEE standards terms* (vol879). Standards Information Network IEEE Press. https://doi.org/10.1099/IEEESTD.2000.322230.

Calhoun, L. G., Johnson, R. E., & Boardman, W. K. (1975). Attribution of depression to internal-external and stable-unstable causes: Preliminary investigation. *Psychological Reports, 36*(2), 463–466. https://doi.org/10.2466/pr0.1975.36.2.463.

Chae, M., & Kim, J. (2004). Do size and structure matter to mobile users? An empirical study of the effects of screen size, information structure, and task complexity on user activities with standard web phones. *Behaviour and Information Technology, 23*(3), 165–181. https://doi.org/10.1080/01449290410001669923.

Chen, M., McGlone, M. S., & Bell, R. A. (2015). Persuasive effects of linguistic agency assignments and point of view in narrative health messages about colon cancer. *Journal of Health Communication, 20*(8), 977–988. https://doi.org/10.1080/10810730.2015.1018625.

Cherni, H., Kadri, A., Taruella, A., Joseph, P. A., & Roy, C. L. (2011). Virtual information display for cognitive rehabilitation: Choice of screen size. *Journal of CyberTherapy and Rehabilitation, 4*(1), 73–81. Retrieved from http://www.rvht.net/pubs/JCR%204(1).pdf#page=75.

Corrigan, P. W. (2000). Mental health stigma as social attribution: Implications for research methods and attitude change. *Clinical Psychology: Science and Practice, 7*(1), 48–67. https://doi.org/10.1093/clipsy.7.1.48.

Deacon, B. J., & Baird, G. L. (2009). The chemical imbalance explanation of depression: Reducing blame at what cost? *Journal of Social and Clinical Psychology, 28*(4), 415–435. https://doi.org/10.1521/jscp.2009.28.4.415.

Doherty, G., Coyle, D., & Sharry, J. (May 2012). Engagement with online mental health interventions: An exploratory clinical study of a treatment for depression. In *Proceedings of the SIGCHI conference on human factors in computing systems, USA* (pp. 1421–1430). ACM. https://doi.org/10.1145/2207676.2208602.

Donker, T., Petrie, K., Proudfoot, J., Clarke, J., Birch, M., & Christensen, H. (2013). Smartphones for smarter delivery of mental health programs: A systematic review. *Journal of Medical Internet Research, 15*(11), e247. https://doi.org/10.2196/jmir.2791. http://www.jmir.org/2013/11/e247/.

Dowty, D. R. (1989). On the semantic content of the notion of 'thematic role'. In *Properties, types and meaning* (pp. 69–129). Dordrecht: Springer.

Dowty, D. R. (1991). Thematic proto-roles and argument selection. *Language, 67*(3), 547–619. https://doi.org/10.2307/415037.

Dragojevic, M., Bell, R. A., & McGlone, M. S. (2014). Giving radon gas life through language effects of linguistic agency assignment in health messages about inanimate threats. *Journal of Language and Social Psychology, 33*(1), 89–98. https://doi.org/10.1177/0261927X13495738.

Ducette, J., & Keane, A. (1984). "Why me?": An attributional analysis of a major illness. *Research in Nursing and Health, 7*(4), 257–264. https://doi.org/10.1002/nur.4770070404.

Dunlop, B. W., Kelley, M. E., Mletzko, T. C., Velasquez, C. M., Craighead, W. E., & Mayberg, H. S. (2012). Depression beliefs, treatment preference, and outcomes in a randomized trial for major depressive disorder. *Journal of Psychiatric Research, 46*(3), 375–381. https://doi.org/10.1016/j.jpsychires.2011.11.003.

Fogg, B. J., & Nass, C. (1997). Silicon sycophants: The effects of computers that flatter. *International Journal of Human-Computer Studies, 46*(5), 551–561. https://doi.org/10.1006/ijhc.1996.0104.

Goldstein, B., & Rosselli, F. (2003). Etiological paradigms of depression: The relationship between perceived causes, empowerment, treatment preferences, and stigma. *Journal of Mental Health, 12*(6), 551–563. https://doi.org/10.1080/09638230310001627919.

Grabe, M. E., Lombard, M., Reich, R. D., Bracken, C. C., & Ditton, T. B. (1999). The role of screen size in viewer experiences of media content. *Visual Communication Quarterly, 6*(2), 4–9. https://doi.org/10.1080/15551399909363403.

Hookham, G., Nesbitt, K., & Kay-Lambkin, F. (February 2016). Comparing usability and engagement between a serious game and a traditional online program. In *Proceedings of the australasian computer science week multiconference* (p. 54). ACM. https://doi.org/10.1145/28043043.2843365.

Hou, J., Nam, Y., Peng, W., & Lee, K. M. (2012). Effects of screen size, viewing angle, and players' immersion tendencies on game experience. *Computers in Human Behavior, 28*(2), 617–623. https://doi.org/10.1016/j.chb.2011.11.007.

Jones, K. R., Lekhak, N., & Kaewluang, N. (2014). Using mobile phones and short message service to deliver self-management interventions for chronic conditions: A meta-review. *Worldviews on Evidence-Based Nursing, 11*(2), 81–88. https://doi.org/10.1111/wvn.12030.

Kannisto, K. A., Koivunen, M. H., & Välimäki, M. A. (2014). Use of mobile phone text message reminders in health care services: A narrative literature review. *Journal of Medical Internet Research, 16*(10). https://doi.org/10.2196/jmir.3442.

Khan, S., & Peña, J. (2017). Playing to beat the blues: Linguistic agency and message causality effects on use of mental health games application. *Computers in Human Behavior, 71*, 436–443. https://doi.org/10.1016/j.chb.2017.02.024.

Kim, D., & Kim, D. J. (2012). Effect of screen size on multimedia vocabulary learning. *British Journal of Educational Technology, 43*(1), 62–70. https://doi.org/10.1111/j.1467-8535.2010.01145.x.

Kim, K. J., & Sundar, S. S. (2013). Can interface features affect aggression resulting from violent video game play? An examination of realistic controller and large screen size. *Cyberpsychology, Behavior, and Social Networking, 16*(5), 329–334.

Kim, K. J., & Sundar, S. S. (2016). Mobile persuasion: Can screen size and presentation mode make a difference to trust? *Human Communication Research, 42*(1), 45–70. https://doi.org/10.1111/hcre.12064.

Kirkwood, W. G., & Brown, D. (1995). Public communication about the causes of disease: The rhetoric of responsibility. *Journal of Communication, 45*(1), 55–76. https://doi.org/10.1111/j.1460-2466.1995.tb00714.x.

Kroenke, K., & Spitzer, R. L. (2002). The PHQ-9: A new depression diagnostic and severity measure. *Psychiatric Annals, 32*(9), 1–7. Retrieved from http://www.lphi.org/LPHIadmin/uploads/.PHQ-9-Review-Kroenke-63754.PDF.

Kühn, S., Gleich, T., Lorenz, R. C., Lindenberger, U., & Gallinat, J. (2014). Playing super mario induces structural brain plasticity: Gray matter changes resulting from training with a commercial video game. *Molecular Psychiatry, 19*(2), 265–271. https://doi.org/10.1038/mp.2013.120.

Kuhn, E., Greene, C., Hoffman, J., Nguyen, T., Wald, L., Schmidt, J., ... Ruzek, J. (2014). Preliminary evaluation of PTSD Coach, a smartphone app for post-traumatic stress symptoms. *Military Medicine, 179*(1), 12–18. https://doi.org/10.7205/MILMED-D-13-00271.

Lang, A. (2006). Using the limited capacity model of motivated mediated message processing to design effective cancer communication messages. *Journal of Communication, 56*(Suppl. 1_1), S57–S80. https://doi.org/10.1111/j.1460-2466.2006.00283.x.

Lau, R. R., & Hartman, K. A. (1983). Common sense representations of common illnesses. *Health Psychology, 2*(2), 167–185. https://doi.org/10.1037/0278-6133.2.2.167.

Lebowitz, M. S., Ahn, W. K., & Nolen-Hoeksema, S. (2013). Fixable or fate? Perceptions of the biology of depression. *Journal of Consulting and Clinical Psychology, 81*(3), 518–527. https://doi.org/10.1037/a0031730.

Li, Z., & Wang, H. (2015). *A mobile game for encouraging active listening among deaf and hard of hearing people: Comparing the usage between mobile and desktop game.* Retrieved from http://www.diva-portal.org/smash/get/diva2:847306/FULLTEXT02.

Lombard, M., & Ditton, T. (1997). At the heart of it all: The concept of presence. *Journal of Computer-Mediated Communication, 3*(2). https://doi.org/10.1111/j.1083-6101.1997.tb00072.

Maier, S. F., & Watkins, L. R. (2005). Stressor controllability and learned helplessness: The roles of the dorsal raphe nucleus, serotonin, and corticotropin-releasing factor. *Neuroscience and Biobehavioral Reviews, 29*(4–5), 829–841. https://doi.org/10.1016/j.neubiorev.2005.03.021.

Maniar, N., Bennett, E., Hand, S., & Allan, G. (2008). The effect of mobile phone screen size on video based learning. *Journal of Software, 3*(4), 51–61. Retrieved from http://www.jsoftware.us/vol3/jsw0304-06.pdf.

McGlone, M. S., Bell, R. A., Zaitchik, S. T., & McGlynn, J. (2013). Don't let the flu catch you: Agency assignment in printed educational materials about the H1N1 influenza virus. *Journal of Health Communication, 18*(6), 740–756. https://doi.org/10.1080/10810730.2012.727950.

McGlone, M. S., & Pfiester, R. A. (2009). Does time fly when you're having fun, or do you? Affect, agency, and embodiment in temporal communication. *Journal of Language and Social Psychology, 28*(1), 3–31. https://doi.org/10.1177/0261927X08325744.

McGuire, W. J. (1973). Persuasion. In G. A. Miller (Ed.), *Communication, language, and meaning psychological perspectives* (pp. 242–255). New York: Basic Books.

Millner, A. J., Jaroszewski, A. C., Chamarthi, H., & Pizzagalli, D. A. (2012). Behavioral and electrophysiological correlates of training-induced cognitive control improvements. *NeuroImage, 63*(2), 742–753. https://doi.org/10.1016/j.neuroimage.2012.07.032.

Mohr, D. C., Burns, M. N., Schueller, S. M., Clarke, G., & Klinkman, M. (2013). Behavioral intervention technologies: Evidence review and recommendations for future research in mental health. *General Hospital Psychiatry, 35*(4), 332–338. https://doi.org/10.1016/genhosppsych.2013.03.008.

Oinas-Kukkonen, H., & Harjumaa, M. (2018). Persuasive systems design: Key issues, process model and system features. In *Routledge handbook of policy design* (pp. 105–123). Routledge.

Petty, R. E., Cacioppo, J. T., Sedikides, C., & Strathman, A. J. (1988). Affect and persuasion:" a contemporary perspective". *The American Behavioral Scientist, 31*(3), 355. https://doi.org/10.1177/000276488031003007.

Raptis, D., Tselios, N., Kjeldskov, J., & Skov, M. B. (August 2013). Does size matter?: Investigating the impact of mobile phone screen size on users' perceived usability, effectiveness and efficiency. In *Proceedings of the 15th international conference on Human-computer interaction with mobile devices and services* (pp. 127–136). ACM. https://doi.org/10.1145/2493190.2493204.

Reeves, B., Lang, A., Kim, E. Y., & Tatar, D. (1999). The effects of screen size and message content on attention and arousal. *Media Psychology, 1*(1), 49–67. https://doi.org/10.1207/s1532785xmep0101_4.

Roepke, A. M., Jaffee, S. R., Riffle, O. M., McGonigal, J., Broome, R., & Maxwell, B. (2015). Randomized controlled trial of SuperBetter, a smartphone-based/internet-based self-help tool to reduce depressive symptoms. *Games for Health Journal, 4*(3), 235–246. https://doi.org/10.1089/g4h.2014.0046.

Roesch, S. C., & Weiner, B. (2001). A meta-analytic review of coping with illness: Do causal attributions matter? *Journal of Psychosomatic Research, 50*(4), 205–219. https://doi.org/10.1016/S0022-3999(01)00188-X.

Roth, S., & Bootzin, R. R. (1974). Effects of experimentally induced expectancies of external control: An investigation of learned helplessness. *Journal of Personality and Social Psychology, 29*(2), 253–262. https://doi.org/10.1037/h0036022.

Seligman, M. E. (1972). Learned helplessness. *Annual Review of Medicine, 23*(1), 407–412. Retrieved from https://pdfs.semanticscholar.org/ef52/775276f83a46162a9b364335d9ee5ee73b99.pdf http://www.annualreviews.org/doi/pdf/10.1146/annurev.me.23.020172.002203.

Suenderhauf, C., Walter, A., Lenz, C., Lang, U. E., & Borgwardt, S. (2016). Counter striking psychosis: Commercial video games as potential treatment in schizophrenia? A systematic review of neuroimaging studies. *Neuroscience and Biobehavioral Reviews, 68*, 20—36. https://doi.org/10.1016/j.neubiorev.2016.03.018.

Sundar, S. S., & Kim, J. (2005). Interactivity and persuasion: Influencing attitudes with information and involvement. *Journal of Interactive Advertising, 5*(2), 5—18. https://doi.org/10.1080/15252019.2005.10722097.

Swift, J. K., & Greenberg, R. P. (2012). Premature discontinuation in adult psychotherapy: A meta-analysis. *Journal of Consulting and Clinical Psychology, 80*(4), 547—557. https://doi.org/10.1037/a0028226.

Thompson, M., Nordin, A. I., & Cairns, P. (September 2012). Effect of touch-screen size on game immersion. In *Proceedings of the 26th annual BCS interaction specialist group conference on people and computers* (pp. 280—285). British Computer Society. Retrieved from https://bit.ly/2JUWib9.

Tolentino, G. P., Battaglini, C., Pereira, A. C. V., De Oliveria, R. J., & De Paula, M. G. M. (May 2011). Usability of serious games for health. In *Games and virtual worlds for serious applications (VS-games), 2011 third international conference on* (pp. 172—175). IEEE. https://doi.org/10.1109/VS-GAMES.2011.33.

Weiner, B. (1985). An attributional theory of achievement motivation and emotion. *Psychological Review, 92*(4), 548—573. https://doi.org/10.1037/0033-295X.92.4.548.

Weiner, B. (1995). *Judgments of responsibility: A foundation for a theory of social conduct.* Available from http://librarystory.info/judgments-of-responsibility-a-foundation-for-a-theory-of-social-conduct-text-archive-free-books-bernard-weiner.pdf.

Westra, H. A., Arkowitz, H., & Dozois, D. J. (2009). Adding a motivational interviewing pretreatment to cognitive behavioral therapy for generalized anxiety disorder: A preliminary randomized controlled trial. *Journal of Anxiety Disorders, 23*(8), 1106—1117.

Wilkinson, N., Ang, R. P., & Goh, D. H. (2008). Online video game therapy for mental health concerns: A review. *International Journal of Social Psychiatry, 54*(4), 370—382. https://doi.org/10.1177/0020764008091659.

Witte, K. (1994). Fear control and danger control: A test of the extended parallel process model (EPPM). *Communication Monographs, 61*(2), 113—134. https://doi.org/10.1080/03637759409376328.

World Health Organization.(2019). Retrieved from https://www.who.int/mental_health/management/en/.

Yardley, L., Spring, B. J., Riper, H., Morrison, L. G., Crane, D. H., Curtis, K., ... Blandford, A. (2016). Understanding and promoting effective engagement with digital behavior change interventions. *American Journal of Preventive Medicine, 51*(5), 833—842. https://doi.org/10.1016/j.amepre.2016.06.015.

Zambarbieri, D., & Carniglia, E. (2012). Eye movement analysis of reading from computer displays, eReaders and printed books. *Ophthalmic and Physiological Optics, 32*(5), 390—396. https://doi.org/10.1111/j.1475-1313.2012.00930.x.

The role of interactivity in new media-based health communication: Testing the interaction among interactivity, threat, and efficacy

Kai Kuang

Department of Communication Studies, University of Pennsylvania, Bloomsburg, PA, United States

The development of the World Wide Web and advancements of technology have provided many opportunities for health communication scholars and practitioners to design new media-based health communication initiatives and make use of the low cost, wide reach, and interactive features to facilitate user participation and information processing (e.g., Kim & Stout, 2010), self-efficacy, attitudes toward health issues (e.g., Liu & Shrum, 2002; Street & Rimal, 1997), and the ability to tailor programs and information to the needs and interests of individual users (e.g., Strecher, Greenwood, Wang, & Dumont, 1999). An earlier chapter of this volume reviews the rich literature on the effects of interactivity and argues that such effects need to be taken into consideration together with the content presented in health messages. That is, the effects of interactive, new media-based health promotion initiatives will need to consider both the message content (i.e., what is in the message) and the message modality (i.e., how is the message presented). This chapter reviews the results of an empirical study (Kuang & Cho, 2016) that tested the theoretical framework proposed in a previous chapter and discusses theoretical and empirical implications of the finding.

Specifically, threat and efficacy have been identified as two key constructs in health communication and promotion theory and research in

377

past decades (e.g., Rimal & Real, 2003; Rogers, 1983; Witte, 1992). It is widely recognized that threat perceptions determine the motivation for individuals to engage in self-protective health behaviors, while efficacy perceptions determines whether danger control or fear control process is initiated (Witte, 1992). A rich body of literature exists on the effectiveness of these two constructs in predicting changes in health beliefs, attitudes, and behaviors (e.g., Smith et al., 2008; see Maloney, Lapinski, & Witte, 2011 for a review and Witte & Allen, 2000 for a metaanalysis). However, this area of research has focused exclusively on the content of health messages. These message content constructs may interact with whether the messages are presented on highly interactive or noninteractive formats. The following study (Kuang & Cho, 2016) reviewed in this chapter seeks to answer this question. This chapter begins with an introduction to the study, followed by the method and results. Theoretical and practical implications are presented in the end of this chapter.

Study rationale

According to the theoretical framework proposed in a previous chapter, message content constructs such as threat and efficacy may interact with message modality constructs such as interactivity in influencing the extent to which users engage with the message and process the information (proposition 1), which in turn influences learning and persuasive outcomes (proposition 2). To test these propositions, the study reviewed in this chapter investigated the interaction among threat, efficacy, and interactivity on message engagement, attitude toward recommended action, and behavioral intention. Before the hypotheses and research question of this study are introduced, key terms are defined below.

Threat and response efficacy

A perceived threat is defined as one's cognitions or thoughts about "a danger or harm that exists in the environment" (Witte, 1992, p. 114), which is oftentimes operationalized with its two dimensions: perceived severity and perceived susceptibility (Witte, 1992). Individuals' beliefs about the magnitude and significance of the threat are perceived severity, while individuals' beliefs about their risk of experiencing the threat are perceived susceptibility to the threat.

Persuasion theories such as the protection motivation theory (PMT; Rogers, 1975, 1983) and the extended parallel process model (Witte, 1992) suggest that following the exposure of a threat message, two appraisals are initiated. First, people appraise the threat of a hazard; then, they evaluate the efficacy of recommended action. That is, the level of threat perception will determine whether a message will be accepted and processed or rejected and disregarded. Individuals' evaluations of these two aspects will subsequently influence their belief, attitude, and behavioral intention (Witte, 1992). For instance, individuals with high-threat perception will be more motivated to begin the second appraisal (i.e., the evaluation of the efficacy of the recommended action). Those who perceive threat as trivial or irrelevant would not have the motivation to process the message further (low- or no-threat perception). In this case, the appraisal of efficacy perceptions will not be initiated or will be examined superficially.

Efficacy is defined as an individual's perceptions of his or her ability to produce an outcome or to perform a behavior or the ability of an external entity (e.g., a course of action) to achieve that outcome or behavior (Bandura, 1994, 1998). In health communication and promotion research, the construct of efficacy is often categorized into self-efficacy and response efficacy (e.g., Rogers, 1983; Witte, 1992). Self-efficacy refers to "people's beliefs about their capabilities to produce designated levels of performance that exercise influence over events that affect their lives" (Bandura, 1994, p. 71). In comparison, response efficacy refers to one's belief that to perform a recommended action can indeed avert the threat (e.g., Zhao & Cai, 2009). The study reviewed in this chapter focused on response efficacy, due to the nature of the context (vaccination). Specifically, individuals' levels of response efficacy is a key determinant of their orientation toward perceptions that immunization is effective and safe (e.g.,Russell, Injeyan, Verhoef, & Eliasziw, 2004), which in turn serves as a prior condition for them to consider adopting the recommended action. In addition, in this context, response efficacy serves as a prerequisite for one's evaluation of self-efficacy. If a person does not perceive the vaccination to be effective, he/she is not likely to consider whether they have the ability to get the vaccine. Therefore, this study focused on response efficacy, with the recognition that individuals' ability to get vaccinated (e.g., cost, convenience) does vary.

Theoretical frameworks such as the PMT and empirical evidence support the significance of response efficacy. For example, PMT (Rogers, 1975, 1983) proposes that an individual's assessments of (a) severity of the health event, (b) probability of the event occurring, (c) belief in the efficacy of a coping behavior to remove the threat (i.e., coping response efficacy), and (d) the individual's perceived ability to carry out the recommended action (i.e., self-efficacy) are crucial in influencing health outcomes. Empirical studies in this literature suggest that the perceived efficacy of the recommended action to achieve the desired outcome is the most important predictor of behavioral intentions (e.g., Struckman-Johnson, Gilliland, Struckman-Johnson, & North, 1990; Tanner, Hunt, & Eppright, 1991).

Interactivity

Interactivity has been a matter of interest for several decades, yet it has no universal conceptualization in literature. As a defining feature of online technologies (e.g., Walther, Pingree, Hawkins, & Buller, 2005) and key variable for studying the uses and effects of (new) media technologies (e.g., Jankowski & Hanssen, 1996; Rafaeli, 1988; Sundar, Kalyanaraman, & Brown, 2003), researchers have identified the most important conceptual components of interactivity, which lie in its ability to allow an exchange of information, user responsiveness, and user control (e.g., December 1996; Pavlik, 1996; Walther et al., 2005).

Some conceptualizations of interactivity focus more on the nominal or dichotomous feature of interactivity and offer approaches to designate whether or not a medium or technology is interactive or not, other researchers have moved beyond this and conceptualized interactivity at higher levels of measurement (Sundar et al., 2003). Following this approach, scholars have operationalized interactivity in terms of the functional characteristics an interface has, such as email links, access to extra information links, feedback forms, chat rooms, audio and video downloads, and so on (e.g., Ahern & Stromer-Galley, 2000; Massey & Levy, 1999; Sundar et al., 2003). This approach of operationalizing interactivity proposes that the presence of such functional features on an interface is sufficient evidence of interactivity. Higher number of functions included on an interface means greater interactivity. For example, Sundar et al. (2003) operationalized interactivity in their study as follows: a website for a political candidate with no extra links (low interactivity), the same site with a link to access extra information about the candidate (medium interactivity), and a form function with a link to the candidate's email address to facilitate correspondence with the candidate (high interactivity).

Past research has compared both interactive and noninteractive presentational formats of health information (i.e., dichotomous/nominal approach) as well as presentational formats with varying levels of interactivity (e.g., low- vs. medium- vs. high-interactivity conditions). Specifically, researchers drew comparisons between classroom lessons versus brochures (Burger et al., 2003), interactive computer-assisted instruction programs versus videos versus pamphlet (Champion et al., 2006), conversational and testimonial messages versus didactic presentations (Slater, Buller, Waters, Archibeque, & LeBlanc, 2003), diagrams versus text (Connelly & Knuth, 1998), and telephone tailoring versus print tailoring (Champion et al., 2007). In general, empirical evidence provides support for the effectiveness of interactivity in health promotion initiatives. For example, Tessaro, Rye, Parker, Mangone, and McCrone (2007) examined the effectiveness of a nutrition intervention with rural low-income

women and found that the interactive intervention group had significantly improved performance on nutrition-related information compared
to the control group in 3 months. De Bourdeaudhuij, Stevens, Vandelanotte, and Brug (2007) evaluated an interactive computer-tailored nutrition intervention in a real-life setting and found the interactive
intervention was more effective in reducing total fat intake compared
with a generic intervention and to no intervention. However, there are
also cases where interactive presentational formats are not more effective,
or even less effective than noninteractive presentation formats. A meta-
analysis conducted by Cook and colleagues (Cook et al., 2008) quantified
the associations of Internet-based instruction and educational outcomes.
They found that Internet-based learning was associated with large positive effects compared with no intervention. However, effects compared
with noninteractive instructional methods were heterogeneous and
generally small, suggesting effectiveness similar to traditional methods.
One possible explanation for such heterogeneity is the possible interaction between interactivity and the content of the messages presented in
these studies. The study presented here is one that tested these interaction
effects in the context of meningococcal vaccination.

Specifically, Sundar's (2007) interactivity effects model suggests that
interactivity, as a modality feature, can promote user engagement with
content, which may further influence attitudes (e.g., Liu & Shrum, 2002;
Sundar & Kim 2005; Tremayne & Dunwoody, 2001). That is, the modality
of mediated health messages may influence individuals' psychological
processing of the message (Sundar, 2000), influencing whether automatic
processing or controlled processing is triggered by these modalities.

Along this line of thinking, dual process theories such as the elaboration likelihood model (ELM; Petty & Cacioppo, 1986) and heuristic-
systematic model of information processing (HSM; Eagly & Chaiken,
1993) suggest that, depending on whether information is processed
heuristically or systematically, health messages delivered via interactive
channels may achieve differential effects. For example, high-threat, high-
efficacy message content may persuade through the central route, hence
high versus low-interactive features may not influence information processing but still achieve similar persuasive effects. In comparison, high-
threat, low-efficacy message content could lead to defensive motivation
and fear control processes when presented in low-interactive format,
while in high-interactive format, high-threat, low-efficacy message may
motivate individuals to seek more information, achieving persuasive effects through peripheral route. Building on these theoretical foundations,
this study sought to test the interaction between message content and
message modality on a range of outcomes, including information processing, information seeking, attitude, as well as behavioral intention.

Such interaction effects were tested within the context of meningococcal vaccination, which is introduced next.

Study context and hypotheses

Meningococcal vaccination

Toward this end, the study was conducted in the context of meningococcal vaccination. Vaccines, which protect people against disease by inducing immunity, can avoid suffering, disability, and death before people fall ill (WHO, 2018). The disease of meningitis, also referred to as spinal meningitis, is "an inflammation (swelling) of the protective membranes covering the brain and spinal cord" (CDC, 2018). Oftentimes, an infection of the fluid surrounding the brain and spinal cord can cause the inflammation. As an infectious disease, meningitis tends to spread quickly wherever larger groups of people gather together. Although it is a relatively rare disease, meningitis is potentially fatal. For those who survive the disease, many are left with lifelong health problems, such as learning disabilities, mental retardation, hearing loss, kidney failure, and limb amputations. College students who live in dormitories, especially freshmen, military personnel, and children in childcare facilities are at an increased risk. Most recently, San Diego State University, Oregon State University, and the Five College consortium in Massachusetts all experienced meningitis outbreak (CDC, 2018).

Although facing high risk of getting this highly contagious disease, college students are not well informed of the availability of the meningococcal vaccination. Therefore, it is important to inform college students about the disease (threat) as well as the availability and the effectiveness of the vaccine (response efficacy). Considering college students as the target audience, interactive ways of engaging them in the health messages could potentially be useful. In sum, this study aimed at (a) evaluating the effects of a highly interactive, Internet-based intervention with multiple related web links and email addresses (high interactivity), versus a low-interactive, Internet-based version of identical content with no hyperlinks (low interactivity) and (b) examining the interaction effect among threat, response efficacy, and interactivity in this health promotion initiative. The following hypotheses were proposed:

H1: For participants who read messages that contain low-threat and high response efficacy statements, those who read the message in high-interactive presentational and low-interactive presentational format would not report differential levels of message effectiveness, information seeking intention, behavioral intention, attitude toward meningococcal vaccination, message involvement, and message processing differently.

H2: For participants who read messages that contain low-threat and low response efficacy statements, those who read the message in high-interactive presentational and low-interactive presentational format would report differential levels of message effectiveness, information seeking intention, behavioral intention, attitude toward meningococcal vaccination, message involvement, and message processing differently.

H3: For participants who read messages that contain high threat and high response efficacy statements, those who read the message in high-interactive presentational format would report higher level of message effectiveness, information seeking intentions, behavioral intention and more favorable attitude toward meningococcal vaccination, and higher level of message involvement and message processing than those who read information in low-interactive presentational format.

H4: For participants who read messages that contain high threat and low response efficacy statements, those who read the message in high-interactive presentational format would report higher level of message effectiveness, information seeking intentions, behavioral intention and more favorable attitude toward meningococcal vaccination, and higher level of message involvement and message processing than those who read information in low-interactive presentational format.

Method

To test these hypotheses, this study adopted a 2 (high, low threat) × 2 (high, low response efficacy) × 2 (high interactivity, low interactivity) factorial experimental design. Data were gathered from a large public university from college age students who are at risk of contracting meningococcal meningitis.

Participants completed the study in a lab setting. A brief introduction to the study gave participants a general idea about what the study was about and emphasized the anonymous nature of their responses. They were asked to read the message carefully and fill out the questionnaire. Participants then received a link to a web page consisting of (a) severity of the meningitis, (b) susceptibility of meningitis to college students, and (c) a message about the effectiveness of meningococcal vaccinations. Threat was manipulated in the first two sections, and response efficacy was manipulated in the third section. Interactivity was manipulated by the amount of interactive features presented on the website. The high-interactivity condition was operationalized according to the functional view of interactivity (e.g., Ahern & Stromer-Galley, 2000; Massey & Levy, 1999; Sundar et al., 2003). By selecting a particular hyperlink, participants would be led to another page with the relevant heading. An ideal test of how presentational formats influences individual's choice would examine a situation in which information provided is constant, while the presentational formats vary. Therefore, all eight versions of the stimulus were made to look as similar as possible to avoid potential incidental confounds. The websites that had the same threat and response efficacy level were identical in content and vary only in their levels of interactivity.

All information contained in the messages was accurate, but each message emphasized different aspects. Specifically, information in high versus low threat and response efficacy conditions emphasized different aspects of the same fact. Each message was equated for length and the order of arguments. Participants also answered a series of questions about their demographic information, including age, gender, ethnicity, marital status, and educational level. At the end of the experiment, the researcher debriefed the participants, reiterated the purpose of the study, and corrected any misperceptions that the threat and response efficacy manipulation may have created. Meanwhile, a CDC flier about meningitis and meningococcal vaccination was disseminated to the participants.

Measures

Seven-point Likert scales ranging from 1 (*strongly disagree*) to 7 (*strongly agree*) were used for the following measures unless otherwise noted.

Manipulation checks

The effectiveness of the threat treatment was gauged with the evaluation of severity and susceptibility. More specifically, perceived threat was measured by five items (e.g., "I may be at risk of getting meningitis," "it is possible that I'll contract meningitis"; adapted from Witte, Cameron, McKeon, and Berkowitz, 1996; $\alpha = 0.68$). The effectiveness of the response efficacy manipulation was measured with two items (e.g., "the meningococcal vaccine is effective in preventing meningococcal meningitis"; $\alpha = 0.64$; Witte, Cameron, McKeon, and Berkowitz, 1996). Perceived interactivity was measured with seven items (e.g., "I was in control of my navigation through this website," "this website is interactive"; $\alpha = 0.85$; McMillan & Hwang, 2002).

Message involvement

Each message involvement scale consisted of five items (adapted from Cox and Cox, 1991; e.g., "the message on the website seemed relevant to me," "this message on the website made me think"; $M = 4.65$, $SD = 1.11$, $\alpha = 0.86$).

Message processing

Participants were asked to choose a number that best represents their reading of the message on a scale of one–seven for each of the pairs of phrases, with one being "not at all interested" and seven being "very much interested," and one being "paid little attention" and seven being "paid a lot of attention" ($M = 4.72$, $SD = 1.25$, $\alpha = 0.82$).

Message effectiveness

Each message effectiveness scale consisted of five items (adapted from Dillard, Shen, and Vail, 2007; "the message on the website was persuasive," "I feel that the message on the website made its point effectively"; $M = 4.82$, $SD = 1.19$, $\alpha = 0.90$).

Attitudes toward getting meningococcal vaccination

Each attitude toward behavior scale ranged from one to seven and comprised four pairs of bipolar adjectives including: "good/bad," "positive/negative," "desirable/not desirable," and "beneficial/not beneficial." Items were reverse coded so that higher scores indicated more positive attitude toward getting vaccinated against meningitis ($M = 5.61$, $SD = 1.29$, $\alpha = 0.94$).

Information seeking intention

Four items measured information seeking intention (adapted from Laurent and Kapferer, 1985, e.g., "I will try to keep myself informed about the issue of meningococcal meningitis," "I will pay attention to articles on the issue of the meningococcal meningitis"; $M = 4.23$, $SD = 1.44$, $\alpha = 0.93$).

Behavioral intention

Intention was measured with three items (e.g., "I intend to get meningococcal vaccine at least once in the future," "In the future, I may get meningococcal vaccine occasionally"; $M = 4.46$, $SD = 1.46$, $\alpha = 0.86$).

Previous vaccine experience

Participants were asked if they had ever taken meningococcal vaccination as a control variable (yes = 1, no = 0). The percentage of participants who had previous experience of getting meningococcal vaccination (i.e., item score = 1) was 52.

Demographic information

Participants were asked to provide their demographic information such as sex, age, and ethnicity. 47.5% of the participants were male, while 68.3% of the participants were white. Participants' age ranged from 18 to 32 years old ($M = 20.79$, $SD = 2.40$). Most of the participants were 18–23 years old (90.5%), representing the population who are at a higher risk of contracting meningitis (CDC, 2018).

Key findings

Manipulation checks suggested that manipulations of threat, response efficacy, and interactivity worked effectively. Assuming $P < .05$, the power to detect a predicted medium effect ($f = 0.25$) in the $2 \times 2 \times 2$ factorial ANCOVA studies was 0.96 when $N = 221$, $a = 8$, number of measurements $= 6$, $r = 0.50$, and number of covariates $= 4$. The cell sizes were not equal, and this would not change the power analysis greatly in each case. This study was adequately powered to detect medium-size main effects and interaction effects should they be present.

Message involvement and message processing

To address the hypotheses, a correlation test was first conducted on the scores for all dependent variables. Results showed that message involvement and message processing were highly correlated, Pearson $r = 0.63$, $P < .001$. Therefore, a $2 \times 2 \times 2$ factorial MANCOVA was conducted, with threat (high/low), response efficacy (high/low), and interactivity (high/low) as independent variables, message involvement and message processing as dependent variables, and gender, age, ethnicity, and previous meningococcal vaccination experience as covariates. The results for this MANCOVA test concerning the three-way interaction for response efficacy, threat, and interactivity were not significant, Wilks' Lambda $= 0.980$, $F_{2,208} = 2.090$, and $P = .126$. However, since multivariate F is often not as powerful as univariate or stepdown F, the significance of the results can be lost (Tabachnick & Fidell, 1996). Therefore, it is still important to examine the tests of between-subject effects.

Message involvement

Results revealed that there was a significant three-way interaction effect for response efficacy, threat, and interactivity on message involvement at 0.05 level, $F(1, 220) = 4.153$, $P = .043$, partial $\eta^2 = 0.019$, $\eta^2 = 0.017$, a partial effect size and total effect size between small and medium according to Cohen's standard. This indicated that interactivity would moderate the two-way interaction for response efficacy and threat on message involvement. A further examination of the means plot for message involvement in different response efficacy, threat, and interactivity conditions revealed that the three-way interaction effect influenced the degree to which response efficacy and threat interacted on the scores of message involvement. In other words, the three-way interaction effect partially qualified for the two-way interaction for response efficacy and threat on message involvement.

To better understand the three-way interaction for response efficacy, threat, and interactivity on message involvement, results were split by the factor of interactivity. Results showed that there was no significant two-way interaction effect for response efficacy and threat at low-interactivity condition, $F(1, 100) = 0.601$, $P = .440$, partial $\eta^2 = 0.006$, and $\eta^2 = 0.006$. However, the two-way interaction effect for response efficacy and threat was significant at high-interactivity condition, $F(1, 111) = 4.206$, $P = .043$, partial $\eta^2 = 0.036$, and $\eta^2 = 0.031$. Therefore, interactivity moderated the two-way interaction effect for response efficacy and threat such that the two-way interaction was significant at high-interactivity level, and was not significant at low-interactivity level.

Decomposing the significant two-way interaction effect for response efficacy and threat on message involvement at high-interactivity condition, results indicated that threat exerted a significant simple effect on message involvement when response efficacy was high, $t(68) = 2.018$, $P = .048$, and $d = 0.50$ (unequal variances between groups). However, threat did not have a significant simple effect on message involvement when response efficacy was low, $t(48) = 1.038$, $P = .305$, and $d = 0.30$. Therefore, at high-interactivity level, response efficacy moderated the impact of threat on message involvement such that the simple effect for threat was significant when response efficacy was high, while it was not significant when response efficacy was low.

However, the two-way interaction for response efficacy and threat averaged across interactivity was not significant, $F(1, 220) = 0.412$, $P = .522$, partial $\eta^2 = 0.002$, and $\eta^2 = 0.002$. In addition, age was a significant covariate on participants' message involvement, $F(1, 220) = 15.728$, $P < .001$, partial $\eta^2 = 0.070$, and $\eta^2 = 0.065$. Other covariates did not exert significant impact on message involvement.

Message processing

In addition, there was no significant three-way interaction on message processing at 0.05 level, $F(1, 220) = 1.153$ $P = .284$, partial $\eta^2 = 0.005$, $\eta^2 = 0.005$, a small partial effect size and a small total effect size according to Cohen's standard. No significant two-way interaction between response efficacy and threat was present on message processing, $F(1, 220) = 0.323$, $P = .571$, partial $\eta^2 = 0.002$, and $\eta^2 = 0.001$. Age also exerted a significant impact on message processing as a covariate, $F(1, 220) = 11.149$, $P = .001$, partial $\eta^2 = 0.051$, and $\eta^2 = 0.049$. Other covariates did not exert significant impact on message processing.

In sum, the three-way interaction effect for threat, response efficacy, and interactivity on message involvement were significant, accounting for 1.7% of the variance in individual's message involvement. Interactivity moderated the two-way interaction for response efficacy and threat on message involvement such that the two-way interaction was significant when the risk message was presented in high-interactive format, while it was not significant in low-interactive format. In other words, the simple effect for threat at the two levels of response efficacy vary more than we would expect by chance in high versus low-interactivity conditions. However, the two-way interaction effect for response efficacy and threat averaged across levels of interactivity was not significant. In addition, the three-way interaction effect for response efficacy, threat, and interactivity on message processing was not significant, nor was the two-way interaction effect for response efficacy and threat averaged across interactivity conditions.

Message effectiveness

To address the hypotheses on message effectiveness, a $2 \times 2 \times 2$ factorial ANCOVA was conducted, with threat (high/low), response efficacy (high/low), and interactivity (high/low) as independent variables, message effectiveness as dependent variable, and gender, age, ethnicity, and previous meningococcal vaccination experience as covariates. Most assumptions for conducting ANCOVA test were met, and the ANCOVA test was robust to violations of the assumptions.

Regarding the three-way interaction effect for response efficacy, threat, and interactivity on message effectiveness, results revealed a nonsignificant interaction effect for threat and response efficacy on message effectiveness, $F(1, 220) = 1.625$, $P = .204$, partial $\eta^2 = 0.008$, $\eta^2 = 0.006$, a small partial effect size and total effect size according to Cohen's standard. That was to say, interactivity would not moderate the two-way interaction between response efficacy and threat on message effectiveness.

In reference to the two-way interaction effect for response efficacy and threat on message effectiveness, results revealed a nonsignificant interaction effect for threat and response efficacy on message effectiveness, $F(1, 220) = 0.106$, $P = .745$, partial $\eta^2 = 0.001$, $\eta^2 = 0.001$, a very small partial effect size and total effect size according to Cohen's standard. This indicated that the impact for threat on message effectiveness would not differ more than we would expect by chance at different levels of response efficacy. In other words, threat would not moderate the impact of response efficacy on message effectiveness.

In addition, results revealed a significant main effect for response efficacy on perceived message effectiveness, $F(1, 220) = 4.751$, $P = .030$, partial $\eta^2 = 0.022$, $\eta^2 = 0.019$, a partial effect and total effect between small and medium size according to Cohen's standard. A further examination of the marginal means indicated that participants who read high response efficacy messages would perceive the message as more effective ($M = 4.98$) than those who read low response efficacy messages ($M = 4.64$). Besides, age was a significant covariate on participants' message effectiveness, $F(1, 220) = 25.943$, $P < .001$, partial $\eta^2 = 0.110$, and $\eta^2 = 0.104$. Other covariates did not exert significant impact on message effectiveness.

In sum, there was no significant three-way interaction effect for response efficacy, threat, and interactivity on message effectiveness. In addition, the two-way interaction effect between response efficacy and threat on message effectiveness was not significant, either. However, the main effect for response efficacy on message effectiveness was significant, which accounted for 1.9% of the variances in scores on message effectiveness.

Attitude, information seeking intention, and behavioral intention

To address the hypotheses on attitude, information seeking intention, and behavioral intention, a correlation test was conducted on the scores for attitude, information seeking intention, and behavioral intention. Results showed that the three variables were correlated, Pearson $r_1 = 0.30$, $p_1 < .001$ (attitude and information seeking intention), $r_2 = 0.66$, $p_2 < .001$ (attitude and behavioral intention), and $r_3 = 0.45$, $p_3 < .001$ (information seeking intention and behavioral intention). Therefore, a $2 \times 2 \times 2$ factorial MANCOVA was conducted, with threat (high/low), response efficacy (high/low), and interactivity (high/low) as independent variables, attitude, information seeking intention, and behavioral intention as dependent variables, and gender, age, ethnicity, and previous meningococcal vaccination experience as covariates. Most assumptions for conducting MANCOVA test were met, and MANCOVA test was robust to violations of assumptions. The results for this MANCOVA test concerning the three-way interaction for response efficacy, threat, and interactivity (Wilks' Lambda $= 0.987$, $F_{3,207} = 0.937$, and $P = .424$) and two-way interaction for response efficacy and threat (Wilks' Lambda $= 0.989$, $F_{3,207} = 0.800$, and $P = .495$) were presented in the following three parts: attitude, information seeking intention, and behavioral intention.

Attitude

With regard to the three-way interaction, results revealed that there was no significant three-way interaction effect for response efficacy, threat, and interactivity on attitude, information seeking intention, and behavioral intention at 0.05 level, $F(1, 220) = 2.276$, $P = .133$, partial $\eta^2 = 0.011$, and $\eta^2 = 0.008$. This showed that interactivity did not moderate the interaction effect for response efficacy and threat on attitude.

Concerning the two-way interaction effect for response efficacy and threat on attitude, results showed that no two-way interaction was present, $F(1, 220) = 0.214$, $P = .644$, partial $\eta^2 = 0.001$, and $\eta^2 = 0.001$. This indicated that the impact for threat on attitude would not differ more than we would expect by chance at different levels of response efficacy. In other words, threat would not moderate the impact of response efficacy on attitude. In addition, participants' previous experience of getting meningococcal vaccinations was a significant covariate on participants' attitude, $F(1, 220) = 73.815$, $P = .000$, partial $\eta^2 = 0.261$, and $\eta^2 = 0.244$. Other covariates did not exert significant impact on attitude.

Information seeking intention

No three-way interaction effect for response efficacy, threat, and interactivity on information seeking intention was present, $F(1, 220) = 0.102$, $P = .749$, partial $\eta^2 = 0.000$, and $\eta^2 = 0.000$. The two-way interaction effect between response efficacy and threat on information seeking intention would not differ more than we would expect by chance at different levels of interactivity. In other words, interactivity does not moderate the two-way interaction between response efficacy and threat.

Regarding the two-way interaction for response efficacy, results revealed that there was no significant two-way interaction effect on information seeking intention, $F(1, 220) = 0.290$, $P = .591$, partial $\eta^2 = 0.001$, $\eta^2 = 0.001$, a small partial effect size and total effect size. This indicated that the impact for threat on information seeking intention would not differ more than we would expect by chance at different levels of response efficacy. In other words, threat would not moderate the impact of response efficacy on information seeking intention.

In addition, results revealed a significant main effect for response efficacy on participants' information seeking intention, $F(1, 220) = 5.185$, $P = .024$, partial $\eta^2 = 0.024$, $\eta^2 = 0.020$, a partial effect and total effect between small and medium size. Specifically, an examination of the marginal means showed that participants who read low response efficacy message would report higher level of information seeking intention ($M = 4.42$) than those who read high-efficacy message ($M = 4.00$). Efficacy exerted a significant main effect on information seeking intention.

Besides, participants' previous experience of getting vaccinated was a significant covariate on participants' information seeking intention, $F(1,$

$220) = 11.636$, $P = .001$, partial $\eta^2 = 0.053$, and $\eta^2 = 0.046$. Age also had a significant impact on information seeking intention, $F(1, 220) = 8.879$, $P = .003$, partial $\eta^2 = 0.041$, and $\eta^2 = 0.035$. Gender impacted participants' information seeking intention significantly, $F(1, 220) = 10.182$, $P = .002$, partial $\eta^2 = 0.046$, and $\eta^2 = 0.040$. Ethnicity also placed a significant impact, $F(1, 220) = 6.716$, $P = .010$, partial $\eta^2 = 0.031$, and $\eta^2 = 0.026$.

Behavioral intention

There was no significant three-way interaction for response efficacy, threat, and interactivity on behavioral intention, $F(1, 220) = 0.056$, $P = .813$, partial $\eta^2 = 0.000$, and $\eta^2 = 0.000$. Interactivity did not moderate the two-way interaction between response efficacy and threat on behavioral intention.

The two-way interaction effect for response efficacy and threat on behavioral intention was not significant, either, $F(1, 220) = 0.920$, $P = .338$, partial $\eta^2 = 0.004$, and $\eta^2 = 0.003$. This indicated that the impact for threat on behavioral intention would not differ more than we would expect by chance at different levels of response efficacy. Additionally, age served as a significant covariate on behavioral intention, $F(1, 220) = 6.969$, $P = .009$, partial $\eta^2 = 0.032$, and $\eta^2 = 0.022$. In addition, participants' previous experience of getting meningococcal vaccination also had a significant impact on behavioral intention, $F(1, 220) = 76.710$, $P = .000$, partial $\eta^2 = 0.268$, and $\eta^2 = 0.246$.

In sum, there was no significant three-way interaction effect for response efficacy, threat, and interactivity on attitude. In addition, the two-way interaction effect between response efficacy and threat on attitude was not significant, either. For information seeking intention, there was no significant three-way interaction effect for response efficacy, threat, and interactivity. In addition, the two-way interaction effect between response efficacy and threat on information seeking intention was not significant, either. However, the main effect for response efficacy was significant, which accounted for 2% of the variances in scores on information seeking intention. No three-way interaction for response efficacy, threat, and interactivity or two-way interaction between response efficacy and threat was detected on individuals' scores of behavioral intention.

Discussion

The study reviewed in this chapter sought to test the theoretical framework proposed in an earlier chapter of this volume and examine the interaction among message content constructs (i.e., threat and efficacy) and interactivity in health communication initiatives mediated via technology. The applied context was meningococcal vaccination. Furthermore, this study focused on how to effectively utilize the feature of interactivity to better deliver threat and efficacy information about vaccination via Internet-based health promotion initiatives. The findings suggest that interactivity has the potential to improve the efficacy in communicating health risks (i.e., meningitis) and encouraging behavioral intention to get meningococcal vaccination.

The results of the study provided partial support for the predictions regarding the three-way interaction on persuasion. As predicted, interactivity moderated the two-way interaction for threat and response efficacy on message involvement. High-threat and high-efficacy health messages presented in highly interactive format would be the most effective in terms of message involvement in health communication. The finding that interactivity moderated the interaction between response efficacy and threat is also noteworthy. For message involvement, interactivity increased the magnitude of the two-way interaction. The two-way interaction for response efficacy and threat predicted by theory would be enhanced by the interactive feature of the message. Through individuals' active involvement in the learning process and their increased ability to navigate to hyperlinks that connected them to more information based on the relevance of the topic, interactivity enhanced information involvement and processing as they establish associate links between different pieces of information and relate the information to their previous knowledge and experience (Jaffe, 1997; Tremayne & Dunwoody, 2001). As a result, individuals' involvement in the communication process was enhanced. It would, in turn, refine their interpretation of new knowledge through the two-way communication offered by interactive presentational format (Cairncross & Mannion, 2001). In health promotion and education initiatives, therefore, the format of interactivity would function together with content constructs such as threat and response efficacy to influence message involvement in the process.

Previous research has demonstrated that interactive, rather than printed or other noninteractive media, would be more effective in enhancing individuals' comprehension of the information provided and in persuading them to engage in recommended health behaviors (e.g., Burger et al., 2003; De Bourdeaudhuij et al., 2007). Others, however, did not discover significant differences between interactive and noninteractive media (e.g., Kroeze, Oenema, Campbell, & Brug, 2008; Oenema, Tan, & Brug, 2005). It may be explained by the theoretical framework in Chapter 1 and the results of this study that interactivity would work together with other constructs in generating its impact. That is, interactivity does not function by itself—the characteristics of user control, two-way communication, and reciprocal influence will interact with other factors in the message to impact individuals' learning experience and the effectiveness of persuasion. Interactivity, as a unique feature of a message's presentational format, will need to be considered together with message content constructs, such as threat and efficacy, in its influence on the effectiveness of health communication. More research on the interaction effect of interactivity and message content constructs on the process of communication and outcomes of persuasion may help health communicators refine message design strategies for recommended health behaviors and make better use of the Internet-based interactive media, which is more and more easily accessible.

The predicted three-way interaction for response efficacy, threat, and interactivity on other outcomes was not supported in the study. It may be that interactivity plays a more crucial role and has a larger impact on the proximal dependent variables, such as message reception and message involvement than it does on the more distal outcomes of persuasion, such as attitudinal and behavioral change (McGuire, 1985). As ELM and HSM suggest, persuasion can take place through both central and peripheral routes (systematic and heuristic processing). A message that is highly engaging and processed in-depth may or may not lead to persuasive effects (attitudinal or behavioral change). The finding of this study found that message involvement and processing could serve as a mediator in how highly interactive health messages generate persuasive effects, yet more research is needed to unpack when message involvement resulted from the interaction of message content and message modality can more accurately predict health persuasion (and when they cannot). That is, more empirical research is necessary to test the conditions under which proximal outcomes like message involvement and information processing will mediate the three-way interaction's impact on the distal outcomes of persuasion.

Last, the finding that low-threat, low-efficacy message may also lead to higher message involvement and motivate information seeking is noteworthy. While the literature suggests that threat motivates action (e.g., Rimal & Real, 2003; Witte, 1992), when presented in a highly interactive format, low-threat, low-efficacy message may initiate active message scrutiny and message involvement (Block & Keller, 1995; Gleicher & Petty, 1992; Rimal & Real, 2003). If the message is highly interactive, easily accessible features such as hyperlinks, individuals may perceive the functional interface to help extend their perceptual bandwidth (Reeves & Nass, 2000). Future research should examine when and why interactive messages may be particularly useful to initiate protective motivation for those with low-threat and low-efficacy perceptions.

Limitations

It should be noticed that the applied context for this study was meningitis and meningococcal vaccination. Future research can test this three-way interaction on a new risk topic to see whether the results will be replicated. Furthermore, multiple topics can be used as random factors in future studies to test whether this model can be generalized to other topics in risk communication. Also, this study used self-report questions to measure participants' message involvement and message processing, which represented their subjective evaluation of those variables. Future research should include objective measures of message involvement and message processing, such as thought listing and true/false questions to ensure the accuracy of the proximal outcome measurements.

Finally, results revealed that participants' previous experience on the topic of the research had placed a significant impact on their evaluation of measurements. Although their previous knowledge of getting meningococcal vaccination was measured and controlled for as a covariate in the analysis, individuals were only asked whether they themselves had been vaccinated against meningitis. Future studies should include participants' past contact and previous experience with people who contracted meningitis.

Conclusion

Overall, the results of this study provide support for the theoretical framework proposed in Chapter 1 and suggest that interactivity may moderate how message content influences information processing. Whether this impact will lead to or mediate the interaction effect other message content and interactivity's impact on attitudinal and behavioral outcomes needs to be further examined in future research. The results highlight the importance of examining interactivity in combination with message content constructs in Internet- and computer-based health promotion and education initiatives.

References

Ahern, R. K., & Stromer-Galley, J. (June 2000). The interaction effect: An experimental study of high and low interactivity political Websites. In *50th annual conference of the International Communication*. Mexico: Acapulco.

Bandura, A. (1994). Self-efficacy. In V. S. Ramachaudran (Ed.), *Encyclopedia of human behavior* (Vol. 4, pp. 71–81). New York: Academic Press.

Bandura, A. (1998). Health promotion from the perspective of social cognitive theory. *Psychology and Health, 13*, 623–649. https://doi.org/10.1080/08870449808407422.

Block, L. G., & Keller, P. A. (1995). When to accentuate the negative: The effects of perceived efficacy and message framing on intentions to perform a health related behavior. *Journal of Marketing Research, 32*, 192–203. https://doi.org/10.1177/002224379503200206.

Burger, J., McDermott, M. H., Chess, C., Bochenek, E., Perez-Lugo, M., & Pflugh, K. K. (2003). Evaluating risk communication about fish consumption advisories: Efficacy of a brochure versus a classroom lesson in Spanish and English. *Risk Analysis: An International Journal, 23*, 791–803. https://doi.org/10.1111/1539-6924.00356.

Cairncross, S., & Mannion, M. (2001). Interactive multimedia and learning: Realizing the benefits. *Innovations in Education and Teaching International, 38,* 156−164. https://doi.org/10.1080/14703290110035428.

CDC. (October 24, 2018). *Meningitis. Centers for disease control and prevention (CDC).* Retrieved from https://www.cdc.gov/meningitis/index.html.

Champion, V., Skinner, C. S., Hui, S., Monahan, P., Juliar, B., Daggy, J., & Menon, U. (2007). The effect of telephone versus print tailoring for mammography adherence. *Patient Education and Counseling, 65,* 416−423. https://doi.org/10.1016/j.pec.2006.09.014.

Champion, V. L., Springston, J. K., Zollinger, T. W., Saywell, R. M., Jr., Monahan, P. O., Zhao, Q., & Russell, K. M. (2006). Comparison of three interventions to increase mammography screening in low income African American women. *Cancer Detection and Prevention, 30,* 535−544. https://doi.org/10.1016/j.cdp.2006.10.003.

Connelly, N. A., & Knuth, B. A. (1998). Evaluating risk communication: Examining target audience perceptions about four presentation formats for fish consumption health advisory information. *Risk Analysis, 18,* 649−659. https://doi.org/10.1111/j.1539-6924.1998.tb00377.x.

Cook, D. A., Levinson, A. J., Garside, S., Dupras, D. M., Erwin, P. J., & Montori, V. M. (2008). Internet-based learning in the health professions: A meta-analysis. *Journal of the American Medical Association, 300,* 1181−1196. https://doi.org/10.1001/jama.300.10.1181.

Cox, D., & Cox, A. D. (1991). Communicating the consequences of early detection: The role of evidence and framing. *Journal of Marketing, 65,* 91−103. https://doi.org/10.1509/jmkg.65.3.91.18336.

De Bourdeaudhuij, I., Stevens, V., Vandelanotte, C., & Brug, J. (2007). Evaluation of an interactive computer-tailored nutrition intervention in a real-life setting. *Annals of Behavioral Medicine, 33,* 39−48. https://doi.org/10.1207/s15324796abm3301_5.

December, J. (1996). Units of analysis for Internet communication. *Journal of Communication, 46,* 14−38. https://doi.org/10.1111/j.1460-2466.1996.tb01459.x.

Dillard, J. P., Shen, L., & Vail, R. G. (2007). Does perceived message effectiveness cause persuasion or vice versa? 17 consistent answers. *Human Communication Research, 33,* 467−488. https://doi.org/10.1111/j.1468-2958.2007.00308.x.

Eagly, A. H., & Chaiken, S. (1993). *The psychology of attitudes.* Orlando, FL: Harcourt Brace Jovanovich College Publishers.

Gleicher, F., & Petty, R. E. (1992). Expectations of reassurance influence the nature of fear-stimulated attitude change. *Journal of Experimental Social Psychology, 28,* 821−843. https://doi.org/10.1016/0022-1031(92)90033-G.

Jaffe, J. M. (1997). Media interactivity and self-efficacy: An examination of hypermedia first aid instruction. *Journal of Health Communication, 2,* 235−251. https://doi.org/10.1080/108107397127572.

Jankowski, N., & Hanssen, L. (1996). Introduction: Multimedia come of age. In N. Jankowski, & L. Hanssen (Eds.), *The contours of multimedia: Recent technological, theoretical and empirical developments* (pp. 1−20). Luton, UK: University of Luton Press.

Kim, H., & Stout, P. A. (2010). The effects of interactivity on information processing and attitude change: Implications for mental health stigma. *Health Communication, 25,* 142−154. https://doi.org/10.1080/10410230903544936.

Kroeze, W., Oenema, A., Campbell, M., & Brug, J. (2008). The efficacy of web-based and print-delivered computer-tailored interventions to reduce fat intake: Results of a randomized, controlled trial. *Journal of Nutrition Education and Behavior, 40,* 226−236. https://doi.org/10.1016/j.jneb.2007.09.008.

Kuang, K., & Cho, H. (2016). Delivering vaccination messages via interactive channels: Examining the interaction among threat, response efficacy, and interactivity in risk communication. *Journal of Risk Research, 19,* 476−495. https://doi.org/10.1080/13669877.2014.988284.

Laurent, G., & Kapferer, J. N. (1985). Measuring consumer involvement profiles. *Journal of Marketing Research, 22*, 41–53. https://doi.org/10.1177/002224378502200104.

Liu, Y. P., & Shrum, L. J. (2002). What is interactivity and is it always such a good thing? Implications of definition, person and situation for the influence of interactivity on advertising effectiveness. *Journal of Advertising, 31*, 53–64. https://doi.org/10.1080/00913367.2002.10673685.

Maloney, E. K., Lapinski, M. K., & Witte, K. (2011). Fear appeals and persuasion: A review and update of the extended parallel process model. *Social and Personality Psychology Compass, 5*, 206–219. https://doi.org/10.1111/j.1751-9004.2011.00341.x.

Massey, B. L., & Levy, M. R. (1999). Interactivity, online journalism and English-language web newspapers in Asia. *Journalism and Mass Communication Quarterly, 76*, 138–151. https://doi.org/10.1177/107769909907600110.

McGuire, W. J. (1985). The nature of attitudes and attitude change. In G. Lindzey, & E. Aronson (Eds.), *Handbook of social psychology*. New York: Random House.

McMillan, S. J., & Hwang, J. S. (2002). Measures of perceived interactivity: An exploration of the role of direction of communication, user control, and time in shaping perceptions of interactivity. *Journal of Advertising, 31*, 29–42. https://doi.org/10.1080/00913367.2002.10673674.

Oenema, A., Tan, F., & Brug, J. (2005). Short-term efficacy of a web-based computer-tailored nutrition intervention: Main effects and mediators. *Annals of Behavioral Medicine, 29*, 54–63. https://doi.org/10.1207/s15324796abm2901_8.

Pavlik, J. (1996). *New media technology: Cultural and commercial perspectives*. Boston: Allyn & Bacon.

Petty, R. E., & Cacioppo, J. T. (1986). *Communication and persuasion*. New York, NY: Springer-Verlag.

Rafaeli, S. (1988). Interactivity: From new media to communication. In R. Hawkins, J. Weimann, & S. Pingree (Eds.), *Advancing communication science: Merging mass and interpersonal processes* (pp. 110–134). Newbury Park, CA: Sage.

Reeves, B., & Nass, C. (2000). Perceptual user interfaces: Perceptual bandwidth. *Communications of the ACM, 43*, 65–70. https://doi.org/10.1145/330534.330542.

Rimal, R. N., & Real, K. (2003). Perceived risk and efficacy beliefs as motivators of change. *Human Communication Research, 29*, 370–399. https://doi.org/10.1111/j.1468-2958.2003.tb00844.x.

Rogers, R. W. (1975). A protection motivation theory of fear appeals and attitude change. *Journal of Psychology, 91*, 93–114. https://doi.org/10.1080/00223980.1975.9915803.

Rogers, R. W. (1983). Cognitive and physiological processes in fear appeals and attitude change: A revised theory of protection motivation. In R. E. Petty (Ed.), *Social psychophysiology* (pp. 153–176). New York: Guilford.

Russell, M. L., Injeyan, H. S., Verhoef, M. J., & Eliasziw, M. (2004). Beliefs and behaviours: understanding chiropractors and immunization. *Vaccine, 23*, 372–379. https://doi.org/10.1016/j.vaccine.2004.05.027.

Slater, M. D., Buller, D. B., Waters, E., Archibeque, M., & LeBlanc, M. (2003). A test of conversational and testimonial messages versus didactic presentations of nutrition information. *Journal of Nutrition Education and Behavior, 35*, 355–359. https://doi.org/10.1016/S1499-4046(06)60056-0.

Smith, S. W., Rosenman, K. D., Kotowski, M. R., Glazer, E., McFeters, C., Keesecker, N. M., & Law, A. (2008). Using the EPPM to create and evaluate the effectiveness of brochures to increase the use of hearing protection in farmers and landscape workers. *Journal of Applied Communication Research, 36*, 200–218. https://doi.org/10.1080/00909880801922862.

Strecher, V. J., Greenwood, T., Wang, C., & Dumont, D. (1999). Interactive multimedia and risk communication. *Journal of the National Cancer Institute Monographs, 25*, 134–149. https://doi.org/10.1093/oxfordjournals.jncimonographs.a024188.

Street, R. L., & Rimal, R. N. (1997). Health promotion and interactive technology: A conceptual foundation. In R. L. Street, W. R. Gold, & T. Mannings (Eds.), *Health promotion and interactive technology: Theoretical applications and future directions* (pp. 1−18). Mahwah, NJ: Lawrence Erlbaum Associates.

Struckman-Johnson, C. J., Gilliland, R. C., Struckman-Johnson, D. L., & North, T. C. (1990). The effects of fear of AIDS and gender on responses to fear-arousing condom advertisements. *Journal of Applied Social Psychology, 20*, 1396−1410. https://doi.org/10.1111/j.1559-1816.1990.tb01480.x.

Sundar, S. S. (2000). Multimedia effects on processing and perception of online news: A study of picture, audio, and video downloads. *Journalism and Mass Communication Quarterly, 77*, 480−499. https://doi.org/10.1177/107769900007700302.

Sundar, S. S. (2007). Social psychology of interactivity in human-website interaction. In A. Joinson, K. McKenna, T. Postmes, & U. Reips (Eds.), *The oxford handbook of Internet psychology* (pp. 89−102). New York, NY: Oxford University Press.

Sundar, S. S., Kalyanaraman, S., & Brown, J. (2003). Explicating web site interactivity: Impression formation effects in political campaign sites. *Communication Research, 30*, 30−59. https://doi.org/10.1177/0093650202239025.

Sundar, S. S., & Kim, J. (2005). Interactivity and persuasion: Influencing attitudes with information and involvement. *Journal of Interactive Advertising, 5*, 5−18. https://doi.org/10.1080/15252019.2005.10722097.

Tanner, J. F., Jr., Hunt, J. B., & Eppright, D. R. (1991). The protection motivation model: A normative model of fear appeals. *The Journal of Marketing, 55*, 36−45. https://doi.org/10.2307/1252146.

Tabachnick, B. G., & Fidell, l. S. (1996). *Using multivariate statistics*. New York, NY: Harper & Row.

Tessaro, I., Rye, S., Parker, L., Mangone, C., & McCrone, S. (2007). Effectiveness of a nutrition intervention with rural low-income women. *American Journal of Health Behavior, 31*, 35−43. https://doi.org/10.5993/AJHB.31.1.4.

Tremayne, M. W., & Dunwoody, S. (2001). Interactivity, information processing, and learning on the World wide web. *Science Communication, 23*, 111−134. https://doi.org/10.1177/1075547001023002003.

Walther, J. B., Pingree, S., Hawkins, R. P., & Buller, D. B. (2005). Attributes of interactive online health information systems. *Journal of Medical Internet Research, 7*, e33. https://doi.org/10.2196/jmir.7.3.e33.

WHO. (October 24, 2018). *Vaccination greatly reduces disease, disability, death and inequity worldwide*. World Health Organization. Retrieved from http://www.who.int/bulletin/volumes/86/2/07-040089/en/.

Witte, K. (1992). Putting the fear back into fear appeals: The extended parallel process model. *Communication Monographs, 59*, 329−349. https://doi.org/10.1080/03637759209376276.

Witte, K., & Allen, M. (2000). A meta-analysis of fear appeals: Implications for effective public health campaigns. *Health Education and Behavior, 27*, 591−615. https://doi.org/10.1177/109019810002700506.

Witte, K., Cameron, J., McKeon, J., & Berkowitz. (1996). Predicting risk behaviors: Development and validation of a diagnostic scale. *Journal of Health Communication, 1*, 317−341. https://doi.org/10.1080/108107396127988.

Zhao, Z., & Cai, X. (2009). The role of risk, efficacy, and anxiety in smokers' cancer information seeking. *Health Communication, 24*, 259−269. https://doi.org/10.1080/10410230902805932.

Index

Printed in the United States
By Bookmasters